College Technology Survival Kit

Revised Second Edition

Marianne Daugharthy
and Alanna Duley

cognella®

SAN DIEGO

Bassim Hamadeh, CEO and Publisher
Kristina Stolte, Senior Field Acquisitions Editor
Carrie Baarns, Manager, Revisions and Author Care
Kaela Martin, Project Editor
Abbey Hastings, Production Editor
Emely Villavicencio, Senior Graphic Designer
Alexa Lucido, Licensing Manager
Aliza Shalit, Interior Designer
Natalie Piccotti, Director of Marketing
Kassie Graves, Senior Vice President, Editorial
Jamie Giganti, Director of Academic Publishing

cognella® | ACADEMIC PUBLISHING
3970 Sorrento Valley Blvd., Ste. 500, San Diego, CA 92121

TABLE of CONTENTS

PART 2 | Microsoft Word

CHAPTER SIX

PART 4 | Presentation Software 483

CHAPTER TWELVE

CHAPTER THIRTEEN

Part 1

File Management

1. Blackboard

2. Canvas Learning Management System

3. Windows File Management

4. Google Web Applications

5. OneNote

CHAPTER ONE

Blackboard

Introduction

Blackboard was initially released on January 21, 1997, as Blackboard Learning Management System. It was created as a virtual learning environment and course management system. Blackboard, Inc. developed the program as a web-based server software.

Blackboard enables instructors and administrators to better manage and customize courses. One of its main purposes was to develop complete online courses by adding online elements to traditional face-to-face courses to minimize or eliminate face-to-face meetings. This paved the way for those students who were either too busy, lived too far away, didn't want to attend classes, or were otherwise unable to participate in face-to-face classrooms, enabling them to attend college any time of day or night. Nowadays, many students attend online classes in different cities, states, and even countries.

Many different open-source Virtual Learning Environments (VLEs) are used by schools, businesses, and training organizations. Some of the best-known e-learning or VLE platforms designed for education include Blackboard (Figure 1-1); Angel (Figure 1-2);

FIGURE 1-1 Blackboard Logo

FIGURE 1-2 Angel Logo

FIGURE 1-3 Moodle Logo   FIGURE 1-4 Canvas Logo

Moodle (Figure 1-3); Canvas (Figure 1-4); eFront; and Atutor. You may encounter one or more of these during your college journey.

In this section, Blackboard and its uses will be discussed so that the incoming student, either traditional or nontraditional, will learn the basics of how to navigate in Blackboard. This includes reading announcements, participating in online forums, creating and responding to wikis, turning in assignments, getting online help, using web links, and looking up grades. Let's get started!

Your educational institution will provide you with a link to Blackboard. Normally, your username and password will be the same as the ones you would need to access your student account. When you log in to Blackboard, you will see a similar login screen, some showing school colors (Figure 1-5), others more generic (Figure 1-6).

FIGURE 1-5 School Colors Blackboard Login Screen

Once you type in your username and password, a dashboard-type window will open. Depending on your school and your instructor, your dashboard window may appear similar to this example (Figure 1-7).

Note: Your instructor may have a few or many modules on the dashboard sheet. Each class will look slightly different.

FIGURE 1-6 Generic Blackboard Login Screen

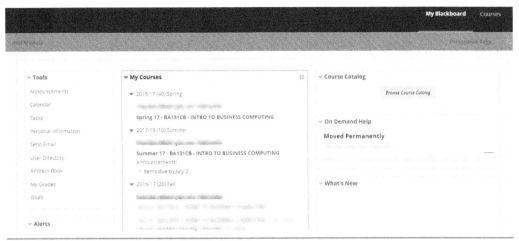

FIGURE 1-7 Blackboard Dashboard

Your classes will be listed under the **My Courses** module. Click on the blue hyperlink below **Courses where you are: Student** to open your class in Blackboard. The left panel of your screen will look similar to Figure 1-8. <u>Note</u>: Each instructor will have different buttons; however, most instructors will have buttons to access *Announcements, Syllabus*, and *Course Schedules*. *Instructor Information* may be included. Other buttons will be named specific to the course at the discretion of the instructor.

Each button will be covered in its own section. This will enable you to easily select the section you want. Some of these buttons you will see only in a face-to-face class; others, you will see only in online or hybrid courses. Then some buttons will be used interchangeably. It is likely you will enroll in a hybrid or online course at least once during your college journey. The hybrid and online buttons may also be used in a face-to-face class. If you have any questions or concerns on how to navigate the Blackboard interface for your class, see your instructor.

Announcements

Many instructors use the Announcements as the entry to your course. Therefore, when you open Blackboard for a specific class, chances are you will be immediately directed to the Announcements. Instructors use this to capture your attention once you check in. Announcements are used to greet the class, inform the class of assignments or exams that will be due in the near future, guide students to use links within the program or on the Internet, announce upcoming events in the class, or pass on other types of information to the class at the discretion of the instructor. These examples don't cover all instances used for announcements.

Additionally, in Blackboard, when an instructor creates an announcement, the instructor may check a box so that Blackboard emails the message in the announcement to the student. Many students either don't check their school email or use an alternate email to communicate with the instructor and the school. When students use an alternative email address rather than the school email, then they do not see the announcement. Many schools prefer the student to use the school email to keep in contact.

If you are currently using Blackboard but are in a different part of the program, you can easily return to **Announcements**. If you click on the (blue) button (link) in the left panel of your screen that reads **Announcements** (Figure 1-9), you will see the latest announcements. You will not be required to respond to these announcements in Blackboard.

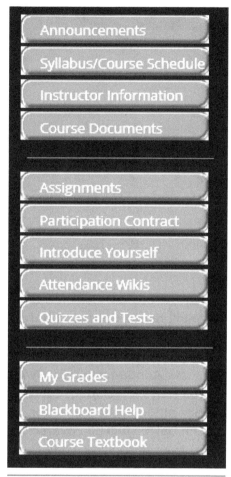

FIGURE 1-8 Blackboard Navigation Buttons

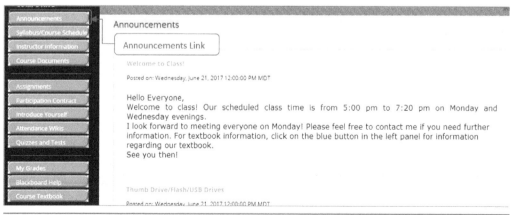

FIGURE 1-9 Announcements Link

Syllabus/Course Schedule

This link is commonly used to access the course syllabus for the class and/or the class schedule for the duration of the class. Sometimes an instructor will group both syllabus and class schedule. When you click on the **Syllabus/Course Schedule** link, you will see a blue

FIGURE 1-10 Syllabus and Course Schedule Link

hyperlink for the Course Syllabus and the Class Schedule (Figure 1-10). In the bottom of the screen, you will see three options. You can *Open, Save,* or *Cancel.* If you just want to view it, click on *Open.* If you would like to save a copy in a specific place, you will click on *Save As.* If you just want to have your computer download the file, then click on *Save.* Otherwise, click on *Cancel.*

If you click *Open,* the program will open the document.

Instructor Information

When you click the Instructor Information (an instructor may use a slightly different name for the link), a window will open with all or most of the following information:

- Instructor name
- Instructor school email address
- Instructor phone number (optional)
- Instructor office location
- Instructor office hours
- Instructor photo (optional)

The instructor may furnish a brief introduction and additional information relating to his or her background in the course subject. This is good information for you to keep in case you might need to contact the instructor in the future.

Course Documents

Some instructors may include a link for additional or supplemental course documents relating to the course subject. The list below will give you a better idea of different types of course documents you may find. Figure 1-11 shows an example of a Course Document window.

Note: These particular course documents will link you to an article on the Internet. To access these web links, just click on the blue hypertext. In Figure 1-12, click on the blue font (this is not a hyperlink, and the font color will vary by instructor) to access the course document.

- Item
- File
- Audio
- Image
- Video

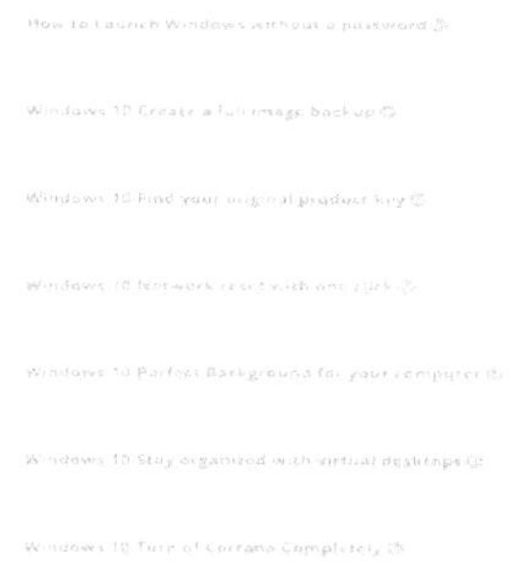

FIGURE 1-11 Course Documents Hyperlinks

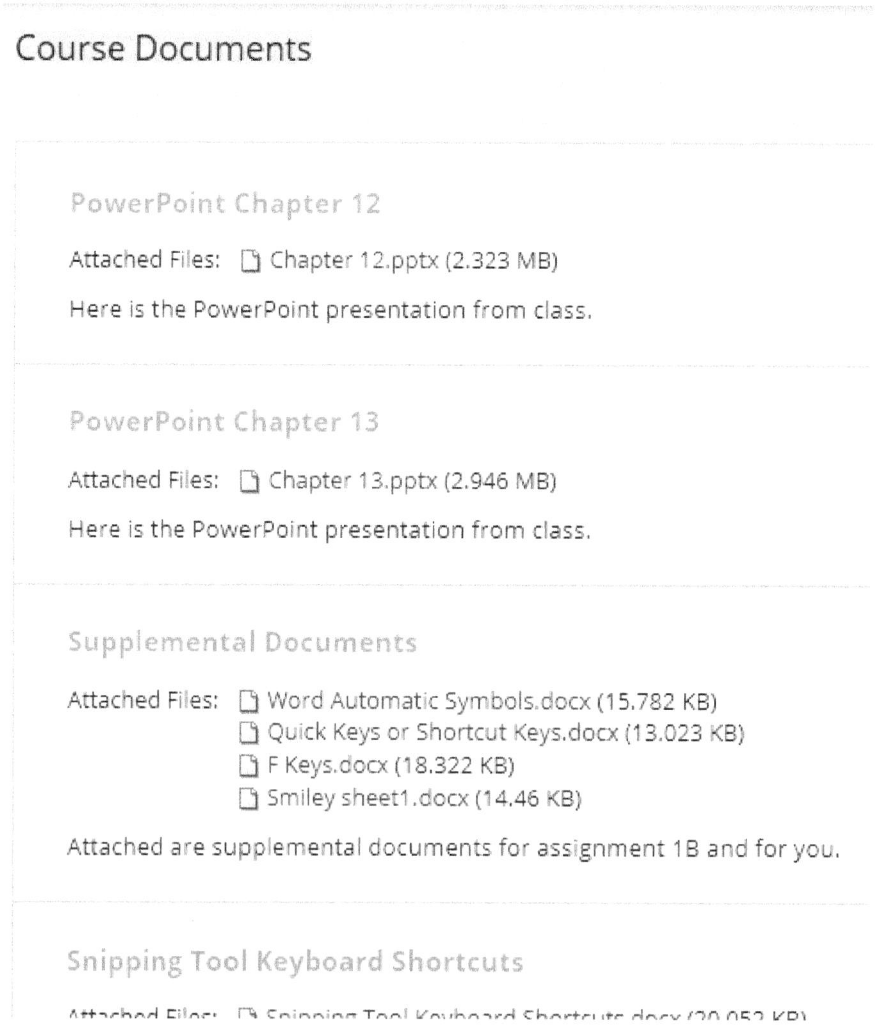

Course Documents

PowerPoint Chapter 12

Attached Files: ☐ Chapter 12.pptx (2.323 MB)

Here is the PowerPoint presentation from class.

PowerPoint Chapter 13

Attached Files: ☐ Chapter 13.pptx (2.946 MB)

Here is the PowerPoint presentation from class.

Supplemental Documents

Attached Files: ☐ Word Automatic Symbols.docx (15.782 KB)
☐ Quick Keys or Shortcut Keys.docx (13.023 KB)
☐ F Keys.docx (18.322 KB)
☐ Smiley sheet1.docx (14.46 KB)

Attached are supplemental documents for assignment 1B and for you.

Snipping Tool Keyboard Shortcuts

Attached Files: ☐ Snipping Tool Keyboard Shortcuts.docx (20.052 KB)

FIGURE 1-12 Course Documents

- Web Link
- Learning Module
- Lesson Plan
- Syllabus
- Course Link
- Flickr Photo
- SlideShare Presentation

In the bottom of the screen, you will see three options. You can *Open; Save,;* or *Cancel*. If you just want to view it, click on *Open*. If you would like to save a copy in a specific place, you will click on *Save As*. If you just want to have your computer download the file, then click on *Save*. Otherwise, click on *Cancel* (Figure 1-13).

FIGURE 1-13 Opening a Document Link

Assignments

Finding Your Assignments in Blackboard
Individual Assignments

Your instructor can add assignments to different areas of your course. You might access assignments from a link on the course menu called ***Assignments*** (Figure 1-14). Or, your instructor might incorporate assignments into each week's content. Ask your instructor if you have questions about how your course is organized.

Be careful with the assignments. An assignment will normally appear after a certain date (generally after a lecture or completion of a certain task). For example, you might have to mark a lecture as reviewed before you may access an assignment. Assignments will appear in Blackboard for a limited amount of time. The instructor will alert you as to when the assignment closes. You will receive an alert either listed in the assignment itself, through **Announcements**, or through your email.

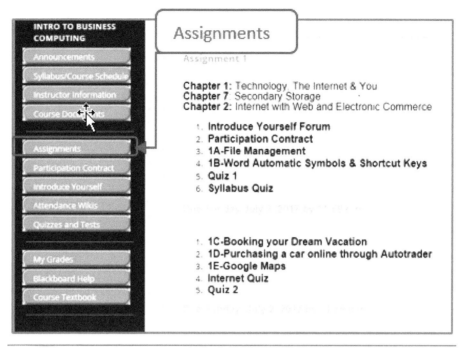

FIGURE 1-14 Assignments Link

Most of the time, if you wait until the last minute, and the assignment does not appear in Blackboard, that means you missed the deadline to complete the assignment. Other assignments may remain open, and you will be able to access them through Blackboard. However, those assignments are generally late, and you may be penalized for a late assignment. Contact your instructor if you don't see an assignment that you think you should.

Once you click on the **Assignments** link, you may see a screen similar to Figure 1-14. This Assignment list begins with Assignment 1 and continues through Assignment 8. In this screen, Assignment 1 lists all the required reading (Chapters 1, 7, and 2) and the associated tasks. Each section of tasks ends with a due date and time. Once you click on the **Assignment 1** hyperlink, the program will take you to a list of each required task (Figure 1-15).

Your instructor may include some attached files. Sometimes you will have a document to begin the assignment with, other times, you will have to create the initial document. Assignment instructions are often included along with any supplemental documents or documentation you will need to complete the task.

FIGURE 1-15 Assignment 1

Submit an individual assignment

Access the assignment.

1. On the **Upload Assignment** page, the *Assignment Information* section provides a review of the instructions, due date, points possible, and the opportunity to download any files provided by your instructor. If your instructor plans to do the assignment in class, it may also be noted in this section. If your instructor has added a rubric for grading, you can view it (Figure 1-16).

Upload Assignment: 1A File Folder Creation

ASSIGNMENT INFORMATION

Due Date	Points Possible
Sunday, July 2, 2017	**10**
11:59 PM	

1. Open the attached directions.

2. Rename document as: *[your initials]* ***1A File FolderCreation*** Save your snip in your Assignment 1 folder.

3. Complete assignment. Save

4. Attach completed assignment to this link in Blackboard.

In Class Lab--This will be completed in class on June 28, 2017.

Due by Sunday, July 2, 2017 by 11:59 p.m.

FIGURE 1-16 Upload Assignment Window—Top Third

2. In the middle section of the Upload Assignment page, if you need to type your submission, you can click on the ***Write Submission*** button to expand the area where you can type your submission. You can use the editor function buttons to format the text. In the lower right of the Write Submission box, you will see Words: 0. As you type your submission, the program will count the number of words. At a glance, you can see if you meet the minimum number of words required for the assignment (Figure 1-17).

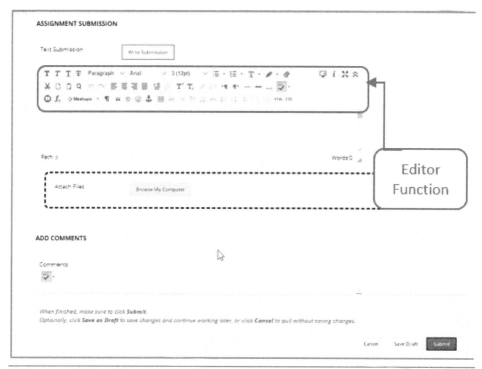

FIGURE 1-17 Write Submission Window

3. Another way to upload a completed assignment is to click the **Browse my Computer** button (next to Attach Files) within the dotted line area. This will upload a file from your computer or thumb drive.

4. OR, you can drag files from your computer to the "hot spot" in the Attach Files area (within the dotted line area). If your browser allows, you can also drag a folder of files. The files will upload individually. If the browser doesn't allow you to submit your assignment after you upload a folder, select **Do not attach** in the folder's row to remove it. You can drag the files individually and submit again.

Note: You can add more than one file to the assignment. Depending on the school's server space allotted to assignment uploads, the program will determine the limit of the number of files or folder size you can upload at a time.

5. Note: If your institution uses an older version of Blackboard Learn, you won't be able to drag files or folders to upload to Blackboard. Ask your instructor for further information regarding the Blackboard version your school is currently using.

6. Your attached file(s) will appear listed below the dotted line area. Just to the right of each listed file, you have the option to **Do Not Attach** if you decide not to attach that particular file **(Figure 1-18)**.

7. Optionally, you can type Comments about your submission. This is normally not required when you turn in an assignment, however, feedback is welcome.

8. Click *Submit*. The Review Submission History page appears with information about your submitted assignment and a success message within a colored banner on the top of the window (Figure 1-19). You will receive a confirmation number. Copy and save this number as proof of your submission. For assignments with multiple attempts, you receive a different number for each submission. If your institution has enabled email notifications for submission receipts, you'll also receive an email with your confirmation number and details each time you submit coursework.

FIGURE 1-18 Attached File

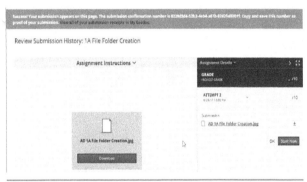

FIGURE 1-19 Submission History and Confirmation Number

9. Double-check to make sure you have attached the correct file. If so, click the *OK* button in the right panel of the window. If not, click on the **Start New** button to reattach your file. If a confirmation number appears in the success banner, be sure to copy it or write it down.

Save an assignment as a draft to submit later
On the **Upload Assignment** page, select *Save Draft* to save your work and continue later. Your text and files are saved on the page. In the banner in the top of the window, you will see **The assignment has been saved** (Figure 1-20). When you return, you can resume working.

FIGURE 1-20 Saving Draft

1. Return to your assignment and select the assignment title (in this example, it will be listed under Assignment 1, ***Assignment 1A File Folder Creation***).
2. On the Review Submission History page, select Continue (Figure 1-21).
3. On the **Upload Assignment** page, make your changes.
4. Optionally, type comments about your submission.
5. Select *Submit*. The **Review Submission History** page appears with information about your submitted assignment.
6. Your instructor may allow only one attempt, a limited number of attempts, or unlimited attempts. Confirm the number of allowed attempts with your instructor.

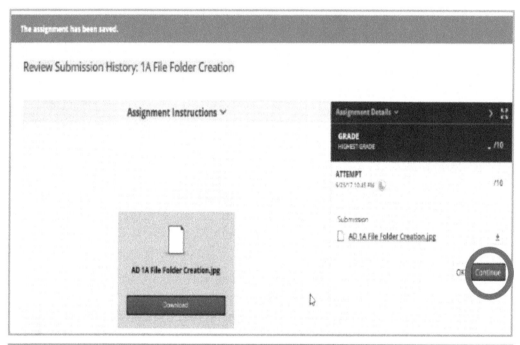

FIGURE 1-21 Continue to Draft

Note: When you finish your assignment, you must select *Submit*. If you do not click on *Submit*, your instructor will not receive your work.

Group Assignments

Your instructor can also create group assignments and provide access to them in the same areas as regular assignments. Group assignments may also appear in the Course View, or left panel (Figure 1-22). Your instructor will have already assigned you to a group and selected this assignment to be a group assignment.

FIGURE 1-22 Group Assignments Button

☺	Assignment submitted. Ready to be graded
☾	Assignment in progress but not submitted
❗	An error has occurred. See your instructor
💬	View feedback from your instructor
Grade	Select the grade to view details

FIGURE 1-23 Grade Status Icons

Submit a group assignment

To turn in the assignment, you will go through the same process as you did for an individual assignment. Your instructor will receive an assignment from each member of your group although this will be invisible to you.

One member submits the group assignment for the entire group. The grade you receive is the same for all members of the group. If you need to resubmit or save a draft, the process will be the same as above when making your submission. You will also receive a confirmation number for your portion of the assignment.

My Grades

Your instructor must grade each assignment and post the grade and provide feedback, if needed. Your assignments are not graded automatically. Normally, an instructor will provide a timetable as to when you can expect to see your grade.

When you click on **My Grades**, the **My Grades** page displays all your grades. **My Grades** is often located on the course menu. The course menu appears on the left side of the course window. If My Grades is not on the course menu, select **Tools** and select **My Grades**. Sometimes an instructor may use both.

On the **My Grades** page, you can view all the coursework and grades for your course. If you have turned in your work but it has not been graded, grade status icons appear (Figure 1-23).

If your assignment has been submitted and graded, the grade appears in the assignment's row.

To view more detail, select the assignment's title to access the **Review Submission History** page.

You can view document details, retrieve a document, and filter and order your view.

1. Select an item's title (blue hypertext in the left of the window) to view details. For example, your instructor can type comments, highlight text, and draw on your document. Select an assignment's title (blue hypertext) to access the assignment's **Review Submission History** page and review the grade, annotations, and feedback in context.

2. If your instructor used a rubric to grade your work, select the View Rubric link to view details (listed in the left panel under the blue hypertext assignment name).

3. If you see a comment balloon (View Feedback icon), click on this to view instructor feedback.

4. You can also retrieve your document anytime you want to save it to a new place on your computer or onto a flash drive. Select an item's title (blue hypertext) to access the assignment's submission history. In the right panel, you can click on the assignment's name and select *Open, Save,* or *Cancel.*

Note: If your file doesn't open automatically in the browser, your institution hasn't turned on inline viewing.

5. To filter your view of your grades, Blackboard has four different options for you to choose from: Near the top of the window, your four options are: All, Graded, Upcoming, and Submitted (Figure 1-24).

6. You can also order grades by Course Order (First assignment to last assignment), Last Activity, Date Due (Latest First), and Date Due (Oldest First). See Figure 1-25.

FIGURE 1-24 Grade Filter Views

My Grades

All   Graded   Upcoming   Submitted   Order by: Course Order
                                                                                     Last Activity
ITEM   LAST ACTIVITY   Due Date (Latest First)
Total   Due Date (Oldest First)
View Description Grading Criteria

Letter Grade
Grading Criteria

Please Introduce Yourself to the Class

FIGURE 1-25 Grade Order

Introduce Yourself (Discussions or Forum)

Discussions is a tool for sharing introductions, thoughts, and ideas within the classroom. Discussion boards may be used in both online and face-to-face courses. In Blackboard, course members (students and instructor) can have the same type of thoughtful discussions that take place in the traditional classroom but offer the advantages of asynchronous communication. It may be slower than synchronous communications as asynchronous communication allows you to take the time to consider your responses carefully. Location and time do not matter in an online discussion.

You can use **Discussions** for these tasks:

- Meet with your peers online for social interaction and collaboration.
- Post questions about homework assignments or course content.
- You may be asked to demonstrate your understanding or application of course material in a discussion.

How to Participate in a Discussion

Your instructor may set up a Discussion or Forum for you to participate in. The class discussion will most likely fall under one of the three bullets listed above. In this example, the instructor set up a Discussion for each of the students to get the chance to meet each other. In the left panel of Blackboard (course menu), click on the blue *Introduce Yourself* button. A Discussion Board dialog box will open (Figure 1-26).

Once the dialog box opens, you will see "Forum" in the left column. In this example, there is only one, but in some courses, you may see more than one. To enter the discussion, click on the name of the forum that appears in blue letters (circled in red). In the center column, you will see the description of the **discussion** along with the instructions for participation, and you may see a due date. In the right column, you will see **Total Posts, Unread Posts**, and **Total Participants**. In this example, there are 27 total posts, 5 unread posts, and 9 total participants

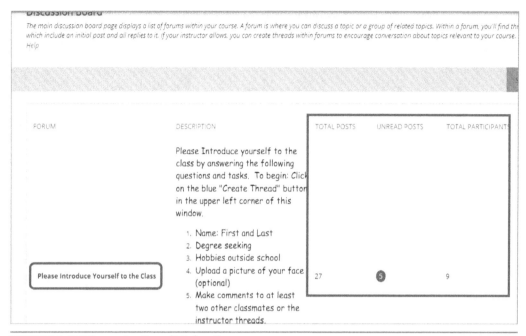

FIGURE 1-26 Discussion Board Dialog Box

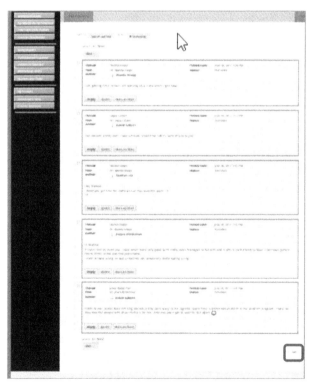

FIGURE 1-27 Five Unread Threads

(in the large red box). For the 5 unread posts, you will notice a white *5* in a red circle. You can click on this to list the unread posts (Figure 1-27).

You will see all five posts or *threads*. In the bottom of each thread, you have the option to *Reply, Quote*, or *Mark as Read* (Figure 1-28).

Once you have clicked on *Reply, Quote*, or *Mark as Read*, then click on *OK* in the lower right of the box (circled in red in Figure 1-27). Once you click on *OK*, Blackboard will return you to the **Discussion Board** page (Figure 1-26).

FIGURE 1-28 Thread Options

Now that you are back on the discussion board, click on the forum name (blue letters). In this next screen, you will create a thread where you will respond to the instructions listed in the Description section. If other threads exist, they will show up in a list.

10. Click on **Create Thread** (middle of screen). See Figure 1-29.

FIGURE 1-29 Create Thread

11. Once the Create Thread dialog box opens, you will see two sections: Forum Description and Message. The Forum Description lists the instructions for participation, and the Message section opens to a box for you to type in your submission. In the Subject box above the Message box, type in your subject. You can use the editor function buttons to format the text (Figure 1-17). In the lower right of the Write Submission box, you will see Words: 0. As you type your submission, the program will count the number of words. At a glance, you can see if you meet the minimum number of words required by the assignment (if necessary).

12. Another way to upload a completed assignment is to click the **Browse My Computer** button (next to *Attach Files*) within the dotted line area. This will upload a file from your computer or thumb drive.

13. A third option available allows you to copy and paste a response in the Message box. However, if you use this option, all of your formatting may go away; this includes bullets, bold and italic formatting, font color, and any other type of formatting.

14. Once you have completed your submission, you have three options: *Cancel, Save Draft*, or *Submit* (Figure 1-30).

15. Once you click on Submit, the list of threads will appear. Your thread will be at the top of the list. Any new threads submitted after yours will appear at the top of the list and yours will move down the list (Figure 1-31).

Message
For the toolbar, press ALT+F10 (PC) or ALT+FN+F10 (Mac).

T *T* **T** T̄ Paragraph ⌄ Arial   ⌄ 3 (12pt)   ⌄ ⋮≣ ▾ ≣ ▾ T ▾ ✎ ▾ ✄

✂ ▯ ▯ Q ↶ ↷ ≡ ≡ ≡ ≡ ⋮≣ ⋮≣ Tˣ Tₓ ∂ ⋯ ¶ ¶ — — ⌣ ✓ ▾

◎ ⊘ ▦ ▣ ƒₓ ❖ Mashups ▾ ¶ ❝ © ☺ ⚓ ▦ ▦ ▦ ▦ ▦ ▦ ▦ ▦ □ □   HTML CSS

Hi Everyone,

I am Sue Smith. My major is Psychology. I want to work with children. I am just beginning my junior year and I know
the next two plus years will just fly. I am looking forward to graduation!

I love to give advice to people. When I was a little girl, I wanted to be Lucy in Peanuts with the Psychological Help for 5
cents sign and the booth. I don't think I could ever truly help poor Charlie Brown.

My other hobbies are guitar playing and playing in team sports such as basketball and softball.

I look forward to meeting everyone!

Path: p   Words:105

*Click **Save Draft** to save a draft of this message. Click **Submit** to submit the post. Click **Cancel** to quit.*   Cancel   Save Draft   **Submit**

FIGURE 1-30 Submission Message Box

16. If you have completed replying to 2 other threads (per assignment), and reading the rest of the unread threads, click *OK* in the lower right of the screen to return to **Discussion Board** page.

17. To exit the Discussion Board page, click on any button in the course menu in the left panel.

18. Click on the ***My Grades*** button in the course menu to see your grades. If you have the yellow icon with the exclamation point, then you have completed the assignment and are waiting for your grade. If you have a blue circle, this means this assignment is still in process and not ready for grading (Figure 1-23). If your grade shows a blue circle, and you believe you completed the assignment, double-check the instructions to make sure you have everything for the assignment turned in. Then, contact your instructor.

19. As long as the **Discussion** is open, you can check in anytime. You can also add more threads and respond to other threads. Keep the conversations going!

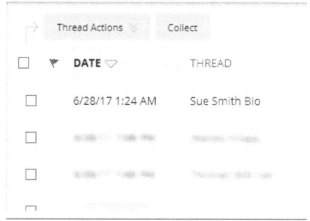

FIGURE 1-31 Threads Listed in Most Recent Order

Wikis

A wiki allows you to collaborate on course-related materials or counts as attendance in an online course. Instructors may require students to submit at least two wikis per week with a minimum number of words as attendance wikis. This tool allows you to modify or contribute to content. In a wiki, your instructor may post a lecture question. The instructor may require you to respond to the content with a minimum number of words and require citations for any researched information or images. Wikis can be seen by the instructor and your classmates: Anyone in the class or group can offer comments or feedback, and the instructor can grade individual work.

Links to wikis may be located on the course menu or on the **Tools** page.

Wikis

A wiki is a collaborative tool that allows you to cont... grade individual work. More Help

Week 1 Attendance Wiki

Type: Course
Last Modified Date: 6/28/17 10:26 PM

FIGURE 1-32 Open a Wiki

Create a Wiki Page

In Blackboard, students are not able to create a wiki, but after your instructor creates the wiki, you can create pages. Click on the *Week 1 Attendance Wiki* hyperlink (Figure 1-32). On the wiki topic page, select **Create Wiki Page** (Figure 1-33). Under WIKI PAGE CONTENT, do the following:

1. Type a name or description in the Name box.
2. In the Content area, type in your response, keeping in mind the minimum number of words specified by your instructor.
3. Click *Submit* when you are done.

Edit a Wiki Page

All course members, including your instructor, can edit a course wiki page, and all course members and the instructor edit wikis in the same way. Likewise, any group member can edit a group wiki page.

When a user is editing a wiki page, the page is locked for a duration of 120 seconds to prevent other users from editing the same page. If you try to edit a page another user is editing, you will be informed that another user is currently editing the page.

Create Wiki Page

Instructions

Hi Class,

This is a weekly wiki created to be an attendance wiki. In other words, you will need to post *twice* on two different days per week. Your week begins on Monday morning at 12:01 am and ends on Sunday at 11:59 p.m. Each wiki needs to be **at least 100 words**, and you are to respond to another student's wiki. You may critique or give feedback to a classmate, but be professional in your approach.

If you have some knowledge you would like to share with the class; this would be a great place to start. Your posts should be interesting.

* indicates a required field.

WIKI PAGE CONTENT

* Name   My Name Attendance

Content
For the toolbar, press ALT+F10 (PC) or ALT+FN+F10 (Mac).

Hi Everyone,

This is my week 1 wiki. I don't really know what to say except that "Hey World, I'm Here!!!!".

Because this is the first week, everything is new in my new class. I guess once we get going, it will be easier to do everything right. I think the instructor will help us and this might even be fun! Especially if everyone joins in and bring up interesting things to talk about. So far this week has been interesting; especially the Internet assignments. I really enjoyed the Google Maps assignment. It was pretty cool! Look! my post is 122 words!

Path: p   Words:122

Click **Submit** to finish. Click **Cancel** to quit without saving changes.   Cancel   Submit

FIGURE 1-33 Create a Wiki Page

1. In the Wiki Details area, select the wiki page you want to edit. In this case, the second one in the list is selected. You can click on the down arrow next to the wiki (Figure 1-34).
2. Or select **Edit Wiki Content** button. The Wiki Page Content dialog box will open (Figure 1-35).

FIGURE 1-34 Selecting and Editing a Wiki

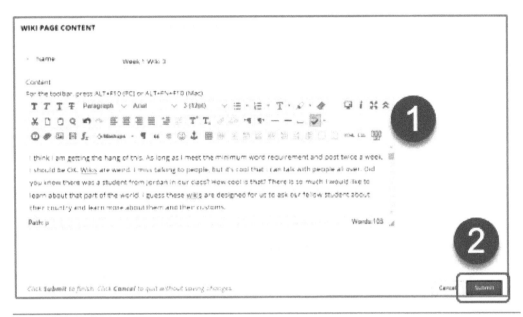

FIGURE 1-35 Editing a Wiki

3. On the **Edit Wiki Page,** make the changes you want. (Changes will be high-lighted in yellow. Words and spaces will not highlight as you edit the wiki.)

4. Select *Submit* to save your work.

Comment on a Wiki Entry

In the Wiki Details area, select the wiki page you want to comment on. Click on the **Comment** button (Figure 1-36) to add your thoughts, and select *Add* when you're finished. The Comment area does not have a word count; however, your instructor may require you to have a word minimum. Open a blank Word document to type your response and use Word's word count. Then copy and paste. Expand the Comments area to view all comments.

View Your Contributions

You can view a list of all the pages and versions you contributed or

FIGURE 1-36 Wiki Comment

modified. Above the *wiki details* box, select ***My Contribution*** (Figure 1-37). On this page, you can view information about your contribution to the wiki in the content frame and the side panel (Figure 1-38).

FIGURE 1-37 My Contribution

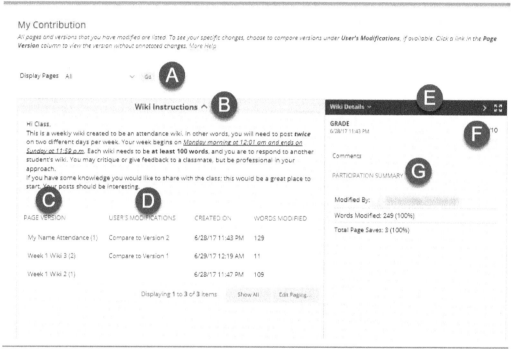

FIGURE 1-38 My Contribution Page

My Contribution Page

1. **Display Pages:** Use the Display Pages list to narrow what appears on the **My Contribution** page. You can click on a specific page, or *All*.
2. **Wiki Instructions:** Expand the section to view the instructions and any outcomes your instructor may have assigned with the wiki.
3. **Page Version:** In the Page Version column, page titles appear with their corresponding version numbers. Select a title to view the page without annotated changes. The page opens in a new window. By default, the most recent page version is listed first.

4. **User's Modification:** In the User's Modifications column, select a link to compare a page to its previous version. The page opens in a new window. Select the Legend tab to view the comparison with a legend or explanation of the formatting used to communicate version differences.
5. **Wiki Details:** In the sidebar, expand to view the information, including how many pages you contributed and edited and how many comments you added to the wiki.
6. **Grade:** This section appears if your instructor enabled grading for the wiki. You can see if your wiki pages have been graded.
7. **Participation Summary:** In this section, you can view Words Modified, which tallies any word added, deleted, or edited in all pages and each page's versions. Words Modified is available as a number count and percentage. **Total Page Saves** is available as a number count and percentage.

View Wiki Grades

1. After your instructor grades wiki contributions, you can view your grade in two places. The grading information appears on the **My Contribution** page and in **My Grades** (*My Grades* button in the course menu).
2. On the Wiki Details page, select *My Contribution*. On the **My Contribution** page, you can view your grade in the **Grade** section. You can also view your instructor's feedback and the date the instructor assigned the grade. (In this example, the wiki had not yet been graded.) See Figure 1-38, item F.

Quizzes, Tests, and Surveys

Locating Your Quiz, Test, or Survey
You may find tests and surveys in any content area, learning module, lesson plan, or folder (Figure 1-39). Generally, instructors will make it easy for you to access quizzes, tests, and surveys. Ask your instructor if you encounter difficulty locating a quiz, test, or survey.

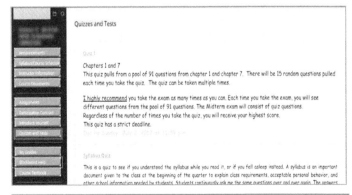

Taking a Quiz, Test, or Survey
Navigate to the quiz, test, or survey, then click on the title (hyperlink). On the next page, click on

FIGURE 1-39 Quizzes, Tests, and Surveys

Begin: Midterm

INSTRUCTIONS

Timed Test   This test has a time limit of 1 hour and 30 minutes.

Timer Setting   This test will save and submit automatically when the time expires.

Force Completion   This test can be saved and resumed at any point until time has expired. The timer will continue to run if you leave the test.

Multiple Attempts   This test allows multiple attempts.

Click **Begin** to start: Midterm. Click **Cancel** to go back.
You will be previewing this assessment and your results will not be recorded.

Click Begin to start. Click Cancel to quit.   Cancel   Begin

FIGURE 1-40 Beginning a Quiz, Test, or Survey

Begin. You also have the option to *Cancel* if you change your mind (Figure 1-40).

Some instructors will require you to type in a password to begin. To enter the exam, type in the password provided by your instructor or test proctor, then click *Submit* (Figure 1-41). Note: Passwords are case sensitive. If you type in the wrong password, you will be prompted to keep entering the valid password until you provide the correct one. After three attempts, if you continue to experience problems with the password, **STOP** and immediately ask your instructor or test proctor for assistance.

Enter Password: Midterm

ENTER PASSWORD: MIDTERM

Password

FIGURE 1-41 Password Screen

If no password is required, Blackboard will take you directly to the first question in the test.

View the Quiz, Test, or Survey Details
At the top of each quiz, test or survey, you can view the information about multiple attempts, the timer, navigation, and any optional description and instructions. You are also informed if you must complete the quiz, test, or survey after you open it. Select the arrows next to the information section to collapse (Figure 1-42) or expand it (Figure 1-43).

Preview Test: Midterm

Test Information

Description

Instructions

Timed Test   This test has a time limit of 1 hour and 30 minutes.This test will save and submit automatically when the time expires.
Warnings appear when **half the time**, **5 minutes**, **1 minute**, and **30 seconds** remain.*[The timer does not appear when previewing this test]*

Multiple Attempts This test allows 2 attempts. This is attempt number 1.

Force Completion This test can be saved and resumed at any point until time has expired. The timer will continue to run if you leave the test.

▼ Question Completion Status:

QUESTION 1   5 points   Save Answer

The GPS device in an automobile uses which communication channel?
○ Infrared
○ Radio Frequency (RF)
○ Microwave
○ Satellite

FIGURE 1-42 Preview Test Window Collapsed

Preview Test: Midterm

Test Information

Description

Instructions

1 Timed Test   This test has a time limit of 1 hour and 30 minutes.This test will save and submit automatically when the time expires.
Warnings appear when **half the time**, **5 minutes**, **1 minute**, and **30 seconds** remain.*[The timer does not appear when previewing this test]*

2 Multiple Attempts This test allows 2 attempts. This is attempt number 1.

3 Force Completion This test can be saved and resumed at any point until time has expired. The timer will continue to run if you leave the test.

4 ▲ Question Completion Status:

| 1 | 2 | 3 | 4 | 5 | 6 | 7 | 8 | 9 | 10 | 11 | 12 | 13 | 14 | 15 | 16 | 17 | 18 | 19 | 20 | 21 | 22 | 23 | 24 | 25 | 26 | 27 | 28 | 29 | 30 | 31 |
| 32 | 33 | 34 | 35 | 36 | 37 | 38 | 39 | 40 | 41 | 42 | 43 | 44 | 45 | 46 | 47 | 48 | 49 | 50 |

FIGURE 1-43 Preview Test Window Expanded

1. **Timed Test**: If your test or survey is timed, the information will appear next to Timed Test in the Test Information window. This will tell you the time limit and whether the test will automatically close when the time expires. Warnings will appear when half the time remains and when 5 minutes, 1 minute, and 30 seconds remain.
2. **Multiple Attempts**: This section will show you the number of attempts and which attempt you are currently working on.
3. **Force Completion**. You can begin the test, save, and resume at any point. If you leave the test, the timer will continue to run. You will have only until the time has expired.
4. The **Question Completion Status** window shows you which questions you have answered and the ones you still need to answer. The window will always remain at the top of the window (Figure 1-44).
   a. View completed questions: The Question Completion Status section displays a saved icon for each question you have answered. You can

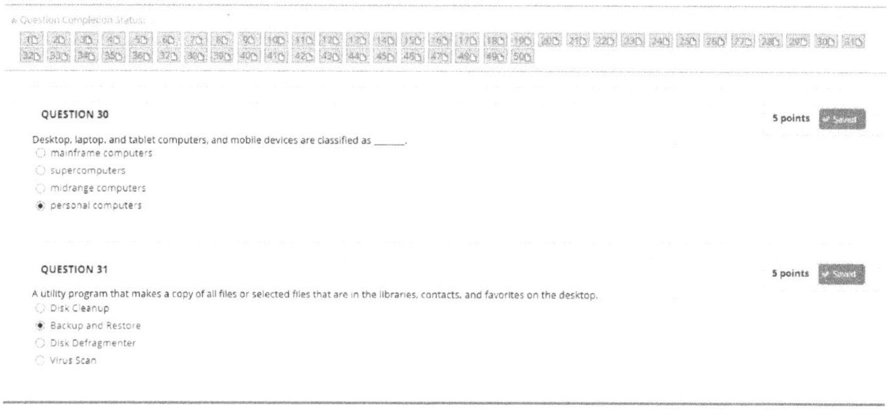

FIGURE 1-44 Question Completion Status

click on a question icon number to jump to that question. Select the arrows next to the status section to collapse or expand it. The window will remain open at the top of the quiz/test/survey as your work. The timer status bar keeps you updated on the remaining time left.

   b. <u>Auto-submit</u>: The test or survey saves and submits automatically when time expires. The Submitted page appears. Automatic submission is the default submission.

3. Continue beyond the time limit: You receive no automatic penalty if you continue beyond the time limit. However, final scoring decisions are made by your instructor. Talk to your instructor if you have questions about this setting. The total time you spend on the test or survey is recorded and available to your instructor when you submit.

   c. If you save and exit, the timer continues to run. For example, you start on Monday, save and exit, and then complete the test on Wednesday. The timer will show that you took 48 hours to complete.

Once you submitted your quiz/test/survey, the window shown in Figure 1-45 will appear. The window will tell you the student name, test name, course, start

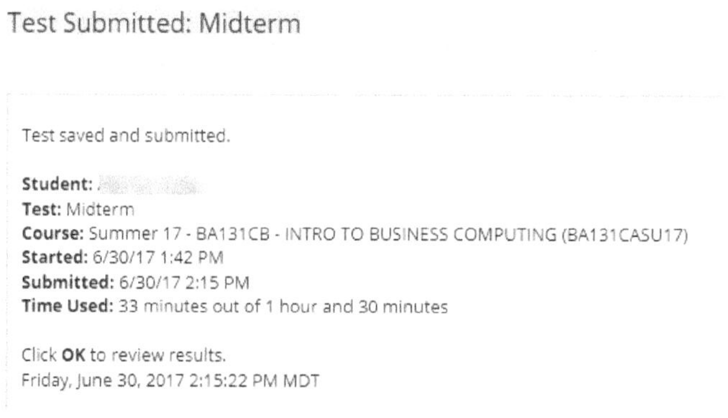

FIGURE 1-45 Test Submitted: Midterm

time, submitted time, elapsed time, and that the test was saved and submitted. In the lower right corner of the window, click *OK* (not shown).

View Your Grade

The Review Test Submission window will pop up (Figure 1-46). You may or may not see your score immediately after you complete the test if all your questions are auto-graded. Your instructor may select a future date to release test scores when all students will have completed the test.

Review Test Submission: Midterm

User	
Course	Summer 17 - BA131CB - INTRO TO BUSINESS COMPUTING
Test	Midterm
Started	7/1/17 12:46 AM
Submitted	7/1/17 12:58 AM
Status	Completed
Attempt Score	215 out of 250 points
Time Elapsed	11 minutes out of 1 hour and 30 minutes
Results Displayed	Submitted Answers

Question 1

Connection devices are the actual connecting or transmission medium that carries the message.

FIGURE 1-46 Review Test Submission: Midterm

After you complete a test, your instructor may select all or some of the following performance results options to show you. For example, your instructor may only show the final score for one test, while for another test the final score, answers submitted, correct answers, and feedback are displayed. Feedback includes one or more of these items:

- Answers submitted
- Correct answers
- Feedback for the questions
- Final score for the test

To access feedback and grade information, select the test name (in this example, "Midterm") in the content area of My Grades (left column). When the **View Attempts** page opens, click the **Grade** link in the Calculated Grade column to access the test, your answers, and any instructor feedback.

Most exams are auto-graded; however, essay, file response, and short-answer questions are not auto-graded. These question types must be manually graded by your instructor. These question types grades will appear once your instructor finishes grading them and releases your grade to you.

Blackboard Help

Blackboard help is normally accessible through your course menu options (Figure 1-47). Once you click on the **Blackboard Help** link, you will be directed to a website for students. Each item you see is a hyperlink to take you to a topic. You have Common Issues and Popular Pages (Figure 1-48). You also have other options to make your search easier. If you click on the purple button with the three lines on it in the upper left corner, this will take you to a screen that shows an outlined list of items you can click on (Figure 1-49). When you click on *Learn*, you will see three options for you to choose from: Student, Instructor, or Administrator (Figure 1-50). If you don't see what you are looking for, there is a search box for you to type in your topic.

If there is no link for Blackboard Help in the course menu, you may access it through the following website: https://help.blackboard.com/Learn.

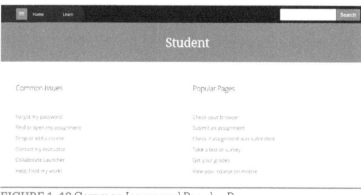

FIGURE 1-48 Common Issues and Popular Pages

FIGURE 1-47 Blackboard Help

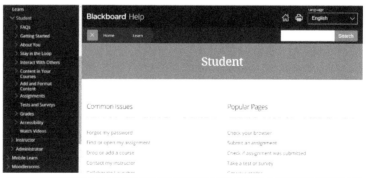

FIGURE 1-49 Student Help with Outline

FIGURE 1-50 Blackboard Learn

Blackboard may also be accessed with your mobile device. Go into Blackboard Help and type in "Mobile Learn" in the search box. If you have further questions, be sure to ask your instructor for assistance.

Course Textbook

Normally, your instructor will make it easy for you to access your textbook information in Blackboard. Many instructors will list textbook information in the syllabus, other instructors will create a course menu link to textbook information, while still other instructors will do both (Figure 1-51). Your textbook information should list information (and a picture!) of the textbook, the ISBN number, price for new and used, where you can purchase it (in the bookstore and online), and if the book is available in an online version (Figure 1-52). Also, you can rent some books online (Figure 1-53). Ask your instructor if you need further information regarding your textbook.

FIGURE 1-51 Course Menu—Course Textbook

FIGURE 1-52 Textbook Purchase Option

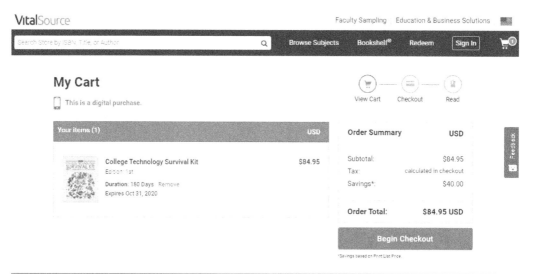

FIGURE 1-53 Textbook Rental Option

CHAPTER TWO

Canvas Learning Management System

Introduction

Welcome to Canvas! Chances are you already have a Canvas account through your institution. Your institution will email your login information to you. If you do not yet have an account, you can create an account when you accept your course invitation.

However, if you are not using Canvas through your institution, you can create your own account. Your instructor will provide you with a join code to link you directly to the course. Canvas email will send you a code that invites you to join the course.

Note: If you need to create an account in Canvas but have not received a join code via Canvas email, please contact your instructor for assistance with logging in.

Accept a Course Invitation

If you have enrolled in or have been invited to a Canvas course, you will receive an email that contains your institution's Canvas URL and your email address to use as your login. To accept the course invitation, click on the **Get Started** button (Figure 2-1).

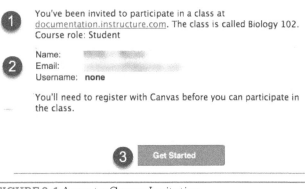

FIGURE 2-1 Accept a Course Invitation

Create a Canvas Account

You will receive a **Welcome Aboard!** Greeting.

   If you do not have a Canvas account, click the **Create My Account** button. If you do have a Canvas Account, then click on the **I Have a Canvas Account** button (Figure 2-2).

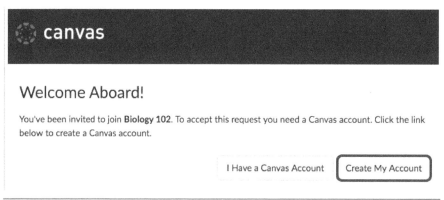

FIGURE 2-2 Welcome Aboard!

I Already Have an Account

If you already have an account, once you click on the **I Have a Canvas Account** button, the following Complete Registration window will open (Figure 2-3):

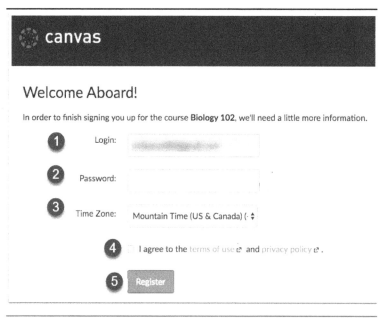

FIGURE 2-3 Canvas Sign-In

1. Click in the Login box and type in your institution email.
2. Click in the Password box and type in your institution password.
3. If necessary, change your time zone.
4. Read the terms of use and privacy policy. If you agree, then click on the check box.
5. Click on the blue **Register** button.

I Need a Canvas Account

If you do not have an account, you can set one up for yourself without an email link.

1. Open a browser and type **canvas.instructure.com** into your browser.

Note: You must have a join code from your instructor or institution to create your account.

2. Click on the **Need a Canvas Account? Click Here. It's Free!** button (Figure 2-4).
3. A Canvas window will open. You will be asked if you are a teacher or a student. Click on the **I'M A STUDENT** button (Figure 2-5).
4. The Student Signup window will appear (Figure 2-6).
   A. Type in the join code provided to you by your instructor.
   B. Type in your full name.
   C. Type in your institution username.
   D. Type in a password.
   E. In the Confirm Password box, type in your password again.
   F. Read the terms of use and privacy policy. If you agree, click in the check box.
   G. Click on the blue **Start Learning** button.

Using Canvas on Your Mobile Device
Canvas Instructure has two native mobile applications for students free for download on both phones and tablets.

FIGURE 2-4 Need a Canvas Account?

FIGURE 2-5 Sign Up Now!

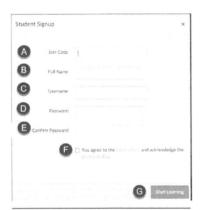

FIGURE 2-6 Student Signup

- **Canvas by Instructure** (iOS 9.0+, Android 4.2+). This app provides access to Canvas while on the go. Depending on your device, not all Canvas features may be available on the app at this time. View *Canvas mobile features* by version and device.
- **Polls for Canvas** (iOS 7.0+, Android 4.0+). If your instructor uses polls in your courses, this app allows you to participate and share your opinion without any extra devices.

Add or Edit My Canvas Profile

Profile

Some institutions may enable a feature in Canvas called **Profile. Profile** allows you to update your ***Profile, Settings, Notifications, Files, ePortfolios***, and any personal links for your account. All users in your courses can view your profile information.

Note: If you do not see the **Profile** tab in your user navigation menu, this feature has not been enabled for your institution.

1. In the Global Navigation menu, click on the **Account** link (1), then click on the **Profile** link (2) (Figure 2-7).
2. Click the ***Profile*** button. You may add the following items:

   - Enter your name.
   - Enter your title.
   - Enter your contact.
   - Enter your biography.
   - Enter links.
   - Profile picture: Click the profile picture icon.

Note: If you want to cancel creating or editing your profile, just click the ***Cancel Editing*** button to the right. Unless otherwise asked to do so, you are not required to complete every field in the Profile box. However, your institution may have some required fields.

Note: If you do not see a placeholder picture with a small pencil in the lower right-hand corner, then your institution has not enabled this feature.

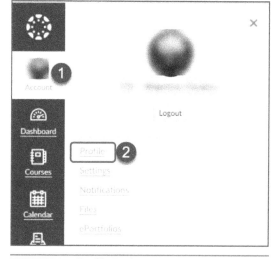

FIGURE 2-7 Profile Link

Settings

The Settings option enables you to connect to web services outside of Canvas.

In the Global Navigation menu, click the Account link (1), and then click the Settings link (2) (Figure 2-8).

If you have previously connected to any web services, click the checkbox underneath the web service to indicate how you wish to be contacted via that service. To add additional services, click the Manage Registered Services link. Click on one of the following services to set up: Google Drive, Skype, LinkedIn, Twitter, or Delicious.

FIGURE 2-8 Settings Link

Note: As created in your user profile, email addresses do not appear as a contact method and are only used for Canvas notifications. Canvas users should contact each other via **Conversations**.

Notifications

Canvas includes a set of default notification preferences you can receive for your courses. Canvas allows you to change the default settings by setting your own notification preferences. These preferences only apply to you.

In the Global Navigation menu, click the Account link (1), and then click the Notifications link (2) (Figure 2-9).

Notifications are sent as one of four delivery types. If you change a setting, the change is made to your account immediately.

1. Notify me right away
2. Daily summary
3. Weekly summary
4. Don't send

FIGURE 2-9 Notifications Link

Notification Preferences

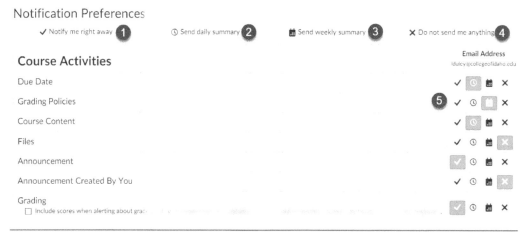

FIGURE 2-10 Notification Preferences

Note: Notification settings apply to all of your courses; you cannot change settings for individual courses.

Note: Canvas sets each notification to a default preference. To change a notification for a contact method, locate the notification and click the icon for your preferred delivery type.

- To receive a notification right away, click the check mark icon (Figure 2-10). These notifications may be delayed by up to one hour in case an instructor makes additional changes.
- To receive a daily notification, click the **Clock** icon.
- To receive a weekly notification, click the **Calendar** icon. You will see the date and time of your weekly notifications posted at the bottom of the notifications page.
- If you do not want to receive a notification, click the **Remove** icon.

Note: Each set notification preference will automatically apply to all of your courses. They cannot be set individually.

Files

In the Global Navigation menu, click the Account link (1), and then click the File link (2) (Figure 2-11).

FIGURE 2-11 File Link

Your files may include personal files, attachments, and photos. Here is a list of the items in the Files window (Figure 2-12):

FIGURE 2-12 Files Window

1. Search for files box.
2. The left panel (2) shows all folders for quick navigation. Some folders may be housed within other folders. To expand all folders, click the arrows next to the folder name. Once you click on the name of a folder, all folder contents will display in the right panel (3, 4, 5, 6, and 7). You can also click folder names in the right panel to view the contents of folders.
3. File Name.
4. Date file was created.
5. Date file was modified.
6. Name of the person who modified the file (if another user modified it, for example).
7. Size of the file.
8. You can add another folder.
9. You can upload another file to your folder.
10. You can also view the published status for your user files.

Note: Files are sorted alphabetically. To sort files, click the name of any column heading.

ePortfolios

ePortfolios are a place where you can display and discuss the significant submissions and experiences that are happening during your learning process. Consider this your brag book. You can use an ePortfolio to do the following (Figure 2-13):

1. Display your favorite papers for more than just your instructor to see.
2. Talk about all the thought and work that went into your class submissions.

FIGURE 2-13 ePortfolios Link

3. Gather an overview of your educational experience as a whole.
4. Share your work with friends, future employers, etc.
5. Build your portfolio to prepare for job interviews.

ePortfolios can be public for everyone to see or private, so only those you allow can view them, and you can change that setting at any time (Figure 2-14).

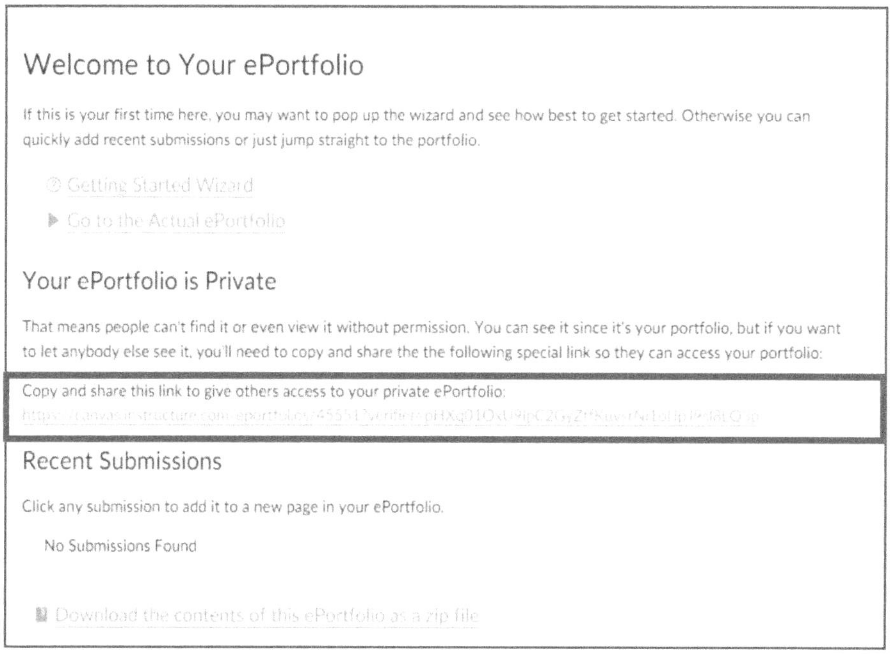

Welcome to Your ePortfolio

If this is your first time here, you may want to pop up the wizard and see how best to get started. Otherwise you can quickly add recent submissions or just jump straight to the portfolio.

⊙ Getting Started Wizard
▶ Go to the Actual ePortfolio

Your ePortfolio is Private

That means people can't find it or even view it without permission. You can see it since it's your portfolio, but if you want to let anybody else see it, you'll need to copy and share the the following special link so they can access your portfolio:

Copy and share this link to give others access to your private ePortfolio:
https://canvas.instructure.com/eportfolios/455/v1?verifier=pHXg0HOxU9jC2Gjj2ttRoverhdsiUp1eJ4tQjp

Recent Submissions

Click any submission to add it to a new page in your ePortfolio.

No Submissions Found

⬇ Download the contents of this ePortfolio as a zip file

FIGURE 2-14 ePortfolio Window

6. Click on **Account** (1) and then click on **ePortfolio** (2).
7. Click on the **Create an ePortfolio** button to begin.
8. The next screen will ask you for an ePortfolio name.

You may click on the optional check box **Make It Public**.

- Then you will see two buttons below: **Make ePortfolio** or **Cancel**.
- The easiest way to set up your ePortfolio is to click on the **Getting Started Wizard**.

The Getting Started Wizard will pop up to show you the basics of your ePortfolio. You can view the *Introduction, Portfolio Sections, Section Pages, Adding Submissions, ePortfolio Settings*, and *Let's Do It*. To close the Getting Started Wizard, click the *Close* icon.

Note: If this is your first time using **ePortfolio**, the Wizard is the easiest way for you to size up what you may want to put in there. In addition, after seeing the examples in the Wizard, you will have a better idea of deciding how you may want to change settings, add submissions, and arrange section pages. It is recommended that you bring some Brag items with you before you begin. Plan to spend a little time with it. If you do it well, it will definitely pay off for you.

Course Home Page

The **Course Home Page** is designed to help you navigate your course and manage your coursework.

Open Course
In the Global Navigation menu, click the **Courses** link, then click the name of the course.

View Course Home Page
The Course Home Page includes (Figure 2-15):

1. Course Navigation
2. Content Area
3. The Sidebar

View Course Navigation
Course Navigation includes links that help you to get to specific locations in the course. Not all links will show up in all courses. Each instructor can hide certain links from your view if the instructor does not plan to use them in your

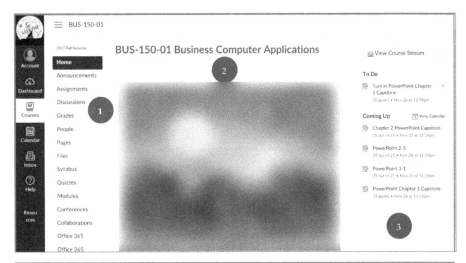

FIGURE 2-15 Course Home Page

course. The active link of the page you are viewing is highlighted in blue. This highlight is designed to help you quickly identify the feature area in Canvas.

You may also see course indicators that show updates to your course grades when your instructor grades your assignments.

View Content Area

You will find all the **Home Page** content and all Canvas content displayed in the content area.

The **Home Page** content can be announcements, the course syllabus, discussions, quizzes, etc. The Course Activity Stream is a list of all recent activity in your course. Your instructor may have also set it up that announcements will show at the top of the page.

View Sidebar

The sidebar shows content for the specific course. It includes additional options.

If your **Course Home Page** displays a page other than the Course Activity Stream, you can view the **Course Activity Stream** by clicking the sidebar **View Course Stream** button. If your instructor set the **Course Activity Stream** as the **Home Page**, this button will not appear.

If your instructor has added you to a group in your course, the **Course Group** section will display links to your course groups.

The **Sidebar** will always show the following (Figure 2-16):

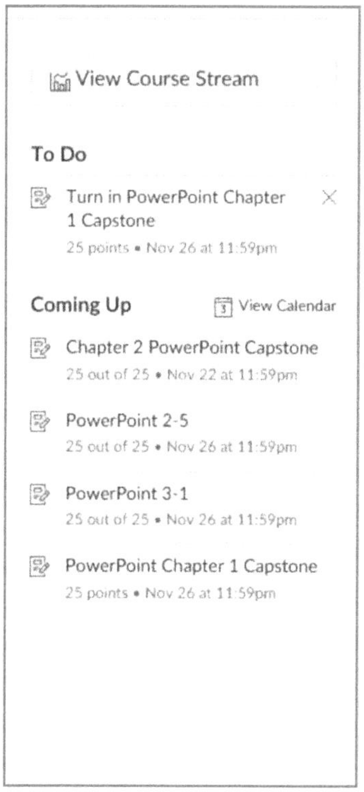

1. **To Do** section. This section shows all assignments with a due date within the next seven days This includes ungraded quizzes and assignments that do not require you to submit them (Figure 2-17).

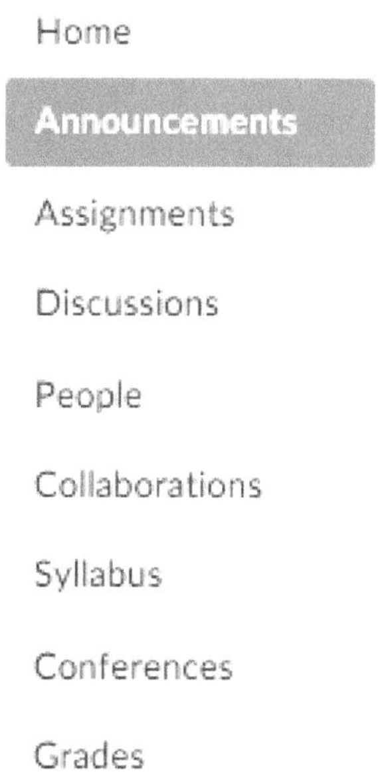

Each item in the To Do list displays the following:

- Assignment name
- Number of points
- Assignment due date

FIGURE 2-16 Sidebar

FIGURE 2-17 Announcements Link

Note: Once the due date has passed, items remain in this section for four weeks. However, ungraded assignments, which do not require an online submission, only display until the due date.

The **Sidebar** can also include a variety of other optional sections depending on how your instructor sets up the **Course Home Page**. Additional sidebar options may include:

1. Coming Up
2. The Assignment lists
3. Calendar and Assignment Groups
4. Recent Feedback

Note: Canvas limits the number of items in the **To Do** section to one hundred. If you have one hundred items and you want to view any new items, you must remove items first. To remove a **To Do** item, click on the ***Remove*** icon (the "X").

Announcements

Open Announcements
In the Course Navigation panel, click the ***Announcements*** link (Figure 2-17).

View Announcements
In Announcements, you can view all the announcements in your course. The announcements are listed with the newest appearing at the top and older announcements listed on the bottom. An announcement contains the following items (Figure 2-18):

1. Announcement name. Click on the announcement name to view your announcement.
2. Name of person who posted the announcement.

FIGURE 2-18 Announcement Window

3. If a discussion has an enabled podcast feed.
4. Search or filter announcements.
5. Your reply to the announcement.
6. Unread/Read announcement.
7. Collapse Replies.
8. Expand Replies.
9. Mark All as Read.

Filter Announcements

To search for an announcement, you have three different options you can use: You can type in an announcement title, a username, or a keyword in the Search title box (Figure 2-19).

FIGURE 2-19 Filter Announcement

Reply to an Announcement

Canvas gives you the option to reply to an announcement if you have a question or comment. This method allows you to reply directly to that announcement. You can reply in both course and group announcements. The steps are the same.

Once you open the announcement, you will see the Reply section under the search area (Figure 2-20).

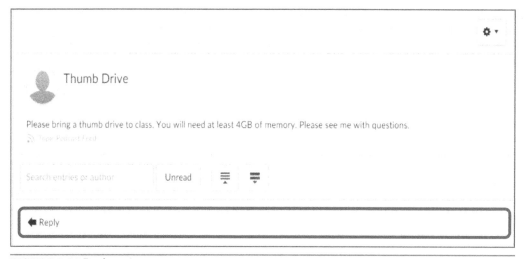

FIGURE 2-20 Reply to Announcement

<u>Note</u>: If the Reply field is not available, then the announcement has been closed for comments and questions and you cannot post a reply.

When you click in the **Reply** box, a Rich Text Box will appear for you to submit your comment or question (1). You have numerous formatting options along with the option to attach a file (lower left of window). Once you complete your response, click on the **Post Reply** button (2) (Figure 2-21).

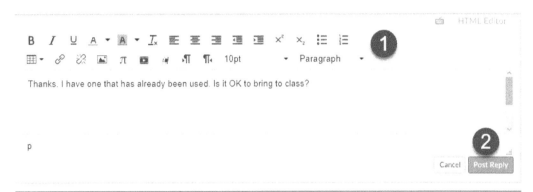

FIGURE 2-21 Reply Submission Window

When you click on the **Post Reply** button, your reply will appear below the reply portion of the announcement (Figure 2-22).

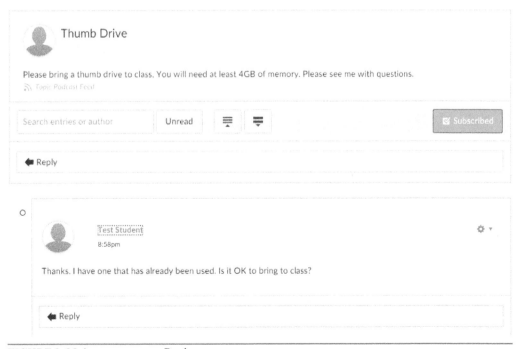

FIGURE 2-22 Announcement Reply

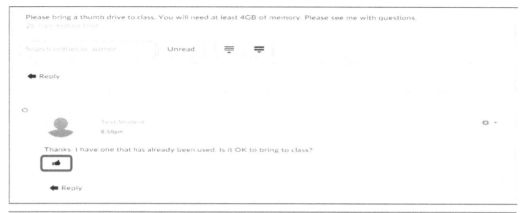

Please bring a thumb drive to class. You will need at least 4GB of memory. Please see me with questions.

Search entries or author   Unread

← Reply

○   Test Student
        8:58pm

Thanks. I have one that has already been used. Is it OK to bring to class?

👍

← Reply

FIGURE 2-23 Like Icon

How to "Like" a Reply

To show that you liked a reply, do the following (Figure 2-23):

1. Click the Announcement name.
2. Locate the reply.
3. Click the **Like** button.

Note: The Like icon by default is gray in color. When you click on the **Like** icon to indicate that you liked the reply, the icon will turn blue. Canvas will also display the total number of likes for a reply.

Note: The Like icon will only work if your instructor allows **Like** in the course.

Assignments

Viewing Assignments

You can view all your course assignments on the **Assignments** page.

1. In the course navigation panel, click on the **Assignments** link (Figure 2-24).
2. Assignments are grouped by overdue assignments, upcoming assignments, undated assignments, and past assignments.
    a. *Overdue Assignments*: Assignments and discussions that are late, are still available, and have not been submitted or graded.
    b. *Upcoming Assignments*: Assignments, discussions, tests, and quizzes that have a due date.

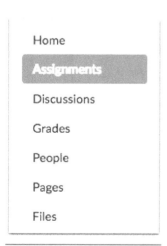

Home

Assignments

Discussions

Grades

People

Pages

Files

FIGURE 2-24 Assignments Link

c. *Undated Assignments*: Assignments, discussions, and quizzes that do not have a due date.

d. *Past Assignments*: Assignments, discussions, and quizzes that are past the due date and are either not available, have been submitted, or have received a grade. Quizzes that are past the due date.

Note: Each assignment has its own icon (Figure 2-25):

- *Assignment*: Page and Student
- *Discussion*: Comment Bubble
- *Quizzes*: Lightning bolt in a circle

The first dates you may see are called availability dates. Sometimes your instructor only wants you to submit an assignment during a specified date range, so the available dates are the range of time that the assignment is accessible to you.

1. If the assignment does not have a date listed, the assignment is open; you can submit the assignment at any time during your course.
2. If the assignment says **Available until** (date), you can submit the assignment until the specified date.
3. If the assignment says **Not Available Until** (date), the assignment is locked until the specified date.
4. If the assignment says **Closed**, the assignment cannot accept submissions.

Note: If a date does not include a time, the listed date defaults to 12 a.m. Therefore, the last day the assignment is available is the full day before the listed date. For instance, if an assignment is available until March 10, you can access the assignment until March 9 at 11:59 p.m.

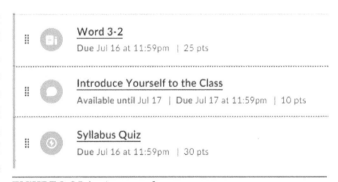

FIGURE 2-25 Assignment Icons

View an Assignment Rubric

Your instructor may include a rubric as part of your assignment. The rubric is a set of criteria that your instructor will use to grade your assignment. Before submitting your assignment, you can use the rubric to evaluate your own work and make sure your assignment fulfills your instructor's requirements.

Note: Not all assignments may include a rubric.

1. Open the **Assignments** links in Course Navigation (Figure 2-26).
2. Click on the name of the chosen assignment. This will open the assignment (Figure 2-27).
3. Scroll down below the assignment instructions to see the Rubric.

The rubric includes criteria (1), ratings (2), and full point values (3). A rubric criterion may include up to five different ratings and individual point values (Figure 2-28).

If a criterion is longer with more details, click the **View Longer Description** link (blue hyperlink).

The rubric may also include an outcome associated with the course. Outcomes are identified by a small flag and are used to assess learning mastery in a course. The outcome also shows the threshold for the outcome, or

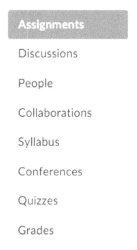

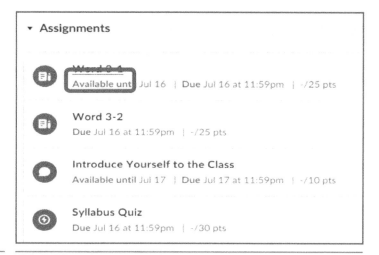

FIGURE 2-26 Assignments Link

FIGURE 2-27 Assignments List

Word 3-1 Rubric	Criteria	Ratings		Pts
Line Spacing		Full Marks 5.0 pts	No Marks 0.0 pts	5.0 pts
Spelling and Grammer		Full Marks 5.0 pts	No Marks 0.0 pts	5.0 pts
Document centered on page		Full Marks 5.0 pts	No Marks 0.0 pts	5.0 pts
Import Completed		Full Marks 10.0 pts	No Marks 0.0 pts	10.0 pts
				Total Points: 25.0

FIGURE 2-28 Ungraded Rubric

the number of points you must achieve to meet expectations. Your instructor may allow you to view outcome results in your course grades.

Submit an Online Assignment

You can submit online assignments in Canvas using several submission type options. There are four submission types: upload a file, submit a text entry, enter a website URL, or submit media.

Your instructors can choose what kind of online submissions they want you to use. If your instructor permits, you may also have the option to resubmit assignments.

Any attachments added as part of a graded assignment submission are also copied to your user files but are not counted against your user quota. However, once the file has been uploaded as a submission, you cannot delete the file. Files are stored in the Submissions folder.

Before submitting your assignment, you may want to review all assignment information, including any assignment rubric.

Cloud Assignment Submissions

You can submit assignments from Google Drive, Dropbox, or another third-party service via your desktop computer in one of two ways:

1. Download the file to your computer and submit as a File Upload.
2. Share the file, copy the file URL, and submit as a Website URL.

Mobile Submissions

You can also submit assignments using your Android or iOS device.

To Submit a File Upload Assignment

1. Click on the **Assignments** link in the Course Navigation panel.
2. Click on the assignment name.
3. Review the assignment instructions and assignment rubric, if applicable.
4. Click on the **Submit Assignment** button (Figure 2-29).

Note: If you cannot see the **Submit Assignment** button, your instructor may not want you to submit your assignment online or the availability date has passed. View the description of the assignment for instructions, or contact your instructor for assistance.

5. When the next window opens, click on the **File Upload** tab. In the Search/ Browse area (1), you can either type in the document path, or you can click on the **Browse** button to search for the file you want to attach (Figure 2-30).

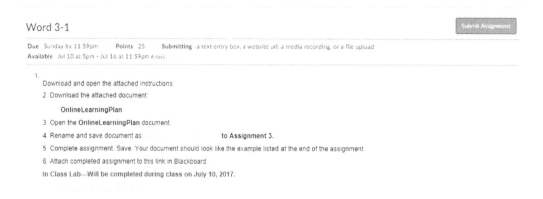

FIGURE 2-29 Submit Assignment Button

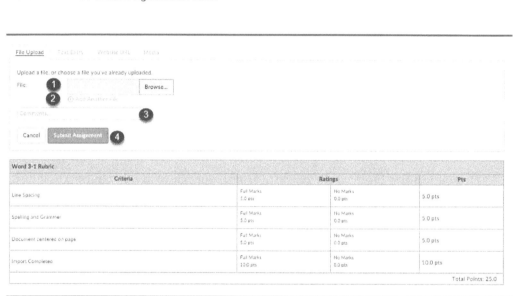

FIGURE 2-30 File Upload Window

6. You can easily add another file (2) if required by your instructor. Just click on the blue hyperlink below the gray *File Name* and *Browse* button area.
7. You can also add optional comments below the *Add Another File* blue hyperlink (3).
8. Click on the *Submit Assignment* blue button, or click *Cancel* if you change your mind (4).

Once you click the *Submit Assignment* button, a new window opens (Figure 2-31). You will see the four following items:
   a. Indicates that you submitted a *file upload*.
   b. The blue Re-submit Assignment button.

FIGURE 2-31 File Upload Submission Window

c. Shows your submission was turned in. Submission details include the date and time of submission and the name of the download.

d. Student comments regarding the assignment.

Your instructor will decide what kinds of submissions are appropriate for each assignment.

Note: Not all file types may be available for your assignment, depending on the assignment submission type set by your instructor.

Submit a Text Entry

1. Click on the **Assignments** link in the Course Navigation panel.
2. Click on the assignment name.
3. Review the assignment instructions and assignment rubric, if applicable.
4. Click on the **Submit Assignment** button (Figure 2-32).

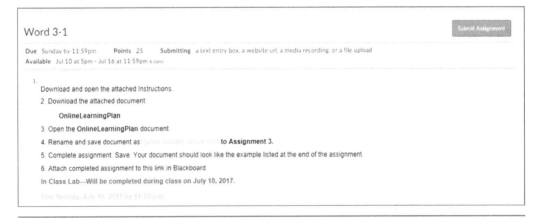

FIGURE 2-32 Submission Window

Note: If you cannot see the **Submit Assignment** button, your instructor may not want you to submit your assignment online, or the availability date has passed. View the description of the assignment for instructions, or contact your instructor for assistance.

1. When the next window opens, click on the **Text Entry** tab.
2. When the Text Entry window appears, you have the option to copy and paste or type your submission in the box. You have many options to use the Rich Text Editor (RTE) which enables you to format your font, paragraphs, numbered and bulleted lists, embed images, add mathematical equations, etc.
3. You can also add optional comments below the Submission window.
4. Click on the **Submit Assignment** blue button, or click *Cancel* if you change your mind (Figure 2-33).

Note: If your assignment has a rubric, it will also appear in the Text Entry window.

5. After you clicked the **Submit Assignment** button, a new window opens. You will see the four following items (Figure 2-34):

   1. This section indicates that you submitted a text entry box, a website URL, a media recording, or a file upload.
   2. The blue button is the **Re-submit Assignment** button.
   3. The information below Submission shows your submission was turned in. Submission details include the date and time of submission, and the name of the download.
   4. Comments show student comments regarding the assignment.

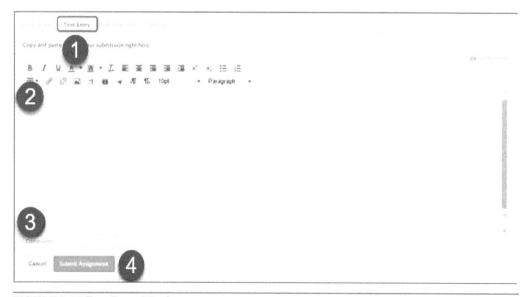

FIGURE 2-33 Text Entry Window

FIGURE 2-34 Text Entry Submission Window

Your instructor will decide what kinds of submissions are appropriate for each assignment.

Note: Not all file types may be available for your assignment, depending on the assignment submission type set by your instructor.

Submit Website URL

1. Click on the **Assignments** link in the Course Navigation panel.
2. Click on the assignment name.
3. Review the assignment instructions and assignment rubric, if applicable.
4. Click on the **Submit Assignment** button (Figure 2-35).

Note: If you cannot see the **Submit Assignment** button, your instructor may not want you to submit your assignment online, or the availability date has passed. View the description of the assignment for instructions, or contact your instructor for assistance.

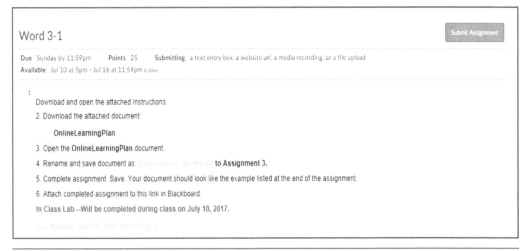

FIGURE 2-35 Submission Window

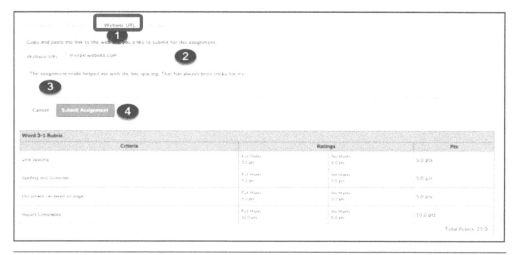

FIGURE 2-36 Website URL Tab

1. When the next window opens, select the **Website URL** tab (Figure 2-36).
2. Type or copy and paste the URL into the Website URL field.
3. You can also add optional comments below the Website URL box.
4. Click on the **_Submit Assignment_** blue button, or click _Cancel_ if you change your mind.

Note: If your assignment has a rubric, it will also appear in the File Upload window.

After you clicked the **_Submit Assignment_** button, a new window opens (Figure 2-37). You will see the four following items:

1. This section indicates that you submitted a text entry box, a website URL, a media recording, or a file upload.
2. This is the blue Re-submit Assignment button.
3. This information indicates that your submission was turned in. Submission details include the date and time of submission, and the name of the download.
4. The **Comments** section shows student comments regarding the assignment.

FIGURE 2-37 Web URL Submission Window

Your instructor will decide what kinds of submissions are appropriate for each assignment.

Note: Not all file types may be available for your assignment, depending on the assignment submission type set by your instructor.

Submit Media Recording

1. Click on the **Assignments** link in the Course Navigation panel.
2. Click on the assignment name.
3. Review the assignment instructions and assignment rubric, if applicable.
4. Click on the **Submit Assignment** button (Figure 2-38).

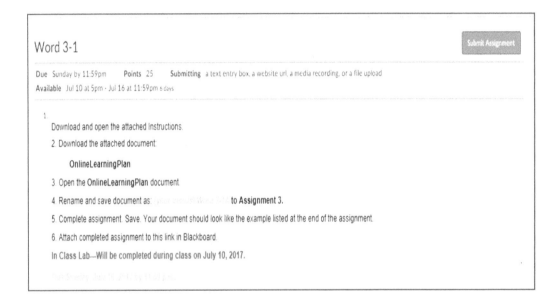

Word 3-1   Submit Assignment

Due Sunday by 11:59pm   Points 25   Submitting a text entry box, a website url, a media recording, or a file upload
Available Jul 10 at 5pm - Jul 16 at 11:59pm 6 days

1.
   Download and open the attached Instructions.
   2. Download the attached document:

       OnlineLearningPlan

   3. Open the OnlineLearningPlan document.

   4. Rename and save document as: your completed Word file to Assignment 3.

   5. Complete assignment. Save. Your document should look like the example listed at the end of the assignment.

   6. Attach completed assignment to this link in Blackboard.

   In Class Lab---Will be completed during class on July 10, 2017.

FIGURE 2-38 Submission Window

Note: If you cannot see the **Submit Assignment** button, your instructor may not want you to submit your assignment online, or the availability date has passed. View the description of the assignment for instructions, or contact your instructor for assistance.

1. Select the **Media** tab (Figure 2-39).
2. Select the choice to **Record** or **Upload Media** in the **Record/Upload Media** field.
3. You can also add optional comments below the **Record/Upload Media** box.
4. Click on the **Submit Assignment** blue button, or click *Cancel* if you change your mind.

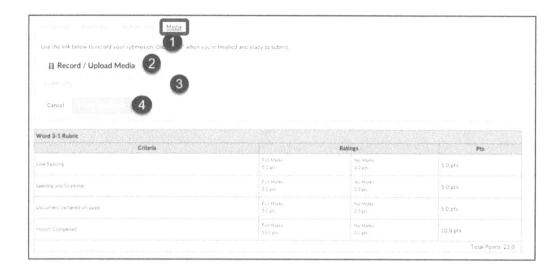

FIGURE 2-39 Media Tab

Note: If your assignment has a rubric, it will also appear in the File Upload window. After you clicked the **Submit Assignment** button, a new window opens (Figure 2-40). You will see the four following items:

1. This section indicates that you submitted a text entry box, a website URL, a media recording, or a file upload.
2. This is the blue Re-submit Assignment button.
3. This information indicates that your submission was turned in. Submission details include the date and time of submission, and the name of the download.
4. The **Comments** section shows student comments regarding the assignment.

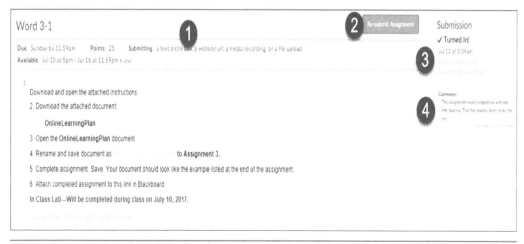

FIGURE 2-40 Media Submission Window

Your instructor will decide what kinds of submissions are appropriate for each assignment.

Note: Not all file types may be available for your assignment, depending on the assignment submission type set by your instructor.

View Submission

After you have submitted your work, you will see information in the Sidebar about your submission. For file uploads, the sidebar provides a link to your submission to download if necessary.

If you choose, you may resubmit another version of your assignment using the **Re-submit Assignment** button. You will only be able to view the details of your most recent submission in the Sidebar, but your instructor will be able to see all of your submissions.

Once the instructor has graded your submission, the **Grades** link in Course Navigation displays a grading indicator. You can also see details about your assignment and links to additional feedback on your **Grades** page.

Discussions

In Course Navigation, click the **Discussions** link (Figure 2-41).

View Discussions

Discussions are organized into three main areas (Figure 2-42):

1. **Pinned Discussions.** These are discussions that your instructor wants you to pay specific attention to and will appear at the top of the **Discussions** page. *You will only see this section heading if there are discussions within this section as designated by your instructor.*

2. **Discussions.** These are current discussions within the course. Discussions are ordered by most recent activity. You will only see this section heading if there are discussions within this section.

3. **Closed for Comments.** These discussions have been manually closed for comments or the discussion is past the available from/until date. These are discussions that are only available in a read-only state and are ordered by most recent activity. You will always see this section heading even if there are no discussions within this section.

Home

Announcements

Assignments

Discussions

Modules

People

Collaborations

Syllabus

Conferences

Quizzes

Grades

FIGURE 2-41 Discussions Link

FIGURE 2-42 Discussion Window

View Individual Discussion

Each discussion will display the discussion name, the date of the last discussion post, the discussion availability dates, the discussion due date (if applicable), whether or not you are subscribed to the discussion, whether or not it is a graded discussion, and the number of unread/total posts in the discussion.

Note: The number of unread/total posts will not appear for group discussions (Figure 2-43).

The first dates you may see are called availability dates. Sometimes your instructor only wants you to submit a discussion during a specified date range, so the available dates are the range of time that the discussion is accessible to you.

1. Name of discussion.
2. Date discussion was posted.
3. If the discussion says **Available until** (date), you can reply to the discussion until the specified date. If the discussion does not have a due date listed, the discussion is open; you can reply to the discussion at any time during your course.
4. If the discussion says **Not Available Until** (date), the discussion is locked until the specified date.
5. You must click on the comment bubble to subscribe to this discussion before you may participate.
6. Indicates read/unread replies.

FIGURE 2-43 Individual Discussions

Note: If a date does not include a time, the listed date defaults to 12 a.m. Therefore, the last day for the discussion is the full day before the listed date. For instance, if a discussion is Available until May 19, you can access the discussion until May 18 at 11:59 p.m.

However, **due dates only apply to graded discussions**. Any replies to discussions after the due date are marked as late; some instructors may deduct points for late replies. You can still reply to late discussions before the **Available Until** date.

Please be aware that the **Due Date** may be *before or on* the **Available Date**. This is **not** common.

Please keep this in mind: **Due Dates** also include a time. If your instructor does not set a specific time, the graded discussion defaults to 11:59 p.m.; however, Canvas does not account for seconds in the due date, so, for instance, a due time of 11:59 p.m. means the graded discussion is marked late at 11:59:01 p.m.

Filter Discussions

There are five ways to filter Discussions (Figure 2-44):

FIGURE 2-44 Filter Discussions

1. Search for a discussion by typing a discussion title, a user name, or a key-word in the **Search title, body, or author** field.
2. View unread discussions by clicking the ***Unread*** button.
3. View your graded discussions by clicking the ***Assignments*** button.
4. Start a new discussion by clicking the ***Add Discussion*** button.
   Note: Some instructors may disable this option.
5. Change the discussions settings to manually mark posts as read by clicking the *Settings* icon (Figure 2-45).

Open Discussion
Click the name of the discussion to view the details.

View Open Discussion
When a discussion is available for participation, you can view the Reply field beneath the discussion topic. To reply to the discussion, click the *Reply* button (Figure 2-46).

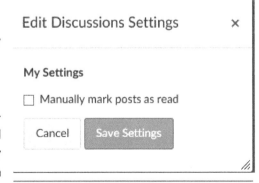

FIGURE 2-45 Settings Icon

If you encounter problems with this assignment, please let me know and I would be very happy to assist.

Search entries or author   Unread

◀ Reply

FIGURE 2-46 View Open Discussion

The discussion also shows the name of the person who created the discussion and the discussion topic.

View a Graded Discussion

If your discussion is a graded discussion, you can view the discussion the same way as regular discussions with additional information:

1. **Graded Discussion** shows points and due date for the graded discussion, if any. Not all graded discussions may have a due date.
2. **Rubric** reflects any grading criteria that your instructor has provided for the graded discussion. A graded discussion may or may not include a rubric. Before you submit your reply, be sure to review the discussion rubric.

If you missed the due date, you may be able to submit a reply to the discussion before the last day of the course. If the graded discussion does not have a due date, you can submit a reply any time before the last day of the course. Ask your instructor if you have questions about the due date.

View Discussion with Required Replies

You may be required to make a reply before you can see the other replies in the discussion. Once you make a reply, any other replies will be visible to you (Figure 2-47).

Search entries or author   Unread

◀ Reply

Replies are only visible to those who have posted at least one reply.

FIGURE 2-47 View Discussion Replies

View Closed Discussion

Your instructor may close any graded or nongraded discussions at any time. Your instructor can manually close the discussion or set the availability until a specific date. Normally, your instructor may make a note in the description topic or syllabus if a discussion is only to be available for a specific period of time.

Once a discussion has been closed for comments, you can still view the details of the discussion topic and any replies, however, you can no longer reply to the discussion.

Calendar

The **Calendar** is a one-stop place to view everything you have to do for all your courses. Canvas provides options for you to view calendar events by day, week, month, or agenda list. The calendar also includes access to the **Scheduler**, which is an optional scheduling tool in Canvas.

Open Calendar

In Global Navigation, click the ***Calendar*** link (Figure 2-48).

View Calendar

The Calendar displays everything you are enrolled in for the reason that the Calendar spans across all of your courses.

FIGURE 2-48
Calendar Link

1. The calendar appears in *Month* view by default (Figure 2-49).
2. In the Navigation bar, you can choose to view the calendar by *Week, Month*, or *Agenda* view.
3. The sidebar shows a quick view calendar for the current month, your list of courses and groups, and undated items for your courses and groups. For the **Calendar Feed,** Canvas will provide you with a web address link to copy and paste into any calendar app that takes iCal feeds (Google Calendar, iCal, Outlook, etc.).

Add Calendar Items

Click on the "**+**" sign to add events to the calendar. Additionally, you can add personal events any time in the navigation bar by clicking the ***Add (+)*** button (Figure 2-50).

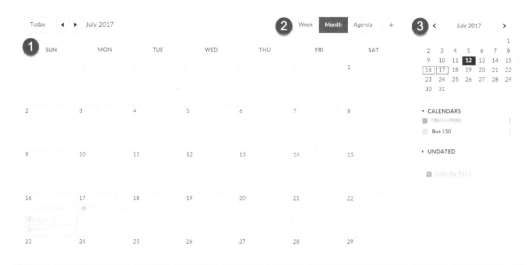

FIGURE 2-49 Calendar Default View

When you click on the **Add** button, the Edit Event window will appear (Figure 2-51). This is where you will type in all your information. If you don't need to enter any additional information, click on **Submit**.

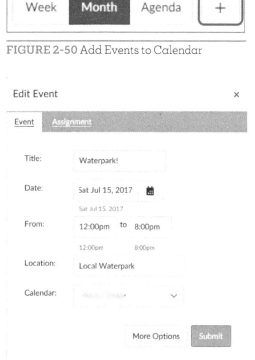

FIGURE 2-50 Add Events to Calendar

However, if you need to add more information, click the **More Options** button; a window will open enabling you to type in a description, directions, meeting agendas, etc., and provide a location and an address at the lower left corner of the window. When you are done entering information, click on **Create Event** (Figure 2-52).

FIGURE 2-51 Edit Event

FIGURE 2-52 New Calendar Event

You can click on any day in the calendar to add an event or click the arrows to navigate to another month, then you can click on a date to add an event to your calendar.

View Calendar List

Canvas identifies each personal, course, and group calendar by a separate color that populates the calendar view. Associated assignments for each course or group will appear within the calendar view (right panel) for each calendar (Figure 2-53).

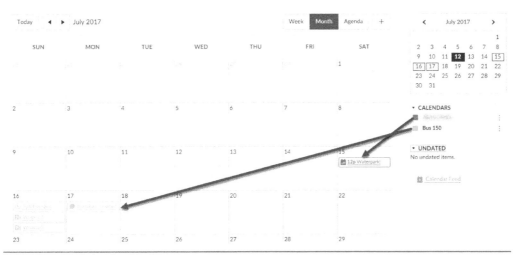

FIGURE 2-53 Calendar List View

By default, the first ten course and group calendars will be selected and appear in the calendar view. Any additional calendars will not be in view. To hide a calendar, click the box next to the name of the calendar.

Note: Canvas will assign an arbitrary color for each calendar unless a custom color is chosen. Each calendar contains fifteen default colors, but you can insert a Hex code to create any color of your choice. Colors set in Dashboard course cards also update in the calendar.

View Undated Events List

Expanding the **_Undated items_** link will show you a list of undated events and assignments. The assignments and events will be separated by icons and by the personal, course, or group calendar color. In this example, the personal notifications are pink and the Bus 150 course notifications are blue. Each course will use a different color for notification, and you also have the option to change the colors if you don't like Canvas's default colors (Figure 2-54).

View Calendar by Month

1. To view events for the current date, click the ***Today*** button (Figure 2-55).
2. In the Month view, click the arrow buttons to move from month to month. View All Assignments and Events.

Assignments are shown with an icon next to the assignment title. The icon reflects the assignment type: Discussion is a conversation bubble, the Assignment icon is a page and a student, the Quizzes icon is a circled lightning bolt, and the Events icon is a calendar page.

Each item on the calendar is color-coded to match the courses or calendars in the sidebar. To view full details for an assignment or event, hover over the item.

Calendar assignments can also be crossed out which is a simple way to keep track of assignments. Assignments are crossed out once the assignment has been submitted. However, assignments that have been awarded a grade but do not contain an actual submission will not be crossed out.

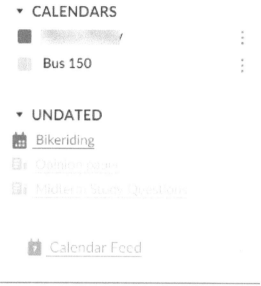

FIGURE 2-54 Undated Events List

FIGURE 2-55 Today and Month View

View All-Day Events

All-day events display the Events icon (calendar page) and do not include a specific event time. The first all-day event is colored blue because it corresponds with Bus 150. The second all-day event is colored pink because it is a personal event (Figure 2-56).

Your calendar view may show entire assignment and event titles as part of the calendar entry. This calendar view is only available in the Month view and can only be enabled by your institution. The wrapped assignment and event title view allows you to view the entire calendar item without having to hover over the title.

FIGURE 2-56 Viewing All Day Events

View Calendar by Week

To view the calendar by week, click the **Week** button. The Week view shows all calendar items by date and time. Note that some assignments may be due at 11:59 p.m., and they will appear at the bottom of the calendar view (Figure 2-57).

All-day events appear at the top of the calendar week (Figure 2-58). These events do not include a specific event time.

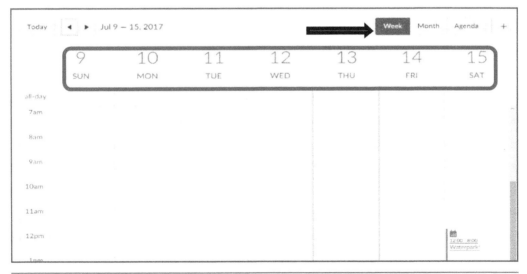

FIGURE 2-57 Calendar View by Week

FIGURE 2-58 All-Day Events

View Calendar Agenda

To view the calendar by agenda, click on the **_Agenda_** button. This will show you the list view of items coming up.

Each personal item will be listed in pink, and all the items for Bus 150 will be listed in blue. The icons will appear to the left of the item under the item's calendar date. (Figure 2-59).

FIGURE 2-59 Calendar Agenda View

Viewing Collaborations

If you've been invited to join a collaboration, you can access the collaboration from Canvas. Collaboration files can also be viewed your online account for the collaboration type (OneDrive or Google Drive, respectively).

Collaborations are web-based tools that you are most likely already familiar with. You can use resources like **_Google Docs links_** to an external site to work collaboratively on tasks like group papers or note-taking. This page gives you an easy place to keep track of those collaborations and also to set them up without having to swap emails.

Google Docs is like Microsoft Word but allows you to work together with others on the same file at the same time without having to constantly email it to everyone. You can choose to receive notifications about collaborations in your Canvas notification preferences. Your instructor will help you set up a Google Drive account for you if you don't already have one.

Note: You and all your collaborators will need a **Google** account in order to participate in any **Google Docs** collaborations.

Note: **Google Drive** allows up to fifty users per collaboration, and all users can view and edit a document at the same time.

Note: Depending on your institution's preference, your **Collaborations** page images may differ from the images in this section. However, functionality of the page remains the same.

Open Collaborations
In Course Navigation, click the **Collaborations** link (Figure 2-60).

View Collaborations
The **Collaborations** page displays all of the collaborations where you have been invited to participate (Figure 2-61). For each collaboration, you can view:

1. The name of the collaboration.
2. The collaboration description.
3. The person who created the collaboration.
4. The date and time the collaboration was created.

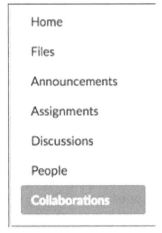

FIGURE 2-60 Collaborations Link

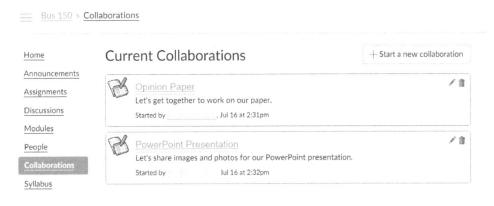

FIGURE 2-61 View Collaborations

Open Collaboration

To open a collaboration, click the name of the collaboration. A blank document resembling a Word document will open in Google Docs.

Note: The collaboration will open in a new tab. You may be asked to sign in to view the file.

Conversations

The Conversations window is split into two panels and displays messages chronologically. You can view and reply to conversations and sort them by inbox type or course. Conversations itself does not have any file size limits; however, attachments added to a conversation are included in the sender's personal files.

Hint: If you right-click on the Inbox link, you can open your Conversation Inbox in a new browser tab to keep it handy while you are doing other tasks in Canvas.

Inbox

In Global Navigation, click the **Inbox** link (Figure 2-62).

If the inbox link includes a numbered indicator, the indicator shows how many unread Conversations messages you have in your Inbox. Once you read the new messages, the indicator will disappear.

FIGURE 2-62
Inbox Link

View Toolbar

The toolbar includes global message options (Figure 2-63).

FIGURE 2-63 Inbox Toolbar

1. Filter conversations by course (Figure 2-64).
2. Inbox drop-down box: allows you to filter by type (Figure 2-65).
3. Compose a new conversation.
4. Reply to a conversation.
5. Reply All to a conversation.

FIGURE 2-64 Filter by Course

6. Archive a conversation.
7. Delete a conversation.
8. Starred drop-down box: Forward, mark as read/unread, and starred conversations.
9. Search for recipients.

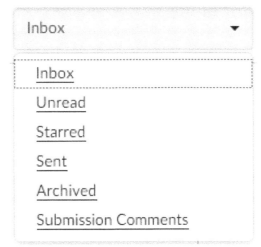

FIGURE 2-65 Inbox Filtering

The **Conversation** Inbox is organized chronologically from newest to oldest with the newest conversations appearing on top and the older conversations at the bottom.

You can manually mark a conversation as read or unread by hovering over the conversation and toggling the circle to the left of the conversation. To "star" a conversation, hover over the conversation and toggle the star to the left of the conversation.

View Conversation Thread
When you select a conversation, all messages in the conversations thread appear in the right Conversations panel.

Manage Conversation Threads
Within each conversation, you can reply, reply-all, forward, or delete the entire conversation thread. You can also hover over an individual message and use the same commands within the individual message.

Select Multiple Conversations
To select multiple messages to archive, delete, mark as read or unread, or star, press the command key (Mac) or the control key (Windows) while clicking each message you want to select.

Note: You can also use the same key command to deselect a message. To select all messages, click the **command + A** keys (Mac) or the **control + A** keys (Windows).

To select a range of messages, click the first message you want to select, hold down the Shift key, and then click the last message you want to select. This action will cause all messages between the first and the last messages to be selected.

The **Discussion Index** page allows you to view all the discussions within a course.

Modules

Your instructor may use **Modules** to organize the course. Modules are designed to control the content and flow of the course. For instance, a module may contain a chapter, or sections of the course, which would include assignments, discussions, pages, quizzes, etc. (Figure 2-66).

Note: If the Modules link is not available, you can still access Module items through other areas of Canvas, such as the **Syllabus** or **Course Home Page**. On the other hand, your instructor may choose to hide all Course Navigation links except for Modules. If other Course Navigation links are not available, your instructor wants you to navigate the course using Modules. Depending on your institution, this may be fairly common.

If your instructor has made Modules available for you, you can click on *Modules* in **Course Navigation**.

Once the Modules window opens, you will be able to view all the modules in your course. In Canvas, modules are organized by order of progression. Each module will contain content items, such as assignments, quizzes, pages, discussions, etc.

To open a specific module, just click on the module name.
Each item within the Module includes three items:

1. Module item name.
2. If the module item is an assignment, then the item includes the due date (if applicable).
3. Number of points the assignment is worth.

Module Icons

Figure 2-67 shows you a list of the icons you may encounter in your Modules.

1. Page
2. Discussion
3. Quiz
4. Assignment
5. Link or External Tool
6. File

Home

Announcements

Assignments

Discussions

Modules

People

Collaborations

Syllabus

Conferences

Quizzes

Grades

FIGURE 2-66 Modules Link

FIGURE 2-67
Module Icons

View Module Requirements

Some modules may include requirements that you must complete. If a module includes requirements, the header shows whether you are supposed to complete all requirements or select one requirement. If you have questions regarding the module requirements, see your instructor for assistance.

Next to the module item, you can view the type of requirement necessary to complete the module item, such as **_View, Mark as done, Contribute, Submit_**, or submit the assignment with a minimum of the score shown. You must complete all required module items before you can progress to the next module. Some modules may require you to complete the module items in order.

Depending on the module item type, requirements include up to five options:

1. **View**: You must view the item to fulfill this requirement.
2. **Mark as done**: You must mark the module item as done before you can progress to the next item.
3. **Contribute**: You must post a reply to the discussion topic or contribute content to a page.
4. **Submit**: You must submit the assignment, graded discussion, or quiz.
5. **Score at least X**: You must submit the assignment with a minimum of the shown score.

View Progression Icons

Module items can also be used to show progression through a module. Modules and/or module items that are not available to you are grayed out.

For any module icon, you can hover over the icon and view the message for the requirement.

Icon meanings may change depending on if your course is using requirements:

- **Orange dash icon**: When next to a module item, the module item is overdue. When next to the module heading, the module requirements have not been met.
- **Green check mark**: The module item has been completed. For requirements, this icon means the module requirement has been met.
- **Blue info icon**: The module item has been submitted but has not yet been graded.
- **Options label**: the module item requires you to choose an assignment path before additional module items can be displayed.
- **White circle**: The module item has not been started.
- **Lock icon**: This module is locked until a future date. This icon means the module cannot be viewed until a prerequisite is completed.
- **Lock message**: This module may contain additional information that cannot be accessed until the name of the assignment in the message is graded.

By using the progression bar at the bottom of the page, you can advance through module items or return to previous modules. To advance to the next module item, click the *Next* button. To return to a previous module item, click the *Previous* button.

If you want to view the name of the next or previous module all you have to do is hover over the *Next* or *Previous* button, respectively. This way you don't have to click on either button.

People

People shows the instructor and all the users enrolled in the course.

In Course Navigation, click the ***People*** link (Figure 2-68).

When the People window opens, you will see the following items (Figure 2-69):

1. You can see the names of all participating and pending enrollment users.
2. Use the *Search people* to find a specific person.
3. Click on the down arrow next to *All Roles* to filter users by role. The filter will also display all users within the selected role (e.g., students).
4. Use the ***Settings*** button to view user groups or registered services in the course.

To search for a specific user, start to type the user's name in the search field (2). Possible results will be listed below (1).

Home

Announcements

Assignments

Discussions

Modules

People

Collaborations

Syllabus

Conferences

Quizzes

Grades

FIGURE 2-68 People Link

FIGURE 2-69 People Window

Filter Users by Role
Click on the ***Roles*** drop-down menu to view the number of users for each role type (Figure 2-70). There are six different options from which to choose. You will likely use the top four the most.

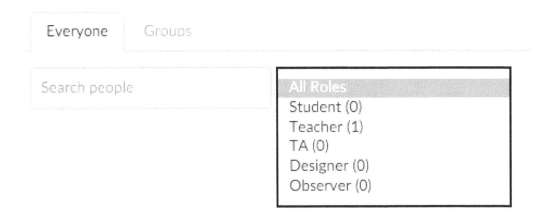

FIGURE 2-70 Filter Users by Role

View User

To learn more about a specific user, just click on the user's name. You can also send this user a message. This will open his or her profile page. If you click your own name, this will provide access to your grades. You may also be able to view your own course analytics.

View User Groups

To view **User Groups**, click the **Group**s tab (Figure 2-71). If your instructor did not create user groups, the list will be empty. This is an easy way to gather information needed to contact group members. Another way is to click on the Settings icon on the right side of the **Everyone** tab (Figure 2-72).

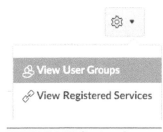

FIGURE 2-71 View User Groups

FIGURE 2-72 Settings Icon

View Registered Services

If other members choose, they can let you see which outside services they've linked to their Canvas account (Figure 2-73). This can make it easier to coordinate group projects and also link up outside of class. If a person has registered a social media account in Canvas, you can see that service listed and communicate with that person through any social media site he or she has registered.

Registered Services

If other members choose, they can let you see which outside services they've linked to their Canvas account. This can make it easier to coordinate group projects and also link up outside of class.

You haven't linked your user profile to any external services. You can link your Canvas account to services like Twitter.

FIGURE 2-73 Registered Services

If you haven't yet registered with web services, you will see the message above. Canvas currently offers the following web services (Figure 2-74):

- Google Drive
- Skype
- LinkedIn
- Twitter
- Delicious

Other Services

Click any service below to register:

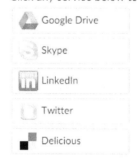

FIGURE 2-74 Web Services

Pages

What are Pages?

Pages are designed to store additional course materials for you to read or required reading outside of assignments, quizzes, etc. Many times, page material may be web articles or links to websites, for example.

To view **Pages**, click the ***Pages*** link in Course Navigation (Figure 2-75).

- Pages store supplemental educational resources that contribute to educational content but may or may not belong in an assignment.
- Pages may include text, video, and links to files and other course or group content.
- Pages may also be linked to other pages.
- Pages may also be used as an online collaboration tool for course or group wikis where only specific users can have access. Canvas keeps the entire history of the page to account for changes over time.

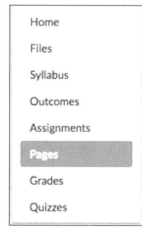

FIGURE 2-75 Pages Link

You can view **Pages** in your course through the **Pages Index** page or through **Modules**.

Note: If you cannot view the Pages Course Navigation link, your instructor has hidden the link in your course.

View All Pages

To view the Pages index, click the ***View All Pages*** button (Figure 2-76). All pages shown (Figure 2-77).

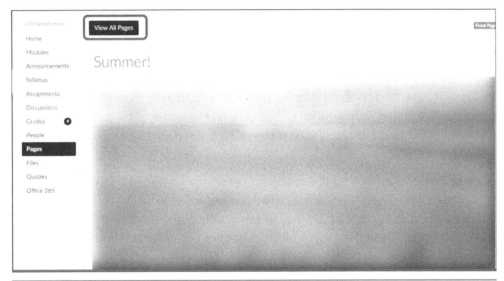

FIGURE 2-76 View All Pages

PAGE TITLE ▲	CREATION DATE	LAST EDIT
5 Devices that make your Computer capable of so much more...	Dec 25, 2017	Dec 25, 2017
8 Critical things to do immediately with a new PC	Dec 25, 2017	Dec 25, 2017
Basic Computer Concepts PowerPoint	Dec 25, 2017	Dec 25, 2017
Budget Laptops--7 ways to avoid buying a piece of junk	Dec 25, 2017	Dec 25, 2017
Conversion Table	Dec 25, 2017	Dec 25, 2017
Facebook is following You....	Dec 25, 2017	Dec 25, 2017
Getting Started with Internet Explorer	Dec 25, 2017	Dec 25, 2017
Happy Easter!	Mar 28, 2018	Mar 28, 2018 by Lana
How to delete your data from your old devices	Dec 25, 2017	Dec 25, 2017
How to launch windows without a password	Dec 25, 2017	Dec 25, 2017
How to securely erase hard drives	Dec 25, 2017	Dec 25, 2017
How to Stop Facebook from Tracking You	Dec 25, 2017	Dec 25, 2017
Internet Reading	Dec 25, 2017	Dec 25, 2017
Internet Reading-2	Dec 25, 2017	Dec 25, 2017
Just for fun---Unnatural Laws	Dec 25, 2017	Dec 25, 2017
Secrets of a former Credit Card Thief	Dec 25, 2017	Dec 25, 2017
Snipping Tool Keyboard Shortcuts	Dec 25, 2017	Dec 25, 2017

FIGURE 2-77 All Pages Shown

Files

Files allow you to store personal files, photos, and links within Canvas. For example, **Files** are useful for your written paper drafts or your part of a group project or even items in progress for your **ePortfolio**. You can do the following with files:

To open Files, click on the **Files** link in the Course Navigation (Figure 2-78).

- You can upload one or multiple files.
- View all details about your files.
- Preview files.

In Canvas, the folder navigation window, file displays, and file names adjust to the width of the browser window.

Canvas provides access to files in three different feature areas (Figure 2-79):

- **User files:** You will find these in your user account.
- **Course files:** These files are located in each course where you are enrolled. However, not all instructors will allow you to view Course Files.
- **Group files:** These files are located in each group in which you are a member.

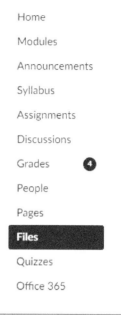

FIGURE 2-78 Files Navigation

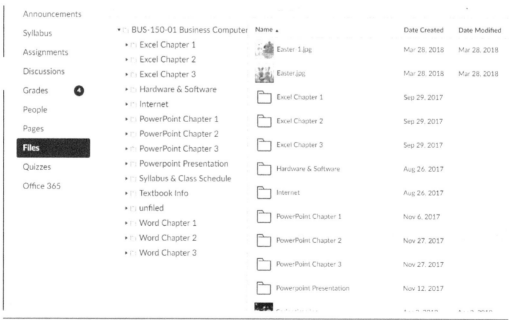

FIGURE 2-79 Files

Quizzes

Viewing Quizzes

1. To open **Quizzes**, click the *Quizzes* link in Course Navigation (Figure 2-80).
2. On the **Quiz Index** page, you can view (Figure 2-81):
   a. The name of each quiz and the availability dates for the quiz.
   b. The due date for the quiz.
   c. Total number of points the quiz is worth.
   d. The number of questions in the quiz.
3. If the quiz says **Available until** (date), you can complete the quiz until the specified date.
4. If the quiz says **Not Available Until** (date), the quiz is locked until the specified date.
5. If the quiz says **Closed**, no more quiz submissions can be submitted.

Note: Quizzes are ordered by due date. Some quizzes may not have a due date.

Availability dates may be the first dates you see. There may be times your instructor wants you to submit a quiz during a specified date range. In other words, the available dates will be the range of time that the quiz will be accessible to you. If the quiz does not have a date listed, the quiz is open; you can complete the quiz at any time during your course.

If you start a quiz but do not submit it, **Quizzes** includes an auto-submit feature that will submit the quiz for you on the **Available until** quiz date. If a quiz does not include an Available until date, the quiz will auto-submit on the last day of the course.

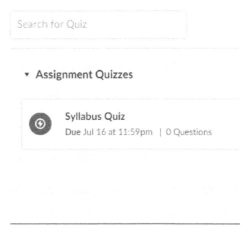

FIGURE 2-80 Quizzes Link

FIGURE 2-81 Quiz Index Page

Home
Announcements
Assignments
Discussions
Modules
People
Collaborations
Syllabus
Conferences
Quizzes
Grades

Grades

The Grades page in a course displays all grades for all course assignments. Additionally, you can also view scoring details, comments, and rubrics, if available.

If your instructor is using multiple grading periods, you can also filter grades by grading period.

Depending on your instructor, some details on the **Grades** page, such as scoring details and the total grade, may be restricted in your course.

Open and View Grades

To view your grades, do the following (Figure 2-82):

1. Click the Grades link in Global Navigation.
2. Click on the course name.
3. In Course Navigation click on the *Grades* link.

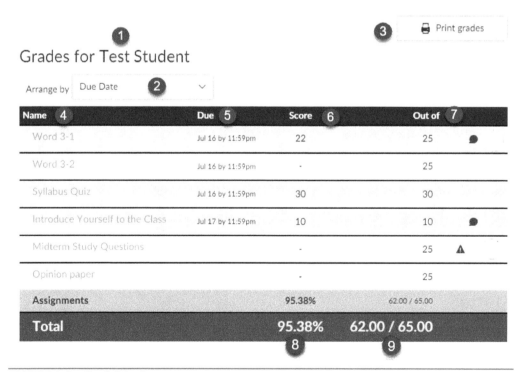

FIGURE 2-82 Grades Link

View Grades

Once you click on the *Grades* link, the Grade window will open (Figure 2-83).

1. **Student Name:** Displays the name of the student.
2. **Arrange By:** You can also sort by *Assignment Group, Due Date, Module*, and *Title. Due Date* is the default. Grades are sorted and displayed chronologically

Print grades

Grades for Test Student

Arrange by Due Date

Name	Due	Score	Out of	
Word 3-1	Jul 16 by 11:59pm	22	25	💬
Word 3-2	Jul 16 by 11:59pm	·	25	
Syllabus Quiz	Jul 16 by 11:59pm	30	30	
Introduce Yourself to the Class	Jul 17 by 11:59pm	10	10	💬
Midterm Study Questions		·	25	⚠
Opinion paper		·	25	
Assignments		95.38%	62.00 / 65.00	
Total		**95.38%**	**62.00 / 65.00**	

FIGURE 2-83 Grade Window

by assignment due date (imminent due dates are listed at the top of the list, and the ones due farther in the future will be displayed farther down in the list). Assignments that are not part of a module will be shown at the end of the assignments list in alphabetical order. However, if modules or assignment groups aren't used in your course, they won't be included as sorting options.

3. **Print Grades:** You can print your grades when you click on this button.
4. **Assignment Name:** When you click on an Assignment link, you will be on the Submission or Re-submission page. This is an easy way to submit assignments.
5. **Due Date:** The day and time the assignment is due.
6. **Score:** The score you earned for the assignment.
7. **Out of:** The total point value of the assignment. You will see various grade icons in the **Out of** column, which indicate the type of assignment you submitted. If you see an icon, that means the assignment has not been graded by your instructor. Once your instructor grades your assignment, your score will replace the icon.
8. **Assignment Score:** This is your grade percentage out of 100%.
9. **Out of Score:** This is your total number of points divided by total points possible.

Grading Icons

You may see the following icons, which represent different assignment submission types on your Grades page (Figure 2-84). This is what they represent:

1. **Document Icon:** Your file has been uploaded and submitted, but your assignment is not yet graded.
2. **Discussion Icon:** Your instructor has included a comment with your assignment.
3. **Link Icon:** A URL has been submitted but not yet graded.
4. **Muted Icon:** Your score is temporarily hidden while your instructor is grading. During this time, you will not be able to view your grade, submission comments, or quiz responses. You will be able to see your grade, submission comments, and quiz responses once your instructor unmutes the assignment.
5. **Filmstrip Icon:** Your media recording has been submitted but not yet graded.
6. **Quiz Icon:** Your quiz has been submitted but not fully graded. This icon will also display if a quiz has been edited

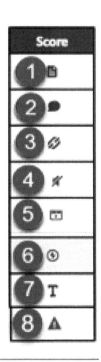

FIGURE 2-84
Grading Icons

and includes major changes that affect the quiz score and may require a grader to manually grade the quiz.

7. **Text Icon:** Your text entry has been submitted but not yet graded.
8. **Black Warning Icon:** This icon alerts you that points earned from this assignment will not count toward your final grade. Unless your instructor indicates otherwise, you should still submit this assignment.

Canvas displays different colors with different meanings on the **Grades** page. The following list will tell you what each color represents. Here you can see what each color represents (Figure 2-85):

- Gray background: Graded assignment.
- White background: Nongraded assignment.
- Gray text: The assignment has been dropped as part of an assignment group calculation and will not factor into your total score.

Note: In Figure 2-85, note that assignment Word 3-2 has a white background. The other three assignments (Word 3-1, Syllabus Quiz, and Introduce Yourself to the Class) each has a gray background.

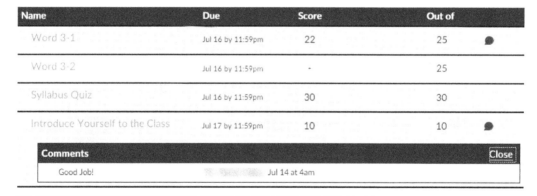

Name	Due	Score	Out of	
Word 3-1	Jul 16 by 11:59pm	22	25	💬
Word 3-2	Jul 16 by 11:59pm	-	25	
Syllabus Quiz	Jul 16 by 11:59pm	30	30	
Introduce Yourself to the Class	Jul 17 by 11:59pm	10	10	💬

Comments		Close
Good Job!	Jul 14 at 4am	

FIGURE 2-85 Grading Comments

View Grading Comments

If your instructor has included a comment in your assignment, the assignment will display a Comment Icon (Figure 2-85). If you want to view your comments, just click on the icon. If you have more than one comment, your comments will be organized chronologically. When you are done reading your comments, just click on the *Close* link.

View Scoring Details

Another feature of Canvas may enable you to view scoring details (Figure 2-86).

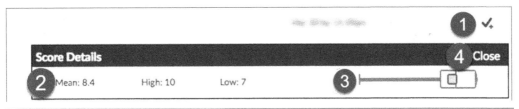

FIGURE 2-86 Scoring Details

Note: Not all schools have this feature.

If you can see scoring details, look at the upper right-hand corner of the box, and you will see the check mark. Once you click on the check mark (1), you can view the mean, high, and low scores from the class (2).

The horizontal gray line graph (3) extends from the lowest score for any student in the course to the highest score. The thicker, white box ranges from the 25th percentile to the 75th percentile, with the assignment mean marked inside the white box by a gray line. Your score appears as a blue box in this plot.

To see the scoring details, there must be more than five other students who have already submitted that assignment in the course. If you don't see it, then that means that fewer than five of your classmates have submitted the assignment. Click the **Close** link ▣ (4) to close the Scoring details box.

If your assignment has a rubric, it may include a rubric icon which means the assignment included a rubric for grading purposes. To view the rubric, click on the rubric icon. Click on *Close* to close the rubric link.

FIGURE 2-87 View Assignment Groups

View Assignment Groups

If there are **Assignment Groups** in your course, the **Grades** page will list them (1) (Figure 2-87). Assignment groups allow instructors to organize assignments, discussions, and quizzes into groups and apply specific grading rules or weights to those groups. You can view the percentage score for each group (2) and the points you've earned versus the total points possible (3).

Note: Your instructor may restrict Assignment group percentages.

CHAPTER THREE

Windows File Management

Introduction

Managing your files on your computer is an important part of effectively maintaining your computer. It is very easy to fill up your hard drive with a lot of files and have no idea of where the files are located. It is also easy to accidentally delete important files and render your computer unusable. In this lesson, you will learn the basics of managing the files in your computer.

Learning Objectives

In this chapter, you will be learning the basics of managing your files on your computer. Once you finish this chapter, you will be able to easily navigate the ins-and-outs of Windows File Management.

1. Navigate Windows File Explorer
2. Create file folders
3. Save files
4. Delete files
5. Copy, paste, and move files

File Explorer Ribbon

Windows provides you with a means of managing the files on your hard drive with File Explorer. The Ribbon that is available in File Explorer provides you with the means of managing your files, folders, and other information on your hard drive, cloud devices, and flash drives.

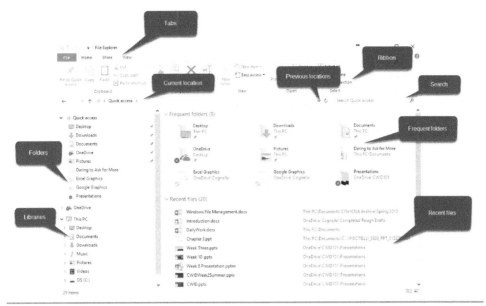

FIGURE 3-1 File Explorer Main Screen

The Ribbon contains several useful groups such as the Clipboard group, Organize group, New group, Open group, and Select group.

To start our study of **File Explorer,** you will want to get a view of the layout of the display. In previous versions of Windows, this is referred to as **Windows Explorer**. Understanding the various parts of the Window will help you to navigate the various parts of **File Explorer**. When you open **File Explorer,** you will see the display shown in Figure 3-1.

Like many of the other **Windows** applications and programs, you will see that **File Explorer** has many of the same elements. You will find a **Title** bar, tabs for

Student Checkup File Explorer

Purpose
As you begin to provide organization to your files, it is helpful to know the various parts of File Explorer. In this exercise, you will match the parts of the File Explorer display with the parts listed.

File Needed: **File Explorer Exercise**
Note: This exercise is also located at the end of this chapter.

Completed File Name: **(Your initials) Student Checkup FE**
1. Download the attached document and save the document (Your initials) Student Checkup FE.
2. A copy of the exercise file is also located at the end of the chapter.

performing various functions, scroll bars, and a ribbon with options that will allow you to manage information on your hard drive. These functions also work with your flash drives and cloud storage. In Figure 3-2, you can see that OneDrive is in the quick access portion of the navigation pane and in the frequent folders.

FIGURE 3-2 Ribbon—Home Tab

Home Tab

The **Home tab** contains many of the commonly used functions on the ribbon for **File Explorer**. The ribbon contains a **Clipboard** group. In this group, you will find a **Pin to Quick Access** icon. This icon will allow you to pin frequently used folders to the quick access area. You can also unpin a folder from the **Quick Access pane** by placing your mouse pointer on the folder, **right-clicking,** and selecting *Unpin from Quick Access*.

When you are not using **Quick Access,** your display will most likely resemble Figure 3-4 below. In this display, you will see a navigation pane on the left that allows you to navigate through the various folders on your computer. Windows initially sets up default libraries for storing documents, audio, video, and graphic files. Files are automatically placed in these folders based upon the file extension.

FIGURE 3-3 Unpin Folder

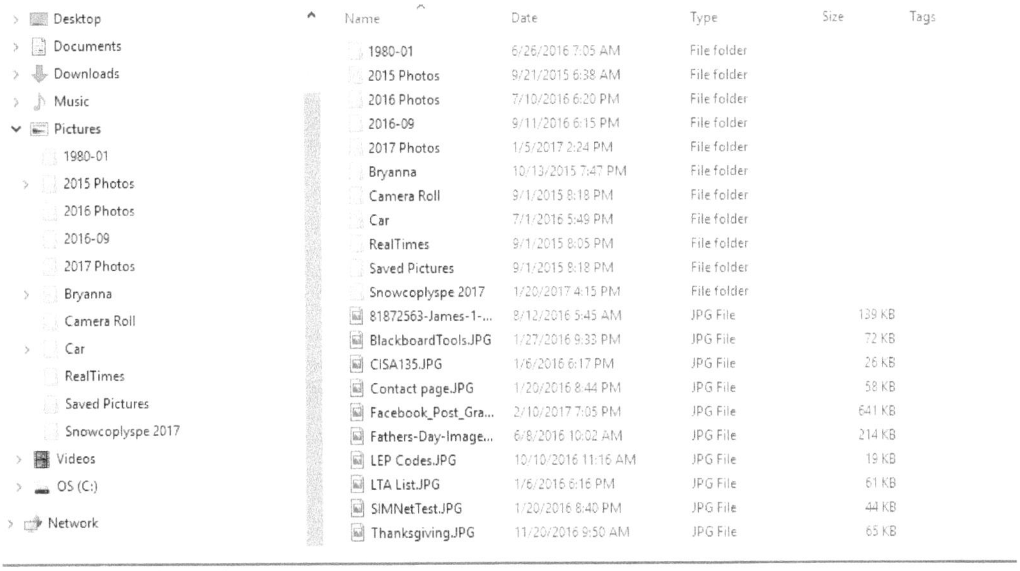

	Name	Date	Type	Size	Tags
> Desktop					
> Documents	1980-01	6/26/2016 7:05 AM	File folder		
> Downloads	2015 Photos	9/21/2015 6:38 AM	File folder		
> Music	2016 Photos	7/10/2016 6:20 PM	File folder		
∨ Pictures	2016-09	9/11/2016 6:15 PM	File folder		
1980-01	2017 Photos	1/5/2017 2:24 PM	File folder		
> 2015 Photos	Bryanna	10/13/2015 7:47 PM	File folder		
2016 Photos	Camera Roll	9/1/2015 8:18 PM	File folder		
2016-09	Car	7/1/2016 5:49 PM	File folder		
2017 Photos	RealTimes	9/1/2015 8:05 PM	File folder		
> Bryanna	Saved Pictures	9/1/2015 8:18 PM	File folder		
Camera Roll	Snowcoplyspe 2017	1/20/2017 4:15 PM	File folder		
> Car	81872563-James-1-...	8/12/2016 5:45 AM	JPG File	139 KB	
RealTimes	BlackboardTools.JPG	1/27/2016 9:33 PM	JPG File	72 KB	
Saved Pictures	CISA135.JPG	1/6/2016 6:17 PM	JPG File	26 KB	
Snowcoplyspe 2017	Contact page.JPG	1/20/2016 8:44 PM	JPG File	58 KB	
> Videos	Facebook_Post_Gra...	2/10/2017 7:05 PM	JPG File	641 KB	
> OS (C:)	Fathers-Day-Image...	6/8/2016 10:02 AM	JPG File	214 KB	
	LEP Codes.JPG	10/10/2016 11:16 AM	JPG File	19 KB	
> Network	LTA List.JPG	1/6/2016 6:16 PM	JPG File	61 KB	
	SIMNetTest.JPG	1/20/2016 8:40 PM	JPG File	44 KB	
	Thanksgiving.JPG	11/20/2016 9:50 AM	JPG File	65 KB	

FIGURE 3-4 File Explorer

The **Downloads** folder is available to store any files that you download and do not assign a save location. You can also store files on your desktop for quick retrieval. This is especially helpful in a work environment where you access the same files daily. Even as a student, you can save school files on your desktop and remove them when you are finished with them.

As you look at Figure 3-4, you will notice in the navigation pane that some of the file folders and libraries have a > beside the folder. This lets you know that there are more folders within that folder or library. Clicking on the > will open the folder for you to see additional folders. In the graphic above, you can see that the Pictures library is open and selected. The folders in the library are displayed beneath the library name, and because the library is selected, they are also displayed in the file list on the right. In addition to the folders, you will also see some photos that are not placed in any specific folder. You will want to remember that when you click on a folder in the navigation pane, the folder will open. If you want to open a folder in the file list on the right, you will need to double-click on that folder to open it. You can also use the double-click to open a file right from File Explorer. We will go into more detail on that shortly.

Now that you have had a brief explanation of the different items in **File Explorer**, the tools on the **Home** tab will make more sense and become much more useful. In the **Clipboard** group, you will have many common tools available, with a couple tools that are unique to **File Explorer.** Cut, Copy, and Paste are tools that most people will use often. These tools will allow you to easily manage files and, where necessary, make copies of these files for other purposes.

Organize Group

The next group on the **Home** tab is the **Organize** group. Here you have the tools at your fingertips to help manage the numerous files that will collect on your computer. Files and folders can be moved on your computer using **Move to** and by making copies of files using **Copy To**. Both features work the same and you can see in Figure 3-5 that when you click on either one, a list of the active folders are made available, and you can choose from one of these folders.

Other tools that are available in the **Organize** group include **Delete** and **Rename**. There are times when it becomes necessary to clean out all of the unneeded files from the computer. For example, you had to write a term paper, and you have numerous revisions of that paper stored on your computer. It is probably not necessary to keep all the revisions; rather, you may just want to keep the final version of the paper. The delete function will allow you to quickly and easily delete these unnecessary files.

Rename is a function that will allow you to quickly and easily rename you files. For example, suppose you were writing a paper for class and realized that your instructor has specific naming conventions for files to be submitted in class. The **Rename** function will allow you to quickly change the name of the file.

All of the functions listed above can be accomplished using other methods in **File Explorer**. As you will quickly learn, Microsoft provides numerous methods for accomplishing the same task. In some cases, it may be faster to drag and drop files into a different folder. Some people will prefer to click on a file and then press the delete key to remove it from their computer.

FIGURE 3-5 Copy To and Move To

New Group

The next group on the **Home** tab is the **New** group. This group will allow you to create new folders and items within your File Explorer. One thing users learn quickly is the need for organization on their computers. Feel free to use file names that make sense. You can have file names with up to 256 characters in them. This means there is no need for cryptic file names. You might also want to think about the folders you will want to create to track your files. The exercise at the end of the chapter will help you get your creative juices flowing.

View Tab

The **View tab** is an interesting and useful tab in the management of your files. With the **View** tab, you can look at more information concerning the files you have on your computer. In the **Panes** group, you can select which panes you want to have available in File Explorer. The **Navigation Pane** has a number of viewing options for viewing the folders and libraries on your computer. The **Preview Pane** allows you to see a preview of a file. This pane is extremely helpful when you are working with photographs and graphic files. It is here that you can see what type of graphic you are looking at. Many digital cameras simply put a number on the photograph you have taken, so the preview will allow you to see the photo file. Other files can also be displayed in the preview pane.

FIGURE 3-6 View Tab

The **Details Pane** provides you with specific information on the file. Some of these details are editable, and this can make it much easier to find a file or similar files. For photos, you can rate the photo, and if you are an avid photographer, you can add in additional photographic information.

FIGURE 3-7 Preview Pane and Details Pane

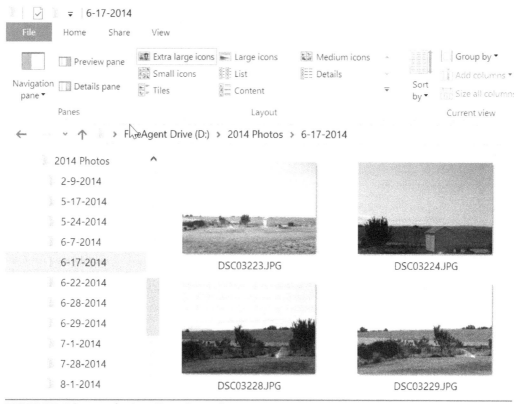

FIGURE 3-8 Layout Options Extra Large Icons

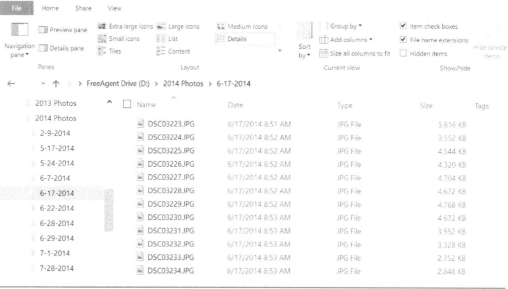

FIGURE 3-9 Layout Options Details

The next group on the **View** tab is the **Layout** group. This group serves a great many purposes when managing files. The **Layout** group will allow you to select the format in which file information is displayed. In Figure 3-8, one of the layout options is to display with extra-large icons. In many cases, the details option is helpful in determining the date of a document or other file information. Figure 3-9 provides a look at **Details** layout style.

Search

No matter how meticulous you are, no matter how careful, there will come a time when you need to find a file on your computer. Time constraints, other people using your computer, and a host of other things, such as your fingers getting in the way, mean that you are going to need to find a file. File Explorer provides a way of searching for these files.

To search for a file, you can enter the file name or even part of a file name in the search box as noted in Figure 3-10. Once you have entered part of the file name or the whole file name, you will want to click on the magnifying glass, and the system will search for the file you are looking for.

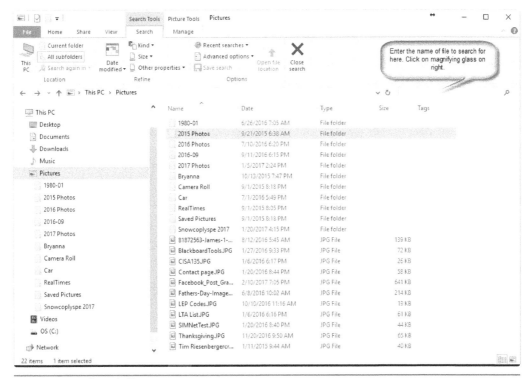

FIGURE 3-10 Search Feature

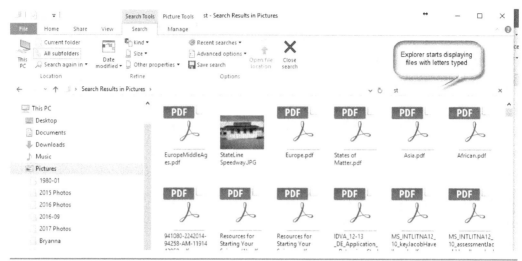

FIGURE 3-11 Completed Search

In Figure 3-11, you can see that a search was done for files that have the letters "st" in the file name. Notice that a list of files is presented that includes a photo and several PDF files. To open the file, simply double-click on the file you wish to open.

When you conduct a search in **File Explorer**, you will see some contextual tabs displayed, depending upon the types of files that are found in your search. The first tab is the **Search Tools,** which will help you to refine your search. The other contextual tab that is displayed is the **Picture Tools** tab, which allows you to manage graphic files in File Explorer.

There are many more options and things you can do with **File Explorer**. There are other tips and tricks that you can employ, such as sorting folder information by date or alphabetically. The use of these skills is learned as you explore the **File Explorer** environment.

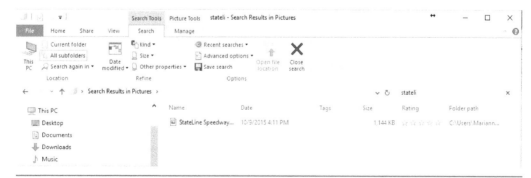

FIGURE 3-12 File Explorer Contextual Tabs

Purpose

Managing files on your computer is important. As a student, you need to be able to find various assignments that you will be required to do in class. In this assignment, you will demonstrate your understanding of how to create folders and manage classroom files.

File Needed: **None**

Completed File Name: **(Your initials) Student Checkup WFM**

You may use any of the following media:

1. Flash drive
2. Local hard drive
3. Microsoft OneDrive
4. Google My Drive
5. **Select** the media you are going to use to complete this assignment.
6. **Create** the following folder using the **new folder button—Basic Computers–101**
7. **Create** a folder like the one above for your other classes.
8. **Open** one of the folders and create the following folders:
   a. Week 1
   b. Week 2
   c. Week 3
   d. Week 4
   e. Week 5
   f. Week 6
   g. Week 7
   h. Week 8
   i. Week 9
   j. Week 10
   k. Week 11
   l. Week 12
   m. Week 13
   n. Week 14
   o. Week 15
9. Within each of the weekly folders, you can organize all your work for the class and easily reference this information as needed. Additional folders can be created for each class that you are taking, creating an organized digital file cabinet of your work.
10. Using the **Snipping Tool** for Windows or **Grab** for MAC, take a screen shot of your file folders. Save your screen shot as (your initials) Student Check WFM.

File Explorer Exercise

In this exercise, you will match the parts of the following File Explorer graphics to their parts listed.

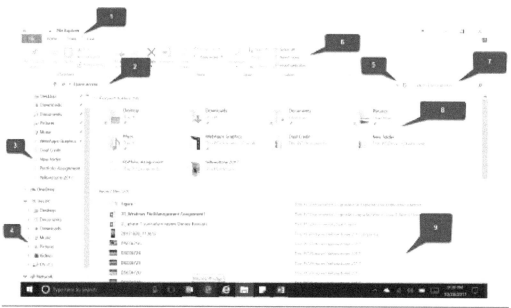

IMG 3.1 File Explorer Exercise

Place the name of the File Explorer part on the corresponding line.

1.   A. Recent files
2.   B. Libraries
3.   C. Current location
4.   D. Folders
5.   E. Previous locations
6.   F. Search
7.   G. Tabs
8.   H. Frequent folders
9.   I. Ribbon

CHAPTER FOUR

Google Web Applications

Introduction

As the Internet has grown over the past twenty years, web applications have also become a presence for users of all types. Web applications provide users with a variety of tools to accomplish many tasks. Many of these applications are free and only require the use of a computer, tablet, or smartphone and access to the Internet. Along with the use of these productivity apps, cloud storage is often available to the user free of charge. In this chapter, we will highlight the many common web applications found on Google.

FIGURE 4-1 Google Main Page

Learning Objectives

- Google Applications

Google

Most people are familiar with Google as a search engine. Google has also made a name with its many applications that are available free of charge to the casual user, educational institutions, and business entities. As a student, Google will provide students with the ease of creating, collaborating, editing, and publishing classroom work. To make use of the Google web apps, you will need to create a Google account. If your educational institution makes use of Google for education, your student email account will then also be your account for Google. Making use of the Google Chrome browser will also make the Google experience much easier and smoother.

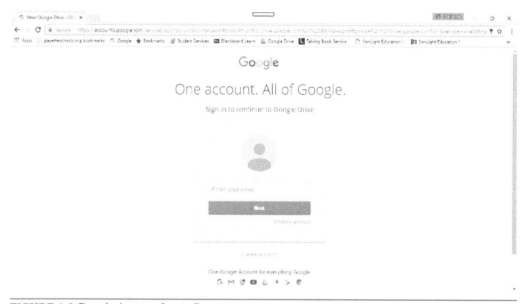

FIGURE 4-2 Google Account Login Page

To begin using the Google applications, enter www.google.com to go to the Google main page. If you already have a Google account, you can go ahead and log in to your account. If you do not have an account, click on the **Create Account** link at the bottom of the web page to create an account.

Creating a Google Account

To access the Google applications and other features, you will first need to create a Google account. Google education accounts have some distinctive features that are not available on personal accounts. Please check with your learning institution to see if they are using Google education accounts for students. If they are, you will be provided with a Google account with login information. The following instructions will provide you with the steps necessary to create a personal account.

1. Open your favorite web browser and go to Google using the URL https://accounts.google.com.

2. If you do not have an account, click on the **Create Account** link below the sign-in box.

3. You will then be directed to provide the necessary information to create an account.

FIGURE 4-3 Creating a Google Account

Note: You may use a current email account for your Google account. You may also have more than one Google account, and Google will allow you to access all your Google accounts from one place.

4. Sign into your account, and begin exploring the features provided in Google.

Google Applications

At this point, you have been introduced to Google and have set up your account along with logging into the site. As we begin to explore Google, you will find that there are many applications that are available for your use. Let us look at some of the features that you have available.

The free Google account will provide you with 15 GB of free cloud storage. This is very handy for people who are on the go. You are now free from having to carry a flash drive to store your files while traveling. If you have an Internet connection, you will have access to your files that are stored on Google. When you initially log in to your Google account, you will go to your Google drive account by default.

As you can see in Figure 4-4, there are many things available to you, the user. At the top of the display there is a search feature that will allow you to search your Google Drive for specific files. You also still have the three icons on the right that allow you to manage your account, set notifications, and access other Google applications. The next bar on the top provides you with the ability to create new documents. Clicking on the **New** button provides you with the option of selecting the type of file you wish to create or even to create a new folder for

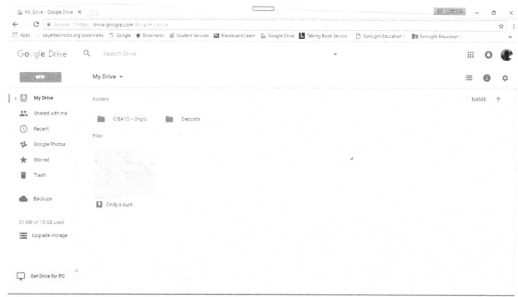

FIGURE 4-4 Google Drive

organizing your specific files. You can also upload files and folders from your computer to your Google drive. The **More** link provides you with other useful Google products such as Google Forms.

My Drive, the next link on the web page, looks identical to the **New button** with the difference being that it is designed for you to select specific items on your **Google Drive**. You also can create a new folder and to upload files and folders. The next item on the bar is the hamburger. The hamburger allows you to easily switch from a tile look to a list look or back. The circle with an "i" lists information on what changes you have made in your Google files.

The last item on the bar is a cog. This cog will allow you to adjust your settings and other features that you use with **Google Drive**. The settings option is just what it says. You can see how much space you have used and what is available for your account. Checking the *Convert uploaded files*

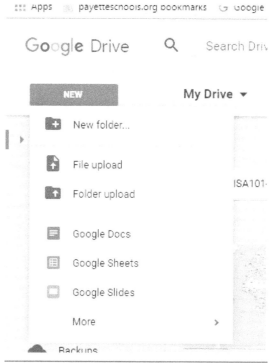

FIGURE 4-5 Google Tools

FIGURE 4-6 My Drive File Details

to Google Docs editor format will ensure that you can easily edit a Word document in **Google Docs**, for example.

You can change language settings. These settings include changing the language to Japanese, for example. If you understand another language, you can also set up Google to accommodate that language. This can also be handy if you are learning a new language. Remember, though, that in most cases, language translators will be in the formal version of the language, such as Castilian Spanish.

Other settings include an option to sync Google Docs, Sheets, and other files to your computer so that you can edit offline. The **Density** setting provides you with three densities for the layout of your Google Drive. There is also an option to create a Google Photos folder. It is a handy way to put all your photos on Google into a specific folder.

The **Notifications** option allows you to specify where you want any account-related notifications to be sent. The final item is the **Manage Apps**.

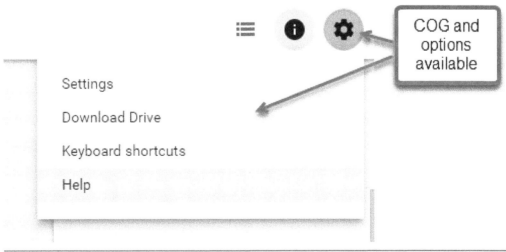

FIGURE 4-7 COG Options

Here you can see specific information and options related to the apps you have added to your account. Google has many apps that you can choose from, and this feature allows you to control those apps and even disconnect the app from your Google account if desired.

You will also notice that there is an option to connect more apps to your account. The following graphic shows you a sample of some of the many apps that are available for your use. Most of these apps are free, so feel free to

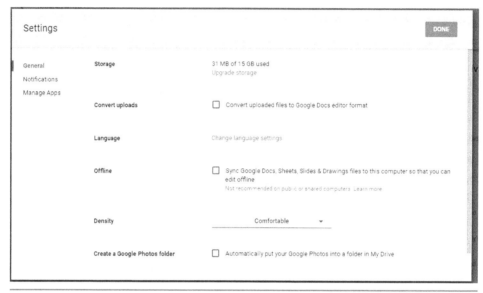

FIGURE 4-8 General Settings Page

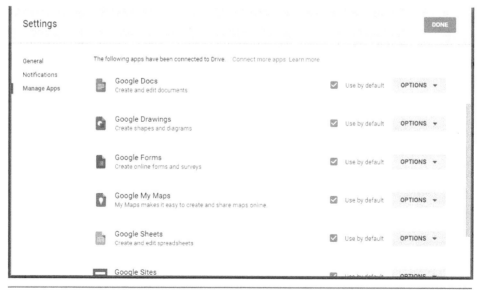

FIGURE 4-9 Notifications Settings Page

Connect apps to Drive   ✕

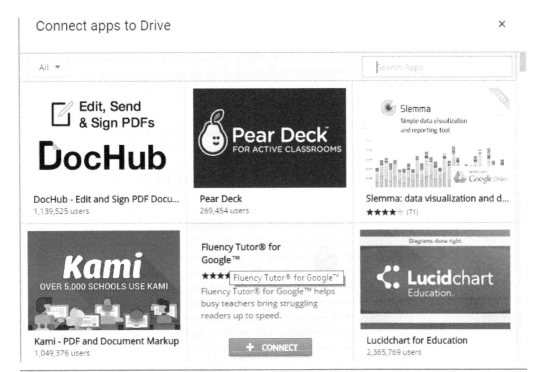

FIGURE 4-10 Connect to Apps Drive

explore and try them out. Lucidchart, for example, is an excellent app that will allow you to create organizational charts, floor plans, flow charts, and entity relationship diagrams.

Another feature in the cog is **Download Drive**. This option will allow you to set up your **Google Drive** to link seamlessly to your computer, making for easy access to your documents. Like any other program that you will use in Windows or any other operating system, Google has its predefined short cut keys. Google has provided a list of these shortcut keys under the settings icon. There is also a help feature that will provide added instruction on the various features in **Google Drive**.

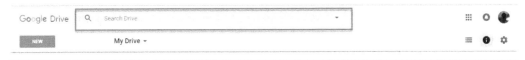

FIGURE 4-11 Google Search Feature

Across the top of the **Google Drive** page you will see a **Search Drive** option. This option will allow you to search your **Google Drive** account for a specific document. The drop-down menu will provide you with the ability to search the drive using the search tools available. When you select the Docs tool, Google will

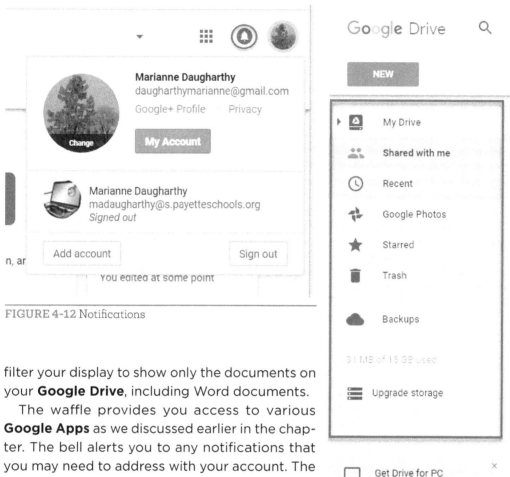

FIGURE 4-13 Navigation Pane

filter your display to show only the documents on your **Google Drive**, including Word documents.

The waffle provides you access to various **Google Apps** as we discussed earlier in the chapter. The bell alerts you to any notifications that you may need to address with your account. The final option on this bar is your profile icon. Here you can add a picture of yourself or something else. You can also manage your profile and the information that is available to others. The Google privacy policy is also available. To change your picture, click on the picture and then select the picture you desire to use. You may need to crop the picture to fit the space provided.

Looking down the left side of the display, you will find the navigation pane. This pane will allow you to access many of the same features that you could access across the top as well as other features. Options in the navigation pane include **My Drive**, where you can view the files and folders on your Google drive. *Shared with me* allows you to see which specific files are shared with you. *Recent* shows the files you have recently worked on. **Google Photos** is just what it means, photos that are stored on your Google drive. *Starred* identifies files and folders that are starred. A file or folder may be starred for whatever reason you decide. *Trash* holds all files that you have deleted. There may be times when you delete something that you did not intend to delete, and this will provide you an avenue for retrieving these items.

Office Productivity Google Apps

A Google account is initially set up with several default applications (apps). Default apps include Google Docs, Slides, and Sheets. These are common office productivity applications, and while these are not as robust as suites such as Microsoft Office, they serve a valuable function in that they provide tools for those who cannot afford them or want to use something different than commercial software.

Google Docs

The first app is **Google Docs. Google Docs** is a web-based word processor. It has many common features found in other word processors such as Microsoft's Word. In Figure 4-14, you can see that the **Google Docs** app will provide you with tools to print, font options, alignment options, and outline and bullet features. The tabs across the top will provide you with many other document-editing options such as Insert features, Tool, and Table features.

FIGURE 4-14 Google Docs Blank Doc

Google Sheets

The next app is **Google Sheets. Google Sheets** is designed to provide you with a method for completing mathematical calculations. Many businesses make use of similar spreadsheet programs to manage their day-to-day finances. Spreadsheet applications have other uses; for students, spreadsheet applications will be useful in completing courses such as Economics and Statistics. Figure 4-15 shows one of the many uses of spreadsheets.

Google Slides

In school and in business, presentations are a common occurrence. Being a skilled presenter is an important skill for students and professionals. **Google Slides** is another application that is part of the Google Office Suite. With **Google**

FIGURE 4-15 Google Sheets

Slides, information can be displayed to provide a visual representation of the presentation. There are a variety of slide formats that will allow you to insert graphics, videos, and text information. Figure 4-16 shows the title slide of a presentation.

In this short lesson, you have learned about some of the features of Google and some of the applications that are available. There are many more applications that are available to Google users. Some other applications that may be of interest to students are Google Scholar, Google Earth, and Google Maps. Google Forms can provide students with a way for studying for exams. Take time to explore the many applications that are available.

FIGURE 4-16 Google Slides

Here you will get a chance to test your understanding of the material covered in the chapter. You will need access to a computer with access to the Internet.

In this project, you will work with the Google Office Productivity Applications.

File Needed: **None**

Completed File Names: **(Your initials) Student Checkup Google Docs 1-1 (Your initials) Student Checkup Google Sheets 1-1 (Your initials) Student Checkup Google Slides 1-1**

1. **Go** to Google.com, and **create** a personal Google account.
2. **Log in** to your Google account.
3. **Go** to the Google Docs application.
4. **Create** a simple one-page Google Doc describing some of the potential uses for Google Docs in college and outside of college.
5. **Save** your Google Doc as (Your initials) Student Checkup Google Docs 1-1. Download a copy and post this document to the location your instructor has provided.
6. **Go** to the Google Sheets application.
7. **Create** a Google Sheet highlighting the common expenses that a student would incur going to college.
8. **Save** your Google Sheet as (Your initials) Student Checkup Google Sheets 1-1. **Download** a copy and **post** this document to the location your instructor has provided.
9. **Go** to the Google Slides application.
10. **Search** the Google applications. Find three applications that you would be interested in trying.
11. In your Google Slides show, create a presentation highlighting the three applications that you wish to try.
12. **Save** the presentation as (Your initials) Student Checkup Google Slides 1-1.
13. **Download** a copy and **post** it to the location your instructor has provided.

CHAPTER FIVE

OneNote

Introduction

OneNote is a relatively new product from Microsoft. OneNote allows you to create a digital notebook of things that are important to you. There are many powerful features available in OneNote, such as sharing, using it across multiple devices, placing documents within the notebook, and even recording lectures. With a tablet, you can also write on your notebook, taking handwritten notes. OneNote will even convert your handwritten notes into searchable text. Let's look at this innovative tool.

Parts of the OneNote Screen

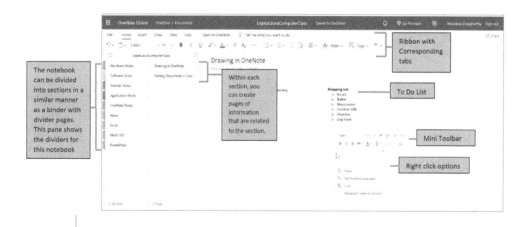

FIGURE 5-1 OneNote Page Layout

Uses for OneNote

The flexibility of OneNote makes it excellent for a variety of uses. Users have shared that they have used OneNote to manage shopping lists for a household. Using the Sharing function in OneNote, any member of a household can check the shopping list, pick up the items, and cross them off the list all while using a smart phone.

Students can make use of OneNote for taking classroom notes, including recording class lectures. Articles, online information, photos, and notes can easily be placed and organized in OneNote. Research projects for a class can be managed in OneNote, and projects that require collaboration in student groups can also take place using the sharing features. Real-time collaboration can provide exciting changes as members work together from various locations.

In the business world, meetings can be managed through OneNote. By selecting the meeting details located on the home tab, meeting information located in Outlook can quickly be added to the notebook, providing a starting point for taking important meeting notes. These notes can then be shared with other members of the meeting.

With some creativity, other uses of the OneNote notebook can be generated. The sky is the limit, and many more uses can found for OneNote.

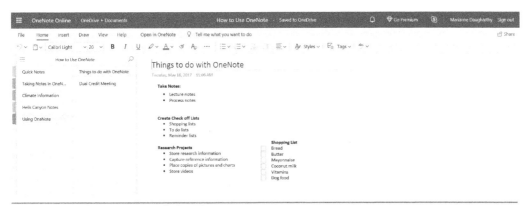

FIGURE 5-2 Things to Do with OneNote

Devices

Because OneNote is cloud based, a variety of devices can be used. The most commonly used devices might be the smart phone, laptop, or desktop computer. The laptop provides portability and access to OneNote information from any location where there is an Internet connection. Additionally, tablets also provide this capability to the OneNote user. Computers with touch screens will allow greater flexibility and use of drawing and annotating features in the OneNote notebook. Finger drawing or the use of a stylus will allow the user to add greater visual enhancements to the notes in the notebook.

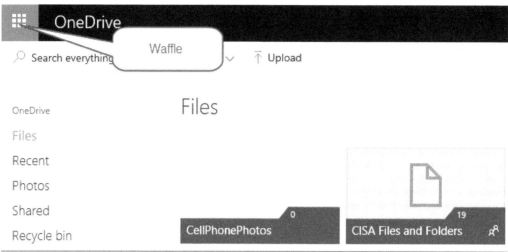

FIGURE 5-3 OneDrive Waffle

Create a OneNote Notebook

To create a OneNote notebook, log in to your OneDrive account or your college student Microsoft email accounts.

1. Click on the **Waffle** located in the upper left corner of the display. Figure 5-3 shows the location of the waffle on the OneDrive or the Microsoft Online email.

2. Once you have selected the waffle, OneDrive or the Microsoft email will present you with a list of the available applications for the OneDrive account. Figure 5-4 shows the available apps for this specific OneDrive account.

3. To use OneNote, click on the OneNote application and then **Open** a new notebook or an existing notebook.

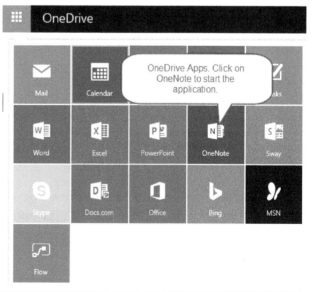

FIGURE 5-4 OneDrive Applications

Sharing OneNote Notebooks

Collaboration in college is a major part of any academic program. Students who are working in groups, as part of a study team, or need to share their notebooks with instructors, will need to be able to share information as required.

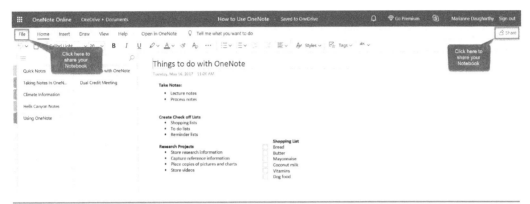

FIGURE 5-5 Sharing OneNote

To share a notebook, you can use one of the two following methods. Figure 5-5 shows you the two methods for sharing a notebook.

1. Click on the **File** tab.
2. Click on **Share** in the navigation pane.

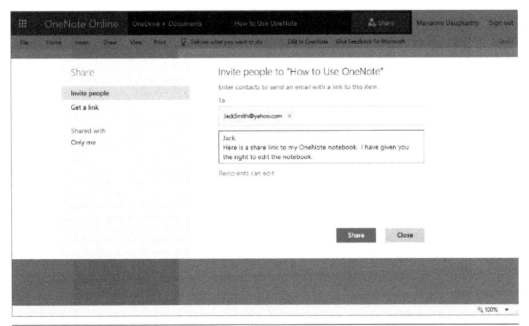

FIGURE 5-6 Email Invite

3. Click on **Share with People**.
4. As shown in Figure 5-6, click on **Invite People**.
5. Enter the email address of the person or persons you want to invite to use your notebook.
6. Add a short message to go with your email.
7. Another option is to use the **Get a Link** feature. This will generate a web link that you can use to share with others or embed in a web page.

Figure 5-7 displays information that lets you know who has access to your OneNote notebook. You can change who has permission to access your notebook at any time. You can also control the type of access a person has from read only to edit permission.

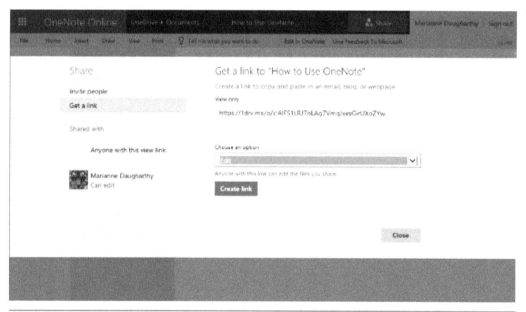

FIGURE 5-7 Shared With

Taking Notes Using OneNote

One of the uses of OneNote is providing students with a method of taking notes for class. As students, you need to have an easy access place to keep your notes for studying and research. OneNote provides you with a tool that will store your notes and research and allow easy access through any device with an Internet connection. You can take notes in your personal style. Notes can be typed, hand-written (if you have a touch screen), and annotated. Web pages can be linked and photos inserted along with related documents and materials. The power of OneNote to keep materials in one place makes it easy for students to have

FIGURE 5-8 Note Taking in OneNote

class-related materials in one place and ready when needed. Figure 5-8 provides you with an example of one of many methods for taking notes.

Meeting Notes in OneNote

OneNote provides you with a method of managing notes for meetings. Because OneNote is integrated with other Microsoft products, OneNote will populate a page in your notebook with initial meeting information by adding meeting details.

To add meeting notes, first start off by clicking on the meeting notes option on the **Home** tab. Referring to Figure 5-9, you can see where the Meeting Details icon is located on the **Home** tab.

Once you have clicked on this icon, your Notebook will ask you to add the meeting details. These details come from your calendar entries. The more detail in your calendar entry the more details in your meeting details. Once you have entered the meeting details, you will be able to add notes as the meeting takes

FIGURE 5-9 Creating Meeting Notes

FIGURE 5-10 Meeting Details

place. Figure 5-10 displays the results of adding the meeting details to your notebook. Please note that depending on the version of OneNote the steps may differ slightly.

Synching OneNote with the Cloud and Other Devices

With OneNote, you can use your notebook online or offline. When using One-Note online, your notes are automatically saved as you enter them. There is no need to save anything. If you click, as in Figure 5-11 on the right, you will see that there is no save option for the notebook. When using other devices such as your smartphone, OneNote entries are also automatically saved for you.

FIGURE 5-11 Syncing OneNote

OneNote for Class

Another feature that you may see in college is the use of OneNote **Class Notebook**. This version of OneNote is designed for use in the classroom. Instructors can create a classroom notebook where students can collaborate, download assignments, access classroom materials, and many other activities based upon what your instructor sets up for your class. Each student has his or her own section within the notebook that is only accessible by the student and the instructor. Students cannot access another student's section in the classroom notebook unless that student shares their login information. Figure 5-12 provides you a sample of what a OneNote notebook looks like. The instructor view that you see here shows the notebook, sections, and students who are invited by the instructor to use the notebook.

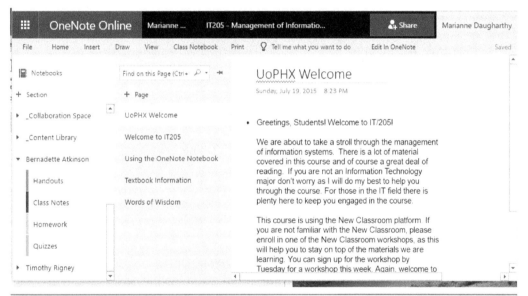

FIGURE 5-12 OneNote for Class

Student Chapter Project

In this exercise, you will create your own personal OneNote notebook for class. OneNote is an excellent tool that will provide you with the means of managing the volumes of information that you as a student will accumulate. Having a classroom notebook will provide you with the ability to manage class notes in a one-stop shop accessible on any device that has access to the Internet.

File Needed: **None**

Completed File Name: **(Your initials) ComputerNotebook**

1. Log in to your OneNote account. Many students will be able to access their OneNote accounts through the student email system, if the college or university is using Microsoft email accounts for students.
2. Create a new notebook and name your notebook (your initials) ComputerNotebook.
3. Create the following sections and pages in your notebook:
   a. Hardware notes
   b. Software notes
   c. OneNote notes
      i. Drawing in OneNote
      ii. Putting documents in OneNote—add the following documents to your notebook.
   d. Internet notes
   e. Application notes
   f. Word
      i. Create an MLA page in the Word section of your notebook.
      ii. Go to the following website: https://owl.english.purdue.edu/owl/resource/747/01/.
      iii. Find the MLA Sample Paper and download a copy.
      iv. Insert the MLA Sample Paper into your notebook using the **File Printout** option on the **Insert** tab.
   g. Excel
      i. Create a Climate Change page in the Excel section of your notebook.
      ii. Go to the following web page www.usclimatedata.com.
      iii. Find the climate information from your state and local town.
      iv. Insert this web information in your notebook by copying and pasting the link.
      v. Press **CTRL+A** to select the information on the web page.
      vi. Press **CTRL+C** to copy the information on the web page.
      vii. Go to your notebook Climate Change page, and press **CTRL+V** to paste the information to your notebook. Try clicking on the various hyperlinks on the notebook page and observe what happens.
   h. PowerPoint
4. Share your OneNote notebook with your instructor.

Part 2

Microsoft Word

CHAPTER SIX

Word Part I

Introduction

Through the years, Microsoft Word has seen numerous releases, with the most recent release of Microsoft Office 2021 in October 2021. Word is the word processor of choice for many businesses and in many educational institutions. As a student, you will be required to write many essays, reports, and other documents for submission to your instructors. In this chapter, we will cover the basics of Word that all students need to know. In the following chapters, we will dive into formatting papers using the Modern Language Association (MLA) and the American Psychological Association (APA) styles. As a student, you may run across other styles such as *Chicago Manual of Style*. While we will not go into this format, the skills you learn using MLA and APA styles will allow you to easily adapt to other writing standards. In all cases, if you are unsure about formatting an element, please always consult with your instructor.

> Microsoft Word has been around for over thirty-eight years. It's first release was in 1983.

Learning Objectives

In this chapter, you will learn the basics of formatting a Word document. When you complete this chapter, you should be able to do the following:

1. Create, Save, Open, and Format a Word Document.
2. Copy, Paste, Move, Undo, Redo, and Other Editing Features.

3. AutoCorrect and AutoComplete functions.
4. Font, Paragraph, Styles, and Editing Groups.
5. Insert Tab—Pages, Tables, Illustrations, Headers and Footers.
6. Design Tab—Themes and Document Formatting.
7. Review Tab—Spelling and Grammar.

Word Layout

Before getting started in creating documents in Word, let's take a few minutes and explore the layout of Word. When you open any Word document, you are presented with a basic layout for the document. The assorted elements on the screen stay the same with only the ribbon changing as you select the different tabs. Even between versions of Word, the layout is basically the same for each document that you create. Now let's look at the various parts of the Word document. Below in Figure 6-1, you can see the various elements of a Word document.

The Title bar contains many important things for you as a user of Word. One of the tools for you to use is the **Quick Access Toolbar**. In this toolbar, you can see the Save icon, and, in this case, the Save feature will save the presentation to cloud storage, undo, redo, and slide show icons. The icon with the down arrow is a feature that will allow you to customize this area of the ribbon. To customize the Quick Access bar, click on the down arrow. On the right, Figure 6-2, you will see the options that are available for the Quick Access bar. From this drop-down list, simply click on the options you wish to add to the Quick Access bar.

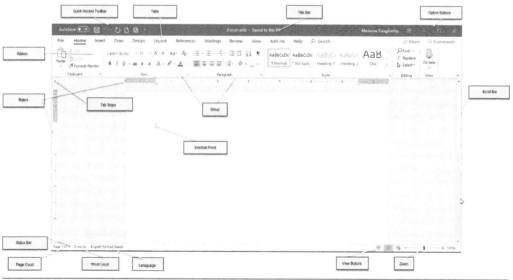

FIGURE 6-1 Word Parts

Clicking on the checked options will deselect the items you do not wish to have on the Quick Access bar.

The Ribbon

When you open Word, one of the first things you see is the ribbon. The ribbon is one of the main tools that all users will employ when using Word or any of the MS Office programs.

The ribbon is located on every tab in Word. It is from the ribbon that you will access all the key features of Word. Figure 6-3 below shows a picture of the

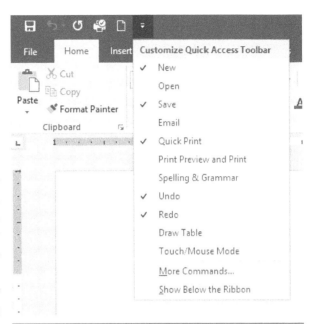

FIGURE 6-2 Quick Access Toolbar

ribbon, using the home tab. Each tab will change the tools that are available to you on the ribbon. Try clicking on each of the tabs of the ribbon to see what options are available on the ribbon. As you work through the materials within this chapter, and other chapters in the textbook, you will be learning about each of the individual tools located on the ribbon that will help you make the most efficient use of the programs as a college student. As a starting point for introducing you to the ribbon, let's take a quick look at the **File** tab.

When you first open Word, or any Microsoft Office application, the first screen you will see are the options available on the **File** tab. The **File** tab is also referred to as the **Backstage**; both terms can be used interchangeably. In the **Backstage**, you will have the option of opening an existing document or creating a new document. Other options will include the ability to print, save, manage account settings, and manage document properties. As we move through the next section of the chapter, you will learn about the many features available in the **File** tab. In Figure 6-4, you will see a sample of the **File** tab and the information contained for a document that is currently open.

FIGURE 6-3 Home Tab on the Ribbon

FIGURE 6-4 File Tab for Open Document

When you place your mouse pointer on the ribbon and use your scroll wheel, Word will move forward or backward through the tabs.

1. Create, Save, Open, and Format a Word Document

For those who are familiar with word processors and Word, this will be a review. Before you can accomplish any task in Word, you must Create or Open a Word document. For a new document, it goes without saying that you will create the document while, at other times, you will be editing existing documents as you prepare the document for class. You may even find yourself making a copy of a document to edit for another class or project. The key is that with Word, you will be working with various documents.

New Documents—Creating a New Document

To get started using Word, you need to create a new document. This initial document will be created using the **Normal Template** *(Normal.dotx)*. This will be the starting format of your new document. Once you have the document created, you can then go and change the design of the document or you can choose from one of many other predesigned document styles. For our first documents, we will make use of the Normal Template and use the default settings of the document. When you initially open Word, you will be presented with a blank document.

FIGURE 6-5 New Document

Creating a New Document

1. Click on the **File** tab.
2. Click on **New**.
3. Select the **Blank document**. This will create your first new document, see Figure 6-5.

If you look at the Title Bar, you will notice that your document will have a name of "Document" followed by a number. When you close your document or use one of the save methods, you will be asked to provide a document name.

A new document can also be created by pressing both the CTRL+N keys at the same time.

Saving a Document

Once a document is created, a generic title will be assigned to the document. This title will be dependent upon how many documents you have created prior to the last closing of Word. The initial document will be titled **Document1.** When you create additional new documents, the number will increment. When you close Word and then open Word, the numbering will begin from **Document1** again. There are several formats available for saving documents in Word. The following table is a list of commonly used document formats available in Word.

Saving a Document

1. Click the File tab.
2. Select *Save* or *Save As* (Figure 6-6).
3. Click the location where you wish to save the document by selecting the location or browsing the computer for the desired location.
4. Enter the name of the document in the Enter File Name here field.
5. Click *Save* to save the document.

TABLE 6-1 Word File Extensions

Format	Extension	Use
Standard Word Document	.docx	This is the standard Word document for versions 2007–2016 including Office 365.
Word 97–2003 Document	.doc	For all versions of Word prior to 2007. This extension is always an excellent choice when you do not know if other recipients have a compatible version of Word.
Word Template Document	.dotx	This extension is used for new documents that are to be used as a template for future documents.
Portable Document Format	.pdf	This creates a document that is typically noneditable. This type of document is typically smaller in size and is frequently used in web pages and legal documents.
Rich Text Format (RTF)	.rtf	This document format is a flexible style that can be used by various word processors.
Open Document Format	.odt	This format is used by free document processors such as Open Office, Start Office, and Google Docs.
Test File	.txt	This is a very simplified text document. It is frequently used when moving information or data between different programs from different software vendors.

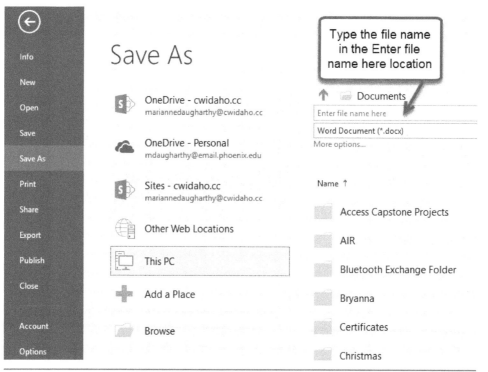

FIGURE 6-6 Saving a Document

If you do not see the location you wish to save your document in, click the More Options link. You will be able to browse your computer for the desired location to save your document (Figure 6-7).

> When working on any document, it is wise to save your work periodically. This can be done easily by pressing CTRL+S at the same time. The work you just completed will then be saved, thereby, reducing the chance of lost work in the event of the unexpected happening.

Saving a Document with a Different File Name

There are times when you will want to save a document that you are working on with a different file name. Many people also use this feature when they desire to create revisions of a project. Word provides a method for easily accomplishing this task.

1. Click on the **File** tab.
2. Click the *Save As* link to display the Save As options.

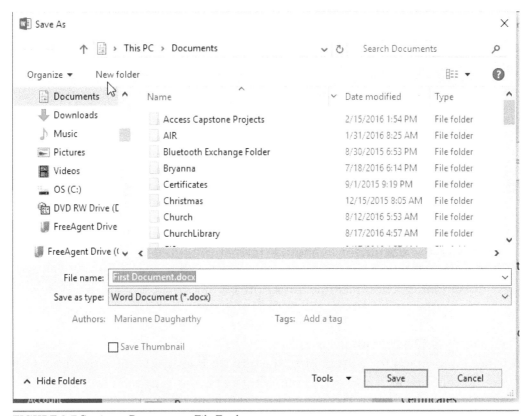

FIGURE 6-7 Saving a Document—File Explorer

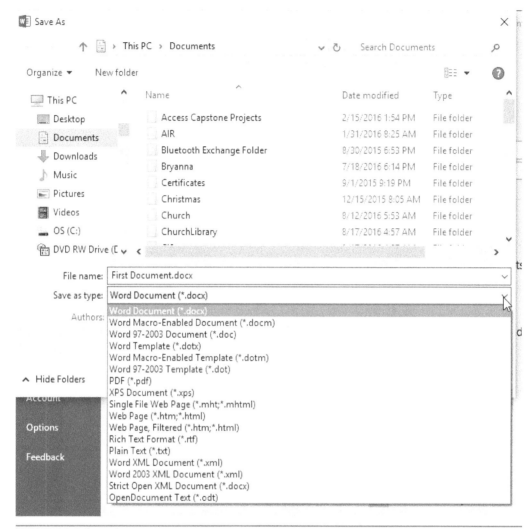

FIGURE 6-8 Save As

3. Enter the new document name and then click the *Save* button.
4. To save the document in another format (Figure 6-8) or location select the ***More Options*** link and browse to the location you desire to save the document in. Then click the *Save* button.

Opening a Document

It is not uncommon for a student to have to go back and edit a document or make corrections and add additional information as a project evolves. Many times, this can be later in the day or on a different day. You will need to open the document you were working on to make changes and corrections.

The easiest method for opening a document is to use the recent documents list in the Backstage view of Word. You can also browse for a document that you may have not opened in a while. Use **Opening a Document:**

1. Click the **File** tab.
2. Select the file to be opened by clicking on the desired file name.
3. If you do not see the file, click on the location/drive you wish to browse for your file (Figure 6-9). As a rule, Windows will by default save all documents in the documents library unless you specify otherwise.

Helpful Tools

Before moving on with other features of Word, there are a few items that will be helpful to you as you create any document. The first tool is the **Show/Hide** tool. Located in the Paragraph group of the Home tab, this tool allows you to see the formatting marks within your document. This tool

FIGURE 6-9 Opening a Document

is a simple tool that by clicking on it, you will turn on the tool, and by clicking again, you will turn it off. The following Figure 6-10 shows some of the formatting marks that are revealed with the Show/Hide tool. Additional features that the Show/Hide will present to you are Page Breaks and Section Breaks.

You can turn on and off the Show/Hide feature from your keyboard by pressing CTRL + Shift + 8 keys at the same time.

Working with text will be another aspect of creating any document. When creating a document, you will want to be aware of your paragraph formatting.

Selecting Text

Using the F8 key you can select text as follows:
Press F8 and the arrow keys to select text.
Press F8 twice to select a word.
Press F8 three times to select the sentence.
Press F8 four times to select the paragraph.
Pres F8 five times to select the entire document.
Pres ESC to turn off the F8 functions.

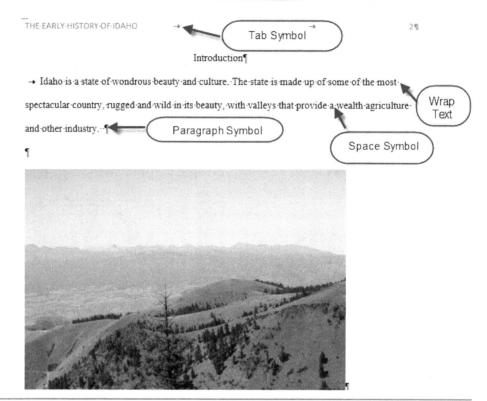

FIGURE 6-10 Show/Hide

As was discussed in the above section about the Show/Hide tool, Word will automatically wrap paragraphs. This means that as you type your work, you will not want to press the enter key at the end of each line. Instead, continue typing your paragraph and press the enter key at the end of the paragraph. This will save you a tremendous amount of frustration in the formatting of your work. Another point to remember is that Word treats each press of the enter key as a paragraph. This means that if you press enter after the title of your paper, Word will think that this is a paragraph.

The third item that you need to know about is selecting text. As you create your document, you will want to select text for several reasons. Sometimes it is a simple word change, and other times you will want to move the selected text to another part of the document. Text can be selected in several ways. The note box to the right will provide you with several ways to select text within your document.

You can also select text using your mouse pointer. This is accomplished by referring to Table 6-2.

TABLE 6-2

Item to Select	Using
Word	Select the word by double-clicking on the word.
Line	1. You can use your mouse pointer to **click and drag** to select the text. 2. Place your mouse pointer in the left margin area of the document and **click** once.
Multiple lines	1. You can use your mouse pointer to **click and drag** to select the text. 2. Place your mouse pointer in the left margin area of the document and **click and hold** the left mouse button. Drag the mouse up or down to select the text.
Sentence	Press the **CTRL** key. While holding the key down, click any place in the sentence you desire to select.
Paragraph	Place your mouse pointer in the left margin area of the document and click twice.
Entire document	1. Place your mouse pointer in the left margin area of the document and click three times. 2. Press **CTRL+A** to select the entire document.
Noncontiguous text	1. Select the first item of text, then, holding down the **CTRL** key, select the next text using your mouse pointer. 2. If you want to select various words, you can hold down the **CTRL** key and then **double-click** on the other words you wish to select.

Student Checkup Word 6-1

Here you will get a chance to test your understanding of the material covered in the chapter. You will need access to a computer with Word. Using the OneDrive Word App will be a viable alternative if you do not have access to a computer with a full version of Office 2019, Office 2021, or Office 365.

In this project, you will start by opening a blank Word document. Here you will begin creating a project on the Hells Canyon Power Complex and Recreational Area covers the states of Idaho and Oregon.

File Needed: **None**
Completed File Name: **(Your initials) Student Checkup Word 6-1**

1. Create a New Document.
   a. Click the **File** tab and choose **New**. Click on the blank document.
2. Save the document.
   a. Click on the File tab. In the link on the left side in the Backstage, click on *Save As* (Figure 6-11).
   b. Select the location where you want to save your document.

c. Change the file name to (your initials) Student Checkup 6-1 in the File name area.

d. Click Save to save the file, and close the Save As dialog box.

3. Type the following into your document.

4. Save your document by pressing CTRL+S.

5. Close the document. You will be using this document again in future Checkups. Post this document as instructed by your instructor.

New

Search for online templates

Suggested searches: Business Industry P

Blank document

FIGURE 6-11 New Blank Document

Keyboard Shortcuts

CTRL+C—Copy
CTRL+V—Paste
CTRL+X—Cut

Hells Canyon Power Complex and Recreational Area The Snake River is one of the longest rivers in the Pacific Northwest. With a length of 1,078 miles, it is the longest tributary of the Columbia River basin. Hells Canyon lies on the Snake River. The canyon itself is 10 miles wide and extends from river mile 254 and ends at river mile 238. The canyon has a depth of 7,993 feet and is known as North America's deepest gorge. The river in the gorge flows past scenic vistas such as the Seven Devils Mountains in Idaho. Accessibility to the area by car is limited due to the rugged terrain of the area. There is a main road that allows visitors to the area to drive from Brownlee Dam, past Oxbow Dam, to the end at Hells Canyon Dam. The drive itself is approximately 40 miles long. The adventurist can take a boat trip further down the river during the summer months.

2. Copy, Paste, Move, Undo, Redo, and Other Editing Features

No matter how skilled you are as a writer, you will need to revise your work. Many times, as you read your work, you will find that you need to move things around, delete information, or paste information from another source. In this section, we will cover some of the commonly used tools to improve the overall readability of your work.

Copy

Copying text is a key step when working with documents. Using the **Copy** function will allow you to easily accomplish this task by combining it with the paste feature. Information may also be copied from other documents, spreadsheets, or into other files.

Paste

In most cases, the **Paste** function is combined with the **Copy** function. The **Paste** function allows you to paste information that has been copied or cut from the document into another location in the document or into another document.

Using Copy and Paste

1. In a document, select the text, paragraph, or graphic you wish to copy and paste (Figure 6-10).
2. Select **Copy** from the home tab, or press **CTRL + C** on your keyboard to copy the desired item.
3. The next step will be to paste the word in the location desired (Figure 6-11).
4. Because we simply copied the word from one place to another, we need to delete the other word so the sentence will make sense.
5. Another method is to simply select the word or text and, then, holding the left mouse button down, drag the text to the desired location in the document (Figure 6-12).

Move

During the editing process of the assignment, it is determined that the information needs to be moved to another section of the document for clarity and better understanding. The **Move** function will allow the writer to easily move text within the document to another location. This function is commonly known as the drag and drop method of moving text.

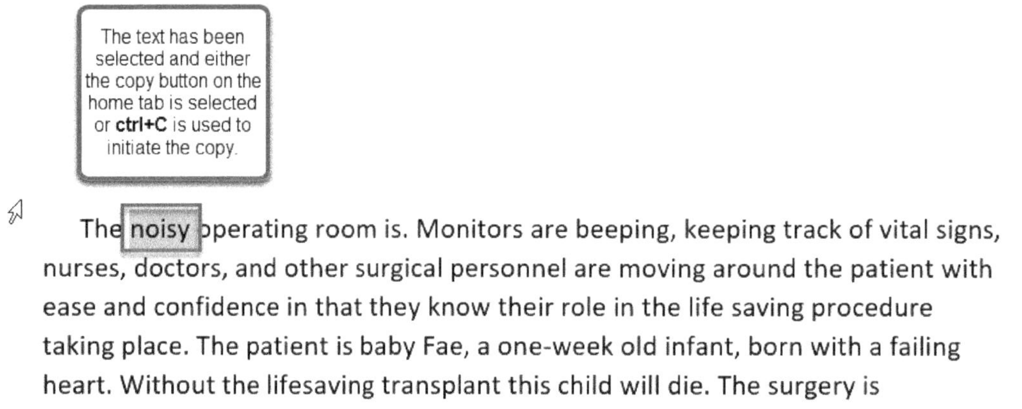

> The text has been selected and either the copy button on the home tab is selected or **ctrl+C** is used to initiate the copy.

The noisy operating room is. Monitors are beeping, keeping track of vital signs, nurses, doctors, and other surgical personnel are moving around the patient with ease and confidence in that they know their role in the life saving procedure taking place. The patient is baby Fae, a one-week old infant, born with a failing heart. Without the lifesaving transplant this child will die. The surgery is

FIGURE 6-12 Select Text

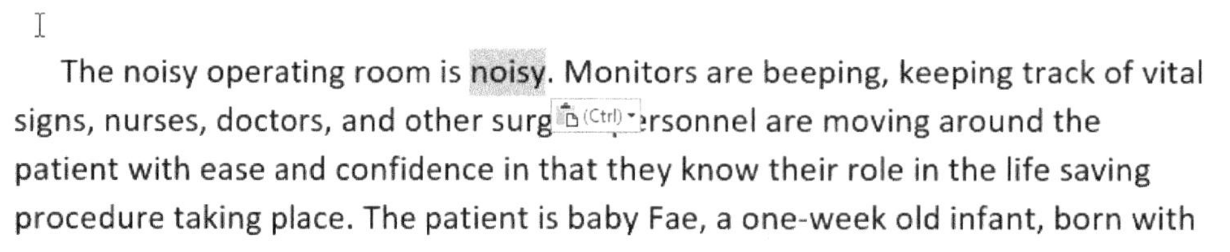

The noisy operating room is noisy. Monitors are beeping, keeping track of vital signs, nurses, doctors, and other surg (Ctrl) ersonnel are moving around the patient with ease and confidence in that they know their role in the life saving procedure taking place. The patient is baby Fae, a one-week old infant, born with

FIGURE 6-13 Move Text

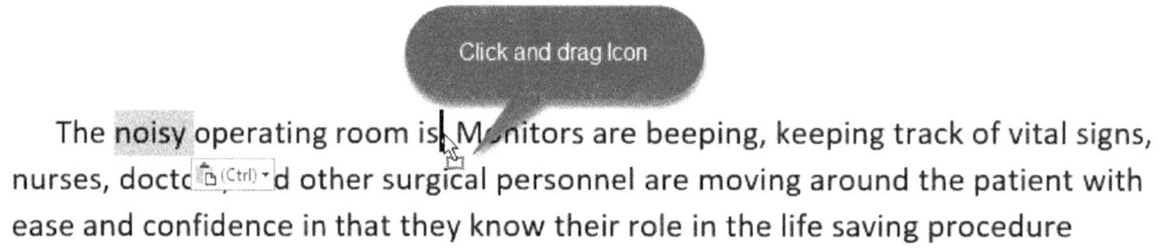

> Click and drag Icon

The noisy operating room is Monitors are beeping, keeping track of vital signs, nurses, docto (Ctrl) d other surgical personnel are moving around the patient with ease and confidence in that they know their role in the life saving procedure

FIGURE 6-14 Drag and Drop

Undo

We have all had the proverbial "oops" situation where our fingers got in the way of each other and we did something we did not want to do. The **Undo** feature allows the editor of the document to quickly undo errors within the document while the document is opened. Once the document has been closed, all stored undo items are no longer available.

Redo

Occasionally, when working with the Undo feature, an item was undone that should not have been. The **Redo** feature will allow you to redo the last item that was undone.

With both the Undo and Redo, if you have not made any corrections, they will not be available. You will know that they are unavailable because the tools will be grayed out.

Format Painter

Many times, people find it is much easier to simply enter all the information into a document and then go back and apply specific formatting. The **Format Painter** allows the ease of copying formatting from one item to another. The feature also allows the application of repeated formats throughout the document.

To use the **Format Painter,** select the text with the format you wish to apply elsewhere in the document. Click on the **Format Painter**. Now, move to the text you wish to apply the format to and select the text. The **Format Painter** will format the text with the same format as the text first selected. If you have a large amount of text that needs to have the same formatting, **double-click** on the **Format Painter** and then you can move from one item to the next to set the formatting. When you are finished with the **Format Painter**, click on the **Format Painter** to turn it off.

Clipboard

When information has been copied, it is stored on the **Clipboard** for the time the document is opened. During this time, you can easily apply information stored on the clipboard to the document.

Options on the Clipboard allow for you to paste an item in the document or clear all items from the clipboard. Items are retained on the clipboard until you close your document.

To paste an item in your document, select the **Clipboard** from the Home Tab. Click on the dropdown arrow next to the item and select paste. Word will pastes the item into the document where your insertion point is currently located.

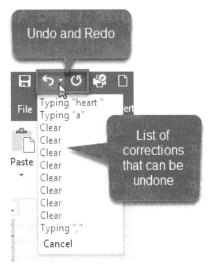

FIGURE 6-15 Undo and Redo

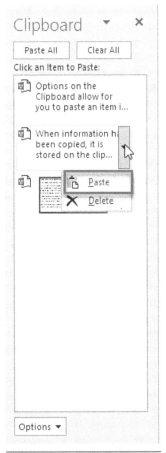

FIGURE 6-16 Clipboard

3. AutoCorrect and AutoComplete Functions

AutoCorrect

The **AutoCorrect** function helps reduce the worry about mistakes by providing a method for correcting common typographical errors. For example, if you know that you spell a word incorrectly all the time and in the same manner, you can set up an AutoCorrect item to automatically correct your mistake when it happens. The AutoCorrect function will also correct common errors such as not capitalizing the word "I" no matter where it is in a sentence. With modern text messaging, this is a common error that tends to drift into academic writing. The AutoCorrect function will correct this error for you. Any time that AutoCorrect is employed, you will have the opportunity to accept the suggestion when Word displays a dialogue box.

AutoFormat

Word's **AutoFormat** will provide automatic formatting within the document: for example, the formatting of fractions, such as ½. Here you can see that the fraction is correctly formatted for the document. Not all fractions are auto-matically formatted in this manner, such as 5/10. Bulleted lists and other formatted items are also automatically formatted in the document.

FIGURE 6-17 AutoComplete

AutoComplete

Word has many features to help users quickly and effectively create documents. The **AutoComplete** feature will automatically complete dates. For example, begin typing the month December; notice in Figure 6-16 that Word will display the full spelling of the month of December. To accept the word, press the **ENTER** key,

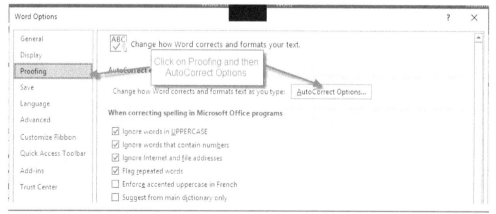

FIGURE 6-18 Custom Auto Correct

and Word will insert the word in your document. If you keep typing the current date, then Word will prompt you with the current date, and by pressing enter, you can enter the full date.

AutoCorrect Custom Entries

Word allows you to create **AutoCorrect** custom entries for your document. As mentioned earlier, if you make the same spelling error, you can set up the **AutoCorrect** functions to make the correction automatically for you. ***Creating Custom AutoCorrect Entries:***

1. Start by clicking on the **File** tab.
2. Now click on the ***Options*** button.
3. Click on the ***Proofing*** button.
4. Enter the text you typically type incorrectly in the Replace box, and then, in the next box, enter the correct spelling of the text.
5. Click on the ***Add*** button.
6. Click on **OK** twice.

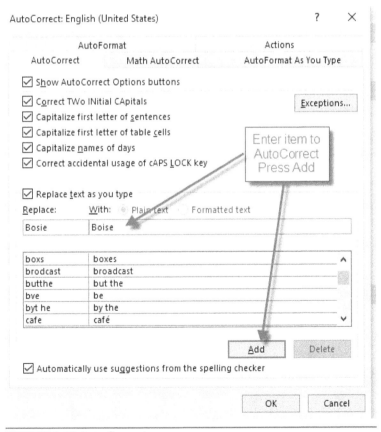

FIGURE 6-19 Auto Correct

Here you will get a chance to test your understanding of the material covered in the chapter. You will need access to a computer with Word. Using the OneDrive Word App will be a viable alternative if you do not have access to a computer with a full version of Office 2019, Office 2021, or Office 365.

In this project, you will continue working on the project you started in the previous checkup. You will be using additional tools that you have learned as you continue to work on the project on the Hells Canyon Power Complex and Recreational Area covering the states of Idaho and Oregon.

File Needed: **(Your initials) Student Checkup Word 6-1**

Completed File Name: **(Your initials) Student Checkup Word 6-2**

1. Open your document from the previous Student Checkup.
2. Select the first sentence in the document. At the end of the first sentence, Press **Enter**.
3. Press **CTRL+END** to place your insertion point at the end of the document.
4. Enter the following text into your document.

Within Hells Canyon there are a number of recreational sites for outdoor enthusiasts. Camping is available all along the canyon. The first campground is located at Brownlee Dam, at the Woodhead campground and picnic area. The campground supports both recreational vehicles and tents. Visitors will find many amenities such as showers, boat ramps and parking, fish cleaning stations, and plenty of beaches for swimming.

Once one goes past the Brownlee Dam and drives towards the Oxbow dam, other camp grounds can be found along the river. These campgrounds are more primitive but will support recreational vehicles and tents for camping. Boat ramps along the river allow fisher men and boaters with a way to easily launch into the river. Fishing is abundant along the river between the dams. Sightseers will see plenty of wildlife from mountain goats, to hawks, and bald eagles. The canyon is rugged and its beauty is in its ruggedness.

The summer provides Idahoans, Oregonians, and many visitors from around the world with plenty of opportunities to enjoy a vast and rugged area known as Hells Canyon Power Complex and Recreational Area. There are many different types of activities available in the canyon. Camping, hiking, fishing, kayaking, and other outdoor activities are available all along the river. Wildlife is plentiful in the canyon and many visitors delight in seeing mountain goats grazing along the steeps of the canyon. Other wildlife such as eagles, deer, and antelope can be seen. This paper will present you with a view of a canyon and recreational area that provides everyone with a glimpse of many different natural marvels.

5. Press **CTRL+S** to save your document.
6. Place your mouse pointer in the left margin of the paper next to the last paragraph, and click twice, selecting the last paragraph.
7. Click on the **Home** tab.
8. Click on the **Cut** icon or on your keyboard press **CTRL+X**.
9. Place your mouse pointer at the beginning of the paragraph that starts "The Snake River" and press **CTRL+V** or Paste on the Home tab. This will paste the paragraph you just copied.
10. Click on the View tab and click on the checkbox next to the Ruler in the show group.

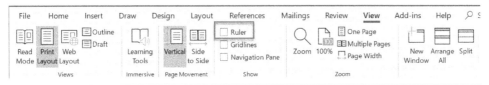

FIGURE 6-20 View Tab—Ruler

11. Set left tab stops. Make sure that the tab stop is set to left as in Figure 6-21a. If your tab stop is not on left, then click on the tab icon until the left tab stops appears.
12. Using your mouse pointer, place it at the ¼ inch mark on the horizontal ruler and click to insert a left tab stop, as in Figure 6-21.
13. Place your mouse pointer at the beginning of the second paragraph that begins with "The summer provides," and click and press the **TAB** key.
14. Repeat the step above with the remaining paragraphs. Figure 6-21b provides you with a view of how the project should look at this point.

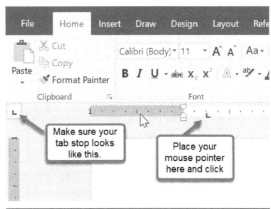

FIGURE 6-21A Setting Tabs

15. Save your document as **(Your initials) Student Checkup Word 6-2**, and submit your assignment as directed by your instructor.

Hells Canyon Recreational Area and Power Complex

The summer provides Idahoans, Oregonians, and many visitors from around the world with plenty of opportunities to enjoy a vast and rugged area known as Hells Canyon Recreational Area. There are many different types of activities available in the canyon. Camping, hiking, fishing, kayaking, and other outdoor activities are available all along the river. Wildlife is plentiful in the canyon and many visitors delight in seeing mountain goats grazing along the steeps of the canyon. Other wildlife such as eagles, deer, and antelope, can be seen. This paper will present you with a view of a canyon and recreational area that provides everyone with a glimpse of many different natural marvels.

The Snake River is one of the longest rivers in the Pacific Northwest. With a length of 1,078 miles, it is the longest tributary of the Columbia River basin. Hells Canyon lies on the Snake River. The canyon itself is 10 miles wide and extends from river mile 254 and ends at river mile 238. The canyon has a depth of 7,993 feet and is known as North America's deepest gorge. The river in the gorge flow past scenic vistas such as the Seven Devils Mountains in Idaho. Accessibility to the area by car is limited due to the rugged terrain of the area. There is a main road that allows visitors to the area to drive from Brownlee Dam, past Oxbow Dam, to the end at Hells Canyon Dam. The drive itself is approximately 40 miles long. The adventurist can take a boat trip further down the river during the summer months.

Within Hells Canyon there are a number of recreational sites for outdoor enthusiasts. Camping is available all along the canyon. The first campground is located at Brownlee Dam, at the Woodhead campground and picnic area. The campground supports both recreational vehicles and tents. Visitors will find many amenities such as showers, boat ramps and parking, fish cleaning stations, and plenty of beaches for swimming.

Once one goes past the Brownlee Dam and drives towards the Oxbow dam, other camp grounds can be found along the river. These campgrounds are more primitive but will support recreational vehicles and tents for camping. Boat ramps along the river allow fisher men and boaters with a way to easily launch into the river. Fishing is abundant along the river between the dams. Sightseers will see plenty of wildlife from mountain goats, to hawks, and bald eagles. The canyon is rugged and its beauty is in its ruggedness.

FIGURE 6-21B Completed Assignment

4. Font, Paragraph, Styles, and Editing Groups

When you initially create a Word document, your document is based upon the *Normal Template*. This means that your paper will be set up with specific fonts, line spacing, and styles that the developers felt were the most commonly used. The college writing styles will require that you make changes to

FIGURE 6-22 Font Group

several elements of the normal template. In this section, we will cover how to make these changes.

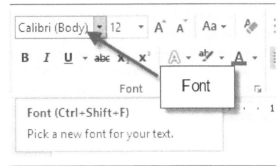

FIGURE 6-23 Fonts

Font Group

The font group provides you with a means of enhancing the look of your document. The use of color, bold, italics, and underlining are just a few of the many features available in the font group.

Starting with the first item in the font group, you will find that you can select from hundreds of different fonts. Calibri is the default font on the normal template. The drop-down menu allows you to select one of the various fonts available. You can also start typing in the font name you with to use, and Word will attempt to find specified font. You will also notice that a list of recently used fonts is available for ease of use.

The next option of importance is the size of the font. The normal template also uses an 11 pt. font size as the default. Font sizes are measured in points. As a rule, 72 pts. equal one inch. This information is important when working on posters, flyers, or other documents where the size of the font is used and measured on a flyer or poster.

Next to the drop-down menu for the font size, you will see the graphic to the right. This function will allow you to increase or decrease your font size by simply clicking on the up or down arrow. This tool is handy when you want to make quick size adjustments to your text. This can be used with a single letter, a whole word, a paragraph, or the whole document.

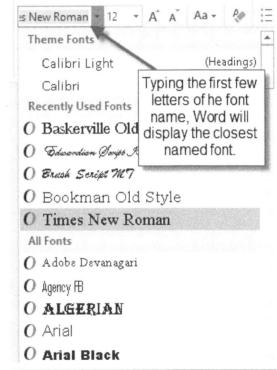

FIGURE 6-24 Font Styles

FIGURE 6-25 Font Size

FIGURE 6-26 Font Enhancements

FIGURE 6-26 Font Enhancements

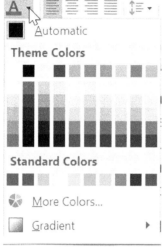

FIGURE 6-27 Font Color

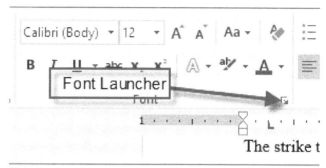

FIGURE 6-28 Font Launcher

The font group includes other formatting options. Bold, italics and underlining are used to highlight specific text in a document and bring attention to the reader of valuable information. The strike through option allows the author or reviewer to annotate an item that should be removed from the document. The subscript and superscript make easy formatting of such items as the molecular structure of water, H_2O, or a mathematical formula such as $X = A^2(B3 + 8)$. Clicking on the subscript and superscript will turn the function on or off.

The remaining options in the font group include text effect, highlighting, and font color. All three options contain a drop-down menu that is provided for you to select the specific feature in each option.

You will notice in each of the groups on the ribbon there is an icon in the lower right corner of the group. This is referred to as the launcher. The launcher will allow you to view more options that are related to each group. The font launcher will provide you with many more options for formatting the font of a document. To access the launcher, click the icon in the lower right corner of the group.

Once you launch the font group launcher, you will be presented with a pop-up menu that provides you with the options for the font group. In the pop-up menu, you will see a preview window that shows you what the font will look like in your document as you make desired changes to the font.

FIGURE 6-29 Font

In Figure 6-29, you can see that the Times New Roman font was selected. A bold emphasis was added to the font, with a color change and a double underline added to the font. In the preview box, you can see what the font will look like before applying it to the document. The advanced

FIGURE 6-30 Paragraph Group

tab allows for further formatting of the font. If you do not want the changes, press the *Cancel* button, and no changes will be applied.

Paragraph Group

Paragraph formatting is a very important part of any document. Many times, students miss some of the excellent paragraph formatting tools available in Word and endure extra, unnecessary time in formatting papers to formatting standards because of a lack of understanding related to formatting paragraphs.

When creating a document and, specifically, a paragraph, you do not want to press the enter key at the end of each line. In the paragraph, Word will wrap the text until you get to the end of the paragraph, and then, you will press the enter key. Pressing the enter key at the end of each line will result in many problems with the correct formatting of your sentences in the paper.

Starting at the top left of the paragraph group, you will see the first three features. Each of these features is designed to allow for the creation of lists (bulleted and numbered) and outlines. Each of the features has a drop-down option to allow you to choose from one of the many available formats or to alter the format you are currently using. Selecting the bullets, a library of different bullet types is presented. The library shows you a sample of the most commonly used bullets. There is also an option for defining your own bullet style with the use of other fonts/symbols such as Wingdings, or even a picture.

The next option is the numbering option. When you are working on a document and you start typing a numbered list, Word will automatically assume that

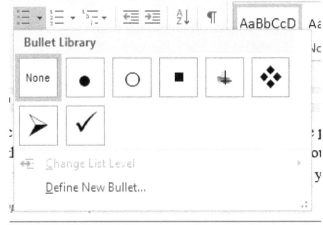

FIGURE 6-31 Bullet Library

FIGURE 6-32 Numbering Library

FIGURE 6-33 List Library

you want to create such a list and will indent the numbered list and create spacing between the number and the information being entered in the document. There are many other numbering styles, and clicking on the down arrow will take you to the library of available numbering options.

The next option is the multilevel or outline list. This list is frequently used by students to create outlines for term papers. The library for the multilevel list contains many different options for creating such a list.

In all the above listings, bullets, numbered listings, and multileveled listings, the use of the tab key and the shift tab are useful in the formatting of information in these listings. By pressing the tab key, the listing will be indented a predetermined number of spaces to the right. To move the indent back to the left, pressing the **SHIFT+TAB** key will change the indent of the listing. The following listing is done using the number listing along with the tab and **SHIFT+TAB** keys.

1. Red
   a. Mauve
   b. Pink
3. Blue
   a. Light blue
   b. Aqua
3. Yellow

The above listing was started by typing in the number 1 and a period. Word started the listing and continued with the listing format. Looking at the ribbon, the number listing option is dark gray when it is active.

Selecting the numbered items, you see that Word highlights the numbers for the list but does not easily allow you to adjust the number in the list. This could be a problem if you have multiple lists within a document and need to adjust the numbering to begin at 1 for each list. To do this, select the list you need to change the number on, and right-click on one of three options:

1. Restart at 1.
2. Continue numbering.
3. Set numbering value.

Each will help you set the design of the numbering format in the desired format.

As sub items in the list are added to the first level, Word changes the numbering of the list with the tabbed indent for the level. The levels in this listing were managed by using the tab and **SHIFT+TAB** keys. If additional levels were needed, Word would appropriately change the level numbering format.

The next feature within the paragraph group is the increase and decrease indent functions.

1. Red
   a. Mauve
   b. Pink
2. Blue
   a. Light blue
   b. Aqua
3. Yellow

FIGURE 6-34 Outline

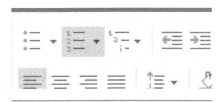

FIGURE 6-35 Number List

FIGURE 6-36 Right-Click Options

There are times when it is necessary to increase the indent of information within a document. Such times could include setting off information from the body of the document, such as a long quote. The increase indent will increase all the information until a decrease indent is applied, returning the paragraph closer to the left margin.

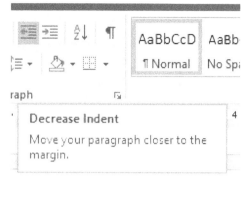

FIGURE 6-37 Decrease Indent

Note: Word retains the formatting of the paragraph above unless you change it in the next paragraph. This also applies if you insert a new paragraph between two paragraphs.

The last option on the first line of the paragraph group is the **Show/Hide** feature. This feature allows you to see the formatting styles applied to the document and where paragraphs begin and end. In the graphic, you can see an example of what Word displays when Show/Hide is selected.

The second line of the paragraph group contains alignment options, line and paragraph spacing options, shading, and borders. The alignment options are just as they sound. They allow for the alignment of the line or paragraph on the paper. As a default, Word aligns all paragraphs to the left margin. The default setting is one inch from the left and right edges of the paper.

The second alignment option is align center. Here the line or paragraph is centered on the line across the paper. This is useful for section headers, allowing for a clean break between sections of a paper. Many formatting styles also require that the title of the paper be placed on the first page of the document and that, that title is centered.

The third option is align right when information is right-aligned, the paragraph is lined up on the right margin of the paper. With many of the college formatting styles, a page header is required on each page, and this header is to be aligned to the right of the paper.

The Early History of Idaho¶

Cassie Drewett¶

College of Western Idaho.................Section Break (Next Page).................

FIGURE 6-38 Show/Hide Section Break

FIGURE 6-39 Line and Paragraph Spacing

The final alignment option is the justify option. This is frequently used in printed publications such as newspapers and magazine articles. The text is presented with an even right and left alignment of the paragraph. In the publishing of newspapers, this alignment makes it easier for the graphics department to easily typeset the article to be printed. This alignment function is not frequently used in academic writing.

There are three other options available in the font group. Line and paragraph spacing, shading, and borders. Line and paragraph spacing allow for a clean look between paragraphs and lines. In academic writing, many of the commonly used formats require that the paper be double-spaced. The author can easily adjust the line spacing within the document. In Figure 6-39, you can see that the spacing in the document is set to 2.0 for double-spacing. There are also options for removing the spacing before and after the paragraph or line.

The shading feature allows you to select text in a paragraph or the paragraph and shade that text. Theme colors and standard colors are presented for your choice. If you do not care for these colors, you can select the more colors option and select a color of your choice.

Borders can be placed around text and paragraphs. The borders function will allow the use of borders to highlight text. Horizontal lines can also be created here, making it easy to place information into sections.

The paragraph launcher allows the author to provide multiple paragraph settings in one place. For example, when writing an academic paper, the launcher allows the author to assign paragraph specifications early in the document. Such specifications would include line spacing, alignment, spacing before and after the paragraph, and special indentations. The author also has the option of setting this information as the default for the specific document now, saving time and effort in the development of the paper format.

Short cut keys that will help you adjust alignment using your keyboard:
Left align—CTRL+L
Center align—CTRL+E
Right align—CTRL+R
Justify—CTRL+J

Styles Group

The styles group is the group that adds style to your document. There are various formatted headings, titles, and emphasis styles that can be used within the paper. The **More** button allows you to see all the available styles for the document and other features such as clear formatting, create style, and apply style.

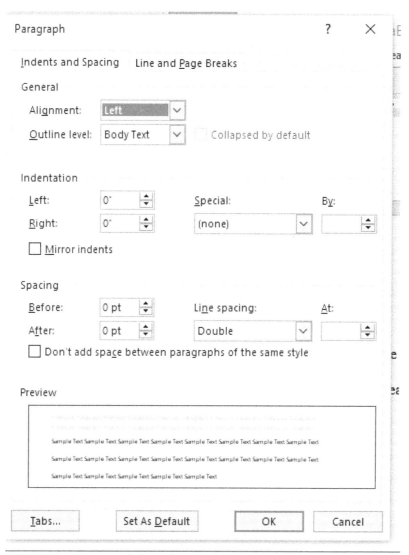

FIGURE 6-40 Paragraph Launcher

When applying a style to a document, you will be given the choice of applying the style to the document only or globally to all Word documents.

Editing Group

The next group on the home tab is the editing group. The **Find** and **Replace** features in the editing group are the two most frequently used options of this group. **Find** allows you to easily find information within the document. In Figure 6-41, the word "Idaho" was selected in the find option. The navigation pane is activated, all instances are highlighted, and the author can easily see and locate the correct instance of the word from the navigation page.

FIGURE 6-41 Find

The other commonly used feature of the editing group is the **Replace** function. Here the author can select replace, and Word will present you with the option to enter the text you wish to replace and what you wish to replace the text with. Figure 6-42 shows you how the replace feature works.

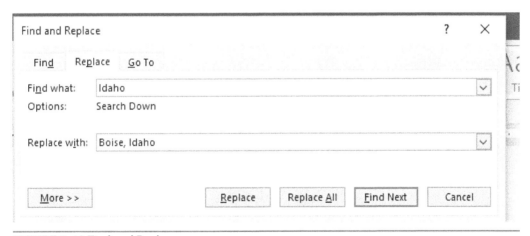

FIGURE 6-42 Find and Replace

Insert and Design Tabs

In this section of the chapter, we will cover some of the other tools located in the Insert and Design tabs of Word. Each of the tabs has several groups of tools available to you to enhance the look of your document. We will start with the Insert tab and then move to the Design tab.

5. Insert Tab—Page, Tables, Illustrations, Header & Footer

Insert Tab

The Insert tab is just as its name implies. This tab allows you to insert assorted items into your document. These items can include cover pages, tables, and illustrations. Other items you can insert from the Insert tab include hyperlinks, online videos, and text boxes. In this section, we will cover several of the more commonly used tools included in each of the various groups on the Insert ribbon.

Pages Group

This group contains three elements useful to all writers whether the writer is creating a term paper or creating an employee handbook. Starting at the bottom of the elements is the page break. Many times, it is important to create a page break within a document. For example, a title page or a works-cited page is needed. These pages must be on their own pages, and there should not be any other information on those pages. Creating a page break within the document will allow this to take place.

FIGURE 6-43 Page Break

Creating a Page Break

1. Ensure that your insertion point is in the document where you want the page break to be placed.
2. Click on the **Insert** tab.
3. Click the **Page Break** located in the **Pages** group.

The next item is the blank page. As a student, you may not come across any assignments that require the inclusion of a blank page within the document. The Blank Page function will allow you to easily insert a blank page.

The third item in the Pages group is the Cover Page. Cover pages are frequently required on many different assignments. Word provides users with several types of cover pages. Using the drop-down menu will present you with a variety of cover pages and other options, such as more options from Office.com and removing cover pages. These cover pages will not work for APA-formatted documents. Formatting of APA cover pages will be covered in a later chapter.

Creating a Cover Page

A cover page can be created at any time in a document. Word is programmed to automatically place the cover page at the beginning of your document.

1. Click on the **Insert** tab.
2. Click on the drop-down arrow next to the **Cover Page** option.

3. Select the built-in cover page that you wish to use. If these do not work, explore the other cover page options from Office.com.

Tables

Tables are used to represent various pieces of information in an organized fashion. Tables can be created directly in Word or linked from an Excel spreadsheet. Word allows you to apply a style to the table or create a simple table with no borders. The table below is a sample of what can be created simply in Word.

Classes	Days	Times
CISA-101	Mon–Wed	3:30–4:45
CWID-101	Mon–Wed	5:00–6:45
Math 125	Tue–Thu	3:30–4:45
History 101	Tue–Thu	5:00–6:45

When you create a table, you will also see the two contextual tabs that are related to the design and layout of your table.

Creating a Table

1. Click on the **Insert** tab.
2. Click on the **Table** drop-down menu.
3. Using your mouse, highlight the number of rows and columns you need for the table. Do not worry if you need more than what is available on drop-down menu. You can easily add more columns and rows.
4. Once the table has been selected, the two contextual tabs will be available for further design of the table you are creating.
5. Click on the **Design** contextual tab.
6. Using the **Table Styles** group, Click on the **More** button and select the table style desired.
7. If you are using a plain table, use the **Borders** drop-down menu to set the borders for the table if desired.

The **Layout** tab will allow the modification of the table. The Rows & Columns group allows you to insert or delete rows and columns within the table. The Merge group will provide you with the

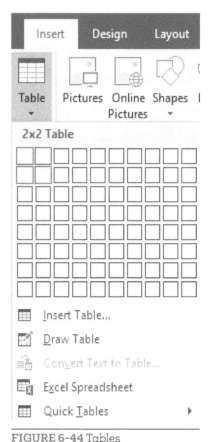

FIGURE 6-44 Tables

ability to merge cells within a table, split cells, or split the table. The alignment group will provide you with the ability to align information in one of nine positions within each cell.

Illustrations Group

The Illustrations group provides you with a means of adding in graphics, picture, and other illustrations to your document. The use of graphics and illustrations can enhance your document and make a point easier to understand for the reader.

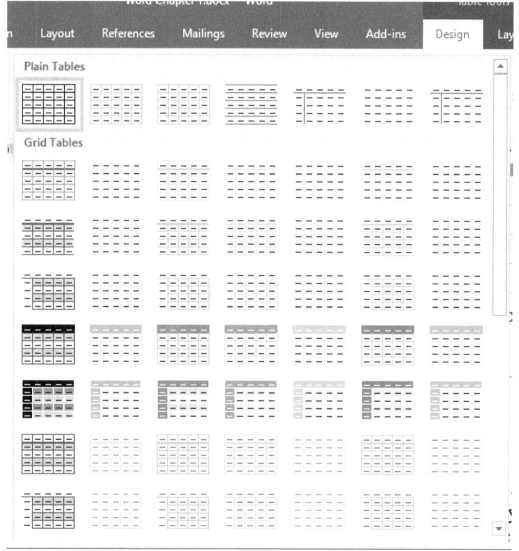

FIGURE 6-45 Table Tools Design Tab

Pictures

The pictures feature will allow you to select a picture that you have taken or one in your pictures library and insert it into your document. When you insert a picture or other graphic, a contextual tab will be available providing you with other formatting options. The following steps will guide you in inserting a picture to your document.

FIGURE 6-46 Table Tools Layout Tab

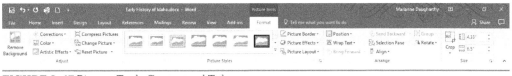

FIGURE 6-47 Picture Tools Contextual Tab

Insert Pictures

1. Click on the Pictures icon in the Illustrations group.
2. **Browse** your computer to the picture you want to insert.
3. Click the **Insert** button once you have selected your picture.
4. For online pictures click on the **Online Pictures** icon.
5. In the image search box, enter the type of picture you are searching for.
6. Select the picture from the results.

FIGURE 6-48 Insert Pictures

Once you have selected the picture you want to insert, the Picture Tools contextual tab will appear. This tab will appear any time you select your picture. It is important to set the text wrapping with your picture. This will anchor your picture and allow you to move the picture

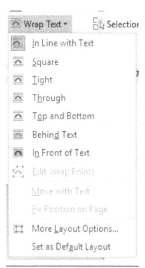

FIGURE 6-49 Search for Pictures

FIGURE 6-50 Wrap Text

within your document. This tool is one that you will also want to use if you are inserting pictures from the Internet or other sources.

You can also create a page break by pressing the **CTRL+ENTER** keys to create a page break within your document.

Shapes

Within the Illustrations group is another tool that allows users to insert and use different shapes within a document. For students who are studying Computer Science, for example, the use of shapes will allow for the creation of flow charts to show the flow of a program or process being designed. For the business major, the use of shapes will allow for the creation of an organizational chart. The following simple organizational chart was made using Word shapes.

Charts like the simple organizational chart below can be created by using the shapes available in Word. The shapes were selected, text entered, and lines chosen to place each position in the correct order.

When a shape is placed in a document, the Drawing Tools contextual tab will be available to allow additional formatting of each shape.

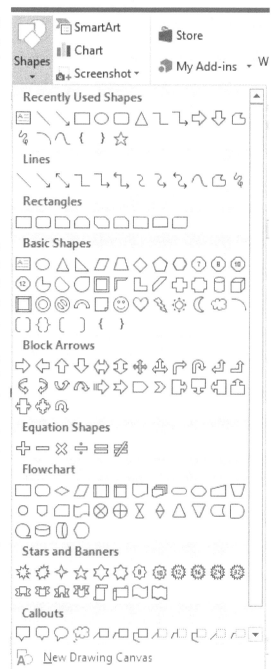

FIGURE 6-51 *Shapes*

SmartArt

SmartArt is another tool that will allow authors to add more visual information to a document. Process, cycle, hierarchy, and a host of other SmartArt

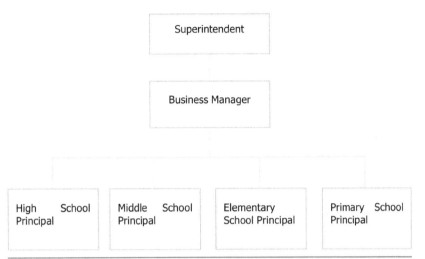

IMAGE 6-1 Flow Chart

FIGURE 6-52 Drawing Tools Contextual Tab

graphics are available to create graphical representations of information that will provide a clearer picture of information within a document.

The organizational chart created in the previous section using shapes can be created in the SmartArt using the hierarchy SmartArt.

SmartArt has a contextual tab that is available when working with SmartArt objects. The contextual tab contains two tabs, the design and format tab, each designed enhance the SmartArt object inserted in the document.

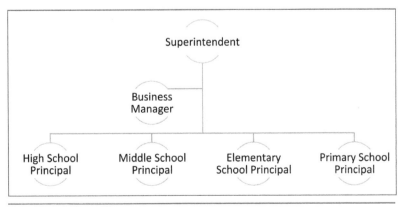

IMAGE 6-2 Flow Chart

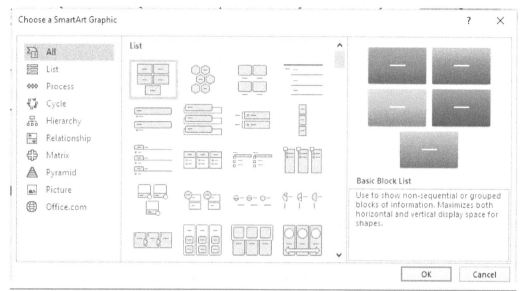

FIGURE 6-53 SmartArt

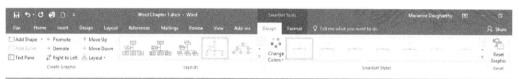

FIGURE 6-54 SmartArt Tools

Header & Footer Group

Each document that is created in Word contains a header and footer area for each page. These headers and can easily be modified to fit several different formats and styles. When combined with other Word features such as section breaks, you will find great flexibility in creating documents with numerous appendices and front matter.

FIGURE 6-55 Header and Footer

Header

In most documents, the header is where such items as the page number is located. In MLA and APA formatted documents, there is specific information that is also contained within the header. You can access the header by one of two methods. The first method is to click on the **Insert** tab and then select the header in the Header and Footer section.

There are options available by clicking on the drop-down arrow next to the header option. There are options available with various preformatted headers, additional header styles from Office.com, and editing features.

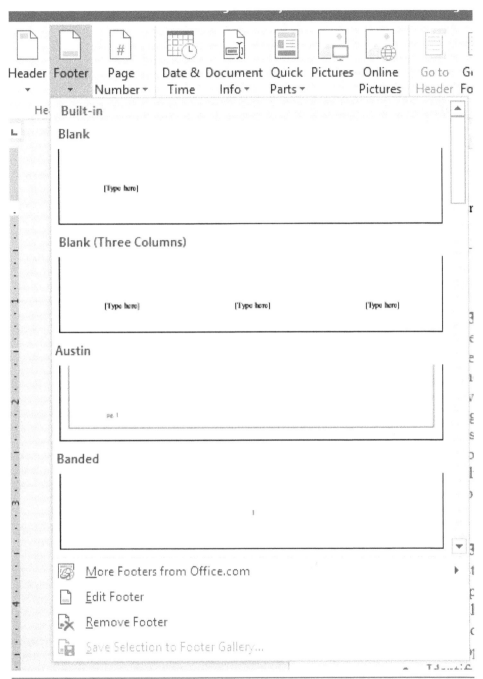

FIGURE 6-56 Footer Options

Second, you can also access the header by double-clicking in the header area located at the top of the document.

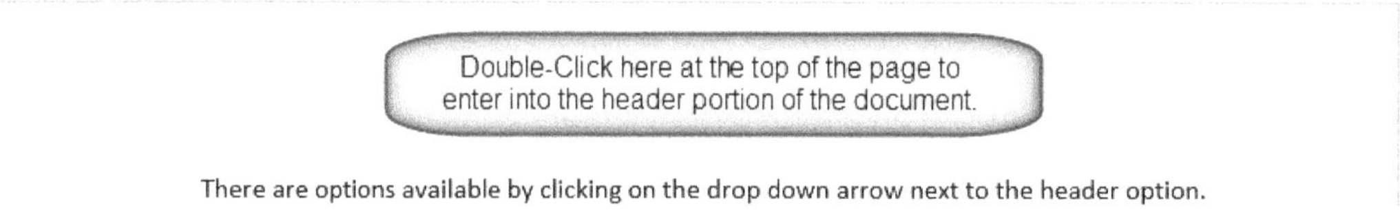

Double-Click here at the top of the page to
enter into the header portion of the document.

There are options available by clicking on the drop down arrow next to the header option.

IMAGE 6-3 Flow Chart

Footer

Now that you have worked with a header. the footer is easy. The footer operates in the same manner as the header. Simply select the Insert tab and select the footer or double-click in the footer area of the document.

Working with Headers and Footers

Headers and footers both work in the same way. We have discussed opening the header and footer, now let's look at working with both. When you are in either the header or footer, the Header and Footer Tools contextual tab appears. This is where you will find many useful tools for working with both.

Headers and footers are preformatted in Word with tab formatting. Any other formatting you must either setup or select from the diverse options available. Default tab stops are set up for the center and right alignment of text entered in these locations.

Changing the style of your header and footer is very straight forward. The header and footer tools we will be using here are in the Header and Footer group. The header and footer icons are the first two tools that you will make use of. If you selected the header or footer through the Insert tab, the drop-down menu for these two tools is the same.

In the dropdown menu, there are a variety of preformatted styles for the headers and footers. By clicking on one, you will change the style of the footer or the header. The headers are more elegant and graphical compared with the counterpart in the footer. The styles in both are meant to complement each other when used together.

Page Number

For many students, a tremendous amount of time is spent formatting the page numbering of a document. This can be frustrating, at best, because students have not been taught how to access the header and footer of a document.

Many students will manually put the page number in on the first line of the page, then they become frustrated because the page number does not stay where it was first inserted into the document. Other issues such as a paragraph spanning two pages also add to formatting frustration. The page number option will solve this issue. When the page number is used, Word will insert a page

FIGURE 6-57 Page Number Options

number in the header that will automatically update as the document is edited. Additionally, the page number inserted will always be in the specified place in the document. This function is frequently used with a plain header or footer although there are elegant options available. You will find a drop-down menu that will provide you with several styles. For papers created that follow MLA or APA formatting, a plain number will be the choice needed for these styles. In Figure 6-57, you can see an example of the various page numbering options that are available.

Here you will get a chance to test your understanding of the material covered in the chapter. You will need access to a computer with Word. Using the OneDrive Word App will be a viable alternative if you do not have access to a computer with a full version of Office 2019, Office 2021, or Office 365. **Note: Blue text represents typed text.**

In this project, you will continue working on the project you started in the previous checkup. You will be using additional tools that you have learned as you continue to work on the project on the Hells Canyon Power Complex and Recreational Area covering the states of Idaho and Oregon.

Files Needed: **(Your initials) Student Checkup Word 6-2**
Hells Canyon Photos.zip

Completed File Name: **(Your initials) Student Checkup Word 6-3**

1. Open your file from the last student checkup.
2. Click the file tab, and save your file as **(Your initials) Student Checkup Word 6-3**.
3. From your document, press **CTRL+A** to select the whole document.
4. On the Home tab, change the font of the whole document to Arial and the Font size to 12 pt.
5. Select the first line by placing your mouse pointer in the left margin near the line. Click once.
6. Using the Styles group on the home tab, click on Title style.
7. With the first paragraph still selected, click on the Font Launcher.

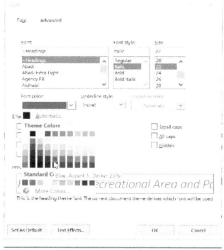

FIGURE 6-58 Font Launcher

FIGURE 6-59 Date Parameter

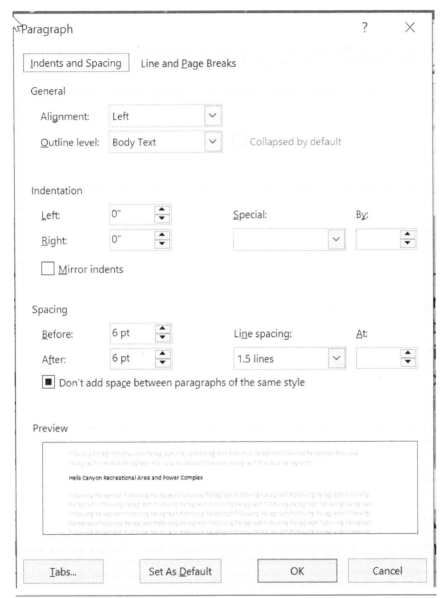

Paragraph ? ✕

Indents and Spacing | Line and Page Breaks

General

Alignment: Left ⌄

Outline level: Body Text ⌄ Collapsed by default

Indentation

Left: 0" ▲▼ Special: By:
⌄ ▲▼

Right: 0" ▲▼

☐ Mirror indents

Spacing

Before: 6 pt ▲▼ Line spacing: At:

After: 6 pt ▲▼ 1.5 lines ⌄ ▲▼

■ Don't add space between paragraphs of the same style

Preview

Previous Paragraph Previous Paragraph Previous Paragraph Previous Paragraph Previous Paragraph Previous Paragraph Previous Paragraph Previous Paragraph Previous Paragraph Previous Paragraph

Hells Canyon Recreational Area and Power Complex

Following Paragraph Following Paragraph

Tabs... | Set As Default | OK | Cancel

FIGURE 6-60 Paragraph Launcher

8. Change the Font size to **22** pt., Font Style Italic, and Font Color Blue, Accent 1, Darker 25%. Press **OK**.
9. Press **CTRL+A** to select the whole document.
10. Click the Paragraph Launcher.
11. Change the Spacing before and after to 6 pt.
12. Change the Line Spacing to 1.5 lines.

13. Click **OK**.
14. Select the **Insert** tab, and click on the Cover page.
15. In the Date parameter, click on the drop-down menu and select the current date.
16. In the Title parameter, enter Hells Canyon Power Complex and Recreational Area. Ensure that the title is left aligned.
17. Delete the Subtitle.
18. Ensure that your name is in the Author parameter.
19. Enter your school name in the Company Name.
20. Press **CTRL+END** to move to the end of the document. Select the Insert tab.
21. Select SmartArt. Choose List and then scroll down until you find Horizontal Picture List and press **OK**.

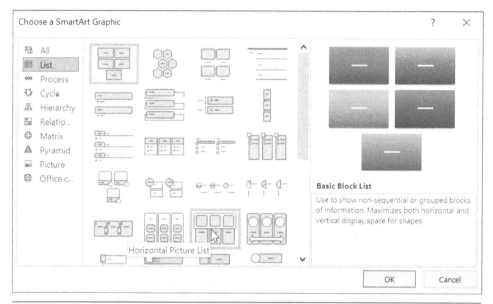

FIGURE 6-61 SmartArt

22. Enter the information in Figure 6-62 into the SmartArt graphic. Go online to select photographs for the graphic. Use 'Brownlee Dam', 'Oxbow Dam', and 'Hells Canyon Dam' as your search parameters.

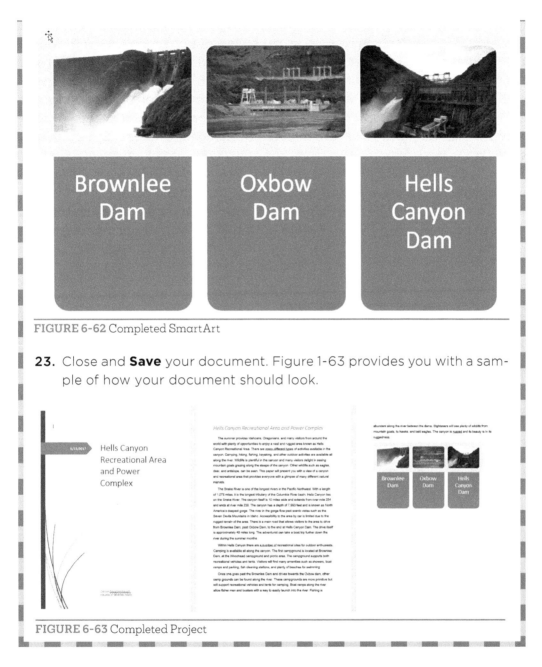

FIGURE 6-62 Completed SmartArt

23. Close and **Save** your document. Figure 1-63 provides you with a sample of how your document should look.

FIGURE 6-63 Completed Project

6. Design Tab—Themes and Document Formatting

The Design tab allows you to select from several design features. While the Normal Template is the default layout when you open a new document, there are times when you might want to venture to the other design formats. This section will provide you with directions on how to make these changes.

Themes

Earlier in this chapter, you learned about styles. In this section, we will discuss the features that initially set up those preformatted styles. The first item on the Design tab is the document formatting group, which contains the themes, styles, colors, and fonts. These themes provide you with a variety of options when designing and setting up your paper. Color and font styles have been chosen for each theme, and you have the freedom to change the color scheme and font style for the design theme.

The default theme is the Office theme. For most work, this theme is the acceptable theme. The colors and fonts are standard for both the college and business environments. The styles menu provides you with a variety of unique styles that can be used with a theme. A **More** button allows you to see more styles for a theme.

FIGURE 6-64 Design Themes

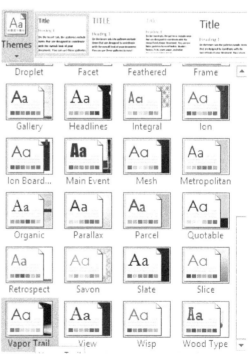

FIGURE 6-65 Available Design Themes

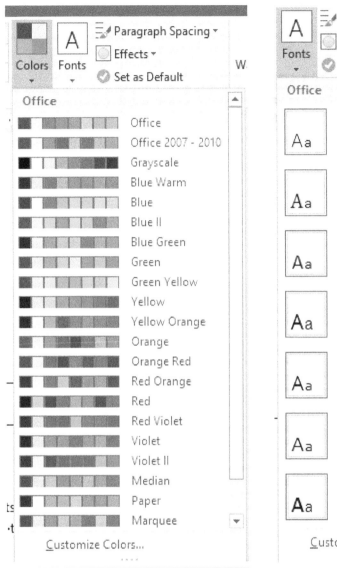

FIGURE 6-66 Color Options

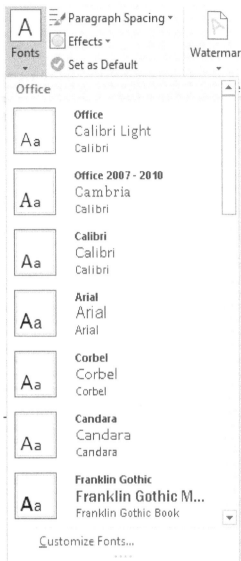

FIGURE 6-67 Font Options

Changing Themes

To change a theme, use the following steps:

1. Select the **Design** tab.
2. Click on the drop-down arrow.
3. Click on the desired theme.

If you have started your document, you can see a live preview of what the theme looks like as you hover over a specific theme in your document.

Colors and Fonts

Many companies and organizations have their own set of colors that are used in their documents. The colors option in the Design Tab provides you with a list of coordinated color groups. You also can create your own color combinations by using the customize colors option on the drop-down menu.

To change colors:

1. Click on the **Colors** drop-down arrow.
2. Find the color scheme you want, and click on it to select the scheme.

As with the themes, Word will provide you with a live preview of the color scheme in your document as you hover over each of the color selections.

Fonts work in the same manner as the Colors option. You also can create your own Font combinations by using the customize font option on the drop-down menu.

To change Fonts:

1. Click on the **Fonts** drop-down arrow.
2. Find the color scheme you want and click on it to select the scheme.

7. Review Tab—Spelling and Grammar

With any paper before turning it in for grading, you need to check the paper for spelling and grammar errors. Word provides you with some tools that will allow you to easily spot problems as you are writing the paper. The **Review Tab** (Figure 6-68) contains tools that will help you ensure your paper has the correct spelling and grammar. Other features that we will cover later include the Comments group, the Tracking group, and the Changes group. Right now, we just want to cover the Proofing group, specifically Spelling and Grammar. Let's start by looking at the clues Word provides you while you write your paper.

FIGURE 6-68 Review Tab

When you are writing a paper, you will see, on occasion, a word underlined with a red wavy line. This is an indication of a spelling error. In some cases, the indicated

By·Cassie·Daughenbaugh¶

FIGURE 6-69 Spelling Error

spelling error is not a spelling error. Names and foreign words are commonly highlighted as incorrectly spelled. In Figure 6-69, you can see that the last name of the author is underlined as a spelling error. If you know that the highlighted word is correctly spelled, you can right-click on the word and click on the **Ignore** or **Ignore All.** From this point on, Word will ignore all occurrences of this word. If it is a word that you use often, consider adding the word to the dictionary. Figure 6-70 depicts the options available on a right click. If the word is a common word or a word in the dictionary, click on the correct spelling of the word when you use the right-click function.

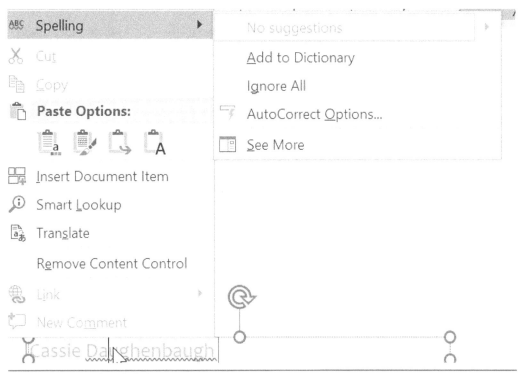

FIGURE 6-70 Right-Click Options

Spelling errors are not the only issues students have to face. Grammatical errors are another area that needs to be addressed. Grammatical errors are identified using a double blue underline. Grammatical errors can range from punctuation issues to the correct format of words such as "cannot." Figure 6-71 shows an example of a grammatical error. Grammatical errors can also be corrected by using a right click. As with the right click on spelling errors, you can click on the correction of choice when displayed.

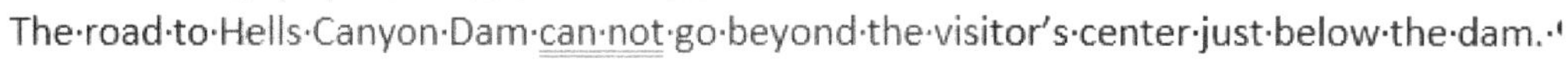

The·road·to·Hells·Canyon·Dam·<u>can·not</u>·go·beyond·the·visitor's·center·just·below·the·dam.·

FIGURE 6-71 Grammatical Error

Another error type that Word highlights are errors of **clarity and conciseness**. These errors are highlighted with a dotted red underline. In Figure 6-72, you can see that the text is underlined, showing that the phrase could be written with more clarity and in a more concise manner. The phrase would be changed to "many," "several," or "a few." As the author, you can choose from any of the three choices or leave the phrase as is.

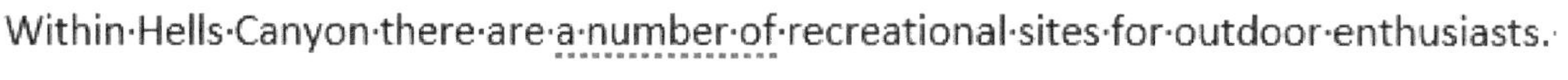

Within·Hells·Canyon·there·are·<u>a·number·of</u>·recreational·sites·for·outdoor·enthusiasts.·

FIGURE 6-72 Clarity and Conciseness

Another option you have for checking your paper is to select the **Spelling and Grammar** (Figure 6-73) icon in the **Proofing** group. This option will go through your paper and highlight each item potentially in error providing you with options for correcting each item in error. Word will display an editor pane to display all the errors or problems to be corrected. In Figure 6-74, you can see how Word provides you with choices to correct the issue. To make the correction, click on the correction of choice.

FIGURE 6-73 Proofing Group

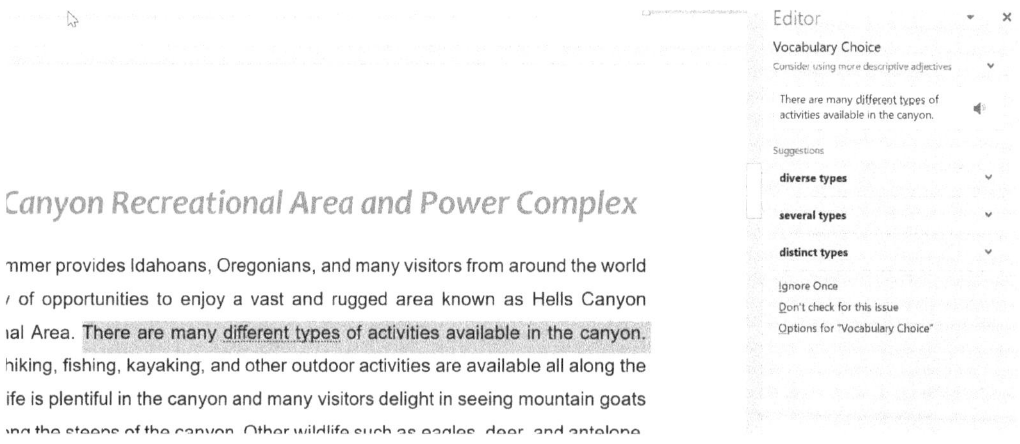

FIGURE 6-74 Spelling and Grammar

Here you will get a chance to test your understanding of the material covered in the chapter. You will need access to a computer with Word. Using the OneDrive Word App will be a viable alternative if you do not have access to a computer with a full version of Office 2019, Office 2021, or Office 365.

In this project, you will continue working on the project you started in the previous checkup. You will be using additional tools that you have learned as you continue to work on the project on the Hells Canyon Power Complex and Recreational Area covering the states of Idaho and Oregon.

File Needed: **(Your initials) Student Checkup Word 6-3**
Completed File Name: **(Your initials) Student Checkup Word 6-4**

1. Open the document you created in the last Student Checkup.
2. Save the current document as **(Your initials) Student Checkup Word 6-4**.
3. Select the **Design** Tab.
4. In the Themes drop-down menu, change the theme to Metropolitan.
5. Using the Document Formatting group, select the document formatting style Black and White (Classic), the sixth option from the left.
6. Using the **Theme Fonts**, change the font to **Candara**. Ensure that your title on your cover page is left-aligned.
7. Select the **Insert** tab.
8. In the **Header and Footer** group, click on the **Header** drop-down menu and select **Slice 2**.
9. Using the Header and Footer Tools contextual tab, click on **Go To Footer**.
10. In the Insert group, click on the **Date and Time**, select the date format, September 1, 2021, the third option from the top. (The date itself will differ: it automatically updates every day.) Ensure that you have the **Update Automatically** box checked.
11. Click *OK*.
12. Click Close Header and Footer.
13. Select the **Review Tab**, click on the **Spelling & Grammar** icon. Make the following corrections:
    a. *different types*—change to diverse types
    b. *a number of*—change to several
14. Save your document, and submit to your instructor.

15. Your completed project should resemble Figure 6-75 below.

FIGURE 6-75 Completed Document

Chapter Projects

In this chapter, you have been introduced to many of the necessary basics that will allow you to begin creating Word documents for school and outside of school. **Note: Blue text represents typed text.**

File Needed: **Word Chapter 6 Project 1 (Arlington)**

Completed File Name: **(Your Initials) Word Chapter 6 Project 1 (Arlington).**

1. Open an existing document.
   a. Open the document titled Word Chapter 6 Project 1.
2. Save the document using **Save As**.
   a. Using **Save As**, save the document with the following file Name: (Your Initials) Word Chapter 6 Project 1.
3. Select your whole document by pressing **CTRL+A.**
4. Change the line spacing of your document to 1.5.
5. Set the paragraph before and after spacing to **6** pt.
6. With your document still selected, change the font of the document to Times **New Roman** with a **12** pt. font size.
7. Press **CTRL+S** to **save** your document.
8. Select the first line of the paper, the title, and apply the **Title** style to it. Center align the title.
9. Select the second line and apply the **subtitle,** center align the text, and increase the font size to **14** pt.

10. Select the line, "The Changing of the Guard" and apply the **Heading 1** style to it.
11. Change the document theme to **Slice** (Design tab/Themes).
12. Change the Document Formatting to **Casual** and colors to **Slipstream** (Design tab/Document Formatting). Note the style sets are in alphabetical order from left to right).
13. Select everything in the document except the title and the subtitle. Change the paragraph formatting by setting the Indentation under the special option to First Line by .25 inches.
14. Select the entire document except the title, subtitle, and the Heading 1 "Changing of the Guard".
15. In the first line of the new page, type **References** and press ENTER.
16. Set the style to heading 1, and center the text.
17. In the following line enter the following information: http://www.arlingtoncemetery.mil/Explore/Changing-of-the-Guard.
18. **Save** your document.
19. Go to Backstage view (File tab). Click on Info, then click on the down arrow next to Properties. Click on Advanced Properties. In the Title box, type in 'Arlington Cemetery' and in the Author box, type in your name.
20. Change the title of the document to Arlington Cemetery.
21. Enter your name in the author field. Click **OK**, and return to the document.
22. Click on the **Insert** tab, and insert a cover page using the Filigree style.
23. In the subtitle, enter "**The Tomb of the Unknown Soldier**."
24. Select today's date, and delete the Company Name and Company Address fields.
25. From the Title on page 2, delete the comma after 'Arlington Cemetery' and the words 'Washington D.C.'.
26. On the **Insert** tab, in the **Header and Footer** group, click on the **Header** drop-down menu and select **Filigree**.
27. In the **Header and Footer Tools** group (Header & Footer Tools/Design tab/Options group), click on the **Different First Page** check box (if not already selected).
28. Select the first page footer, and then select the Filigree footer style.
29. Select the second page footer, then and select page number; use **Plain Number Style 3** from the Bottom of Page options. Close Header and Footer.
30. Move your cursor in front of the title on page 2. Select the Home tab. Click on Replace in the Editing group. Make the following changes:
    a. *is located in*—change to "is in" (1 replacement).
    b. *At this time*—change to "Now" (1 Replacement).
    c. *dignitaries*—change all to "dignitaries" (1 Replacement).

d. *soliminity*—change all to "solemnity" (2 Replacements).

e. (3 Replacements).

f. *time honored*—change to "time-honored"

g. *united states* to *United States*. (1 Replacement).

h. Click **OK** when you receive the "spell-check complete" message.

31. **Save** your document, and submit it as directed by your instructor.

32. Figure 6-76 provides you with an example of the completed project.

FIGURE 6-76 Completed Chapter 6 Project 1

In this chapter, you have been introduced to many of the necessary basics that will allow you to begin creating Word documents for school and outside of school. **Note: Blue text represents typed text.**

File Needed: **Word Chapter 6 Project 2 (Yellowstone)**

Completed File Name: **(Your Initials) Word Chapter 6 Project 2 (Yellowstone).**

1. Open an existing document.
   a. Open the document titled: Word Chapter 6 Project 2 (Yellowstone).
2. Save the document using **Save As**.
   a. Using Save As, save the document with the following file name: **(Your Initials) Word Chapter 6 Project 2 (Yellowstone)**.
3. Select your whole document by pressing **CTRL+A.**
4. Change the line spacing of your document to 1.5.
5. Set the paragraph before and after spacing to 6 pt.
6. Change the paragraph formatting. In the **Indention** section, set the **Special** option to **First Line** by 0.25".
7. With your document still selected, change the font of the document to Arial with a 12 pt. font size.
8. Press **CTRL+S** to **save** your document.
9. Change the color for the theme to **Red Orange** (Design tab/Document Formatting group, Colors).
10. Change the color for the theme to **Red/Orange.**
11. Select the first line of the paper, the title, and apply the **Title** style to it. Center align the title.
12. Go to the end of your document, and insert a hard page break.
13. In the first line of the new page, type "**References**," and press enter.
14. Set the style to heading 1 and center the text.
15. In the following line enter the following information: https://www.nps.gov/yell/learn/historyculture/yellowstoneestablishment.htm.
16. **Save** your document.
17. Go to Backstage view (File tab). Click on Info, then click on the down arrow next to Properties. Click on Advanced Properties.
18. Change the title of the document to "**Yellowstone National Park**."
19. Enter your name in the Author field. Delete any other information except for Title and Author fields. Click **OK** and return to the document.
20. Click on the **Insert** tab, and insert a cover page using the Integral style. Ensure that your title is right aligned.
21. In the subtitle enter **Land of Fire and Ice**.
22. Select the abstract field and delete it; delete the word "Abstract."

23. Below your name insert your course information.
24. Click on the picture and delete it. Replace it with a picture of Yellowstone. Use the search parameter of "Yellowstone National Park". Resize picture to 4.18" tall by 4 wide or as close as you can.
25. Go to the next page.
26. In the **Header and Footer** group (**Insert** tab), click on the **Header** drop-down and select ***Filigree***.
27. In the **Header and Footer Tools** group (Header & Footer Tools/Design tab/Options group), click on the **Different First Page** check box (if not already selected).
28. In the **Header and Footer Group** on the **Design** tab, click on Footer or double-click in the footer on page 2.
29. Click on the drop-down arrow under **Footer**.
30. Click on **Page Number**, then **Bottom of Page**. Select 'Tildes'.
    a. If page number is "1", click on the **Page Number** icon. Then click on **Format Page numbers**. If page number is "1", select the number 1 and then Under the **Page Number** section, click in circle next to **Start At**, then type in '2' in the box. Close **Header and Footer**.
31. In the first paragraph of the body of the paper, change "It was at the beginning" of the first sentence to "**Yellowstone National Park is**." (1 Replacement).
32. Move your cursor in front of the title on page 2. Select the Home tab. Click on Replace in the Editing group. Make the following changes:
    a. *time period*—change to "period" (2 replacements)
    b. *Recent news*—change to latest (1 Replacement)
    c. *Gant* to *Grant*. Close the Find and Replace dialog box. (1 Replacement).
33. **Save** your document, and submit as instructed by your instructor.
34. Figure 6-77 provides you with an example of the completed project.

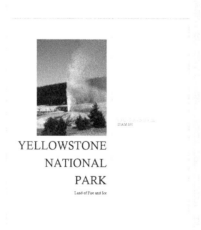

FIGURE 6-77 Completed Project

were made to the protection of the huge park. The biggest threat came from poachers. Bison were almost poached to extinction, and the punishment for poaching was banishment from the park. The efforts of Emmerson Hough and George Bird Grinnell created a national outcry that spurred Congress to create and pass the National Park Protection Act. This act gave the Army the authority and ability to protect all parts of the park.

Today visitors can visit the park and enjoy the many features and treasures of the park. The most famous attraction is Old Faithful Geyser. This geyser derives its name from the predictability of its eruptions. The actual eruptions occur every 60 to 90 minutes and can be predicted within 10 minutes of the eruption. Scientists have noted that the length of an eruption will also determine how soon the geyser will erupt again. A short eruption will lead to a shorter period between eruptions, while a longer eruption will produce a longer period. Because of the frequency of the eruptions, Old Faithful is a favorite of most visitors.

From Old Faithful, walkways are provided for visitors to view other hydrothermal points of interest. Visitors can stroll from the Old Faithful Visitors center out to the Morning Glory pool. Along this leisurely stroll, visitors pass by various geysers that may be just sending up steam, bubbling, or erupting. Latest news reports stated that Steamboat geyser is erupting for the first time since 2014. This geyser's eruptions are totally unpredictable.

As visitors tour the park, they are treated to many fantastical sights. Mud pots and hot springs dot the country side. Lakes and ponds, along with rivers provide fishermen with opportunities for enjoying a leisurely day of fishing. Bison can be seen throughout the park taking a stroll along the roads. Bear and wolf populations are also abundant throughout the park. Deer and moose can be seen in the early mornings and evenings. Bald eagles are frequently seen along the rivers and near lakes. Park managers work to keep the populations in balance while protecting the public from any entanglements with the wildlife.

Yellowstone National Park is one of the crowning jewels of the United States. The measures that Congress has taken help to ensure that the park is available to all who wish to enjoy its treasures.

References

https://www.nps.gov/yell/learn/historyculture/yellowstoneestablishment.htm

---

FIGURE 6-77 *(Continued)*

CHAPTER SEVEN

Word Part II

Introduction

In the previous chapter on Word, you were introduced to the basics of Word. You learned about the various features and tools available to you and gained a basic understanding of each of these tools. There are many more tools available in Word, and in this chapter, we will apply more hands-on experiences and delve deeper into the features available in Word.

Learning Objectives

In this chapter, you will apply the basics of formatting a Word document and further explore the various tools available in Word. When you complete this chapter, you should be able to do the following:

1. Layout Tab—
   a. Access the Page Setup features do manage the margins, page orientation columns, and breaks within your paper.
   b. Use the Arrange features to control the positioning of items on the page.
2. References Tab—
   a. Use the Table of Contents feature to add a table of contents to your document.
   b. Use the Research tools to do additional research on your work.
   c. Use the Citations & Bibliography tools to create a table of contents, insert and manage source information.
   d. Use the Captions group, create captions for graphics used in the document.

3. Review Tab—
   a. Use the Proofing group to access the Thesaurus and word count in the document.
   b. Use the Comments group to insert and delete comments and move between comments.
   c. Use the Tracking group to track changes, review changes made by a reviewer, accept and reject changes.
4. View Tab—
   a. Using the Views group to move between the different views of a document.
   b. Using the Show group to show the ruler and gridlines on a document.
   c. Using the Zoom group change the amount of information that is displayed on the computer screen.
   d. Using the Window group to display two documents side by side.

1. Layout Tab

As you know, your default document is built on the Normal template. For most documents, this template is very effective. For formal academic writing, changes are needed to the document to make it acceptable for assignment submission. The layout tab will provide you with the tools to modify your document to meet college and university standards. In most cases, you will be using MLA and APA formatting standards.

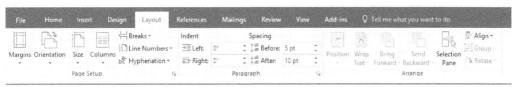

FIGURE 7-1 Layout Tab

Page Setup

Whether you are in school or working for a company, you will find various page setup requirements. In college, you will see formatting styles such as MLA and APA formatting requirements. In the work world, it will vary from company to company. The features covered here will help you to work with any formatting style requirements. The options you will most commonly use are the Margins, Orientation, Columns, and Breaks.

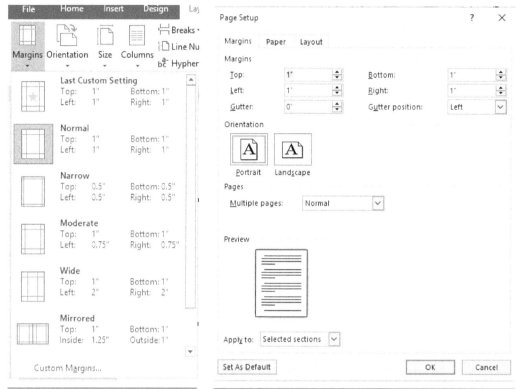

FIGURE 7-2 Margins   FIGURE 7-3 Custom Margins

Margins

Margin settings will vary depending upon the style requirements. In APA formatting, margin settings will be 1 ½ inches for the left margin, and 1 inch for the other three margins. MLA formatting requires margin settings will be 1 inch on all four sides. Adjusting these settings is quick and simple in Word.

Click on the Layout tab. In the page setup group, you will select the margins feature. The drop-down menu will provide you with several common margin settings and the option to set your own margins. For MLA formatting, you can simply use the normal default setting of 1 inch. If you desire to use a different margin setting that is not listed, use the following instructions.

1. In the margins drop-down menu, you will find many predefined margin settings. The normal setting is a 1-inch margin on all sides of the paper. You can select one of the margin settings by **clicking** on the desired setting. There are times, though, when the predefined margin settings will not work for the paper you are working on. To create other margin settings, click on the **Custom Margins** option located at the bottom of the margins drop-down menu.

2. Make the desired changes to the margin(s) by either typing in the margin size or use the up and down spin arrows. The up and down spin arrows will increment the margin size by .10 of an inch.
3. Click **OK**.

Page Orientation

In nearly every assignment that you will complete, the orientation of your paper will be portrait. There are times, however, that it makes sense to change the orientation of a page to landscape. You may even have papers where you need to incorporate the use of both portrait and landscape orientation in the same document. In Word, this can be easily accomplished.

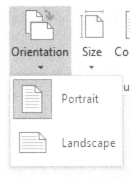

FIGURE 7-4 Page Orientation

Changing Page Orientation

As a rule, Word creates all new documents with a portrait orientation. To use a different orientation, you will need to tell Word to change it.

1. Click on the **Orientation** drop-down menu.
2. Click on the desired orientation.

For a paper that uses multiple orientations, you will need to make use of section breaks to allow you the use of both orientation styles.

1. Place your mouse pointer at the end of the page where you will want the change in orientation to begin.
2. Click on the **Layout** tab and then the **Breaks** drop-down menu.
3. Click on **Next Page**. This will insert a section break along with a page break.
4. Click on **Orientation** and select landscape.
5. Create your page(s) and then repeat steps 2–4 to return the orientation of your paper back to portrait.

Changing page orientation will allow you to easily include spreadsheet information, photos, and other material in your paper in a more appropriate page layout.

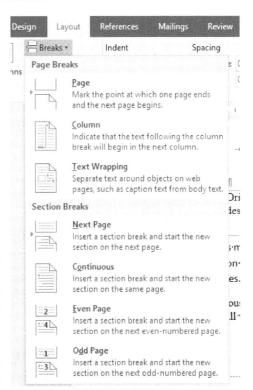

FIGURE 7-5 Page Breaks to Page Multiple Orientations

Columns

There are times when it is necessary to create lists of information that are related. The use of columns will provide you with an easy method of displaying information in an organized format. Making a list of class information would be easier displayed using columns.

Class Name	Meets	Time
Introduction to Computers	Mon and Wed	3:30-4:45
Connecting with Ideas	Mon and Wed	5:00-6:15
Math 125	Tue and Thu	3:30-4:45
Science 101	Tue and Thu	5:00-6:15

Setting Up Columns

The use of columns is accomplished by using a couple of functions.

FIGURE 7-6 Columns

1. Prior to setting up the columns as above, a Continuous Section break is inserted into the document.
2. Press **Enter** to start a new line.
3. Click on the **Columns** drop-down menu and select the number of columns.
4. Enter the information in the first column then insert a Column break from the breaks drop-down menu.
5. Enter the information in the next column. In the example above, there are three columns, so another Column break is needed at the end of the second column. Enter the information in column three.
6. Once all column information is entered, select the **Breaks** drop-down menu again and insert another **Continuous Section** break.
7. Select the **Columns** drop-down menu and select **One** column. You are now ready to move on with the rest of your paper.

Breaks

The use of breaks allows you to do different things with your paper. If you are writing an APA formatted paper, you will need to make use of section breaks to control the formatting of the different page styles required. We will learn more about this type of formatting in the next chapter. When you need to insert columns, change the page orientation within the document, add in columns, or use different page numbering, using different breaks will provide you the means of accomplishing these tasks. In Figure 7-7, you can see the variety of Page and Section Breaks that are available to use in a document. Along with the different breaks, you will also see what each type of break is designed to accomplish. The most common breaks are the Page, Column, Next Page, and Continuous breaks. Earlier in the chapter, you were introduced to the Column Break which you needed to use to create a three-column section in the paper.

Along with the Column Break, you also needed to use a Continuous Section Break to tell Word that you needed to set aside a specific area in the paper to handle the columns. The Continuous Section Break allows you to break a page into different sections to handle information in different formats. As you work through the different exercises in this chapter and the next, you will have the opportunity to try many of the different types of breaks.

FIGURE 7-7 Page and Section Breaks

File Needed: **(Your initials) Student Checkup Word 6-4**
Completed File Name: **(Your initials) Student Checkup Word 7-1**

1. Open your student checkup file from project 6-4.
2. Save the file as (Your initials) Student Checkup Word 7-1.
3. Using the **Layout** Tab change the left margin to 1.25 inches.
4. Go to the end of the document and place your insertion point at the end of the last paragraph, before the SmartArt graphic. Using the Breaks function, select a Next Page Section Break. The SmartArt graphic will now be on a new page.
5. Change the Orientation from Portrait to Landscape. Select the SmartArt and center it horizontally on the page.
6. Press **CTRL+End** to move to the end of the document. Press the Enter key to create a new paragraph.
7. Using the **Breaks** function, select a Next Page Section Break.
8. Change the Page Orientation to Portrait.
9. Using **WordArt**, select any **WordArt** style of your choice. Type in '**Idaho Hells Canyon Campsites**' as the title. Center the title at the top of the page. Change the **SmartArt** font size to **28** pt. Press **ENTER** three times to create three new blank lines.
10. Under the WordArt, put your cursor on the third blank line and ensure that it is left-aligned.
11. Using the information in Figure 7-8, create a list of the following beginning with **Campsite Names**, then all the campsite names listed below, then **Number of Campsites**, then all the numbers listed below, and then **Hiking**, then the following "Yes". This will appear in a long list of items in one column. This is OK.
12. Select all the information you just entered in the list. In the **Layout** tab, click on **Columns**, next click on **Three Columns**. Your list should be adjusted to three columns. If you still have only 1 column, place your cursor in the list in front of **Number of Campgrounds**. On the **Layout** tab, click on **Breaks**. Then click on **Column**. Then place your cursor in the list in front of **Hiking**. On the **Layout** tab, click on **Breaks**. Then click on **Column**. If needed, adjust the left margin on the ruler so that all information in the first and second columns are on one line for each entry.
13. For the first entry of each column, make the following changes.
    a. Dark Teal, Text 2, Lighter 10%
    b. Underline and Bold the text
    c. Left Align the Text
    d. If necessary, adjust the right column margin so that all information in the first and second columns are on one line for each entry.

14. Save your document and submit to your instructor as directed. Figure 7-9 shows you how the last two pages of the document should look when you have completed this assignment.

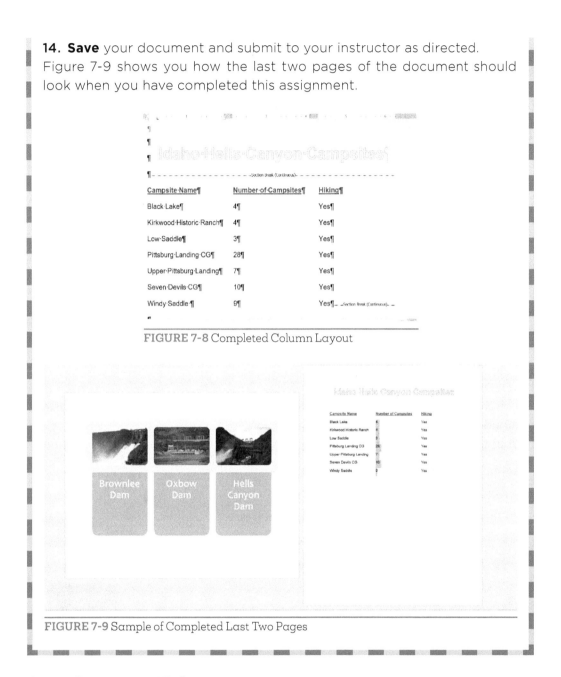

FIGURE 7-8 Completed Column Layout

FIGURE 7-9 Sample of Completed Last Two Pages

2. References Tab

In any assignment, you will need to deal with references. These references can come in the form of in-text citations as you cite the work of an author you are quoting or paraphrasing. Captions are used to provide additional meaning to graphics that you might include in your paper, the table of contents and bibliography provide organization and legitimacy to your paper. All tools play a role in the use of references in your papers. They are a required element of any academic paper and, even in the business world, you will find these tools in use.

We cover the tools that you will use as a student. You can easily take these tools and expand upon them outside of the academic environment.

Table of Contents

Depending upon your learning institution and the style of paper used, you may be required to create a table of contents for longer assignments. The use of the table of contents helps your reader to easily follow the flow of your paper from major point to major point. Microsoft Word makes it easy to add in a table of contents to your paper.

When you create your paper, making use of the heading styles found on the Home tab is the first step in setting up your paper for Word to automatically create your Table of Contents. As you create each major section of your paper, use the appropriate header to identify the section.

FIGURE 7-10 Table of Contents

Footnotes

Footnotes provide a method for putting additional information on the bottom of a page, amplifying information concerning something on the page. Word will format the Footnote at the end of the page with an appropriate font size, annotations, and footing at the bottom of the page. Figure 7-11 shows you an example of a footnote.

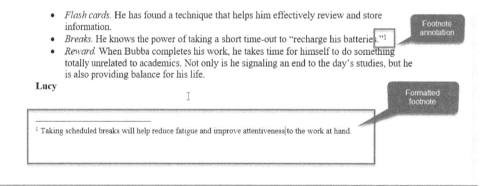

FIGURE 7-11 Footnote Sample

Creating a Footnote

To insert a Footnote, place your insertion point at the location you wish to create a Footnote.

1. On the References tab click **Insert Footnote**.
2. Type in your Footnote in the location that Word places your insertion point.

Another feature in the Footnotes group is the Insert Endnote. An Endnote is used to put a citation or comments related to the specific item at the end of the document. Endnotes work in the same manner as Footnotes with the only difference being the location of the note.

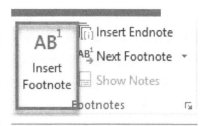

FIGURE 7-12 Insert Footnote

Citations and Bibliography

As a college student, you will be writing numerous papers and doing research for these assignments. Instructors are going to require that you provide an in-text citation and a reference page entry for any items you paraphrase or quote in your paper. The Citations and Bibliography group will provide you a way for easily creating these required items in the document.

Creating Citations

1. Click on the **Style** drop-down menu to select the writing style that is required for your class. This first step will streamline the information presented that will be required for the citation and reference page entry (Figure 7-13). In the figure, you will see the two most commonly used styles in academics highlighted.
2. As you work on your assignment, you will want to create the **In-text Citation** and the **Source** at the same time. This will enable you to quickly and easily reuse the source again if you have other citations for the item.
3. Now you will want to ensure that the insertion point is positioned at the end of the text where you will be inserting the **In-text Citation.** Now you will want to click on the **References** tab and click on the **Insert Citation** drop-down arrow. You will then be presented with two choices as in Figure 7-14.

FIGURE 7-13 Styles

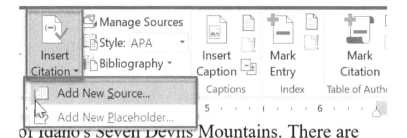

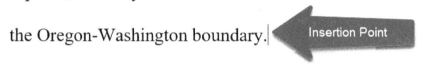

oɪ ɪuaɪɪo s Seven Devils Mountains. There are

expanse, and only three roads that lead to the

the Oregon-Washington boundary.

Insertion Point

FIGURE 7-14 Inserting Citation

4. To insert the citation, you will want to first click on the **Add New Source** option first. This will allow you to enter and build all the citation and reference page information initially. By doing this, you will be able to add in additional citations within your paper from the same source as needed.

5. In the **Create Source** screen, you will enter all the information for your source. Word will then create your **In-Text Citation** from the information you enter. You will see that there are many distinct types of publications currently available. You will need to select the appropriate type of source for your reference. For our example, a website was used as the source. In Figure 7-15, you will see that the information on the source has been inserted. Additionally, because this source is being created as an APA source, the accessed date was also filled in.

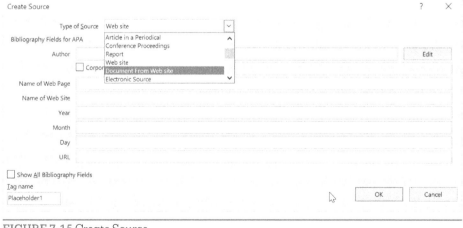

FIGURE 7-15 Create Source

6. Clicking on the **Show All Bibliography Fields** will present you with all of the additional fields available for the style you are working with. The asterisk (*) lets you know which fields you should have filled in for your reference to be as complete as possible. More information in this case is always better. Additionally, if you ever have a question on the proper formatting of references or in-text citations, please make sure that you contact your instructor for additional guidance.

7. When you have completed entering your source information, you will see that Word has also inserted your **In-Text Citation** into your document as in Figure 7-17.

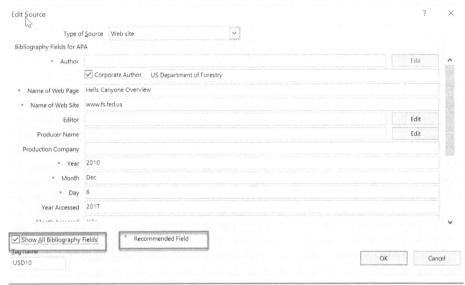

FIGURE 7-16 Create Source Information

8. When you need to insert an **In-Text Citation** from the same source, be sure that you insertion point is in the correct place for the citation. Click on the **Insert Citation** drop-down menu, and select the source from the list of sources associated with the document. Figure 7-18 shows you an example of the source list to choose from.

FIGURE 7-17 In-Text Citation

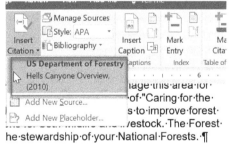

FIGURE 7-18 In-Text Citation from Stored Source

Captions

When using pictures and graphics in a document, you will want to provide a caption with the graphic. The caption will provide information about the graphic.

Inserting Captions

1. Insert the graphic or picture into your document.
2. Wrap the text on the graphic or picture. In Figure 7-19, a Top and Bottom text wrap was selected.
3. Click on the graphic. You know that the graphic is selected because the sizing handles will be available (Figure 7-20).
4. Click on the **References** tab, and then click on the **Insert Caption** icon.
5. Enter the caption information for the caption in the pop-up (Figure 7-21).
6. Once you have entered your caption information, press the **Enter** key.
7. Now you can make modifications to you caption. For some, this will mean aligning the caption to the right or to the center of the caption box.
8. Figure 7-22 shows the picture with the associated caption.
9. Another good practice to do with the caption is to group the picture and the caption together. To group, you will want to select the caption and press the

FIGURE 7-19 Set Text Wrapping

FIGURE 7-20 Sizing Handles

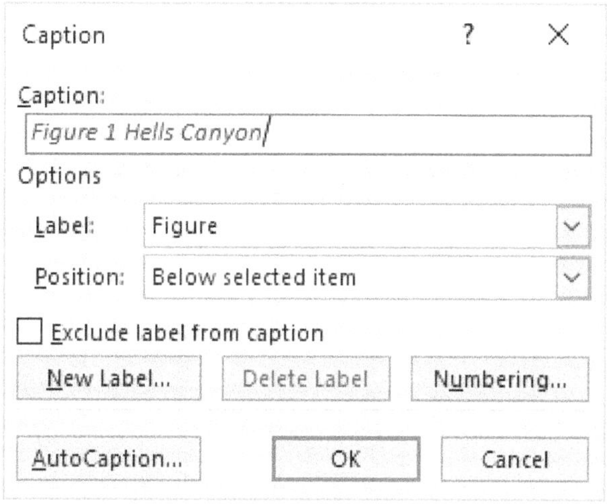

FIGURE 7-21 Insert Caption

Figure·1·Hells·Canyon¶

FIGURE 7-22 Inserting Captions

CTRL key and select the picture. Click on the **Picture Tools** or **Drawing Tools** contextual tabs. In the Arrange group, you will find an icon labeled **Group**. Click on the **Group** icon, and then click on **Group**. This will tie the two items together, and if you must move them, they will retain their formatting. If you need to separate them, click on the **Ungroup** icon.

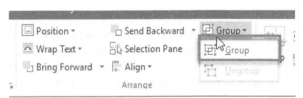

FIGURE 7-23 Grouping Picture and Caption

Here you will get a chance to test your understanding of the material covered in the chapter. You will need access to a computer with Word. Using the OneDrive Word App will be a viable alternative if you do not have access to a computer with a full version of Office 2019, Office 2021, or Office 365.

This is the second of our checkups for Chapter 2. In this checkup, you will continue modifying the document you have been working on, adding in more features and information and making it a more complete document.

File Needed: **(Your initials) Student Checkup Word 7-1**
Completed File Name: **(Your initials) Student Checkup Word 7-2**

1. **Open** the document you created in the last checkpoint.
2. **Save** the document as (Your initials) Student Checkup Word 7-2.
3. Go to the following web page: https://web.archive.org/web/20101206120003/http://www.fs.fed.us/hellscanyon/overview/index.shtml.
4. In your document on page two, move to the end of the second paragraph, place your insertion point at the end of the sentence ending with "during the summer months," and press the **Enter** key, starting a new paragraph.
5. If your new line is not indented, press the **Increase Indent** on the Home tab.
6. From the web page above, copy and paste the paragraph and graphic beginning with "**Hells Canyon, North America's deepest ...**" and ending with "**Oregon-Washington boundary**" on the new line you just created in your document.
7. Ensure that the other formatting of the paragraph matches that of the rest of the text in your document. Click anywhere in the paragraph above. Click on the **Format Painter (paintbrush)** icon (**Home** tab), then place your cursor at the beginning of the new paragraph and click and hold down your left mouse button and "roll" it over all the text in the new paragraph. Ensure that your paragraph font matches the rest of the document. Also ensure that the paragraph is left-aligned.
8. Place your insertion point between the last word in the paragraph (after the word 'boundary') but before the period.
9. Select the **References** tab.
10. For the style, make sure that it is set to APA.
11. Click on the **Insert Citation,** and then **Add New Source**.
12. Enter the following information:
    a. Type of Source—Web site
    b. Corporate Author—U.S. Department of Forestry
    c. Name of Web Page—Hells Canyon Overview
    d. Name of Web Site—www.fs.fed.us
    e. Year—2010

    f. Month—December

    g. Day—06

    h. Year Accessed—Current year

    i. Month Accessed—Current month

    j. Day Accessed—Current Day

    k. URL:https://web.archive.org/web/20101206120003/http://www.fs.fed.us/hellscanyon/overview/index.shtml

Note: if any placeholder item(s) above from a - k do not appear in the **Create Source** window where you enter your citation information, click on **the Show All Bibliography Fields** checkbox. For the URL, you can copy it from the address line on the web site.

13. Move to the beginning of your document.

14. Place your insertion point at the beginning of the first paragraph, "The summer provides," press **Enter**.

15. Move your insertion point to the new line above, and press the **Backspace** key once.

16. Click on **Heading 2** in the **Styles** group.

17. Select **Heading 2**, and enter "**Introduction**".

18. Move to the paragraph that begins with "Hells Canyon, North America's," and press **Enter.**

19. Move your insertion point to the new line above, and press the **Backspace** key once.

20. Click on the **Home** tab.

21. Select **Heading 2**, and enter "**U.S. Forestry Service**". If your U.S. Forestry Service does not align with the left margin, click on the graphic and move it down. You may also have to resize the picture to be smaller to make it fit.

22. Move to the beginning of page 2, and place your insertion point right before the title "Hells Canyon Power Complex and Recreational Area".

23. Select the **References** tab, select **Table of Contents**, and then select **Automatic Table 2.**

24. Press **CTRL+Enter** to create a page break.

25. Scroll down in your document to the picture. Click on the picture to select it.

26. Click on either the **Layout Options (Wrap Text)** icon that appears to the upper right of the picture, then click **Square**. Or, click on the **Picture Tools Format** tab and select **Wrap Text** and then select **Square**. The text will wrap around the graphic.

27. With the picture still selected, click on the **References** tab and select **Insert Caption.** Enter the caption information as shown in Figure 7-24. Press **OK**.

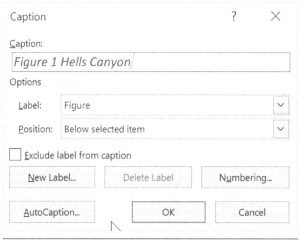

FIGURE 7-24 Caption Information

28. **Center align** the caption to fit underneath the graphic. Right-click on the graphic and select "**Remove Link**". **Group** the picture and caption (**Picture Tools** tab/**Arrange** group/**Group Objects** button).

29. **Save** your document and submit to your instructor as instructed.

Completed document for this assignment.

FIGURE 7-25 Completed 7-2 Checkup Project

3. Review Tab

The **Review** Tab is a tool that will allow you to check your document for spelling and grammar errors. Other tools on this tab include a Thesaurus, tools for providing comments, and tracking tools that will allow you to mark up your paper with corrections. Many instructors will use the Tracking Changes to provide students with feedback on their papers. The **Changes** group allows you to accept or reject the recommended changes.

Proofing Group

The first group on the **Review** tab is the **Proofing** group. This group provides you with tools to proof your assignment. We have already worked with this group in the last chapter, and we will cover more of the features included in this group.

FIGURE 7-26 Review Tab

First in the **Proofing** group is the **Spelling & Grammar** tool. With this tool, you can go back after you have finished writing your assignment and select the **Spelling & Grammar** tool to have Word check your paper for errors. While you are writing your paper, you can correct errors as you see them using the **Right Click** function. Simply click on the word or phrase in error, **right click,** and then decide if you want to accept the recommendation from Word for the correction. Figure 7-27 provides you with an example of using this technique. In the figure, you can see that you have two choices here of accepting the change or ignoring the error. Figure 7-28 is an example of how the **Spelling & Grammar tool** displays errors and corrections.

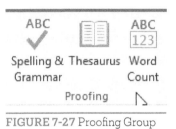

FIGURE 7-27 Proofing Group

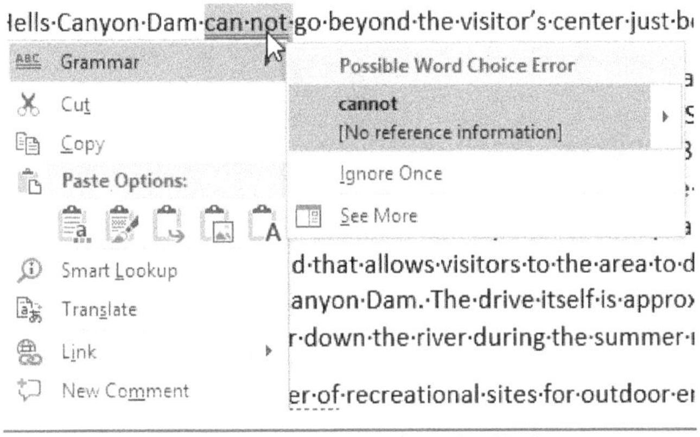

FIGURE 7-28 Correcting Errors with Right Click

The next option in the **Proofing Group** is the **Thesaurus**. When writing a paper there may be times when you need to find a different word for a phrase or sentence. The **Thesaurus** will provide you with alternative words that may be more effective in getting your point across. To use the **Thesaurus**, select the word you wish to find another similar word for. Click on the **Review** tab, and then click on the **Thesaurus**. From the list that is provided, select a word that fits your desired changes.

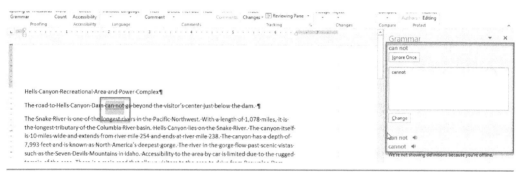

FIGURE 7-29 Spelling and Grammar

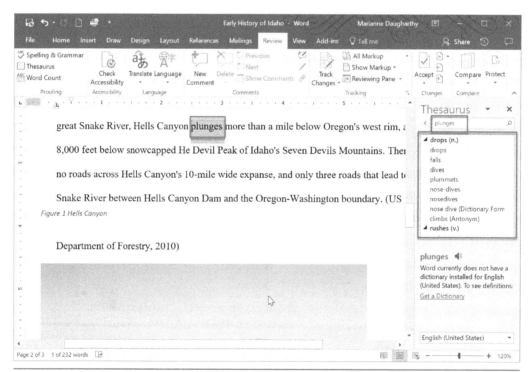

FIGURE 7-30 Thesaurus

The final option in the **Proofing** group is the **Word Count** option. This option will help you to ensure that your paper meets word count requirements of an assignment. Clicking on **Word Count** will provide you with a simple display of the **Word Count** and other statistics surrounding the document. Figure 7-31 provides you with a sample of the information that is provided with the Word Count.

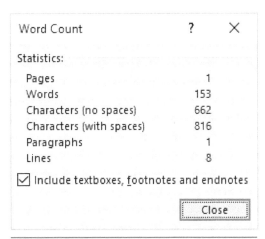

FIGURE 7-31 Word Count

Comments Group

The **Comments** group is used to manage comments inserted in the document. Instructors frequently use the comments function to insert grading comments to students. Students can use the comments function to suggest comments on group assignments or in doing peer reviews of other student assignments. Figure 7-32 shows you the options available for the **Comments** group. In the **Comments** group, you can create a new comment. Comments can be deleted, and the previous and next function will move you through the document to the various comments in the document. The **Show Comments** feature will show the comments in the document.

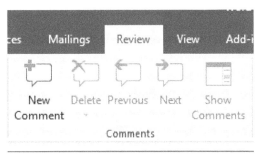

FIGURE 7-32 Comments Group

Figure 7-33 shows an example of comments within the document. Notice that with an active comment, the other comment functions become active. Additionally, there is an option to reply to the comment or resolve the issue surrounding the comment.

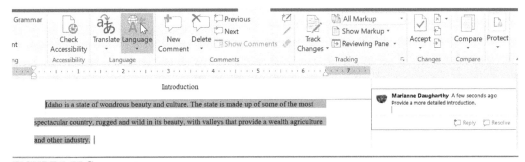

FIGURE 7-33 Comments

Track Changes

When working on a group project or a project that has many drafts, keeping track of the changes can be invaluable. The **Track Changes** function allows the tracking of the various changes throughout the life of the document. Each person who makes a change to the document will be identified by a different color. You can click on the **Launcher** and adjust the color settings and other tracking settings for track changes. The **Advanced Options** button allows you to make changes such as colors for various changes. The **Change User Name** allows you to change the name of the person making the changes or even using the Office programs.

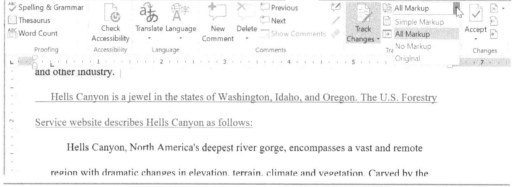

FIGURE 7-34 Track Changes

The last step in working with the **Track Changes** is to **Accept** or **Reject** the changes. This function is in the **Changes** group. It allows you to put the finishing touches on the paper and button up all corrections and modifications to the paper. **Previous** and **Next** buttons allow you to move through your document to the changes that have been made in the document.

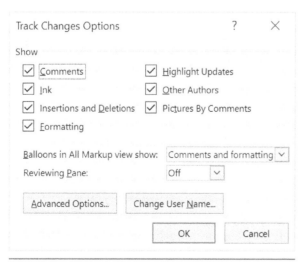

FIGURE 7-35 Track Changes Launcher

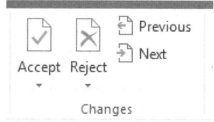

FIGURE 7-36 Changes Group

4. View Tab

The final tab in this chapter is the **View** tab. The **View** tab provides you with tools that will make viewing your document from various positions value to you. On the ribbon, you will find several groups that will assist you in looking at your document.

FIGURE 7-37 View Tab

Views

The Views group allows you to see how the document would look in different format. For example, if you want to put your document on the web, the **Web Layout** will show you how the document will look as a web page.

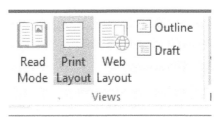

FIGURE 7-38 Views Group

If you have been making use of the various headings, you can use the **Outline** view. This view will allow you to easily move paragraphs or whole sections of your document around.

The most common view is the **Print Layout** view. This is the view that you will want to use when creating and editing your document. It is also the view that will show you how your document will look when you print it.

FIGURE 7-39 Show Group

Show

The **Show** group provides you with tools that will make formatting your paper much easier. The two tools that you will frequently use here are the **Ruler** and **Gridlines**; the **Show Ruler** provides a vertical and horizontal ruler. This ruler helps you to see the position of information on the paper. When you look at the rulers, you will see that the horizontal ruler is the same width of a letter size piece of paper, 8.5 inches by 11 inches. The margins that you have set are the white space outside of the typing area. Using the horizontal ruler, you can set various tab stops, adjust table columns, and, if you are using the column feature, you can adjust them on the ruler, too.

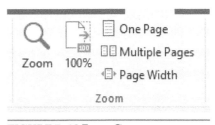

FIGURE 7-40 Zoom Group

The **Gridlines** option will display gridlines on your document. Gridlines are set 1/8th of an inch apart within the document. The use of gridlines is useful when you need to align or place graphics or pictures in your document.

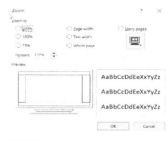

Zoom

The **Zoom** group (Figure 7-40) allows you to increase or decrease the size of your document on the screen.

FIGURE 7-41 Zoom Options

The magnifying glass will increase the size of the display. This is done by selecting the size of the display using the **Zoom** display that pops up when you select the **Zoom** icon as in Figure 7-41.

Other **Zoom** options include a 100% icon that will set the display to a normal-sized view. You can also select an option of seeing only one page of the document or multiple pages of the document at one time. The **Page Width** icon will adjust the width of the document displayed to the width of the computer monitor.

Window

The **Window** group provides you with a way to view multiple sections of your document at one time or two documents as the same time. For this section, we will just cover the **Split** option and the **View Side by Side**. These two options are commonly used and can be time saving when creating and editing a document.

The **Split** option allows you to split the document so that you can work in one section of the document and view another section of the document. This feature is handy when you want to create a table or SmartArt based upon information located in another part of the document. Figure 7-43

FIGURE 7-42 Window Group

provides you a sample of what a split document looks like. The split area can be adjusted by sliding the line between the split up or down.

There are times when you need to setup your display to see two documents at the same time. It can be a challenge to have to switch back and forth between documents. The View **Side by Side** will allow you to see two documents at the same time next to each other. It is best to have the documents at the point you wish them both to be. Once you activate the **Side by Side** function, the documents will move together as you adjust your position in the documents. Figure 7-44 provides you with sample of what documents look like when set to **Side by Side.**

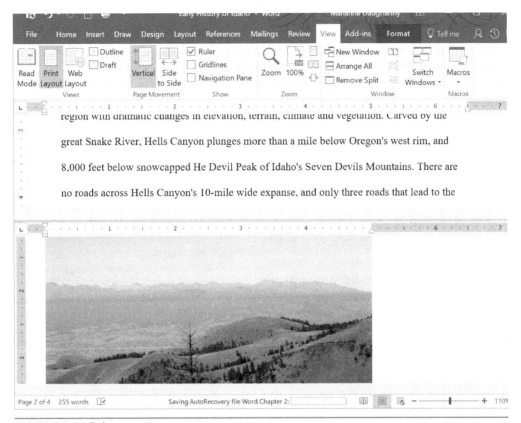

FIGURE 7-43 Split

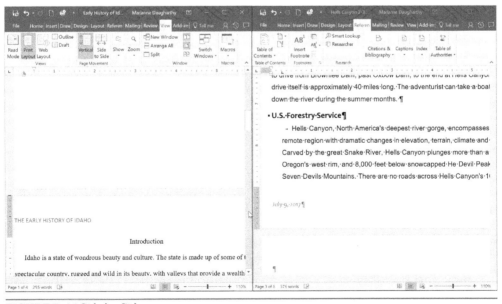

FIGURE 7-44 Side by Side

Reference Pages

One of the last things you will need to do as you complete your document is make sure that you have created your **Reference** page or **Works Cited** page. If you have been managing your sources as you have created your paper, then this will be easily completed with a few clicks of your mouse.

1. Click **CTRL+End** to move to the end of your document.

2. Click **CTRL+Enter** to create a hard page return. Your reference page should always be on a page of its own; the hard page return will prevent information from spilling on to your reference page if you decide to add more information to your paper.

3. Click on the **References** tab. In the **Citations & Bibliography** group, make sure that you have selected the correct paper style. If, by some chance, you created all your sources in the wrong style, do not worry as Word will auto-matically adjust for the selected style. Figure 7-45 shows you a list of reference styles that are available in Word. Most colleges and universities will make use of APA and MLA formatting styles.

4. Next, select the **Bibliography** drop-down, and select the appro-priate **Reference** page style as in Figure 7-46.

5. Word will create the necessary reference page entries using the sources you used in your document. You will need to check each source for accu-racy and possibly make minor formatting corrections based upon your institution's policies.

FIGURE 7-45 Select Style

FIGURE 7-46 Insert Bibliography

6. When you have completed creating your reference page, you will have a page similar to the one in Figure 7-47.

REFERENCES

U.S. Department of Forestry. (2010, December 06). *Hells Canyon Overview*. Retrieved July 9, 2017, from www.fs.ded.us: https://web.archive.org/web/20101206120003/http://www.fs.fed.us/hellscanyon/overview/index.shtml

FIGURE 7-47 References

Student Checkup Word 7-3

Here you will get a chance to test your understanding of the material covered in the chapter. You will need access to a computer with Word. Using the OneDrive Word App will be a viable alternative if you do not have access to a computer with a full version of Office 2019, Office 2021, or Office 365. **Note: Blue text represents typed text.**

This is the third of our checkups for Chapter 2. In this checkup, you will continue modifying the document you have been working on, adding in more features and information and making it a more complete document.

File Needed: **(Your initials) Student Checkup Word 7-2**
Completed File Name: **(Your initials) Student Checkup Word 7-3**

1. **Open** the document from the previous checkup.
2. **Save** the document as (Your initials) Student Checkup Word 7-3.
3. Turn on Track Changes (Review tab/Tracking group/Track Changes). Click on Track Changes. Change Markup to Markup.
4. In the second paragraph, in the body of the paper, change "flow" in the phrase, "The river in the gorge flow past scenic vistas," to "**flows**".
5. In the introductory paragraph, use the Thesaurus to look up other meanings for plentiful. Replace plentiful with abundant.
6. Select the last paragraph on page 3, which begins "Once one goes past," and add a new comment. In the comment box enter **Find additional information about recreational activities and details about the power complex.**
7. Click on the **View** tab, and turn on the **Ruler** and **Gridlines**.
8. Using the Zoom function, set the zoom to 200%.
9. Move to the end of your document. Click on the **Layout** tab, **Breaks**, **Section break** new page. Change the **Columns** to one.

10. Place your insertion point at the beginning of the new page.
11. Ensure that the Citations and Bibliography style is set to APA (**References** tab/**Citations & Bibliography** group). Insert a reference page in **APA** style (**References** tab/**Citations & Bibliography** group/**Bibliography**). Click on the drop-down arrow to the right of **Bibliography** and from the list, select the second option: **References**.
12. **Save** your document, and post as instructed by your instructor for grading.

Here you have a sample of the updated pages for your project.

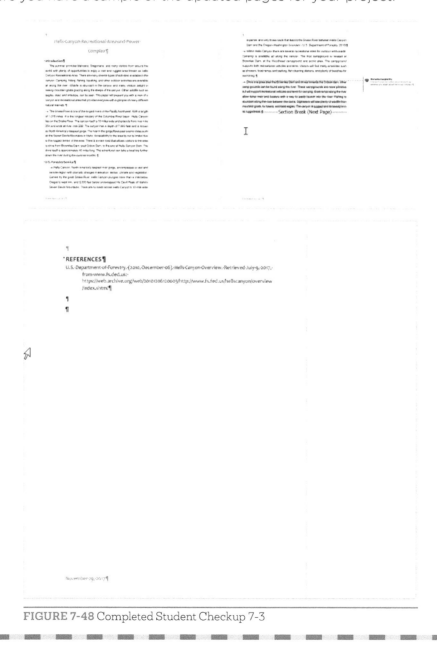

FIGURE 7-48 Completed Student Checkup 7-3

Chapter Projects

Here you will get a chance to test your understanding of the material covered in the chapter. You will need access to a computer with Word. Using the OneDrive Word App will be a viable alternative if you do not have access to a computer with a full version of Office 2019, Office 2021, or Office 365. **Note: Blue text represents typed text.**

You will take the data file provided and format the file into a nicely designed and laid out paper.

File Needed: **Word Chapter 7 Project 1 Data File**

Completed File Name: **(Your Initials) Word Chapter 7 Project 1 (Washington D.C.).**

1. **Open** the Word Chapter 7 Project 1 (Washington D.C.) file.
2. **Save** the file as (Your Initials) Word Chapter 7 Project 1 (Washington D.C.).
3. Using the **Layout tab,** change the **margins** to **1 inch** all sides.
4. Select the whole document, and change the line spacing to double spacing. Set the before and after spacing to 6 pt. and indentation to first line at .25.
5. Change the font to **Arial** and **12 pt**.
6. Using the **Review** tab, run spell check and accept the recommended changes.
7. Move to the top of the document and set the style to **Title** and center align the first line of the paper.
8. While still at the beginning of the paper, insert the **Facet** cover page.
9. For the cover page title, enter **The Splendors of Washington D.C.**
10. **Delete** the **Document Subtitle, Abstract,** and **email address**.
11. Change the author name to your name.
12. On page 2, **edit** the page header to include the Facet Even page header. If page number is "1", select the number 1 and then click on the **Page Number** icon. Then click on **Format Page numbers**. Under the **Page Number** section, click in circle next to **Start At**, then type in '2' in the box. Close **Header and Footer**.
13. **Close** the header.
14. Place your insertion point at the end of the third paragraph (ending with President Roosevelt) and before the period.
15. **Select** the **References** tab.
16. For the style, make sure that it is set to **APA.**

17. Click on the **Insert Citation** and then **Add New Source**.
18. Enter the following information:
    a. Type of Source—Web site
    b. Corporate Author—Washington D.C.
    c. Name of Web Page—Visiting the Franklin Delano Roosevelt Memorial
    d. Name of Web Site—www.Washington.org
    e. Year—2017
    f. Year Accessed—Current year
    g. Month Accessed—Current month
    h. Day Accessed—Current Day
    i. URL:https://washington.org/DC-guide-to/franklin-delano-roosevelt-memorial
19. Press **CTRL+End** to move to the end of the document.
20. Press **CTRL+Enter** to create a page break.
21. From the **References** page, insert a **Bibliography,** using the **References** choice.
22. Make sure the reference page is double-spaced, references have a hanging indent, and the word **Reference** is centered.
23. **Save** your project, and submit to your instructor, as directed, for grading.

Completed Chapter 7 project 1.

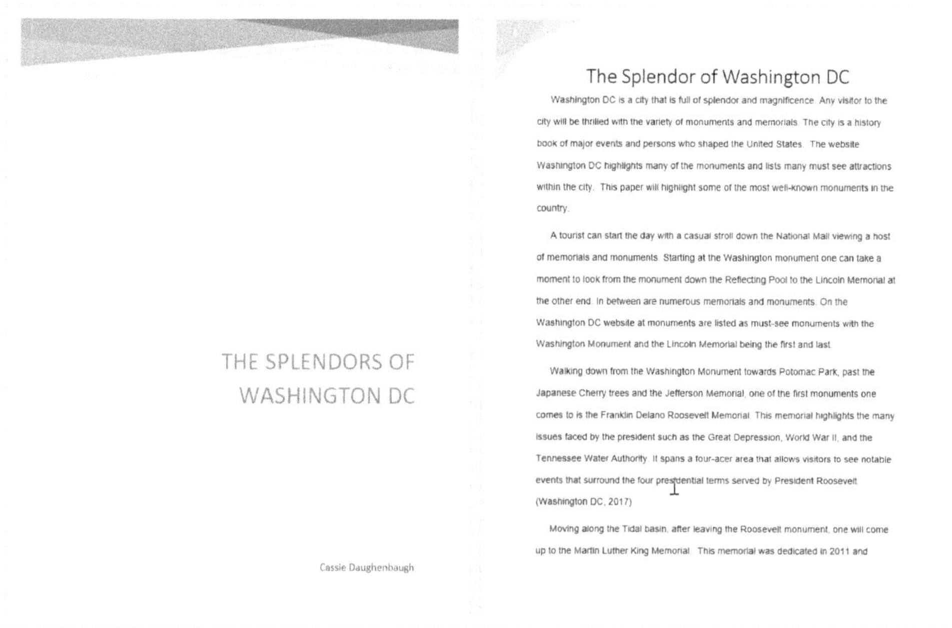

THE SPLENDORS OF
WASHINGTON DC

Cassie Daughenbaugh

The Splendor of Washington DC

Washington DC is a city that is full of splendor and magnificence. Any visitor to the city will be thrilled with the variety of monuments and memorials. The city is a history book of major events and persons who shaped the United States. The website Washington DC highlights many of the monuments and lists many must see attractions within the city. This paper will highlight some of the most well-known monuments in the country.

A tourist can start the day with a casual stroll down the National Mall viewing a host of memorials and monuments. Starting at the Washington monument one can take a moment to look from the monument down the Reflecting Pool to the Lincoln Memorial at the other end. In between are numerous memorials and monuments. On the Washington DC website at monuments are listed as must-see monuments with the Washington Monument and the Lincoln Memorial being the first and last.

Walking down from the Washington Monument towards Potomac Park, past the Japanese Cherry trees and the Jefferson Memorial, one of the first monuments one comes to is the Franklin Delano Roosevelt Memorial. This memorial highlights the many issues faced by the president such as the Great Depression, World War II, and the Tennessee Water Authority. It spans a four-acer area that allows visitors to see notable events that surround the four presidential terms served by President Roosevelt (Washington DC, 2017).

Moving along the Tidal basin, after leaving the Roosevelt monument, one will come up to the Martin Luther King Memorial. This memorial was dedicated in 2011 and

FIGURE 7-49 Completed Chapter 7 Project 1

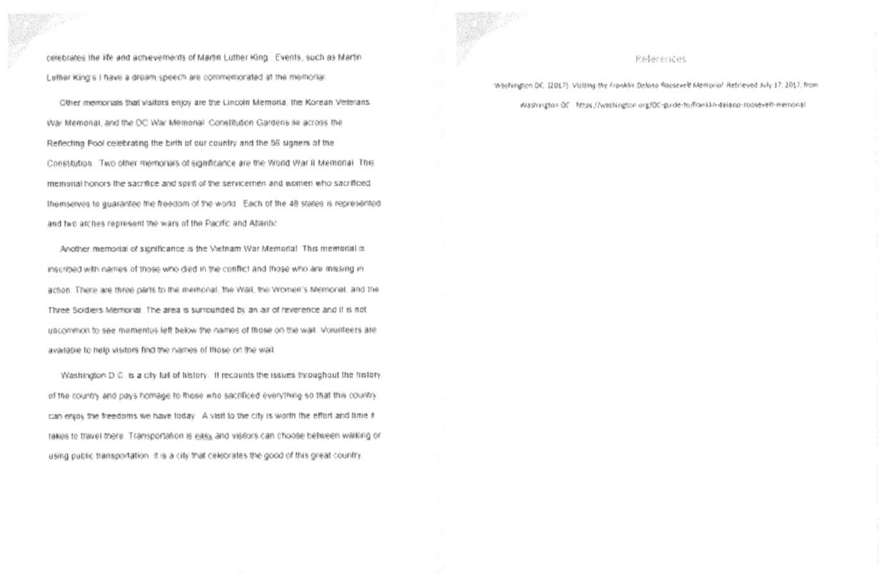

celebrates the life and achievements of Martin Luther King. Events, such as Martin Luther King's I have a dream speech are commemorated at the memorial.

Other memorials that visitors enjoy are the Lincoln Memorial, the Korean Veterans War Memorial, and the DC War Memorial. Constitution Gardens are across the Reflecting Pool celebrating the birth of our country and the 56 signers of the Constitution. Two other memorials of significance are the World War II Memorial. The memorial honors the sacrifice and spirit of the servicemen and women who sacrificed themselves to guarantee the freedom of the world. Each of the 48 states is represented and two arches represent the wars of the Pacific and Atlantic.

Another memorial of significance is the Vietnam War Memorial. This memorial is inscribed with names of those who died in the conflict and those who are missing in action. There are three parts to the memorial, the Wall, the Women's Memorial, and the Three Soldiers Memorial. The area is surrounded by an air of reverence and it is not uncommon to see mementos left below the names of those on the wall. Volunteers are available to help visitors find the names of those on the wall.

Washington D.C. is a city full of history. It recounts the issues throughout the history of the country and pays homage to those who sacrificed everything so that this country can enjoy the freedoms we have today. A visit to the city is worth the effort and time it takes to travel there. Transportation is easy, and visitors can choose between walking or using public transportation. It is a city that celebrates the good of this great country.

References

Washington DC. (2017). Visiting the Franklin Delano Roosevelt Memorial. Retrieved July 17, 2017, from Washington DC. https://washington.org/DC-guide-to/franklin-delano-roosevelt-memorial

FIGURE 7-49 *(Continued)*

Student Chapter 7 Project Word 2

Here you will get a chance to test your understanding of the material covered in the chapter. You will need access to a computer with Word. Using the OneDrive Word App will be a viable alternative if you do not have access to a computer with a full version of Office 2019, Office 2021, or Office 365. **Note: Blue text represents typed text.**

You will take the data file provided and format the file into a nicely designed and laid out paper.

File Needed: **Word Chapter 7 Project 2**—the file you created in the last chapter Completed File Name: **(Your Initials) Word Chapter 7 Project 2 (Yellowstone).**

1. Open the Word Chapter 6 Project 2 (Yellowstone) file.
2. Save the file as (Your Initials) Word Chapter 7 Project 2 (Yellowstone).
3. Place your insertion point at the end of the first paragraph, ending with (NPS.gov).
4. Select (NPS.gov) and delete it. If you accidently deleted the period, place a period at the end of the new citation.
5. Select the **References** tab.
6. For the style, make sure that it is set to APA.
7. Click on the **Insert Citation**, and then **Add New Source**.

8. Enter the following information: (If all fields listed below do not appear in the **Create Source** do not appear, click on the checkbox to the left of **Show All Bibliography Fields**. If you accidently deleted the period, place a period at the end of the new citation.
   a. Type of Source—Web site
   b. Corporate Author—National Park Service
   c. Name of Web Page—National Park Service
   d. Name of Web Site—Birth of a National Park
   e. Year—2017
   f. Month—May
   g. Day—09
   h. Year Accessed—Current year
   i. Month Accessed—Current month
   j. Day Accessed—Current Day
   k. URL: https://www.nps.gov/yell/learn/historyculture/yellowstone establishment.htm
9. Go to the end of the third paragraph, **delete** the second (NPS.gov).
10. Click on References, Insert Citation and select the citation you just created for the National Park Service to insert the citation. Ensure that you have a period after the closing parentheses of the new citation.
11. Move to page 2 of the paper, and place your insertion point at the end of the first paragraph ending "protect all parts of the park."
12. Press **Enter**. On the new line, select **heading 2** and enter Yellowstone National Park Timeline.
13. Using bullets, enter the following information:
    a. **1870—A group of explorers discussed the preservation of the area around a campfire.**
    b. **March 1, 1872—Yellowstone National Park Protection Act is signed.**
    c. **August 20, 1886—The Army takes over management of the park.**
    d. **August 25, 1916—Park Services Organic Act signed into law.**
    e. **1963—The Park moves to "natural regulation", also known as Ecological Process Management.**
    f. **1988—Fires affected 36% of the park.**
14. Change the bullet style to the arrow.
15. Change the font style to Arial and resize the font to size 12.
16. At the end of the 1963 bullet, enter the following reference information and create the in-text citation.
    a. Source—Web site
    b. Corporate Author—National Park Service
    c. Name of Web Page—National Park Service
    d. Name of Web Site—Modern Management

e. Year—2016

f. Month—June

g. Day—16

h. URL: https://www.nps.gov/yell/learn/historyculture/modernman-agement.htm

i. For date accessed, use the current date you create this document. If all fields listed below do not appear in the **Create Source** do not appear, click on the checkbox to the left of **Show All Bibliography Fields**.

17. Go to the end of the last paragraph in your document (after the period after the word **treasures**). Using **Heading 2**, add the heading **Pictures of Yellowstone**. Press **ENTER**.

18. In the blank line underneath the **Pictures of Yellowstone** heading, add a **SmartArt** picture graphic; choose from one of the many options available (i.e., horizontal Picture List option). Insert three images that you find online of **Yellowstone National Park** into the **SmartArt** -graphic. Add the text that appears in the **SmartArt** graphic in Figure 7.50.

19. Press **CTRL+End** to move to the end of the document.

20. Delete all of the text after the SmartArt graphic. Insert a **Page Break** (**Layout** tab/**Page Setup** group/**Breaks**).

21. From the **References** page, insert a **Bibliography** using the **References** choice.

22. Make sure the reference page is set to double-spaced, your references have a hanging indent, and the word **References** is centered.

23. **Save** your project and submit to your instructor as directed for grading.

Completed Chapter 7 project 2.

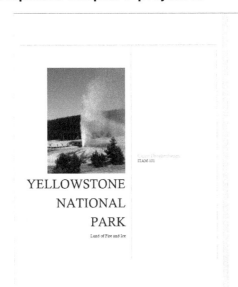

FIGURE 7-50 Completed Chapter 7 Project 2

In 1886 the US Army was the responsibility for the management of the park. Enforcement of the rules and regulations of the park fell to the army and improvements were made to the protection of the huge park. The biggest threat came from poachers. Bison were almost poached to extinction, and the punishment for poaching was banishment from the park. The efforts of Emmerson Hough and George Bird Grinnell created a national outcry that spurred Congress to create and pass the National Park Protection Act. This act gave the Army the authority and ability to protect all parts of the park.

Yellowstone National Park Timeline

> - 1870 – A group of explorers discussed the preservation of the area around a campfire
> - March 1, 1872 – Yellowstone National Park Protection Act is signed
> - August 20, 1886 – The Army takes over management of the park
> - August 25, 1916 – Park Services Organic Act signed into law
> - 1963 – The park moves to "natural regulation" also known as Ecological Process Management. (National Park Service, 2016)
> - 1988 – Fires affected 36% of the park

Today visitors can visit the park and enjoy the many features and treasures of the park. The most famous attraction is Old Faithful Geyser. This geyser derives its name from the predictability of its eruptions. The actual eruptions occur every 60 to 90 minutes and can be predicted within 10 minutes of the eruption. Scientists have noted that the length of an eruption will also determine how soon the geyser will erupt again. A short eruption will lead to a shorter period between eruptions, while a longer eruption will produce a longer period. Because of the frequency of the eruptions, Old Faithful is a favorite of most visitors.

From Old Faithful, walkways are provided for visitors to view other hydrothermal points of interest. Visitors can stroll from the Old Faithful Visitors center out to the Morning Glory pool. Along this leisurely stroll visitors pass by various geysers that may be just sending up steam, bubbling, or erupting. Latest news reports stated that Steamboat geyser is erupting for the first time since 2014. This geyser's eruptions are totally unpredictable.

As visitors tour the park, they are treated to many fantastical sights. Mud pots and hot springs dot the country side. Lakes and ponds, along with rivers provide fishermen

~ 2 ~

with opportunities for enjoying a leisurely day of fishing. Bison can be seen throughout the park taking a stroll along the roads. Bear and wolf populations are also abundant throughout the park. Deer and moose can be seen in the early mornings and evenings. Bald eagles are frequently seen along the rivers and near lakes. Park managers work to keep the populations in balance while protecting the public from any entanglements with the wildlife.

Yellowstone National Park is one of the crowning jewels of the United States. The measures that Congress has taken help to ensure that the park is available to all who wish to enjoy its treasures.

Pictures of Yellowstone

Mud Pots | Bison taking a stroll | Chromatic pools

~ 3 ~

References

National Park Service. (2016, June 16). *National Park Service*. Retrieved March 29, 2018, from Modern Management:

https://www.nps.gov/yell/learn/historyculture/modernmanagement.htm

National Park Service. (2017, May 9). *National Park Service*. Retrieved March 29, 2018, from Birth of a National Park:

https://www.nps.gov/yell/learn/historyculture/yellowstoneestablishment.htm

~ 4 ~

FIGURE 7-50 (*Continued*)

Word Part III

Introduction

In the previous chapters of Word, you learned how to use the program. You gained basic experience that will prepare you to make use of this software to complete college assignments. You will have a variety of assignments and, depending upon your institution and/or instructor, there will be a specific writing format required for written assignments. In this chapter, we will cover the fundamentals of using Word in preparing APA- and MLA-formatted documents.

Learning Objectives

This is where the rubber will meet the road. You will learn in this chapter how to make Word work for you in completing written assignments. This will save you time and reduce frustration as you prepare term papers and other written pieces of work. By the time you finish this chapter, you will complete the following learning objectives:

1. Format an APA paper
2. Format an MLA paper

APA Formatting

APA stands for the American Psychological Association and is a standard of writing that is used by colleges and universities. The complete manual consists of formatting standards that include the position of various elements in the document, proper use of grammar, and formatting of in-text citations and reference page entries.

The American Psychological Association Publication Style came into existence in 1928.

Microsoft Word provides students with the tools necessary for easily and effectively creating the documents that students will need to submit in school. With the knowledge of how to use Microsoft Word effectively, students will spend less time being frustrated with the formatting of assignments using APA formatting guidelines. The first section of this chapter will focus upon on the details of APA formatting. You will learn two ways of creating these documents for your class assignments.

Formatting Using APA Formatting Guidelines

With Microsoft Word, there are two methods for formatting assignments using APA formatting guidelines. For this section, we will cover the long method first as there may be students who do not have the most current version of Microsoft Office or who may be using other word processors. You already have the skills and knowledge from the previous chapters to create these documents, now it is time to put them to work.

Bookmark this website for an excellent sample paper:
https://owl.english.purdue.edu/media/pdf/20090212013008_560.pdf.

Method 1

1. The first step in creating an APA formatted document is to create a new blank document.
2. To make formatting the document easier throughout, you will want to set several things first to save time and energy.
3. Click on the **Paragraph Launcher** and make the following setting changes (Figure 8-1).
   a. Line spacing: **double.**
   b. Before and After spacing: **zero**.

   c. Indentation: **First line: .05.**

   d. Press **OK** when you are finished.

4. Click on the **Font Launcher.**

   a. Set the font to **Times New Roman.**

   b. Set the font size to **12 pt.**

   c. Press **OK** when you are finished.

5. Click on the **Layout** tab.

   a. Click on the **Margins** drop-down box.

   b. Depending upon your institution and instructor preferences, the top, bottom, and right margins should be set at **1 inch**. The left margin may be set at **1 inch** or **1.5 inches**. Always follow the class and institution standards.

6. The next step in preparing your document is to press **Enter** twice and then create a hard page break and repeat. Your document will now have three blank pages.

7. You will want to save your document so that your initial setup will be saved, and you will be ready to start your paper.

8. Now you will want to create your cover page. The information on the cover page is centered both vertically and horizontally.

9. Click on the first page of your document.

10. On the **Home** tab, click **Center Align.**

11. Click on the **Layout** tab (Figure 8-2).

   a. Use **Page Setup Launcher** to set the vertical alignment of your cover page.

   b. Click on the **Layout** tab.

   c. In the **Page** section of the display, click on the **Vertical alignment** drop-down menu.

FIGURE 8-1 Paragraph Settings

FIGURE 8-2 Vertical Alignment

d. Select **Center**.

e. Press **OK.**

12. Move to the second page of your document.

13. Click on the **Layout** tab.

   a. Use **Page Setup Launcher** to set the vertical alignment of your cover page.

   b. Click on the **Layout** tab.

   c. In the **Page** section of the display, click on the **Vertical alignment** drop-down menu.

   d. Select **Top.**

   e. In the **Preview** section of the display, change the **Apply to** from Whole document to **This point forward**.

   f. Press **OK.**

14. **Save** your changes.

15. Now you need to add the information to your cover page.

16. In the first line of your document, enter the title of the paper. You will want to check how many letters your title is, and you can do this by selecting the title and then double-clicking on the word count in the lower left corner of your document.

17. Now you need to add the information to your cover page.

18. The next thing is to create the Running Header. The running header is to be no longer than 50 characters, including punctuation and spaces. In Figure 8-4, you can see that our title is 48 characters long with spaces.

   a. Click on the **Insert tab,** and select **Header**. From the drop-down menu, select **Edit Header**.

   b. Click on the checkbox **Different First Page**. You need to do this because your header will be different on the remaining pages of your document.

FIGURE 8-3 Finding the Word Count

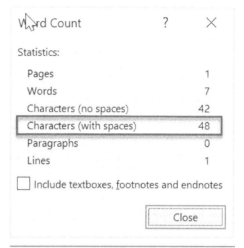

FIGURE 8-4 Number of Characters in Title

FIGURE 8-5 Setting the Page Number

c. In the header area, aligned to the left margin, enter Running head and the title of your paper. Remember this title must be less than 50 characters, including spaces and punctuation. The header must be in all capital letters.

d. **Tab** once or twice until you are on the right margin.

e. Click on **Page Number**, located on the header tab.

f. Use **Current Position** and **Plain Number** (Figure 8-5).

g. Make sure that your header font is set to **Times New Roman** and **12** pt.

h. **Close** the header, and **Save** your document.

19. Now you are ready to finish up the rest of your cover page. Because you have already set your line spacing and other settings, you need to enter the required cover page information. The first line will be the title of your paper, the next line will be your name, and the third line will your college or university.

Now you have a completed the running header and the cover page for your paper. Your headers for the remainder of the document are also ready and will save you a tremendous amount of work in worrying about ensuring the formatting of these important aspects of your paper are correct.

Running Head: HELLS CANYON RECREATIONAL AREA AND POWER COMPLEX   1

Hells Canyon Recreational Area and Power Complex

Cassie R. Daughenbaugh

College of Western Idaho

FIGURE 8-6 Cover Page

Running·Head:·HELLS·CANYON·RECREATIONAL·AREA·AND·POWER·COMPLEX → 1¶

FIGURE 8-7 Running Header

Once you have the basic settings in place and your running header completed, you will need to finish your cover page, set the header for the rest of the document, and then write the body of your paper. The last item you will do to complete your document is to place your references on the last page of the document. Thus, you created three blank pages to work with.

Let us begin with the pages that will comprise the body of your document. On page two, the first thing you will want to do is to get your header set up. You will want to go back into the header first thing and make use of the following settings.

1. In the header area, aligning the header to the left margin, you can copy and paste the title of your paper from the running header.
2. Now you will want to **tab** once or twice, depending upon the length of your title, to place your insertion point on the right margin. Now, select **Page Number**, choose **Current Position**, and then **Plain Number**.
3. Your page header will look like the first page, with the difference being that you do not have the words "**Running head:**" preceding the title (Figure 8-8).
4. Save your document.

HELLS·CANYON·RECREATIONAL·AREA·AND·POWER·COMPLEX → 2¶

FIGURE 8-8 Page Header

Abstract

There are a few more steps, and you will be ready to start working on the body of your paper. Depending upon your instructor and institution, you may be required to provide an abstract of your paper. At this point, you are now on the second page of the document and are ready to begin this step. The abstract should be between 150 and 250 words in length. You can always check the word count of your abstract by selecting the text and checking the word count in the lower right corner of your document. The abstract provides a brief overview of the paper. It is here that you will identify any specific acronyms and key terms that will be used within your paper. The first blank line of the abstract will contain the word "Abstract." It is not bolded or italicized. Figure 8-9 provides you an example of the abstract page of the document. When you have finished with your **Abstract**, press **CTRL+Enter** to create a hard page break and begin with the body of your paper.

After creating a new blank page, you can begin to write the body of your paper. Since you have already set your page up prior to writing, you will be able to easily begin creating the main body of your paper.

To begin the body of your document, you will need to place the title of the paper at the top of the page. The title is centered, but not bolded or underlined. Paragraphs are indented .5 inches from the left margin and aligned to the left. Another formatting issue that you will need to keep in mind when working with APA formatting includes block indenting quotes greater than 40 words. This is accomplished by using the **Increase Indent** on the Home tab. You will want to be sure that you include the in-text citation at the end of your block indent. Make sure that you have the source entered in with your document because you are required to have a reference for each item identified in your paper.

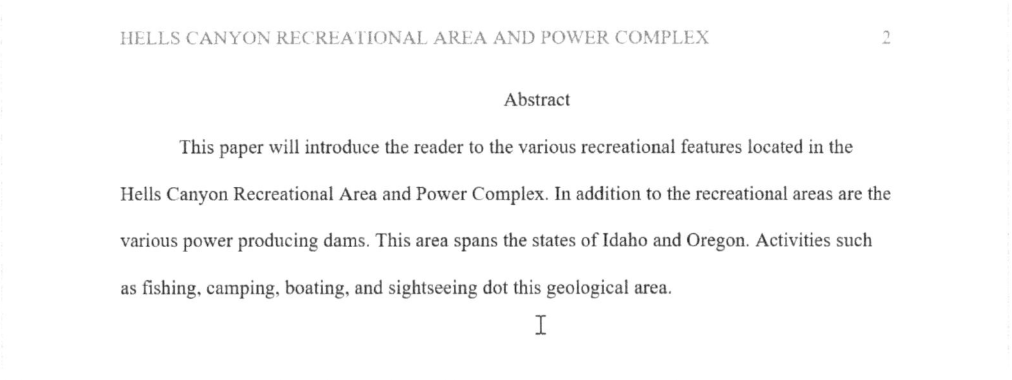

HELLS CANYON RECREATIONAL AREA AND POWER COMPLEX   2

Abstract

This paper will introduce the reader to the various recreational features located in the

Hells Canyon Recreational Area and Power Complex. In addition to the recreational areas are the

various power producing dams. This area spans the states of Idaho and Oregon. Activities such

as fishing, camping, boating, and sightseeing dot this geological area.

FIGURE 8-9 Abstract

Other formatting specifics can be found in the **Sample Paper** that you can obtain from the link at the beginning of this section and from the *Publication Manual* of the American Psychological Association. The last thing you will need to do when you finish writing your paper is to insert your references. The last page created at the beginning of this lesson is where the reference page will go. If you do not have a blank last page with a hard page break on the previous one, you will need to create a page. From there you can go to the **References** tab and prepare to insert your **Reference** page. First, make sure that the style is set to **APA Sixth Edition**. Then, all you need to do is ensure you are on the last blank page and click the **Bibliography** drop-down menu and select the middle option labeled **References**. Word will insert the formatted reference page entries on this last page.

Once you have created your reference page, you will need to make a few corrections. Click in your reference page. Select all the entries and change the spacing to **double**. Change the font to **Times New Roman** and **12** pt., and center align the title "**References**." Figure 8-10 shows you an example of a formatted reference page.

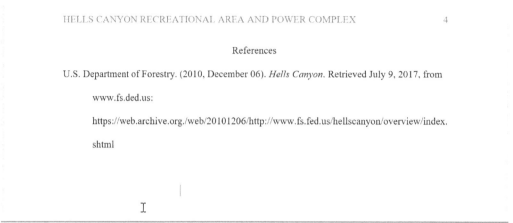

FIGURE 8-10 Reference Page

Method 2

This method is not available on all versions of Microsoft Word. However, it makes the APA formatting even easier and more streamlined. For this method, you will want to create a new document, but instead of creating a blank document, you will want to insert in the search bar "APA." Figure 8-11 provides you an example of the search criteria for the APA template. You will see that there are three choices. For most situations, you will choose the first style, **APA style report**, to create your paper.

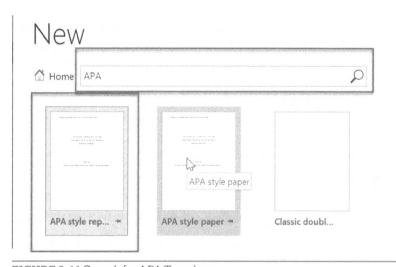

FIGURE 8-11 Search for APA Template

Running head: [SHORTENED TITLE UP TO 50 CHARACTERS]   1

[Title Here, up to 12 Words, on One to Two Lines]

[Author Name(s), First M. Last, Omit Titles and Degrees]

[Institutional Affiliation(s)]

Author Note

[Include any grant/funding information and a complete correspondence address.]

FIGURE 8-12 APA Template Cover Page

The template is already set up for you to begin working on your paper. You will see fields that you just simply need to click in and enter your information. With each field, you are given tips for what type of information you need to enter in that field. Figure 8-12 provides you with a picture of the cover page.

To enter information in the template, simply click on the field or tab from field to field. Figure 8-13 shows fields being entered on the cover page.

FIGURE 8-13 Entering Information into Template

For the rest of the document, all you need to do is to enter the information in each of the fields. You will need to go into your header and enter the title of the paper. Remember that the title is fifty characters or less, including punctuation and spaces. In the body of the template, you will be provided with additional guidelines on using headers.

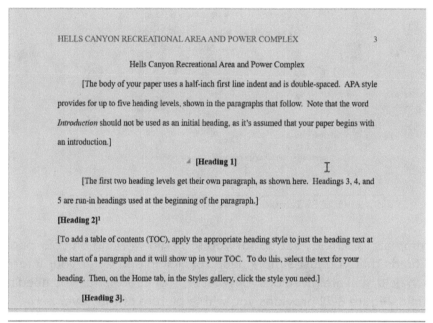

FIGURE 8-14 Template Body

With these advances in technology, Microsoft has made the formatting of these documents much easier and less time consuming. As a student, you are responsible for ensuring that all elements are correctly formatted. The template and the Sample APA will help you to easily ensure that all elements are in place and provide you with help in accomplishing this.

Student Checkup Word 8-1

Here you will get a chance to test your understanding of the material covered in the chapter. You will need access to a computer with Word. Using the OneDrive Word App will be a viable alternative if you do not have access to a computer with a full version of Office 2019, Office 2021, or Office 365.

This chapter concentrates on creating assignments formatted using APA and MLA formatting guidelines. This assignment will give you a chance to try your hand formatting work using the APA formatting style.

File Needed: **Hells Canyon Project Chapter 8 Student Data File**

Completed File Name: **(Your Initials) Student Checkup Word 8-1 APA**

1. Open the Hells Canyon Project 8 Student Data File.
2. Save the document as (Your initials) Student Checkup Word 8-1.
3. Insert a page break at the line that begins with Abstract of your document and at the last line of your document. You should have three pages now, with the first and last pages being blank.
4. Select the whole document.
5. Using the **Paragraph Launcher,** make the following changes:
   a. Under **General,** set the **Alignment** to **Left.**
   b. Under **Indentation,** set **Special** to **First Line By 0.5.**
   c. Under Spacing, set **Before** and **After** to **0** pt. and **Line Spacing** to Double. Click on **OK** to close.
   d. Go to the **Layout** tab. In the **Page Layout** group, click on **Margins.** Change all margins to *Normal.* (1" all around).
6. Make the following changes to the font: **Times New Roman** and **12** pt. font style.
7. Deselect the whole document by clicking anywhere in the document.
8. On the top of the first page, place your insertion at the end of the first paragraph after *geographical area.* Insert a **Page Break.**
9. Click in front of the word **Abstract.** On the **Layout** tab, in the **Page Setup** group, click on **Breaks.** Then click on **Section Break Next Page.**
10. Turn on the **Show/Hide** button (**Home** tab, **Paragraph** group). Place your cursor at the beginning of the words **Section Break (next page).** Click on the **Layout** tab, **Page Setup Launcher.** Click on the **Layout** tab. In the **Page** section, change the **Vertical Alignment** to **Center.** In the **Preview** section, next to the **Apply to:** click the drop-down arrow to select **This Section.** Click **OK.**
11. Type the following: First line: **Hells Canyon Recreational Area and Power Complex.** Second line: Your **First and Last name.** Third line: **Your Educational Institution.** Select all three lines and horizontally **Center** the text. Click on the **Show/Hide** button to turn it off.
12. On the second line of the page, enter **Your Name** and then on the third line, enter **Your Learning Institution.**
13. Select all of the text from page 2 (beginning with **Abstract**) through the end of the document (including the last blank page). Check to ensure that the page layout is set to **Top** (**Layout** tab/**Page Setup**

group/**Layout** tab/**Page** section). In the **Preview** section next to the **Apply to**: click the drop-down arrow to select **Selected Sections**. Delete any blank lines at the top of each page, if needed.

14. Move to the header of the first page. Double-click in the header area. On the **Header & Footer Tools Design** tab, **Options** group, ensure that the checkbox next to **Different First Page** is checked. In the left side of header, type in the following: "**Running Head: HELLS CANYON REC-REATIONAL AREA AND**". Press **TAB** once to take you to the right side of the header. In the **Header & Footer** group, click on the drop-down arrow below **Page Number**. Click on **Current Position**, then select **Plain Number** under the **Simple** section. If your page number shows up as a "**0**", select it. Return to the **Page Number** drop-down arrow and select **Format Page Numbers**. Under **Page Numbering**, click on the radial button next to **Start At** and type in "**1**". Select all the header font and change the font to Times New Roman, size 12.

15. Move to the header on page 2. On the Ribbon, go to the **Header & Footer/Design** tab/**Navigation** group. If the **Link to Previous** button is selected, de-select it. If there is any text in your header, select it and delete it. Then in the left header, type in **HELLS CANYON RECREATION-AL AREA AND POWER COMPLEX.** Then tab once to the right header and insert a page number in the **Current Position**. If the page number shown is not a "**2**", go back to the **Page Number** drop-down arrow and select **Format Page Numbers**. Under **Page Numbering**, click on the radial button next to **Start At** and type in "**2**". Select all the header font and change the font to **Times New Roman** size **12**. Note: You may have to repeat this step for the headers for page 3 and beyond. And also change all the header font to **Times New Roman** size **12**.

16. In the body of the paper, make the following corrections:
    a. Select the first line on page 2 "**Abstract**" and center align. Remove the first line indentation.
    b. Move to the end of the first paragraph on page two, and place your insertion point after the phrase "geological area." Insert a hard page break.
    c. On page three, delete any unnecessary blank lines at the top of the page.
    d. Select the first line on page 3 "**Hells Canyon Recreational Area and Power Complex**". Center align. Remove the first line indentation. **Bold** text.
    e. Bold the text.

f. Select the first paragraph following the text **"U.S. Forestry Service"** and increase the first line indent to **1.0"**. Increase the hanging indent to **0.5"** for the entire paragraph.

17. Move to page 5 and remove an extra page breaks and blank lines.

18. Move to the top of page 4. Place your cursor after the word "**boundary"** and before the period. Enter the following information as a new citation in the **Add New Source** box.

    a. Type of source—Web site
    b. Name of Web Page—Hells Canyon
    c. Name of Web Site—www.fs.fed.us
    d. Year—2010
    e. Month—December
    f. Day—06
    g. Year Accessed—2017
    h. Month Accessed—July
    i. Day Accessed—09
    j. URL: https://web.archive.org./web/20101206/http://www.fs.fed.us/hellscanyon/overview/index.shtml

19. In the **Citations & Bibliography** group, ensure that the Style is set to **APA**.

20. Move to the last page of your document, page 5. Click on the **Bibliography** drop-down menu and select the middle selection, **References,** and insert a reference page.

21. Center the word **References.**

22. Ensure that all references are left-aligned with a hanging indent of 0.5" and double-spaced. Use Times New Roman size 12 pt. font style to match the rest of your document (See Figure 8-15).

23. Perform a **Spell Check** starting at the beginning of your document. For "**steeps**", click on **Ignore Once**. For "**10-mile wide**", accept the recommended correction. Double-check the formatting of your document and make sure that your final copy resembles the document in Figure 8-15.

24. **Save** your document and submit as instructed by your instructor.

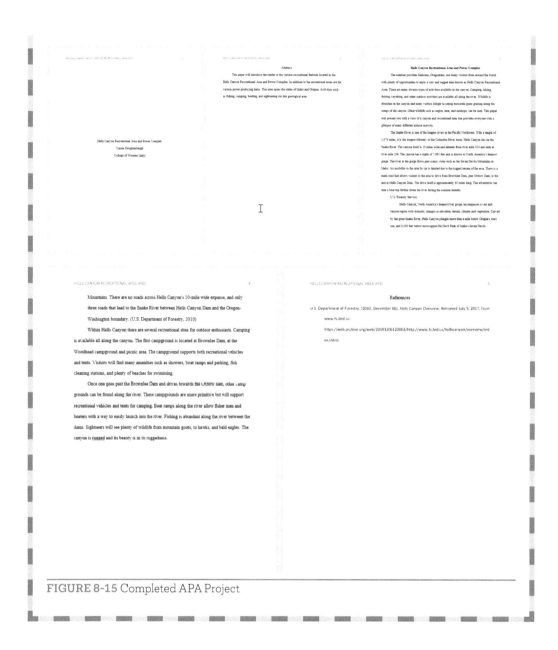

FIGURE 8-15 Completed APA Project

MLA Formatting

MLA formatting stands for the Modern Language Association style of formatting written assignments. MLA is used by many learning institutions including colleges, universities, and secondary K–12 schools. The style is straightforward, and it is easy to grasp a solid understanding of it. In this section, we will cover the basics of MLA formatting.

Formatting Papers Using MLA Formatting Guidelines

After completing the previous section of this chapter and the previous chapters on Word, you have gained all the skills necessary to complete assignments in MLA formatting style. For this section, we are going to take the most direct route for completing any assignments using MLA. Remember that no matter what tools you use, you will be required to ensure that your formatting is correct.

> **Bookmark this website for an excellent sample paper:**
> https://owl.english.purdue.edu/media/pdf/20170627162500_747.pdf.

Creating an MLA Formatted Paper

1. For this section, we are going to take the most direct route.
2. To create an MLA document, you will first create a new document. When creating a new document, search for an MLA template. Figure 8-16 shows the results of a search for MLA templates. For this example, the first template was selected.
3. With the template open, you will first want to click on each of the fields and then fill in the information.
4. First, you will want to open the header and enter your last name. Close the header.
5. The next step will be to fill in the fields that are pro-vided. There is no fancy formatting. The paper is double-spaced. The font is **Times New Roman** with a **12** pt. font.

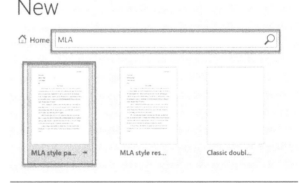

FIGURE 8-16 New MLA Document

The template has fields and helpful information for inserting graphics and tables. Additionally, instructions are included for long quotes and the Works Cited page.

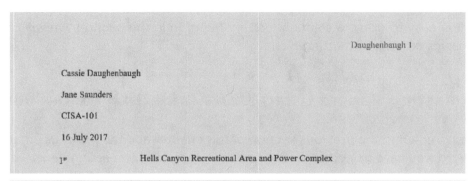

Daughenbaugh 1

Cassie Daughenbaugh

Jane Saunders

CISA-101

16 July 2017

1"   Hells Canyon Recreational Area and Power Complex

FIGURE 8-17 MLA Document Information

6. The last item on the template is the Works Cited page. The information on the template is provided for you to create the references located on the page. You can use this template, or you can use the Citations & Bibliography tool to create your Works Cited page.

Student Checkup Word 8-2

Here you will get a chance to test your understanding of the material covered in the chapter. You will need access to a computer with Word. Using the OneDrive Word App will be a viable alternative if you do not have access to a computer with a full version of Office 2019, Office 2021, or Office 365.

This chapter concentrates on creating assignments formatted using APA and MLA formatting guidelines. This assignment will give you a chance to try your hand at formatting work using the MLA formatting style.

File Needed: **Hells Canyon Project Chapter 8 Student Data File**

Completed File Name: **(Your Initials) Student Checkup Word 8-2 MLA**

1. Open the Hells Canyon Project Chapter 8 Student Data File.
2. Save the document as (Your Initials) Student Checkup Word 8-2 MLA.
3. Open the header on page 1. Press **TAB** twice. Type in your last name and one space. insert a page number in the **Current Position**. If the page number shown is not a "**1**", go back to the **Page Number** drop-down arrow and select **Format Page Numbers**. Under **Page Numbering**, click on the radial button next to **Start At** and type in "**1**". Select all the header font and change the font to **Times New Roman** size **12**.

Repeat for the header on page 2, except you will change the page numbers to "2".

4. Delete the word "Abstract" and the following paragraph.

5. Press **CTRL+A** to select your entire document. Add a 0.5" first line indentation. Change the font to **Times New Roman** size **12**. Remove any before and after spacing, and ensure that the entire document is **left**-aligned. Set the margins to **Normal**.

6. Place your cursor at the top of the document in front of the words "**The Summer provides ...**". Press the **ENTER** key 6 times. Align all 6 lines to the left margin. Type in the following:

First line: Your first and last name.
Second line: the instructor's name.
Third line: Course Information.
Fourth line: Current date.
Fifth line: Leave Blank
Sixth line: **"Hells Canyon Recreational Area and Power Complex"**. Center-align. This is the title.

7. Select the first paragraph following the text **"U.S. Forestry Service"** and increase the first line indent to **1.0"**. Increase the hanging indent to **0.5"** for the entire paragraph.

8. At the end of the above paragraph (after the word "boundary" and before the period), create an in-text citation by adding a new source using the following reference information:
   a. Type of source—Web site
   b. Name of Web Page—Hells Canyon
   c. Name of Web Site—www.fs.fed.us
   d. Year—2010
   e. Month—December
   f. Day—06
   g. Year Accessed—2017
   h. Month Accessed—July
   i. Day Accessed—09
   j. URL: https://web.archive.org./web/20101206/http://www.fs.fed.us/hellscanyon/overview/index.shtml

9. In the **Citations & Bibliography** group, ensure that the Style is set to **MLA**.

10. Press **CTRL+END** to go to the end of your document.

11. Insert a new page or press **CTRL+ENTER** for a new page.
12. Create a **Works Cited** page. In the **Citations & Bibliography** group, click on the drop-down next to **Bibliography**. Select **Works Cited**.
13. Ensure that all references are left-aligned with a hanging indent of 0.5" and double-spaced. Use Times New Roman size 12 pt. font style to match the rest of your document (See Figure 8-18).
14. Perform a **Spell Check** starting at the beginning of your document. For "**steeps**", click on **Ignore Once**. For "**10-mile wide**", accept the recommended correction. Double-check the formatting of your document and make sure that your final copy resembles the document in Figure 8-18..

FIGURE 8-18 Completed MLA Project 8-2

Chapter Projects

Student Chapter 8 Project Word 1

Here you will get a chance to test your understanding of the material covered in the chapter. You will need access to a computer with Word. Using the OneDrive Word App will be a viable alternative if you do not have access to a computer with a full version of Office 2019, Office 2021, or Office 365.

In this project, you will take data files provided to you and convert the file to an APA and MLA formatted documents.

File Needed: **Word Chapter 8 Project 1 APA**

Word Chapter 8 Project 1 MLA

Completed File Names: **(Your initials) Student Chapter 8 Word 1 APA (Your initials) Student Chapter 8 Word 1 MLA**

MLA Project

1. Open Word Chapter 8 Project 1 MLA file.
2. **Save** the file as (Your initials) Student Chapter 3 Word 1 MLA.
3. Select the whole document.
4. Set the paragraph spacing to double with no spacing above or below the paragraph. Set the indentation for Special to first line at .05.
5. Set your font to **Times New Roman** at **12** pt. Set margins as **Normal**.
6. In the **header**, tab to the **right margin**. Type in your last name and press the **Spacebar** once. Insert a page number in the **Current Position**. Ensure that your page number is '**1**". Select your last name and page number and change the font to **Times New Roman**, size **12**. Ensure that you have a header on pages 1 & 2.
7. Click in front of the paper title. Add four blank lines. Move to the top of your document. On the first line, type in your first and last name, second line: instructor name; third line: Course name and number; fourth line: current date.
8. Select the first 5 lines of your document (including your paper title). Remove the indentation. Ensure that these first 4 lines are aligned to the left margin. Also make sure that the paper title is center-aligned on the page.
9. **Center-align** the title. In your title, change **DC** to **D.C.**
10. Use the following reference information and insert an in-text citation at the end of paragraph three (after **Roosevelt** and before the period). Click on the **References** tab and ensure that your **Citation & Bibliograph Style** is set to **MLA**.
    a. Source—Web site
    b. Author—Washington D.C.
    c. Name of Web Site—www.washington.org
    d. Year—2017
    e. Year Accessed—2017
    f. Month Accessed—July
    g. Day Accessed—02
    h. URL: https://washington.org/DC-guide-to/franklin-delano-roosevelt-memorial

    i. Block indent the entire paragraph, including the citation. Select the entire paragraph. Set your indention to 1", and your hanging indent to 0.5". This is a direct quote that Is over 40 words long.

11. Create a **Works Cited** page on the last blank page of your document. Use the third option: **Works Cited. Double-space** your citation and References heading and ensure the font is changed to **Times New Roman**, size **12**. **Center-align** the words **Works Cited**, and change the font color to **Black.**

12. Run a **Spelling and Grammar** check. Accept all recommendations except for **four-acer**. You will need to manually type in **four-acre**. Click on **Resume**. For the word **commerated**, change the spelling to **commemorated**.

13. **Save** your document and post according to the instructions provided by your instructor.

Completed MLA chapter project.

FIGURE 8-19 Completed MLA Project

APA Project

1. Open Word Chapter 8 Project 1 APA file.
2. **Save** the file as (Your initials) Student Chapter 8 Word 1 APA.
3. Select the whole document and make the following corrections:
    a. Change the font to **Times New Roman** at **12** pt.
    b. Double space the entire document.
    c. Set the Special indentation to First line at 0.5 inches.

    d. No spacing before or after each paragraph.

    e. Change margins to **Normal** (1" all around).

4. Save your document.

5. Go to the top of your document. Place your cursor in front of the title (The Splendor of Washington D.C.). Insert a **Section Break Next Page**.

6. Go the end of your document and insert a page break.

7. Go back to the first page. and enter the following information on a different line for each item.

    a. **The Splendor of Washington D.C.**

    b. Your Name

    c. Your School

8. Select the above lines, and center align them.

9. Select the **Layout** tab, and launch the Page Setup.

10. In the Page Setup window, select the **Layout** tab.

11. In the Page section, in the Vertical alignment drop-down menu, select the Center option and **Apply to** the selected section of the document.

12. Insert a header on the first page with the following information:

    a. Check **Different First Page** in the header tools.

    b. Left-aligned enter: Running head: THE SPLENDOR OF WASHING-TON D.C.

    c. Add a right-aligned plain page number.

    d. Go to the second page and enter the following header information: THE SPLENDOR OF WASHINGTON D.C.

    e. Tab over to the right margin. Insert a plain page number in the current position. It should be "2". If it is not a "2", re-format the page number.

    f. Close the Header/Footer tab.

13. On the second page of the document, remove the indentation and **center-align** the paper title. **Change DC to D.C.**

14. Use the following reference information and insert an in-text citation at the end of paragraph three (after **Roosevelt** and before the period). Click on the **References** tab and ensure that your **Citation & Bibliograph Style** is set to **APA**.

    a. Source—Web site

    b. Corporate Author—Washington D.C.

    c. Name of Web Site—www.washington.org

    d. Year—2017

   e. Year Accessed—2017

   f. Month Accessed—July

   g. Day Accessed—02

   h. URL: https://washington.org/DC-guide-to/franklin-delano-roosevelt-memorial

15. Create a **References** page on the last blank page of your document. Use the second option: **References. Double-space** your citation and References heading and ensure the font is changed to **Times New Roman**, size **12**. **Center-align** the word **References**, and change the font color to **Black.**

16. Run a **Spelling and Grammar** check. Accept all recommendations except for **four-acer**. You will need to manually type in **four-acre**. Click on **Resume**. For the word **commerated**, change the spelling to **commemorated**.

17. **Save** your document, and post according to the instructions provided by your instructor.

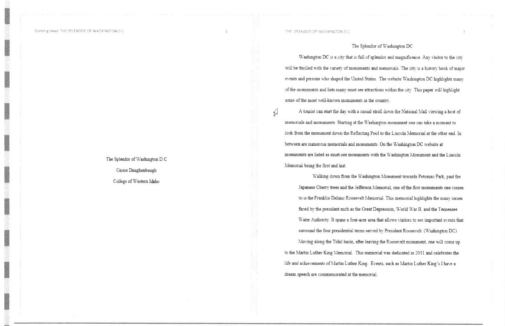

FIGURE 8-20 Completed APA Project

Other memorials that visitors enjoy are the Lincoln Memoria, the Korean Veterans War Memorial, and the DC War Memorial. Constitution Gardens is across the Reflecting Pool celebrating the birth of our country and the 56 signers of the Constitution. Two other memorials of significance are the World War II Memorial. This memorial honors the sacrifice and spirit of the servicemen and women who sacrificed themselves to guarantee the freedom of the world. Each of the 48 states is represented and two arches represent the wars of the Pacific and Atlantic.

Another memorial of significance is the Vietnam War Memorial. This memorial is inscribed with names of those who died in the conflict and those who are missing in action. There are three parts to the memorial, the Wall, the Women's Memorial, and the Three Soldiers Memorial. The area is surrounded by an air of reverence and it is not uncommon to see mementos left below the names of those on the wall. Volunteers are available to help visitors find the names of those on the wall.

Washington D.C. is a city full of history. It recounts the issues throughout the history of the country and pays homage to those who sacrificed everything so that this country can enjoy the freedoms we have today. A visit to the city is worth the effort and time it takes to travel there. Transportation is easy and visitors can choose between walking or using public transportation. It is a city that celebrates the good of this great country.

References

Washington DC. 2017. 02 July 2017. <https://washington.org/DC-guide-to-franklin-delano-roosevelt-memorial>.

FIGURE 8-20 (*Continued*)

Student Chapter 8 Project Word 2

Here you will get a chance to test your understanding of the material covered in the chapter. You will need access to a computer with Word. Using the OneDrive Word App will be a viable alternative if you do not have access to a computer with a full version of Office 2019, Office 2021, or Office 365.

In this project, you will take data files provided to you and convert the file to an APA and MLA formatted documents.

File Needed: **Word Chapter 7 Project 2**

Completed File Name: **(Your initials) Student Chapter 8 Word 2 MLA**

MLA Project

1. Open Word Chapter 7 Project 2 file.
2. **Save** the file as (Your initials) Student Chapter 8 Word 2 MLA.

3. Using the document you just saved, change the formatting to an MLA formatted document.

4. Remove the cover page. (**Insert** tab/**Cover Page**/**Remove Cover Page**).

5. Change the design theme to Office.

6. Select the whole document, and set the line spacing to double.

7. Select the entire document. Change the font to **Times New Roman**, size **12**. Place your cursor in front of the title. Press **ENTER** four times. Left align the new four lines (the first four lines should **not** be indented). In the first line, type in your first and last name. In the second line, type in your instructor's name. In the third line, type in course name, and in the fourth line, type in the current date.

8. Change the entire document font to **Times New Roman**, size **12**. Set the margins to **Normal**.

9. In the **header**, tab to the **right margin**. Type in your last name and press the **Spacebar** once. Insert a page number in the **Current Position**. Ensure that your page number is '**1**". Select your last name and page number and change the font to **Times New Roman**, size **12**. Ensure that you have a header on pages 1 & 2.

10. Run Spelling & Grammar check; accept all recommended corrections. Click in front of the paper title. Add four blank lines. Move to the top of your document. On the first line, type in your first and last name, second line: instructor name; third line: Course name and number; fourth line: current date. In the **header**, tab to the **right margin**. Type in your last name and press the **Spacebar** once. Insert a page number in the **Current Position**. Ensure that your page number is '**1**". Select your last name and page number and change the font to **Times New Roman**, size **12**. Ensure that you have a header on the remaining pages in your document.

11. On the **References** tab, **Citation & Bibliography** group, ensure that the **Style** is set to **MLA**.

12. **Delete** all the text on the **References** page (page 5). In its place, add a **Works Cited** page at the end of your document. Insert a **Page Break** if necessary. Format **Works Cited** as **Times New Roman**, size **12** font and double-spaced. Change the font color of **Works Cited** to **black.**

13. Run a **Spelling and Grammar** check. Accept all recommended corrections. **Grinell** is a proper name. You may ignore it once during the spell check.

14. **Save** your document, and post according to the instructions provided by your instructor.

FIGURE 8-21 Completed MLA Project

CHAPTER EIGHT Word Part III | 229

Here you will get a chance to test your understanding of the material covered in the chapter. You will need access to a computer with Word. Using the OneDrive Word App will be a viable alternative if you do not have access to a computer with a full version of Office 2019, Office 2021, or Office 365.

In this project, you will take data files provided to you and convert the file to APA and MLA formatted documents.

File Needed: **Word Chapter 7 Project 2**

Completed File Name: **(Your initials) Student Chapter 8 Word 3 APA**

APA Project

1. Open Word Chapter 7 Project 2 file.
2. **Save** the file as (Your initials) Student Chapter 8 Word 3 APA.
3. Using the document you just saved, change the formatting to an APA formatted document.
4. Change the design theme to Office.
5. Remove cover page. Create an APA cover page. In line one, type in the paper title, line 2, type in your name, and line 3, type in your educational institution. Add in your Running Head and page number. Align the vertical alignment of the cover page to **Center**.
6. Select entire document (including cover page) and change font to **Times New Roman**, size **12** font, double-space entire document. Remove any before and after spacing. Margins need to be set to **Normal**.
7. Click in the page 2 header. Click on the **Link to Previous** button to turn it off. Change the header on page **2** to **Yellowstone National Park** with a plain page number on the right margin. Ensure that the page number is **2**. Change the font to **Times New Roman**, size **12**.
8. Click in the page 3 header. Delete the existing header. Change the header on page 3 to **Yellowstone National Park** with a plain page number on the right margin. Ensure that the page number is **2**. Change the font to **Times New Roman**, size **12**. Ensure that pages 4 & 5 both have the same header as page 3, and that the page numbers are correct.
9. Click in the Footer on page 3. Delete the footer.
10. Click in the **References** on page 5. On the **Layout** tab in the **Page Setup** launcher, change the vertical page alignment to **Top.** Under

Preview, select **This Section**. Ensure that the word **References** is double-spaced with no before and after spacing, **Times New Roman** size **12** font, and the font color is black.

11. Run a **Spelling and Grammar** check. Accept all recommended corrections**. Grinell** is a proper name. You may ignore it once during the spell check.

12. **Save** your document, and post according to the instructions provided by your instructor.

FIGURE 8-22 Completed APA Project

Part 3
Excel

CHAPTER NINE

Excel Part I

Introduction

In the previous section of this book, we covered the use of Microsoft Word and many of its features. This section will cover the use of Microsoft Excel and the use of spreadsheets. Spreadsheets serve many purposes and provide an avenue for representing data in various formats. We will look at how to put data into a spreadsheet and how to transform that data into useful information.

Learning Objectives

In this section, you will learn the basics of formatting an Excel Worksheet or Spreadsheet. When you complete this section, you should be able to do the following:

1. Create, Save, Open, and Format an Excel Workbook.
2. Data Entry, Editing, Adjusting Rows and Columns, and the Fill Handle.
3. Cut, Copy, Paste, Office Clipboard, Merge & Center, and AutoComplete functions.
4. Sum Function, Themes, Mini Toolbar, and Format Painter.
5. Formatting a workbook using the Ribbon, Cell Styles, and Themes.
6. Insert, Delete, Hide, and Unhide columns and Rows. Modify worksheets.
7. Finalizing a Workbook.

The Ribbon: Introducing the File Tab and the *Home* Tab

When you open an Excel workbook, you will notice many differences between Word's and Excel's Ribbons. You will also see that many features on the Ribbon you learned about in Word are identical or similar to Excel. This will make navigating Excel much easier and allow you to easily expand your understanding of Microsoft Office applications. Let's start off with the File tab and look at the features that are unique to Excel.

File Tab or Backstage

The **File** tab or Backstage view in Excel is very similar to the File tab in Word. The **Info** option is where you would view information regarding your workbook, such as ***Protect Workbook, Inspect Workbook, Manage Workbook,*** and ***Browser View Options*** (Figure 9-1).

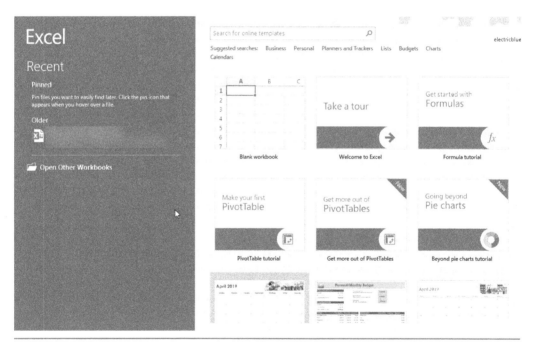

FIGURE 9-1 File Tab

The ***Open*** feature allows you to open other workbooks from your PC or online.

The ***Save*** feature will allow you to save your workbook. This is commonly referred to an *update save*. Normally, this feature will save your updates since the last time you saved your workbook; however, if you hadn't saved it previously, it will ask you where you want to save your workbook, and it will also ask you for a name (same as ***Save As***).

The **Save As** feature is normally where you navigate to save your workbook for the first time. You will choose a location on your computer, alternative drive, or in the cloud where you want to save your workbook and a name for your workbook.

The **Print** feature is where you navigate to print your workbooks. Other options include selecting the printer you want to use and the page settings.

The **Close** feature allows you to close your workbook safely.

The remaining features include **Share, Export, Publish, Account, Feedback**, and **Options**. Take a few moments to explore those, too.

The back arrow in the upper left of the Backstage will take you back to your workbook (Figure 9-2).

FIGURE 9-2 Back Button

Home Tab

The **Home** tab in Excel is similar to the **Home** tab in Word, with a few differences that we will cover here. When you initially look at the Excel *Home* tab, at the far left you will see that the *Clipboard* and *Font* groups are the same as in Word (Figure 9-3).

Excel has an *Alignment* group instead of a *Paragraph* group. Excel works by putting data in cells, and, unlike Word, aligns data in the cells. Other changes in the *Home* tab are the *Number*, *Styles*, and *Cells* groups. These groups are unique to Excel. There are a few differences between Excel and Word in the *Editing* group. Let's jump into the features that will be most important to you as a student or a casual user.

FIGURE 9-3 *Home* Tab

Alignment Group

The *Alignment* group allows you to position data within the cell.

Within the Alignment group, you will find alignment tools that allow you to left, center, and right align data within the cell. These are horizontal alignments (Figure 9-4).

The other positioning tools are top, middle, and bottom align. These are vertical alignments. Excel by default aligns text to the left of the cell and numeric information to the right of the cell.

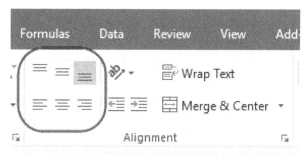

FIGURE 9-4 Text Alignments

The next portion of the *Alignment* group includes the **Increase Indent** and **Decrease Indent** tools (Figure 9-5). Once text is entered in the cell, the indent can be adjusted with the increase and decrease indent tools. The other option is the orientation. In setting up headers and other column markers, you can adjust the orientation of the information.

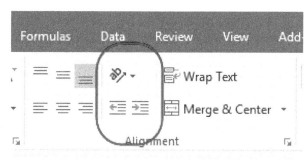

FIGURE 9-5 Increase and Decrease Indents

The **Wrap Text** feature will allow you to wrap text within a cell (Figure 9-6). Normally, text entered in the cell will display across the cell. If there is no information in the cell adjacent, then the text will display in the next cell. The ***Wrap Text*** feature will use the cell space more efficiently by wrapping longer text strings entered in the cell.

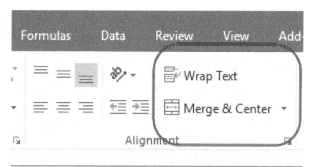

FIGURE 9-6 Wrap Text

The **Merge & Center** feature will merge the information across several cells and center the information across the cells. You also have the options to *Merge Across, Merge Cells*, or *Unmerge Cells* (Figure 9-7).

Number Group

Numeric information may be represented in a variety of formats, from numbers, to currency, and dates.

Dollar Sign: Formats a number as Currency.
Percent: Formats a number as a percentage.
Comma: Formats as a thousand separator.

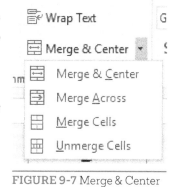

FIGURE 9-7 Merge & Center

Increase Decimal: Shows more decimal points for a more precise value.

Decrease Decimal: Shows fewer decimal points. It will round a number up or down (Figure 9-8).

The drop-down arrow in the **General** text box will allow you to select a variety of numeric formats quickly. You may select the desired format by clicking on one of the many preformatted styles (Figure 9-9).

General: alphanumeric (letters or numbers). Text will appear exactly as typed.

Number: Formats as a number with two decimals (default).

Currency: Formats as a number with a dollar sign, comma, and two decimals (default). Zeros appear as zeros. The dollar sign is displayed immediately to the left of the number.

Accounting: Formats as a number with a dollar sign, comma, and two decimals (default). Zeros appear as a dash. The dollar sign is displayed to the far left of the cell.

Short Date, Long Date, Time, Percentage, Fraction, and **Scientific** appear as shown on right.

When you click on the ***More Number Formats*** option at the bottom of the list, you will get the same dialog window as you would if you clicked on the launcher option (see below).

The launcher option (diagonal arrow in lower right-hand corner of the Number group) will allow you to easily choose a format category and then further adjust the formatting of the number. You can change the type of currency or the number of decimal points represented (Figure 9-10).

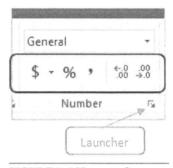

FIGURE 9-8 Numeric Group

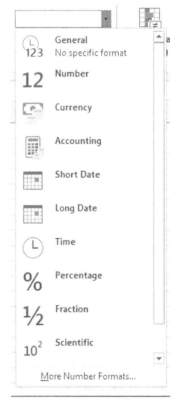

FIGURE 9-9 General Text Box

Styles Group

The *Styles* group in Excel is very different from the *Styles* group in Word. Excel has three buttons in the Styles group. In contrast to applying styles to documents using alphanumeric characters, Excel applies styles to workbook using both alphanumeric and number characters.

Conditional Formatting is used to spot trends and patterns in your data using bars, colors, and icons to visually highlight important values (Figure 9-11).

FIGURE 9-10 Format Cells Launcher Option

Highlight Cell Rules: Includes the options of Greater Than, Less Than, Between, Equal To, Text that Contains, A date Containing, and Duplicate Values.

Top/Bottom Rules: Includes the options of Top 10 Items, Top 10%, Bottom 10 Items, Bottom 10%, Above Average, and Below Average.

Data Bars: You have the option to select one of six gradient data bars or of six solid data bars.

Color Scales: You have the option to select one of twelve color scale choices.

Icon Sets: There are four Icon Sets. You have the option to choose an icon set from the Directional group, the Shapes group, the Indicator group, and the Ratings group.

New Rule ...: An option for you to create your own new rule if you do not find a preset one in the Conditional Formatting groups.

FIGURE 9-11
Conditional Formatting

Clear Rules: Clears rules from selected cells or the entire workbook.

Manage Rules: A dialog box contains the options to create a new rule, edit a rule, or delete a rule.

Format as Table: Quickly converts a range of cells to a table with its own style (Figure 9-12). You can change the table style to any of the available styles in each of the Light, Medium, and Dark styles.

Additionally, you also have the option to create your own new table style or pivot table style.

Cell Styles: Colorful styles enable your data to stand out and add formatting for numeric and alphanumeric cells (Figure 9-13).

You have the options to color-in your cells. The color palette you have will

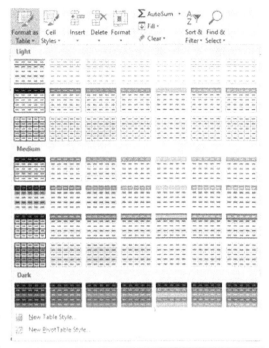

FIGURE 9-12 Format as Table

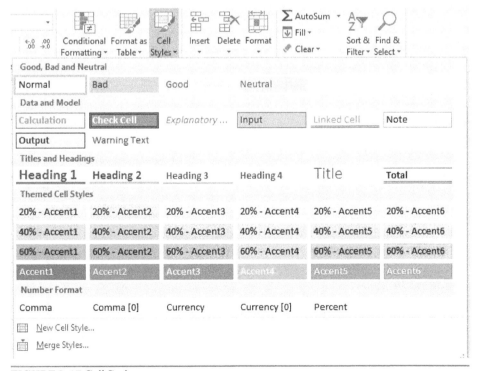

FIGURE 9-13 Cell Styles

depend on whether you selected the default theme or if you selected one on the Design tab.

Additional features include adding ***Titles and Headings*** and totals for accounting worksheets.

Other optional sections include **Good, Bad,** and **Neutral; Data or Model; Number Format; New Cell Styles;** and **Merge Styles**.

Cells Group

Insert: Allows you to insert rows, columns, or worksheets to your workbook (Figure 9-14).

Delete: Allows you to delete rows, columns, or worksheets from your workbook.

Format: Allows you to change row height, column width, organize sheets, hide and unhide cells, and protect cells or entire worksheets (Figure 9-15).

Editing Group

The *Editing* group allows you to perform editing within your worksheet quickly (Figure 9-16).

The **AutoSum** feature provides a quick list of the most used formulas in Excel (Figure 9-17).

Sum: Will add together all numbers above or to the left of the active cell. The formula will stop adding cell values when a range includes an alphanumeric value or an empty cell.

Average: Will average all numbers above or to the left of the active cell. The formula will stop averaging values in cells when a range includes an alphanumeric value or an empty cell.

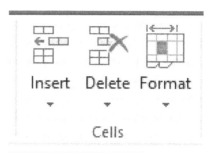

FIGURE 9-14 Cells Group

FIGURE 9-15 Format Icon

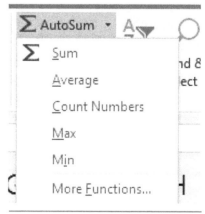

FIGURE 9-17 AutoSum

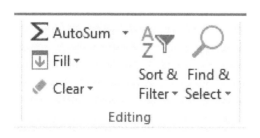

FIGURE 9-16 Editing Group

Count Number: Will count all numbers above or to the left of the active cell. The formula will stop counting cell contents in cells when a range includes an alphanumeric value or an empty cell. This formula will not sum a range of numbers.

Max: Will return the largest number in a range of numbers.

Min: Will return the smallest number in a range of numbers.

More Functions: Will open the Insert Function dialog box. This is where you can select additional formulas in Excel.

The **Fill** button continues a series or pattern into neighboring cells in any direction (Figure 9-18).

Down: Continues a series or pattern downward.

Right: Continues a series or pattern to cells to the right.

Up: Continues a series or a pattern upward.

Left: Continues a series or a pattern to the left.

Series: Will fill as a trend by incrementing steps.

Justify: Will justify the series.

Flash: Automatically fills in values. Enter a couple of samples you want to output, and keep the active cell in the column you want filled in.

The **Clear** feature will allow you to clear various elements in the worksheet, such as formats that you placed in the worksheet (Figure 9-19).

Clear: Removes all formats and contents.

Clear Formats: Removes all formats and keeps contents.

Clear Contents: Removes all content and keeps formats.

Clear Comments: Clears all cell comments.

Clear Hyperlinks: Clears cell hyperlinks.

The **Sort & Filter** feature will allow you to sort information quickly in your worksheet (Figure 9-20).

Sort Smallest to Largest: Sorts from A to Z.

Sort Largest to Smallest: Sorts from Z to A.

Custom: Allows you to perform one or more sorts within a sort.

FIGURE 9-18 Fill Button

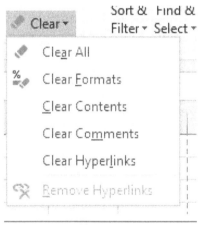

FIGURE 9-19 Clear Feature

Filter: Allows you to turn on filtering for a specified range of cells. Click the down arrow in the column header to narrow down the data.

Clear: Clears your most recent sort or filter.

Reapply: Will redo your most recent sort or filter.

The **Find & Select** feature allows you to quickly find and select specific information (Figure 9-21).

Find: Allows you to find all the occurrences of your search, or you can find the next occurrence.

Replace: Allows you to replace one replacement occurrence, replace all, find all, or find next.

Go To ...: Will provide a short list of options where you may go to.

Go To Special ...: Will provide a select list of options.

Formulas: Will show all cells containing formulas.

Comments: Will show all cells containing comments.

Conditional Formatting: Will show all cells containing Conditional Formatting.

Constants: Will show all cells containing a constant or absolute value.

Data Validation: Will show all cells with Data Validation rules.

Select Objects: Select objects including ink, shapes, and text areas. This is especially useful when working with objects behind the text.

Selection Pane: See a list of all your objects. This makes it easier to select objects, change their order, or change their visibility.

FIGURE 9-20 Sort & Filter

1. Create, Save, Open, Edit, and Print an Excel Workbook

New Workbooks

When you open Excel, you will likely select the first workbook option, a Blank Workbook. This style of workbook allows you the freedom and flexibility of styling your data in a format that

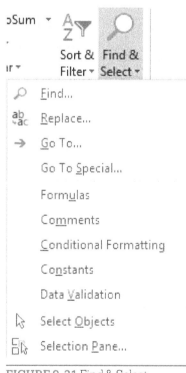

FIGURE 9-21 Find & Select

is meaningful to you. Excel also has numerous other professionally formatted workbook styles from which you can choose. Figure 9-22 shows you some of the choices available to you for creating a new workbook.

FIGURE 9-22 Creating a Workbook

Saving a Workbook

When you create a new workbook, Excel will assign a generic title to the workbook. This title will be dependent upon how many workbooks you have created prior to closing Excel. The initial workbook will be titled ***Book 1—Excel***. When you create additional new workbooks, the number will increment.

When you close Excel and reopen Excel, the numbering will begin from ***Book 1—Excel*** again. Similar to Word, there are several formats available for saving workbooks in Excel. The following table is a list of commonly used workbook formats available in Excel.

Saving a New Workbook

1. Click the **File** tab.
2. Select **Save** or **Save As**. You may also press **CTRL+S** to save a workbook (Figure 9-23).
3. Click the location where you wish to save the document by selecting the location or browsing the computer for the desired location.

TABLE 9-1 List of Commonly Used Workbook Formats

Format	Extension	Use
Excel Workbook	.xlsx	This is the standard Excel workbook for versions 2007–2016, including Office 365.
Excel 97–2003 Workbook	.xls	This Excel workbook is compatible with older versions (1997, 2000, 2003) of Microsoft Excel.
Excel Macro-Enabled Workbook	.xlsm	This Excel workbook contains embedded macros.
Excel Template	.xltx	This extension is used for a new workbook that is to be used as a template for future workbooks.
Excel Macro-Enabled Template	.xltm	Sample or model Excel workbook(s) that contains embedded macros.
Portable Document Format	.pdf	This creates a workbook that is typically non-editable. This workbook can be opened and viewed with free software.
Text (tab-delimited)	.txt	This is data only with columns separated by a tab character. File may be opened by many applications.
OpenDocument Spreadsheet	.ods	Workbook for Google Docs and the Open Office Suite.

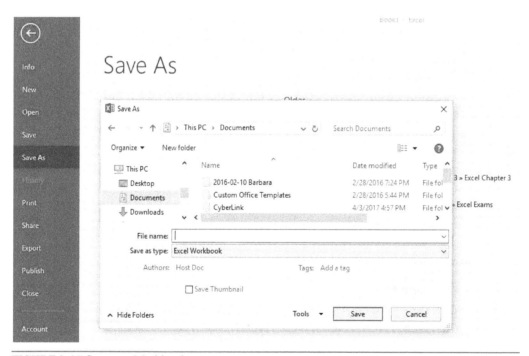

FIGURE 9-23 Saving a Workbook

4. Enter the name of the workbook in the **File Name** box field. In the **Save as type** box below the **File Name** box field, click the down arrow on the right side of the box and select the type of file you want. Most of the time, you will select *Excel Workbook*.
5. Click **Save** to save the workbook (Figure 9-24).

FIGURE 9-24 Saving a Workbook for the First Time

6. If you do not see the location where you wish to save your document, click the ***Browse*** button. You will be able to browse your computer for the desired location to save your workbook.

Saving a Workbook with a Different File Name
There are times when you will want to save a workbook that you are working on with a different file name. Many people also use this feature when they desire to create revisions of a project. Excel provides a method for easily accomplishing this task.

1. Click on the **File** tab.
2. Click the ***Save As*** link to display the Save As options.

3. Enter the new document name, and then click the **Save** button.
4. To save the document in another format or location, select the **Browse** button and browse to the location where you would like to save the document. Then click the **Save** button.

Opening an Existing Workbook

It is common for a student to have to go back and edit a workbook or make corrections and add additional information as a project evolves. Many times, this can be later in the day or on a different day. You will need to reopen the workbook you were working on to make changes and corrections.

The easiest method for opening a workbook is to use the recent workbook list in the Backstage view of Excel. You can also browse for a workbook that you may have not opened in a while.

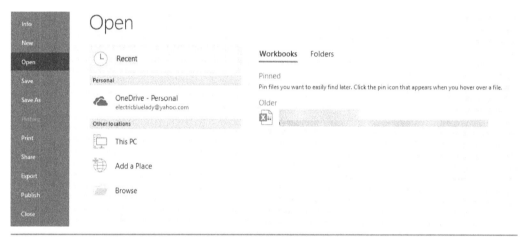

FIGURE 9-25 Opening an Existing Workbook

1. Click the File tab (Figure 9-25).
2. Select the file to be opened by clicking on the desired file name.
3. If you do not see the file, click on the location/drive you wish to browse for your file on. As a rule, Windows will, by default, save all files in the Documents Library (on your computer's hard drive) unless you specify otherwise.

A single worksheet has up to 1,048,576 rows and 16,384 columns. The cell reference of the last cell in a worksheet is XFD1048576.

2. Data Entry, Editing, Adjusting Rows and Columns, and the Fill Handle

Entering and Editing Data in an Excel Workbook

When you open a new or saved Excel Workbook, note the following:

1. An Excel workbook contains a finite number of sheet tabs. Each sheet is called a worksheet or spreadsheet. The number of tabs you may have in a workbook will vary. The allowed number of tabs in a worksheet is limited by available memory (default is one sheet).
2. An Excel worksheet consists of numbers and rows. Columns are labeled with letters and rows are labeled with numbers. Data is entered into a **cell**, which is the intersection of a column and a row. Each cell is identified by a **cell reference**, or **cell address**. A cell reference will always begin with a letter (column), then the number (row), i.e., **A1**.

Cell A1 is also referred to as the **Home** cell. Cell A1 is at the intersection of column A and row 1. You can reference (go to) cell A1 three ways:

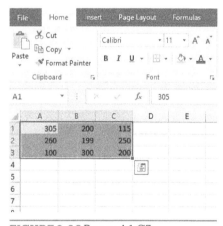

1. Click on cell A1 in your worksheet.
2. Type **A1** in the Name box above column A.
3. Press the **CTRL + Home** keys to return to cell A1.

A rectangular group of cells is called a **range**. The range address A1:C3 identifies nine cells in three columns and three rows (Figure 9-26).

FIGURE 9-26 Range A1:C3

To navigate to any cell in the worksheet, you can do the following:

1. Enter the cell reference in the Name Box (Figure 9-27).
2. Press **Tab** to move to the right across columns or press **Shift + Tab** to move left across columns.
3. Press **Enter** to move down one cell, or press **Shift + Enter** to move up one cell.
4. If necessary, use the scroll bar on the right then click on the cell.

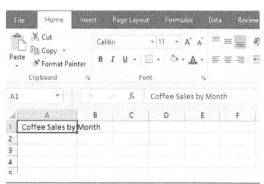

FIGURE 9-27 Name Box

Types of Data

In Excel, there are three types of data. Data in a worksheet may be **_Labels_**, **_Values_**, or **_Dates/Times_**.

Label is text that displays a name, a main title, row or column titles and other similar descriptive information. However, labels are not included in calculations. Labels are left-aligned in a cell.

Value is a number that can be used in a calculation or is a result of a calculation. Values are right-aligned in the cell.

Dates/Times is displayed either as a time (9:30 AM) or as a date (12/25/2025). Dates/Times are right-aligned in the cell by default.

When you type in alphanumeric data (data that includes alphabetic characters and numbers), Excel automatically treats that data as a label. If you want to type numerical data that will not be used in calculations, you can type an apostrophe (') before the data. Examples would include employee numbers, part numbers, and phone numbers.

When a label in a cell is longer or wider than the cell, the label spills into an empty adjacent cell. If an adjacent cell or cells are not empty, Excel will truncate or cut off the data in the cell. However, the contents of the selected cell may be seen in the Formula Bar, or you can widen the column to see the cell's contents in its entirety.

> When you type in a Social Security number with hyphens, Excel will automatically identify it as a label.

Entering Data in a Cell

To enter data, click the cell with the pointer to select and activate the cell. The pointer will appear as a thick solid white cross when you select data in a worksheet. The **active cell** will display a solid border around the cell, and the active cell's address will appear in the Name Box.

1. Left-click on the desired cell and type in the data.
2. Press **Enter** to complete the entry and to move to and activate the cell below.
3. Press **Tab** to complete the entry and activate the cell to the right.
4. Press any keyboard directional arrow key to complete the entry and activate the cell in the direction of the arrow.
5. Press **CTRL + Enter** to complete the entry and keep the current cell active.
6. Click the **_Enter_** button in the Formula Bar (it will appear as a check mark and will turn green when you move the mouse over it) to complete the entry and keep the cell active.

Editing Cells

You can edit cells as you type or after the entry is complete. To delete characters to the left of the insertion point, press the **Backspace** key. You can also use arrow keys to move the insertion point. Press the **Delete** key to erase characters to the right of the insertion point. You can also edit a completed entry. To do this, you can double-click the cell, press **F2**, or (**FN+F2**).

Clear or Replace Cell Contents

To clear data from a cell, select the cell and press **Delete** or click the **Clear** button (*Home* tab, *Editing* group). The **Clear** button has five options: Clear All, Clear Format, Clear Contents, Clear Comments, and Clear Hyperlinks (Figure 9-28).

TABLE 9-2 Five Common Excel Pointers

5 Common Excel Pointers	
✛	Select data in the worksheet
+	Autofill Handle
◄‖► ‖	Column and Row Resizer
✛	Move Pointer
15	Resize Pointer

1. **Clear All:** Deletes formatting and content.
2. **Clear Formats:** Deletes formatting and keeps data.
3. **Clear Contents:** Deletes data and keeps formatting.
4. **Clear Comments:** Deletes the comment in the cell. Excel allows one comment per cell.
5. **Clear Hyperlinks:** Deletes the hyperlink in the cell. Excel allows one hyperlink per cell.

To replace data in a cell, select the cell and type in the new data. You can press Enter, click the **Enter** button (the check mark button in the Formula Bar), or press tab or an arrow key.

If you want to clear the contents from a range of cells, select the range of cells, then press Delete. Otherwise, you can click on the **Clear** button and select one of the three available options listed above.

FIGURE 9-28 Clear Feature

Change Column Width or Row Height

The five different ways to change the width of a column:

1. Select the column you want to change by clicking on the letter. Then on the *Home* tab on the Ribbon, go to the Cells group. Click on Format then click on Column Width. A small column width box will appear. Type in the desired width (Figure 9-29).

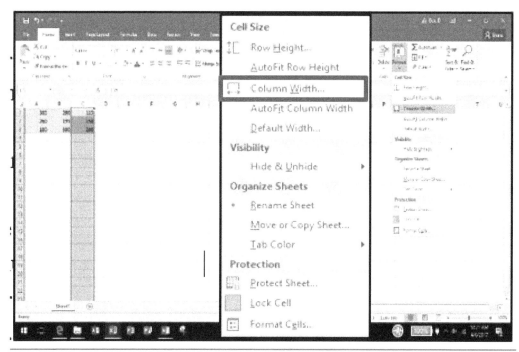

FIGURE 9-29 Changing Column Width

2. Right-click on the letter of the column you want to change. Click on Column Width. A small column width box will appear. Type in the desired width.
3. Select the column you want to change by clicking on the letter. Press and hold your left mouse key. Use your mouse to move back and forth to make your column the right width.
4. Select the column you want to change by clicking on the line dividing it by the next column on the right. You will get a black cross with a double arrow crossbar. Once you get the black cross, hold down your left mouse button and drag the black cross where you want the column width to be.
5. Select the column you want to change by clicking on the line dividing it by the next column on the right. Once you get the black cross, double-click with your left mouse to auto-size the column.

The five different ways to change the height of a row:

1. Select the row you want to change by clicking on the number. Then on the *Home* tab on the Ribbon, go to the Cells group. Click on Format, and then click on Row Height. A small row height box will appear. Type in the desired width (Figure 9-30).

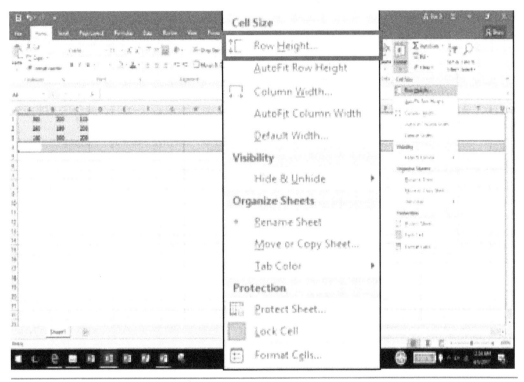

FIGURE 9-30 *Changing Row Height*

2. Right-click on the number of the row you want to change. Click on Row Height. A small row height box will appear. Type in the desired width.
3. Select the row you want to change by clicking on the number. Press and hold your left mouse key and use your mouse to move up and down to make your row the right height.
4. Select the row you want to change by clicking on the line dividing it by the next row above or below. You will get a black cross with a double arrow crossbar. Once you get the black cross, hold down your left mouse button and drag the black cross up and down to where you want the row height to be.
5. Select the row you want to change by clicking on the line dividing it by the next row above or below your selected row. Once you get the black cross, double-click with your left mouse to auto-size the row.

The Fill Handle

A **series** is a list of labels or values that follow a pattern. Excel has some built-in label series. An example of a label series is the months of the year, days in a week. Excel also recognizes patterns in number series, such as 5, 10, 15, 20 ... and can complete the series with the **Fill Handle** (Figure 9-31). If Excel is unable to recognize the series, the *Fill Handle* copies the data.

In a cell, a fill handle is a small, green square in the lower right corner of the cell or selected range. When you place your mouse in the lower right corner of the cell or selected range, your white cross selector turns into a small, heavy black cross. Then you click on the black cross and drag across or down the cell range for the series or to copy data. Once you release the pointer (mouse) button, the data is completed and the **Auto Fill Options** button displays near the end of the series. The button provides other options for how to complete the series. Normally, you do not need to make changes.

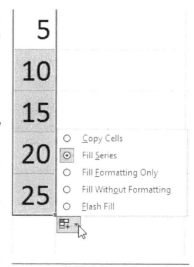

FIGURE 9-31 Fill Handle

For Excel's built-in series, such as the days of the weeks and months of the year, you will only need to enter the first item of the series, such as January. For other series, including numbered series, you need to enter and select at least two items for Excel to recognize the pattern.

Use the Fill Handle to Create a Series

1. Type in the first item in the series (in this example, type "Sunday"). Press Enter.
   a. Press **CTRL+Enter** to keep the cell active. If you accidently move from the cell, just reselect the cell again.
   b. To identify a custom series, type two or three entries and select all cells with data that identify the series.
2. Point to the *Fill Handle* to display the *Fill pointer* (Figure 9-32).
3. Click and drag the *Fill* pointer through the last cell for the series.
   a. A series can be horizontal or vertical.
   b. Instead of dragging the *Fill* pointer through the last cell for the series, you can double-click the *Fill* pointer to complete the series data.
4. Release the pointer button.
   a. The series is complete, and the **AutoFill Options** button appears.

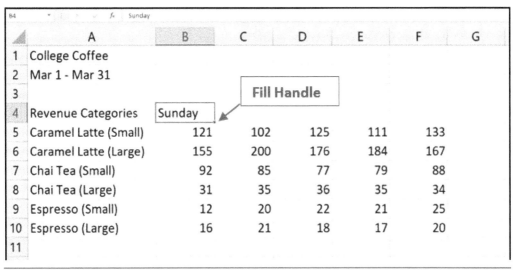

FIGURE 9-32 Fill Handle

5. Click the **AutoFill Options** button.
   a. Choose your desired option (Figure 9-33).

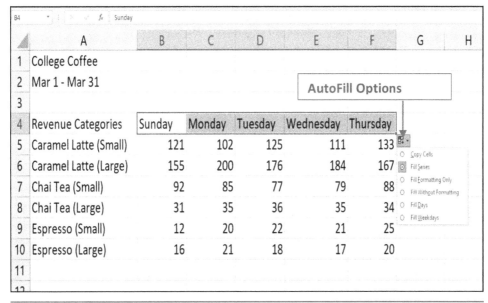

FIGURE 9-33 AutoFill Options

6. Press **ESC** (located in the upper left corner of your keyboard) to remove the **AutoFill Options** button or continue to the next task.

3. Cut, Copy, Paste, Office Clipboard, Merge & Center, and AutoComplete Functions

Cut, Copy, and Paste Cell Contents

Excel has the same *Cut, Copy*, and *Paste* commands as other Windows applications, such as Word. The **Cut** command moves data from one location to another. The **Copy** command duplicates cell contents to another cell or range of cells. The **Paste** command places either cut or copied data from the *source cell* or range and pastes it in a *destination cell* or *destination range*. The cut or copied data is usually stored on the *Office Clipboard* located in the Clipboard group on the *Home* tab.

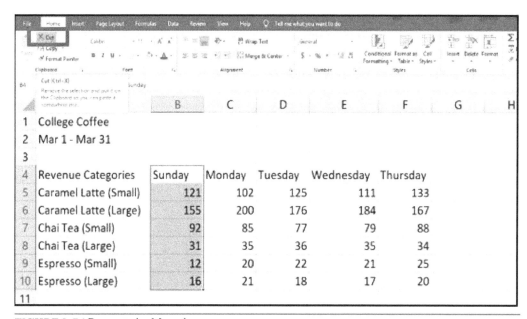

FIGURE 9-34 Range to be Moved

Use Cut and Paste to Move Data

1. Select the cell or range to be moved (Figure 9-34).
2. Click the **Cut** button (*Home* tab, *Clipboard* group).
3. Select the destination cell where you want your data to begin. You will need to select the top left cell in a destination range.
4. Click the **Paste** button (*Home* tab, *Clipboard* group).
   a. If the destination cells are not blank, Excel will overwrite the existing data with the pasted data (Figure 9-35).

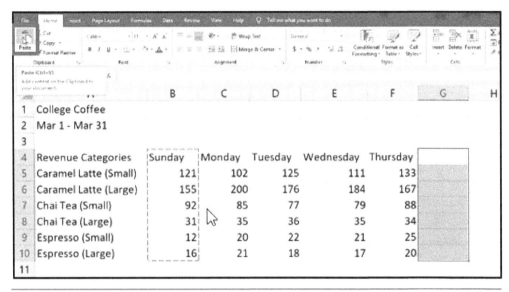

FIGURE 9-35 Range Moved

Drag and Drop Method to Move Data

1. Select the cell or range of cells you want to move.
2. Point to any border of the selection to display a move pointer (4-pointed black cross).
3. Click and drag the selection to the new location.
    a. The destination address will show as a preview (Figure 9-36).
4. Release the pointer button.

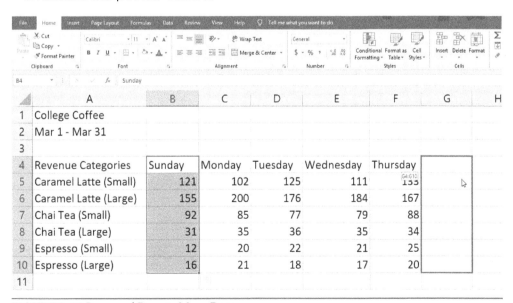

FIGURE 9-36 Drag and Drop to Move Data

Drag and Drop Method to Copy Data

1. Select the cell or range of cells you want to copy.
2. Point to any border of the selection to display a move pointer (4-way pointed black cross).
3. Press **CTRL** to display the copy pointer.
   a. The copy pointer appears as a white arrow with a tiny plus sign.
4. Drag the selection to the destination cell or cells (Figure 9-37).
   a. The copied cells will show as a preview. Release the pointer button and then release the **CTRL** key.
5. If you need to make another copy, continue to press the **CTRL** key and drag to the next location.
6. Release the pointer button and then release the **CTRL** key.

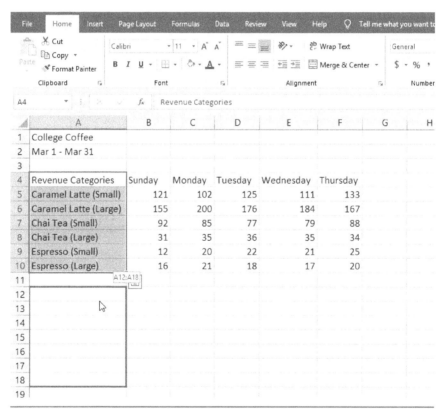

FIGURE 9-37 Drag and Drop to Copy Data

Office Clipboard

The **Office Clipboard** is a virtual place within an application to store cut or copied data from Office Applications. The data is available for pasting in any application. The Office Clipboard can hold up to twenty-four items, with the most recent cut or copied item appearing at the top of the pane (Figure 9-38).

When you want to paste an item in your clipboard into your workbook, all you need to do is click on the destination cell (where you want the item to go), then hover on the desired item in the clipboard. A short drop-down list will appear, providing you the option to either paste or delete the item. On the **Clipboard**, you have two buttons. The *Paste All* will paste every item in your clipboard into your workbook. The *Clear All* option will clear your clipboard (Figure 9-39).

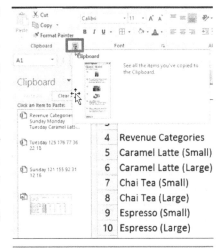

FIGURE 9-38 Office Clipboard

Merge & Center

The **Merge & Center** command combines or merges two or more cells into one cell and centers the data within the combined cell. Excel provides this command as a quick way to center a main label over multiple columns. The **Merge & Center** button also has three other options (Figure 9-40).

Merge Across: This option allows you to merge a range of cells with data, but the data will not be merged across the selection.

Merge Cells: This option allows you to merge a blank range of cells.

Unmerge Cells: This option allows you to unmerge a merged range of cells.

1. Select the cells to be merged and centered. In this case, select cells A1 through F1 (Figure 9-40).
2. The data must be in the leftmost cell of the range to be merged. College Coffee appears in cell A1. You can also merge the cells first and then enter the dataClick the **Merge & Center** button. The title "College Coffee" will appear in the center in the range (Figure 9-41).
3. Select cells A2 through F2. Click the **Merge & Center** button.

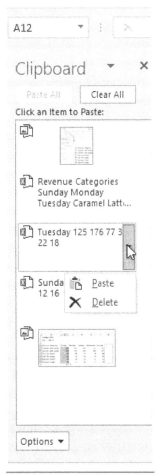

FIGURE 9-39 Clipboard

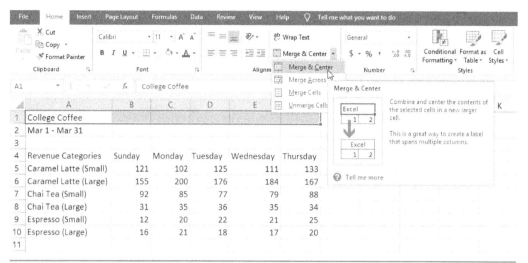

FIGURE 9-40 Merge & Center

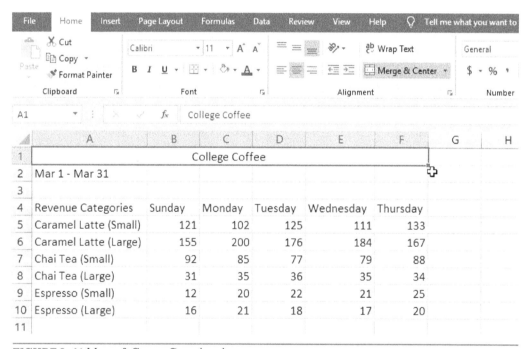

FIGURE 9-41 Merge & Center Completed

AutoComplete

AutoComplete displays a suggested label in a column where the first character or two that you type matches a label already in the column. It allows you to quickly and accurately complete repetitive data. It will only work for alphanumeric data, not for a column of numbers or values.

For example, a column that lists college names might be repeated many times. You will type in the first occurrence. On the second and succeeding occurrences of the college name, Excel will complete the label once you type in the first letter (Figure 9-42). Only the "Si" in "Sierra" has been typed in. If the suggestion is correct, press Enter. Otherwise, you can type in one more letter to have Excel pull up the next remaining college name that begins with the first letter you typed in.

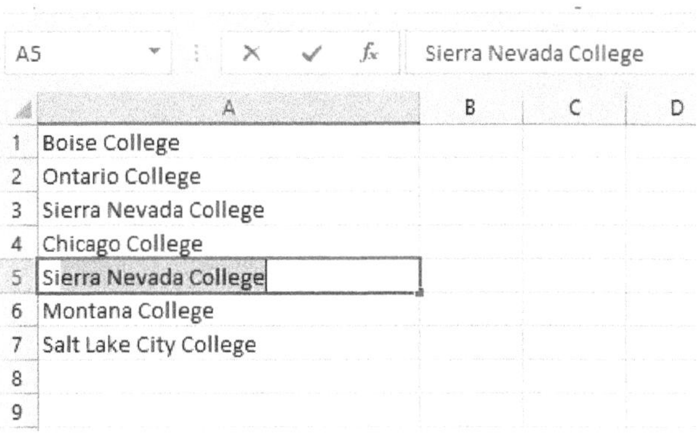

FIGURE 9-42 AutoComplete

Student Checkup Excel 9-1

Here you will get a chance to test your understanding of the material covered in the section so far. You will need access to a computer with Excel. Using the OneDrive Excel App will be a viable alternative if you do not have access to a computer with a full version of Excel or Office 365. **Note: Blue text represents typed text.**

In this project, you will open a blank Excel workbook that tracks revenue for one week for Bill's Bikes and BBQ. You will add labels and values to complete the report and change row heights and column widths. You will also use the ***Merge & Center*** button and the Fill Handle tool.

File Needed: **None**. You will create a **new blank workbook.**

Completed File Name: **(Your Initials) Student Checkup Excel 9-1**

1. Open a blank workbook.
   a. Open Microsoft Excel. Left click on **Blank workbook**.
2. Save the workbook for the first time.
   a. Click on the **File** tab. In the list on the left side in the Backstage, click on **Save As** (Figure 9-43).
   b. Select a location where you want to save your workbook.
   c. Change the file name to ***(Your initials) Student Checkup Excel 9-1*** in the *File name* area.
   d. Click **Save** to save the file and close the *Save As* dialog box.

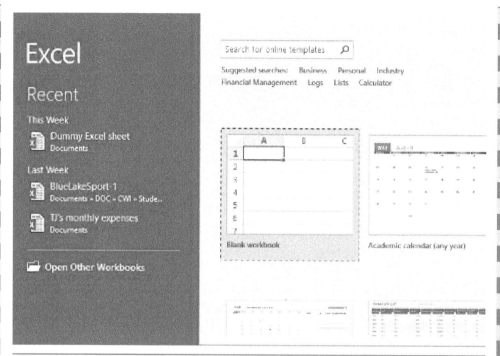

FIGURE 9-43 Opening an Excel Blank Workbook

3. Enter label data into your worksheet (Figure 9-44).

   a. Click cell **A1** and type **Bills Bikes and BBQ**. Press **Enter**.

   b. In cell **A2**, type in **May 1–May 7**. Press **Enter**.

   c. In cell **A5**, type in **BBQ Ribs**. Press **Enter**.

   d. In cell **A6**, type in **BBQ KBOBs**. Press **Enter**.

   e. In cell **A7**, type in **BBQ Corn on the Cob**. Press **Enter**.

   f. In cell **A8**, type in **BBQ Crab Cakes**. Press **Enter**.

   g. In cell **A9**, type in **BBQ Chicken**. Press **Enter**.

   h. In cell **A10**, type in **BBQ Steak**. Press **Enter**.

   i. In cell **A11**, type in **Total**, and press **Enter**.

   j. In cell **B4**, type in **Monday**, and press **Enter**.

	A	B	C
1	Bills Bikes and BBQ		
2	May 1 - May 7		
3			
4		Monday	
5	BBQ Ribs		
6	BBQ KBOBs		
7	BBQ Corn on the Cob		
8	BBQ Crab Cakes		
9	BBQ Chicken		
10	BBQ Steak		
11	Total		

FIGURE 9-44 Enter Labels

4. Enter value data into your worksheet.

5. Type the values shown in cells **B5:H10** below (Figure 9-45).

	A	B	C	D	E	F	G	H	I
1	Bills Bikes and BBQ								
2	May 1 - May 7								
3									
4		Monday							
5	BBQ Ribs	4123	3240	3575	3460	3665	6333	6800	
6	BBQ KBOB	1099	888	1051	1080	1210	3677	4021	
7	BBQ Corn	1035	1100	1158	1168	1299	3995	4254	
8	BBQ Crab	5200	5675	5640	5550	5850	7569	7789	
9	BBQ Chick	6150	6340	6299	6315	6145	8192	8352	
10	BBQ Steak	5880	6095	5980	6195	6255	8265	8512	
11	Total								
12									

FIGURE 9-45 Enter Value Data

6. Use the Fill Handle to complete a series.
   a. Click **B4**.
   b. Point to the *Fill Handle* (small, green square in the lower right corner of the cell) until the *Fill* pointer (a thin, black plus sign) appears.
   c. Click and drag the *Fill* pointer to reach cell **H4**.
   d. Release the pointer button or left mouse button.
   e. Click in cell **I4**. Type in **Totals**.
   f. Select the cell range **B4:I4**. Click the **Center** button (*Home* tab, *Alignment* group).

7. Change row height and column width.
   a. Change Row **4** height to **19.50** pts.
   b. Auto-size Column **A** width.
   c. Auto-size Column **D** width.

8. Merge & Center
   a. Select the cell range **A1:I1**. Click on the **Merge & Center** button (*Home* tab, *Alignment* group).
   b. Select the cell range **A2:I2**. Click on the **Merge & Center** button.

9. Save and close the workbook (Figure 9-46).
   a. Press **CTRL+S**, or click on the **File** tab, then click on **Save**, or click on the **Save** button on the **Quick Access** Toolbar in the upper left corner above the Ribbon in your worksheet.

⏴	A	B	C	D	E	F	G	H	I
1				Bill's Bikes and BBQ					
2				May 1 - 7					
3									
4		Monday	Tuesday	Wednesday	Thursday	Friday	Saturday	Sunday	Total
5	BBQ Ribs	4123	3240	3575	3460	3665	6333	6800	
6	BBQ KBOBs	1099	888	1051	1080	1210	3677	4021	
7	BBQ Corn on the Cob	1035	1100	1158	1168	1299	3995	4254	
8	BBQ Crab Cakes	5200	5675	5640	5550	5850	7569	7789	
9	BBQ Chicken	6150	6340	6299	6315	6145	8192	8352	
10	BBQ Steak	5880	6095	5980	6195	6255	8265	8512	
11	Total								
12									

FIGURE 9-46 Student Checkup Excel 9-1 Complete

4. Sum Function, Themes, Mini Toolbar, and Format Painter

A **function** is a predetermined formula that performs calculations using specific values in a particular order. The following are some of Excel's most widely used functions (Figure 9-47).

Sum: Adds the values in a cell range.

Average: Returns the average value in a cell range.

Count Numbers: Counts the number of values in a cell range.

Max: Returns the highest value in a cell range.

Min: Returns the lowest value in a cell range.

FIGURE 9-47 Functions

Excel 2019 provides hundreds of functions. Excel breaks down all the functions by category. The following table lists the fourteen Excel function categories (Table 9-3).

A **formula** calculates a result for numeric data in a cell. The terms "function" and "formula" are commonly used interchangeably.

TABLE 9-3 Excel 2019 Function Categories

Excel 2019 Function Categories
Database
Cube
Date and Time
Engineering
Financial
Information
Logical
Lookup and Reference
Math and Trigonometry
Statistical
Text
User-Defined that are installed with Add-Ins
Web

To use the **SUM** Function:

1. Click the cell for the total (destination cell).
2. Click the **AutoSum** button (*Home* tab, *Editing* group). It resembles an epsilon (Σ). The range that is being added will be shown with a moving, green-dashed box.
   a. The formula will appear in the destination cell (C11) and also in the Formula Bar (Figure 9-48).
3. Press **Enter** to accept the range and complete the function. The formula will appear in the cell and the formula bar as *=sum(B5:B10)*.
   a. If this is not the correct formula, drag the pointer to select a different range before pressing **Enter**.
   b. If you have an adjacent row or column of values to the formula cell, you can double-click the **AutoSum** button to complete the function.

To display formulas instead of results, click the Show Formulas button on the Formulas tab or press CTRL+~.

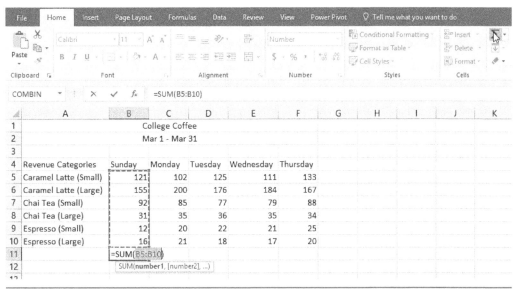

FIGURE 9-48 AutoSum

When using functions, Excel has **syntax** rules. Excel syntax contains the required elements and order of those elements for the function to work. Every function begins with the equals sign (=) followed by the name of the function and one opening and one closing parenthesis. For example, =sum(). You enter the argument(s) for the function within the parenthesis. An argument is the cell reference or value required to complete the function. A function can contain one or more arguments. For example, the function *=sum(B5:B10)* contains two arguments while the function *=sum(B5,B6,B7,B8,B9,B10)* contains six arguments. Both functions will return the same value.

Steps to use the **Fill Handle** to copy a function:

1. Click the cell with the function to be copied.
2. Point to the *Fill Handle* green box in the lower right corner of the cell.
3. Click and drag the *Fill* pointer across the cells where the function should be pasted (Figure 9-49).
4. If you prefer, you may use the regular copy and paste commands to copy a formula or function to be pasted.

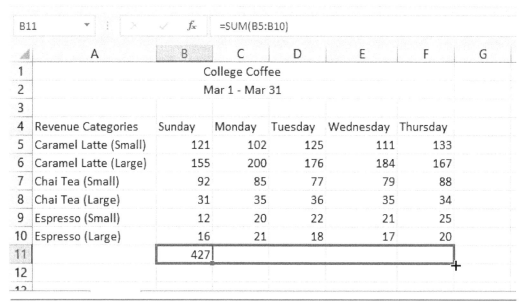

FIGURE 9-49 Fill Handle

Editing a Function Argument

You can edit the function or formula in the cell or in the Formula Bar referenced by a function or formula. Once you edit the function or formula, the results are automatically recalculated. Another way is to use **Range Finder**. Range Finder is an Excel feature that highlights and color-codes cells as you enter or edit a function or a formula.

In the Formula Bar (Figure 9-50), you can retype the formula *=sum(B5:B10)* to *=sum(B5:B11)*, or you can click in the cell itself and retype the formula. To activate the *Range Finder*, click in the Formula Bar. The Range Finder will highlight

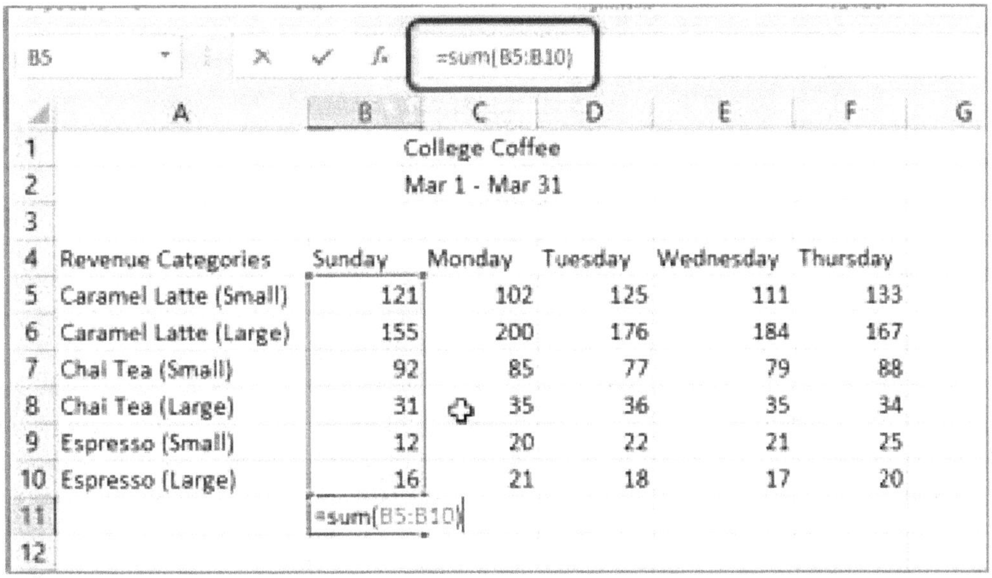

	A	B	C	D	E	F	G
1			College Coffee				
2			Mar 1 - Mar 31				
3							
4	Revenue Categories	Sunday	Monday	Tuesday	Wednesday	Thursday	
5	Caramel Latte (Small)	121	102	125	111	133	
6	Caramel Latte (Large)	155	200	176	184	167	
7	Chai Tea (Small)	92	85	77	79	88	
8	Chai Tea (Large)	31	35	36	35	34	
9	Espresso (Small)	12	20	22	21	25	
10	Espresso (Large)	16	21	18	17	20	
11		=sum(B5:B10)					
12							

FIGURE 9-50 Formula Bar

the range within the formula. At each corner of the range, you will see four blue boxes. You can click and drag on any of the four boxes to expand or shrink the argument range. Excel will automatically recalculate the results.

Excel follows the same ***Order of Operations*** as you would use in math. To use math in Excel, refer to Table 9-4 in your formulas as you would use math operators. The bolded columns represent customary arithmetic operations. The non-bolded columns represent the equivalent in Excel.

TABLE 9-4 Excel Arithmetic Operators

Excel Arithmetic Operators		Comparison Operators	
Addition	+ (plus sign)	**Equals**	=
Subtraction	- (minus sign)	**Greater Than**	>
Multiplication	* (asterisk)	**Less Than**	<
Division	/ (forward slash)	**Greater Than or Equal to**	>=
Exponentation	^ (caret)	**Less Than or Equal to**	<=
		Not Equal to	<=>

Table 9-5 shows the Order of Operations normally used when solving problems in ordinary math.

TABLE 9-5 Order of Operations

Order of Operations
1. Parenthesis and other grouping objects.
2. Exponents.
3. Multiplication and Division from left to right.
4. Addition and Subtraction from left to right.

Formatting a Worksheet

Anytime you open a new workbook in Excel 2016, the workbook uses a default **theme** named *Office*. A *theme* is a collection of colors, fonts, and special effects. The Office default theme applies the 11 pt. Calibri font and the General number format to all cells.

You can easily customize Font Style, Font Size, and Font Color. As you hover over each font, Excel shows you a Live Preview of the selected data with the new font applied.

1. Select the cell or range you want to format.
2. Click the Font drop-down list [*Home* tab, *Font* group.
   a. Excel will display a list of available fonts.
3. Point to a font name. Live Preview will show the selected data with the new font.
4. Once your select a font, then you can click on the **Font Size** drop-down list (*Home* tab, *Font* group). If your desired font size (displayed in points) is not displayed, you can type it in the blue area in the displayed font size box. Excel will accept half-size points. For example, you can type in 11.5 (Figure 9-51).
5. Click the **Increase Font Size** button to adjust the font size or **Decrease Font Size** button to adjust the font size in 1-pt. increments (*Home* tab, *Font* group).

FIGURE 9-51 Fonts

6. You can also click on **the Bold**, **Italic**, or **Underline** buttons to apply one style or multiple styles (*Home* tab, *Font* group).
7. Click the Font Color drop-down list (the arrow at the right of the button) to select a color (*Home* tab, *Font* group).
   a. To apply the most recent font color selected, click on the **Font Color** button (not the arrow).

The Mini Toolbar

The **mini toolbar** appears when you right-click a cell or when you make a selection of a range. It includes common commands from the *Font, Alignment*, and *Number* groups. It is *very* handy and it can be a great timesaver (Figure 9-52).

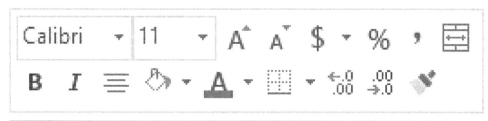

FIGURE 9-52 Mini Toolbar

The Format Painter

The **Format Painter** is another great timesaver that Excel provides. It copies formatting and styles from one cell to another cell or range. Here is how to use the Format Painter:

1. Select a cell that contains the formatting you want to copy. In this example, cell B5 has been selected.
   a. <u>Four changes</u> were made to the cell. The data was italicized, it was formatted as bold, the data was indented, and finally, the font color was changed to blue.
2. Click the **Format Painter** button once (*Home* tab, *Clipboard* group). The pointer will change to a thick, white cross with a tiny paintbrush.
3. Click the cell or drag across the range to be formatted (Figure 9-53).
4. Release the pointer button. You just replaced four steps with only one step.

FIGURE 9-53 Format Painter

5. Double-click the *Format Painter* for multiple areas in the worksheet. To turn off the *Format Painter*, you can either click on the **Format Painter** button or press the **ESC** key.

Format Numbers

In Excel, you can format values with currency symbols, commas (thousands separator), decimal points, and percent signs to enable the reader to quickly recognize and understand those values. The *Number* group on the *Home* tab includes command buttons for *Accounting*, *Percent*, and *Comma styles*. Two other buttons appear in the Number group: The *Increase Decimal* or *Decrease Decimal* (Figure 9-54).

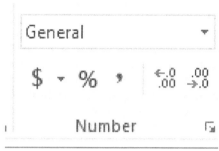

FIGURE 9-54 Format Numbers

Steps to Format Numbers:

1. Select the cell or a range of numbers.
2. Click a command button (*Home* tab, *Number* group).
   a. Click the **General** drop-down list to choose a format.
   b. Press **CTRL+1** to open the Format Cells dialog box and click the Number tab to select a format.
   c. Click the **Number** launcher (*Home* tab) to open the Format Cells dialog box.
3. Click the **Increase Decimal** or **Decrease Decimal** button to choose the number of desired decimal places.

> When a cell displays a series of hash tags, or pound sign symbols (#####), you need to widen the column to see the value.

5. Formatting a Workbook Using the Ribbon, Cell Styles, and Themes

Borders and Fill

A **border** is an outline for a cell or a range. Borders can be used to separate main or column headings, to emphasize data, or group data. **Fill** or shading is a background color or pattern to highlight or draw attention to data.

Steps to add **Borders** and **Fill** using the Ribbon:

1. Select the cell or range.
2. Click the arrow next to the **Borders** button (*Home* tab, *Font* group).

3. Select a border option from the list (Figure 9-55).
   a. To remove a border, choose **No Border**.
4. Click the **Fill Color** button (looks like a bucket) (*Home* tab, *Font* Group).
   a. Click the **Fill Color** button to apply the most recently selected color.
   b. Click the down-arrow to the right of the **Fill Color** button to select another color.
   c. Click the down-arrow to the right of the **Fill Color** button to select **No Fill** if you want to remove a fill and revert to the original sheet.
   d. Click **More Colors** to build a custom color (Figure 9-56).

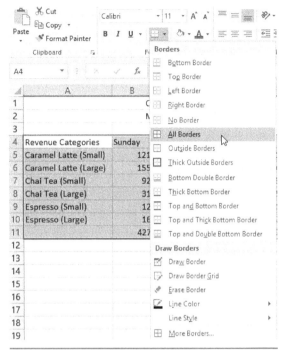

FIGURE 9-55 Borders

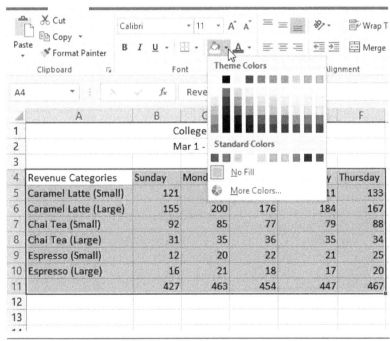

FIGURE 9-56 Fill Button

The Format Cells dialog box has a Border tab and Fill tab. You can choose different line styles, colors, or different positions for the border. From the fill tab, you can choose colors, patterns, or gradients for your cell backgrounds.

Steps to add **Borders** and **Fill** using the Format Cells dialog box:

1. Select the cell or range.
2. Click the **Font** launcher (*Home* tab, Font group) to open the Format Cells dialog box.
   a. You may also press **CTRL+1** to open the Format Cells dialog box.
   b. You may also right-click a cell in the range and select **Format Cells**.
3. Click the **Border** tab (Figure 9-57).
   a. Click *None* to remove all borders.
   b. Click a color. (Choose a color *before* choosing a line; otherwise, you will need to select the color again *after* you choose a line.)
   c. Select a line in the Styles box.

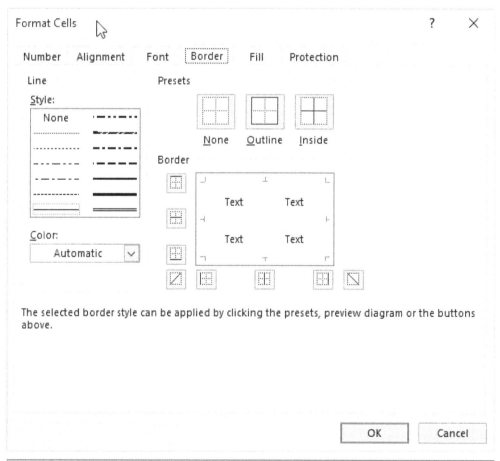

FIGURE 9-57 Borders Tab

4. Click **Outline** in the *Presets* area to apply an outline border.
   a. The Preview area shows the border.
   b. Build a custom border by clicking the desired icons in the *Border* area or by clicking the desired position in the *Preview* area.
5. Click the Fill tab (Figure 9-58).
   a. Select a color tile in the *Background Color* area.
      i. Optional: Select a color from the *Pattern Color* list and select a pattern from the *Pattern Style* list.
      ii. Optional: Click ***Fill effects*** to apply a gradient. Choose two colors: a shading style and a variant.
6. Click *OK* to close the Format Cells dialog box.

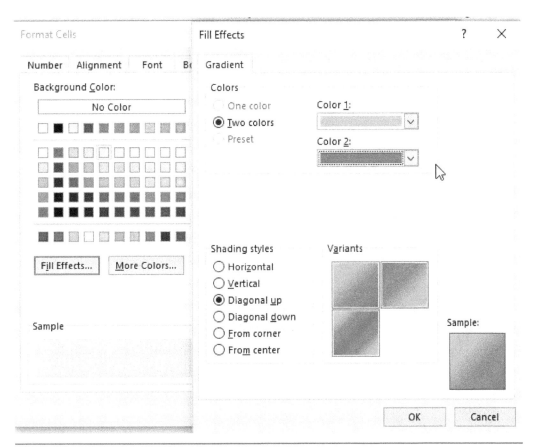

FIGURE 9-58 Fill Tab—Fill Effects

Cell Styles

A **cell style** is a set of formatting elements that includes font style, size, color, alignment, borders, fills, and number formats. Once you have applied a cell style, it will overwrite individual formatting already applied. You can also individually change any of the attributes (Figure 9-59).

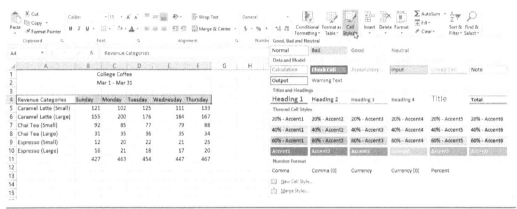

FIGURE 9-59 Cell Styles

Steps to apply **Cell Styles**:

1. Select the cell or range.
2. Select the ***Cell Styles*** button to open the **Cell Styles** gallery (*Home* tab, *Styles* group).
3. Point to a style name to see a *Live Preview* in the worksheet.
4. Choose your Titles and Headings.
5. Choose your Themed Cell Styles.
6. Choose your Number Format.
7. Choose any other buttons you would need. <u>Note</u>: the colors will vary depending on the theme.
   a. Click **Normal** in the *Good, Bad, and Neutral* group to remove any cell styles.

Workbook Themes

A workbook **theme** is a professionally designed set of fonts, colors, and effects. When you change the workbook theme, data formatted with theme settings are reformatted with the new theme fonts, colors, and effects. You can change the theme to restyle a worksheet quickly without having to edit cell formats individually throughout the sheet. After you select a theme, you can further customize it by selecting a theme color and a theme font. The ***Color*** button provides a color palette, and the ***Fonts*** button provides a list of fonts.

Excel's themes gallery lists built-in themes. You can also find additional themes online. You can also create and save your own theme.

Steps to change the workbook theme:

1. Click the **Theme** button (*Page* Layout tab, *Themes* group). The Themes gallery opens.
2. Point to a theme name. *Live Preview* displays the worksheet with new format settings (Figure 9-60).
3. Click a theme icon to apply a different theme.
   a. Click the **Fonts** button list to see the new theme font names at the top of the list.
   b. Click the **Colors** button to see new theme colors.

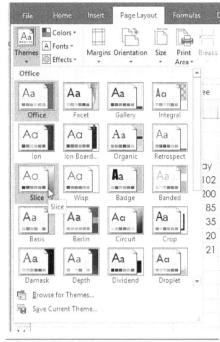

FIGURE 9-60 Themes Gallery

When you choose a workbook theme, the colors in the palette in the Cell Styles will differ, depending on the selected theme.

1. Click the **File** tab and choose **Open**. If you have just started Excel and the file name appears in the Recent list in the Excel *Start* page, click the name to open it. Otherwise,
2. Click **Open Other Workbooks** at the bottom of the *Start* page.
3. Locate the folder where your file is stored.
4. Open **(Your initials) Student Checkup Excel 9-1.** (Click *Enable Editing* if the workbook has opened in Protected View).
5. File/Save As (**Your initials**) **Student Checkup Excel 9-2.**
6. Calculate daily totals using *SUM*.
   a. Click cell **B11**.
      i. Click the ***AutoSum*** button (*Home* tab, *Editing* group).
   b. Press **Enter** to accept the suggested range and to complete the formula, or you can just double-click the **AutoSum** button in cell **B11**.
7. Copy a function using the *Fill Handle* horizontally.
   a. Click cell **B11**.
      i. Point to the *Fill Handle* in the lower right corner of the cell. Click and drag the *Fill* pointer to cell **H11** (Figure 9-61). Release the pointer button.
      Widen column if necessary. If you see "######" in any of your columns, just widen the column.
8. Double-click the **AutoSum** button (Home tab, **Editi**.)
9. Copy a function using the *Fill Handle* vertically.
   a. Click cell **I5**.
      Point to the **Fill Handle** in the lower right corner of the cell. Click and drag the **Fil**l pointer to cell I11 (Figure 9-61). Release the pointer button. If you see "**######**" in any column, just widen the column.
10. Apply Cell Styles.
    a. Select cell **A1** and click the ***Cell Styles*** button. (*Home* tab, *Styles* group).
    b. Click **Title** in the *Titles and Headings* group. Apply **Bold** formatting.
    c. Select cell **A2** and click the ***Cell Styles*** button.
    d. Click **Heading 1** in the *Titles and Headings* group.

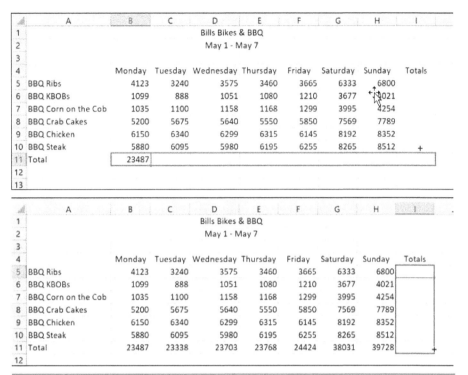

	A	B	C	D	E	F	G	H	I
1				Bills Bikes & BBQ					
2				May 1 - May 7					
3									
4		Monday	Tuesday	Wednesday	Thursday	Friday	Saturday	Sunday	Totals
5	BBQ Ribs	4123	3240	3575	3460	3665	6333	6800	
6	BBQ KBOBs	1099	888	1051	1080	1210	3677	4021	
7	BBQ Corn on the Cob	1035	1100	1158	1168	1299	3995	4254	
8	BBQ Crab Cakes	5200	5675	5640	5550	5850	7569	7789	
9	BBQ Chicken	6150	6340	6299	6315	6145	8192	8352	
10	BBQ Steak	5880	6095	5980	6195	6255	8265	8512	
11	Total	23487							
12									
13									

	A	B	C	D	E	F	G	H	I
1				Bills Bikes & BBQ					
2				May 1 - May 7					
3									
4		Monday	Tuesday	Wednesday	Thursday	Friday	Saturday	Sunday	Totals
5	BBQ Ribs	4123	3240	3575	3460	3665	6333	6800	
6	BBQ KBOBs	1099	888	1051	1080	1210	3677	4021	
7	BBQ Corn on the Cob	1035	1100	1158	1168	1299	3995	4254	
8	BBQ Crab Cakes	5200	5675	5640	5550	5850	7569	7789	
9	BBQ Chicken	6150	6340	6299	6315	6145	8192	8352	
10	BBQ Steak	5880	6095	5980	6195	6255	8265	8512	
11	Total	23487	23338	23703	23768	24424	38031	39728	
12									

FIGURE 9-61 Copying Functions using Fill Handles

e. In Cell **A4**, type in **Revenue Categories**.
f. Select the range **A4:A11**, press and hold down the **CTRL** key and select cells **B4:I4** to add them to the selection. Then release the **CTRL** key and the left mouse button.
g. Click on the ***Cell Styles*** button and select **Light Blue, 20%-Accent 5** in the **Themed Cell Styles** categories.
h. While the ranges **A4:A11** and **B4:I4** are still selected, click the ***Bold*** button.
i. Resize ranges **A4:A11** and **B4:I4** to **12** pt. font. Resize columns if necessary.
j. Click any blank cell to deselect cells and view the styles.
11. Change the theme, and apply font attributes.
   a. Click the ***Themes*** button (*Page Layout* tab, *Themes* group), and choose *Gallery* theme. Note: If you do not have the *Gallery* theme, use a theme of your choice.
   b. Click the **Font** drop-down list (*Themes* group) and select **Georgia** in the **Fonts** section. Note: If you do not have **Georgia** font, use **Arial** font.

c. Select the range **B5:I11**.

d. Click the **Font Size** drop-down list and choose **12** pt.

12. Use the Format Painter.

    a. Click cell **A4**. Resize font size **14**.

    b. Click the **Format Painter** button once (*Home* tab, *Clipboard* group).

    c. Drag to paint cells **B4:I4**, and release the pointer button.

    d. Center align range **B4:I4**.

    e. **AutoFit** column widths **A4:I4**, if necessary.

13. Apply number formats and align text.

    a. Select the range **B5:I5**.

        i. On the *Home* tab, *Number* group, click on the down arrow next to **General**. Select **Accounting**.

        ii. While the range **B5:I5** is selected, click the **Decrease Decimal** button (*Home* tab, *Number* group) twice.

        iii. Select the range **B11:I11**.

        iv. On the **Home** tab, click on **Cell Styles**. Click on **Total**.

        v. While the range **B11:I11** range is still selected, click on the down arrow next to **General**. Select **Accounting** (*Home* tab, *Number* group).

        vi. Click the **Decrease Decimal** button two times while the range **B11:I11** is selected.

        vii. Resize range **B11:I11** to size **14** pt. font. Resize columns if necessary.

    b. Select the range **B6:I10**.

        i. Click on the **Comma** in the *Home* tab, *Number* group.

        ii. While the range **B6:I10** is still selected, click the **Decrease Decimal** button twice (*Home* tab, *Number* group).

14. Add Border formatting.

    a. Select the range **A4:I11**. Click on the **Border** button arrow (*Home* tab, *Font* group).

        i. Select **All Borders**. The "Total"' row in row 11 will be overwritten with the *All Borders* format.

    b. Select the range **B11:I11**.

        i. Click on the down arrow next to the **Borders** button (*Home* tab, *Paragraph* group).

        ii. At the bottom of the list, click on **More Borders** … .

        iii. The **Format Cells** dialog box will open.

        iv. Click the **Border** tab (unless the dialog box opens with the **Border** tab on top).

    v. In the Border Preview area, click the bottom border icon to remove the border (Figure 9-62).

    vi. Click the double-solid-line style (second column, seventh style) in the border Style group.

    vii. Click on the down arrow in the **Color** box. Select **Red, Accent 1** (first row, 5th color).

    viii. In the Preview area, click the bottom border icon to reset the border (Figure 9-63). **It should appear as a red double line.**

    ix. Click **OK** to close dialog box.

  c. Save your workbook.

15. Click the **File** tab and **click** Close, or press **CTRL+W** to close the workbook (Figure 9-64).

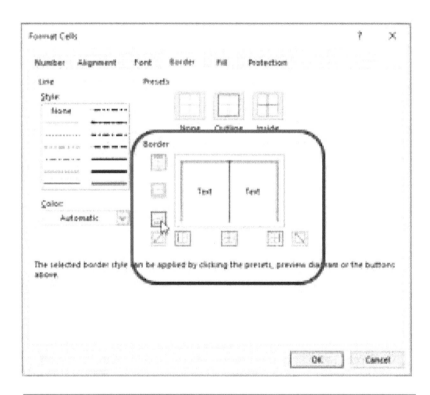

FIGURE 9-62 Formatting Borders

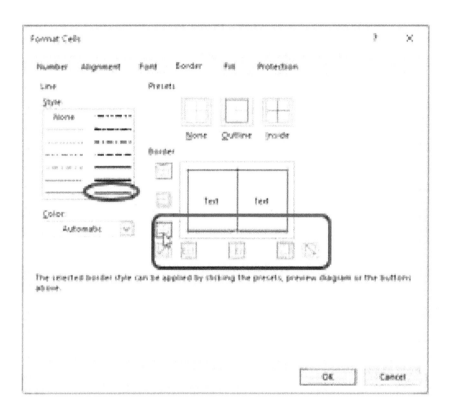

FIGURE 9-63 Formatting Borders

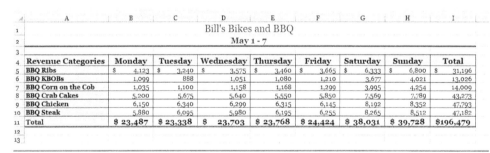

	A	B	C	D	E	F	G	H	I
1				Bill's Bikes and BBQ					
2				May 1 - 7					
3									
4	**Revenue Categories**	**Monday**	**Tuesday**	**Wednesday**	**Thursday**	**Friday**	**Saturday**	**Sunday**	**Total**
5	BBQ Ribs	$ 4,123	$ 3,240	$ 3,575	$ 3,460	$ 3,665	$ 6,333	$ 6,800	$ 31,196
6	BBQ KBOBs	1,099	888	1,051	1,080	1,210	3,677	4,021	13,026
7	BBQ Corn on the Cob	1,035	1,100	1,158	1,168	1,299	3,995	4,254	14,009
8	BBQ Crab Cakes	5,200	5,675	5,640	5,550	5,850	7,569	7,789	43,273
9	BBQ Chicken	6,150	6,340	6,299	6,315	6,145	8,192	8,352	47,793
10	BBQ Steak	5,880	6,095	5,980	6,195	6,255	8,265	8,512	47,182
11	Total	$ 23,487	$ 23,338	$ 23,703	$ 23,768	$ 24,424	$ 38,031	$ 39,728	$196,479
12									
13									

FIGURE 9-64 Student Checkup Excel 9-2 Complete

6. Insert, Delete, Hide, and Unhide Columns and Rows, Modify Worksheets

Wrap Text

The *Wrap Text* command allows you to display a label on multiple lines within a cell, splitting the label between words to fit the width of the column. You can control where the label splits by inserting a manual *line break*. Press **ALT+Enter** after the word where you want the new line to begin. If you need to expand the Formula bar, click on the **Formula Bar** *expand* or *collapse* button at the right edge of the Formula bar (Figure 9-65).

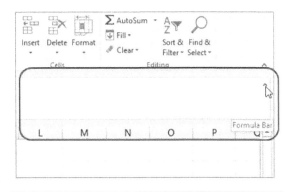

FIGURE 9-65 Formula Bar Expanded

Wrap Text in a Cell

1. Select the cell within the label.
2. Click on the **Home** tab.
3. Click the **Wrap Text** button in the *Alignment* group (Figure 9-66).

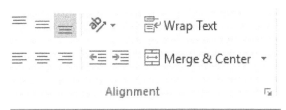

FIGURE 9-66 Wrap Text

   a. To control the split, click the desired location to split in the **Formula Bar** or in the cell. Press **ALT+Enter** to insert a manual line break and then press **Enter** to finish.
4. When complete, adjust the column width and row height as desired.

Insert and Delete Columns and Rows

Excel enables you to insert or delete rows or columns in a worksheet. When you do, Excel moves existing data to make room for new data or fill the gap left by deleted data. Excel automatically updates formulas or functions. Excel will insert row(s) above the selected row and will insert columns(s) to the left of the selected column.

   If you want to insert multiple rows or columns, first select the number of rows or columns that you want to insert. For example, if you want to add 2 rows above row 4, you will want to select rows 4 and 5 (4:5) to insert 2 rows above the original row 4. For columns, if you want to insert two columns to the left of column A, select columns A and B (A:B).

1. *Insert columns*
   a. Right-click the column or row heading(s) of the column(s) or row(s) you want to insert.
      I. You may select multiple columns or rows as you need.
      II. You may select nonadjacent columns or rows.
   b. Click ***Insert*** in the shortcut menu.
      I. Excel will insert a new column to the left of the current column.
2. *Insert rows*
   a. Right-click the row heading number(s) below the row where a new row should appear.
   b. Click ***Insert*** from the shortcut menu (Figure 9-67, bottom).
   c. Excel will insert a row above the selected row.

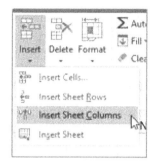

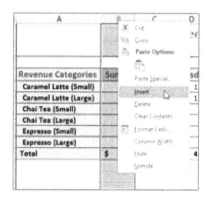

FIGURE 9-67 Insert Columns

When you delete a column or row, <u>data is deleted and remaining columns and rows shift to the left or up</u>. Most formulas or functions are updated if you delete a row or column that is within the argument range. To delete multiple columns or rows, select them and use the **Delete** command.

Try This!

To insert columns, select the column heading(s), click the ***Insert*** button (*Home* tab, *Cells* group), and select **Insert Sheet Columns** (Figure 9-67, top).

To insert rows, select the row number heading(s), click the ***Insert*** button (*Home* tab, *Cells* group), and select **Insert Sheet Rows** (Figure 9-67, top).

<u>Note</u>: If you press the **Delete** key after you selected the column or rows you want to delete (instead of using the **Delete** command), Excel will only delete the cell contents, leaving empty rows or columns in your worksheet.

Steps to Delete a Column or a Row:

1. *Delete columns*
   a. Right-click the column heading(s) of the columns you want to delete.
      i. You may select multiple columns as you need.
      ii. You may select non-adjacent columns.
   b. Click **Delete** in the shortcut menu (Figure 9-68, bottom).
      i. Excel will delete the column and shift all the remaining columns right of the deleted column to the left.
2. *Delete rows*
   a. Right-click the row heading number(s) you want to delete.
   b. Click **Delete** in the shortcut menu.
      i. Excel will delete the row(s) and shift the remaining rows up.

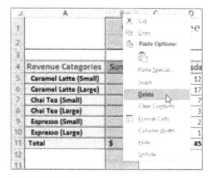

FIGURE 9-68 Delete Columns

Try This!

To delete columns, select the column heading(s), click the **Delete** button (*Home* tab, *Cells* group), and select **Delete Sheet Columns** (Figure 9-68, top).

To delete rows, select the row number heading(s), click the **Delete** button (*Home* tab, *Cells* group), and select **Delete Sheet Rows** (Figure 9-68, top).

Hide and Unhide Columns or Rows

If your worksheet has more data than necessary for your current task, you can hide data to optimize space. An easy example is your checkbook, which has several years' worth of data. Instead of deleting this data (not recommended), you can hide it instead. The **Hide and Unhide** commands apply to columns or rows but not individual cells. Excel creates a tiny gap between the column or row headings. Additionally, column or row headings will not appear to be consecutive, so you can quickly identify what is hidden.

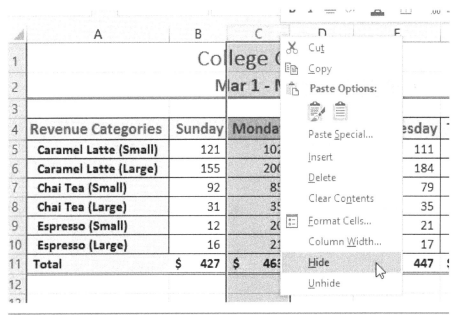

FIGURE 9-69 Hide Columns or Rows

Hide and Unhide Columns or Rows

1. *Hide Columns and Rows*
    a. Right-click the column or row heading(s) of the column(s) or row(s) you want to hide.
        I. You may select multiple columns or rows as you need.
        II. You may select nonadjacent columns or rows.
    b. Click **Hide** (Figure 9-69).
        I. Excel hides the entire column(s) or row(s).
        II. Excel maintains formula references in hidden cells.
2. *Unhide Columns and Rows*
    a. Drag from the column to the left of the hidden column to one column to the right of the hidden column.
    b. Drag from the row above hidden rows to one row below hidden rows.
    c. Right-click one of the selected row or column headings.
    d. Click **Unhide** (Figure 9-70).

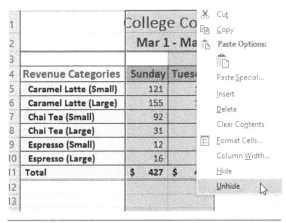

FIGURE 9-70 Unhide Columns or Rows

> To hide or unhide columns or rows, select the column or row headings, click the Format button (***Home* tab, *Cells* group**), choose Hide & Unhide, and select either Hide or Unhide.

Modify Worksheets

Each worksheet in an Excel workbook has a worksheet tab located near the bottom left of the Excel window that displays the name of the sheet. The sheet name default is *Sheet 1*. A new workbook starts with one sheet, but the number of worksheets you can have in an Excel workbook is limited only by the size of memory on the computer. Excel makes it easy to insert and delete sheets, rename them, and change the tab color. You can also move, hide, or copy sheets.

Three ways to insert a worksheet:

FIGURE 9-71 Insert Worksheets

Insert Worksheets

1. Click the ***New Sheet*** button (plus sign) to the right of the worksheet tabs (Figure 9-71).
   i. Excel inserts a new worksheet to the right of the active sheet.
2. Click the arrow on the ***Insert*** button (*Home* tab, *Cells* group) (Figure 9-72). Select **Insert Sheet**.
   a. Excel inserts a new worksheet to the left of the active sheet.
3. Right click a tab and select **Insert** (Figure 9-72).
   a. The Insert dialog box opens. Select **Worksheet** and click *OK*.
   b. Excel inserts the new worksheet to the left of the active sheet.

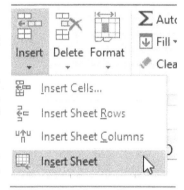

FIGURE 9-72 Insert Sheet

Two ways to delete worksheets:

Delete Worksheets

1. Right-click a worksheet tab and choose **Delete** (Figure 9-73).
   a. Excel deletes the worksheet.
2. Click the arrow on the ***Delete*** button (*Home* tab, *Cells* group) and select **Delete Sheet**.
   III. Excel deletes the worksheet.

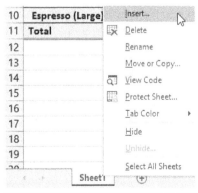

FIGURE 9-73 Delete Sheet

Rename Worksheets and Change Tab Color

New worksheets are, by default, named *Sheet1, Sheet2*, and so on. Excel enables you to rename a worksheet to identify its contents or purpose. When you rename a tab with a longer name, Excel shows the entire name. If you have several worksheets, Excel provides tab-scrolling buttons located to the left of the left-most tab name. You can move forward and backward through the tabs.

To further distinguish or identify a particular worksheet, or distinguish all worksheets within a workbook, you can apply a tab color, or different tab colors, for each tab. The chosen theme color palette includes tiles for your theme color palette and standard colors and also an option to select or build a custom color.

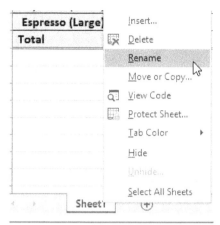

FIGURE 9-74 Rename Sheet

Rename a Worksheet

1. Double-click or right-click the Worksheet tab and select **Rename** (Figure 9-74).
2. Type the new name on the tab and press **Enter**.
3. Then click on the **Format** button (*Home* tab, *Cells* group) and select **Rename Sheet** (Figure 9-75).

Apply a Tab Color

1. Right-click the worksheet tab.
2. Choose Tab Color from the menu to open the palette (Figure 9-76).
3. You can click on the **Format** button (*Home* tab, *Cells* group) and select **Tab Color** (Figure 9-76).

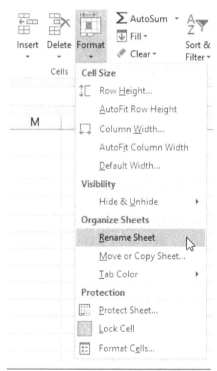

FIGURE 9-75 Rename Sheet

Modify the Appearance of the Workbook

Excel provides four different views so that you can adjust how you see data in a worksheet to save time. You can view all four buttons in the Ribbon on the **View** tab, *Workbook Views* group (Figure 9-77). You can also view three of the

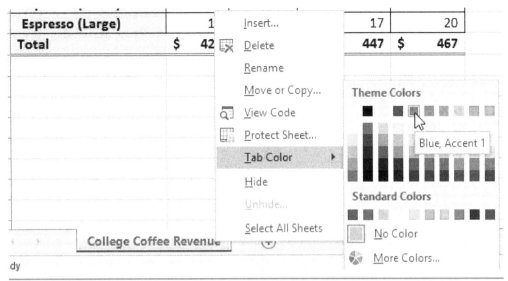

FIGURE 9-76 Adding a Tab Color

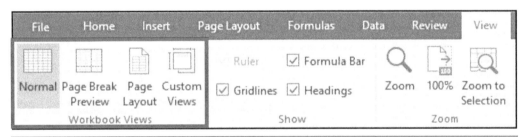

FIGURE 9-77 Worksheet Views on the View Tab

four workbook views using the status bar located in the lower right corner of the worksheet (Figure 9-78). The three excel views shown are **Normal**, *Page Layout*, and **Page Break Preview**.

1. **Normal** view is the default view. It is used to create and modify a worksheet (Figure 9-79).
2. **Page Layout** view opens the header and footer areas, indicates margin areas, and shows rulers (Figure 9-80).
3. **Page Break Preview** displays printed pages with dashed or dotted lines to mark where new pages start (Figure 9-81).

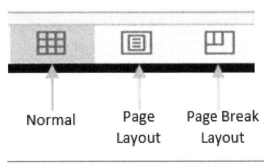

FIGURE 9-78 Worksheet Views on the Status Bar

4. **Custom View** saves your current display and print settings as a custom view that you can quickly apply in the future. This view is not commonly used by Excel beginners.

FIGURE 9-79 Normal View

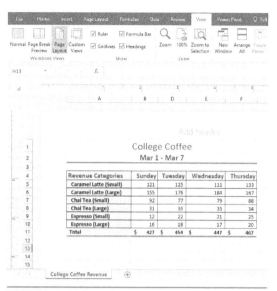

FIGURE 9-80 Page Layout View

Zoom Options

The *Zoom* Options allow you to change the magnification of a sheet. To see more of the data at once, ***zoom out*** (move the Zoom slider to the left), or to get a closer look at the content, ***zoom in*** (move the Zoom slider to the right).

The Zoom Options are located in two places in Excel. The first place is in the *Status Bar*, just to the right of *Workbook Views* (Figure 9-82), or on the *View* tab on the Ribbon in the *Zoom* group.

In the Status Bar, when you click on the **Zoom In** button (plus sign), the magnification will be increased in 10% increments with each click. When you click on the **Zoom Out** button (minus sign), the magnification decreases in 10% increments.

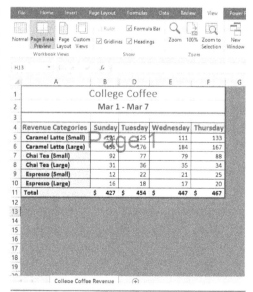

FIGURE 9-81 Page Break Preview

Excel workbooks default to 100% view. The slider will be in the center, and 100% will appear to the right of the plus sign. You can also click on the slider, hold

FIGURE 9-82 Worksheet Views and Zoom Slider

down your left mouse button, and slide the slider to the left or right to find your desired magnification.

In the *Zoom* group on the View tab, you will see three different versions of *Zoom* (Figure 9-83).

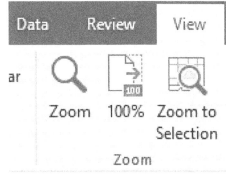

FIGURE 9-83 Zoom Group on View Tab

1. *Zoom* tile (Magnifying Glass). When you click on this tile, a dialog box will appear listing commonly used magnifications plus an option to *Fit Selection*, or *Custom*. The *Custom* setting allows you to type in your desired magnification.
2. The 100% tile. Reverts the magnification to 100%.
3. *Zoom to Selection*. Zooms the sheet so the selected range of cells fills the entire window. This can help you focus on a specific area of the sheet.

View Multiple Worksheets

The **New Window** command (**View** tab, *Window* group) will open a second window for your worksheet so you can work in different places at the same time (Figure 9-84).

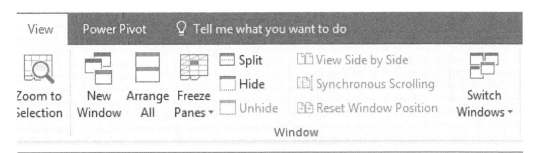

FIGURE 9-84 View Tab, Windows Group

7. Finalizing a Workbook

At this point, you will want to make sure your workbook is ready to be turned in or for sharing. A quick spell-check can help locate misspelled words, incorrect context, or possible grammar errors. Using **Page Setup**, **Margins**, **Page Orientations**, **Paper Size**, and **Headers** and **Footers** will enable you to put the finishing touches on your workbook.

Spell-Check

The spell-Check command (Review tab, *Proofing* group) is a tool that scans a worksheet and locates words that do not match entries in the main Office directory; it can also find duplicate words (Figure 9-85). Once you use the Office dictionary, this dictionary is shared among all Office applications. For example, if you add a word to the dictionary in Microsoft Word, it is shared with Microsoft Excel. Proper names are a good example of unusual words added to the Office dictionary. You have the option to spell-check the entire workbook or just a selected range. Table 9-6 (below) lists and describes the Spelling dialog box options.

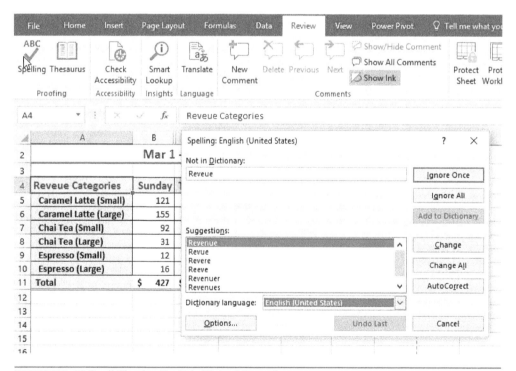

FIGURE 9-85 Spell Check—English (United States)

TABLE 9-6 Spell Check Options

Option	Action
Ignore Once	Skips the occurrence of the label.
Ignore All	Skips all occurrences of the same spelling of the label.
Add to Dictionary	Adds the label to the default dictionary.
Change	Changes the label to the highlighted entry in the Suggestions box.
Change All	Same as *Change* but changes the same label throughout the worksheet.
Delete	Appears to *Repeated* word. Click to delete one occurrence of the label.
AutoCorrect	Adds the label to the *AutoCorrect* list.
Options	Opens the Excel Options dialog box to the Proofing tab or changing default settings.
Undo Last	Reverses the most recent correction.
Cancel	Discontinues spell check.

The Page Setup Dialog Box

The Page Setup dialog box provides several command groups for controlling how a worksheet will print. On the **Page Layout** tab, the commands are from the *Sheet Options, Scale to Fit*, and *Page Setup* groups. To open the Page setup dialog box, go to the *Page Layout* tab, *Page Setup* group. Then click on the Page Setup launcher (Figure 9-86).

The **Page Setup** dialog box has four tabs (Table 9-7).

Margins, Page Orientations, and Paper Size

The **Margins** button (*Page Layout* tab, *Page Setup* group) lists *Normal, Wide, Narrow*, and *Custom Margins*.

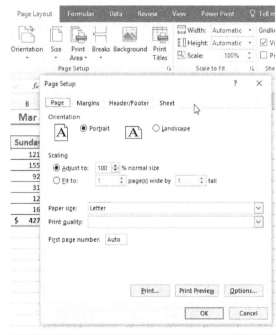

FIGURE 9-86 Page Setup Dialog Box

When you select **Custom Margins**, the Page Setup dialog box (Figure 9-87) opens, and you can set custom margins on the Margin tab.

TABLE 9-7 Page Setup Settings

Tab	Available Settings
Page	Set the orientation to Portrait or Landscape. Use Scaling to shrink or enlarge the printed worksheet to the paper size. Choose a Paper size or set Print quality. Define the First page number.
Margins	Adjust Top, Bottom, Left, Right worksheet margins. Set Header and Footer top and bottom margins. Center on page horizontally or vertically.
Header/Footer	Choose a preset header or footer layout. Create a custom header or footer. Specify first and other page headers. Set header and footers to scale with worksheet and to align with margins.
Sheet	Identify a Print area other than the entire worksheet. Identify Pint titles to repeat on each page. Print Guidelines, Row and column headings, Comments, and Error Messages.

The **Orientation** button (*Page Layout* tab, *Page Setup* group) offers two choices, *Portrait*, or *Landscape*. A portrait page is taller than it is wide. A landscape page is wider than it is tall.

The **Size** button (*Page Layout* tab, *Page Setup* group) provides a list of paper sizes from which you may choose; however, your printer must be able to accommodate the size.

Headers and Footers

A **header** is information that prints at the top of each page. A **footer** is data that prints at the bottom of each page. Headers and footers display identifying information such as your name,

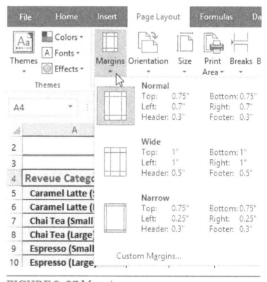

FIGURE 9-87 Margins

the workbook name, and the date. In Excel, each header or footer has three sections: left, middle, and right. In the left section, Excel left-aligns text; in the middle section, Excel centers text, and in the right section, Excel right-aligns text. Excel also provides a list of predefined headers and footers, or you can create your own.

You can also remove a header or footer. One way you can remove a header is to open the Page Setup box (Figure 9-86) then click on the Header/Footer tab, then select (**none**) from the *Header* or *Footer* drop-down list. Another way is to click the header or footer section and delete the text.

Print Area

A **print area** is the data that prints when you give a *Print* command. Excel defaults to print the entire worksheet, but you can select any range of cells as a print area. You can add adjacent data to a work area; however, Excel prints nonadjacent ranges on separate pages, and you can clear a print area to return to the default (Figure 9-88).

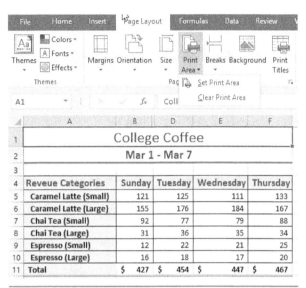

FIGURE 9-88 Selected Print Area

To Set a Print Area

1. Select the cells you want to print.
2. Click on the **Print Area** command (*Page* Layout tab, *Page Setup* group).
3. Prior to printing, you can view the print area in the Backstage view for the Print command and in Page Break review.

To Delete a Print Area

1. Click the ***Print Area*** button (*Page Layout* tab, *Page Setup* group).
2. Select **Clear Print Area**.

Preview and Print a Workbook

The **Print** command in the Backstage view provides a preview so that you can make last minute changes before you print.

1. Click on ***Print Preview*** to check your worksheet.
2. Click on ***Show Margins*** to display margin and column markers.
3. Click ***Zoom to Page*** to toggle between zoom sizes.
4. Set the number of copies.

5. Click *Printer* button to choose the printer name.
6. Click the **Settings** arrow.
7. Specify which pages to print.
8. Double-check and verify page orientation, paper size, margins, and scaling. To make changes, click on the blue **Page Setup** link at the bottom of the list in the **Settings** area (Figure 9-89).
9. Click **Print**. The data is sent to the printer, and then the Backstage view closes.

FIGURE 9-89 Print Menu

Press **CTRL+P** to open the **Print** command in the Backstage view. This keyboard combination also works while you are on the Internet.

Student Checkup Excel 9-3

In this project, you will open an existing Excel workbook that tracks revenue for one week for Bill's Bikes and BBQ. You will add a sheet, hide a row and add data. Additionally, you will spell-check your worksheet, and finalize your workbook for distribution. **Note: Blue text represents typed text.**

File Needed: **(Your Initials) Student Checkup Excel 9-2**

Completed Project File Name: **(Your initials) Student Checkup Excel 9-3**

1. Open **(Your Initials) Student Checkup Excel 9-2**. This is the workbook you completed in Student Checkup Excel 9-2.
2. Save the workbook as **(Your Initials) Student Checkup Excel 9-3.**
3. Rename **Sheet1** to **Restaurant Revenue**. (Right-click on the tab and select **Rename**.)
4. Change the tab color to **Red, Accent 1**. (Right-click on the tab, and select **Tab Color**.)
5. Insert a new row after row 7 (this will be your new row 7). **BBQ Corn on the Cob** will now be in row 8.
6. Enter the following data in cells **A7:H7**. Notice as you type in the data, the data will automatically format to match the rest of the data. Also,

note that the totals change too. If the program adds $ signs to the cells, just click on the **Comma**, then click **Decrease Decimal** twice.

7. If cell **I7** does not populate automatically, click on cell **I6** and autofill it down to cell **I7**.

8. Hide row **8** (BBQ Corn on the Cob). (Right-click on the number 8 [row] and select **Hide**.) Widen column **I** if necessary.

| 7 | BBQ Pulled Poork | 7,099 | 6,888 | 6,571 | 6,329 | 6,722 | 8,989 | 9,558 |

IMG 9.1

9. Check spelling.
   a. Press **CTRL + *Home***. This will take you to the beginning of the workbook (cell A1).
      Click the ***Spelling*** button (*Review* tab, *Proofing* group).
      Make any indicated changes.
10. Change page setup options.
    a. Click the ***Page Layout*** tab.
    b. Click the **Orientation** button and select **Landscape** (*Page Layout* tab/*Page Setup* **group)**.
    c. Click the **Page Setup launcher** to open the **Page Setup** dialog box (*Page Layout* tab/*Page Setup* group). The **launcher** is the diagonal arrow in the lower right of the *Page Setup* group box.
       i. On the **Page** tab, under the **Scaling** area, click the down arrow next to the ***Fit to*** button.
       ii. Set the **Fit to option to 1 page wide and 1 page tall**.
       iii. Click on the **Margins** tab.
       iv. In the **Center on Page** area, click in the check box next to **Horizontally**.
    d. Click on the **Header/Footer** tab.
       i. Click the **Header** drop-down list and select **(Your Initials) Student Checkup Excel 9-3**. You will see the file name displayed in the center section of the header.
       ii. Click the **Footer** drop-down list and select **Restaurant Revenue** to insert the sheet name in the center section of the footer.
    Note: This will place your information in the center header and center footer portions of your sheet.
11. Click the ***Print Preview*** button to preview your worksheet.

12. Print your worksheet. (Not required for assignment.)
   a. Click the **File** tab to access **Backstage**. Select *Print*. **Print Preview** will display how your worksheet will print.
   b. Select your printer.
   c. Click *Print* to print the worksheet.
13. Save and close your workbook (Figure 9-90).

Student Checkup Excel 9-3.xlsx

Bills Bikes & BBQ
May 1 - May 7

Revenue Categories	Monday	Tuesday	Wednesday	Thursday	Friday	Saturday	Sunday	Totals
BBQ Ribs	$ 4,123	$ 3,240	$ 3,575	$ 3,460	$ 3,665	$ 6,333	$ 6,800	$ 31,196
BBQ KBOBs	1,099	888	1,051	1,080	1,210	3,677	4,021	13,026
BBQ Pulled Pork	7,099	6,888	6,571	6,329	6,722	8,989	9,558	52,156
BBQ Corn on the Cob	1,035	1,100	1,158	1,168	1,299	3,995	4,254	14,009
BBQ Crab Cakes	5,200	5,675	5,640	5,550	5,850	7,569	7,789	43,273
BBQ Chicken	6,150	6,340	6,299	6,315	6,145	8,192	8,352	47,793
BBQ Steak	5,880	6,095	5,980	6,195	6,255	8,265	8,512	47,182
Total	$30,586	$30,226	$ 30,274	$ 30,097	$ 31,146	$47,020	$ 49,286	$ 248,635

Restaurant Revenue

FIGURE 9-90 Student Checkup Excel 9-3 Completed

Excel Project 9-1

You have been hired to create an Excel workbook for Sam's Sub Shop that tracks daily expenses for categories that include meats, cheeses, veggies, condiments, and bread. Sam also wants you to include chips, brownies, and beverages. Your workbook will track weekly expenses for a month. **Note: Blue text represents typed text.**

File Needed: **None**. You will create a **new blank workbook**.

Completed assignment name: **(Your Initials) Excel Project 9-1**

1. Create and save a workbook.
   a. Click the **File** tab to open the Backstage view.
   b. Select **New** and then click **Blank workbook**.
   c. Click the *Save* button on the Quick Access toolbar to open the Save As dialog box.
   d. Select the folder to save the workbook or **Browse** to a location on OneDrive, your computer, or external media.

e. Name your workbook as **(Your Initials) Excel Project 9-1.**

　　f. Click **Save.**

2. Enter data with spelling errors. Type the following items exactly as you see them.

　　a. In cell **A1**, type **Sam's Sub Shoppe**. Press **Enter.**

　　b. In cell **A2**, type **July 2025**. Press **Enter.**

　　c. In cell **A4** type **Expense Catagorys**. Press **Enter.**

3. Adjust the width of column A.

　　a. Point to the border line between column **A** and column **B** headings. Your pointer will change to display a two-pointed arrow.

　　b. Double-click to AutoFit column A, *or*

　　c. Left-click, hold down your mouse, and drag your mouse to the right until the column appears wide enough for the text.

4. Enter values and labels as shown in Figure 9-91.

	A	B	C	D	E
1	Sam's Sub Shoppe				
2	Jul-20				
3					
4	Expens Catagorys	Week 1	Week 2		
5	Meats	4800	4500	5200	5500
6	Cheeses	2100	1950	2200	2300
7	Veggies	555	425	595	600
8	Condements	51	45	55	60
9	Bread	2325	2135	2445	2650
10	Chips	1000	850	1025	1050
11	Brwnies	775	790	800	850
12					

FIGURE 9-91 Labels & Values to be Entered with Errors

5. Use the *Fill Handle* to fill a series and copy data.

　　a. Select cells **B4:C4**.

　　b. In the lower right of cell **C4**, drag the *Fill Pointer* to cell **E4**.

　　c. In cell **F4**, type in **Totals**. Press **Enter**.

6. **Merge and Center** labels.

　　a. Select cells **A1:F1,** then click on the ***Merge & Center*** button (*Home* tab, *Alignment* group).

    b. Select cells **A2:F2,** then click on the ***Merge & Center*** button (*Home* tab, *Alignment* group).

    c. Select cells **B4:F4**. Click the ***Center*** button (*Home* tab, *Alignment* group).

7. Select cell **A2**. Format the date with the <u>March 14, 2012</u>, format (*Home* tab, *Number* group).

    a. Click the **Number Format** down arrow (the word *Custom* appears next to it).

    b. Select **More Number Formats**.

    c. On the **Number** tab, in the left panel, select **Date**.

    d. In the **Type** box, select the date <u>March 14, 2012</u>. Your date will appear as "July 1, 2025".

    e. Click **OK** to close dialog box.

8. Select a workbook theme.

    a. Click the **Themes** button (***Page Layout*** tab, *Themes* group).

    b. Choose the **Slice** theme from the gallery. <u>Note</u>: If your computer does not have the **Slice** theme, then select a theme of your choice.

    c. In the **Themes** group, click on the down arrow next to **Fonts**. Click on *Century Gothic*. <u>Note</u>: If your computer does not have the *Century Gothic* font, select **Arial** font instead.

9. Adjust the width of column **A**. Select method **a, b, or c** to adjust the column width.

    a. Select cell **A1,** and click the ***Cells Styles*** button or the ***More*** button (*Home* tab, *Styles* group).

    b. Select **Title**. Select **Bold** font. Change font size to **20** pt.

    c. Select cell **A2**, and click the ***Cells Styles*** button or the ***More*** button (*Home* tab, *Styles* group).

    d. Select **Heading 2**. Change font size of cell **A2** to size **16** pt. font.

    e. Select cells **A4:F4**. Hold down your **CTRL** key, and then select cells **A5:A12.** You have selected two ranges.

    f. Click the ***Cells Styles*** button, then, under the *Themed Cell Styles* group, select **Light Blue, 20%-Accent 1** (*Home* tab, *Styles* group).

    g. With the ranges **A4:F4** and **A5:A12** still selected, click the **Bold** button (*Home* tab, *Font* group) or press **CTRL B**. Resize columns if necessary.

    h. Select cell **A12**. Type **Totals,** and press **Enter**.

10. Apply borders.

    a. Select the range **A4:F12**.

    b. Click on the down arrow next to the ***Borders*** button (*Home* tab, *Font* group).

    c. Click on **All Borders**.

11. Apply font attributes.
    a. Select range **A4:F12**.
    b. Click the **Font size** drop-down list (*Home* tab, *Font* group) and select **14**. Resize columns if necessary.
    c. Select cells **A5:A11**.
    d. Click the ***Increase Indent*** button (*Home* tab, *Alignment* group) once.
    e. Select Cell **A12,** and click the ***Align Right*** button (*Home* tab, *Alignment* group).
    f. If necessary, resize column **A**.
12. Use the *SUM* function, and copy a formula using the *Fill Pointer*.
    a. Select cell **B12**.
    b. Click the ***AutoSum*** button twice (*Home* tab, *Editing* group). Press **Enter**.
    c. Select cell **B12** (you may have to click outside the cell and select **B12** again), and drag (*autofill*) the *Fill Pointer* to cell **E12**.
    d. Select cell **F5**.
    e. Double-click the ***AutoSum*** button (*Home* tab, *Editing* group).
    f. Select cell **F5** (you may have to click outside the cell and select **F5** again), and drag (*autofill*) the Fill Pointer to cell **F12**.
13. Format Numbers.
    a. Select ranges **B5:F5** and **B12:F12**.
    b. Click the ***Accounting Number Format*** button ($ sign) (*Home* tab, *Number* group). Excel will adjust the column widths to accommodate the values.
    c. Click the ***Decrease Decimal*** button (*Home* tab, *Number* group) twice. The column widths will not adjust. If the columns are too narrow or wide, go ahead and resize them for a better fit.
    d. Select cells **B6:F11**.
    e. On the *Home* tab in the Number group, click on the comma (,), then click twice on the ***Decrease Decimal*** button.
14. Format the **Total** row and add **Borders.**
    a. Select the range **A12:F12,** and click the ***Cells Styles*** button or the ***More*** button (*Home* tab, *Styles* group).
    b. Click the ***Cells Styles*** button**,** and select **Total** in the *Themed Cell Styles* group.
    c. Select the range **A12:F12**. Change font size to **16** pt. Resize columns if necessary.
    d. While the range **A12:F12** is still selected, click on the down arrow next to the ***Borders*** button (*Home* tab, *Font* group).

e. Click on **More Borders …** (Here we will add vertical borders to the Totals row.)

f. On the **Border** tab in the **Border** area, click on the *Left Vertical Border* button, *Center Vertical Border* button, and the **Right Vertical Border button**. Select **Black, Text 1** color if not already selected.

g. Click **OK.**

15. Change row heights.

   a. Right-click the heading for row **4**. (At the far left of your screen, to the left of column **A**, right-click on the **4**.)

   b. In the shortcut menu, choose **Row Height** and type **30** as the new row height.

   c. Right-click the heading for row **12.**

   d. In the shortcut menu, choose **Row Height** and type **25** as the new row height.

16. Insert a row and change column width.

   a. Select cell **A9** (Bread), and then right-click row heading **9.** (Click on the **9** for the row.)

   b. Choose **Insert** from the shortcut menu. This new row will be your new row 9. Rows 10–12 will shift down.

   c. In cell **A9**, type **Soft Drinks & Waters.**

   d. Resize column **A** to fit the text.

   e. Enter the following data in row **9**.

   | 9 | Soft Drinks & Waters | 1585 | 1350 | 1600 | 1750 |

Note: If necessary, when you are in cell **E9**, you may need to press your right arrow key to populate cell **F9**.

17. Rename the sheet and set the tab color.

   a. Right-click the **Sheet1** tab.

   b. Click on *Rename*.

   c. Type **July 2025 Expenses,** and press *Enter*.

   d. Right-click the **July 2025 Expenses** tab.

   e. Select **Tab Color**. Choose **Blue** under **Standard Colors**.

18. Spell-check your worksheet.

   a. Press **CTRL + Home** to move to cell **A1** or click in cell **A1**.

   b. Click the *Spelling* button (*Review* tab, *Proofing* group).

   c. Accept the first spelling suggestions for every error except for "*Catagorys*." For "*Catagorys*," select the first spelling suggestion. It should be changed to "*Catagories*."

d. For "Condements" and "Brwnies," accept the first spelling suggestions.

e. Click **OK.**

19. Change page setup options.

a. Click the ***Page Layout*** tab, and click the ***Page Setup*** launcher.

b. On the **Page** tab, select the **Landscape** radio button.

c. Click the **Margins** tab.

d. Select the **Horizontally** box under *Center on Page*.

e. Click the **Header/Footer** tab.

f. Click the **Header** drop-down list, and choose **(Your Initials) Excel Project 9-1** to insert the name in the **center** header section.

g. Click the **Footer** drop-down list, and choose **July 2025 Expenses** to insert the name in the **center** footer section.

h. On the **Header/Footer** tab, click on the ***Print Preview*** button *or* click on the **File** tab, then click on **Print**.

i. Save and close workbook (Figure 9-92).

j. Turn in your assignment.

Excel Project 9-1.xlsx

Sam's Sub Shoppe
July 1, 2020

Expense Categories	Week 1	Week 2	Week 3	Week 4	Totals
Meats	$ 4,800	$ 4,500	$ 5,200	$ 5,500	$ 20,000
Cheeses	2,100	1,950	2,200	2,300	8,550
Veggies	555	425	595	600	2,175
Condiments	51	45	55	60	211
Soft Drinks & Waters	1,585	1,350	1,600	1,750	6,285
Bread	2,325	2,135	2,445	2,650	9,555
Chips	1,000	850	1,025	1,050	3,925
Brownies	775	790	800	850	3,215
Totals	$ 13,191	$ 12,045	$ 13,920	$ 14,760	$ 53,916

July 2020 Revenue

FIGURE 9-92 Project 9-1 Completed

Patrick's Planes, Trains, and Cars has hired you to prepare a workbook reflecting monthly sales data for the first 6 months of 2022. Your tasks will include editing and formatting data, perform calculations, and prepare the workbook for the company CFO. **Note: Blue text represents typed text.**

File Needed: **PatrickPlanesTrains&Cars.xlsx**

Completed assignment name: **(Your Initials) Excel Project 9-2.xlsx**

1. Open **PatrickPlanesTrains&Cars.xlsx** from your student data files. If the workbook has opened in Protected View, click **Enable Editing** in the yellow security bar.
2. Save the workbook as **(Your Initials) Excel Project 9-2**.
3. Apply the **Berlin** theme to the worksheet.
4. Edit worksheet data.
   a. Edit cell **A4** to **Revenue Items**.
   b. Edit cell **B7** to **1400**.
   c. Edit cell **F12** to **1000**.
5. Use the *Fill Handle* to complete a series.
   a. Select cell **B4**.
   b. Use the *Fill Handle* to complete the series to **June** in column **G**. **Center** Align.
   c. Type **Total** in cell **H4**. **Center**-align (if needed).
   d. *Autofit* the columns so that the complete label displays.
6. Merge & Center.
   a. Merge & Center range **A1:H1**.
   b. Merge & Center range **A2:H2**.
7. Delete row **14** (**Clearance** row).
8. Use **SUM** and the **Fill Handle** to calculate totals. Choose method a, b, or c below to calculate totals.
   a. Use the **AutoSum** button to build a *SUM* function in cell **H5** (*Home* tab, *Editing* group).
   b. Use the *Fill Handle* to copy the formula in cell **H5** to cell **H13**.
   c. Select the range **B14:H14** and click on the **AutoSum** button. The *SUM* formula is inserted, and you will see a **Quick Analysis** options button appear.
   d. Press **ESC** (upper left of your keyboard) to ignore the *Quick Analysis* options.
9. Format labels and values.
   a. Select cell **A1**. Click on the **Cell Styles** button. In the *Titles and Headings* group, click on **Title**. **Bold** title.

    b. Select cell **A2**. Click on the **Cell Styles** button. In the *Titles and Headings* group, click on **Heading 2**.

    c. Format cells **A4:H4** as **Bold**.

    d. Increase the row height of row **4** to **21 (28 pixels)**.

    e. Format cells **A5:A13** as **Bold**. Press the **Increase Indent** button one time (*Home* tab, *Alignment* group). **AutoFit** column **A**.

    f. Click on cell **A14**. **Bold**. **Right Align**.

    g. Select the range **B5:H5**. Format as *Accounting*. Click the **Decrease Decimal** button twice (*Home* tab, *Number* group).

    h. Select the range **B6:H13**. Format the cells as **Comma** style. Click the Decrease Decimal button twice.

    i. Select the range **B14:H14**. Click on the **Cell Styles** button [*Home* tab, *Styles* group]. In the *Titles and Headings* area, click on **Total**. Format as *Accounting*. Click the **Decrease Decimal** button twice.

    j. *AutoFit* all columns if needed.

10. Rename a worksheet.

    a. Double-click or right-click on *Sheet1*.

    b. Type in **January – June 2025**.

    c. Press **ENTER**.

11. Change the page orientation from *Portrait* to *Landscape* (*Page Layout* tab, *Page Setup* group).

12. Center the page horizontally (*Page Layout* tab, *Page Setup* group).

    a. Click on the Page Setup launcher.

    b. Click on the Margins tab.

    c. In the Center on Page area, click on the Horizontally box. Click OK to close dialog box.

13. Finalize and prepare the workbook for distribution.

    a. Click the **Insert** tab, then click on the **Header & Footer** button (*Insert* tab, *Text* group).

    b. Click in the **Right header** section. A **Design** tab will appear beneath the *Header & Footer* tab. Insert the sheet name. The **Sheet Name** button will appear in the *Header and Footer Elements* group, in the header it will appear as "&[Tab]". This is correct.

    c. Scroll down and click in the **Left footer** section. Type in your first name and last name.

    d. Click on the Right footer section. Insert the **File Name** button. The **File Name** button is located in the *Header and Footer Elements* group. In the header it will appear as "&[File]". This is correct.

    e. Click in any cell in your worksheet to exit the **Headers & Footers**. Return to **Normal** view. To do this, you can click on the *View* tab and click on *Normal View* in the *Workbook Views* group. Otherwise, go to the bottom right of your worksheet. You will see three buttons for three different views. The **Normal** button is the left button. It looks like a grid.

f. Click on the **View** tab. In the *Show* group, click on the **Gridlines** checkbox to deselect it (Figure 9-93).

14. Save and close your workbook. Turn in your assignment.

January - June 2022

Patrick's Planes, Trains, & Cars
January - June 2022 Monthly Sales

Revenue Items	January	February	March	April	May	June	Total
Model Planes	$ 3,000	$ 3,100	$ 2,950	$ 3,200	$ 3,100	$ 3,200	$ 18,550
Model Plane Parts	800	850	750	800	700	750	4,650
Model Plane Accessories	1,400	1,100	1,500	1,750	1,900	1,200	8,850
Model Trains	4,000	4,100	3,900	4,200	4,300	3,700	24,200
Model Train Parts	1,500	1,600	1,300	1,200	1,100	1,350	8,050
Model Train Accessories	2,000	2,100	1,900	2,000	2,150	2,100	12,250
Model Cars	3,500	3,600	3,100	3,300	3,500	3,100	20,100
Model Car Parts	1,000	900	800	850	1,000	800	5,350
Model Car Accessories	2,900	1,100	1,000	2,000	2,100	1,950	11,050
Totals	$ 20,100	$ 18,450	$ 17,200	$ 19,300	$ 19,850	$ 18,150	$ 113,050

Axxxxx Dxxxx   4/24/2020   AD Excel Project 9-2

FIGURE 9-93 Project 9-2 Completed

Excel Project 9-3

Tony and Guido's Pizza is the newest pizzeria in town. As a friend of Tony and Guido, you have volunteered to help them set up a workbook to help them keep track of their sales. As payment, you will happily accept some of their excellent pizza. Tony and Guido would like you to set up their restaurant worksheet by pizza type and pizza size and then add up total weekly sales, showing the totals for each pizza size. **Note: Blue text represents typed text.**

File Needed: ***Tony&GuidosPizza.xlsx***

Completed File Name: ***(Your Initials) Excel Project 9-3.xlsx***

1. Open the **Tony&GuidosPizza.xlsx** from your student data files. If the workbook has opened in Protected View, click *Enable Editing* in the yellow security bar.

2. Save the workbook as **(Your Initials) Excel Project 9-3**.

3. Apply the **Retrospect** theme to the worksheet. <u>Note</u>: If your computer does not have the Retrospect theme, then select one of your own.

4. Edit worksheet data.
   a. Delete **Sheet2** tab. Right-click on **Sheet2**. Select ***Delete***.
   b. Edit cell **D6** to 1600.
   c. Edit cell **C9** to 1500.
   d. Edit cell **E16** to 1960.

5. Use the *Fill Handle* to complete a series.
   a. Select cells **B4 & C4**.
   b. Use the *Fill Handle* to complete the series to **Week 4** in column **E**. Center align.
   c. Type **Total** in cell **F4**. If necessary, center align.
   d. Change row **4** height to size 19.50 (26 pixels).
   e. Select the range **A4:F4**. Click on the ***Cell Styles*** button (*Home* tab, *Styles* group). In the *Themed Cell Styles* area, select **Accent 1**. Resize font to size **12** pt. Apply **Bold** formatting.
   f. Resize column **A** to size 18 (131 pixels).
   g. Select cell **A5**. Apply **Bold** formatting. Change font color to **Orange, Accent 1.**
   h. While you are still in cell A5, double-click on the **Format Painter** (*Home* tab, *Clipboard* group), click in cells **A10** and **A15**. Click again on the ***Format Painter*** to turn it off.

6. Merge & Center.
   a. **Merge & Center** range **A1:F1**.
   b. **Merge & Center** range **A2:F2**.

7. Format Text.
   a. Select cell **A1**. Click the ***Cell Styles*** button. In the *Titles and Headings* group, click on **Title**.
   b. in Cell **A1**, change the **Font Color** to **Orange Accent 1**.
   c. In cell **A1,** change the **Font Size** to **20** pt.
   d. In cell **A1,** apply **Bold** formatting.
   e. Select cell **A2**. Press the ***Cell Styles*** button. In the *Titles and Headings* group, click on **Heading 2**. Change **Font Color** to **Orange, Accent 1.**

f. Format cells **A6:A9** as **Bold**.

    i. Press the ***Increase Indent*** button one time (*Home* tab, *Alignment* group).

g. **Format cells A11:A14 as Bold**.

    i. Press the ***Increase Indent*** button one time (*Home* tab, *Alignment* group).

h. **Format cells A16:A19 as Bold**.

    i. Press the ***Increase Indent*** button one time (*Home* tab, *Alignment* group).

    ii. If necessary, **AutoFit** column **A** to show your complete labels.

8. Use *SUM* and the *Fill Handle* to calculate totals.

a. Use the ***AutoSum*** button to build a *SUM* function in cell **F6** (*Home* tab, *Editing* group).

b. Use the *Fill Handle* to copy the formula in cell **F6** to Cell **F9**.

c. Use the ***AutoSum*** button to build a *SUM* function in cell **F11** (*Home* tab, *Editing* group).

d. Use the *Fill Handle* to copy the formula in cell **F11** to Cell **F14**.

e. Use the ***AutoSum*** button to build a *SUM* function in cell **F16** (*Home* tab, *Editing* group).

f. Use the *Fill Handle* to copy the formula in cell **F16** to Cell **F19**.

g. Select cell **B20**. Type in the formula **=sum**(**B6:B19**). Press **Enter**. The value in **B20** should be **$15,300**. Select cell **B20** again. **Autofill** the contents of **B20** through cell **F20**.

9. Merge Cells and Border formatting.

a. Select cells **A5:F5**. Click on the down arrow next to **Merge & Center**. Click on *Merge Across*.

b. Select cells **A10:F10**. Click on the down arrow next to **Merge & Center**. Click on *Merge Across*.

c. Select cells **A15:F15**. Click on the down arrow next to **Merge & Center**. Click on *Merge Across*.

d. Select the range **A4:F20**.

e. Click on the down arrow next to the ***Borders*** button.

f. Click on ***More Borders ...***

g. In the **Format Cells** dialog box**,** double-check that the **Border** tab is on top.

h. On the **Border** tab in the color group, select **Orange, Accent 1**. (You do not need to change the line style.)

i. In the **Presets** area, click on the ***Outline*** and ***Inside*** buttons.

j. Click *OK* to close the Format Cells dialog box.

10. Format values and labels.
    a. Select cells **B6:F6**. Format as **Accounting**. Click the *Decrease Decimal* button twice.
    b. Select cells **B11:F11**. Format as *Accounting*. Click the *Decrease Decimal* button twice.
    c. Select cells **B16:F16**. Format as *Accounting*. Click the *Decrease Decimal* button twice.
    d. Select the range **B7:F9**. Use *Comma* formatting. Click the *Decrease Decimal* button twice.
    e. Select the range **B12:F14**. Use *Comma* formatting. Click the *Decrease Decimal* button twice.
    f. Select the range **B17:F19**. Use *Comma* formatting. Click the *Decrease Decimal* button twice.
    g. Select cells **A20:F20**. Click the *Fill Color* button. Click on *Orange, Accent 1*.
    h. Change range **A20:F20** font color to **white.** Apply **Bold** formatting.
    i. Select range **B20:F20** and apply *Accounting* format, zero decimals (click on the *Decrease Decimal* button twice). Resize range **B20:F20** font to size **12** pt.
    j. Select the range **F6:F9**. Apply **Bold** formatting.
    k. Select the range **F11:F14**. Apply **Bold** formatting.
    l. Select the range **F16:19**. Apply **Bold** formatting.
11. Insert Rows.
    a. Insert a new row 9.
    b. In cell **A9,** type Large.
    c. Enter the data from **IMG 9.2** (below) in row **9**.
    d. Click on cell **F8**. Use the **Fill Handle** in the lower right of the cell to drag the formula down to cell **F9**.
    e. Insert a new row **15**.
    f. In cell **A15**, type **Large**.
    g. Enter the data from **IMG 9.3** (below) in row **15**.
    h. Click on cell **F14**. Use the **Fill Handle** in the lower right of the cell to drag the formula down to cell **F15**
       Note: Excel may automatically fill in the formula for you.
    i. Insert a new row **21**.
    j. In cell **A21**, type **Large**.
    k. Enter the data from **IMG 9.4** (below) in row **21**.
    l. Click on cell **F20**. Use the **Fill Handle** in the lower right of the cell to drag the formula down to cell **F21**
       Note: Excel may automatically fill in the formula for you.
    m. The grand total value in cell **F23** should be **$80,105**.

12. Insert Data into the Workbook.
    a. In cell **A9**, type **Large**.
    b. Enter the following data in row **9**.
    c. Click on cell **F8**. Use the *Fill Handle* in the lower right of the cell to drag the formula down to cell **F9**.

	A	B	C	D	E
9	**Large**	1,400	1,300	1,400	1,450

IMG 9.2

    d. In Cell **A15**, type **Large**.
    e. Enter the following data in row **15**.
    f. Click on cell **F14**. Use the *Fill Handle* in the lower right of the cell to drag the formula down to cell **F15**.
       Note: Excel may automatically fill in the formula for you.

	A	B	C	D	E
15	**Large**	1,500	1,550	1,585	1,565

IMG 9.3

    g. In cell **A21**, type **Large**.
    h. Enter the following data in row **21**.
    i. Click on cell **F20**. Use the *Fill Handle* in the lower right of the cell to drag the formula down to cell **F21**.
       Note: Excel may automatically fill in the formula for you.
    j. The value in cell **F23** should be **$80,105**.

	A	B	C	D	E
21	**Large**	1,250	1,265	1,295	1,255

IMG 9.4

13. Rename a worksheet.
    a. Double-click on *Sheet1*.
    b. Type in **May 2025 Sales**.
    c. Change the tab color to **Orange, Accent 1**.
14. Change the paper orientation from Portrait to Landscape (*Page Layout* tab, *Page Setup* group).
15. Center the page horizontally (*Page Layout* tab, *Page Setup* group).
    a. Click on **Page Setup** launcher.
    b. Click on the **Margins** tab.

   c. In the Center on Page area, click on the **Horizontally** box.

   d. Click *OK* to close the dialog box.

16. Finalize and prepare the workbook for distribution.

   a. Click the *Insert* tab and click on **Header & Footer** button (*Insert* tab, *Text* group).

   b. Click in the **Right Header** section, insert the **Sheet Name** field. (A **Design** tab will appear under the **Header & Footer** tab.) The **Sheet Name** button will appear in the *Header and Footer Elements* group.

   c. Click in the **Right Footer** section. Insert the **Page Number** field. The **Page Number** button is located in the *Header and Footer Elements* group on the *Design* tab. "&[Page]" will appear. This is correct.

   d. Click in the **Left Footer** section. Type in your first and last name.

   e. Click any cell (outside of the header and footer) in your worksheet and return to Normal view (Figure 0-94).

17. Save and close your workbook. Turn in your assignment.

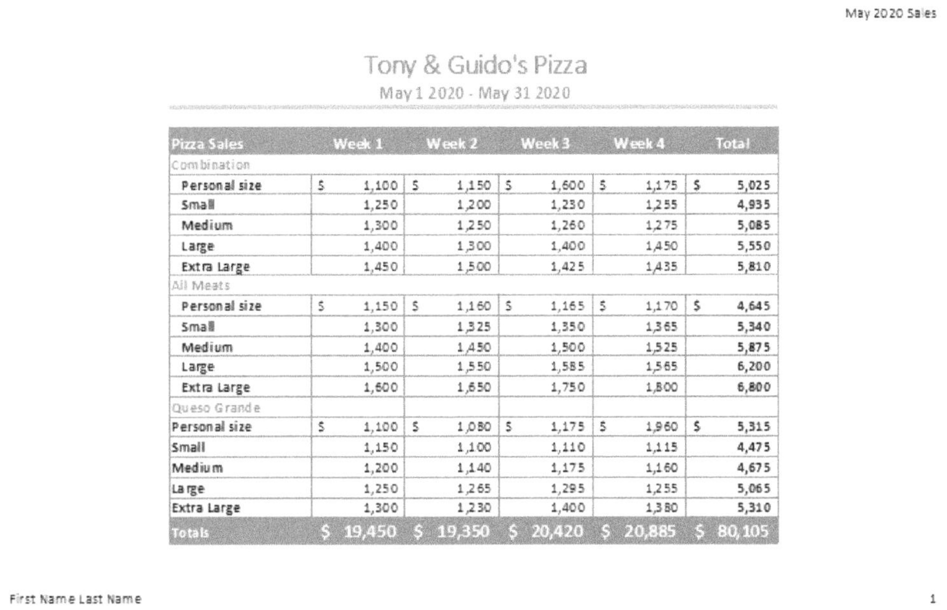

May 2020 Sales

Tony & Guido's Pizza
May 1 2020 - May 31 2020

Pizza Sales	Week 1		Week 2		Week 3		Week 4		Total	
Combination										
Personal size	$	1,100	$	1,150	$	1,600	$	1,175	$	5,025
Small		1,250		1,200		1,230		1,255		4,935
Medium		1,300		1,250		1,260		1,275		5,085
Large		1,400		1,300		1,400		1,450		5,550
Extra Large		1,450		1,500		1,425		1,435		5,810
All Meats										
Personal size	$	1,150	$	1,160	$	1,165	$	1,170	$	4,645
Small		1,300		1,325		1,350		1,365		5,340
Medium		1,400		1,450		1,500		1,525		5,875
Large		1,500		1,550		1,585		1,565		6,200
Extra Large		1,600		1,650		1,750		1,800		6,800
Queso Grande										
Personal size	$	1,100	$	1,080	$	1,175	$	1,960	$	5,315
Small		1,150		1,100		1,110		1,115		4,475
Medium		1,200		1,140		1,175		1,160		4,675
Large		1,250		1,265		1,295		1,255		5,065
Extra Large		1,300		1,230		1,400		1,380		5,310
Totals	$	19,450	$	19,350	$	20,420	$	20,885	$	80,105

First Name Last Name   1

FIGURE 9-94 Project 9-3 Completed

CHAPTER TEN

Excel Part II

Introduction

In this Excel section, you will learn the basics of creating charts. Also, you will learn how to meaningfully design, edit, filter, and edit source data. You will also learn how to use shapes, add WordArt, and choose pictures to enhance your charts. **Note: Blue text represents typed text.**

Learning Objectives

Excel Part 2 showcases the most commonly used charts by students which include column charts, bar charts, pie charts, and combination charts. When you complete this section, you should be able to do the following:

1. Create Excel charts and chart sheets.
2. Use quick chart layouts and chart styles to design your charts.
3. Edit chart elements, such as titles, data labels, and legends.
4. Switch Rows and Columns, Filter Source Data, and Edit Source Data.
5. Use shapes, WordArt, and pictures to enhance a chart.
6. Create Pie charts, Combination charts, and Treemap charts.
7. Use Sparklines in a worksheet.

Insert Tab and the Page Layout Tab

Insert Tab
The ***Insert tab*** (Figure 10-1) is most commonly accessed when you add tables, pictures, shapes, charts, text boxes, hyperlinks, Word Art, Symbols, and Headers

and Footers. You will use it to mostly build tables and charts. You may also add Sparklines to a chart.

FIGURE 10-1 Tab

Tables Group
The Tables group allows you to create Pivot Tables and regular tables.

A **PivotTable** enables you to easily arrange and summarize complex data. **Recommended PivotTables** provide a customized set of PivotTables that best suit your data (Figure 10-2).	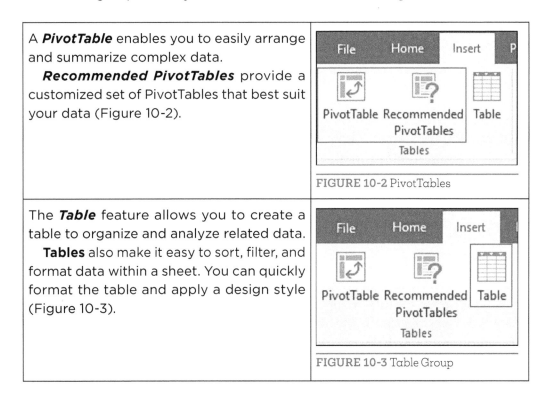 FIGURE 10-2 PivotTables
The **Table** feature allows you to create a table to organize and analyze related data. **Tables** also make it easy to sort, filter, and format data within a sheet. You can quickly format the table and apply a design style (Figure 10-3).	FIGURE 10-3 Table Group

Illustrations Group
The **Illustrations** group is where you insert pictures from your computer and online sources, including social media. You can also insert shapes, SmartArt, or take a screen shot of any open window on your computer and place it in your worksheet.

The **Pictures** feature allows you to insert pictures from your computer or from other computers you are connected to (Figure 10-4).	FIGURE 10-4 Pictures
Online Pictures enables you to find and insert pictures from a variety of online sources. In Office 2019 and 2021, you may also insert pictures from web pages and from online sources such as Bing.com, Facebook, Flickr, and OneDrive (Figure 10-5).	FIGURE 10-5 Online Pictures
The **Shapes** feature enables you to insert ready-made shapes into your worksheet (Figure 10-6). Some of the **Shapes** categories include *lines, rectangles, basic shapes, block arrows, equation shapes, flowchart, stars and banners,* and *callouts.*	FIGURE 10-6 Shapes
The **Icons** feature enables you to insert an icon to communicate using symbols (Figure 10-7).	FIGURE 10-7 Icons
The **3D Models** feature inserts a 3D model that you can rotate and see from all angles (Figure 10-8).	FIGURE 10-8 3D Models
A **SmartArt** graphic may be inserted into a worksheet to visually communicate information (Figure 10-9). **SmartArt** graphics range from graphical lists and process diagrams to more complex graphics such as *Venn diagrams* and *organization charts.*	FIGURE 10-9 SmartArt

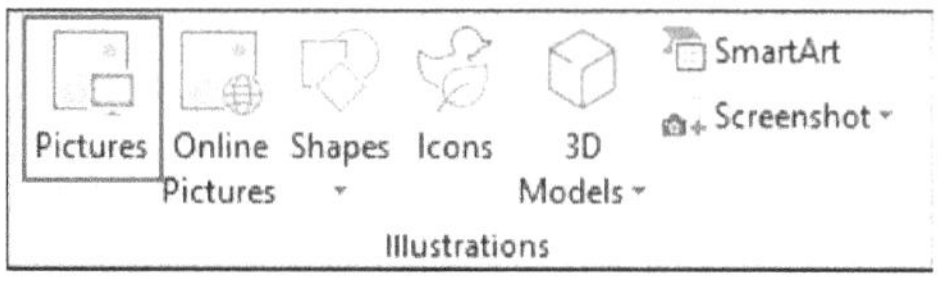

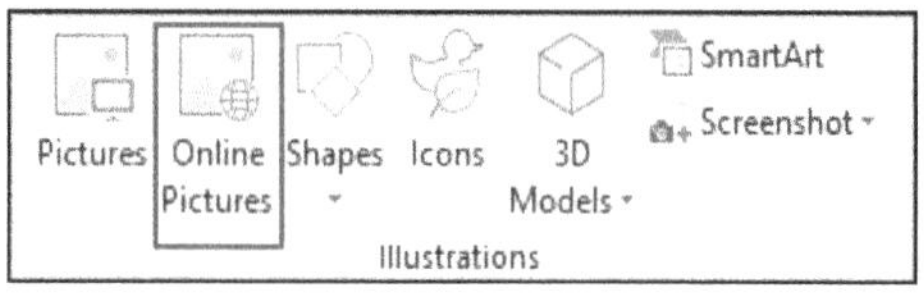

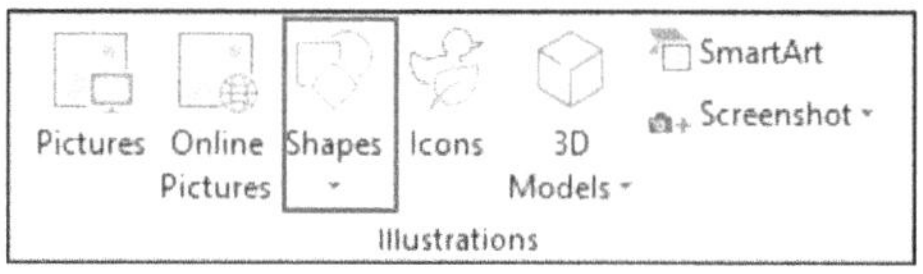

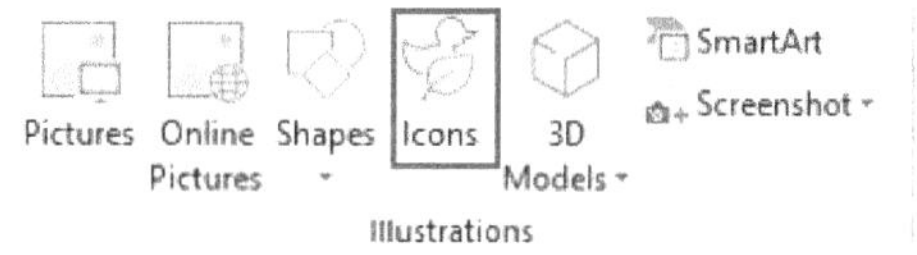

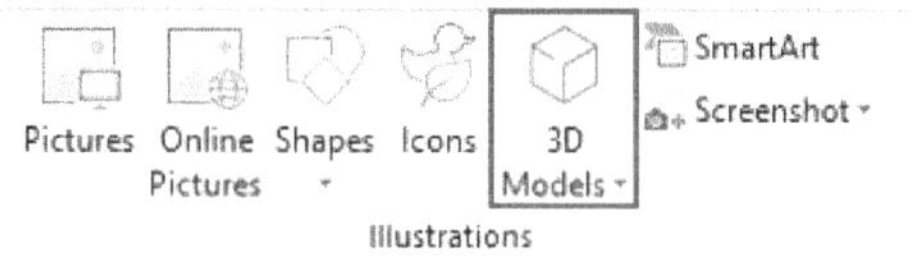

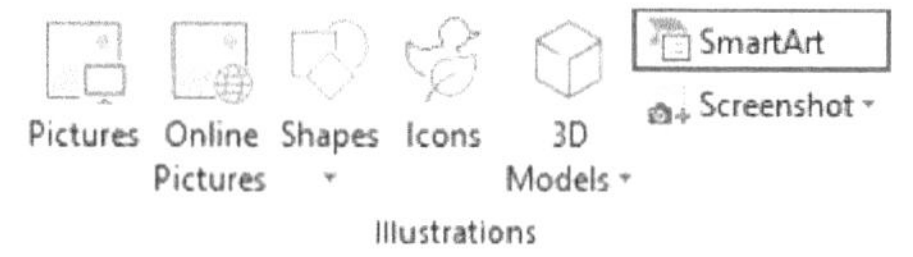

Screenshot or ***Screen Clipping*** enables you to quickly add a snapshot of any open window on your desktop to your worksheet. A **screenshot** enhances readability and captures information for your audience without leaving the program that you are working in (Figure 10-10).	 FIGURE 10-10 Screenshot

Charts Group

The *Charts* Group enables you to visually represent your data in a worksheet. Excel provides several categories of charts from which to choose. Stumped by which chart to choose? Click on ***Recommended Charts*** to let Excel help you.

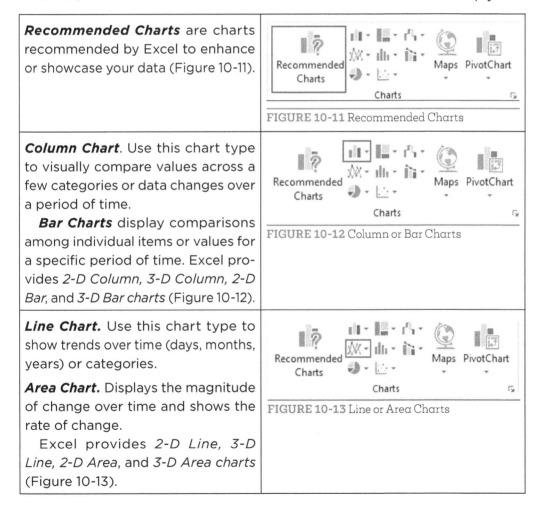

Recommended Charts are charts recommended by Excel to enhance or showcase your data (Figure 10-11).	FIGURE 10-11 Recommended Charts
Column Chart. Use this chart type to visually compare values across a few categories or data changes over a period of time. ***Bar Charts*** display comparisons among individual items or values for a specific period of time. Excel provides *2-D Column, 3-D Column, 2-D Bar*, and *3-D Bar charts* (Figure 10-12).	FIGURE 10-12 Column or Bar Charts
Line Chart. Use this chart type to show trends over time (days, months, years) or categories. ***Area Chart.*** Displays the magnitude of change over time and shows the rate of change. Excel provides *2-D Line, 3-D Line, 2-D Area*, and *3-D Area charts* (Figure 10-13).	FIGURE 10-13 Line or Area Charts

Pie or Doughnut Chart. Use this chart type to show proportions to a whole. Use it when the totals of your numbers are 100%. Excel provides *2-D Pie, 3-D Pie*, and *Doughnut* charts (Figure 10-14).	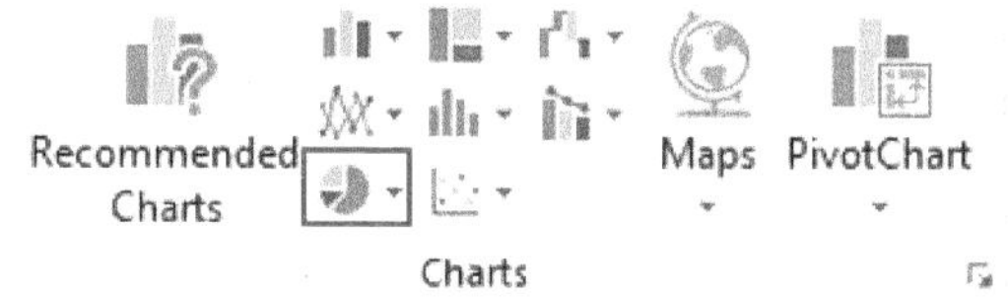 FIGURE 10-14 Pie or Doughnut Charts
Hierarchy Charts. Use this chart to compare parts to a whole or when several columns of categories form a hierarchy. Excel provides *Treemap* and *Sunburst* charts (Figure 10-15).	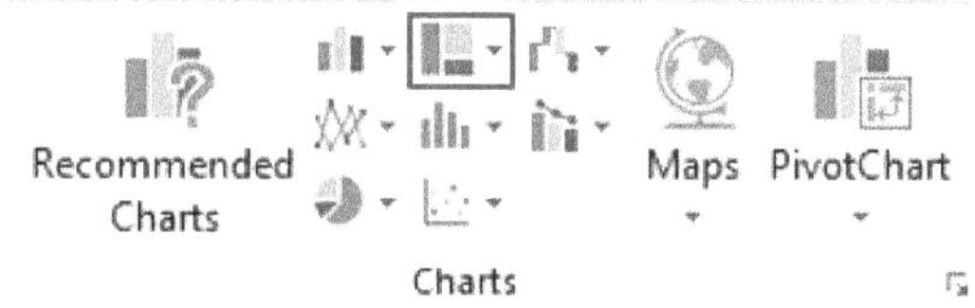 FIGURE 10-15 Hierarchy Charts
Statistical Charts. Use this chart type to show statistical analysis of your data. Excel provides Histograms and Box & Whisker (Figure 10-16).	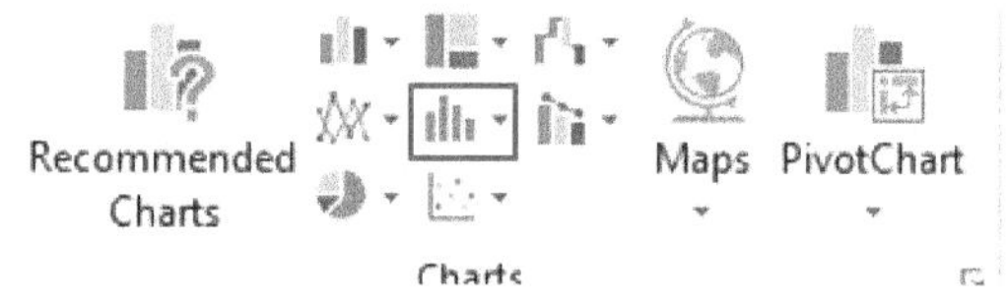 FIGURE 10-16 Statistical Charts
Scatter (X, Y) or **Bubble Charts.** Use these charts to show the relationships between sets of **values** (Figure 10-17).	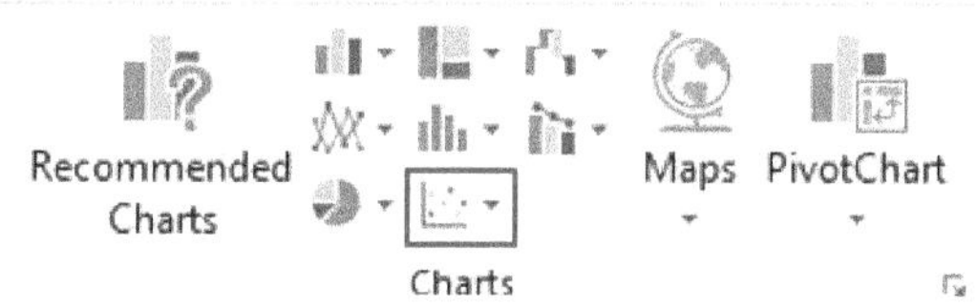 FIGURE 10-17 Scatter & Bubble Charts
Waterfall & Stock Charts. **Waterfall.** Use this chart type to show cumulative effect of a series of positive and negative values. For example, use it when you have data representing inflows and outflows such as financial data (Figure 10-18). **Stock Chart.** Use this chart type to show a trend of a stock's performance over time.	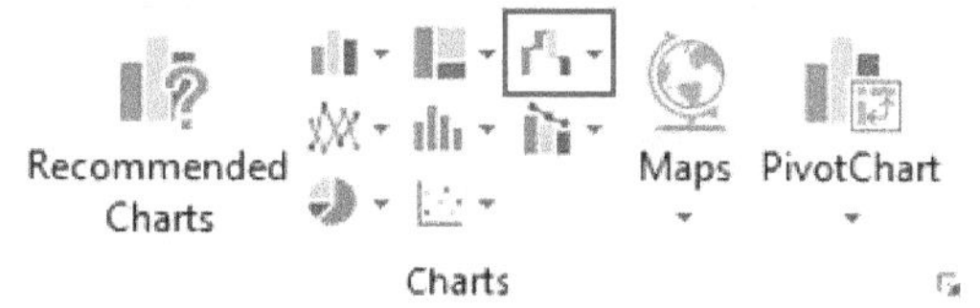 FIGURE 10-18 Waterfall & Stock Charts

Combo Chart. Use this chart type to highlight different types of information. Use it when the range of values in a chart varies widely or you have mixed types of cells (Figure 10-19).	 FIGURE 10-19 Combo Chart
Maps. Use this chart type to compare values and show categories across geographical regions (Figure 10-20). Use it when you have geographical regions in your data, like countries/regions, states, counties or postal codes.	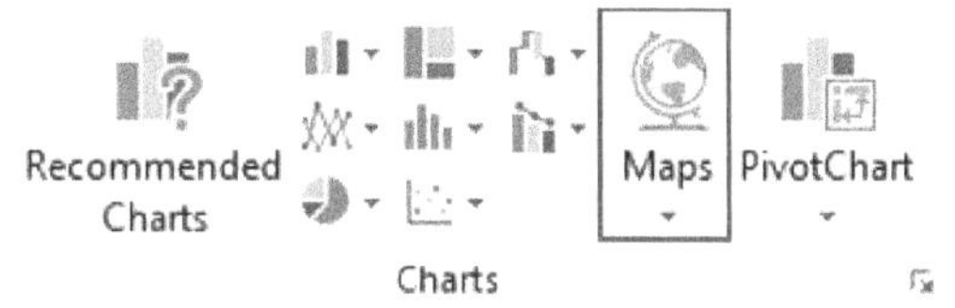 FIGURE 10-20 Maps
PivotChart. Use Pivot Charts to summarize data and explore complicated data (Figure 10-21).	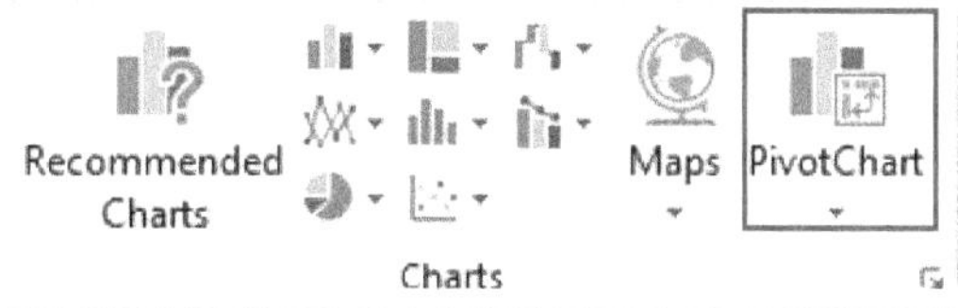 FIGURE 10-21 PivotChart
3D Map. **See your geographic data on a 3D map, visualized over time.** Use it for insights, animate over time and create a video (Figure 10-22).	 FIGURE 10-22 3D Map

Sparklines Group

Sparklines are mini charts placed in single cells, each representing a row of data in your selection.

There are three types of **Sparkline** charts (Figure 10-23): 1. Line 2. Column 3. Win/Loss	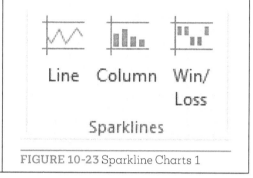 FIGURE 10-23 Sparkline Charts 1

Filters Group

The **Filters** group enables you to sort data visually and interactively.

Slicer Filter. Enables you to filter data visually (Figure 10-24). *Slicers* make it easier to filter tables, Pivot-Tables, PivotCharts, and cube functions.	 FIGURE 10-24 Slicer Filter
Timeline Filters enable you to filter dates interactively (Figure 10-25). *Timeline Filters* make it faster and easier to select time periods in order to filter tables, PivotTables, PivotCharts, and cube functions.	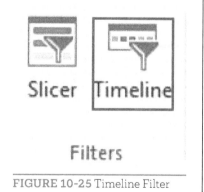 FIGURE 10-25 Timeline Filter

Links Group

The **Links** group enables you to set up one or multiple *hyperlinks* in your workbook for quick access to webpages and files.

Hyperlinks give you quick access to webpages and files. *Hyperlinks* can also take you to different places in your workbook (Figure 10-26).	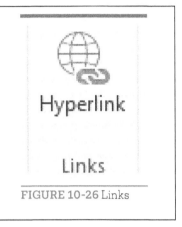 FIGURE 10-26 Links

Text Group

The **Text** group contains five different options. You can insert a **text** box, insert a **Header & Footer**, enhance your font with **WordArt**, add a **Signature line**, and place an **Object** in your workbook.

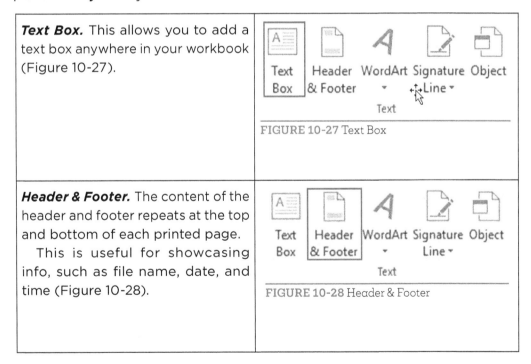

Text Box. This allows you to add a text box anywhere in your workbook (Figure 10-27).	FIGURE 10-27 Text Box
Header & Footer. The content of the header and footer repeats at the top and bottom of each printed page. This is useful for showcasing info, such as file name, date, and time (Figure 10-28).	FIGURE 10-28 Header & Footer

WordArt. Adds artistic flair to your workbook using a WordArt text box (Figure 10-29).	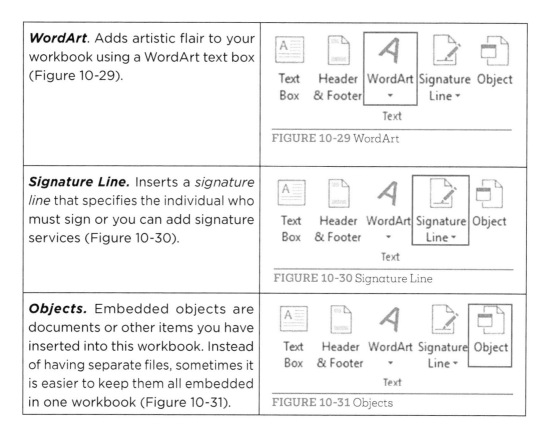 FIGURE 10-29 WordArt
Signature Line. Inserts a *signature line* that specifies the individual who must sign or you can add signature services (Figure 10-30).	FIGURE 10-30 Signature Line
Objects. Embedded objects are documents or other items you have inserted into this workbook. Instead of having separate files, sometimes it is easier to keep them all embedded in one workbook (Figure 10-31).	FIGURE 10-31 Objects

Symbols Group

The Symbols group contains the Equation and the Symbols tiles.

Equation. Add common mathematical equations to your workbook, such as the area of a circle or the quadratic equation. (Figure 10-32). You can also build your own equations using the library of math symbols and structures.	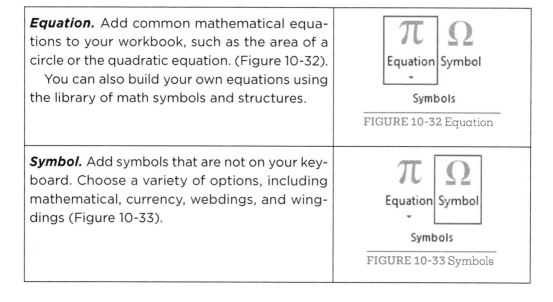 FIGURE 10-32 Equation
Symbol. Add symbols that are not on your keyboard. Choose a variety of options, including mathematical, currency, webdings, and wingdings (Figure 10-33).	FIGURE 10-33 Symbols

Page Layout Tab

The **Page Layout** tab (Figure 10-34) is used to set up your workbook using margins, orientations, and size; enhance it with different themes, add backgrounds, show or print gridlines and headings, and arrange and align objects in your workbook.

FIGURE 10-34 Page Layout Tab

Themes Group

The **Themes** group enables you to give your workbook instant style and personality.

Themes. Each theme uses a unique set of fonts, colors, and effects to create a consistent look and feel (Figure 10-35).	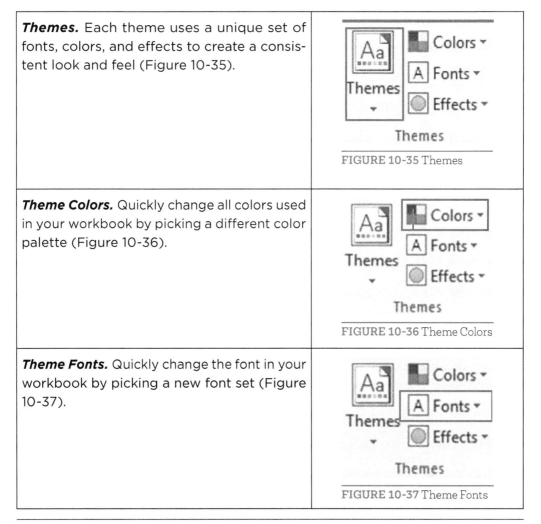 **FIGURE 10-35** Themes
Theme Colors. Quickly change all colors used in your workbook by picking a different color palette (Figure 10-36).	**FIGURE 10-36** Theme Colors
Theme Fonts. Quickly change the font in your workbook by picking a new font set (Figure 10-37).	**FIGURE 10-37** Theme Fonts

Theme Effects. Quickly change the overall look of objects in your workbook. Each option uses various borders and visual effects, such as shading and shadow, to give your objects a different look (Figure 10-38).	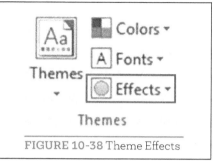 FIGURE 10-38 Theme Effects

Page Setup Group

The **Page Setup** group is where you go to in Excel to finalize your workbook prior to printing or distribution.

Adjust Margins. Set the margin size for worksheet or current section (Figure 10-39). You can choose from several commonly-used margin formats or customize your own (Figure 10-40). The three most common margin settings are Normal, Wide, and Narrow. These settings are the most commonly used when creating workbooks and worksheets.	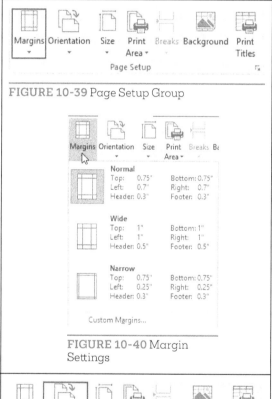 FIGURE 10-39 Page Setup Group FIGURE 10-40 Margin Settings

Orientation. Excel provides two different page orientations (Figure 10-41).
 	
  Portrait. The width is smaller than the height.
 	
  Landscape. The width is larger than the height.

	FIGURE 10-41 Orientation

Page Size. Excel provides you with 36 built-in page sizes. This includes sheets, envelopes, and index cards, featuring measurements in inches and millimeters (Figure 10-42).	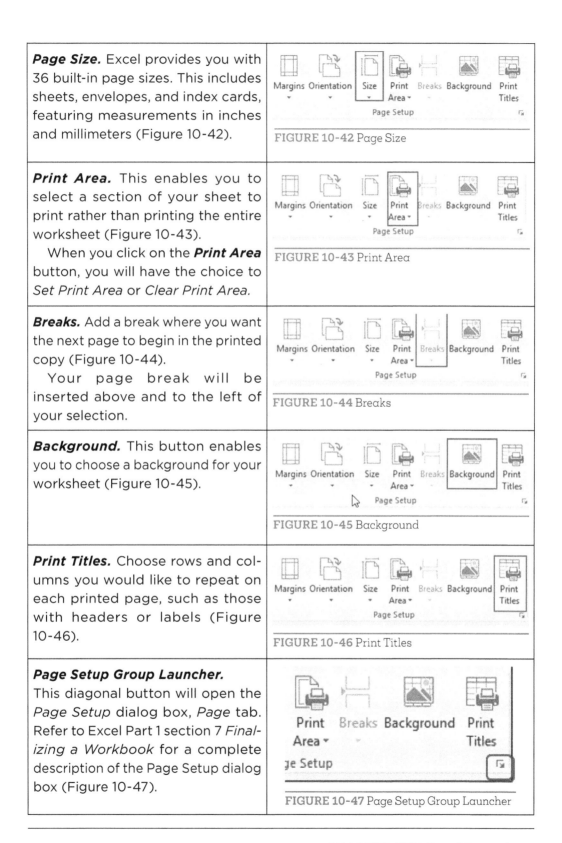FIGURE 10-42 Page Size
Print Area. This enables you to select a section of your sheet to print rather than printing the entire worksheet (Figure 10-43). When you click on the **Print Area** button, you will have the choice to *Set Print Area* or *Clear Print Area*.	FIGURE 10-43 Print Area
Breaks. Add a break where you want the next page to begin in the printed copy (Figure 10-44). Your page break will be inserted above and to the left of your selection.	FIGURE 10-44 Breaks
Background. This button enables you to choose a background for your worksheet (Figure 10-45).	FIGURE 10-45 Background
Print Titles. Choose rows and columns you would like to repeat on each printed page, such as those with headers or labels (Figure 10-46).	FIGURE 10-46 Print Titles
Page Setup Group Launcher. This diagonal button will open the *Page Setup* dialog box, *Page* tab. Refer to Excel Part 1 section 7 *Finalizing a Workbook* for a complete description of the Page Setup dialog box (Figure 10-47).	FIGURE 10-47 Page Setup Group Launcher

Scale to Fit Group

The **Scale to Fit** group enables you to shrink the width or height of your printout to fit a page, or you can stretch or shrink your printout to a percentage its actual size.

Width. This setting lets you set the width of your page to the number of pages you want. Automatic is the default setting (Figure 10-48).	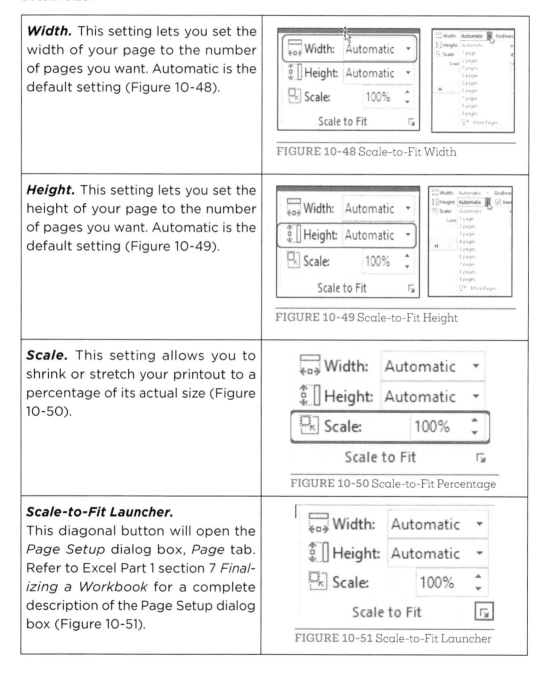 FIGURE 10-48 Scale-to-Fit Width
Height. This setting lets you set the height of your page to the number of pages you want. Automatic is the default setting (Figure 10-49).	FIGURE 10-49 Scale-to-Fit Height
Scale. This setting allows you to shrink or stretch your printout to a percentage of its actual size (Figure 10-50).	FIGURE 10-50 Scale-to-Fit Percentage
Scale-to-Fit Launcher. This diagonal button will open the *Page Setup* dialog box, *Page* tab. Refer to Excel Part 1 section 7 *Finalizing a Workbook* for a complete description of the Page Setup dialog box (Figure 10-51).	FIGURE 10-51 Scale-to-Fit Launcher

Sheet Options Group

Sheet Options give you the choice to either view or print gridlines in your worksheet or view and print headings in your worksheet.

Gridlines. This enables you to either view or print gridlines in your worksheet (Figure 10-52).	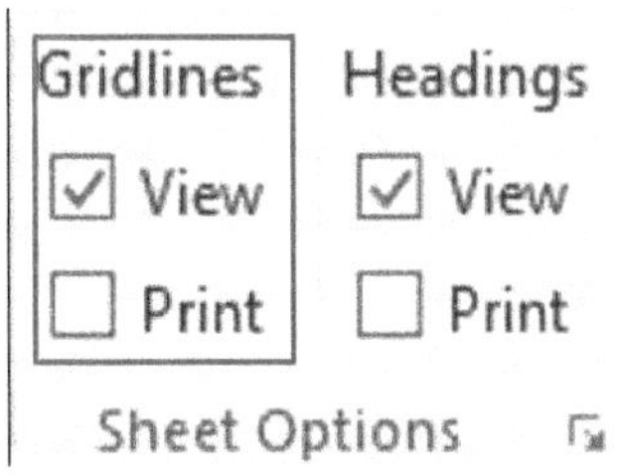 FIGURE 10-52 Gridlines Options
Headings. This enables you to either view or print headings in your worksheet (Figure 10-53).	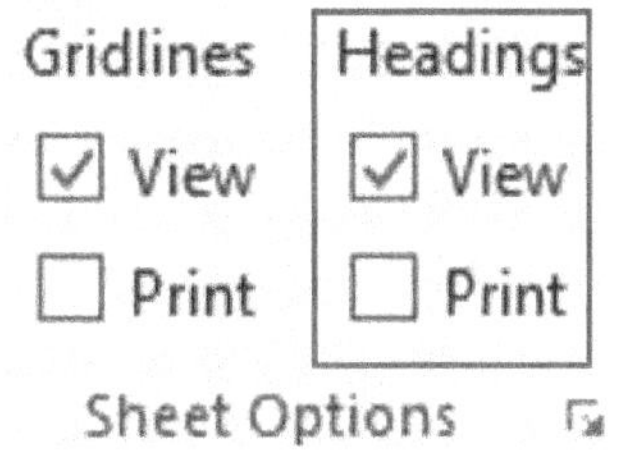 FIGURE 10-53 Header Options
Sheet Options Launcher. This diagonal button will open the *Page Setup* dialog box, *Sheet* tab. Refer to Excel Part 1 section 7 *Finalizing a Workbook* for a complete description of the Page Setup dialog box (Figure 10-54).	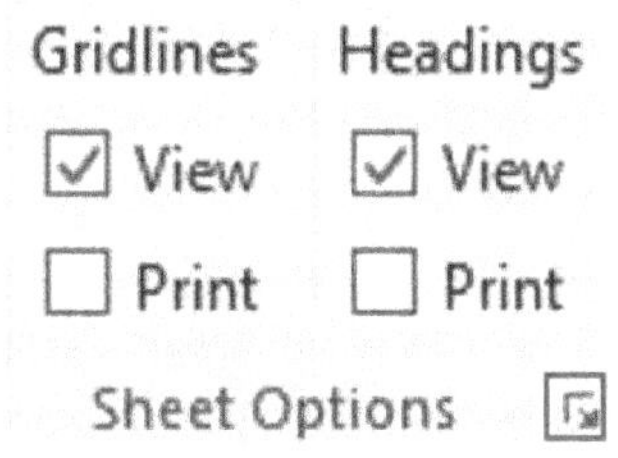 FIGURE 10-54 Sheet Options Launcher

Arrange Group

The **Arrange** group enables you to align, group, rotate, and send shapes and other objects in front of data or behind data. Or, you can see a list of all of your objects. Using any of these options in the **Arrange** group provides a more professional look with a finishing touch.

The **Bring Forward** button provides 2 options (Figure 10-55). *Bring Forward* will bring the selected object forward one level. *Bring to Front* will bring it in front of all the objects.	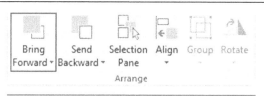 FIGURE 10-55 Bring Forward
The **Send Backward** button provides 2 options (Figure 10-56). *Send Backward* will send the selected object back one level. *Send to Back* will send the object behind all other objects.	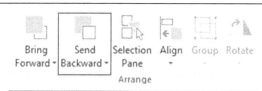 FIGURE 10-56 Send Backward
Selection Pane shows you a list of all your objects (Figure 10-57). This makes it easier to select objects, change their order, or change their visibility. Up and down arrows are available to move objects, with two buttons to show objects or hide objects. If you want to show or hide one or more objects but not all objects, just left click on the "eye" to the right of each listed object.	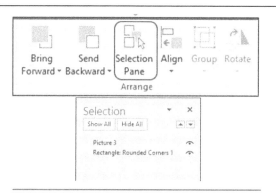 FIGURE 10-57 Selection Pane
Align Objects. The **Align Objects** button changes the placement of your selected objects on the page (Figure 10-58). This aligns objects to the margins or to the edge of the page. You can also align them relative to one another. **Align Left.** Horizontally left aligns all selected objects on the left side in a straight line. **Align Center.** Horizontally center aligns all selected objects.	

Align Right. Horizontally right aligns all selected objects on the right side in a straight line.

Align Top. Vertically top aligns all selected objects on the top side in a straight line.

Align Middle. Vertically center aligns all selected objects.

Align Bottom. Vertically aligns all selected objects on the bottom side in a straight line.

Distribute Horizontally. To make this work, you need at least 3 objects to select. This distributes equal space between objects in a horizontal line.

Distribute Vertically. To make this work, you need at least 3 objects to select. This distributes equal space between objects in a vertical line.

Snap to Grid. This is a computer function used to organize files or objects automatically. It uses an invisible grid to line up the items on the screen along perfect horizontal and vertical lines.

Snap to Shape. Use this function to snap shapes or other objects to grid lines that go through the vertical and horizontal edges of other shapes or objects.

View Gridlines. This button acts as a toggle button. When you open your workbook, you will see a grid in the background. If you do not want to see a grid background, click on the **View Gridlines** button. To turn the grid background back on, click on the **View Gridlines** button again.

FIGURE 10-58 The Align Button

Group button. The **Group** button allows you to group together *two items at a time*. This is commonly used when you wish to add a caption to a picture. Prior to grouping, the picture and caption are two separate objects. Once your group both objects, they become one object (Figure 10-59).

If you wish to group three items, group the first two items to become one. Then select the first grouped item and the third object and group them again.

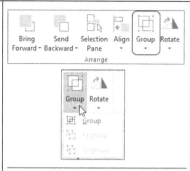

FIGURE 10-59 Group Button

Rotate. This button enables you to rotate your object (Figure 10-60).

Rotate Right 90°. Flips your object to the right one time (Figure 10-61).

Rotate Left 90°. Flips your object to the left one time (Figure 10-61).

Flip Vertical. Will flip your object upside down (Figure 10-61).

Flip Horizontal. Will flip your object over. This is useful if you need a mirror image of your object or if you prefer the mirror image over the original (Figure 10-61).

More Rotation Options ... Opens the *Format Picture* dialog box. In the third box down, you can select your own degree of rotation (Figure 10-62).

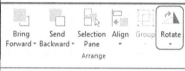

FIGURE 10-60 Rotation Options

FIGURE 10-61 Rotation Options

FIGURE 10-62 More Rotation Options

1. Create Excel Charts and Chart Sheets

Create a Chart Object and a Chart Sheet

One of the best features of Excel is the ability to easily create and format charts to visually represent numeric data in a worksheet. These charts make it easier for you and your audience to identify trends, recognize patterns, and make comparisons. Charts in Excel are dynamic. A dynamic chart is linked to its data; when you update the chart's source data, Excel automatically updates your chart. Depending on your needs, you may display a chart in the workbook alongside its data, or you can place your chart on its own page.

Create a Chart Object

A **chart object** may be a title, legend, axes, data labels, data tables, trendlines, and gridlines, (Figure 10-74). These objects may be accessed by clicking on the green plus in the upper right corner of the chart, or may be clicked on in the chart. A third way to access chart objects is to go to the Ribbon. Click on *Chart Tools* tab, *Design* Tab, *Chart Layout* group, *Add Chart Element* button. Each object can also be sized and positioned in a worksheet, and you can size and position each chart element within the chart.

    Source data are the cells that contain values and labels to be graphed into a chart. However, you do not usually include sums, averages, or similar calculations. In Figure 10-63, notice that the source data includes the series names in column A, range (A4:A10), the category names in row 4, (range B4:F4), and six values for each day, Sunday through Thursday. Each of the values is a ***data point***, a cell containing a value. A group of data points or values is a ***data series***. In this example, there are six data series, one for each revenue category (each a different coffee and size). Each data series has a name or label.

    The text label that describes a data series is a ***category label***. In Figure 10-63, the category labels are the names of the days. When creating a chart, the best way to arrange data is with labels and values in adjacent cells and no empty rows. If you omit labels for the source data, there will be no labels in the chart

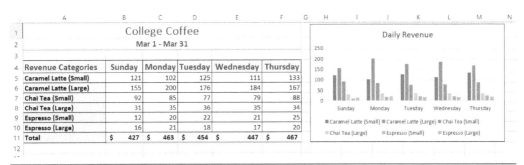

FIGURE 10-63 Chart Object and Its Source

to describe the data. If you have an empty row within the source data, it will be graphed with a value of zero (0) and will distort the chart's ability to illustrate a trend or comparison.

When you select contiguous source data (all cells are next to each other), the **Quick Analysis** button will appear in the lower right corner of the selection (Figure 10-64). The Quick Analysis tool is a speedy way to select a recommended chart type, format, totals, Tables, and Sparklines. Additionally, you will notice the appearance of commonly used **Conditional Formatting** options, (*Home* tab, *Conditional Formatting* group), and the **Clear** options (*Home* tab, *Editing* group).

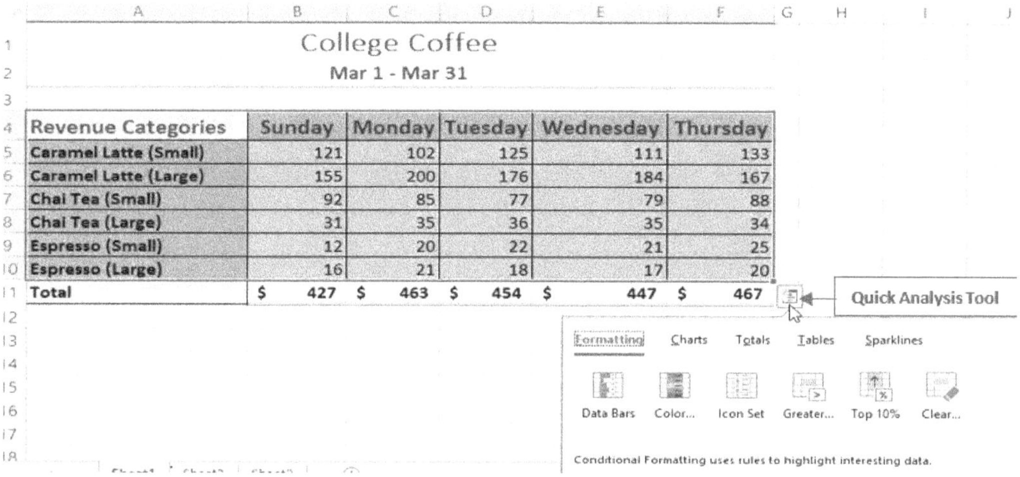

FIGURE 10-64 Quick Analysis Tool

Excel has many chart types, and most types have subtypes or variations. Table 10-1 below names each Excel chart type and Data Example. Please refer to the Charts Group section in this section.

Size and Position a Chart Object

Once you click on a chart object, it becomes active and is surrounded by eight selection handles. A selection handle is a small circle shape located on each corner and in the middle of each side. Once your chart object is selected, the Range Finder highlights the source data in the worksheet. When you point to a selection handle, you will see a two-pointed resize arrow. Click and drag a corner handle to size the height and width proportionally.

If you need to move the chart object, point to the chart border to display a four-pointed move pointer. You can drag the chart object to the desired location. When the chart is activated or selected, the Chart Tools Design and Format tabs will be available in the Ribbon (Figure 10-65), and three Quick Chart Tools are

TABLE 10-1 Chart Types and Data Examples

Chart Type	Data Example
Column	Daily sales data for each type and size of coffee.
Bar	Number of cups of coffee sold for each type and size of coffee.
Pie	Revenue or expenses by coffee type for a specified amount of time.
Line	Number of all coffees sold over a weekly period.
Area	Daily sales of each coffee type and size over a weekly period.
Combo Chart	Line chart comparing the sales of one coffee type and size versus total sales.
X, Y (Scatter or bubble)	Number of times a patron purchases a coffee, cost to make coffee, and retail prices.
Waterfall	Use this chart to show when you have data inflows (coffee sales) and outflows (coffee expenses). Used as a financial tool.
Funnel	Total Coffee values show progressively smaller or larger values.
Stock	The opening, closing, and high price for coffee stock each day for a specified time.
Surface	Displays optimum combinations of two sets of data on a surface.
Radar	Displays the frequency of multiple data series relative to a center point.
TreeMap	Revenue stream sales displayed in a block by each coffee type and size.
Sunburst	Coffee sales by day, type, and size, resembling a sun.
Histogram	Number of coffees by type and size in each day category.
Box & Whisker	Displays the distribution of data with minimum, mean, maximum and outlier values.

available in the top right corner of the object: *Chart Elements* (green plus sign), *Chart Styles* (paint brush), and *Chart Filters* (funnel).

Chart Tools Design Tab

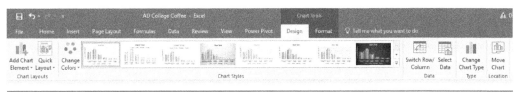

FIGURE 10-65 Chart Tools Design Tab

Add Chart Element (Figure 10-66).

*A**x**es.* You can add *Primary Horizontal, Primary Vertical*, or other options.

*A**x**is Titles.* You can add *Primary Horizontal, Primary Vertical*, or other options.

Chart Title. You have the options of *Above Chart, Centered Overlay*, or *more options*.

Data Labels. You have the options of *Center, Inside End, Inside Base, Outside End, Data Callout, None,* and more options.

*Data Ta**b**le.* You can show a data table with *Legend Keys, No Legend Keys*, or *None.*

Error Bars. You can choose from *Standard Error, Percentage, Standard Deviation*, or *More Error Bars Options.*

Gridlines. These gridlines will appear behind your chart. You have the option to choose *Primary Major Horizontal, Primary Major Vertical, Primary Minor Horizontal, Primary Minor Vertical,* and *more Gridline options.*

Legend. You can choose where you want to place your legend in your chart: *Right, Top, Left Bottom, None,* or *More Legend Options.*

*L**i**nes*. *Works only with Line Charts.* Excel provides *Drop Line, High-Low Lines,* or *None* options.

Trendline. Works only with 2-D charts. Excel provides *Linear, Exponential, Linear Forecast, Moving Average, None,* or *More Trendline Options.*

*U**p**/Down Bars*. *Excel provides Up/Down Bars, None, or More Options.*

FIGURE 10-66 Chart Elements

Quick Layout. Excel provides numerous different chart layouts using a mix of chart elements for each chart type (Figure 10-67).

Column Charts (shown). 11 different *Quick Layout* options for both 2-D and 3-D charts.

Bar Charts. 10 different *Quick Layout* options exist for 2-D charts; 9 different *Quick Layout* options for 3-D charts.

Line Chart. 12 different *Quick Layout* options exist.

Pie Chart. 7 different *Quick Layout* options for both 2-D and 3-D exist.

Area Chart. 8 different *Quick Layout* options for both 2-D and 3-D charts.

X-Y Scatter. 11 different *Quick Layout* options.

Bubble. 11 different *Quick Layout* options.

Map. 4 different *Quick Layout* options.

Stock. 7 different *Quick Layout* options.

Surface. 5 different *Quick Layout* options.

Radar. 4 different *Quick Layout* options.

Treemap. 7 different *Quick Layout* options.

Sunburst. 6 different *Quick Layout* options.

Histogram. 3 different *Quick Layout* options.

Box & Whisker. 5 different *Quick Layout* options.

Waterfall. 5 different *Quick Layout* options.

Funnel. 4 different *Quick Layout* options.

Combo. 11 different *Quick Layout* options.

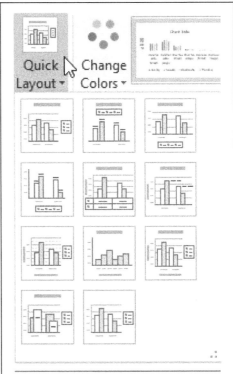

FIGURE 10-67 Quick Layout

Chart Styles Group

Excel provides a color palette from which you can choose from numerous color combinations to help you customize color and style in your chart. Additionally, Excel provides a gallery of Chart Styles for you to change the overall visual style of the chart.

Change Colors. This selection allows you to customize color and chart style (Figure 10-68).

Excel provides 2 different color categories from which to choose:

Colorful. Varied color palette.

Monochromatic. Different shades of the same color.

Note: The **Change Colors** selection in this example is based on the **Office Theme**. Each theme will show a different color palette for the Colorful options and for the Monochromatic options.

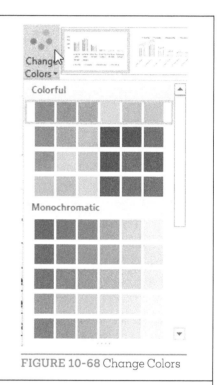

FIGURE 10-68 Change Colors

Chart Styles. This selection allows you to change the overall visual style of your chart (Figure 10-69).

Depending on the selected chart style, the number of style options will vary.

FIGURE 10-69 Chart Styles

Data Group (Chart Tools/Design Tab)

When you create a chart, Excel selects which data is charted on the X axis and which data is charted on the Y axis. Sometimes Excel's selections do not effectively or concisely display the data as desired. To assist with this issue, within the Data group, Excel features the option to Switch Row/Column with one click.

However, if you need to make changes other than switch rows or columns, Excel features the **Edit Data** button. This button enables you to make range data changes.

Switch Row/Data. Data being charted on the X axis will move to the Y axis and vice versa. In other words, the data on the X and Y axes will be swapped (Figure 10-70).	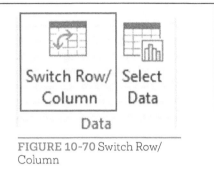 FIGURE 10-70 Switch Row/ Column
Edit Data. Changes the data range included in the chart (Figure 10-71). 　The *Edit Data* dialog box has three parts: 　**Chart data range.** Your source data range appears in gray. If you look at your actual source data, you will notice a green moving dashed line outlining your source data range. You can manually type in your changes in the *Chart data range* box. 　**Legend Entries (Series).** This is where you may either select or deselect to show a series in your legend. 　**Horizontal (Category) Axis Labels.** This is where you may either select or deselect the categories you wish to show in your chart.	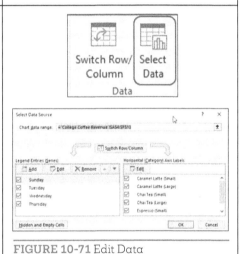 FIGURE 10-71 Edit Data

Type Group

The type group makes it easy for you to change your chart type. For instance, you can create a chart as a **2-D column** chart, but after you made your chart, you believe you can better display your data with a different chart type, for example, a **bar** chart.

Change Chart Type

Once you click on the **Change Chart Type** button, the *Change Chart Type* dialog box will open. You will be able to choose the new chart type you want (Figure 10-72).

With the Change Chart Type dialog box, Excel has two different tabs to choose charts. You can click on the Recommended Charts tab. Excel will display recommended charts. If you click on All Charts (shown), you may choose your own. The left panel shows all the different chart types. The charts that appear across the upper third of the dialog box show the chart subtypes from which you may choose. Excel will display your choices below the chart subtypes.

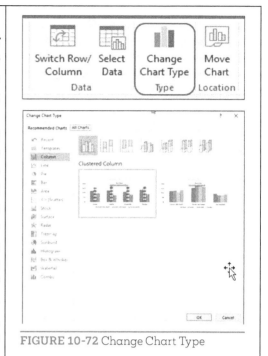

FIGURE 10-72 Change Chart Type

Location Group

Move Chart. This will move your chart to another worksheet or tab in the workbook.

You are provided with two options (Figure 10-73).

New Sheet. This option is to move your chart to a new sheet. If you select this option, Excel will ask you for a new sheet name, then move the chart to fill up the new worksheet.

Object In. Excel will show the current worksheet in the box. By clicking on the down arrow on the right of the Object In box, you may place your object (chart) in a worksheet of your choice unless you only have one worksheet in your workbook.

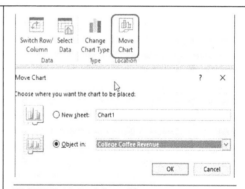

FIGURE 10-73 Move Chart

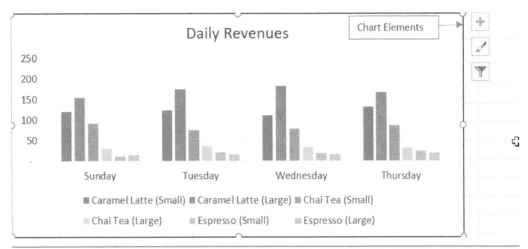

FIGURE 10-74 Chart Elements Option

Create a Chart Sheet

A chart sheet is an Excel chart that is displayed on its own sheet in the workbook. The chart sheet does not have rows, columns, and cells, but the chart is linked to its data on the source worksheet.

Once you create a chart object, you may either keep the chart object in the same worksheet with the chart's data on its source worksheet, or you can move it to its own sheet. To do so, click on the **Move Chart** button on the *Chart Tools, Design tab*. Excel will use the default sheet names *Chart1, Chart2*, and so on, but in the Move Chart dialog box, you can type in your choice of name for the new tab.

> Select your data, and then press the **F11 (FN+F11)** function key to create an automatic column chart sheet.

Although the **Quick Analysis** button tool does not appear for noncontiguous data, source data for a chart does not need to be contiguous. You can select nonadjacent data and you can open **Recommended Charts** in the *Charts* group on the *Insert tab* or you can select a chart type of your choice.

Here are the steps to create a Chart Sheet for noncontiguous cells.

1. Select the values and labels for the chart.
2. Select the first range. Press the **CTRL** key and select each range (Figure 10-75).

3. Click the **Recommended Charts** button (*Insert tab*, *Charts* group).
   a. The Insert Chart dialog box will open.
   b. Click on the **All Charts** tab to select your desired chart type. You can click the thumbnail for a chart type to preview your chart. Click **OK.**
   c. The chart object is active. The *Chart Tools* tabs become available.

	A	B	D	E	F
1	College Coffee				
2	Mar 1 - Mar 7				
3					
4	Reveue Categories	Sunday	Tuesday	Wednesday	Thursday
5	Caramel Latte (Small)	121	125	111	133
6	Caramel Latte (Large)	155	176	184	167
7	Chai Tea (Small)	92	77	79	88
8	Chai Tea (Large)	31	36	35	34
9	Espresso (Small)	12	22	21	25
10	Espresso (Large)	16	18	17	20
11	Total	$ 427	$ 454 $	447 $	467
12					

FIGURE 10-75 Chart Sheet for Noncontiguous Cells

4. If desired, click the **Move Chart** button (*Chart Tools, Design* tab, *Location* group).
5. Click the **New Sheet radio** button (Figure 10-76).
6. Type in a name for the chart sheet.
7. Click **OK.**

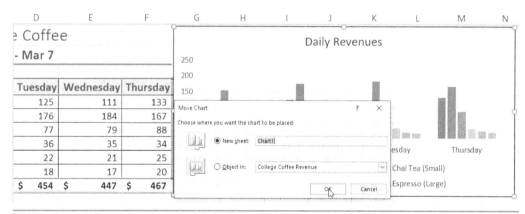

FIGURE 10-76 Move Chart to New Worksheet

2. Use Quick Chart Layouts and Chart Styles to Design Your Charts

When you create a new chart, Excel provides it with a default layout, color, and style. Excel also has various tools to help you customize and enhance the appearance of your chart. The *Chart Tools, Design* tab includes commands for selecting a chart layout, a chart style, or changing the chart's color theme.

A **chart layout** is a set of elements and a location of those elements. Each element is an individual part of the chart, including a legend, main title, and axis titles. When you click on the **Quick Layout** button (*Chart Tools, Design* tab, *Chart Layouts* group), it opens a gallery of predefined layouts (Figure 10-77). As you point to each chart layout in the gallery, *Live Preview* will redraw the chart. When a chart layout adds an element, such as a title, it will display a generic label like "Chart Title." If you like a specific chart layout, you can add a new element, delete an element, or edit an element.

Apply a Quick Layout to a Chart:

1. Select your chart object or the chart sheet tab.
2. Click the **Quick Layout** button (Chart Tools, Design tab, *Chart Layouts* group).
   a. The galley displays thumbnail images of each layout. Quick Layouts are named Layout 1 through the last number.
3. Point to a layout to preview it in your chart.
4. Click the thumbnail you want for your chart.
5. Your chart will be reformatted with the selected *Quick Layout* elements.

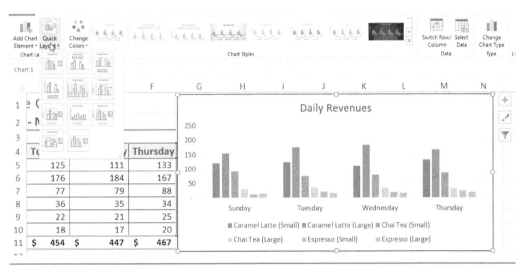

FIGURE 10-77 Quick Layouts

Chart Styles

Once you have selected or customized a Quick Layout for your chart, you may want to apply a Chart Style to enhance your chart.

1. Select the chart object or the chart sheet tab.
2. Point to a style thumbnail to see a preview of the chart.
3. Click on the thumbnail to select a style.
4. Excel will redraw your chart with the selected style (Figure 10-78).

Chart Colors

The workbook theme (*Design* tab, *Document Formatting* group) and the chart style together form the basis for a chart's color scheme. The *Chart Styles* group (*Chart Tools, Design* tab) includes a **Change Colors** button with optional color palettes. Excel divides these palettes into *Colorful* and *Monochromatic*.

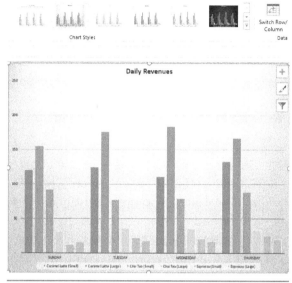

FIGURE 10-78 Chart Styles

1. Select the chart object or the chart sheet tab.
2. Click the **Change Colors** button (*Chart Tools, Design* tab, *Chart Styles* group).
3. Point to a palette to see a Live Preview in the chart.
4. Click on the thumbnail to select a palette.
5. Excel will format your chart with the selected color palette (Figure 10-79).

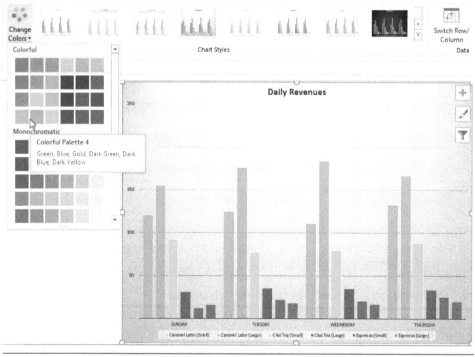

FIGURE 10-79 Chart Colors

Print a Chart

Excel provides you with the option to print a chart object on the same page with the worksheet data, or it can be printed separately. To print a chart with the data, deselect the chart object by clicking in a worksheet cell. At this point, you will need to size and position the chart and cell to fit a printed page. Use the Page Setup commands to select a page orientation or optional headers or footers.

To print only the chart object in its own sheet, select it and use regular Print and Page Setup options. By default, a selected chart object will print scaled to fit a landscape page. A chart sheet (a chart moved from the original chart source data) will also default to print in landscape orientation fit to the page.

1. Click any cell in the worksheet. Size and position the chart object as desired.
2. Click the **File** tab to open the *Backstage* view (Figure 10-80).
3. Select **Print**.
4. Choose print settings as desired.
   a. Set margins and scale the sheet to fit the page.
5. Click **Print**.

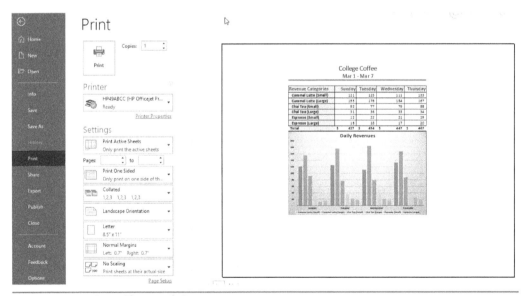

FIGURE 10-80 Print Chart with Data

In this project, you will open an existing workbook for Bill's Bikes and BBQ. You will create a column chart that tracks revenue and a bar chart to track revenues using noncontiguous data. **Note: Blue text represents typed text.**

File Needed: **(Your Initials) Student Checkup Excel 9-3**

Completed File Name: **(Your initials) Student Checkup Excel 10-1**

1. Open **(Your Initials) Student Checkup Excel 9-3**. This is the workbook you completed in Student Checkup **Excel 9-3** in Excel Part 1.
2. Save the workbook as **(Your Initials) Student Checkup Excel 10-1.**
3. Create a column chart.
   a. Select the range **A4:H11** on the **Restaurant Revenue** sheet. These will be your labels and values for your chart.
4. Click the **Quick Analysis** button (to the right of cell H12) (Figure 10-81). Then, a new box will open. Click on **Charts** (Figure 10-81).
5. Click on Clustered Column (Figure 10-82).

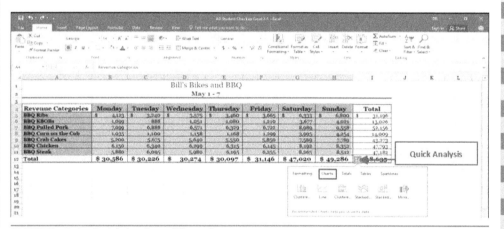

FIGURE 10-81 Quick Analysis/Chart Option

Size and position your chart.
6. Click in a blank area in your chart.
   a. Click in a blank corner of your chart (upper left or right corners work best), to display a 4-way cross (move) pointer.
   b. Press and hold your left mouse button. Drag the chart so that the top left corner of the chart is in the upper left corner of cell **A14.**

c. Point to the lower right of your chart (lower right selection handle) to display a resize arrow (double arrow).

d. Drag the pointer to reach cell **I30.**

e. Change your chart title to **Daily Revenues**. Resize title font to size **20. Bold** title text.

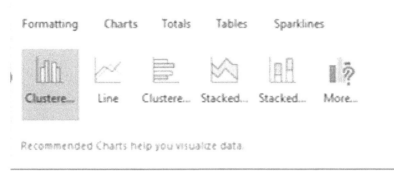

FIGURE 10-82 Quick Analysis Charts

Choose a Quick Layout.

7. Select the chart if necessary (click in a blank area).

a. Click the **Quick Layout** button (*Chart Tools, Design* tab, *Chart Layouts* group).

b. Click **Layout 3** (Figure 10-83).

c. Click in a blank area of your chart (upper right or left corner).

d. Click on Shape Outline (*Chart Tools/Format* tab/*Shape Styles* group)

e. Click on the down arrow and select **Red, Accent 1** (first row, 5th color).

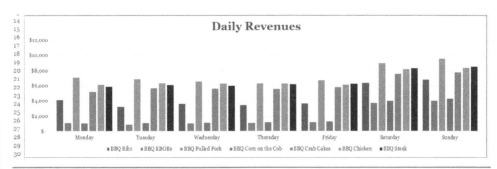

FIGURE 10-83 Chart Positioned and Sized—Layout 3

8. Create a chart using nonadjacent ranges, and move your chart to a new tab.
   a. Select range **A4:A11** (Revenue Categories through BBQ Steak).
   b. Press and hold down the **Ctrl** key and select cells **G4:H11.**
   c. Go to *Insert tab*, select *column chart*, then select *3-D Clustered Column Chart.*
   d. Click the ***Move Chart*** button (*Chart Tools, Design* tab, *Location* group).
   e. Click the ***New sheet*** radio button.
   f. Type in **Saturday & Sunday Revenues.**
   g. Click **OK.** The new chart sheet is activated.
9. Choose a chart style.
   a. Click the ***More*** button to open the *Chart Styles* gallery (*Chart Tools, Design* tab, *Chart Styles* group).
   b. Select **Chart Style 3**.
10. Click on the ***Change Chart Type*** button (*Chart Tools, Design* tab, *Type* group).
    a. In the left panel of the **Change Chart Type** dialog box, click on **Bar.**
    b. Click on the **3-D Clustered Bar** chart. Select the first chart.
    c. Click **OK** to close dialog box.
11. Rename chart title to **Saturday & Sunday Revenues** (triple-click in your title, then type in title name). Resize chart title font to size 24 pt.
    a. Click on the **Chart Legend** below the chart. (Sunday and Saturday). Bold and resize font to size **14** pt.
    b. Click on the **Y** axis (BBQ Steak ...). Bold and resize font to size **12** pt.
    c. Click on the **X** axis ($2,000, $4,000, etc.). Bold and resize font to size **12** pt.
12. Preview your charts before you print.
    1. Click on the Saturday & Sunday Revenues worksheet.
13. Click the **File** tab to access the *Backstage* area. Select **Print**. *Print Preview* will display how your worksheet will print (Figure 10-84).
14. Select your printer.
15. Click **Print** to print the worksheet.
16. Save and close your workbook (Figure 10-85).

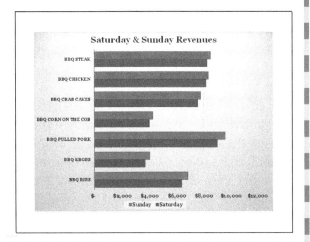

Print

Copies: 1

Print

Printer

HP49ABCC (HP Officejet Pr...
Ready

Printer Properties

Settings

Print Active Sheets
Only print the active sheets

Pages: [ ] to [ ]

Print One Sided
Only print on one side of th...

Collated
1,2,3 1,2,3 1,2,3

Landscape Orientation

Letter
8.5" x 11"

Normal Margins
Left: 0.7" Right: 0.7"

Page Setup

FIGURE 10-84 Backstage Print

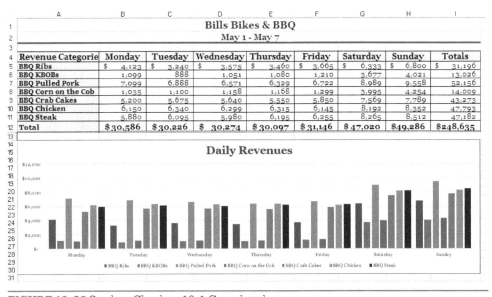

FIGURE 10-85 Student Checkup 10-1 Completed

3. Edit Chart Elements, Such as Titles, Data Labels, and Source Data

A **chart element** is a separate, clickable, editable object. The Chart Layout and style affects which elements will be in your chart, but you can add, remove, format, size, and position elements as you design your chart.

Add and Remove Chart Elements

When you point to a chart element, a ScreenTip pops up and describes it. Once you click the element (such as a legend), it becomes active and is surrounded by selection handles. Clicking on an element is one way to select it; another way is to select an element from the **Chart Elements** drop-down list on the *Chart Tools, Format* tab. The name of the selected element will appear in the **Chart Elements** box (Figure 10-86).

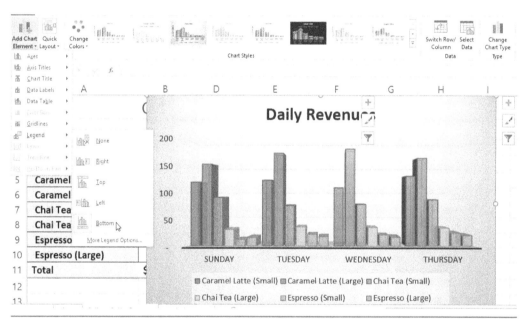

FIGURE 10-86 Add and Remove Chart Elements

In addition, you can show or hide chart elements. To do so, click on the **Chart Elements** button in the upper right of the chart (green plus sign). Once you click on the green plus sign, the *Chart Elements* pane opens with a list of available elements for the chart type. You can select or deselect chart elements by clicking in the checkboxes next to each element (Figure 10-87).

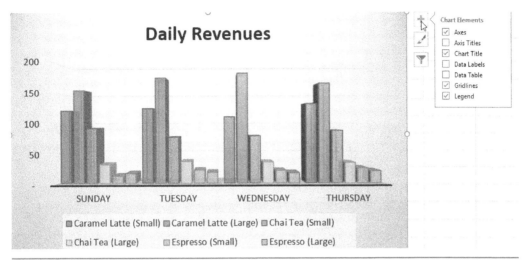

FIGURE 10-87 Chart Elements Pane

Add Chart Titles and Axes Titles to a Chart

Chart titles by default are positioned over the top of the chart. Axes titles by default are positioned to the left of the chart (Y axis), and the X axis is positioned below the chart. Excel allows you to select a title or axis and move it wherever you want in the chart. Normally, you would use a chart title to describe the meaning of your chart; however, the axes can be optional, depending on how well the chart represents the data.

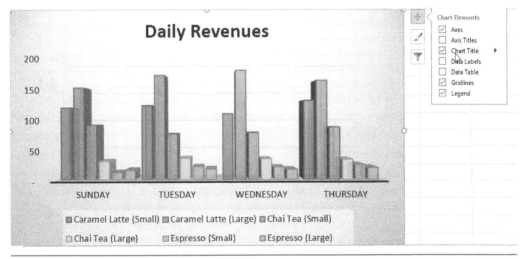

FIGURE 10-88 Insert a Chart Title

Steps to insert a Chart Title:

1. Click in your chart.
2. Click the **Chart Elements** button in the top right corner of the chart (green plus sign).
3. Select the *Chart Title* box.
4. The *Chart Title* placeholder appears above the chart (Figure 10-88).
5. Click the *Chart Title* arrow in the *Chart Elements* pane to select a position for the title.
6. Triple-click the *Chart Title* placeholder text to select it.
7. Type a title to replace the placeholder text.

To edit placeholder text, you can select the object and type text in the *Formula* bar and press **Enter**, or you can click on the **Enter** button (green check mark) in the *Formula* bar. Although the label appears in the formula bar as you type, you will not be able to see it on the chart until you press Enter (Figure 10-89).

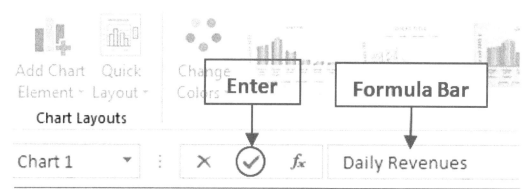

FIGURE 10-89 Formula Bar

When you select an element, you can also format it with font attributes from the *Font* and *Alignment* groups (*Home* tab). If you want to apply a format to a portion of the text, click to place an insertion point inside the element and select the characters you want to change.

If you want to remove a chart element, select it and press **Delete**. You can also resize the chart element by selecting it and then clicking on one of the size handles and drag it until you reach the desired size.

Note: If you remove chart elements, it will make more room for your chart. You may want to keep in mind how you want to balance the number of elements you need to represent your chart, but you don't want your chart to look too busy or difficult to understand.

When you double-click on an element, its **Format** pane will open with format and design choices for that element.

Add Data Labels to a Chart

Data labels display the number represented by a market on a chart, such as a pie slice, column, bar, or other marker on the chart. It is recommended that data labels be used when there are not too many data series in the chart. You want to avoid cluttering a chart which would make it more difficult for your audience to quickly understand.

Data labels are displayed from the **Chart Elements** button on the chart or *Chart Tools, Design* tab, *Chart Layouts* group.

Add Chart Labels:

1. Select your chart of the chart sheet tab.
2. Click the **Chart Elements** button in the top right corner of the chart.
3. Select the **Data Labels** box.
4. Point to **Data Labels** in the pane and point to its arrow.
5. Choose a location for the data labels (Figure 10-90).

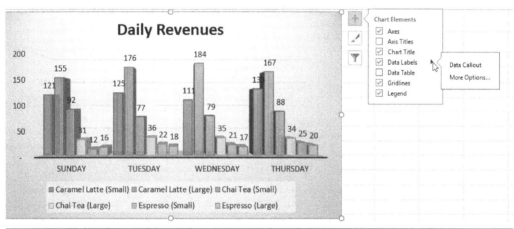

FIGURE 10-90 Data Labels

Add a Data Table to a Chart

A chart data table is located just below the chart. It is a columnar display of the values for each data series in a chart. A data table can be used to provide chart data to your readers. It is an easy way to display both a chart and data in a logical readable form.

If you would like to include a data table with your chart, it is very easy to add one. Here are the steps to include a data table with your chart:

1. Click on your chart object or chart sheet tab.
2. Click on the **Add Chart Element** button on the *Chart Tools, Design* tab, *Chart Layout* group.
3. You will see three options: One is to show your data table With *Legend Keys* (Figure 10-91), another is with *No Legend Keys* (Figure 10-92), and the last is *More Data Table Options*. With your mouse, hover over each option and choose which one will best fit your chart.
4. Click on your choice.

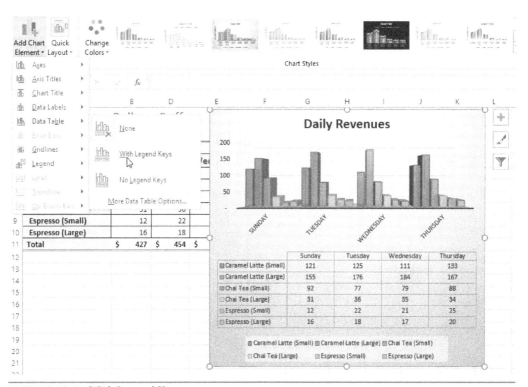

FIGURE 10-91 With Legend Keys

A third way to add a data table to your chart is to click on the **Quick Layout** button, *Layout 5* (*Chart Tools, Design* tab, *Chart Layouts* group). See Figure 10-93. This option will add an Axis Title to the left of the chart. Also, the chart's original legend will disappear. Compare Figure 10-93 to Figure 10-91 and Figure 10-92. This option appears to be a cleaner way to show your data table without legend replication. If you want to keep the *Axis Title*, click on it to rename it or, if you do not want to have an *Axis Title* next to your chart, you can click on it and delete it.

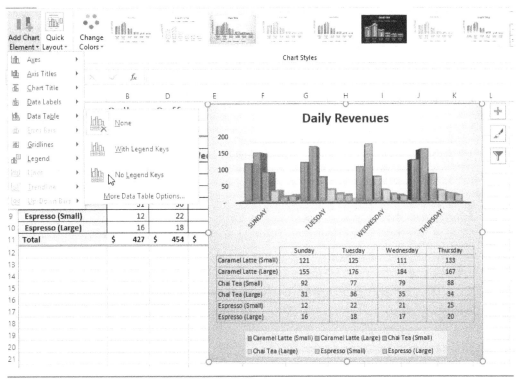

FIGURE 10-92 Without Legend Keys

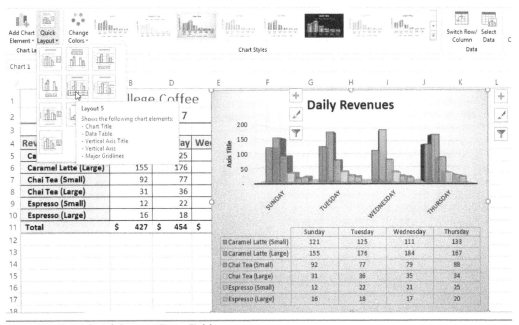

FIGURE 10-93 Quick Layout Data Table

Add a Trendline to a Chart

A **trendline** is a chart element that plots patterns using a moving average of the current data in your chart. Depending on the type of trendline selected, it will use a straight or curved line and can extend beyond current data to predict future trends. A trendline may be used for most charts; however, **a trendline cannot be displayed on a stacked chart, pie chart, or a 3-D chart**. A trendline traces for one data series at a time. If you have multiple data series, as in a typical column chart, you can add a trendline for each series.

Insert a Trendline into a Chart:

1. Click the chart or the chart sheet tab.
2. Change chart type to "Clustered Column."
3. Click on a single data point (in a column chart, click on the colored bar of what you want to show as a trendline. In this example, Caramel Latte (Small) was selected. All four Caramel Latte (Small) bars will be shown as selected.
4. Click the **Chart Elements** button (*Chart Tools, Design* tab, *Chart Layouts* group).
5. Click on the **Trendline** option.
6. Click on your **Trendline** choice (Figure 10-94).
   1. An Add Trendline dialog box will pop up. This is where you can select one or more series to create trendlines (Figure 10-95).

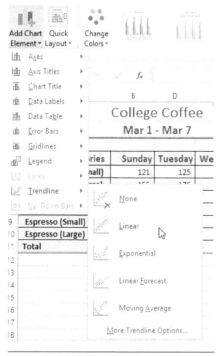

Note: If you only have one series in your chart, Excel will automatically add a trendline to that series.

FIGURE 10-94 Trendline Options   FIGURE 10-95 Trendline Options

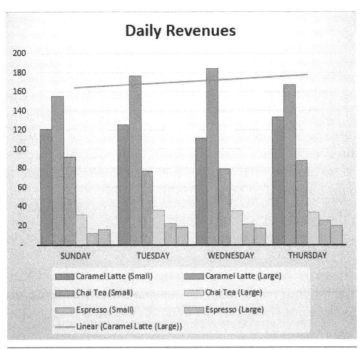

FIGURE 10-96 Chart with One Trendline

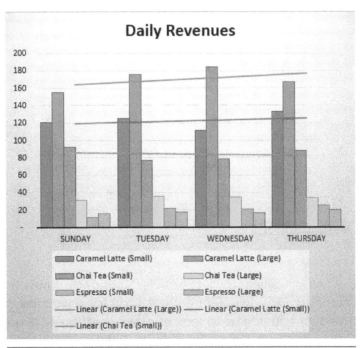

FIGURE 10-97 Chart with Three Trendlines

4. Switch Rows and Columns, Filter Source Data, and Edit Source Data

Switch Row and Column Data

When you select data and build a chart, Excel will plot the data series based on the number of rows and columns selected in the worksheet and the chart type. Excel will determine if the labels are along the bottom or the side of the chart, based on your choices. Excel provides you with the option to change which data series will be plotted on the X axis and which will be plotted on the Y axis.

It is easy to switch row and column data.

1. Click on the chart or the chart sheet tab.
2. Click the **Switch Row/Column** button (*Chart Tools, Design* tab, *Data* Group).
3. The X axis and Y axis data will be flipped in your chart (Figure 10-98).
4. If you change your mind, just click on the **Switch Row/Column** button to toggle back to your original row and column data (Figure 10-99).

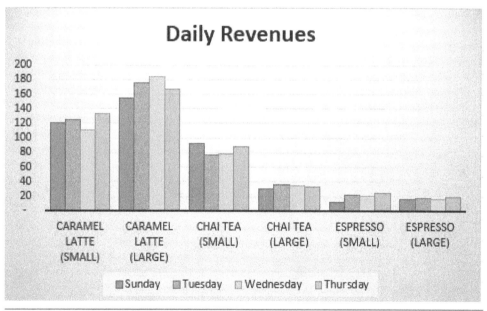

FIGURE 10-98 X Axis and Y Axis Changed

Sometimes, when you select a chart type for your data, it may not depict the data as you intended. Or, you select a chart type for your data and then you change your mind, or you decide to look at other chart types. Excel provides a button called **Change Chart Type** (*Chart Tools, Design* tab, *Type* group).

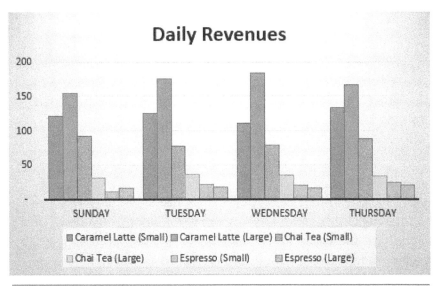

FIGURE 10-99 *Original Chart*

To change the chart type, do the following:

1. Click the chart or chart sheet tab.
2. Click the ***Change Chart Type*** button.
3. Click the **Recommended Charts** tab.
4. Click **All Charts** tab if you prefer another chart type not listed in the **Recommended Charts** tab.
5. Click on a thumbnail image to preview the chart in the dialog box.
6. Select a chart type and click **OK** (Figure 10-100).

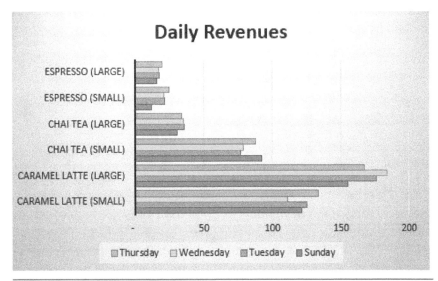

FIGURE 10-100 *Chart Type Changed*

Filter Source Data

When you create a chart in Excel, Excel automatically displays all categories and data series. However, Excel also provides you the option to filter or refine which data is displayed by hiding categories or series. A filter is a requirement or condition that identifies which data is shown and which is hidden. Although chart filters do not change or delete the original underlying data, chart filters will enable you to display and focus on particular data.

To filter source data, do the following:

1. Select your chart or chart sheet tab.
2. Click the **Chart Filters** button in the top right corner of the chart.
3. The Chart filters pane will display a check mark for the series and categories that are shown.
4. Deselect the box for a category or series to be hidden.
5. Click **Apply** (Figure 10-101).
6. Click the **Chart Filters** button to close the pane.
7. If you want to unhide category or series data, click on the check boxes to display the data again. Your underlying data will not change.

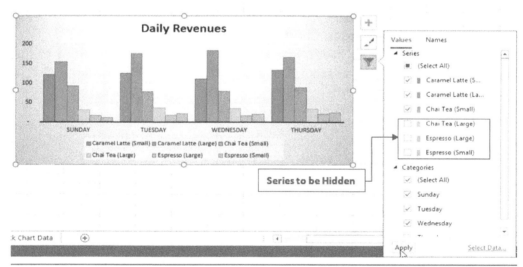

FIGURE 10-101 Chart Filters Pane

Edit Source Data

Sometimes you may want to display all your data but make changes. You can add another column or a data series. You can also delete data. To add or delete a data series in a chart, select the chart and drag the sizing arrow (Figure 10-102) in the lower right corner of the highlighted cell range to expand or shrink the data range. Removing cells from the data range deletes that data series from the chart.

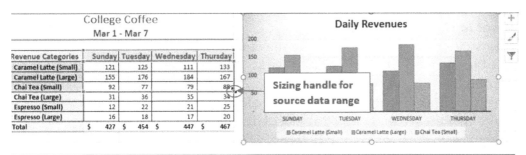

FIGURE 10-102 Revenue Categories Removed from Chart

FIGURE 10-103 Tab

Current Selection group

The **Current Selection** group allows you to choose *Chart Elements, Format Selection*, or *Reset to Match Style*.

Chart Area The combo box for the **Chart Area** allows you to quickly select an element in the chart if you want to make changes to it (Figure 10-104).	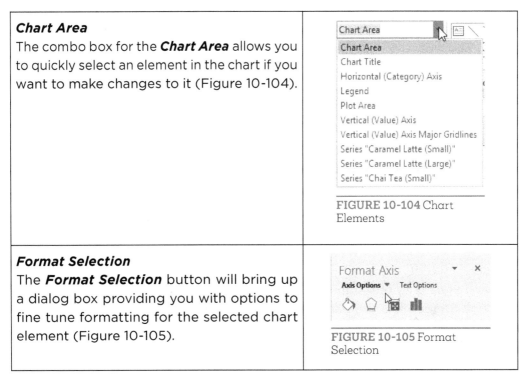 FIGURE 10-104 Chart Elements
Format Selection The **Format Selection** button will bring up a dialog box providing you with options to fine tune formatting for the selected chart element (Figure 10-105).	FIGURE 10-105 Format Selection

Reset to Match Style Clears the custom formatting of the selected chart element back to the overall visual style applied to the chart (Figure 10-106). This ensures that the selected chart element matches the overall theme of the workbook. In other words, this button is your "undo" if you previously formatted a chart element and wanted to change it back.	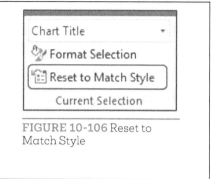 FIGURE 10-106 Reset to Match Style

Insert Shapes Group

In this group, Excel provides a convenient way to add shapes to your chart.

Shapes Click on the down arrow to open a gallery of shapes. There are 9 categories from which to choose (Figure 10-107).	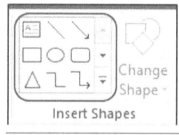 FIGURE 10-107 Shapes
Change Shapes This button provides options to change your shape with a single click. (Figure 10-108).	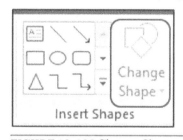 FIGURE 10-108 Change Shapes

Shape Styles Group

A **Shape Style** is a predesigned set of borders, fill colors, and effects for a chart element. Shape fill is the background color, and shape outline is the border around the element. Shape effects include shadows, glows, soft edges, or 3-D bevels.

Shape Styles Group This opens a gallery of two categories consisting of **Shape Styles** and **Presets.** This is an easy way to apply a built-in Theme Style to your chart (Figure 10-109).	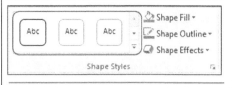 **FIGURE 10-109** Shape Styles Group
Shape Fill Fills the selected shape with a solid color, gradients, picture, or texture. When you click on the down arrow next to the button, a color palette will appear (Figure 10-110).	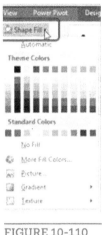 **FIGURE 10-110** Shape Fill
Shape Outline This button enables you to pick the color, width, and line style for the outline of your shape (Figure 10-111).	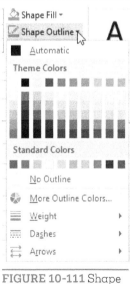 **FIGURE 10-111** Shape Outline

Shape Effects Applies a visual effect to the selected shape, such as shadow, glow, reflection, or 3-D rotation (Figure 10-112).	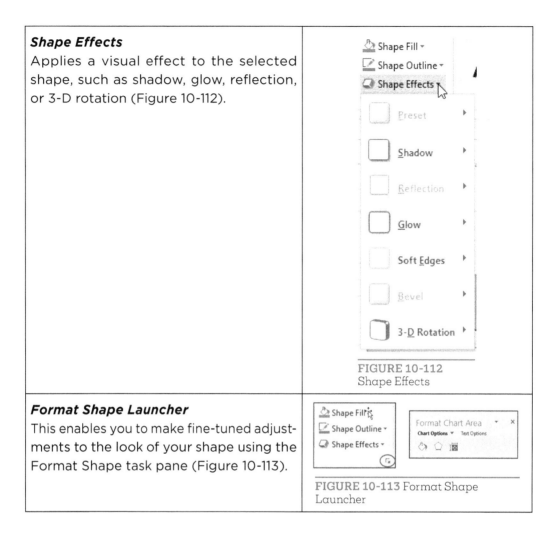 **FIGURE 10-112** Shape Effects
Format Shape Launcher This enables you to make fine-tuned adjustments to the look of your shape using the Format Shape task pane (Figure 10-113).	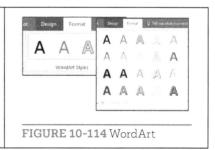 **FIGURE 10-113** Format Shape Launcher

WordArt Styles Group

WordArt Styles provide a quick way to add pizazz to any text object in your chart.

WordArt Excel has custom built-in options for you to enhance your font. WordArt is normally used for chart titles, axes, legends, and sometimes for text boxes. The font colors in WordArt are based on the theme you chose for your workbook (Figure 10-114).	**FIGURE 10-114** WordArt

Text Fill Fills the text with a solid color, gradient, picture, or pattern (Figure 10-115).	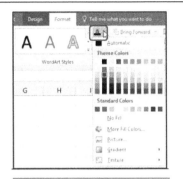 **FIGURE 10-115** Text Fill
Text Outline Customizes the outline of your text by choosing the color, width, and line style (Figure 10-116).	 **FIGURE 10-116** Text Outline
Text Effects Turns your text into a work of art! Add a visual effect such as shadow, reflection, or glow to your text (Figure 10-117).	 **FIGURE 10-117** Text Effects
Format Text Effects-Text Box Show the Format Text Effects task pane to change text properties (Figure 10-118).	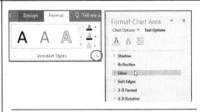 **FIGURE 10-118** Format Text Effects

Accessibility Group

Alt Text Accessibility Create a text description of objects for screen readers in one to two sentences (Figure 10-119). *For example:* how would you describe this object and its context to someone who is blind?	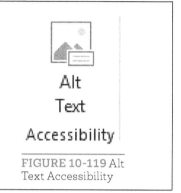 Alt Text Accessibility FIGURE 10-119 Alt Text Accessibility

Arrange Group

The **Arrange** group provides you with ways to move objects forward and backward. The Arrange group also has different *Align* options and allows you to *Group* objects or *Rotate* objects as needed.

Bring Forward Brings the selected object forward one level so that it's hidden behind fewer objects (Figure 10-120).	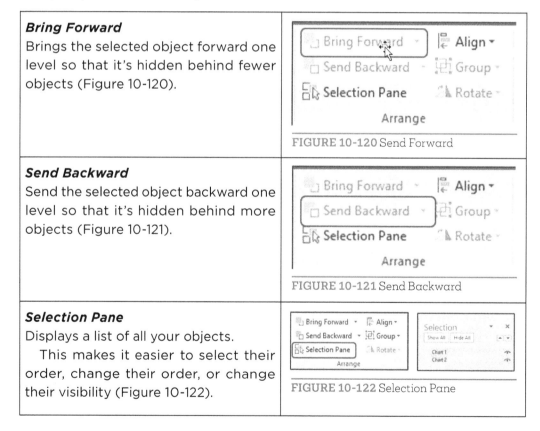 FIGURE 10-120 Send Forward
Send Backward Send the selected object backward one level so that it's hidden behind more objects (Figure 10-121).	FIGURE 10-121 Send Backward
Selection Pane Displays a list of all your objects. This makes it easier to select their order, change their order, or change their visibility (Figure 10-122).	FIGURE 10-122 Selection Pane

Align Objects. The **Align Objects** button changes the placement of your selected objects on the page (Figure 10-123).

This aligns objects to the margins or to the edge of the page. You can also align them relative to one another.

Align Left. Horizontally left aligns all selected objects on the left side in a straight line.

Align Center. Horizontally center aligns all selected objects.

Align Right. Horizontally right aligns all selected objects on the right side in a straight line.

Align Top. Vertically top aligns all selected objects on the top side in a straight line.

Align Middle. Vertically center aligns all selected objects.

Align Bottom. Vertically aligns all selected objects on the bottom side in a straight line.

Distribute Horizontally. To make this work, you need at least 3 objects to select. This distributes equal space between objects in a horizontal line.

Distribute Vertically. To make this work, you need at least 3 objects to select. This distributes equal space between objects in a vertical line.

Snap to Grid. This is a computer function used to organize files or objects automatically. It uses an invisible grid to line up the items on the screen along perfect horizontal and vertical lines.

Snap to Shape. Snaps shapes or other objects to grid lines that go through the vertical and horizontal edges of other shapes or objects.

View Gridlines. This button acts as a toggle button. When you open your workbook, you will see a grid in the background. If you do not want to see a grid background, click on the **View Gridlines** button. To turn the grid background back on, click on the **View Gridlines** button again.

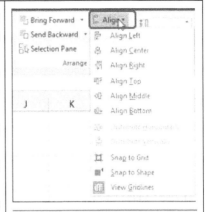

FIGURE 10-123 Align Objects

Group Join objects together to move and format them as if they were a single object (Figure 10-124). 　*For example*: You can group a picture and a caption. 　Excel provides the Group, Regroup, and Ungroup options.	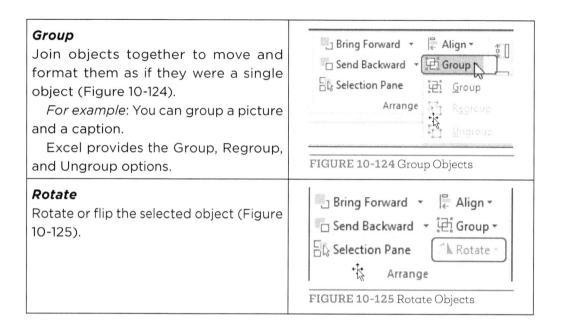 FIGURE 10-124 Group Objects
Rotate Rotate or flip the selected object (Figure 10-125).	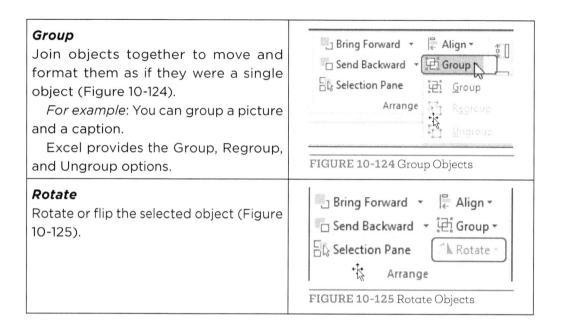 FIGURE 10-125 Rotate Objects

Size Group

The Size group enables you to fine-tune the height and width of your object.

Shape Height Change the height of the object or picture (Figure 10-126).	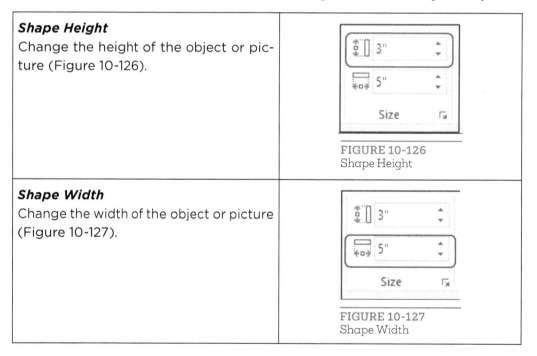 FIGURE 10-126 Shape Height
Shape Width Change the width of the object or picture (Figure 10-127).	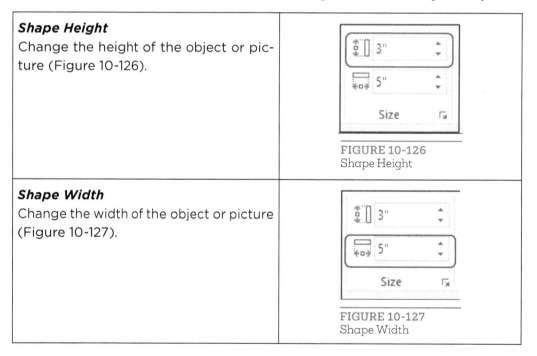 FIGURE 10-127 Shape Width

Size and Properties Show the Size and Properties dialog in which you can specify the size and positioning of the object and specific alternative text (Figure 10-128).	
	FIGURE 10-128 Size and Properties

Apply a Shape Style

A **shape style** is a predesigned set of borders, fill colors, and effects for a chart element. **Shape fill** is the background color, and **shape outline** is the border around the element. **Shape effects** include shadows, glows, soft edges, or 3-D bevels. These commands may be found in the *Shape Styles* group on the *Chart Tools, Format* tab.

Excel groups *Shape Styles* in a gallery as either *Theme Styles* or *Presets*. When you point to an icon, a *ScreenTip* appears with a descriptive name. When you find one you like, click on the icon to apply it to your selected chart element. It is easy to apply a shape style to your selected chart element.

Here is how to apply a Shape Style:

1. Make sure your chart is selected.
2. Click on **Chart Elements** drop-down arrow (*Chart Tools, Format* tab, *Current Selection* group) to select your chart element. In this example, **Chart Area** has been selected.
3. Click on the **More** down arrow (*Chart Tools, Format* tab, *Shape Styles* group).
4. Click a shape style icon.
5. The **Chart Area** has been reformatted (Figure 10-129).

Apply Shape Fill, Outline, and Effects

Excel provides a *fill color* gallery, *outline color and width* options, and *special effects* to enhance your chart elements by displaying more in-depth and realistic views. Although Excel uses built-in style settings according to your selected theme, you may still override these built-in style settings to your liking.

For *fill color*, you can choose from the gallery to select a standard color or a custom color. Once your color is selected, you can refine it to use as a gradient, which is a variegated blend of the color. Other options include selecting a picture or a texture.

FIGURE 10-129 Applying a Shape Style

Steps to apply Gradient Fill to a Chart Element:

1. Make sure your chart is selected.
2. Select the chart element.
3. Click on the Chart Elements drop-down arrow (*Chart Tools, Format* tab, *Current Selection* group) to select your chart element. In this example, **Chart Area** has been selected.
4. Click on the *Shape Fill* down arrow (*Chart Tools, Format* tab, *Shape Styles* group).
5. When the *Shape Fill* gallery opens, you have the option to select from Theme colors, Standard colors, No Color, or More Fill colors.
6. Once you select your Theme Color, Standard Color, or custom color, then reopen the *Shape Fill* gallery and select Gradient.
7. At this point, you have four options: No Gradient, Light Gradient, Dark Gradient, or more Gradients (Figure 10-130).
8. Hover over selected options. You will be able to preview each option. Click on your preferred gradient.
9. Click on another cell in the worksheet or another chart element to see your gradient.

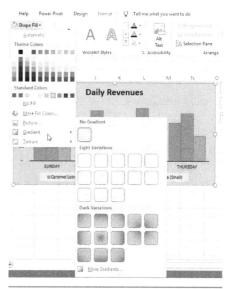

FIGURE 10-130 Applying Gradient Fill

Chart Element Outline

A **Chart Element Outline** is a border that surrounds the element. An outline enhances an element by creating definition. Excel provides solid and dashed lines as well as weight and thickness for outlines. Plus you may add a color to your outline. Excel also provides a gallery of weights to help you visualize the width. To view your outline effect, deselect the chart object.

Steps to Apply a Chart Element Outline:

1. Make sure your chart is selected.
2. Click on **Chart Elements** drop-down arrow (*Chart Tools, Format* tab, *Current Selection* group) to select your chart element. In this example, **Chart Title** has been selected.
3. Click on the **Shape Outline** down arrow (*Chart Tools, Format* tab, *Shape Styles* group).
4. When the *Shape Outline* gallery opens, you have the option to select from Theme Colors, Standard Colors, No Color, or More Fill Colors.
5. Once you select your Theme Color, Standard Color, or custom color, reopen the **Shape Outline** gallery and move down to Weight (Figure 10-131).
6. Select your line weight. If you desire, you can reopen the Shape Outline gallery and move down to Dashes if you prefer a dashed line.
7. Click on another cell in the worksheet or another chart element to see your outline.

FIGURE 10-131 Applying a Chart Element

Chart Element Effects

Excel offers special effects to provide elements with a realistic three-dimensional look. Bevels and shadows are two effects used to enhance larger elements. Excel also offers **Presents, Glow, Soft Edges,** and **3-D-Rotation**.

Steps to apply a **Chart Element** Effect:

1. Make sure your chart is selected.
2. Click on *Chart Elements* drop-down arrow (*Chart Tools, Format* tab, *Current Selection* group) to select your chart element. In this example, **Chart Area** has been selected.
3. Click on the *Shape Effect* down arrow (*Chart Tools, Format* tab, *Shape Styles* group).
4. When the *Shape Effects* gallery opens, you will have the option to select from *Presets, Shadow, Glow, Soft Edges, Bevel,* and *3-D Rotation*.
5. Select your **Shape Effect**. In this example, Preset3 was the selected **Shape Effect** (Figure 10-132).
6. Once you click on your **shape effect**, your selection will appear. If you change your mind, just click on **Shape Effects** again and reselect your **Shape Effect**.

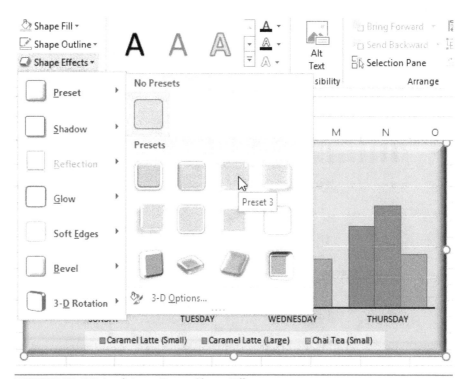

FIGURE 10-132 Applying a Preset Shape Effect

Format Task Pane

In Excel, every chart element has a *Format* task pane that contains shapes, fill, and color options and provides custom commands for the element. Use one of two ways to open the *Format* pane: double-click on the element or right-click it and choose **Format** (*Element name*) from the menu.

In Figure 10-133, the selected element is the legend. In the Format Legend dialog box, you can choose the Fill and Border icon (bucket); effects of shadow, glow, and soft edges (pentagon icon); and Legend Options (column chart icon), which include placement options for your legend. Toward the top right corner of the Format Legend dialog box, you can click on the down arrow and either Move, Size, or Close.

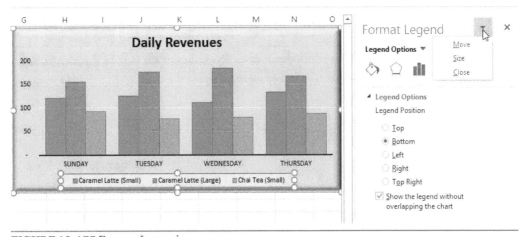

FIGURE 10-133 Format Legend

Each element will have a slightly different dialog box. Depending on the selected element, each dialog box will have more or fewer options but will offer similar commands for all elements.

The steps to use the **Format Task Pane** for a *Format Chart Title* element are as follows:

1. Double-click the **Title** chart element.
2. Click on the **Border** option (green font).
3. Under the **Border** heading, click on *Gradient Line*.
4. Click on *Presets gradient* icon down arrow.
5. Click on *Radial Gradient—Accent 6* (Lower right corner green option).
6. Then choose your **Type**. Options include *Linear, Radial, Rectangular,* or *Path*.
7. Select your **Direction**.
8. Choose your **Angle**.

9. The *Gradient Stops* enable you to create shades of your color. The more stops you have, the more graduated your color will be. The fewer stops you have will give you more of a single solid color.

10. In the *Color* box, click on the down arrow next to the bucket and select your color.

11. Explore the remaining options (Figure 10-134).

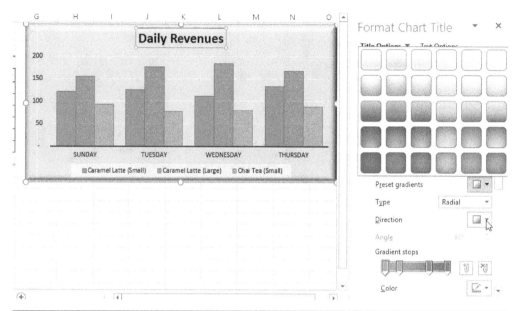

FIGURE 10-134 Formatting Chart Title

5. Use Shapes, WordArt, and Pictures to Enhance a Chart

You can enhance your charts with pictures, shapes, or **WordArt**. You can use pictures as a fill for a chart element, or you can insert pictures as separate design objects on the chart. If you want to highlight a particular data point on a chart, you can insert an arrow, or you can add a text box to highlight specific important information in your chart, usually not clearly depicted by the chart. **WordArt** is often applied to a chart title to create a highly visible and distinctive look.

Fill the Shape with a Picture

You can insert a picture or **clip art** to fill in the chart area, plot area, or a marker, such as bars, columns, or pie slices. It's tempting to get overly creative when adding pictures or clip art, but when it comes to using pictures or clip art, sometimes less is more. A picture or clip art is best used to emphasize a specific data point or as a background for solid or gradient colored bars or columns. You will want to avoid making the chart appear busy. A less cluttered chart is easier for your audience to view and, ultimately, to understand.

You can insert a picture or clip art from the **Fill** command on the Format task pane for the element. Once you have inserted your picture or *clip art*, the task pane displays Stretch and Stack options. The **Stretch** option enlarges and elongates a single copy of the picture or *clip art* to fill the element. When you select the **Stack** option, the stack sizes and repeats the image to fill the area. One final option is the **Stack and Scale**. This setting is used for precise matching of the number of images used per unit of value.

Steps to use a picture as a chart area background are as follows:

1. Double-click the chart area background. For best results, double-click in one of the four corner areas of the chart.
2. The **Format Chart Area** dialog box will appear on the right side of your screen.
3. Click on **Fill**.
4. Click on **Picture or texture fill**.
5. Under the **Insert picture from** area click either the **File, Clipboard**, or **Online** button.
6. When you click *File*, your Pictures folder located on your computer hard drive will open and display a gallery of your pictures. Click on your desired picture and then click **Insert**.
   a. When you click **Clipboard**, any pictures currently on your Clipboard will display. Click on your desired picture. Excel will insert the picture. If you have no pictures on your clipboard, the button will appear as grey.
   b. When you click on *Online*, Excel will open an Insert Picture dialog box with either Bing or Google searches displayed.
   c. Type in your picture topic. Click on the small magnifying glass. Select your picture, then click **Insert** (Figure 10-135).

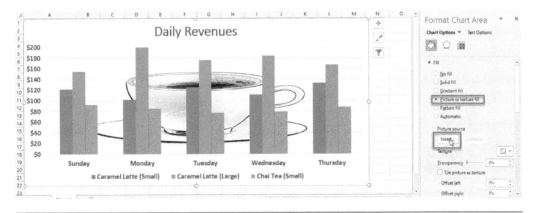

FIGURE 10-135 Inserted Background Picture

If you would prefer to use a texture, click on the down arrow next to the **Texture** icon. Click on your desired texture.

Steps to use a picture as Fill:

1. Double-click the data point desired (this will be a column or bar).
2. The **Format Data Series** dialog box will appear on the right side of your screen.
3. Click on *Fill*.
4. Click on *Picture or texture fill*.
5. Under the *Insert picture from* area, click either the *File, Clipboard*, or *Online* button.
6. When you click *File*, your Pictures folder located on your computer hard drive will open and display a gallery of your pictures. Click on your desired picture and then click *Insert*.
7. When you click *Clipboard*, any pictures currently on your Clipboard will display. Click on your desired picture. Excel will insert the picture. If you have no pictures on your clipboard, the button will appear grey.
8. When you click on *Online*, Excel will open an **Insert Picture** dialog box with either Bing or Google searches displayed.
9. Type in your picture topic. Click on the small magnifying glass. Select your picture and then click *Insert.* In this example, "coffee cup" was the topic typed in (Figure 10-136).
10. Click on *Stack* option.
11. Notice that the stacked coffee cups columns have a border. To add a border, in the Format Data Series dialog box, double-click on the bucket and then click on *Border*.
12. Select the type of border line, color, and weight to add more definition to your chart.

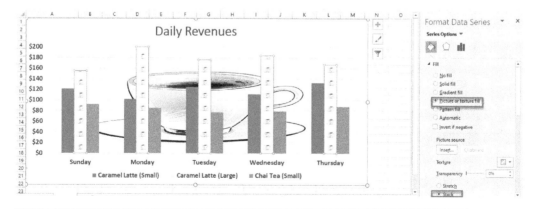

FIGURE 10-136 Inserted Image as Stacked

Insert Shapes

Inserting a shape or text box into a chart enables you to provide additional information to augment your findings or to highlight or emphasize a point on your chart. Shapes may be placed anywhere on your chart but are normally placed in areas of a chart that do not obscure any data. Once you insert a shape, you can select and click on it to move it or change its size. Once you select the shape, the **Drawing Tools Format** tab above the Ribbon becomes available with commands to alter the appearance of the shape. There, the **Format Shape** task pane will also appear in the right panel of your screen.

Steps to insert a shape into a chart:

1. Select the chart object or the chart sheet tab.
2. Click the **More** button (*Chart Tools, Format* tab, *Insert Shapes* group).
3. Select your desired shape. The *Format Shape* dialog box will open.
    1. Click the location in your chart where you want your shape to be.
4. Resize shape to your preferred size. Use the size handles to resize your shape.
5. If you want to format your shape, you can either use the Format Shape dialog box, appearing in the right panel of your screen, or you can click on the *Drawing Tools, Format* tab to select lines, colors, and effects.

In this example, a "Best Seller" text box was added and a right-pointing green arrow (Figure 10-137).

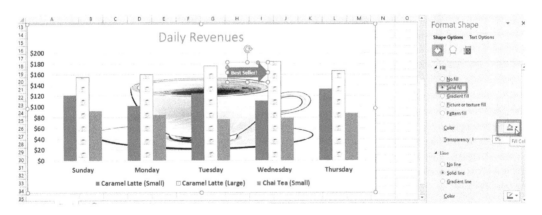

FIGURE 10-137 Add and Format Shapes to a Chart

Add WordArt to a Chart

In a chart, WordArt is commonly used for main titles. WordArt may also be used on the axe's labels, legend labels, and data labels, depending on the text size of the element. WordArt is a text box with present font style, fill, and effects. Your chosen theme for your worksheet will determine the colors in the WordArt choices as well as your chart colors. If you prefer to change a WordArt style, you can individually change its fill, outline, and effects.

Steps to add **WordArt** to a chart:

1. Select the chart title element.
2. Click on the ***More*** button to open the WordArt Styles gallery (*Chart Tools, Format* tab, *WordArt Styles* group).
3. Point to your desired style to see a *ScreenTip* with a description.
4. Click your preferred style (Figure 10-138).
5. Resize the title by changing the font size.

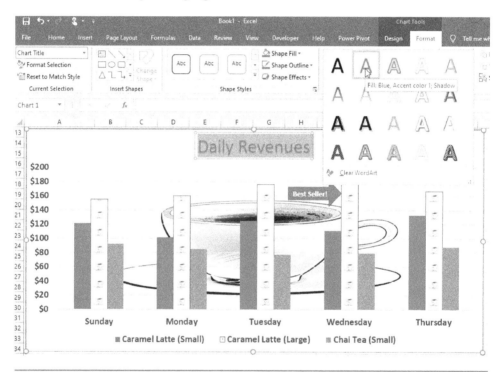

FIGURE 10-138 Adding WordArt to a Chart

In this project, you will open an existing workbook for Bill's Bikes and BBQ. You will change the chart theme, filter, edit, and format Bill's Bikes and BBQ charts. You will switch row and column data, remove chart elements, and change the chart type. Finally, you will format the charts for enhanced visual appeal. **Note: Blue text represents typed text.**

File Needed: **(Your Initials) Student Checkup Excel 10-1**

Completed File Name: **(Your initials) Student Checkup Excel 10-2**

1. Open **(Your Initials) Student Checkup Excel 10-1**. This is the workbook you completed in Student Checkup **Excel 10-1.**
2. Save the workbook as **(Your Initials) Student Checkup Excel 10-2.**
3. Click on the **Restaurant Revenue** tab.
4. Change theme to **Wood Type** (*Page Layout* tab, *Themes* group).
5. Click in a blank corner of your column chart.
   a. Triple-click on the chart title.
   b. Rename chart title to **Top Three Sellers**.
   c. Resize chart title font to **28** pt.
   d. To the Chart Title, apply *WordArt* style **Fill: Black, Text color 1; Shadow** (*Chart Tools, Format* tab, *WordArt Styles* group).
   e. Under **Series**, click in the check boxes to de-select all options except for **BBQ Pulled Pork, BBQ Chicken,** and **BBQ Steak**.
   f. Under **Categories,** click in the check boxes to de-select all options except for **Saturday** and **Sunday**.
   g. Under *Categories*, click on the check boxes to deselect the following days: Monday, Tuesday, Wednesday, Thursday, and Friday. You should only have Saturday and Sunday checked. Alternatively, you may click on the **Select All** check box to deselect it and then click on Saturday and Sunday.
   h. Click on *Apply* (Figure 10-139).
   i. Click on the circle at the bottom of your chart, and drag it down to the top of row 36.

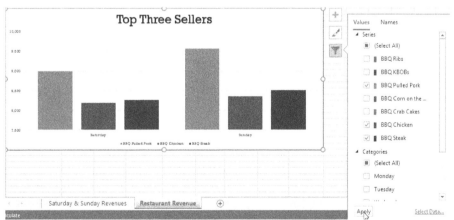

FIGURE 10-139 Filtering a Chart

6. Switch Rows and Columns.
   a. Click in a blank area in the upper right corner of the Three Top Sellers chart.

Click the **Switch Row/Column** button (*Chart Tools, Design* tab/*Data* group).

BBQ Pulled Pork, BBQ Chicken, and *BBQ Steak* should be your **X** axis, and *Saturday* and *Sunday* should be your **Legend (Figure 10-140).**

    b. Click the **Switch Row/Column** button (**Chart Tools**, **Design** tab, **Data** group).

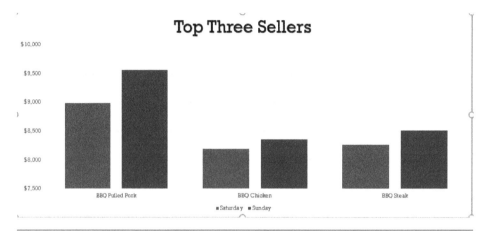

FIGURE 10-140 Chart after Switch Rows/Columns Applied

7. Click on **Quick Layout** button and select **Quick Layout 3** (*Chart Tools, Design* tab, *Chart Layouts* group).
    a. Select the **Legend** (It should be *Saturday, Sunday*). Resize the legend font to size **14** pt. **Bold** text.
    b. Select the **X** axis. (It should be *BBQ Pulled Pork, BBQ Chicken, BBQ Steak*). Resize the **X** axis font to size **14**. **Bold** text.
    c. Select the **Y** axis. (It should be number values). Resize the **Y** axis font to size **14** pt. **Bold** text.
        i. If you don't have any "$" for your **Y** axis values, right-click the **Y** axis. From the shortcut menu, select **Format Axis**. Once the **Format Axis** task pane opens, scroll down all the way to the bottom. Click on **Number**. Under **Category**, format as *Currency*, no decimals, and with a dollar sign **($)**.
    d. Close the Format Axis pane.
8. Apply shape styles and outlines to chart elements.
    a. Select **Plot** area to select the plot area of the chart. To do this, click between the lines in the chart.
    b. Right-click in the **Plot** area. Click on **Format Plot Area** ...

c. Click on the **bucket and** then click on **Fill.**

d. Under **Fill,** click on **Picture or Texture Fill.**

e. Under **Picture Source,** select **Insert.**

f. In the **Insert Pictures** dialog box, you will have the following three choices:
   - From a File
   - Online Pictures
   - From Icons

g. Select <u>Online</u> pictures (Bing Image Search, etc.). When the **Online Pictures** box appears, type in: **Brick Wall** then press **Enter**. (Figure 10-141).

h. Select a brick wall image of your choice. Click **Insert**.

i. Close the **Format Plot Area** task dialog box.

FIGURE 10-141 Formatting Plot Area

9. Double-click or right-click on one of the **Sunday** series to open the **Format Data Series** task pane.

a. Click the **Fill and Line** button (bucket).

b. Click on **Fill**. Then click on **Picture and Texture Fill**.

c. Under **Picture Source**, click on **Insert**. In the **Insert Pictures** dialog box, click on Online Pictures in the dialog box. Type in **BBQ Steak or BBQ Steak Clip Art**. Press **Enter**.

d. Select and insert a BBQ steak image of your choice.

e. Scroll down in the **Format Data Series** task pane. Click on **Stack**.

f. With the Sunday series still selected, click on **Border** (below the **Fill** section) in the **Format Data Series** task pane (in the right of the screen).

g. Under **Border**, click on *Solid Line*.

h. Click on the down arrow to the right of **Color** (in the **Border** section). Select **Black, Text 1**.

i. Change the width to **2.0** pt.

10. Click on one of the **Saturday** series to open the *Format Data Series* task pane.

   a. Click the *Fill and Line* button (bucket).

   b. Click on *Fill*. Then click on *Solid Fill*.

   c. Click the down arrow next to the **Color** button. Select **Orange, Accent color 1**.

   d. In the **Format Data Series** task pane, click on *Border* (below the **Fill** section).

   e. Under **Border**, click on *Solid Line*.

   f. Click on the down arrow to the right of **Color** (in the **Border** section). Select **Black, Text 1**.

   g. Change the width to **2.0** pt.

   h. Close the **Format Data Series** task pane.

11. Click on the **Saturday and Sunday Revenues** tab.

12. Click on the chart in a blank area in the upper right or left corner.

   a. Click on the *Change Chart Type* button. In the left panel, on the **All Charts** tab, select *Column*. Then select *3-D Clustered Column* chart (fourth chart on the left above the two Clustered Column charts displayed). Click **OK**.

   b. Select the **Chart Title**. Apply *WordArt* Fill: **Orange, Accent color 1; Shadow** (*Chart Tools, Format* tab, *WordArt Styles* group). Resize *WordArt* text to size **28** pt. and **bold** text.

   c. Select the **Legend**. Resize the legend font to size **16** pt**. Bold** text (Home tab, *Font* group).

   d. Select the **X** axis. Resize the **X** axis font to size **11** pt.

   e. Select the **Y** axis. Resize the **Y** axis font to size **11** pt.

13. Save and close the workbook (Figure 10-142).

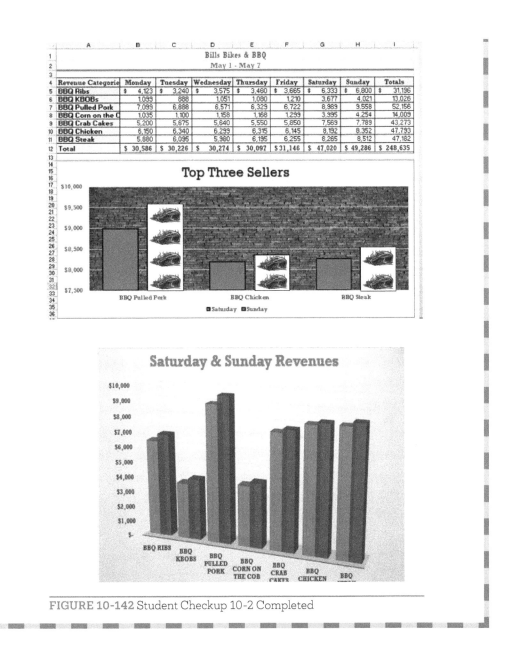

Revenue Categorie	Monday	Tuesday	Wednesday	Thursday	Friday	Saturday	Sunday	Totals
BBQ Ribs	$ 4,123	$ 3,240	$ 3,575	$ 3,460	$ 3,665	$ 6,333	$ 6,800	$ 31,196
BBQ KBOBs	1,099	688	1,051	1,080	1,210	3,677	4,021	13,026
BBQ Pulled Pork	7,099	6,888	6,571	6,329	6,722	8,989	9,558	52,156
BBQ Corn on the C	1,035	1,100	1,158	1,168	1,299	3,995	4,254	14,009
BBQ Crab Cakes	5,200	5,675	5,640	5,550	5,850	7,569	7,789	43,273
BBQ Chicken	6,150	6,340	6,299	6,315	6,145	8,192	8,352	47,793
BBQ Steak	5,880	6,095	5,980	6,195	6,255	8,265	8,512	47,182
Total	$ 30,586	$ 30,226	$ 30,274	$ 30,097	$ 31,146	$ 47,020	$ 49,286	$ 248,635

FIGURE 10-142 Student Checkup 10-2 Completed

6. Creating Pie and Combination Charts

Create and Design a 3-D Pie Chart, Doughnut Charts, and Funnel Charts

In a pie chart, the entire pie represents 100%. Each slice of pie represents a percentage of the whole. Perhaps you have a slice each of apple, cherry, blueberry, pumpkin, lemon meringue, and banana crème. All of these together represent your entire pie. Each slice of the pie can be a different percentage of the pie, but all together the pieces must add up to 100%. When working with a pie chart, each slice of the pie is a series. Pie slices are identified by **category**, and the percentages represent the total of a **series**. Note: When working with pie charts, limit the number of categories because a pie chart with a large number of slices is more difficult to interpret. In other words, *less is more*.

1. Prior to building the pie chart for College Coffee, complete the following steps:
   a. Click in cell **G4**. Type in Totals. Press **Enter.**
   b. In cell **G5,** double-click on the **AutoSum** button (Home tab/*Editing* group).
   c. Autofill through cell **G10**.
   d. Click in cell **F11**. Autofill through cell **G11**.
   e. Click on cell **A1**. Click on **Merge & Center**. This will unmerge your cells.
   f. While still in cell **A1**, select across through cell **G1**.
   g. Click on **Merge & Center**. This will re-merge your cells.
   h. Click on cell **A2**. Click on **Merge & Center**. This will unmerge your cells.
      i. While still in cell **A2**, select across through cell **G2**.
      ii. Click on **Merge & Center**. This will re-merge your cells.
   i. If you are missing your blue line in **A2**, click on **Cell Styles** on your Home tab and reselect **Heading 1**.
   j. Now you are ready to build a pie chart! ☺

Revenue Categories	Sunday	Tuesday	Wednesday	Thursday	Totals
College Coffee					
Mar 1 - Mar 7					
Caramel Latte (Small)	121	125	111	133	592
Caramel Latte (Large)	155	176	184	167	882
Chai Tea (Small)	92	77	79	88	421
Chai Tea (Large)	31	36	35	34	171
Espresso (Small)	12	22	21	25	100
Espresso (Large)	16	18	17	20	92
Total	$ 427	$ 454	$ 447	$ 467	$ 2,258

FIGURE 10-143 Selecting Non-Adjacent Ranges for a Pie Chart

2. Here are the steps to build a pie chart: You will be working with categories and series totals.
   a. Select range **A4:A10**. Press and hold down the **Ctrl** Key. Select range **G4:G10** (Figure 10-143).
   b. Click on the *Insert tab*.
   c. Click on the down arrow next to the **Pie** chart icon (*Insert tab*, *Charts* group).
   d. Select **3-D Pie** option.
      i. Excel will display your pie chart (Figure 10-144).
      ii. Click the ***Move Chart*** button (Chart Tools, Design tab, *Location* group).
      iii. Click the ***New Sheet*** button.

iv. Type in Revenue Pie Chart for the chart sheet.

v. Click **OK.** You will notice you now have two tabs in your workbook.

3. To

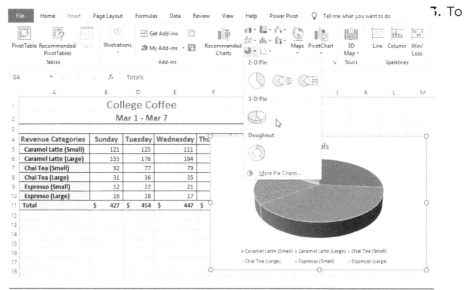

FIGURE 10-144 Pie Chart

make a **Doughnut** chart, follow the steps above for a pie chart. On step 4, select **Doughnut** chart instead of 3-D Pie chart (Figure 10-145a).

4. To make a **Funnel** chart, follow the steps above for a pie chart. On step 3, select **Funnel** chart instead of **3-D Pie** Chart. You will find the **Funnel** chart on the *Insert tab/Charts* group/*Insert Waterfall, Funnel, Stock, Surface or Radar chart* (Figure 10-145b).

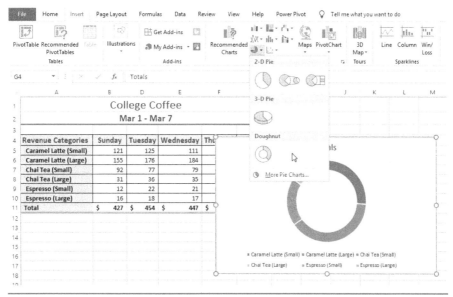

FIGURE 10-145A Doughnut Chart

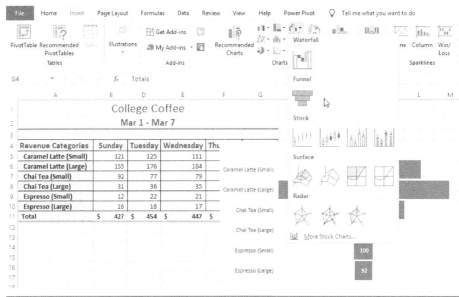

FIGURE 10-145B Funnel Chart

Pie Chart Elements and Options

Sometimes when you create a pie chart, you need to rotate it so that a particular piece shows up in the front of the pie. Other times, you may need to emphasize or promote one piece over the other pieces in a pie. This causes the piece to move away from the pie; however, the pie chart itself shrinks.

To rotate a **Pie Chart**:

1. Click in the center of the pie to select the entire pie.
   a. The **Format Data Series** task pane opens.
2. Click the *Series Options* button (this will be the green column chart icon).
3. Drag the vertical slider to set the *Angle of First Slice*.
4. The percentage is shown in the entry box.
5. You can also type in a percentage or use the spinner arrows to set a value. In this case, type in **110**, or you can use the Angle of First Slice slider or the up and down arrows.

To explode a pie slice:

1. Click the slice (data point) you want to explode. <u>Best practice</u>: Click in the center of the pie and then click in the slice.
2. The Format Data Point task pane opens.
3. Drag the vertical slider to set the Pie Explosion.
4. The percentage is shown in the entry box.
5. You can type in a percentage or use the spinner arrows to set a value. In this case, type in **30**, or use the Point Explosion slider or the up and down arrows.

6. The larger the percentage, the farther the slice is from the rest of your pie. Usually a percentage around 30% to 40% looks more professional (Figure 10-146).

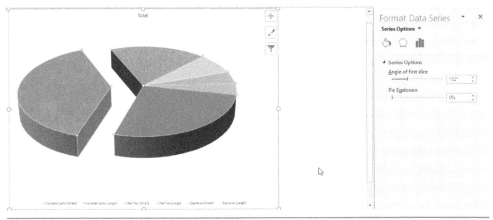

FIGURE 10-146 Angle of First Slice Change with Exploded Pie Slice

To explode the entire pie:

1. Click in the center of the pie.
   a. Drag the vertical slider to set the Pie Explosion.
2. The percentage is shown in the entry box.
   a. You can type in a percentage or use the spinner arrows to set a value. In this case, type in **30**, or use the Point Explosion slider or the up and down arrows.
   b. The larger the percentage, the greater the distance between all pie slices. Usually a percentage around 30% to 40% looks more professional (Figure 10-147).

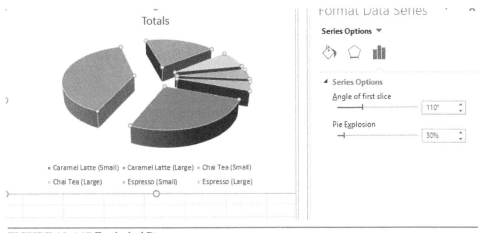

FIGURE 10-147 Exploded Pie

To rotate a doughnut chart and to explode the doughnut, do the following:

1. Select the doughnut.
   a. Double-click the doughnut piece shape.
2. The **Format Data Series** task pane opens.
   a. Or, you can right-click on a doughnut piece and choose **Format Data Series**.
2. Click the ***Series Options*** button.
3. Drag the vertical slider to set the *Angle of First Slice*.
4. The percentage is shown in the entry box.
5. You can also type in a percentage or use the spinner arrows to set a value.
6. Drag the vertical slider to set the **Doughnut Explosion**. The entire doughnut will explode. *You will not be able to explode only one piece as you can in a pie chart.*
7. The percentage is shown in the entry box.
8. You can type in a percentage or use the spinner arrows to set a value.
9. The larger the percentage, the farther the pieces are blown apart.
10. Usually a percentage around 30% to 40% looks more professional.
11. Drag the horizontal slider to set **Doughnut Hole** size.
12. You can type in a percentage or use the spinner arrows to set a value.
13. The larger the percentage, the larger the doughnut hole.
14. Usually a percentage around 40% to 60% looks more professional (Figure 10-148).

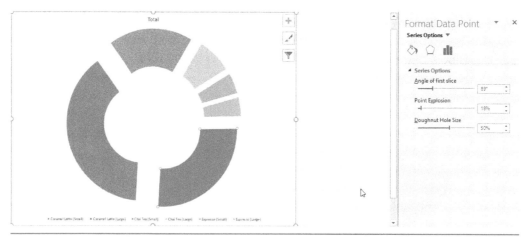

FIGURE 10-148 Doughnut Exploded

Create a Combination Chart

A combination chart is a combination of two chart types, such as a line chart and a column chart. Its purpose is to compare unlike items. Best practices for this type of chart is to keep the number of series low because too many data series complicate what your audience sees. The College Coffee Shop can use a combination chart to compare revenue from a small caramel latte to total revenue. To focus on the comparison, one series is shown as a line and the other as a column. The line and column combination is the most common. However, you can use a line and an area combination.

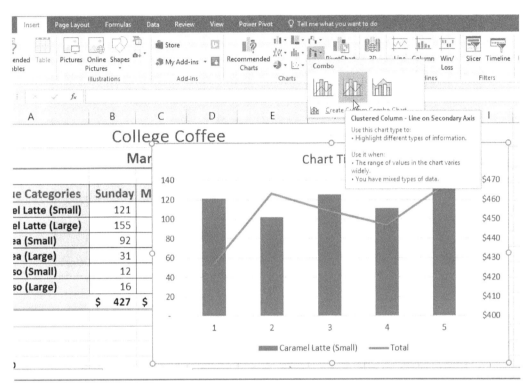

FIGURE 10-149 Combo Chart

Here is how to create a Combination (Combo) chart:

1. Select the cell ranges **A5:E5** and **A11:E11** for the chart. The cell ranges need not be contiguous. In this example, the Small Caramel Latte revenue for Sunday through Thursday is compared to the total revenue for Sunday through Thursday.
2. Click the Insert **Combo Chart** button (*Insert tab*, *Charts* group).
3. Excel will display suggested combinations.
    a. Point to one of the suggested combinations to see a description and a *Live Preview*.
2. Select the chart subtype.
3. A combo chart object displays in the worksheet (Figure 10-149).
    a. If desired, you can move the chart to its own sheet.

You can use several series to compare to the Total in a combination chart. As explained above, the more data series used to compare to the total will tend to make the chart more complicated. As an example, the chart shown in Figure 10-150 depicts *Caramel Latte (Large), Chai Tea (Large)*, and *Espresso (Large)* compared to the *Total*. This chart is beginning to look a bit complicated.

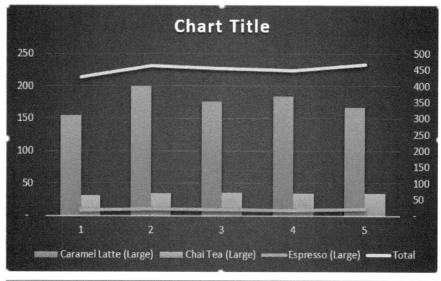

FIGURE 10-150 Multi-Series Combo Chart

Create a Treemap Chart

A Treemap chart represents a way to show how certain items contribute to a revenue stream which enables an individual or business to determine the larger and smaller revenue streams. Each item is represented as a block, with the larger revenue stream as a larger box and smaller revenue streams as smaller blocks. This allows you to decide what your more profitable items are versus your least profitable items. This provides a way to make solid business decisions about whether a product should be promoted or discontinued. Many restaurants, retail stores, supermarkets, etc., use this type of chart to sort out sales winners and sales losers.

To create a Treemap chart, do the following:

1. Select the cell range **A5:E10**.
2. Click on the **Insert tab**. Then choose the **Insert Hierarchy chart** button. Click on the down arrow. Select **Treemap** (Figure 10-151).
3. Move chart to its own sheet. Click on the **Move Chart** button (*Chart Tools/ Design/Location/Move Chart*). Name the sheet **Treemap Chart**.

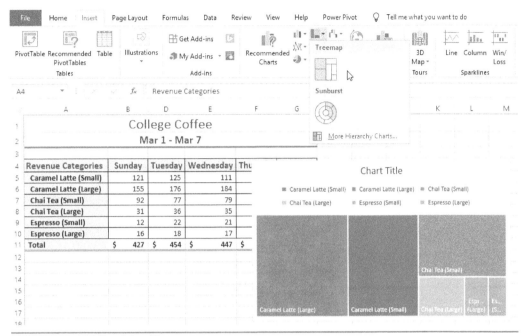
FIGURE 10-151 TreeMap Chart

4. Click on **Quick Layout**. Select **Quick Layout 5** (*Chart Tools, Design, Chart Layouts, Quick Layout*).
5. Click on one of the data labels in one of the boxes, (e.g., *Chai Tea [Small]*). This will select all data labels. Resize font size to **12** pt. **Bold** text.
6. Click on the **Chart Title**. Change *chart title* to be **Revenue Streams,** then press **Enter**, then type **Mar 1–Mar 7**.
7. Resize chart title font to size **28** pt. font. **Bold** text.
8. Click on **Legend**. Delete **Legend**.
9. Click on **Chart Style 7**.
10. Click in the white area in the upper right hand of your chart (but not on the line). Add a black border around your chart. (*Chart Tools* tab, *Format* tab, *Shape Styles* group, *Shape Outline*). See Figure 10-152.

At a glance, this chart shows you that the Caramel Lattes are the best sellers, and the Espresso drinks are the worst best sellers. It also shows that the small Chai Teas significantly outsell the large Chai Teas.

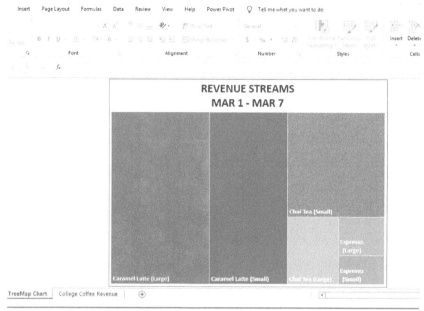

FIGURE 10-152 Revenue Stream TreeMap Chart

7. Creating Sparkline Charts

Sparklines are miniature charts created in a cell or a cell range. These miniature charts are useful when you do not want to add a separate chart object or sheet. A **Sparkline** chart is an embedded chart created from a selected data range and placed in a location range, usually adjacent to the data.

Sparkline Styles

There are three different Sparkline types: *Line, Column*, and *Win/Loss*. Once you create a Sparkline, a new tab will appear above the Ribbon called **Sparkline Tools/Design** tab (Figure 10-153).

FIGURE 10-153 Sparkline Tools Tab

In the *Type* group, you will notice the three different types of Sparklines. You can easily change the type of Sparkline chart by clicking on one of these. In this instance, you can see a Column Sparkline chart was created. You can quickly change to a Line or a Win/Loss type.

In the *Show* group, you can have the charts show the *High Point, Low Point, Negative Points, First Point,* and *Last Point*. The default color for these choices is red. For the Column Sparkline charts, you will notice that you will not be able to click on the **Markers** box. This box is used for the **Line** Sparkline charts.

In the *Style* group, you can click on the **More** button and you will have thirty-six options for each of the three types of Sparkline charts. To the right of the **Sparkline Style** gallery is another button that you can use to change your Sparkline color to a color not listed in the thirty-six options and also to choose the line weight (thickness) for your Sparkline. Finally, below that button, you will see the ***Marker*** button. A **marker** for a Sparkline is the data point value. This button allows you to select *High points, Low points, First Points, Last Points,* and *Negative Points.* Each one will allow you to select a different color to create emphasis.

In the *Group* group, you have the options to change *Horizontal* and *Vertical Axis* values. This is not commonly used. To the right of the ***Axis*** button, you have the option to *Group/Ungroup* and then *Clear.* You can clear selected Sparkline or clear a selected Sparkline group.

To create a **Sparkline** chart in a worksheet:

1. In the **College Coffee** worksheet, insert a blank column between columns **F** and **G**.
2. Select the cell range **A5:F10** as data to be graphed.
3. Click the ***Column Sparkline*** button (*Insert tab/Sparklines* group).
4. A **Create Sparklines** dialog box will pop up. In the **Data Range** box, the information you see confirms your data range you want to use for the Sparklines. The second box is where you want your **Sparklines** to go. In this case, we want the **Sparkline** charts to appear in the range **G5:G10.** Click **OK.** See Figure 10-154.

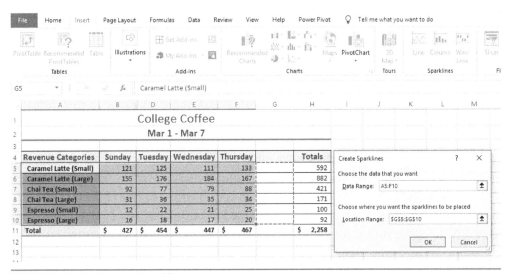

FIGURE 10-154 Create Sparklines

5. At this point, you can determine what type of **Sparkline** chart you want. Also, in the following figure, I have changed the *row height* of rows **5-10** from **15** pt. to **24** pt.
6. In the *Show* box, I clicked on the **High Point** box, and the program changed the high column in each Sparkline to red (*Sparkline Tools, Design* tab, *Show* group, *High Point*). See Figure 10-155.

Feel free to experiment with colors, markers, **Sparkline** chart types, etc. For instance, the Caramel Latte (Large)—the best seller—actually had the highest sales on Wednesday; however, the Chai Tea (Small)—the next best seller—had its highest sales on Monday.

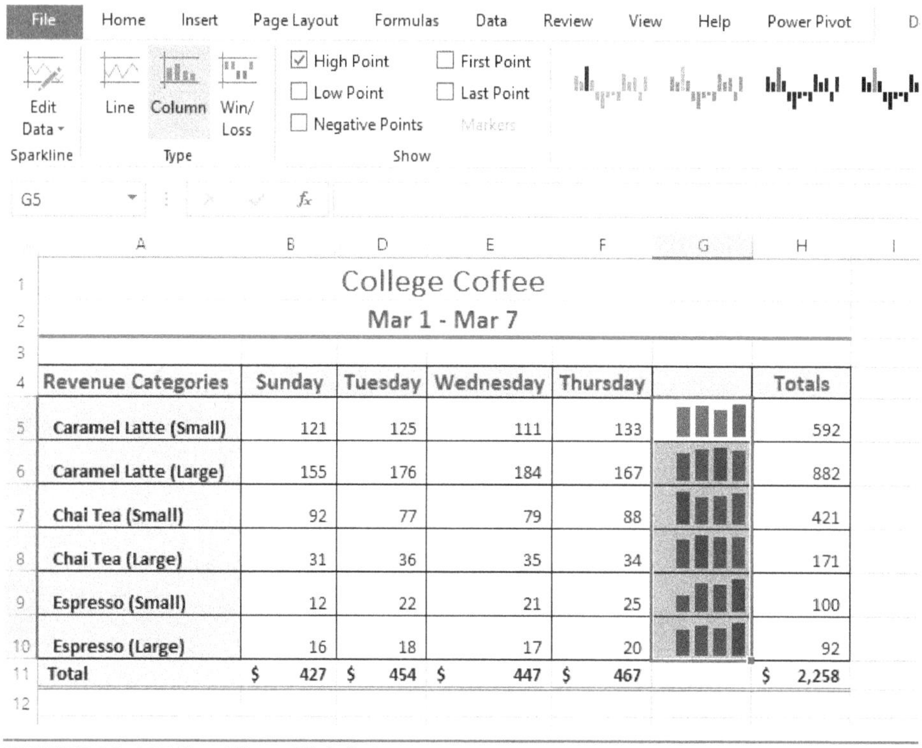

FIGURE 10-155 Sparklines High Point

If you wish to clear your **Sparklines**, click on the eraser in the *Group* Group. You can choose between deleting *Selected Sparklines* or *Selected Sparkline Groups*. What is the difference? If you choose *Selected Sparklines*, you can choose your specific coffees/teas, such as Caramel Latte (Small), Chai Tea (Large), Espresso (Small), and Espresso (Large). Be sure to hold down your **CTRL** key when selecting your adjacent and nonadjacent **Sparklines**. Or if you prefer to clear them all, then you can click on ***Selected Sparkline Groups***. If you clear them all, be sure to delete the column and change the row heights back to the original heights if necessary.

In this project, you will open an existing workbook for Bill's Bikes and BBQ. You will create a pie chart to show the proportion of each revenue category. You will also insert a combination chart sheet to compare the sales of Pulled Pork BBQ Monday through Friday with Total Revenue. Finally, you will format the charts for enhanced visual appeal. **Note: Blue text represents typed text.**

File Needed: **(Your Initials) Student Checkup Excel 10-2**

Completed File Name: **(Your initials) Student Checkup Excel 10-3**

1. Open **(Your Initials) Student Checkup Excel 10-2**. Save as **(Your Initials) Student Checkup Excel 10-3.**
    a. Create a 3-D pie chart.
2. Create a **3D**- pie chart.
    a. On the **Restaurant Revenue** tab, select nonadjacent ranges **A4:A11** and **I4:I11**.
    b. Click on the **Insert** tab and then click on the drop-down arrow next to the pie chart (**Insert** tab, **C**harts group).

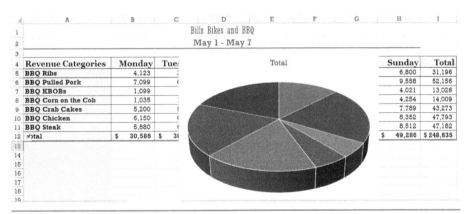

FIGURE 10-156 Pie Chart

    c. Click on **3-D** pie (Figure 10-156).
    d. Move the pie chart to its own sheet. Click on the **Move Chart** button (**Chart Tools**, **Design** tab, **Location** group).
    e. Once the **Move Chart** dialog box opens, click on the **New Sheet** radio button. In the box, type in **Total Revenue Pie Chart**.
    f. Click on **Chart Style 2** (**Chart Tools**, **Design** tab, **Chart Styles** group).

g. Triple-click on the **Title** element. Type in **TOTAL REVENUE.** Resize font to size **24** pt. Close the **Format Chart Title** task pane.

h. Right-click in the upper left or right corner of the chart. Left-click on **Format Chart Area**. If necessary, click on the Fill (the bucket).

i. Click on *Gradient Fill*. Keep the default gradient fill (Figure 10-157).

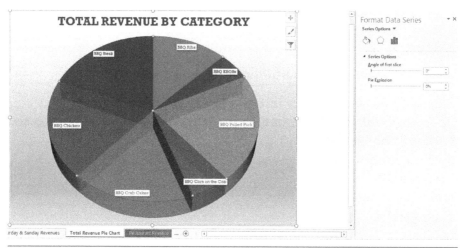

FIGURE 10-157 Pie Chart with Default Labels

j. Click in the center of the pie to select the entire pie. Click on the green plus sign in the upper right of the chart. Move your mouse over to the arrow to the right of **Data Labels**. Click on the arrow. Then click on **Data Callout** (Figure 10-158).

k. Click on one of your labels. Resize the font to size **14** pt. and **bold** text.

l. Then click on *More Options ...* (under **Data Callout**). Under the **Label Options** area, click in the **Percentage** check box, if unchecked. Make

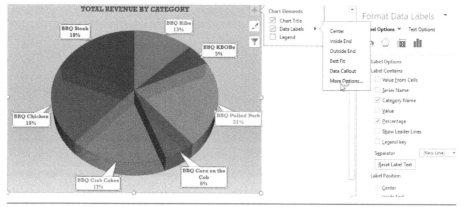

FIGURE 10-158 Pie Chart with Callout Labels

sure that only the **Category Name** and **Percentage** check boxes are checked (Figure 10-158). <u>Note</u>: If a chart requires numbers, such as dollar figures, you will place a check in the **Values** checkbox instead of **Percentage** (Figure 10-158).

m. Click in the center of the pie to select all slices.

n. In the Format Data Series dialog box, click on the **Series Options** button (it looks like a column chart) (Figure 10-159).

   i. Under Series Options, change the *Angle of First Slice* to **30** degrees.

   ii. Click on the **Pulled Pork BBQ** slice (you may have to click on it twice. Just make sure that only the BBQ Pulled Pork slice has the circles around it).

   iii. Change the **Point Explosion** to **35%.**

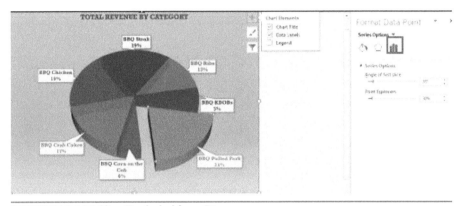

FIGURE 10-159 Slice Exploded from Pie

o. Close the **Format Data Point** pane.

p. Right-click in a blank area in the upper left or right corner of your chart.

q. Left-click on **Format Chart Area** to open the task pane.

r. Make sure the *bucket* is selected.

s. Scroll down to the bottom of the pane. You will see **Border**. Left-click on **Border**. You will need to scroll down again to see the items under **Border**.

t. Under **Border**, click on **Solid Line**.

u. Next to color, click on the down arrow next to the *bucket*. Select **Dark Red, Accent 2** (First row, 6th color).

v. Close the **Format Chart Area** task pane.

3. Create a Combination Chart. In this chart, you will compare **the BBQ Pulled Pork** and **BBQ Crab Cakes** series to the **Total**.

   a. On the **Restaurant Revenue** sheet, select nonadjacent ranges **A7:H7**, **A9:H9**, and **A12:H12**. Select the first range, hold down your **CTRL** key, and then select the second range and the third range. Once you have selected the third range, you can let go of the **CTRL** key.

   b. Click on the *Insert tab*. In the *Charts* group, click on the down arrow next to the **Combo Chart** button.

   c. Click on the second option (*Clustered Column—Line on Secondary Axis*).

   d. Move the combo chart to its own sheet. Click on the ***Move Chart*** button (*Chart Tools, Design* tab, *Location group*).

   e. Once the **Move Chart** dialog box opens, click on the **New Sheet** radial button (**Chart Tools**, **Design** tab, **Location** group). In the box, type **Combo Chart**. Click **OK** to close dialog box.

   f. If not already selected, click on **Chart Style 1** (*Chart Tools, Design* tab, *Chart Styles* group).

   g. Triple-click on the ***Title*** element. Type in **BBQ Pulled Pork & BBQ Crab Cakes**. Press **Enter**. Type in **vs Totals**. Resize font to size **24** pt. Click outside of chart title to deselect it.

   h. Click in the upper left or right corner of the chart. Right-click. Left-click on *Format Chart Area*.

   i. Click on ***Fill***.

   j. Click on Picture or ***Texture Fill*** radio button. Click on the down arrow to the right of the ***Texture*** button. Select the *Stationery* texture (Fourth row down, first option).

   k. Close the **Format Chart Area** task pane.

   l. Click on the **Y** axis.

   m. Resize font to size **14** pt. **Bold** font.

   n. Right-click on the **Y** axis. Left-click on ***Format Axis*** on the shortcut menu.

   o. In the **Format Axis** task pane, make sure the **Axis Option** button is selected (green column chart icon), then scroll down to the bottom. Click on ***Number***.

   p. Scroll down. In the Category box under **Number**, click on the down arrow and select **Currency**.

   q. Just below the **Category** box, check to make sure that **0** appears in the **Decimal Places** box, and that the **$** appears in the **Symbol** box below the decimals.

   r. Close the **Format Axis** task pane.

---

s. Click on the **Z** axis. Resize font to size **14** pt. **Bold** font.

t. Select the **Legend** below the chart. Resize font to size **14** pt. **Bold** font.

u. Right-click in a blank area in the upper left or right corner of your chart. Click on **Format Chart Area.**

v. The **Format Chart Area** task pane will appear.

w. Make sure the bucket icon is selected.

x. Scroll down to the bottom of the pane. You will see **Border**. Left-click on *Border*. You will need to scroll down again to see the items under **Border**.

y. Under **Border**, click on *Solid Line*. Next to color, click on the down arrow next to the *bucket*. Select **Black, Text 1** (First row, 2nd color).

z. Close the **Format Chart Area** task pane.

4. **Save** and close the **workbook** (Figure 10-160).

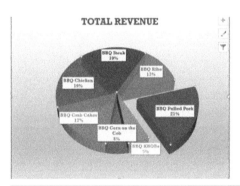 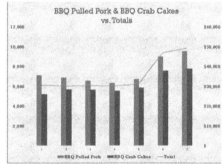

FIGURE 10-160 Student Checkup Excel 10-3 Completed

Excel Project 10-1

Sam of Sam's Sub Shoppe has a request for you to create some charts for his business. He was very impressed with the workbook you had created in Excel Part 1. He would like you to create a column chart to track his expenses for his sub sandwiches that includes meat, cheeses, veggies, and bread. Additionally, he would like you to add a linear trendline to help him project his future meat expenses. Finally, he would like you to create a bar chart to track expenses for his miscellaneous items. **Note: Blue text represents typed text.**

File Needed: **(Your Initials) Excel Project 9-1.xlsx**

Completed File Name: **(Your Initials) Excel Project 10-1.xlsx**

1. Open *(Your Initials) Excel Project 9-1.xlsx*. Rename as **(Your Initials) Excel Project 10-1.xlsx.**
2. Create a **2-D Column** chart.
   a. Select range **A4:E12**.
   b. Click on the *Insert tab*.
   c. Click on the **More** button (down arrow on the right side of the **Column** chart button) (*Insert tab*, *Charts* group).
   d. Select the first *2-D Column* option.
   e. Click in the upper left corner of the chart. Move the upper left corner of the chart to cell **A16**.
   f. Using the middle right handle in the chart, stretch the chart through column **F**.
   g. Click on the **Switch Row/Column** button (*Chart Tools, Design* tab, *Data* group).
   h. In the **Chart Styles** group, select chart style 8. It will have a dark charcoal color background.
   i. Click on the X-Axis and click on **Bold**.
   j. Click on the Y-Axis and click on **Bold**.
   k. Click on the Legend and click on **Bold**.
   l. Triple-click on the chart title. Rename chart title as **Weeks 1–4 Expenses**. Click outside the title to deselect it.
   m. Filter the source data.
      i. Click in a blank area in your chart.
      ii. Click on the **Chart Filters** button (funnel) in the top right corner of the chart. <u>Note</u>: you must be in **Normal** view for the filter, paint brush, and green cross buttons to appear.
      iii. Under **Series**, de-select the following items: *Condiments, Soft Drinks & Waters, Chips,* and *Brownies*. You should only have check marks next to *Meats, Cheeses, Veggies,* and *Bread*. Click on **Apply** (Figure 10-161).
3. Insert a **Trendline**.
   a. Click on one of the **Meats** series (blue bars).
   b. Click on **Add Chart Element** (*Chart Tools, Design* tab, *Chart Layouts* group).
   c. Click on **Trendline**.
   d. Click on **Linear**.

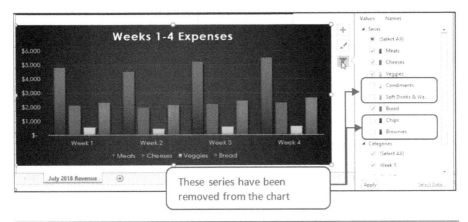

FIGURE 10-161 Chart Filters Applied

    e. Right-click on your trendline.

       i. Click on **Format Trendline.**

      ii. In the **Format Trendline** task pane, click on the bucket.

     iii. In the **Insert Trendline** task pane, under the **Trendline Options**, click on the **Fill & Line** icon (bucket). Under **Line**, click on **Solid Line**.

     iv. Next to the **Colo**r icon, click on the down arrow to the right. Click on **Light Turquoise, Background 2** (first row, third color).

      v. Close the **Format Trendline** task pane.

Note: You can only insert a trendline in a **2-D** chart.

4. Insert a **Bar Chart**.

    a. Select range **A4:E12**.

    b. Click on the *Insert tab*.

    c. Click on the ***More*** button (down arrow on the right side of the ***Column*** chart button) (*Insert tab*, *Charts* group).

    d. Select the first *3-D Bar* option.

    e. **Move Chart** to a new sheet (*Chart Tools, Design* tab, *Location* group).

    f. Click on the ***New Sheet*** radio button. Type in **Bar Chart** in the box. Click on **OK**.

5. Insert a **Quick Layout** for your chart.

    a. Click to select your chart object if necessary.

    b. Click on the ***Quick Layout*** button (*Chart Tools, Design* tab, *Chart Layouts* group).

    c. Click on **Layout 5**. You should have a chart with a data table.

    d. Right-click in the upper right-hand corner of your chart. On the short-cut menu, click on **Format Chart Area** (second from the bottom).

e. When the **Format Chart Area** task pane opens, click on **Fill** and then click on **Gradient Fill**. Use the default color (in other words, the color that appears once you click on **Gradient Fill** should be shades of blue).

f. Click on the **X** axis. Change the font size to **12** pt. and apply **Bold** (*Home* tab, *Font* group). Change the font color to **Black, Text 1**.

   i. If you do not have a **"$"** on your X-axis, right-click on your X-axis. Next, click on **Format Axis**. Make sure the **Axis Options** button is selected (green column chart).

   ii. Scroll down to **Number**. Scroll down to the drop down box below **Category**. Click on the down arrow and select **Currency**. Make sure you have no decimals and the "$" shows in the **Symbol** drop down box.

g. Click on the **Y** axis. Change the font size to **12** pt. and apply **Bold** (*Home* tab, *Font* group). Change the font color to **Black, Text 1**.

h. Click in the *Data Table*. Change the font size to **12** pt. and apply **Bold** (*Home* tab, *Font* group). Change the font color to **Black, Text 1**.

i. Click in the data portion of your chart.

   i. Change the font size to **12** pt. and apply **Bold**.

   ii. Change the font color to **Black, Text 1**.

   iii. In the **Format Data Table** pane, click on **Solid Line** under **Border**. Then change the border color to **White Background**.

j. Note: If you are using Microsoft 365, you may not be able to click in the data table. Instead, you will have to go to *Chart Tools/Format* tab/*Current Selection* and change the selection to Data table.

k. Close the Format Data Table task pane.

6. Triple-click on the chart title. Rename chart title as **Miscellaneous Items**.

   a. Add **WordArt** to the Title.

      i. Click on **Fill: Dark Purple, Accent Color 2, Outline: Dark Purple Accent 2** (*Chart Tools, Format* tab, **WordAr**t group).

      ii. Resize chart title font to size **28** pt. (you may need to reselect the title).

      iii. Click outside the title to deselect it. (Figure 10-162).

      iv. Close the Format Chart Title task pane.

7. Click in a blank corner of your chart and click on the **Switch Row/Column** button (*Chart Tools*, *Design* tab, *Data* group).

8. Filter the source data.
   a. Click the column chart object.
   b. Click on the **Chart Filters** button in the top right corner of the chart.
   c. Deselect the following **categories**: *Meats, Cheeses, Veggies, Condiments*, and *Bread*.
   d. Click on **Apply**. If you chart does not look like Figure 10-163, then go to the Chart Tools, Design tab and click on the **Switch Row/Column** button again in the *Data* group.
9. Right-click in one of the **Soft Drinks & Waters** bars.
   a. Click on the **Format Data Series menu item**.
      i. When the Format Data Series task pane appears, click on the **Bucket** button.
      ii. If necessary, click on **Fill**.
      iii. Click on **Picture** or **Texture Fill** radio button.
      iv. Under **Picture Source**, click on **Insert**.
      v. In the **Insert Pictures** dialog box, select **Online Pictures**.
      vi. Type in Soda Bottles. Press **Enter**.
      vii. Select your picture. Click on it then click on **Enter**.
      viii. In the *Format Data Series* pane, scroll down and click on **Stack**.
      ix. Close *the Format Data Series* task pane.
10. Save and close your workbook. Turn in the assignment. Figure 10-164 shows the completed assignment.

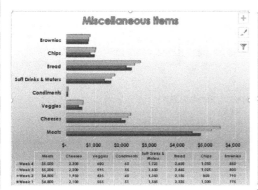

FIGURE 10-162 Bar Chart

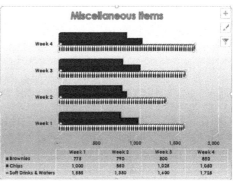

FIGURE 10-163 Switched Bar Chart

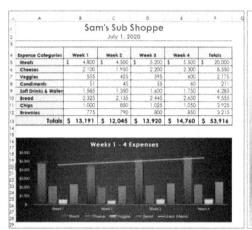
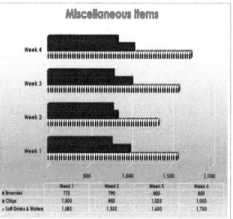

FIGURE 10-164 Excel Project 10-1 Completed

Excel Project 10-2

Patrick's Planes, Trains, and Cars would like you to create two charts to reflect sales for January through June 2020. Your tasks will include creating a 3-D Column chart to show sales for Model Planes, Model Trains, and Model Cars. Additionally, Patrick would like you to create and format a 3-D pie chart showing and comparing sales of parts and accessories. Finally, Patrick would like you to build and format a TreeMap chart showing Patrick his best-selling items and least best-selling items. **Note: Blue text represents typed text.**

File Needed: **(Your Initials) Excel Project 9-2.xlsx**

Completed File Name: **(Your Initials) Excel Project 10-2.xlsx**

1. Open **(Your Initials) Excel Project 9-2.xlsx** from your student data files. If the workbook has opened in Protected View, click Enable Editing in the yellow security bar.
2. Save the workbook as **(Your Initials) Excel Project 10-2**.
3. Create a **3-D Column** chart object.
   a. Select range **A4:G13**.
   b. Click on the *Insert tab*.
   c. Click on the **More** button (down arrow on the right side of the **Column chart** button) (*Insert tab, Charts* group).
   d. Select the first **3-D Column** option.

e. Click in the upper left corner of the chart. Move the upper left corner of the chart to cell **A16**.
f. Using the lower right corner handle in the chart, stretch the chart through column **H** and **row 34**.
g. Click on **the Switch Row/Column** button (*Chart Tools, Design* tab, *Data* group).
h. Select **Chart Style 3**. It has a silver background.
i. Triple-click on the chart title. Rename chart title as **Patrick's Trains, Planes & Cars**. Press **Enter**. Type **January–June 2025 Monthly Sales**. Resize chart title font size to **14**. Click outside the title to deselect it. Close the **Format Chart Area** task pane.
j. Filter the source data.
    i. Click in the upper right corner of your column chart.
    ii. Click on the **Chart Filters** button outside the middle right of the chart.
    iii. Deselect the following series: *Model Plane Parts, Model Plane Accessories, Model Train Parts, Model Train Accessories, Model Car Parts*, and *Model Car Accessories*.
    iv. Click on **Apply.** You should only have three series remaining: *Model Planes, Model Trains*, and *Model Cars*.
k. Click on the **X** axis. Resize font to size **10** pt. Apply **Bold**.
l. Click on the **Y** axis. Resize font to size **12** pt. Apply **Bold**.
m. Click on the **Legend**. Resize font to size **10** pt. Apply **Bold**.
n. Add a solid border around the entire chart. Use **Black, Text 1**. Change border width to **1.5** pt. (*Chart Tools, Format tab, Shape Styles group, Shape Outline*) (Figure 10-165).
o. Close the **Format Chart Area** task pane.

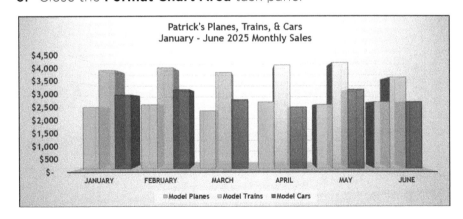

FIGURE 10-165 3D Column Chart

4. Prepare to create a **Funnel** chart.

    a. Before you create your Funnel chart, you will need to sort your data to get the actual funnel. Otherwise, you will get a chart with different sized horizontal bars that won't represent a funnel at all!

        i. Select range **A4:H13**.

        ii. Go to Home tab/*Editing* group. Click on **Sort & Filter**.

        iii. Click on ***Custom Sort***.

        iv. In the upper right of the **Sort** window, make sure the **My data has headers** check box is checked.

        v. In the **Sort** window, click on the down arrow in the **Sort by** box under **Column**.

        vi. Click on ***Total***. Then click ***OK*** (Figure 10-166). You won't need to change the **Sort On box** (should have **Cell Values** in it), but you will need to change the **Order** box to **Largest to Smallest**. <u>Note</u>: **Order** in the **Sort** box defaults to **Smallest to Largest**. This selection will make the horizontal bars in your Funnel chart appear smallest on top and larger on the bottom (Figure 10-167). To make the horizontal bars in your Funnel chart appear as largest on top and smallest on the bottom, click on the down arrow under Order to change it to **Largest to Smallest** (Figure 10-168). You will notice your column chart has changed. That is okay.

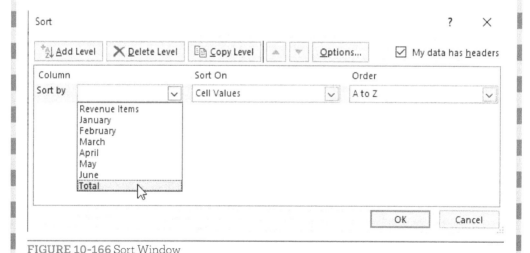

FIGURE 10-166 Sort Window

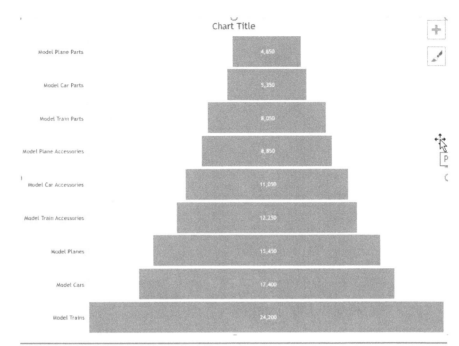

FIGURE 10-167 Funnel Chart Smallest to Largest

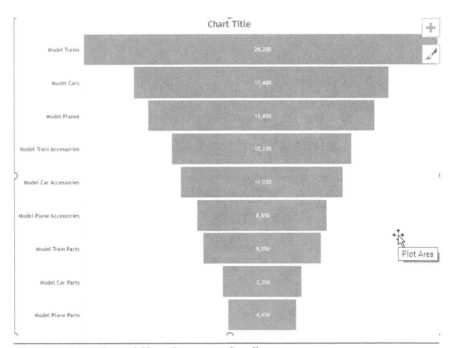

FIGURE 10-168 Funnel Chart Largest to Smallest

2. Select nonadjacent ranges **A4:A13** and **H4:H13**.

    i. Insert a **Funnel** chart (*Insert tab/Charts* group/Insert *Waterfall, Funnel, Stock, Surface* or *Radar* chart).

    ii. Move your Funnel chart to a **New Sheet** (*Chart Tools, Design* tab/*Location* group).

    iii. Click in the ***New Sheet*** radio button. Type in **Funnel Chart.**

    iv. In the **Chart Styles** group, click on **Style 6** (*Chart Tools, Design* tab/*Chart Style* group).

    v. Triple-click in the **Title**. Change the title to **Patrick's Trains, Planes, and Cars**. Press **Enter**. On the second line of the title, type **Totals**.

    vi. Resize the title font to size **20** pt. Click outside the title in a blank chart area.

c. Click on the **Y** axis.

    i. Resize font to size **12** and **bold**.

    ii. Click on the label (value) in one of the horizontal bars. Resize font to size **20** and **bold**.

    iii. Right click on one of the labels. Select **Format Data Label**.

    iv. Click on ***Label Options*** (the green column chart icon).

    v. Click on ***Number***.

d. Under **Category**, click on the down arrow and select **Currency**. Make sure that "**0**" shows in **the Decimal places** box, and a "**$**" in the **Symbol** box.

    i. Close the Format Data Labels task pane.

    ii. Click on the **Legend (Total)** and press **Delete** (Figure 10-169).

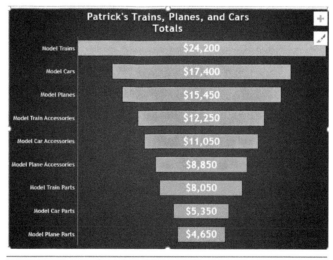

FIGURE 10-169 Completed Funnel Chart

3. Create a **Treemap Chart**.
    a. On the **January–June 2025** worksheet, select range **A4:H13**.
    b. Click on the *Insert tab*.
    c. Click on the down arrow next to the *Insert Hierarchy Chart* button.
    d. Click on *Treemap*.
    e. Click on *Move Chart* (*Chart Tools, Design* tab, *Location* group).
    f. In the **Move Chart** dialog box, click on the *New Sheet radio* button.
    g. Type in Treemap Chart.
    h. Change **Chart Style**.
    i. Select **Chart Style 6**.
    j. Insert a **Quick Layout** for your chart.
        i. Click to select your chart object if necessary.
        ii. Click on the *Quick Layout* button (*Chart Tools, Design* tab, *Chart Layouts* group). Click on **Layout 2**.

FIGURE 10-170 Treemap Chart

    k. Triple-click on your chart title. Change it to **January–June 2025 Revenue Streams**.
       Add **WordArt** to the chart title.
        i. Click on *Fill: Aqua, Accent color 4; Soft Bevel*.

l. Resize *Chart Title* to size **28** pt.

m. Click on one of the data labels. Resize the font to size **14** pt. **Bold** font.

n. Right-click on one of the labels. Left-click on **Format Data Labels** task pane.

o. Click on **More Data Label Options ...**

p. In the Format Data Labels task pane, click on the **Label Options** icon (green column chart).

q. Click on **Label Options**.

r. Under the **Label Contains area**, select the **Category** name and **Value**. Make sure the **Series Name** box is <u>not</u> selected (Figure 10-170).

s. In the **Format Data Labels** pane, scroll down to **Number**. Under **Number**, select **Currency**, **no decimals**, with a "**$**" sign.

t. Close the **Format Data Label** task pane.

u. **Save** and close your workbook. Turn in your assignment. Figure 10-171 is the completed assignment.

Revenue Items	January	February	March	April	May	June	Totals
Model Trains	4,000	4,100	3,900	4,200	4,300	3,700	24,200
Model Cars	3,500	3,600	3,100	3,300	3,500	3,100	20,100
Model Planes	$ 3,000	$ 3,100	$ 2,950	$ 3,200	$ 3,100	$ 3,200	$ 18,550
Model Train Accessories	2,000	2,100	1,900	2,000	2,150	2,100	12,250
Model Car Accessories	2,300	1,100	1,000	2,000	2,100	1,950	11,050
Model Plane Accessories	1,400	1,100	1,500	1,750	1,900	1,200	8,850
Model Train Parts	1,500	1,600	1,300	1,200	1,100	1,350	8,050
Model Car Parts	1,000	900	800	850	1,000	800	5,350
Model Plane Parts	800	850	750	800	700	750	4,650
Totals	$ 20,100	$ 18,450	$ 17,200	$ 19,300	$ 19,850	$ 18,150	$ 113,050

Patrick's Planes, Trains, & Cars
January - June 2025 Monthly Sales

FIGURE 10-171 Excel Project 10-2 Completed

Tony and Guido's Pizzeria would like you to create two charts for them. The first chart will be a column chart showing the biggest sellers for each type of pizza plus a trendline to help them predict sales of their best-selling pizza. Secondly, Tony and Guido would like to see some Sparklines charts to target the best sales days during May for each menu item. In addition, Tony and Guido would like you to create a 3-D pie chart depicting the top sellers. They will make you an offer you can't refuse. **Note: Blue text represents typed text.**

File Needed: **(Your Initials) Excel Project 9-3.xlsx**

Completed File Name: **(Your Initials) Excel Project 10-3.xlsx**

1. Open (**Your Initials**) **Excel Project 9-3.xlsx** from your student data files. If the workbook has opened in Protected View, click Enable Editing in the yellow security bar.
2. Save the workbook as **(Your Initials) Excel Project 10-3.**
3. In range **A6:A10**, add the words **Custom Combo** in front of each pizza size. For example: *Custom Combo Personal size.*
4. In range **A12:A16,** add the words **All Meats** in front of each pizza size. For example: *All Meats Personal size.*
5. In range **A18:A22**, add the words **Queso Grande** in front of each pizza size. For example: *Queso Grande Personal size.*
6. Resize column **A** width to **27** (194 Pixels).
7. Create a *2-D column* chart.
   a. Select ranges **A4:E4**, press and hold down the **Ctrl** key, then select ranges **A6:E10, A12:E16,** and **A18:E22**. Release the **Ctrl** key.
   b. Click on the *Insert tab* and then click on the down arrow next to the **column chart** button.
   c. Select the first chart under **2-D Column**.
   d. If **Week 1, Week 2, Week 3,** and **Week 4** appear in your **Legend**, click on the **Switch Row/Column** button once (*Chart Tools, Desig*n tab, *Data* group). Ensure that **Week 1, Week 2, Week 3,** and **Week 4** appear as your **X** Axis, and all the pizza types should appear as the **Legend**.
   e. Select the chart. Click on the **Chart Filter** (funnel) button. Under **Series**, select **Custom Combo Extra Large, All Meats Extra Large,** and **Queso Grande Extra Large**. Click **Apply**.
   f. Drag the upper left center of the chart to cell **A25**. Click on the lower right handle (circle) of the chart and resize it to extend through column **F** and to the top of row **40**.

8. Format the column chart.

    a. In the *Chart Styles* gallery, select chart style **6**.

    b. Triple-click on the chart title. Rename chart title as **Tony & Guido's Pizzeria**. Press **Enter**. Type **May 1, 2025–May 31, 2025**. Click outside the title to deselect it.

    c. Insert a **Trendline**.

        i. Click on the All Meats Extra Large Pizza series (dark brown bars).

        ii. Click on **Add Chart Element** (*Chart Tools, Design* tab, *Chart Layouts* group).

        iii. Click on **Trendline** (*Chart Tools, Design* tab, *Element* group), then click on **Linear**. (Remove the words (Figure 10-172).

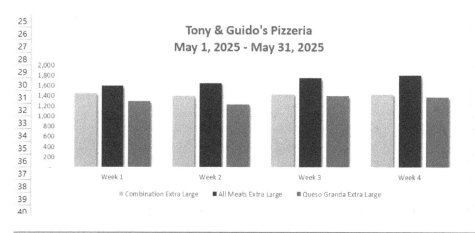

FIGURE 10-172 Tony & Guido's Column Chart

    d. Format chart background and Trendline.

        i. Right-click in a blank corner in your chart.

        ii. Click on **Format Chart Area** at the bottom of the shortcut menu.

        iii. Under **Fill**, click the radio button next to **Gradient Fill**.

    e. Click on the down arrow next to the **preset gradients**. Select the **Top Spotlight, Accent 1** (second row, first color).

    f. If necessary, click on the bucket again in the **Format Chart Area** task pane. Scroll down to **Border**.

    g. Click on **Border**. Scroll back down to Border. Click on **Solid Line**.

    h. Click on the down arrow next to the bucket (just below where you selected your solid line). Click on **Orange, Accent 2** (1st row, 6th color).

i. Move down to the **Width** box. Click on the down arrow and select **1.5** pt.

j. Close **Format Chart Area** task pane.

k. Format chart font and axes.

l. Click on the chart **Title**. Change font color to **Black, Text 1** (font size should be **16** pt.).

m. Click on the **Legend**. **Bold** text, and change font color to Black, Text 1 (font size should be **9** pt.).

n. Click on the **X** axis. Resize font to size **10** pt., **Bold** text, and change font color to **Black, Text 1**.

o. Click on the **Y** axis. Resize font to size **10** pt., **Bold** text, and change font color to Black, Text 1.

   i. Right-click on the **Y** axis. In the shortcut menu, select **Format Axis** at the bottom of the list.

   ii. Under **Format Axis**, click on the **Axis Options** icon (small green column chart icon).

   iii. Move your mouse down to **Number**. If necessary, you may have to scroll down to the bottom of the list.

   iv. Under **Category**, click on the down arrow and select Accounting.

   v. Under the **Accounting** box, make sure that **Decimal Places** has a zero in it, and in the **Symbol** box below, the **Decimal Places** box shows a **$**.

   vi. Close **Format Axis** task pane (Figure 10-173).

p. Insert a **3-D Pie** chart.

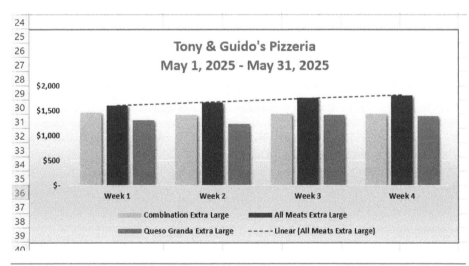

FIGURE 10-173 Trendline Chart

q. Select the following nonadjacent cells: Select cell **A10**. Press and hold down your **Ctrl** key and then select the following cells **F10, A16, F16, A22**, and **F22**. Release the **Ctrl** key.

    i. Click on the ***Insert tab***. Click in the down arrow next to the ***Pie chart*** button. Select the *3-D Pie* chart option.

    ii. Click on ***Move Chart*** (*Chart Tools, Design* tab, *Location* group).

    iii. In the **Move Chart** dialog box, click on the ***New Sheet*** radio button.

    iv. Type in Revenue Pie Chart.

r. Insert a **Quick Layout** for your chart.

    i. Click to select your chart object if necessary.

    ii. Click on the ***Quick Layout*** button (*Chart Tools, Design* tab, *Chart Layouts* group).

    iii. Click on **Layout 1**.

s. Insert a **Chart Style**.

    i. Click to select your chart object if necessary.

    ii. Click on the ***Chart Style More*** button (*Chart Tools, Design* tab, *Chart Styles* group).

    iii. Click on **Chart Style 10**. Delete legend.

t. Format **Chart Title**.

    i. Click in the Chart Title. Type in TOP SELLERS REVENUE. Press Enter. Type in MAY 1, 2025–MAY 31, 2025.

    ii. Resize chart title font to size 24 pt. Bold title text.

    iii. Add WordArt to the chart title.

    iv. Click on ***Fill: Orange, Accent color 1, Shadow.***

u. Format **Data Labels**.

    i. Click in the center of the pie.

    ii. Click on the ***Chart Elements*** button in the upper right side of the chart (*green cross*).

    iii. Click on the arrow to the right of **Data Labels**.

    iv. Click on ***Data Callout***.

    v. Change the **Data Labels** font size to **14** pt. Apply **Bold.** Change font color to **Black, Text 1** (*Home* tab, *Font* group).

    vi. To ensure readability, move any of the labels around if necessary.

v. Explode Pie slice.

    i. Left-click in the center of the pie.

    ii. Left-click in the *All Meats Extra Large* slice.

    iii. Right click in the All Meats Extra Large slice. In the shortcut menu, left-click on ***Format Data Point***.

iv. Once the **Format Data Point** task pane appears, change the *Angle of First Slice* to **300** degrees. Press **Enter**.

v. Change the *Point Explosion* to **30%**. Press **Enter** (Figure 10-174).

vi. Close **Format Data Point** task pane.

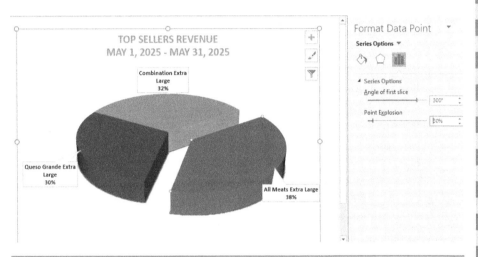

FIGURE 10-174 Exploded Pie Chart

aa. Left click in the center of the pie. Left-click in the **All Meats Extra Large** slice. Right-click in the **All Meats Extra Large** slice.

i. In the shortcut menu, left-click on *Format Data Point*.

ii. Once the *Format Data Point* task pane appears, click on the *paint bucket*, then click on **Fill**.

iii. Click on *Picture* or *Texture fill*.

iv. Click on *Insert* under *Picture Source*.

v. In the **Insert Picture** dialog box, select **Online Pictures**. Type in **Meat Pizza**. Press Enter. Choose a photo or picture of your choice. Click on **Insert**.

ab. Left-click in the **Custom Combo Extra Large** slice.

i. In the shortcut menu, right-click on **Format Data Point**.

ii. Once the **Format Data Point** task pane appears, click on the *paint bucket*, then click on *Fill*.

iii. Click on *Picture or Texture* fill.

      iv. Click on **Insert** *under* **Picture Source**.

      v. In the **Insert Picture** dialog box, select Online Pictures. Type in **Combination Pizza**. Press **Enter**. Choose a photo or picture of your choice. Click on **Insert**.

ac. Left-click in the **Queso Grande Extra Large** slice.

      i. In the shortcut menu, right-click on **Format Data Point**.

      ii. Once the **Format Data Point** task pane appears, click on the *paint bucket* and then click on **Fill**.

      iii. Click on **Picture or Texture** fill.

      iv. Click on **Insert** *under* **Picture Source.**

ad. In the **Insert Picture** dialog box, select **Online Pictures**. Type in **Cheese Pizza**. Press **Enter**. Choose a photo of your choice. Click on **Insert**.

Right-click in the upper right corner of your chart. Once the **Format Chart Area** task pane appears, click on **Fill**.

ae. Click on **Gradient Fill**. Click on the down arrow next to *Preset gradients*. Click on **Light Gradient-Accent 1** (first color in the first row).

af. Scroll down to the bottom of the Format Chart Area task pane. Click on **Border.**

   Under *Border*, click on **Solid Line.**

ag. Click on the down arrow next to the **Color** button (bucket picture).

ah. Under **Standard Colors,** select **Dark Red** (first option).

ai. In the *Width* spinner box, (below the *Color* button), click the up arrow to **1.5** pt. or type in **1.5**.

aj. Close the **Format Chart Area** task pane.

ak. Click in your chart but not in the pie to see your chart outline (Figure 10-175).

10. Insert **Sparklines** for Custom Combo pizza.

   a. Click on the May 2025 Sales tab.

   b. Insert a new column between columns **E** & **F**.

   c. Select range **F6:F10**.

   d. Click on the **Insert tab**. Click on the **Sparklines** button. Click on **Line**.

   e. In the **Location Range** box, make sure that **$F$12:$F$16** appears in the box. Press **OK**.

   f. In the Data Range box, select the ranges **B6:E10**.

   g. In the **Location Range** box, make sure that **$F$6:$F$10** appears in the box. Press **OK**.

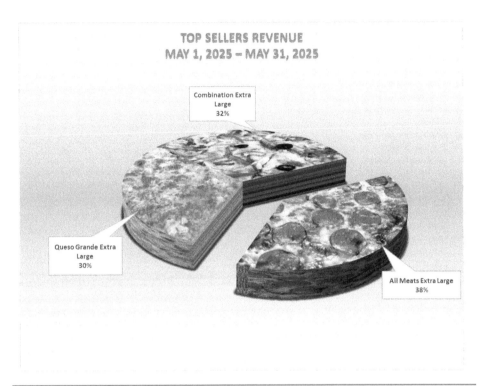

TOP SELLERS REVENUE
MAY 1, 2025 – MAY 31, 2025

Combination Extra
Large
32%

Queso Grande Extra
Large
30%

All Meats Extra Large
38%

FIGURE 10-175 Pizza Pie Chart

11. Insert **Sparklines** for All Meats Pizzas.
    a. Select range **F12:F16**.
    b. Click on the ***Insert tab***. Click on the **Sparklines** button. Click on ***Line***.
    c. The **Create Sparklines** dialog box will pop up.
    d. In the *Data Range* box, select the ranges **B12:E16**.
    e. In the *Location Range* box, make sure that **$F$12:$F$16** shows in the box. Press **Enter**. *Autofill* (drag) down through cell **F16**.
12. Insert **Sparklines** for Queso Grande Pizzas.
    a. Select range **F18:F22**.
    b. Click on the ***Insert tab***. Click on the **Sparklines** button. Click on **Line**.
    c. The Create Sparklines dialog box will pop up.
    d. In the *Data Range* box, Select the ranges **B18:E22**.
    e. In the **Location Range** box, make sure that **$F$18:$F$22** appears in the box. Press **OK**.

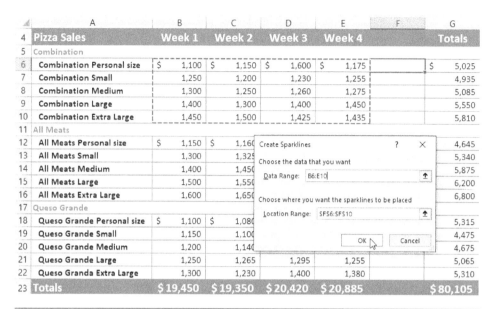

	A	B	C	D	E	F	G
4	**Pizza Sales**	**Week 1**	**Week 2**	**Week 3**	**Week 4**		**Totals**
5	Combination						
6	**Combination Personal size**	$ 1,100	$ 1,150	$ 1,600	$ 1,175		$ 5,025
7	**Combination Small**	1,250	1,200	1,230	1,255		4,935
8	**Combination Medium**	1,300	1,250	1,260	1,275		5,085
9	**Combination Large**	1,400	1,300	1,400	1,450		5,550
10	**Combination Extra Large**	1,450	1,500	1,425	1,435		5,810
11	All Meats						
12	**All Meats Personal size**	$ 1,150	$ 1,160				4,645
13	**All Meats Small**	1,300	1,325				5,340
14	**All Meats Medium**	1,400	1,450				5,875
15	**All Meats Large**	1,500	1,550				6,200
16	**All Meats Extra Large**	1,600	1,650				6,800
17	Queso Grande						
18	**Queso Grande Personal size**	$ 1,100	$ 1,080				5,315
19	**Queso Grande Small**	1,150	1,100				4,475
20	**Queso Grande Medium**	1,200	1,140				4,675
21	**Queso Grande Large**	1,250	1,265	1,295	1,255		5,065
22	**Queso Granda Extra Large**	1,300	1,230	1,400	1,380		5,310
23	**Totals**	**$ 19,450**	**$ 19,350**	**$ 20,420**	**$ 20,885**		**$ 80,105**

Create Sparklines dialog box:
Choose the data that you want
Data Range: B6:E10
Choose where you want the sparklines to be placed
Location Range: $F$6:$F$10
OK   Cancel

FIGURE 10-176 Custom Combo Sparklines

13. Select rows **6-10**. Resize **Row Heights** to **30** (you can drag to resize, or right click anywhere in rows **6-10**, select **Row Height** on the short-cut menu, then type in **30**, then click **OK**.

14. Select rows **12-16**. Resize Row Heights to **30** (you can drag to resize or right-click anywhere in rows **12-16**, select **Row Height** on the shortcut menu, then type in **30,** then type **OK.**

15. Select rows **18-22**. Resize row heights to 30 (you can drag to resize or right-click anywhere in rows **18-22**, select **Row Height** on the shortcut menu, then type in **30**, then type **OK**.

    a. Select range **F6:F10**. Add **Markers** to the lines (*Insert* tab, *Sparklines Tools*, *Show* group, *Markers*).

    b. Select range **F12:F16**. Add **Markers** to the lines.

    c. Select range **F18:F22**. Add **Markers** to the lines.

    d. Resize column **F** width to size **19** (Figure 10-177).

    e. **Save** and close your workbook. Turn in your assignment.

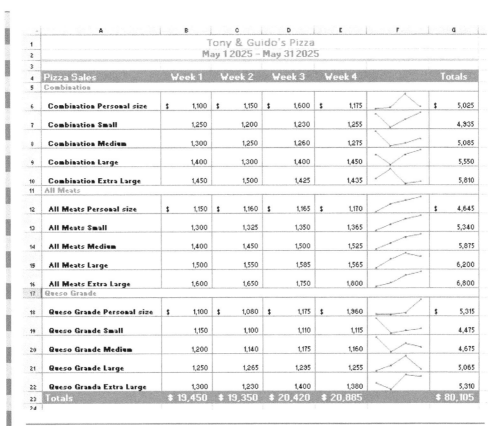

Pizza Sales	Week 1	Week 2	Week 3	Week 4		Totals
Combination						
Combination Personal size	$ 1,100	$ 1,150	$ 1,600	$ 1,175		$ 5,025
Combination Small	1,250	1,200	1,230	1,255		4,935
Combination Medium	1,300	1,250	1,260	1,275		5,085
Combination Large	1,400	1,300	1,400	1,450		5,550
Combination Extra Large	1,450	1,500	1,425	1,435		5,810
All Meats						
All Meats Personal size	$ 1,150	$ 1,160	$ 1,165	$ 1,170		$ 4,645
All Meats Small	1,300	1,325	1,350	1,365		5,340
All Meats Medium	1,400	1,450	1,500	1,525		5,875
All Meats Large	1,500	1,550	1,585	1,565		6,200
All Meats Extra Large	1,600	1,650	1,750	1,800		6,800
Queso Grande						
Queso Grande Personal size	$ 1,100	$ 1,080	$ 1,175	$ 1,360		$ 5,315
Queso Grande Small	1,150	1,100	1,110	1,115		4,475
Queso Grande Medium	1,200	1,140	1,175	1,160		4,675
Queso Grande Large	1,250	1,265	1,295	1,255		5,065
Queso Grande Extra Large	1,300	1,230	1,400	1,380		5,310
Totals	**$ 19,450**	**$ 19,350**	**$ 20,420**	**$ 20,885**		**$ 80,105**

Tony & Guido's Pizza
May 1 2025 – May 31 2025

FIGURE 10-177 Sparklines

CHAPTER ELEVEN

Excel Part III

Introduction

In Excel Part 3, you will learn basic formulas most commonly used by students and new practitioners of Excel. Formulas are the heart of Excel, and learning Excel formulas will make you very powerful when you use it. Becoming proficient with Excel formulas will help you to see mathematics in a new way.

Learning Objectives

When you complete this section, you should be able to do the following:

1. Customize Status Bar: Formulas without formulas.
2. Addition, Subtraction, Multiplication, Division, Averages, Minimum, Maximum, and Modes.
3. Financial and Logical functions: Payment, IF function, and Absolute Value functions.
4. Statistical functions: Standard Deviation, T-Test, and Combinations.
5. Trigonometry functions: Sine, Cosine, and Tangents.
6. Conditional Formatting and Goal Seek.

Formulas Tab

The **Formulas** tab contains hundreds of built-in formulas designed to help you to quickly calculate an array of mathematical problems covering a spectrum of applications and disciplines. This tab also allows you to define names for ease of identifying parts of a function, also to trace precedents and dependents to audit formulas. The ***Show Formula*** button allows you to see all the functions on your worksheet (Figure 11-1).

FIGURE 11-1 Formulas Tab

Function Library

The **Function Library** is the area in Excel where you can either search for a formula or look one up by category. Excel has numerous formulas from which to choose. Likewise, the **Home** tab also shows the **AutoSum** button (*Home* tab, *Editing* group). On all tabs, you can create functions by clicking on the **fx** Insert Function just left of the *Formula Bar*.

The **Insert Function** button opens to the *Insert Function* dialog box. In this dialog box, you can *Search for a function* by typing in the function of your choice. Once you type in a function, click on **Go** button. The **Go** button will provide one or a list of functions below the *Select a function* (Figure 11-2).

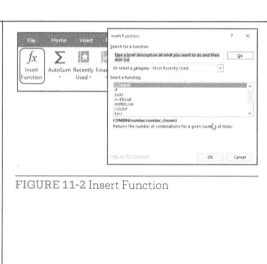

FIGURE 11-2 Insert Function

You can also click on the down arrow next to the *Or select a category* box and a list will appear with the *Most Recently Used* and all the formula categories shown on the ribbon.

This is a great shortcut to use to find a function rather than clicking through each category to find the formula you want.

The **AutoSum** button provides a quick way to access the most commonly used functions in Excel, such as *Sum, Average, Count Numbers, Max*, and *Min*. You may also access *More Functions* at the bottom of the list (Figure 11-3).

The **AutoSum** button may also be used on the *Home* tab.

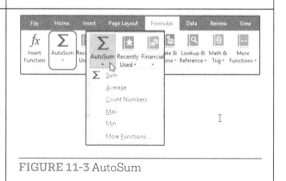

FIGURE 11-3 AutoSum

The **Recently Used** button is a handy timesaver when you have been recently using several functions in a workbook (Figure 11-4).

When you click on the down arrow, for your convenience, Excel lists the 10 most recent formulas used in the workbook.

If you have used *fewer than 10* recent formulas, then Excel will list **all** your most recently used formulas. You also have the option to *Insert Function* if your function does not appear in the list.

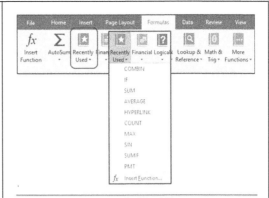

FIGURE 11-4 Recently Used Functions

Financial adds a financial formula to your worksheet. Excel lists **55** different financial formulas for time value of money, interest, payment calculations, and more (Figure 11-5).

When you click on the **Financial** button, a list of Financial functions will appear in alphabetical order with the option to Insert Function if your function does not appear in the list.

FIGURE 11-5 Financial Functions

Logical adds a logical formula to your worksheet. Excel lists **11** different logical formulas (Figure 11-6).

When you click on the **Logical** button, a short list of **11** options appears in alphabetical order with the option to *Insert Function* if your function does not appear in the list.

FIGURE 11-6 Logical Functions

Text Function converts numbers to text using currency formats and joins several text strings into one string, plus other functions (Figure 11-7). Excel lists **28** different **Text Functions** in alphabetical order with the option to *Insert Function* if your function does not appear in the list.	 FIGURE 11-7 Text Functions
Date & Time Function adds a date or time function, calculates the number of days between two dates, plus more to your worksheet (Figure 11-8). Excel lists **24** different **Date & Time Functions** in alphabetical order with the option to *Insert Function* if your function does not appear in the list.	 FIGURE 11-8 Date & Time Function
Lookup & Reference Function enables you to search a horizontal or vertical list for a value, converts a vertical range of cells to horizontal, and vice versa, plus more functions (Figure 11-9). Excel lists **19** different **Lookup & Reference Functions** in alphabetical order with the option to *Insert Function* if your function does not appear in the list.	 FIGURE 11-9 Lookup & Reference
Math & Trig Functions add a math or trigonometry function to your worksheet. Some functions include Sine, Cosine, Tangent, Logs, Absolute Values, plus many more functions commonly used in math class (Figure 11-10). Excel lists **74** different **Math & Trig Functions** in alphabetical order with the option to *Insert Function* if your function does not appear in the list.	 FIGURE 11-10 Math & Trig

More Functions include *Statistical (112 functions), Engineering (54 functions), Cube (7 functions), Information (20 functions), Compatibility (21 functions),* and *Web (3 functions)* categories. Each category is listed in alphabetical order (Figure 11-11).

At the end of each category list, you will see the option to *Insert Function* if your function does not appear in the list.

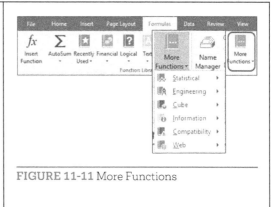

FIGURE 11-11 More Functions

Defined Names

The **Defined Names** group enables you to name Excel cells with an assigned name in any language rather than a cell reference. By naming cells with a real name, Excel makes it easier to visualize and keep track of more complex formulas.

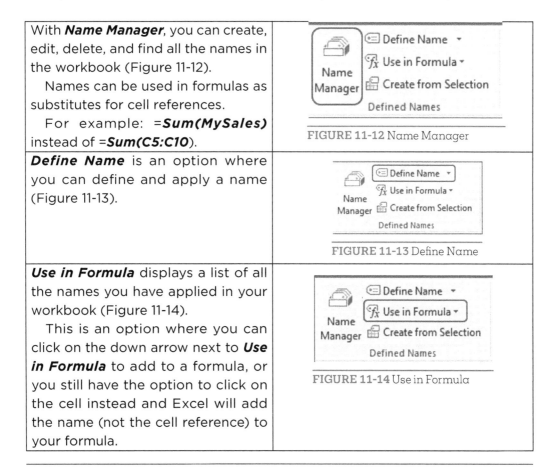

With **Name Manager**, you can create, edit, delete, and find all the names in the workbook (Figure 11-12). Names can be used in formulas as substitutes for cell references. For example: **=Sum(MySales)** instead of **=Sum(C5:C10)**.	FIGURE 11-12 Name Manager
Define Name is an option where you can define and apply a name (Figure 11-13).	FIGURE 11-13 Define Name
Use in Formula displays a list of all the names you have applied in your workbook (Figure 11-14). This is an option where you can click on the down arrow next to **Use in Formula** to add to a formula, or you still have the option to click on the cell instead and Excel will add the name (not the cell reference) to your formula.	FIGURE 11-14 Use in Formula

Create from Selection automatically generates names from the selected cells (Figure 11-15). Many users choose to use the text in the top row or the leftmost column of the selection.	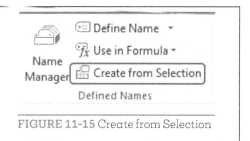 FIGURE 11-15 Create from Selection

Formula Auditing Group

The options in the **Formula Auditing** group allow you to follow the precedents of functions to see which values constitute your function. The ***Trace Dependents*** show arrows that indicate which cells are affected by the currently selected cell. You have further options to ***Remove Arrows*** (Note: Arrows will disappear after a few minutes of inactivity). Excel allows you to ***Error Check*** your functions for common errors and ***Evaluate Formula*** to debug complex functions.

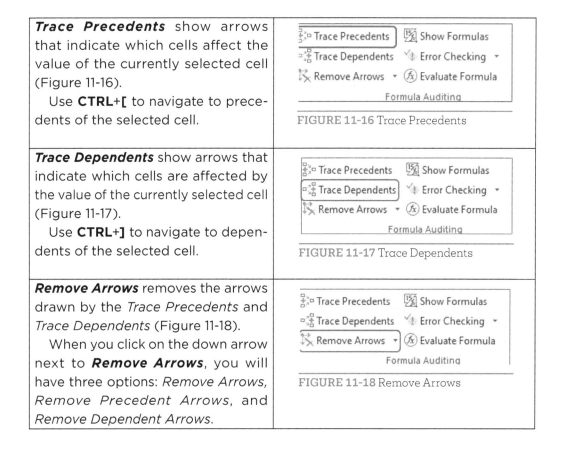

Trace Precedents show arrows that indicate which cells affect the value of the currently selected cell (Figure 11-16). Use **CTRL+[** to navigate to precedents of the selected cell.	FIGURE 11-16 Trace Precedents
Trace Dependents show arrows that indicate which cells are affected by the value of the currently selected cell (Figure 11-17). Use **CTRL+]** to navigate to dependents of the selected cell.	FIGURE 11-17 Trace Dependents
Remove Arrows removes the arrows drawn by the *Trace Precedents* and *Trace Dependents* (Figure 11-18). When you click on the down arrow next to ***Remove Arrows***, you will have three options: *Remove Arrows*, *Remove Precedent Arrows*, and *Remove Dependent Arrows*.	FIGURE 11-18 Remove Arrows

Show Formulas. This button acts as a toggle to show formulas or show values (Figure 11-19). Another way to show formulas is to press **Ctrl** + ˜ (button is located in the upper left of your keyboard under the **Esc** button).	 FIGURE 11-19 Show Formulas
Error Checking. Checks for common errors that occur when using formulas (Figure 11-20). When you click on the down arrow next to **Error Checking**, you will have three options: *Error Checking, Trace Error*, and *Circular Reference*.	 FIGURE 11-20 Error Checking
Evaluate Formula helps you to debug a complex formula evaluating each part of the formula individually (Figure 11-21). Stepping through the formula part-by-part can help you verify it is calculating correctly.	 FIGURE 11-21 Evaluate Formula
Watch Window enables you to add cells to the Watch Window list to keep an eye on their values as you update values in other parts of your worksheet (Figure 11-22)**.** The **Watch Window** stays on top so you can keep watch on these cells even when you are working on other sheets.	 FIGURE 11-22 Watch Window

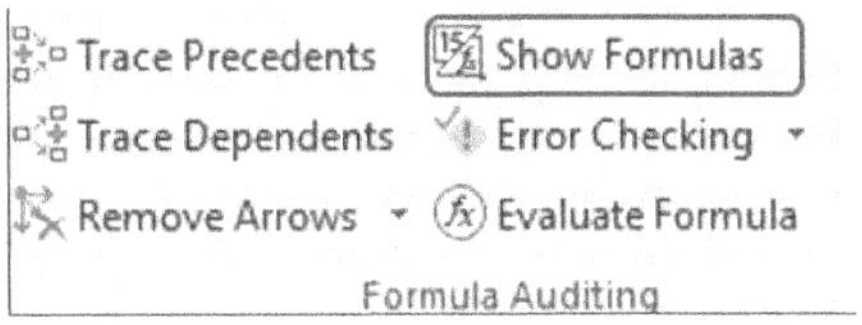

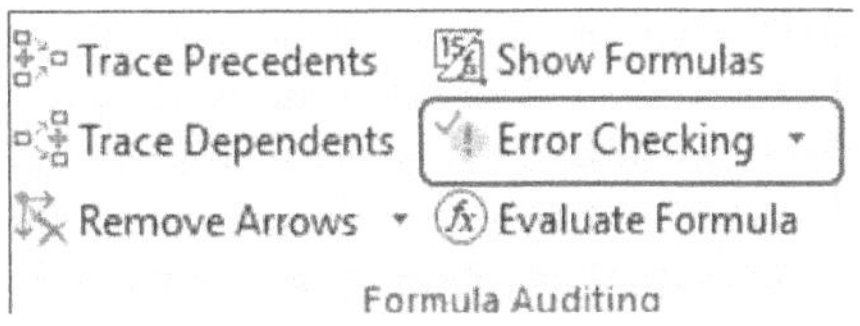

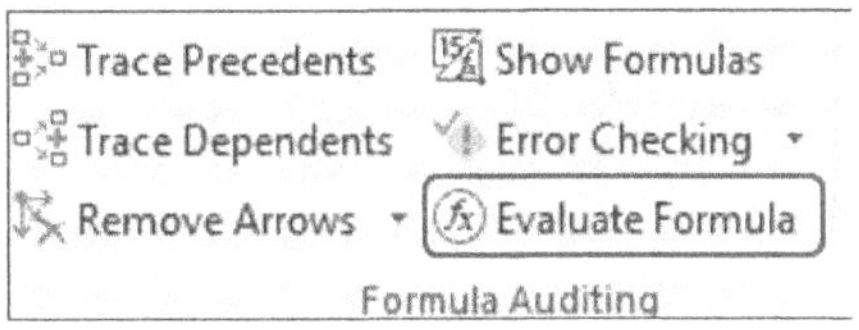

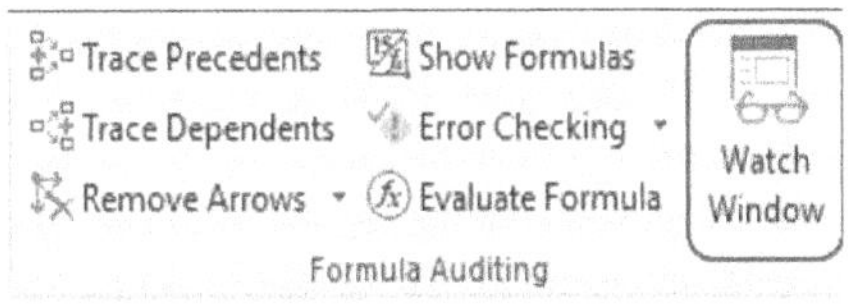

Calculation Group

These buttons will be used if automatic calculation is turned off. However, you have the option to calculate the entire workbook or the active sheet.

Calculation Options. Choose to calculate formulas automatically or manually (Figure 11-23). If you make a change that affects a value, Excel will automatically recalculate it.	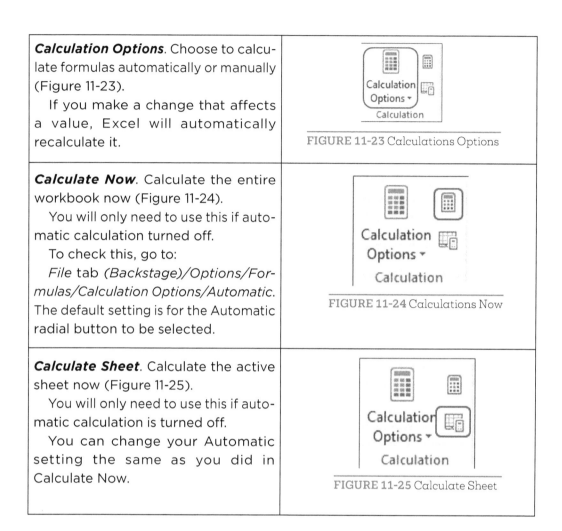 FIGURE 11-23 Calculations Options

Calculate Now. Calculate the entire workbook now (Figure 11-24).
 	
    You will only need to use this if automatic calculation turned off.
 	
    To check this, go to:
 	
    File tab *(Backstage)/Options/Formulas/Calculation Options/Automatic*. The default setting is for the Automatic radial button to be selected.
	FIGURE 11-24 Calculations Now

Calculate Sheet. Calculate the active sheet now (Figure 11-25).
 	
    You will only need to use this if automatic calculation is turned off.
 	
    You can change your Automatic setting the same as you did in Calculate Now.
	FIGURE 11-25 Calculate Sheet

1. AutoCalculate: Formulas without Formulas

If you want to avoid repetitious formula computing for the simple formulas such as *Average, Count, Numerical Count, Min* (Smallest number), *Max* (largest number), and SUM, Excel enables you to customize the **Status Bar** to show values for all of the above listed functions or select functions from the list.

    To show Status Bar:

1. Highlight the range you want to calculate. In this example, range **B5:F10** was selected to be calculated. <u>Note</u>: You need to select *at least two cells with values* for this to work.
2. Right-click on the Status Bar (Figure 11-26).

Within the red square group (Figure 11-26), you can select or deselect each function as desired. You may also select or deselect any other option in the list if you wish.

In this example, all functions within the square are active (selected with a ✓ mark) and read along the bottom of the screen (Figure 11-27).

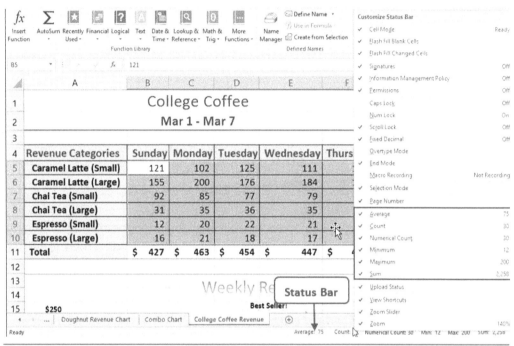

FIGURE 11-26 Status Bar

Average: 75   Count: 30   Numerical Count: 30   Min: 12   Max: 200   Sum: 2,258

FIGURE 11-27 Status Bar Function Results

2. The Most Common Mathematical Functions

These functions may help simplify Math Lab problems and enable you to quickly double-check your work. The Order of Operations is the same as you would use in math. The Excel Arithmetic Operators and Comparison Operators are also very similar to those you would use in math (Figure 11-28). The bolded columns represent customary arithmetic operations. The nonbolded columns represent the equivalent in Excel.

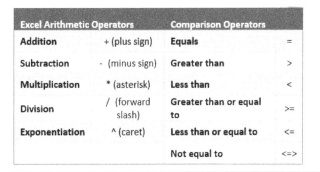

Excel Arithmetic Operators		Comparison Operators		Order of Operations
Addition	+ (plus sign)	Equals	=	
Subtraction	- (minus sign)	Greater than	>	
Multiplication	* (asterisk)	Less than	<	
Division	/ (forward slash)	Greater than or equal to	>=	
Exponentiation	^ (caret)	Less than or equal to	<=	
		Not equal to	<=>	

Order of Operations
1. Parenthesis and other grouping objects.
2. Exponents
3. Multiplication and division from left to right.
4. Addition and subtraction from left to right.

FIGURE 11-28 Arithmetic and Comparison Operators and Order of Operations

Addition

The **Plus sign (+)** is used for addition.

In Figure 11-26 above, note that the total in cell **B11** is **427**. Excel provides several ways you can calculate cell **B11**. <u>Note:</u> Cell **B11** needs to be the *active* cell.

1. =sum(B5+B6+B7+B8+B9+B10). Press **Enter**.

   =sum(B5:B10). Press **Enter**.

   =sum(B5:B10). Type in the equal sign, Sum, and the opening and closing parenthesis After typing in =sum (click on cell **B5**, hold down your mouse and select the cells **B5** through **B10**), type in the closing parenthesis, then press **Enter**.

   Double-click the **_AutoSum_** button located in the *Home* tab, *Editing* group.

   Double-click the **_AutoSum_** button located in the Formulas tab, *Function Library* group.

You may also select the **_fx Insert Function_** on the **Formula Bar**, on **any** tab. The *Function Arguments* dialog box will open. In the *Number1* box, Excel assumes you are adding up the range **B5:B10** in the active cell **B11**. In the center of the dialog box, the total value will appear in the red circle in the middle of the Function Arguments box (Figure 11-29). The Formula result also appears in the lower left of the dialog box. If it is correct, then click on **OK**.

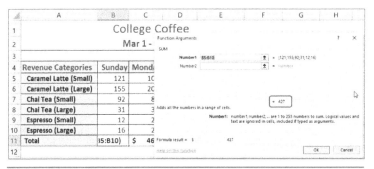

FIGURE 11-29 Function Arguments Dialog Box for SUM

Subtraction

The **minus sign** (−) is used for subtraction.

Performing **Subtraction** in Excel is very straightforward. In the following example, there are several common ways to perform subtraction. Select cell **H11**. You want to subtract Sunday's Total (cell **B11**) from Grand Total (cell **G11**) giving you the totals for Monday, Tuesday, Wednesday, and Thursday.

Note: Cell **H11** needs to be the active cell (Figure 11-30).

	A	B	C	D	E	F	G	H
2				Mar 1 - Mar 7				
3								
4	Revenue Categories	Sunday	Monday	Tuesday	Wednesday	Thursday	Grand Total	
5	Caramel Latte (Small)	121	102	125	111	133	592	
6	Caramel Latte (Large)	155	200	176	184	167	882	
7	Chai Tea (Small)	92	85	77	79	88	421	
8	Chai Tea (Large)	31	35	36	35	34	171	
9	Espresso (Small)	12	20	22	21	25	100	
10	Espresso (Large)	16	21	18	17	20	92	
11	Total	$ 427	$ 463	$ 454	$ 447	$ 467	$ 2,258	=G11-B11
12								

FIGURE 11-30 Subtraction Function

2. Type in the formula: **=G11–B11**. Press **Enter**. (This is when you type in the entire formula). Your answer is **$1,831**.

You may also select the ***fx Insert Function*** on the **Formula Bar**, on **any** tab. The *Function Arguments* dialog box will open.

a. In the *Search for a Function* box, type in **Subtract** then click on **Go**.

The word **IMSUB** should appear as the first (or only) option highlighted in blue in the *Select a Function* box. Click **OK** (Figure 11-31).

In the *Function Arguments* box, in the *Number1* box, either click on cell G11 or type **G11**. In the *Number2* box, click on cell B11 or type **B11**. Then click OK (Figure 11-32).

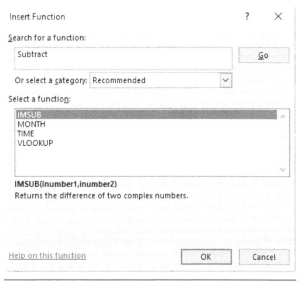

FIGURE 11-31 Insert Subtraction Function

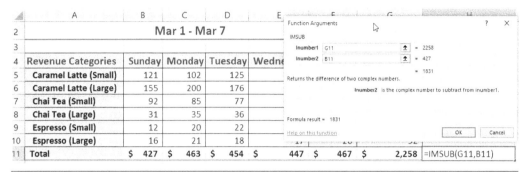

	A	B	C	D	E	F	G	H
2			Mar 1 - Mar 7					
3								
4	Revenue Categories	Sunday	Monday	Tuesday	Wedne			
5	Caramel Latte (Small)	121	102	125				
6	Caramel Latte (Large)	155	200	176				
7	Chai Tea (Small)	92	85	77				
8	Chai Tea (Large)	31	35	36				
9	Espresso (Small)	12	20	22				
10	Espresso (Large)	16	21	18				
11	Total	$ 427	$ 463	$ 454	$ 447	$ 467	$ 2,258	=IMSUB(G11,B11)

FIGURE 11-32 Subtraction Function Arguments

Multiplication

The **asterisk** or "star" **(*)** is used for multiplication.

Performing multiplication in Excel is very easy. In the following example, there are three common ways to perform multiplication. Select cell **H11**. You want to multiply Thursday's Total (cell **F11**) times **5**, giving you the grand total based on equal sales for all 5 days.

Note: Cell **H11** needs to be the active cell (Figure 11-33).

1. =G11*5. Press **Enter**. (This is when you type in the entire formula). Your answer is **$2,335**.

    =G11*5. Press **Enter**. (This is when you click on cell **G11**, type in the asterisk or star key, and type 5). Your answer is **$2,335**.

    You may also select the **fx Insert Function** on the Formula Bar, on **any** tab. The Function Arguments dialog box will open.

	A	B	C	D	E	F	G	H
2			Mar 1 - Mar 7					
3								
4	Revenue Categories	Sunday	Monday	Tuesday	Wednesday	Thursday	Grand Total	
5	Caramel Latte (Small)	121	102	125	111	133	592	
6	Caramel Latte (Large)	155	200	176	184	167	882	
7	Chai Tea (Small)	92	85	77	79	88	421	
8	Chai Tea (Large)	31	35	36	35	34	171	
9	Espresso (Small)	12	20	22	21	25	100	
10	Espresso (Large)	16	21	18	17	20	92	
11	Total	$ 427	$ 463	$ 454	$ 447	$ 467	$ 2,258	=F11*5

a. In the

FIGURE 11-33 Product Function

Search for a Function box, type in Product, then click on **Go**. The word Product should appear as the first (or only) option highlighted in blue in the Select a Function box. Click **OK** (Figure 11-34).

b. In the Function Arguments box, in the Number1 box, either click on cell **F11** or type **F11**. In the Number2 box, type in **5**. Then click **OK** (Figure 11-35).

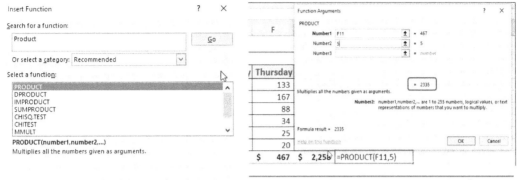

FIGURE 11-34 Insert Function

FIGURE 11-35 Function Arguments—Product

Division

The **slash** (/) is used for division.

Performing **Division** in Excel is very easy. In the following example, there are three common ways to perform division Select cell **H11**. You want to divide Grand Total (cell **G11**) by **5**, giving you average sales for five days.

Note: Cell **H11** needs to be the active cell (Figure 11-36).

1. **=G11/5**. Press **Enter**. (This is when you type in the entire formula). Your answer is **$451.60**.

   =G11/5. Press **Enter**. (This is when you click on cell **G11**, type in the slash key, and type **5**). Your answer is **$451.60**.

   You may also select the **fx** *Insert Function* on the Formula Bar on any tab. The Function Arguments dialog box will open.

2. In the *Search for a Function* box, type in **Division** or **Divide** then click on **Go**.

The word **Quotient** should appear as the first (or only) option highlighted in blue in the *Select a Function* box. Click **OK** (Figure 11-37).

In the *Function Arguments* box, in the *Numerator* box, either click on cell **G11** or type **G11**. In the Denominator box, type in **5**. Then click **OK** (Figure 11-38). This method returns an integer (no decimal points).

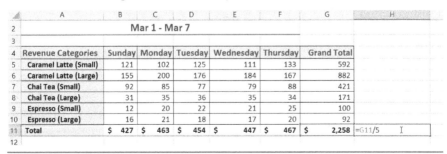

	A	B	C	D	E	F	G	H
2		Mar 1 - Mar 7						
3								
4	Revenue Categories	Sunday	Monday	Tuesday	Wednesday	Thursday	Grand Total	
5	Caramel Latte (Small)	121	102	125	111	133	592	
6	Caramel Latte (Large)	155	200	176	184	167	882	
7	Chai Tea (Small)	92	85	77	79	88	421	
8	Chai Tea (Large)	31	35	36	35	34	171	
9	Espresso (Small)	12	20	22	21	25	100	
10	Espresso (Large)	16	21	18	17	20	92	
11	Total	$ 427	$ 463	$ 454	$ 447	$ 467	$ 2,258	=G11/5
12								

FIGURE 11-36 Division Function

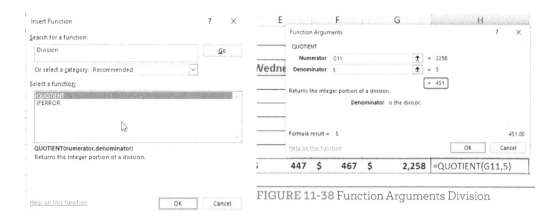

FIGURE 11-38 Function Arguments Division

FIGURE 11-37 Insert Function—Division

Average or Mean

Calculating **Averages** or **Means** in Excel is simple. In the following example, there are several common ways to average a range of numbers. Select cell **H6**. You want to calculate average sales for the range **B6:F6** (*Caramel Latte (Large)*).

Note: Cell **H6** needs to be the active cell (Figure 11-39).

	A	B	C	D	E	F	G	H
2				Mar 1 - Mar 7				
3								
4	Revenue Categories	Sunday	Monday	Tuesday	Wednesday	Thursday	Total	
5	Caramel Latte (Small)	121	102	125	111	133	592	
6	Caramel Latte (Large)	155	200	176	184	167	882	=AVERAGE(B6:F6)
7	Chai Tea (Small)	92	85	77	79	88	421	
8	Chai Tea (Large)	31	35	36	35	34	171	
9	Espresso (Small)	12	20	22	21	25	100	
10	Espresso (Large)	16	21	18	17	20	92	
11	Total	$ 427	$ 463	$ 454	$ 447	$ 467	$ 2,258	

FIGURE 11-39 Average Function

1. **=Average(B6:F6)**. Press **Enter**. Your answer is **176**.
2. **=Average(B6:F6)**. Type in the equal sign, Average, and the opening and closing parentheses. After typing in **=Average** (click on cell **B6**, hold down your mouse, and select the cells **B6** through **F6**), type in the closing parenthesis, then press **Enter**. Your answer is **176**.
3. Click the down arrow on the right side of the **AutoSum** button located on the *Home* tab, *Editing* group. Double-click on **Average**. Change the cells in the parenthesis to be (**B6:F6**). Then press **Enter**. Your answer is **176**.
4. Click the down arrow below the **AutoSum** button located in the *Formulas* tab, *Function Library* group. Double-click on **Average**. Change the cells in the parentheses to be (**B6:F6**). Then press **Enter**. Your answer is **176**.

5. You may also select the *fx* Insert Function on the **Formula Bar** on **any** tab. The Function Arguments dialog box will open.

   a. In the Search for a Function box, type in **Average**, then click on **Go**.

   b. The word **Average** should appear as the first (or only) option highlighted in blue in the Select a Function box. Click **OK** (Figure 11-40).

   c. In the Function Arguments box, in the *Number1* box, either click on range **B6:F6** or type **B6:F6**. Leave the *Number2* box blank. Then click **OK** (Figure 11-40 and Figure 11-41). Your answer shows as **176.4**. You may also round down the result.

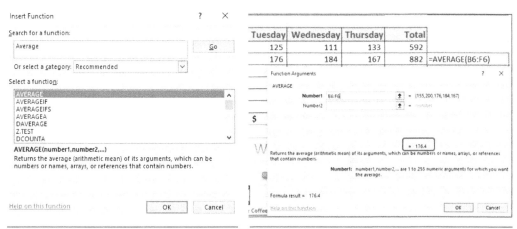

FIGURE 11-40 Insert Function-Average   FIGURE 11-41 Function Arguments—Average

Minimum

Calculating **Minimums** in Excel is easy. In the following example, there are several common ways to derive a minimum value from a range of numbers. Select cell **H11**. You want to find the lowest value in the range **B11:F11** (*Total Row*). In other words, the lowest sales total for the week.

   <u>Note</u>: Cell H11 needs to be the active cell (Figure 11-42).

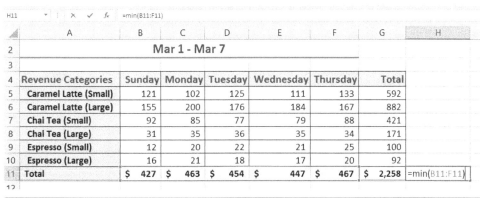

FIGURE 11-42 Minimum Function

1. **=Min(B6:F6)**. Press **Enter**. Your answer is **427**. Sunday had the lowest total sales.
2. **=Min(B11:F11)**. Type in the equal sign, **Min**, and the opening and closing parentheses. After typing in **=Min**, click on cell **B11**, hold down your mouse, and select the cells **B11** through **F11**, type in the closing parenthesis, then press **Enter**. Your answer is **427**.
3. Click the down arrow on the right side of the **AutoSum** button located in the *Home* tab, *Editing* group. Double-click on **Min**. Change the cells in the parentheses to be (**B11:F11**). Then press **Enter**. Your answer is **427**.
4. Click the down arrow below the **AutoSum** button located in the Formulas tab, *Function Library* group. Double-click on **Min**. Change the cells in the parenthesis to be (**B11:F11**). Then press **Enter**. Your answer is **427**.
5. You may also select the **fx** Insert Function on the Formula Bar, on **any** tab. The *Function Arguments* dialog box will open.
   a. In the Search for a Function box, type in **Min**, then click on **Go**.
   b. The word **Min** should appear as the first (or only) option highlighted in blue in the *Select a Function* box. Click **OK** (Figure 11-43).
   c. In the Function Arguments box, in the *Number1* box, either click on range **B11:F11** or type **B11:F11**. Leave the *Number2* box blank. Click **OK** (Figure 11-44). Your answer is **427**.

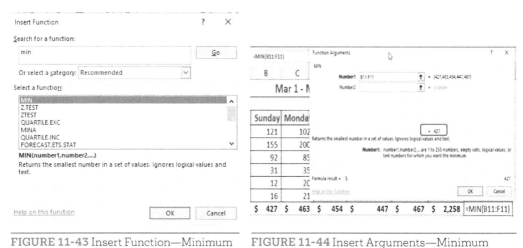

FIGURE 11-43 Insert Function—Minimum   FIGURE 11-44 Insert Arguments—Minimum

Maximum

Calculating **Maximums** in Excel is another common function. In the following example, there are several common ways to return a maximum value from a range of numbers. Select cell **H11**. You want to find the highest value in the range **B11:F11** (*Total Row*). In other words, the highest sales total for the week.

Note: Cell **H11** needs to be the active cell (Figure 11-45).

H11			X	✓	fx	=max(B11:F11)		

▲	A	B	C	D	E	F	G	H
2				Mar 1 - Mar 7				
3								
4	Revenue Categories	Sunday	Monday	Tuesday	Wednesday	Thursday	Total	
5	Caramel Latte (Small)	121	102	125	111	133	592	
6	Caramel Latte (Large)	155	200	176	184	167	882	
7	Chai Tea (Small)	92	85	77	79	88	421	
8	Chai Tea (Large)	31	35	36	35	34	171	
9	Espresso (Small)	12	20	22	21	25	100	
10	Espresso (Large)	16	21	18	17	20	92	
11	Total	$ 427	$ 463	$ 454	$ 447	$ 467	$ 2,258	=max(B11:F11)
12								

FIGURE 11-45 Maximum Function

1. **=Max(B6:F6)**. Press **Enter**. Your answer is **467**. *Thursday* had the highest total sales.
2. **=Max(B11:F11)**. Type in the equal sign, **Max**, and the opening and closing parenthesis. After typing in =Max(click on cell **B11**, hold down your mouse and select the cells **B11** through **F11**), type in the closing parenthesis, then press **Enter**. Your answer is **467**.
3. Click the down arrow on the right side of the ***AutoSum*** button located in the *Home* tab, *Editing* group. Double-click on **Max**. Change the cells in the parenthesis to be (**B11:F11**). Then press **Enter**. Your answer is **467**.
4. Click the down arrow below the ***AutoSum*** button located in the Formulas tab, *Function Library* group. Double-click on **Max**. Change the cells in the parenthesis to be (**B11:F11**). Then press **Enter**. Your answer is **467**.
5. You may also select the ***fx*** Insert Function on the Formula Bar, on **any** tab. The *Function Arguments* dialog box will open.
   a. In the Search for a Function box, type in **Max**, then click on **Go**.
   b. The word **Max** should appear as the first (or only) option highlighted in blue in the *Select a Function* box. Click **OK** (Figure 11-46).
   c. In the Function Arguments box, in the *Number1* box, either click on range **B11:F11** or type **B11:F11**. Leave the *Number2* box blank. Click **OK** (Figure 11-47). Your answer is **467**.

Mode

Calculating a **Mode** in Excel is another common function. In the following example, there are several common ways to return a mode value from a range of numbers. Select cell **H11**. You want to find the mode value in the range **B5:F10**. In other words, you are looking for the number that appears the most times in range **B5:F10**.

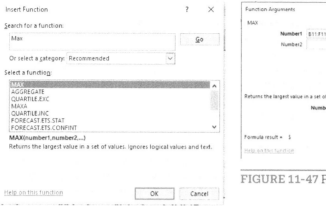

FIGURE 11-47 Function Arguments—Maximum

FIGURE 11-46 Insert Function—Maximum

Note: Cell **H11** needs to be the active cell (Figure 11-48).

H11				fx	=mode(B5:F10)			
	A	B	C	D	E	F	G	H
2				Mar 1 - Mar 7				
3								
4	**Revenue Categories**	**Sunday**	**Monday**	**Tuesday**	**Wednesday**	**Thursday**	**Total**	
5	**Caramel Latte (Small)**	121	102	125	111	133	592	
6	**Caramel Latte (Large)**	155	200	176	184	167	882	
7	**Chai Tea (Small)**	92	85	77	79	88	421	
8	**Chai Tea (Large)**	31	60	36	35	34	196	
9	**Espresso (Small)**	12	23	22	21	25	103	
10	**Espresso (Large)**	16	21	18	17	20	92	
11	**Total**	$ 427	$ 491	$ 454	$ 447	$ 467	$ 2,286	=mode(B5:F10)
12								

FIGURE 11-48 Mode Function

Note: Change the values in the following cells:

1. Cell **C8**: Change value to **60**.
2. Cell **C9**: Change value to **23**.
3. =**Mode(B5:F10)**. Press **Enter**. Your answer is **21**. The value **21** appears twice.
4. =**Mode(B5:F10)**. Type in the equal sign, **Mode**, and the opening and closing parentheses. After typing in =**Mode** (click on cell **B5**, hold down your mouse and select the cells **B5** through **F10**), type in the closing parenthesis, then press **Enter**. Your answer is **21**.
5. You may also select the *fx* Insert Function on the **Formula Bar**, on *any* tab. The Function Arguments dialog box will open.
   a. In the Search for a Function box, type in Mode, then click on **Go**.

b. The word **Mode** should appear as the first (or only) option highlighted in blue in the *Select a Function* box. Click **OK** (Figure 11-49).

c. In the Function Arguments box, in the *Number1* box, either click on range **B5:F10** or type B5:F10. Leave the *Number2* box blank. Click **OK** (Figure 11-50). Your answer is **21**.

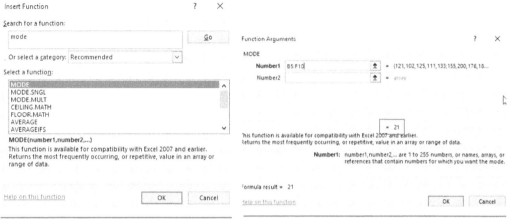

FIGURE 11-49 Insert Function—Mode   FIGURE 11-50 Function Argument—Mode

8. In cell **A18**, type in **Mode of Total Sales**.

9. Resize column **A**.

10. For the following formulas, your range will be **B12:H12**. You will be averaging the totals for Monday–Sunday.

    a. Click on cell **B15**. Type or insert the ***Average*** formula to calculate the average of the range **B12:H12**. Your formula will be: **=average(B12:H12)**. Your answer will be **$35,519**.

    b. Click on cell **B16**. Type or insert the ***Minimum*** formula to calculate the smallest number of the range **B12:H12**. Your formula will be: **=min(B12:H12)**. Your answer will be **$30,097**.

    c. Click on cell **B17**. Type or insert the ***Maximum*** formula to calculate the largest number of the range **B12:H12**. Your formula will be: **=max(B12:H12)**. Your answer will be **$49,286**.

    d. Click on cell **B18**. Type or insert the ***Mode*** formula to return the most recurring value in the range **B12:H12.** Your formula will be: **=mode(B12:H12)**. Note: The "**N/A**" that appears in cell **B18** means that there are no recurring values (modes) in the range **B12:H12** (Figure 11-51).

11. Select range **A15:B18**. Apply **All Borders** formatting.

	A	B	C	D	E	F	G	H	I	J
1				Bills Bikes & BBQ						
2				May 1 - May 7						
3										
4	Revenue Categories	Monday	Tuesday	Wednesday	Thursday	Friday	Saturday	Sunday	Totals	
5	BBQ Ribs	$ 4,123	$ 3,240	$ 3,575	$ 3,460	$ 3,665	$ 6,333	$ 6,800	$ 31,196	
6	BBQ KBOBs	1,099	888	1,051	1,080	1,210	3,677	4,021	13,026	
7	BBQ Pulled Pork	7,099	6,888	6,571	6,329	6,722	8,989	9,558	52,156	
8	BBQ Corn on the Cob	1,035	1,100	1,158	1,168	1,299	3,995	4,254	14,009	
9	BBQ Crab Cakes	5,200	5,675	5,640	5,550	5,850	7,569	7,789	43,273	
10	BBQ Chicken	6,150	6,340	6,299	6,315	6,145	8,192	8,352	47,793	
11	BBQ Steak	5,880	6,095	5,980	6,195	6,255	8,265	8,512	47,182	
12	Total	$30,586	$30,226	$ 30,274	$ 30,097	$31,146	$ 47,020	$49,286	$248,635	
13										
14										
15	Average of Totals	$ 35,519								
16	Minimum of Totals	$ 30,097								
17	Maximum of Totals	$ 49,286								
18	Mode of Totals	#N/A								
19										

FIGURE 11-51 Average, Min, Max, and Mode

12. Click in cell E15. Type in **Total Sales**. Press Enter. Select the range E15:G15. Click on **Merge Across** (*Home* tab, *Alignment* group).

13. Click in cell E16. Type in **Monday's Percentage of Total Sales**. Press Enter. Select the range E16:G16. Click on **Merge Across**.

14. Click in cell E17. Type in **Tuesday's Percentage of Total Sales**. Press Enter. Select the range E17:G17. Click on **Merge Across**.

15. Click in cell E18. Type in **Wednesday's Percentage of Total Sales**. Press Enter. Select the range E18:G18. Click on **Merge Across.**

16. Click in cell E19. Type in **Thursday's Percentage of Total Sales**. Press Enter. Select the range E19:G19. Click on **Merge Across**.

17. Click in cell E20. Type in **Friday's Percentage of Total Sales**. Press Enter. Select the range E20:G20. Click on **Merge Across**.

18. Click in cell E21. Type in **Saturday's Percentage of Total Sales**. Press Enter. Select the range E21:G21. Click on **Merge Across**.

19. Click in cell E22. Type in **Sunday's Percentage of Total Sales**. Press Enter. Select the range E22:G22. Click on **Merge Across**.

20. Click in cell A15 (*Average of Total Sales*). Click on the Format Painter. Click in cell E15. Select range E15:G15. Click on **Merge Across**.

21. Resize column **E** to **18.5** pt. width.

22. Click in cell H15. Type in **=I12** or type **=** and click on cell I12.

23. Click in cell H16. Type in a formula to divide Monday's Total by Total Sales. Your formula is: =B12/H15. Your answer should be .123015666.

    a. Click in cell **H17**. Type in a formula to divide Tuesday's Total by *Total Sales*.

    b. Click in cell **H18**. Type in a formula to divide Wednesday's Total by *Total Sales*.

    c. Click in cell **H19**. Type in a formula to divide Thursday's Total by *Total Sales*.

    d. Click in cell **H20**. Type in a formula to divide Friday's Total by *Total Sales*.

    e. Click in cell **H21**. Type in a formula to divide Saturday's Total by *Total Sales*.

    f. Click in cell **H22**. Type in a formula to divide Sunday's Total by *Total Sales*.

24. Select the range **F16:F22**. Format as a *Percentage* with **NO** decimals. **Center** the percentage values in the cells.

25. Select and **bold** range **H15:H22**. Resize range **H15:H22** to size **12.** Apply **All Borders** formatting.

26. Click on the **Formulas** tab. Click on the ***Show Formulas*** button (*Formulas* tab, *Formula Auditing* group) to see your formulas. Or, you can press the **CTRL** key and the **tilde (~)** key (located in the upper left corner of your keyboard just under the **Esc** key) at the same time to see your formulas (Figure 11-52).

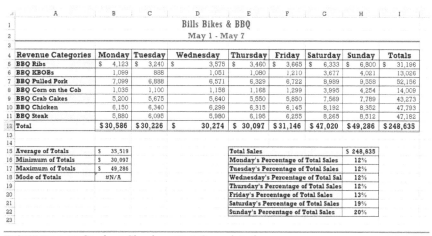

Revenue Categories	Monday	Tuesday	Wednesday	Thursday	Friday	Saturday	Sunday	Totals
				Bills Bikes & BBQ				
				May 1 - May 7				
BBQ Ribs	4123	3240	3575	3460	3665	6333	6800	=SUM(B5:H5)
BBQ KBOBs	1099	888	1051	1080	1210	3677	4021	=SUM(B6:H6)
BBQ Pulled Pork	7099	6888	6571	6329	6722	8989	9558	=SUM(B7:H7)
BBQ Corn on the Cob	1035	1100	1158	1168	1299	3995	4254	=SUM(B8:H8)
BBQ Crab Cakes	5200	5675	5640	5550	5850	7569	7789	=SUM(B9:H9)
BBQ Chicken	6150	6340	6299	6315	6145	8192	8352	=SUM(B10:H10)
BBQ Steak	5880	6095	5980	6195	6255	8265	8512	=SUM(B11:H11)
Total	=SUM(B5:B11)	=SUM(C5:C11)	=SUM(D5:D11)	=SUM(E5:E11)	=SUM(F5:F11)	=SUM(G5:G11)	=SUM(H5:H11)	=SUM(I5:I11)

Average of Totals	=AVERAGE(B12:H12)
Minimum of Totals	=MIN(B12:H12)
Maximum of Totals	=MAX(B12:H12)
Mode of Totals	=MODE(B12:H12)

Total Sales	=I12
Monday's Percentage of Total Sales	=B12/H15
Tuesday's Percentage of Total Sales	=C12/H15
Wednesday's Percentage of Total Sales	=D12/H15
Thursday's Percentage of Total Sales	=E12/H15
Friday's Percentage of Total Sales	=F12/H15
Saturday's Percentage of Total Sales	=G12/H15
Sunday's Percentage of Total Sales	=H12/H15

FIGURE 11-52 Formulas

27. Press the same key combination (**CTRL+Tilde**), or click on the **Show Formulas** button again to revert back to your values (Figure 11-53).
28. Save and close the workbook.

Revenue Categories	Monday	Tuesday	Wednesday	Thursday	Friday	Saturday	Sunday	Totals
				Bills Bikes & BBQ				
				May 1 - May 7				
BBQ Ribs	$ 4,123	$ 3,240	$ 3,575	$ 3,460	$ 3,665	$ 6,333	$ 6,800	$ 31,196
BBQ KBOBs	1,099	888	1,051	1,080	1,210	3,677	4,021	13,026
BBQ Pulled Pork	7,099	6,888	6,571	6,329	6,722	8,989	9,558	52,156
BBQ Corn on the Cob	1,035	1,100	1,158	1,168	1,299	3,995	4,254	14,009
BBQ Crab Cakes	5,200	5,675	5,640	5,550	5,850	7,569	7,789	43,273
BBQ Chicken	6,150	6,340	6,299	6,315	6,145	8,192	8,352	47,793
BBQ Steak	5,880	6,095	5,980	6,195	6,255	8,265	8,512	47,182
Total	$ 30,586	$ 30,226	$ 30,274	$ 30,097	$ 31,146	$ 47,020	$ 49,286	$ 248,635

Average of Totals	$ 35,519
Minimum of Totals	$ 30,097
Maximum of Totals	$ 49,286
Mode of Totals	#N/A

Total Sales	$ 248,635
Monday's Percentage of Total Sales	12%
Tuesday's Percentage of Total Sales	12%
Wednesday's Percentage of Total Sal	12%
Thursday's Percentage of Total Sales	12%
Friday's Percentage of Total Sales	13%
Saturday's Percentage of Total Sales	19%
Sunday's Percentage of Total Sales	20%

FIGURE 11-53 Student Checkup 11-1 Completed

3. Financial Functions, IF Function, TODAY and NOW Functions, and Absolute Value Functions

PMT Function

1. The PMT function is on the Formulas tab, *Financial* category. The PMT function calculates a constant payment amount for a specified period of time at a stated constant interest rate. You can use the PMT function to calculate your monthly payments for a selected payback time if you borrow money to purchase a car, college tuition, or even a mortgage. The PMT function can easily be used for short- and long-term purchases (Figure 11-54).

	A	B	C
1	**New Car or Truck Purchase**		
2	**Estimated Monthly Payments**		
3		**Car**	**Truck**
4	**Loan Amount**	10000	25000
5	**Number of Years to Repay**	3	7
6	**Interest Rate**	0.045	0.065
7	**Monthly Payment**	=PMT(B6/12,B5*12,B4)	=PMT(C6/12,C5*10,C4)

FIGURE 11-54 PMT Function Formula

2. The PMT function has five arguments. Three of them are required: *rate*, *nper*, and *pv*. The other two arguments are optional: *fv* and *type*.
3. The proper syntax for a PMT formula is **=PMT(rate,nper,pv,[fv],[type])**
   - **Rate** is the interest rate, a percentage of the amount borrowed. Most rates are set at a yearly rate. To calculate monthly payments, you must divide the rate by 12.
   - **Nper** is the total number of periods for repayment. If you make monthly payments for 10 years, the *nper* argument is 120. (10 years * 12 monthly payments).
   - **Pv** is the *present value.* This is the amount you borrowed *today.*
   - **Fv** is any future value after the last payment, an amount still owed at the end of the loan. When the **fv** argument is omitted, it means zero or that you paid back the entire amount of the loan plus interest.
   - **Type** indicates if payments are made at the beginning or the end of the period. Because the interest amount is less, most loan payments are made at the beginning of the period. The number 1 is used as a default to set payments at the beginning of the period.

Figure 11-55 shows the completed function.

Note: The **PMT** result is a negative number because the function is calculated from a borrower's point of view. This is money paid out. If you prefer to see a positive number rather than a negative number, just place a minus sign in front of the loan amount in the formula: **=PMT(B6/12,B5*12,-B4)**.

	A	B	C
1	**New Car or Truck Purchase**		
2	**Estimated Monthly Payments**		
3		Car	Truck
4	Loan Amount	$ 10,000	$ 25,000
5	Number of Years to Repay	3	7
6	Interest Rate	4.50%	6.50%
7	Monthly Payment	$ (297)	$ (430)

FIGURE 11-55 Payment Function

You can achieve this same formula by clicking on the **fx** button next to the Formula **Bar** on any tab (Figure 11-56).

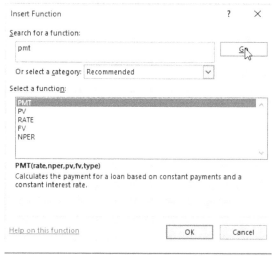

1. In the *Insert Function* dialog box, type **pmt** in the Search for a function box. PMT will appear highlighted in blue at the top of the list. Click on **Go**. Click on **OK** (Figure 11-56).
2. When the *Function Arguments* box opens, click in the *Rate* box. Type in **B6/12** or click on cell **B6** then type in /12 (Figure 11-57).

FIGURE 11-56 Insert Function—PMT

3. In the **nper** box, type in **B5*12** or click on cell **B5** then type in /12.
4. In the **pv** box, type in **B4** or click on cell **B4**. Leave the *fv* and *type* boxes blank.

IF Function

The **IF** function tests a condition or a statement; if it is *true*, then there is a specified result. If it is *false*, there is an alternative result. In the **College Coffee** worksheet, you will use the **IF** formula to determine if each day's revenue is above average. If the day's revenue is above average, you can display "Yes" in the cell, otherwise, you can display "No" in the cell.

An **IF** function has three arguments, and its syntax is

=IF(Logical_Test,value_if_true_if_false)

In plain English, for **College Coffee**, the **IF** function would read like this:

If(Monday's Total Sales >457, "Yes" otherwise "No")

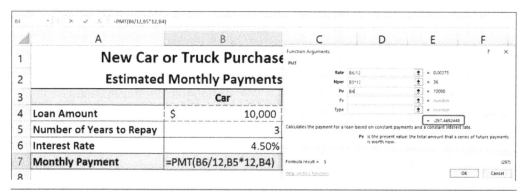

FIGURE 11-57 Rate Box

In this case, *"Yes"* replaces *"True,"* and *"No"* replaces *"False."* If you want to get creative, you can make your function look like this:

If(Monday's Total Sales >457,"Yep," otherwise "Nope")

You can achieve this same formula by clicking on the ***fx*** button next to the Formula Bar on any tab (Figure 11-58). Click in **H4**. Type in **Average Daily Sales**. In cell **H5**, type in the formula **=Average(B11:F11)**. In cell **A12**, type in **Above Average Sales?**

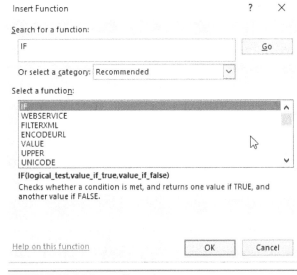

FIGURE 11-58 Insert Function

1. Click in cell **B12**.
2. In the Insert Function dialog box, type IF in the Search for a function box. Click on **Go**. **IF** should appear at the top of the list highlighted in blue. Click on **OK** (Figure 11-58).
3. When the *Function Arguments* box opens, click in the *Logical_test* box. Type in **B11>$H$5** (Figure 11-59). Be sure to add the dollar signs. This number is an absolute value.
4. In the *Value_if_true* box, type in **Yep** (Do not type in any quotation marks. Excel will add those for you).
5. In the *Value_if_false* box, type in **Nope** (Do not type in any quotation marks. Excel will add those for you). Click **OK**. Press **Enter**.
6. Click on cell **B12** again. Move your mouse to the lower right corner of the cell over the green box. Click on the green box and ***Autofill*** through cell **F12**.

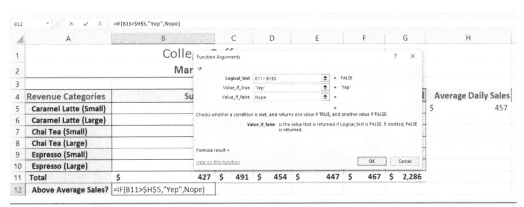

FIGURE 11-59 If Function Arguments

TODAY and NOW Functions

The Date & Time category contains multiple functions for date and time arithmetic, for conversion of dates and times to values, and for controlling how dates and times are displayed.

The **TODAY** function inserts the current date in the cell and updates each time the workbook is opened. The date and time displayed uses the computer's clock. The syntax is **=TODAY()**. The parentheses are required, but there are no arguments. The **NOW** function syntax is **=NOW()** and has no arguments. Both of these functions are volatile which means they change each time the workbook is opened, and the result depends on the current date and time determined by the computer. However, if you type in the date yourself, it will be as a date stamp and will not change when you reopen the workbook.

Once you enter either a **TODAY** or **NOW** function, you can format the results to show either the date or the date and time. The Format Cells dialog box has a *Date* category and a *Time* category with many present styles (Figure 11-60). From the **Number Format** list (*Home* tab, *Number* group), there are two date formats available: *Short Date* and *Long Date* (Figure 11-61).

Excel treats each date as a *serial number*, a unique value assigned to each date. Excel starts by setting January 1, 1900, as number 1, January 2, 1900, as number 2, and so on. January 1, 2018, is number 43101. If you want to see the serial number for any date, apply the *General* format to the cell.

FIGURE 11-60 TODAY Function

FIGURE 11-61 Short Date & Long Date

You can also use the **=Today()** formula to show past dates and future dates. For example, to show a date 270 days in the future, type in =Today()+270 (Figure 11-62).

FIGURE 11-62 Future Date with Today Function

To show a date 30 days in the past, type in =Today()-30 (Figure 11-63).

Time arithmetic is used to calculate the number of days from one date to another. This is commonly used for calculating the number of days from today to Christmas, or today to graduation, for example.

Use the **DAYS** function when you want to calculate the difference between two dates.

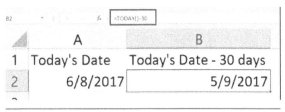

FIGURE 11-63 Past Date with Today Function

Difference in Days

In this example, the start date is in cell **A2**, and the end date is in **B2**. The formula is in **C2**. In cell C2 type in =DAYS(B2,A2). Your result is 207 days. See Figure 11-64.

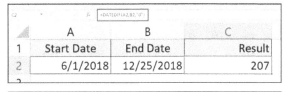

FIGURE 11-64 Difference in Days

Difference in Weeks

In this example, the start date is in cell A1, and the end date is in B1. The "d" returns the number of days. But notice the /7 at the end. That divides the number of days by 7 since there are 7 days in a week.

FIGURE 11-65 Difference in Weeks

Note that this result also needs to be formatted as a number. Press CTRL+1. Then click **Number** > **Decimal places: 2** (Figure 11-65).

Difference in Months

In this example, the start date is in cell **A1**, and the end date is in **B1**. In the formula, the "**m**" returns the number of full months between the two days (Figure 11-66).

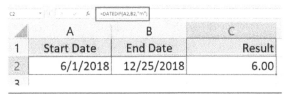

FIGURE 11-66 Difference in Months

Difference in Years

In this example, the start date is in cell A1, and the end date is in B1. The "y" returns the number of full years between the two days (Figure 11-67).

Note: In this example, the start date was changed from 6/1/2018 to 6/1/2017.

	A	B	C
1	Start Date	End Date	Result
2	6/1/2017	12/25/2018	1.00

FIGURE 11-67 Difference in Years

Calculate Time in Accumulated Years, Months, and Days

These formulas are handy if you enjoy time countdowns, have impatient children when it comes to a vacation or a birthday, have the computer calculate how many days you have lived so far, or if you want bragging rights. The following figures show the calculations for years, months, and days. Figure 11-68 shows the results of the formulas, and Figure 11-69 shows you the formulas.

Figure 11-70 shows you a single formula that replaces the three formulas you used to calculate accumulated years, months, and days in Figure 11-69.

You can put all three calculations in one cell like this example. Use ampersands, quotes, and text. It's a longer formula to type, but it's all in one.

	A	B	C	D
1	Start Date	End Date	Formula	
2	7/11/2011	1/1/2018	6	Years
3			5	Months
4			0	days
5				

FIGURE 11-68 Calculation Results

	A	B	C	D
1	Start Date	End Date	Formula	
2	40735	43101	=DATEDIF(A2,B2,"y")	Years
3			=DATEDIF(A2,B2,"ym")	Months
4			=B2-DATE(YEAR(B2),MONTH(B2),1)	days
5				

FIGURE 11-69 Calculation Formulas

C7 =DATEDIF(A2,B2,"y")&" years, " &DATEDIF(A2,B2,"ym")&" months, " &B2-DATE(YEAR(B2),MONTH(B2), 1)&" days"

	A	B	C	D
1	Start Date	End Date	Result	
2	7/11/2011	1/1/2018	6	Years
3			5	Months
4			0	days
5				
6				
7		All in One:	6 years, 5 months, 0 days	

FIGURE 11-70 Single Formula

Tip: Press **ALT+ENTER** to put line breaks in your formula. This makes it easier to read. Also, press **CTRL+SHIFT+U** if you can't see the whole formula. Enjoy!

Absolute Value Functions

An **Absolute Value** or Constant is indicated with dollar signs as in cell **$A$1** in Excel. When an absolute value is copied, it does not change. For example, in the formula **=$A$1 – B12**, **$A$1** would not change when copied anywhere in the workbook. However, the cell **B12** would reflect where the copy is located. You can manually type in the dollar signs in an **absolute reference**, or you can use the **F4 (FN+F4)** function key. When building a formula, enter the cell address and press **F4 (FN+F4)**.

In the following example, cell **B13** is the Absolute Reference cell. In Figure 11-71, the formula in cell **C5 is =B5*B13**. The result in **C5** will be correct. However, when you **autofill** the formula through cell **C10**, you will get dashes or zeros instead of numbers. Figure 11-72 will show **trace precedents** which are arrows that indicate which cells affect the value of the currently selected cell (Formulas tab, *Formula Auditing* group) or use **CTRL+[** to navigate to precedents of the selected cell. These arrows can visually show you where your formula went wrong.

In Figure 11-72, look at cell **C5**. Cell **B5** points to cell **C5**. Cell **B13** also points to cell **C5**. That result is correct. Look at cell **C6**. Cell **B6** points to cell **C6**; however, cell **B14** points to **C6**. The value in cell **B14** is blank or zero. The program tries to multiply cell **C6** by zero. The same thing happens when Excel tries to calculate cell **C7**, **C8**, **C9**, and **C10**. When you **autofill** down, Excel is programmed to move one cell down. This works the same if you were performing an **autofill** across; Excel is programmed to move one cell to the right. Unless cell **B13** has been identified as an **Absolute Reference Absolute Value, or Constant**, Excel will move the formula.

In Figure 11-73, look at the results of **C5:C10**. You now have values in cells where previously the values were blank or zero. If you look in the formula bar, you will notice the formula identifies cell **B13** as an

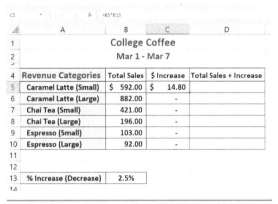

FIGURE 11-71 Formula Results without Absolute Reference

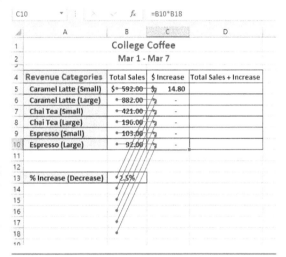

FIGURE 11-72 Trace Precedents without Absolute Reference Formulas

	A	B	C	D
		College Coffee		
		Mar 1 - Mar 7		
	Revenue Categories	Total Sales	$ Increase	Total Sales + Increase
5	Caramel Latte (Small)	$ 592.00	$ 14.80	
6	Caramel Latte (Large)	882.00	22.05	
7	Chai Tea (Small)	421.00	10.53	
8	Chai Tea (Large)	196.00	4.90	
9	Espresso (Small)	103.00	2.58	
10	Espresso (Large)	92.00	2.30	
11				
12				
13	% Increase (Decrease)	2.5%		

C5 — fx =B5*$B$13

FIGURE 11-73 Formulas with Absolute Reference

Absolute Reference. In Figure 11-74, all the arrows point from each value to cell **B13**. This allows you to audit to verify that the formula is referencing the same cell for all the calculations. Figure 11-75 shows the formulas with the *Absolute Reference* for each value.

Figure 11-75 shows you the formulas with the Absolute Reference for each value.

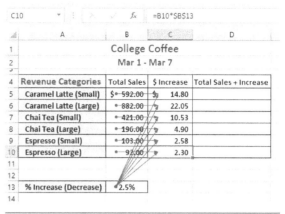

FIGURE 11-74 Trace Precedents with Absolute Reference Formulas

	A	B	C	D
1		College Coffee		
2		Mar 1 - Mar 7		
4	Revenue Categories	Total Sales	$ Increase	Total Sales + Increase
5	Caramel Latte (Small)	='College Coffee Revenue'!G5	=B5*$B$13	=B5+C5
6	Caramel Latte (Large)	='College Coffee Revenue'!G6	=B6*$B$13	=B6+C6
7	Chai Tea (Small)	='College Coffee Revenue'!G7	=B7*$B$13	=B7+C7
8	Chai Tea (Large)	='College Coffee Revenue'!G8	=B8*$B$13	=B8+C8
9	Espresso (Small)	='College Coffee Revenue'!G9	=B9*$B$13	=B9+C9
10	Espresso (Large)	='College Coffee Revenue'!G10	=B10*$B$13	=B10+C10
11				
12				
13	% Increase (Decrease)	0.025		

FIGURE 11-75 Absolute Reference Formulas

File Needed: **(Your Initials) Student Checkup Excel 11-1**

Completed File Name: **(Your initials) Student Checkup Excel 11-2**

1. Open **(Your Initials) Student Checkup Excel 11-1**. This is the workbook you completed in Student Checkup Excel 11-1.
2. Save the workbook as **(Your Initials) Student Checkup Excel 11-2**.
3. Right-click on the **Restaurant Revenue** tab.
   a. Click on **Move or Copy**.
4. In the *Before Sheet* box, click on **Move to End**, then click the check box below next to *Create a Copy*. Then click **OK**.
5. Rename the new sheet as **Net Income**.
6. On the Net Income sheet, select rows **15-51**. Delete those rows. You will be deleting the *Average, Minimum, Maximum,* and *Mode* rows This will also delete the *Top Three Sellers* chart.
7. In cell **A14**, type in **Expense Categories**. Select range **B14:H14**. Click on **Merge Across**.
8. In cell **A15**, type in **Rent**.
9. In cell **A16**, type in **Payroll**.
10. In cell **A17**, type in **Supplies**.
11. In cell **A18**, type in **Ingredients**.
12. In cell **A19**, type in **Insurance**.
13. In cell **A20**, type in **Total Expenses**.
14. In cell **A22**, type in **Net Income**.
15. Apply **All Borders** (*Home* tab, Font group) to the ranges A14:H20 and A22:H22.
16. In cell K4, type in **Estimated Expenses (%)**. **Left-align** text. Select cells K4 and **L$**. **Merge & Center** cells. Resize column **K** to size **18**.

13			
14	**Expense Categories**		
15	**Rent**		
16	**Payroll**		
17	**Supplies**		
18	**Ingredients**		
19	**Insurance**		
20	**Total Expenses**		
21			
22	**Net Income**		

FIGURE 11-76 Expense Categories

17. In cell **K5**, type in **Rent**. In cell **L5**, type in **20%**.
18. In cell **K6**, type in **Payroll**. In cell **L6**, type in **14%**.
19. In cell **K7**, type in **Supplies**. In cell **L7**, type in **11%**.
20. In cell **K8**, type in **Ingredients**. In cell **L8**, type in **7%**.
21. In cell **K9**, type in **Insurance**. In cell **L9**, type in **2%**.
22. In range **K5:L9**, bold all text and increase font size to **12** pt. In range **L5:L9**, center align the percentages.

23. Apply **All Borders** to the range **K4:L9**. Apply **Fill** color (White, Background 1, Darker 15%) to range **K5:K9** (Figure 11-77).

24. Click in cell **B15**. Type in **=B12*$L$5**. Or, type in the **equals** sign, then click on cell **B12**, press the asterisk or star key (*****) then click on cell **L5**. Immediately press the **F4** key. The **20%** for *Rent* is an **absolute value**. Note: Pressing the **F4** key may not work on your computer. If not, just type in the formula with the **$** signs.

Estimated Expenses (%)	
Rent	20%
Payroll	14%
Supplies	11%
Ingredients	7%
Insurance	2%

FIGURE 11-77 Estimated Expenses (%)

25. Click in cell **B16**. Type in **=B12*$L$6**. The **14%** for *Payroll* is an absolute value.

26. Click in cell **B17**. Type in **=B12*$L$7**. The **11%** for *Supplies* is an **absolute value**.

27. Click in cell **B18**. Type in **=B12*$L$8**. The **7%** for *Ingredients* is an **absolute value**.

28. Click in cell **B19**. Type in **=B12*$L$9**. The **2%** for *Insurance* is an **absolute value**.

29. Click in cell **B20**. Type in **=SUM(B15:B19)**. This is your *Total Expenses*.

30. Click in cell **B22**. Type in **=B12-B20**. This is your *Net Income* for Monday.

31. Select range **B15:B22**. Resize font to size **12** pt. Format with no decimals (Figure 11-78).

32. Select cells **B15**, **B20**, and **B22**. Format as **Accounting**, no decimals. (You should have a $)

33. Select range **B16:B19**. Format as **Comma**, no decimals. (You should <u>not</u> have a $).

	A	B
14	**Expense Categories**	
15	**Rent**	=B12*$L$5
16	**Payroll**	=B12*$L$6
17	**Supplies**	=B12*$L$7
18	**Ingredients**	=B12*$L$8
19	**Insurance**	=B12*$L$9
20	**Total Expenses**	=SUM(B15:B19)
21		
22	**Net Income**	=B12-B20
23		

FIGURE 11-78 Format with No Decimals

34. Highlight the range **B15:B22**. Move your mouse to the green box in the lower right corner of cell **B22**. Once your mouse pointer turns to a black cross (you may have to move your mouse a bit), hold down your left mouse button and drag **(*Autofill*)** through cell **H22** (Figure 11-79).

35. If you do get decimal numbers, be sure to remove the decimals.

14	Expense Categories							
15	Rent	$ 6,117						
16	Payroll	$ 4,282						
17	Supplies	$ 3,364						
18	Ingredients	$ 2,141						
19	Insurance	$ 612						
20	Total Expenses	$ 16,516						
21								
22	Net Income	$ 14,070						
23								
24								

FIGURE 11-79 AutoFilling Absolute Value Formulas

36. Select the range **B22:H22**. Resize font to size **14**. Apply **Bold** to the range.

37. While range **B22:H22** is still selected, apply **Total Formatting** (*Home* tab, *Styles* group, *Cell Styles*). Resize font to size **14 and** apply **Bold** to the range.

38. After you have performed the ***Autofill***, you will have populated all of your formulas (Figure 11-80).

14	Expense Categories							
15	Rent	$ 6,117	$ 6,045	$ 6,055	$	6,019	$ 6,229	$ 9,404	$ 9,857
16	Payroll	4,282	4,232	4,238		4,214	4,360	6,583	6,900
17	Supplies	3,364	3,325	3,330		3,311	3,426	5,172	5,421
18	Ingredients	2,141	2,116	2,119		2,107	2,180	3,291	3,450
19	Insurance	612	605	605		602	623	940	986
20	Total Expenses	$ 16,516	$ 16,322	$ 16,348	$	16,252	$ 16,819	$ 25,391	$ 26,614
21								
22	Net Income	$ 14,070	$ 13,904	$ 13,926	$	13,845	$14,327	$ 21,629	$ 22,672

FIGURE 11-80 Populated Values

39. Click on the Show Formulas button (Formulas tab, Formula Auditing group). Your formulas should look like Figure 11-81.

14	Expense Categories							
15	Rent	=B12*$L$5	=C12*$L$5	=D12*$L$5	=E12*$L$5	=F12*$L$5	=G12*$L$5	=H12*$L$5
16	Payroll	=B12*$L$6	=C12*$L$6	=D12*$L$6	=E12*$L$6	=F12*$L$6	=G12*$L$6	=H12*$L$6
17	Supplies	=B12*$L$7	=C12*$L$7	=D12*$L$7	=E12*$L$7	=F12*$L$7	=G12*$L$7	=H12*$L$7
18	Ingredients	=B12*$L$8	=C12*$L$8	=D12*$L$8	=E12*$L$8	=F12*$L$8	=G12*$L$8	=H12*$L$8
19	Insurance	=B12*$L$9	=C12*$L$9	=D12*$L$9	=E12*$L$9	=F12*$L$9	=G12*$L$9	=H12*$L$9
20	Total Expenses	=SUM(B15:B19)	=SUM(C15:C19)	=SUM(D15:D19)	=SUM(E15:E19)	=SUM(F15:F19)	=SUM(G15:G19)	=SUM(H15:H19)
21								
22	Net Income	=B12-B20	=C12-C20	=D12-D20	=E12-E20	=F12-F20	=G12-G20	=H12-H20

FIGURE 11-81 Populated Formulas

40. Add a new sheet (click on the circled plus to the right of the Net Income Sheet). Rename sheet as **Payment.**

41. In cell **A1**, type in **Bill's Bikes and BBQ**. Select cells **A1:B1**. **Merge & Center**. Format **as Heading 1** (**Home** tab, Styles group). Resize column **A** to **17.5** pt. Resize column **B** to **12** pt.

42. In cell **A2**, type **Loan Amount**.
43. In cell **A3**, type **Term in Months**.
44. In cell **A4**, type **Interest Rate**.
45. In cell **A5**, type **Payment**.
46. In cell **B2**, type $**15,000**. This is the amount that you want to borrow. This is your *Present Value* or pv.
47. In cell **B3**, type **60** (five years). This is the number of months that you want to pay off the loan.
48. In cell **B4**, type in **5%**. This is the *annual* interest rate. To calculate the monthly rate, this number will need to be divided by 12.
49. Click in cell **B5**. Click on the *fx* on the formula bar. When the **Insert Function** dialog opens, type in **PMT** in the **Search for a Function** box.
50. Click on **Go**.
51. In the **Select a Function** area, **PMT** should be highlighted in blue.
52. Click **OK** (Figure 11-82a).
53. In the **Rate** (Interest Rate) box, click on cell **B4** press / then type in **12**. It should look like **B4/12**.
54. In the **Nper** (Term in Months) box, click on cell **B3**.
55. In the **Pv** (Loan Amount) box, click on cell **B2**.

FIGURE 11-82A Insert Function Dialog Box

56. In the middle right of the **Function Arguments** box, you will see your answer. Your answer is **-283.0685047** (Figure 11-82b). Note: Alternatively, you can type the following formula in cell **B5**: **=PMT(B4/12,B3,B2)**. You will get the same answer. Click **OK**. The number will appear as a negative number. A negative number represents money that you pay out.

57. Round your **Payment** up to 2 decimals, if necessary.

58. Save and close.

59. Attach this assignment to the link in Canvas or Blackboard.

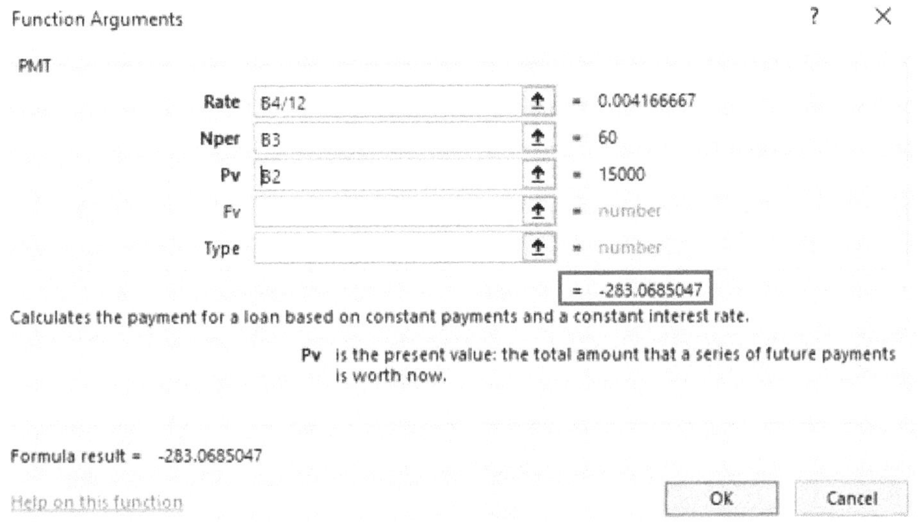

Function Arguments			?	X

PMT

Rate	B4/12	⬆	= 0.004166667
Nper	B3	⬆	= 60
Pv	B2	⬆	= 15000
Fv		⬆	= number
Type		⬆	= number

= -283.0685047

Calculates the payment for a loan based on constant payments and a constant interest rate.

Pv   is the present value: the total amount that a series of future payments is worth now.

Formula result =   -283.0685047

Help on this function   OK   Cancel

FIGURE 11-82B Function Arguments PMT Dialog Box

4. Statistical Functions: Standard Deviations, T-Test, Combinations

Standard Deviations

Standard deviations are based on a sample. The standard deviation is a measure of how widely values are dispersed from the average value (the mean).

To calculate a standard deviation in Excel 2010 and later, you will use the following formula:

STDEV.S(number1,[number2], …)

The **STDEV.S** function syntax has the following arguments:

- **Number1.** This is Required. The first number argument corresponding to a sample of a population. You can also use a single array or a reference to an array instead of arguments separated by commas.

- **Number2**. This is <u>Optional</u>. Number arguments 2 to 254 corresponding to a sample of a population. You can also use a single array or a reference to an array instead of arguments separated by commas.
- **STDEV.S** assumes that its arguments are a sample of the population. If your data represents the entire population, then compute the standard deviation using **STDEV.P**.
- The standard deviation is calculated using the "n-1" method.
- Arguments can either be numbers or names, arrays, or references that contain numbers.
- Logical values and text representations of numbers that you type directly into the list of arguments are counted.
- If an argument is an array or reference, only numbers in that array or reference are counted. Empty cells, logical values, text, or error values in the array or reference are ignored.
- Arguments that are error values or text that cannot be translated into numbers cause errors.
- If you want to include logical values and text representations of numbers in a reference as part of the calculation, use the **STDEVA** function.
- **STDEV.S** uses the following formula, where **x** is the sample mean **AVERAGE**(number1, number2, ...) and **n** is the sample size.

$$\sqrt{\frac{\sum (x - \bar{x})^2}{(n-1)}}$$

Open a new workbook and type in the following information beginning in cell **A1 through cell A10** (Figure 11-83).

1. Click on cell **A13**.
   a. Click on the *fx* button in the Formula Bar on any tab.
   b. Type in STDEV.S. Click **GO**.
   c. When **STDEV.S** appears at the top of the list, click on **OK** (Figure 11-84).
   d. In the *Number1* box, either type in A2:A10 or select the range **A2:A10**.
   e. Leave the *Number2* box blank.
   f. Click **OK**.
   g. Your answer is **2.60** (Figure 11-85).

	A
1	Data 1
2	3
3	4
4	5
5	8
6	9
7	1
8	2
9	4
10	5
11	
12	
13	=STDEV.S(A2:A10)
14	

FIGURE 11-83 Data Array

FIGURE 11-84 STDEV.S

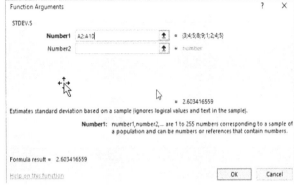

FIGURE 11-85 STDEV.S Function Arguments

Histogram or Pareto Charts

A **Histogram** or **Pareto** (sorted histogram) is a column chart that shows frequency data.

To create a **Histogram** in Excel, you use the **Histogram** tool of the *Analysis ToolPak*. It uses two columns of data to create a histogram: one for data you want to analyze and one for bin numbers that represent the intervals by which you want to measure the frequency.

Make sure you load the *Analysis ToolPak* to add the **Data Analysis** command to the **Data** tab. Then you'll be ready to create a histogram. Here's how:

1. Open a new Workbook. Rename it as (**Your initials**) Stats.
2. On *Sheet1*, type in Data 1 in cell A1 and the numbers in range **A2:A10** (Figure 11-86).
3. Click on the Data tab.
4. Click on **Data Analysis** (Figure 11-87).

FIGURE 11-86
Data List

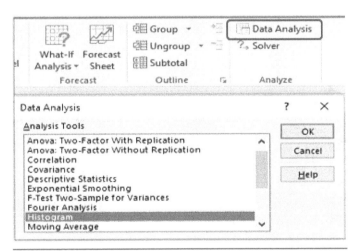

FIGURE 11-87 Data Analysis

5. Click on **Histogram** (Figure 11-88). Click **OK**.
6. Select the Input Range **A2:A10** or type in $A$2:$A$10.
7. Under Output Options, click the **New Worksheet Ply Radio** button: Type in Pareto Chart for the *New Worksheet* name.
8. Click the check box next to either Pareto (sorted Histogram) or **Cumulative Percentage**.

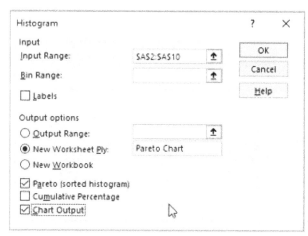

FIGURE 11-88 Histogram

9. If you want both the Bin list and a chart, click in the **Chart Output** checkbox.

If you want to customize your chart, you can change text labels, and click anywhere in the histogram chart to use the Chart Elements, Chart Styles, and Chart Filter buttons on the right of the chart (Figure 11-89).

	A	B	C	D	E	F	G
1	Bin	Frequency	Bin	Frequency			
2	1	1	6.333	4			
3	3.667	2	3.667	2			
4	6.333	4 More		2			
5	More	2	1	1			
6							

PARETO CHART

Frequency

FIGURE 11-89 Pareto Chart

T-Test

T-TEST to determine whether two samples are likely to have come from the same two underlying populations that have the same mean.

   T.TEST(array1,array2,tails,type)

The **T.TEST** function syntax has the following arguments:

- *Array1*. **Required**. The first data set.
- *Array2*. **Required**. The second data set.
- *Tails*. **Required**. Specifies the number of distribution tails. If tails = 1, **T.TEST** uses the one-tailed distribution. If tails = 2, **T.TEST** uses the two-tailed distribution.
- *Type*. **Required**. The kind of T-Test to perform (Figure 11-90).
- If array1 and array2 have different numbers of data points, and type = 1 (paired), **T.TEST** returns the #N/A error value.

If Type equals	This test is performed
1	Paired
2	Two-sample equal variance
3	Two-sample unequal variance

FIGURE 11-90 T-Test Types

- The tails and type arguments are truncated to integers (no decimals).
- If tails or type is nonnumeric, **T.TEST** returns the #VALUE! error value.
- If tails is any value other than 1 or 2, **T.TEST** returns the #NUM! error value.
- **T.TEST** uses the data in array1 and array2 to compute a non-negative t-statistic. If tails=1, **T.TEST** returns the probability of a higher value of the t-statistic under the assumption that *array1* and *array2* are samples from populations with the same mean. The value returned by **T.TEST** when tails=2 is double that returned when tails=1 and corresponds to the probability of a higher absolute value of the t-statistic under the "same population means" assumption.

	B
1	**Data 2**
2	6
3	19
4	3
5	2
6	14
7	4
8	5
9	17
10	1

FIGURE 11-91 Data 2 List

Open your (**Your Initials**) Stats workbook and, on *Sheet1*, type in the following information starting in cell **B1** (Figure 11-91).

1. Click on the *fx* button in the Formula Bar on any tab.
2. Type in T.Test. Click on **GO** (Figure 11-92).
3. When **T-Test** appears at the top of the list, click on **OK**.
4. In the *Array1* box, either type in **A2:A10** or select the range **A2:A10**.
5. In the *Array2* box, either type in **B2:B10** or select the range **B2:B10**.
6. In the *Tails* box, type in **2**.
7. In the *Type* box, type in **1** (Figure 11-93).
8. Click **OK**. Your answer is **0.196** (rounded to three decimal points).

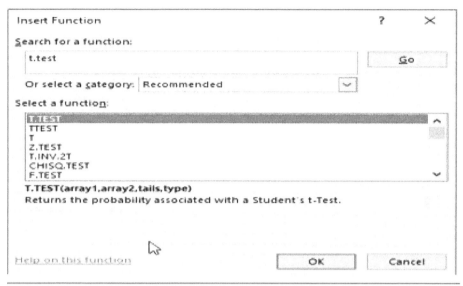

FIGURE 11-92 Input Function T.TEST

Function Arguments   ?   ×

T.TEST

    Array1   A2:A10   ↥   = {3;4;5;8;9;1;2;4;5}
    Array2   B2:B10   ↥   = {6;19;3;2;14;4;5;17;1}
     Tails   2   ↥   = 2
      Type   1   ↥   = 1

                                        = 0.196015785

Returns the probability associated with a Student's t-Test.

              Type is the kind of t-test: paired = 1, two-sample equal variance
                    (homoscedastic) = 2, two-sample unequal variance = 3.

Formula result = 0.196015785

Help on this function   OK   Cancel

FIGURE 11-93 Function Arguments

Combinations

Combinations returns the number of combinations for a given number of items. Use **COMBIN** to determine the total possible number of groups for a given number of items.

        COMBIN(number, number_chosen)

The **COMBIN** function syntax has the following arguments:

- **Number Required**. The number of items.
- **Number_chosen Required**. The number of items in each combination.
- Numeric arguments are truncated to integers (in other words, no decimals).
- If either argument is nonnumeric, **COMBIN** returns the #VALUE! error value.
- If number < 0, number_chosen < 0, or number < number_chosen, **COMBIN** returns the #NUM! error value.
- **A combination is any set or subset of items regardless of their internal order.** Combinations are distinct from permutations, for which the internal order is significant.
- The number of combinations is as follows, where number = n and number_chosen = k:

$$\binom{n}{k} = \frac{P_{k,n}}{k!} = \frac{n!}{k!(n-k)!}$$

Here is a fun example of how to use the **COMBIN** Formula:

You have a small bag of plain M&M'S. Once you open the bag, you begin to separate the M&M'S by color. As you are sorting colors, you are curious as to how many combinations you can make using six different colors with two M&M'S per group. Note: No combination can have two M&M'S of the same color.

	A
1	M&M Colors
2	Red
3	Blue
4	Yellow
5	Orange
6	Green
7	Brown

FIGURE 11-94
M&M'S Color List

1. Open a new Excel workbook. Rename as (**Your Initials**) Combinations.
2. On *Sheet1*, beginning cell **A1**, type in the list shown at the right (Figure 11-94).
3. Notice that in cells **A2:A7**, you have six different colors. Next, click in cell **A10**.
4. Click on the **fx button** in the Formula bar on any tab.
5. Type in COMBIN. Click on **GO**.
6. When **COMBIN** appears at the top of the list, click on **OK** (Figure 11-95).
   a. In the *Number* box, type in 6 (this is the total number of items).

FIGURE 11-95 Insert Function—COMBIN

b. In the *Number_ Chosen* box, type in **2** (the number of items in each combination (Figure 11-96). Click **OK**.

c. Your answer is **15**.

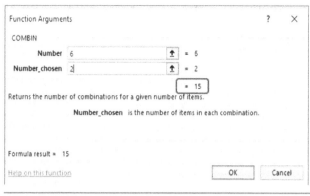

FIGURE 11-96 Function Arguments—COMBIN

Figure 11-97 shows you the formula and the list of your 15 different combinations. These were typed in. The formula only returned the value of **15**.

You may use combinations to combine people in groups, toys, marbles, colors, or just about anything else.

Another thing to keep in mind is that the larger the total *number of items* and the *number chosen* will greatly increase the number of combinations. For example, in the previous formula, there were six total items, and the number chosen was two. Try this: Change the total number of items to **10** and the number chosen to **5**. All of a sudden, the number of combinations grows to **252**.

FIGURE 11-97 M&M'S Color Combinations

5. Sine, Cosine, and Tangents

Sine, Cosine, and Tangent are the main functions used in Trigonometry and are based on a Right-Angled Triangle. Why do we use these functions?

Because they let us work out angles when we know sides.
And they let us work out sides when we know angles.

Let's begin by giving a **name** to each side of a right triangle (Figure 11-98):

"Opposite" is opposite to the (right) angle θ.
"Adjacent" is adjacent (next to) to the (right) angle θ.
"Hypotenuse" is the long side.

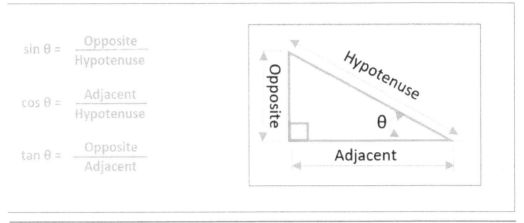

$$\sin\theta = \frac{\text{Opposite}}{\text{Hypotenuse}}$$

$$\cos\theta = \frac{\text{Adjacent}}{\text{Hypotenuse}}$$

$$\tan\theta = \frac{\text{Opposite}}{\text{Adjacent}}$$

FIGURE 11-98 Right Triangle

Excel provides easy formulas to calculate Sine, Cosine, and Tangent. Let's calculate all three:

What are the **sine**, **cosine**, and **tangent** of 30°?

(The classic 30° triangle has a **hypotenuse** of length 2, an **opposite** side of length 1, and an **adjacent** side of √3. See Figure 11-99.

Sine: =sin(radians(30)). Result is **0.5**.
Cosine: =cos(radians(30)). Result is **0.866**.
Tangent: tan(radians(30)). Result is **0.577**.

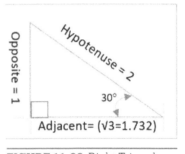

FIGURE 11-99 Right Triangle

6. Conditional Formatting and Goal Seek

Conditional Formatting

Conditional Formatting will enable you to spot trends and patterns with a quick glance. With the use of data bars, color scales, and icon sets, you can visually highlight important values. Other options of Conditional Formatting include Highlight Cells Rules (Figure 11-100) and Top/Bottom Rules (Figure 11-101). These options allow you to highlight specific needs, or you can create your own.

Let's try it:

1. Open the **Boise Idaho Weather** Workbook.
2. Select the range **B3:M6**.
3. Click on the **Conditional Formatting** button (*Home* tab, *Styles* group).
4. Click on the **Color Scales** button. Click on the *Red—Yellow—Green Color Scale* (2nd option, top row). See Figure 11-102.

FIGURE 11-100 Conditional Formatting
Highlight Cells Rule

FIGURE 11-101 Conditional Formatting
Top/Bottom Rules

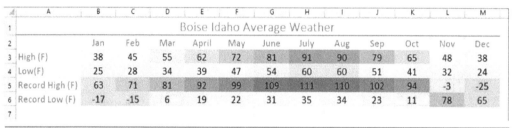

	A	B	C	D	E	F	G	H	I	J	K	L	M
1		Boise Idaho Average Weather											
2		Jan	Feb	Mar	April	May	June	July	Aug	Sep	Oct	Nov	Dec
3	High (F)	38	45	55	62	72	81	91	90	79	65	48	38
4	Low(F)	25	28	34	39	47	54	60	60	51	41	32	24
5	Record High (F)	63	71	81	92	99	109	111	110	102	94	-3	-25
6	Record Low (F)	-17	-15	6	19	22	31	35	34	23	11	78	65
7													

FIGURE 11-102 Boise Average Weather

5. Re-select the range **B3:M6**.
6. Click on the **Conditional Formatting button** (*Home* tab, *Styles* group).
7. Click on the **Clear Rules** button. Then click on *Clear Rules from Selected Cells*. This will clear your formatting (Figure 11-104).

FIGURE 11-103 Copy a
Worksheet

FIGURE 11-104 Clear Condi-
tioning Formatting Rules

8. While the range **B3:M6** is still highlighted, click on the ***Conditional Formatting*** button.
9. Click on ***Top/Bottom*** button. Then click on ***Above Average***. This will show you the temperatures that are above average. Excel will highlight the temperatures that are above average. A small dialog window will pop up and give you options on how you would like to format your cells, plus a Custom Format where you can choose fonts, font colors, bold, italics, background color, and borders to highlight your data (Figure 11-105).
10. Choose your format for your highlighted cells.

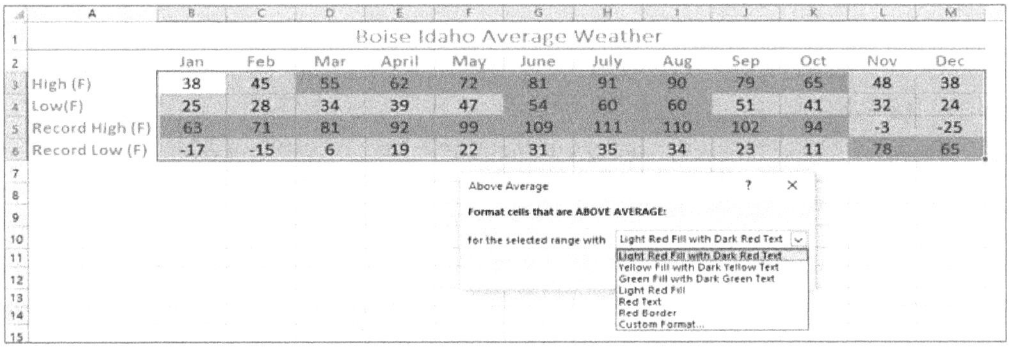

FIGURE 11-105 Boise Above Average Temperatures

Conditional Formatting will prove to be a valuable tool for you to learn and remember. You will find countless ways to use it and, if you own a business or plan to own a business someday, you will find this as a handy tool to help you track inventory levels, cash inflows and outflows, and anything else where you will need to quickly spot trends or patterns.

Goal Seek

You can use Goal Seek to find the result you want by adjusting an *input* value.

If you know the result that you want from a formula but are not sure what input value the formula needs to get that result, use the **Goal Seek** feature.

For example, suppose that you need to borrow some money. You know how much money you want, how long you want to take to pay off the loan, and how much you can afford to pay each month. You can use Goal Seek to determine what interest rate you will need to secure in order to meet your loan goal.

Because you want to calculate the loan interest rate needed to meet your goal, you use the **PMT** function. The **PMT** function calculates a monthly payment amount. In this example, the monthly payment amount is the goal that you seek.

Here are the steps to do this task:

1. Open a new, blank worksheet. Save it as **(Your Initials)** Goal Seek.
2. First, add some labels in the first column to make it easier to read the worksheet (Figure 11-106).
   a. In cell A1, type **Loan Amount**.
   b. In cell A2, type **Term in Months**.
   c. In cell A3, type **Interest Rate**.
   d. In cell A4, type **Payment**.
   e. Next, add the values that you know.
   f. In cell B1, type **12000**. This is the amount that you want to borrow. ($12,000).
   g. In cell B2, type **120** (ten years). This is the number of months that you want to pay off the loan.

	A	B	C
1	Loan Amount	12000	
2	Term in Months	120	
3	Interest Rate		
4	Payment		
5			

FIGURE 11-106 Setting Up Payments

Note: Although you know the payment amount *that you want,* you do not enter it as a value because the payment amount is a result of the formula. At this step, let the formula calculate the value. Instead, you add the formula to the worksheet and specify the payment value at a later step when you use **Goal Seek**.

Next, add the formula for which you have a goal. For the example, use the PMT function:

   a. In cell B4, type **=PMT(B3/12,B2,B1)**. This formula calculates the payment amount of $100 per month. In this example, you want to pay $125 each month. You don't enter that amount here because you want to use Goal Seek to determine the interest rate, and **Goal Seek requires that you start with a formula** (Figure 11-107).

The formula refers to cells **B1** and **B2**, which contain values that you specified in preceding steps. The formula also refers to cell **B3**, which is where you will specify that **Goal Seek** put the interest rate. The formula divides the value in **B3** by 12 because you specified a monthly payment; however, the **PMT** function assumes an annual interest rate.

Because there is no value in cell **B3**, Excel assumes a **0%** interest rate and, using the values in the example, returns a payment of **$100.00**. **You can ignore that value for now.**

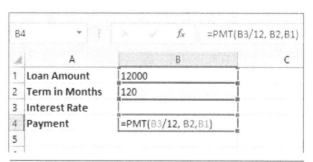

FIGURE 11-107 Payment Formula

This is how you use **Goal Seek** to determine the interest rate

1. Click on cell **B4**.
2. On the Data tab, in the *Forecast* group, click **What-If Analysis**, and then click *Goal Seek* (Figure 11-108).
   a. In the *Set cell* box, enter the reference for the cell that contains the formula that you want to resolve. In the example, this reference is cell **B4** (Payment).
   b. In the *To* value box, type the formula result that you want. In the example, this is −125. Note that this number is negative because it represents a payment.
   c. In the *By changing cell* box, enter the reference for the cell that contains the value that you want to adjust. In the example, this reference is cell **B3** (Interest rate).
   d. Click **OK** (Figure 11-109).

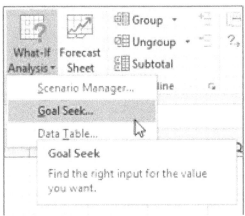

FIGURE 11-108 Goal Seek

FIGURE 11-109 Goal Seek Values

Note: The cell that Goal Seek changes must be referenced by the formula in the cell that you specified in the **Set cell** box.

Goal Seek has found a solution (Figure 11-110). Click **OK** to close the *Goal Seek Status* dialog box. Your solution is **0.046093655**. Click on cell **B3** and reformat the Interest Rate as Percentage with **2** decimal places (*Home* tab, *Number* group). Your answer should be **4.61%**.

FIGURE 11-110 Goal Seek Solution

In this project, you will open an existing workbook for Bill's Bikes and BBQ. You will use Conditional Formatting and Goal Seek to help Bill see sales trends and to calculate sales margins. **Note: Blue text represents typed text.**

File Needed: **(Your Initials) Student Checkup Excel 11-2**
Completed File Name*: **(Your initials) Student Checkup Excel 11-3**

1. Open (Your Initials) Student Checkup 11-2.
2. Save the workbook as **(Your Initials) Student Checkup Excel 11-3.**
3. Open the **Restaurant Revenue** tab.
4. Add a **Standard Deviation** formula.
5. Click in cell **A19**. Type in **Standard Deviation of Totals**. Use the **Format Painter** to format cell **A19** like cell **A18,** if necessary. Resize column **A** to fit. Apply **All Borders** formatting to **A19:B19**.
6. In cell **B19**, use the **STDEV.S** formula to determine the standard deviation of range **B12:H12**.
   a. Click on the **fx** button next to your formula bar. In the **Insert Function** dialog box, type in **STDEV.S**. In the **Number1** box, your range should be **B12:H12.** Your answer should be **8662.032724.** Click **OK**. If necessary, click the **Decrease Decimal** button so that you have **2** decimals.
   b. Format your answer as an **Accounting** formatting with two decimals.
7. Add an Average **of Values** formula.
8. Click in cell **A21**. Type in **Average of Values**. Use the **Format Painter** to format cell **A21** to look like cell **A15,** if necessary.
9. In cell **B21**, use the **average** formula to calculate the average of range **B5:H11**. Your answer should be **$5,074**. Use the **Format Painter** to format cell **B21** to look like **B15**, if necessary.
10. Add a **Combination** Formula. Bill's customers usually order two different items for a meal. Bill sells seven different items. How many different combinations can be made?
    a. Click in cell **A22**. Type in **Number of Menu Combinations**. Use the **Format Painter** to format cell **A22** like cell **A15**. Resize column **A** if necessary.

b. In cell **B22**, use the **COMBIN** formula to calculate the number of combinations. Type in **=Combin(7,2)**. You should have **21** different combinations. **Center** value in cell.

11. Apply **All Borders** formatting to range **A21:B22**.

Note: You can't have two of the same item in one combination.

12. Select the range **B5:H11**.

13. Click on the **Conditional Formatting** button (*Home* tab, *Styles* group).

14. Click on the **Icon Sets** button. Click on the **3 Arrows (Colored)**. This is the first option under **Directional**. See Figure 11-111.

	A	B	C	D	E	F	G	H	I	J
1				Bills Bikes & BBQ						
2				May 1 - May 7						
3										
4	Revenue Categories	Monday	Tuesday	Wednesday	Thursday	Friday	Saturday	Sunday	Totals	
5	BBQ Ribs	$ 4,123	$ 3,240	$ 3,575	$ 3,460	$ 3,665	$ 6,333	$ 6,800	$ 31,196	
6	BBQ KBOBs	1,099	888	1,051	1,080	1,210	3,677	4,021	13,026	
7	BBQ Pulled Pork	7,099	6,888	6,571	6,329	6,722	8,989	9,558	52,156	
8	BBQ Corn on the Cob	1,035	1,100	1,158	1,168	1,299	3,995	4,254	14,009	
9	BBQ Crab Cakes	5,200	5,675	5,640	5,550	5,850	7,569	7,789	43,273	
10	BBQ Chicken	6,150	6,340	6,299	6,315	6,145	8,192	8,362	47,793	
11	BBQ Steak	5,880	6,095	5,980	6,195	6,255	8,265	8,512	47,182	
12	Total	$30,586	$30,226	$ 30,274	$ 30,097	$31,146	$ 47,020	$ 49,286	$248,635	
13										
14										
15	Average of Totals	$ 35,519			Total Sales			$ 248,635		
16	Minimum of Totals	$ 30,097			Monday's Percentage of Total Sales			12%		
17	Maximum of Totals	$ 49,286			Tuesday's Percentage of Total Sales			12%		
18	Mode of Totals	#N/A			Wednesday's Percentage of Total Sales			12%		
19	Standard Deviation of Totals	$ 8,662			Thursday's Percentage of Total Sales			12%		
20					Friday's Percentage of Total Sales			13%		
21	Average of Values	$ 5,074			Saturday's Percentage of Total Sales			19%		
22	Number of Menu Combinations	21			Sunday's Percentage of Total Sales			20%		
23										

FIGURE 11-111 Conditional Formatting Directional Arrow Icons

15. Reselect the range **B5:H11**.

16. Click on the Conditional Formatting button (*Home* tab, *Styles* group).

17. Click on the **Clear Rules** button. Then click on *Clear Rules from Selected Cells*. This will clear your formatting.

18. While the range **B5:H11** is still highlighted, click on the **Conditional Formatting** button.

19. Click on **Top/Bottom** button. Then click on *Below Average*. Excel will highlight the below average sales values. A small dialog window will pop up. Click on the down arrow next to the *For the Selected Range With* box.

20. Select *Green Fill with Dark Green Text*. All the values that are below average (the average is **$5,074** which was calculated in cell **B21** (Figure 11-112).

21. While the range **B5:H11** is still selected, click on the **Conditional Formatting** button (*Home* tab, *Styles* group).

Revenue Categories	Monday	Tuesday	Wednesday	Thursday	Friday	Saturday	Sunday	Totals
BBQ Ribs	$ 4,123	$ 3,240	$ 3,575	$ 3,460	$ 3,665	$ 6,333	$ 6,800	$ 31,196
BBQ KBOBs	1,099	888	1,051	1,080	1,210	3,677	4,021	13,026
BBQ Pulled Pork	7,099	6,888	6,571	6,329	6,722	8,989	9,558	52,156
BBQ Corn on the Cob	1,035	1,100	1,168	1,168	1,299	3,995	4,254	14,009
BBQ Crab Cakes	5,200	5,675	5,640	5,550	5,850	7,569	7,789	43,273
BBQ Chicken	6,150	6,340	6,299	6,315	6,145	8,192	8,352	47,793
BBQ Steak	5,880	6,095	5,980	6,195	6,255	8,265	8,512	47,182
Total	$ 30,586	$ 30,226	$ 30,274	$ 30,097	$ 31,146	$ 47,020	$ 49,286	$ 248,635

FIGURE 11-112 Conditional Formatting Below Average Sales

22. Click on the **Clear Rules** button. Then click on *Clear Rules from Selected Cells*. This will clear your formatting.
23. With the range **B5:H11** still selected, click on the **Conditional Formatting** button.
24. Click on **Highlight Cells Rules** button. Then click on *Greater Than*. A small dialog window will pop up. Type **5074** in the box under Format Cells that are GREATER THAN. The **$5,074** is the **Average of Values** number that you have in cell **B21** in your **Restaurant Revenue** sheet.
25. In the right side of the **With** box, click on the down arrow and select *Yellow Fill with Dark Yellow* Text. Click **OK** (Figure 11-113).

Revenue Categories	Monday	Tuesday	Wednesday	Thursday	Friday	Saturday	Sunday	Totals
BBQ Ribs	$ 4,123	$ 3,240	$ 3,575	$ 3,460	$ 3,665	$ 6,333	$ 6,800	$ 31,196
BBQ KBOBs	1,099	888	1,051	1,080	1,210	3,677	4,021	13,026
BBQ Pulled Pork	7,099	6,888	6,571	6,329	6,722	8,989	9,558	52,156
BBQ Corn on the Cob	1,035	1,100	1,168	1,168	1,299	3,995	4,254	14,009
BBQ Crab Cakes	5,200	5,675	5,640	5,550	5,850	7,569	7,789	43,273
BBQ Chicken	6,150	6,340	6,299	6,315	6,145	8,192	8,352	47,793
BBQ Steak	5,880	6,095	5,980	6,195	6,255	8,265	8,512	47,182
Total	$ 30,586	$ 30,226	$ 30,274	$ 30,097	$ 31,146	$ 47,020	$ 49,286	$ 248,635

FIGURE 11-113 Conditional Formatting GREATER THAN

26. While the range **B5:H11** is still selected, click on the **Conditional Formatting** button (*Home* tab, *Styles* group).
27. Click on the **Clear Rules** button. Then click on *Clear Rules from Selected Cells*. This will clear your formatting.
28. While the range **B5:H11** is still highlighted, click on the **Conditional Formatting** button.
29. Click on **Data Bars**. Under the *Gradient* group, click on the *Light Blue Data Bar* (Figure 11-114).

Revenue Categories	Monday	Tuesday	Wednesday	Thursday	Friday	Saturday	Sunday	Totals
			Bills Bikes & BBQ					
			May 1 - May 7					
BBQ Ribs	$ 4,123	$ 3,240	$ 3,575	$ 3,460	$ 3,665	$ 6,333	$ 6,800	$ 31,196
BBQ KBOBs	1,099	888	1,051	1,080	1,210	3,677	4,021	13,026
BBQ Pulled Pork	7,099	6,888	6,571	6,329	6,722	8,989	9,558	52,156
BBQ Corn on the Cob	1,035	1,100	1,158	1,168	1,299	3,995	4,254	14,009
BBQ Crab Cakes	5,200	5,675	5,640	5,550	5,850	7,569	7,789	43,273
BBQ Chicken	6,150	6,340	6,299	6,315	6,145	8,192	8,352	47,793
BBQ Steak	5,880	6,095	5,980	6,195	6,255	8,265	8,512	47,182
Total	$ 30,586	$ 30,226	$ 30,274	$ 30,097	$ 31,146	$ 47,020	$ 49,286	$ 248,635

FIGURE 11-114 Conditional Formatting Data Bars

30. Click on the Conditional Formatting button (*Home* tab, *Styles* group).
31. Click on the **Clear Rules** button. Then click on *Clear Rules from Selected Cells*. This will clear your formatting.
32. With the range **B5:H11** is still highlighted, click on the **Conditional Formatting** button.
33. Click on **Color Scales**. Click on the **Red – White – Green Color Scale** (First row, fourth icon). See Figure 11-115.

Revenue Categories	Monday	Tuesday	Wednesday	Thursday	Friday	Saturday	Sunday	Totals
			Bills Bikes & BBQ					
			May 1 - May 7					
BBQ Ribs	$ 4,123	$ 3,240	$ 3,575	$ 3,460	$ 3,665	$ 6,333	$ 6,800	$ 31,196
BBQ KBOBs	1,099	888	1,051	1,080	1,210	3,677	4,021	13,026
BBQ Pulled Pork	7,099	6,888	6,571	6,329	6,722	8,989	9,558	52,156
BBQ Corn on the Cob	1,035	1,100	1,158	1,168	1,299	3,995	4,254	14,009
BBQ Crab Cakes	5,200	5,675	5,640	5,550	5,850	7,569	7,789	43,273
BBQ Chicken	6,150	6,340	6,299	6,315	6,145	8,192	8,352	47,793
BBQ Steak	5,880	6,095	5,980	6,195	6,255	8,265	8,512	47,182
Total	$ 30,586	$ 30,226	$ 30,274	$ 30,097	$ 31,146	$ 47,020	$ 49,286	$ 248,635

FIGURE 11-115 Conditional Formatting Color Scales

34. Add a new worksheet. Name it **Goal Seek**.
35. Click in cell **A2**. Type in the formula for **Today**. The formula is: **=today()**. Format as a short date. Resize font to **12** pt. **bold**, and **center** align.
36. On the **Restaurant Revenue** worksheet, copy the range **A5:A11** and paste it in to range **A5:A11** in the **Goal Seek** sheet. Resize Column **A** if necessary.
37. In cell **B4** type in **Cost**. In cell **C4**, type in **Retail**.
38. Click on cell **A5**. Apply the Format Painter (*Home* tab, *Clipboard* group) to range **A4:C4**. Center **Cost** and **Retail** in cells.
39. Select range **A4:C11**. Apply **All Borders** formatting.

40. Enter the following values in ranges **B5:B11 (Cost)** and **C5:C11 (Retail)**. Format as *Currency* (Figure 11-116).

41. Click on cell **D4**. Type in Margin. Click on cell **C4** then click on **Format Painter** and click on cell **D4**.

42. Select range **D5:D11**. Apply **All Borders** formatting.

43. Click on cell **D5**. Type in **=(C5-B5)/C5**. Press **Enter**. Format **D5** as a percentage. **Center** the value in the cell.

44. Reselect cell **D5** if necessary. Move your mouse to the lower right corner of the cell. Click on the green square, hold down your left mouse key, and drag (**Autofill**) down through cell **C11** (Figure 11-116a).

45. Click on the **Formulas** tab. Then click on *Show Formulas* in the *Formula Auditing* group (Figure 11-116b).

	A	B	C	D
1				
2	6/19/2019			
3				
4		**Cost**	**Retail**	**Margin**
5	**BBQ Ribs**	$3.50	$7.00	50%
6	**BBQ KBOBs**	$2.75	$5.00	45%
7	**BBQ Pulled Pork**	$3.00	$5.50	45%
8	**BBQ Corn on the Cob**	$0.50	$1.50	67%
9	**BBQ Crab Cakes**	$3.75	$7.00	46%
10	**BBQ Chicken**	$2.50	$6.00	58%
11	**BBQ Steak**	$3.50	$8.00	56%

FIGURE 11-116A Cost and Retail Values

	A	B	C	D
1				
2	**=TODAY()**			
3				
4		**Cost**	**Retail**	**Margin**
5	**BBQ Ribs**	3.5	7	=(C5-B5)/C5
6	**BBQ KBOBs**	2.75	5	=(C6-B6)/C6
7	**BBQ Pulled Pork**	3	5.5	=(C7-B7)/C7
8	**BBQ Corn on the Cob**	0.5	1.5	=(C8-B8)/C8
9	**BBQ Crab Cakes**	3.75	7	=(C9-B9)/C9
10	**BBQ Chicken**	2.5	6	=(C10-B10)/C10
11	**BBQ Steak**	3.5	8	=(C11-B11)/C11

FIGURE 11-116B Formulas and Margin Calculations

46. Click on cell **F4**. Type in **New Retail Price to make 75% Margin**. Left align. Resize column to fit.

47. Click in cell **D5**.

a. On the **Data** tab, in the *Forecast* group, click *What-If Analysis*, and then click *Goal Seek*.

b. In the *Set cell* box, click on cell **D5**.

c. In the *To value* box, type in **75%**.

d. In the *By changing cell* box, click on cell **C5** ($7.00)**. Click **OK.** The program will add the "$" symbol (Figure 11-117).

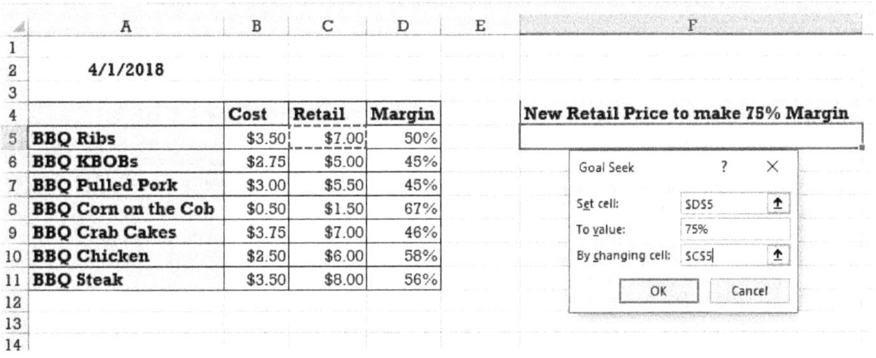

FIGURE 11-117 Goal Seek

48. Your answer should be **$13.99**. If necessary, decrease decimals to 2 decimal. Click **OK**.

49. In cell **F5**, type in **$13.99. Bold** and **Center**. See Figure 11-118A. Note: In Figure 11-118a, the new retail price has been highlighted in yellow. This means that Bill will need to charge $13.99 to make a 75% margin.

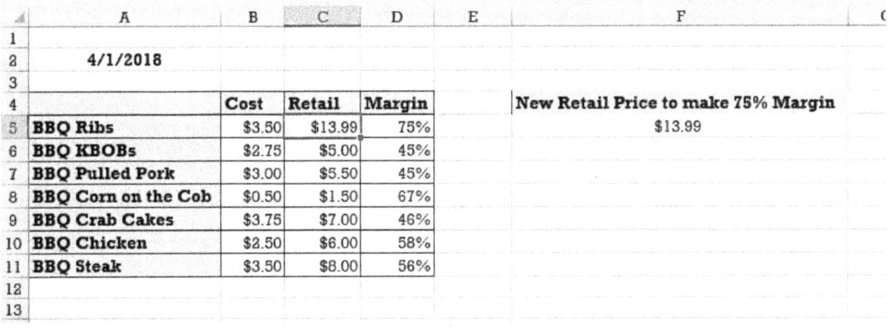

FIGURE 11-118A New Retail Price

50. Click on your **Restaurant Revenue** tab. Move this tab to the far left so it is the first tab (Click on the tab, hold down your left mouse and drag to the left to move the tab).

51. Move the **Saturday & Sunday Revenues** tab to the right of **Restaurant Revenue** tab as the second tab. Change the tab color to **Yellow** under **Standard Colors**.

52. Move the **Net Income** tab to the right of **Saturday & Sunday Revenues** tab as the third tab. Change the tab color to **Green** under **Standard Colors**.

53. Move the **Payment** tab to the right of the **Net Income** tab as the fourth tab. Change the tab color to **Purple** under **Standard Colors**.

54. Move the **Goal Seek** tab to the right of the **Payment** tab as the fifth tab. Change the tab color to **Blue** under **Standard Colors**.

55. Move the **Total Revenue Pie Chart** tab to the right of the **Goal Seek** tab as the sixth tab. Change the tab color to **Light Green** under **Standard Colors**.

56. The **Combo Chart** tab should be the last tab. Recolor the tab to Red under Standard Colors.
    Note: Your tabs should be in the following order from left to right: **Restaurant Revenue** (Orange, Accent 1 tab), **Saturday & Sunday Revenues** (Yellow tab), **Net Income** (Green tab), **Payment** (Purple tab), **Goal Seek** (Light Blue tab), **Total Revenue Pie Chart** (Light Green tab), and **Combo Chart** (Red tab). (Figure 11-118b).

57. Save and close. Turn in your assignment.

FIGURE 11.118B Tab Order and Colors

Excel Project 11-1

You have finally learned enough Excel to begin to feel comfortable creating a personal budget. You know that if you use an Excel template, making a personal budget will be easy. You want to create a simple, yet effective, budget including a chart. Note: You may use ***realistic fictional data*** instead of personal real data.

File Needed: **Monthly College Budget**
Completed File Name: **(Your Initials) Monthly College Budget.xlsx**

1. Open the **Monthly College Budget** workbook**.**
2. Save as **(Your Initials) Monthly College Budget.xlsx.** Your worksheet will look like Figure 11-119.
3. Scroll down and you will see a graphic for **Cash Flows**. Under the **Cash Flows** graphic, you will see a slider bar. You can slide the bar from January to December. The selected month will appear in the doughnut charts.
4. The **Monthly Cash after Expenses** area reflects your Income minus your expenses. These numbers will calculate on their own when you enter figures in the sections that follow. **Do not change these formulas**.

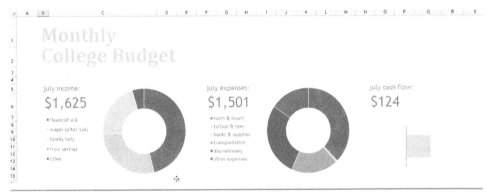

FIGURE 11-119 Monthly College Budget

5. Under **Monthly Income**, you can type in your own figures. If you need to add a row, just insert a row above or below where you want it to be. You can type in your category and your monthly amounts. The program is set up to automatically update your totals.
6. Under **Monthly Expense**, you have the following subcategories: *Room & Board, Tuition & Fees, Books & Supplies, Transportation, Discretionary*, and *Other Expenses*. At the bottom of the worksheet, you will see **Total Expenses**. Total Expenses is the sum of all of your expenses.
7. In the **Monthly Income** section, insert your figures for each category and for each month. The program will automatically calculate everything as you go along. Insert a row to add a category if needed. If a category is listed that you don't need, just delete the row.

8. In the **Monthly Expense** subcategories, insert your figures for each one and for each month. The program will automatically calculate everything as you go along. Insert a row to add a category if needed. If a category is listed that you don't need, just delete the row.

Note: Do not change anything in the cells with the **light grey background** or in the **Total Income** and **Total Expense** rows.

9. This is meant to be a tool to help you take charge of your personal money management.

10. Save and close your workbook. Turn in the assignment.

Excel Project 11-2

In the last project, you had to face creating a budget to see how well you have been managing your money. However, you have had your eye on a brand new red sports car. The current price for this sports car is $36,000. You have been dreaming of driving it off the dealer lot with a big smile and a manageable way to pay off the loan for the car. Luckily, you have received an early $5,000 cash gift for graduation. You would like to apply the $5,000 gift and your old trade-in clunker as down payments and make payments to build up your credit while you pay off the car. You have negotiated with the dealer, and the dealer has offered you a 5% interest rate over 72 months. **Note: Blue text represents typed text.**

File Needed: **Dream Car.xlsx**
Completed File Name: **(Your Initials) Excel Project 11-2.xlsx**

1. Open the **_Dream Car.xlsx_** workbook.
2. Save as **(Your Initials) Dream Car.**
3. Set range names for the workbook.
4. On the **_Car Loan_** worksheet, select cells **B5:C11** (Figure 11-120).
5. Click the **_Create from Selection_** button _(Formulas_ tab, _Defined Names_ group).
   a. In the pop-up dialog box, make sure the **_Left Column_** button checkbox is the _only_ checkbox checked. Click **OK**.
6. Select the range **E5:F7**.
7. Click the **_Create from Selection_** button (Formulas tab, _Defined Names_ group).
   a. In the pop-up dialog box, make sure the **_Left Column_** button check box is the _only_ checkbox checked. Click **OK.**

8. Select cells **E10:F11.** Repeat the steps in 5a above.
   a. Your formulas will now have names in English instead of cell references such as B5 or C11.

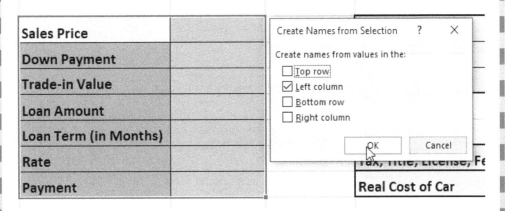

Sales Price			Create Names from Selection ? X
Down Payment			Create names from values in the:
Trade-in Value			☐ Top row
Loan Amount			☑ Left column
Loan Term (in Months)			☐ Bottom row
Rate			☐ Right column
Payment			OK Cancel

Tax, Title, License, Fe

Real Cost of Car

FIGURE 11-120 Naming Cells

9. Click in cell **C5**. Type in **$36,000** *(Sales Price)*. Press **Enter.**
10. Click in cell **C6**. Type in **$5,000** (**Down Payment**). Press **Enter**.
11. Click in cell **C7**. Type in **$1,500** (**Trade-in value**). Press **Enter**.
12. Click in cell **C8** (Loan Amount). Type in = then click on ***Sales Price*** (cell **C5**) then type in **–** then click on ***Down Payment*** (cell **C6**) then type in – then click on ***Trade-In value*** (cell **C7**). Your formula will look like this: **=Sales_Price – Down_Payment – Trade-In value**. Your **Loan Amount** should equal **$29,500.00**.
13. Click in cell **C9** (Loan Term (in Months). Type in **72**.
14. Click in cell **C10** (Rate). Type in **5%** (Figure 11-121).
15. Insert a *PMT* function.
16. Click on cell **C11**.
    a. Click the ***Financial*** button (*Formulas* tab, *Function Library* group) and select **PMT**.
    b. In the Payment **Function Arguments** box, click the **Rate** box, and then click cell **C10** in the **Car Loan** worksheet. The range name *Rate* is added to the box. Type **/12** immediately after **Rate** to divide by 12 for monthly expenses.
    c. In the Payment **Function Arguments** box, click the ***Nper*** box and click cell **C9** in the **Car Loan** worksheet. The range name *Loan_ Term_in_Months* is added to the box.
    d. Click on the **Pv** box. Type in a minus sign in front of Loan_Amount in the **Pv** box. Click on cell **C8** (**Loan Amount**). Your answer will appear as a positive number.

e. Leave the *Fv* and ***Type*** boxes empty.

f. Click **OK**. Your loan payment will be **$475.10** (rounded).

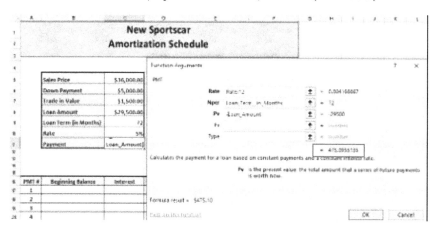

FIGURE 11-121 PMT Function

17. Create a *total interest* formula.
    a. Click cell **F5** (**Total Interest**). The formula is the **Payment** times the total number of payments (**Loan Term (in Months)**). Then you subtract the **Loan Amount**.
    b. Type = and click cell **C11** (**Payment**).
    c. Type * to multiply and click cell **C9** (**Loan_Term_(in_Months)**).
    d. Type in a – sign to subtract.
    e. Click cell **C8** (**Loan_Amount**). Your formula will be: **=Payment*Loan Term (in Months)-Loan Amount**. Your answer should be **$4,706.88** (See Figure 11-122).

18. Create a *total principal* formula and the *total loan cost* (interest plus principal).
    a. Click cell **F6** (**Total Principal**). The formula is =**Payment** * **Loan Term (in Months), - Total Interest**.
    b. Type = and click cell **C11** (**Payment**).
    c. Type * to multiply, and click on cell **C9 (Loan Term (In Months))**.
    d. Type in a – sign to subtract.
    e. Click cell **F5** (**Total Interest**). Press **Enter**. Your answer should be **$29,500.00** (See Figure 11-122).

19. The Total Principal is the same amount as the **Loan Amount** you have calculated in cell **C8.** In this case, your answer is **$29,500.00**.

20. Click in cell **F7**. Type = click cell **F5**, type + click cell **F6**, then press **Enter**.

21. Your formula is =**F5+F6**. Your *Total Cost* of the loan is **$34,206.88** (Figure 11-122).

22. Click in cell **F10**. Type in **$2,660**. This is your tax, title, and dealer fees for the car. (This number is based on a sales price of $36,000 and 6% sales tax. Sales tax = $2,160.00, Tax title, and dealer fees = $500.00)
21. In cell **F11**, the **Real Cost of Your Car** is **$41,866.88. Yikes! (This is the Total Cost of Loan + Down Payment +Trade-in Value + Tax, Title, License, Fees.)**

	A	B	C	D	E	F
4						
5		Sales Price	$36,000.00		Total Interest	$4,706.88
6		Down Payment	$5,000.00		Total Principal	$29,500.00
7		Trade-in Value	$1,500.00		Total Cost of Loan	$34,206.88
8		Loan Amount	$29,500.00			
9		Loan Term (in Months)	72			
10		Rate	5%		Tax, Title, License, Fees	$2,660.00
11		Payment	$475.10		Real Cost of Car	$36,866.88
12						
13						

FIGURE 11-122 Calculated Values

22. Click in cell **F10**. This is your sales tax, title, license, and fees for the car. Depending on where you live, the numbers will differ from this assignment. In my state, these are the current figures:
    Sales tax=6% =Sales Price*6% ($36,000*6%) or $2, 160.00
    Estimated title, license, and fees: $500.00
    F10 value = $2160.00 + $500.00 or **$2,660.00**.
    Note: this value does not include auto insurance.
23. Click in cell **F11**. The real cost of the car is equal to Total Cost of Loan (F7) + Tax, Title, License, Fees (F10). In this example, your numbers are $34,206.88 + $2,660.00 or $36,866.88. **The Real Cost of the car is $36,866.88.**
25. Create an amortization schedule.
    a. Calculate *Beginning Balance* (cell **B17**).
        i. Click cell **B17**. The beginning balance is the total cost of the loan.
        ii. Type **=** then click on cell **F4** (Total Cost of Loan). **DO NOT** type in $36,866.88 (Real Cost of Car) OR type in "**F7**". *To make the formulas work, you must click in each cell in the equations.* Press **Enter.**
26. Calculate *Interest Payment.*
    a. Click in cell **C17**.
    b. Type in the following formula: **=B17*(Rate/12). (Click on cell C9 for the Rate.)** Your answer should be **$142.53**.

Sales Price	36000
Down Payment	5000
Trade-in Value	1500
Loan Amount	=Sales_Price-Down_Payment-Trade_in_Value
Loan Term (in Months)	72
Rate	0.05
Payment	=PMT(Rate/12,Loan_Term__in_Months,-Loan_Amount)

Total Interest	=Payment*Loan_Term__in_Months-Loan_Amount
Total Principal	=Payment*Loan_Term__in_Months-Total_Interest
Total Cost of Loan	=Total_Interest+Total_Principal

Tax, Title, License, Fees	2660
Real Cost of Car	=Total_Cost_of_Loan+F10

FIGURE 11-123 Formulas

27. *Calculate Principal Payment.*
   a. Click in cell **D17**.
   b. Type in the following formula: **= Payment-C17. (Click on cell C11 for the Payment.)** Your answer should be **$332.57**.
28. *Calculate Total Payment.*
   a. Click in cell **E17**.
   b. Type in **=**. Click on cell **C17**. Press your **plus** key. Click on cell **D17**. The formula is: **= C17 + D17**. Your **Total Payment** in cell **E17** should be **$475.10**.
29. Calculate the *Ending Balance.*
   a. Click in cell **F17**.
   b. Type in **=**. Click on cell **B17**. Press your **minus** key. Click on cell **E17**. The formula is: **= B17 – E17**. Your **Ending Balance** in cell **F17** should be **$33,731.78**.
30. Calculate the new Beginning Balance for the second payment.
   a. Click on cell **B18**.
   b. Type in **=**. Click on cell **F17**. The formula is: **=F17**. The new **Beginning Balance** in cell **B18** should be **$33,731.78**.
   Note: When completing these formulas, be sure to click in the cells as noted in the formulas. **DO NOT type in the cell references (such as B17, E17, etc.).** These cells contain the formulas you need to make the amortization table work correctly.

TABLE 11-1 Formulas

B17 (Beginning Balance)	=Total_Cost_of_Loan
C17 (Interest)	=B17*(Rate/12)
D17 (Principal)	=Payment - C17
E17 (Total Payment)	=C17 + D17
F17 (Ending Balance)	=B17-E17
B18 (Beginning Balance)	=F17

31. Click on cell **B18**. Move your mouse to the lower right corner of cell **B18**. Position it over the green box, and then double-click. Column **B** will populate with **zeros** through row **88**. Cell **A88** will contain the value **72**, representing the last payment.

32. Select cells **C17:F17**. Move your mouse to the lower right corner of cell **F17**. Position it over the green box, and then double-click. Columns **C** through **F** will populate with your amortization values.

33. Your amortization table is complete. Scroll down to your last **Ending Balance** in cell **F88**. Your balance should be zero! See Figures 11-124 and 11-125.

34. If your balance is not zero, check the following: Make sure your preliminary numbers (those that were given for you) are typed in correctly. You may also check your formulas by comparing them to the formulas in the completed assignment.

35. Save and turn in assignment.

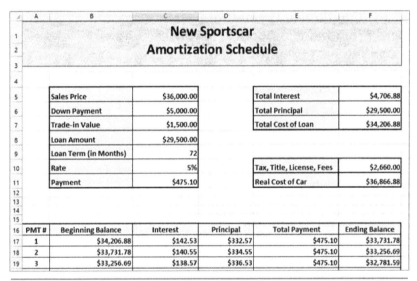

FIGURE 11-124 Values and Completed Amortization Table

FIGURE 11-125 Completed Amortization Table Formulas

As you read through Excel Part 3, you discovered that you were intrigued with the Conditional Formatting section. Seeing the examples listed in the section were very interesting, but you would like to try some other type of conditional formatting along with formulas that would trigger a conditional formatting based on your requirements.

In this assignment, you will use other **Conditional Formatting** techniques to enable you to successfully use this tool to help you spot trends, highlight specific values, and add some data bars and icons to highlight your data. **Note: Blue text represents typed text.**

File Needed: **Conditional Formatting.xlsx**
Completed File Name: **(Your Initials) Conditional Formatting.xlsx**

1. Open the **Conditional Formatting.xlsx** workbook.
2. Save as **(Your Initials) Conditional Formatting.**
3. Use **Conditional Formatting** to highlight information.
   a. Select the range **B4:G11** on the **Odd & Even** tab.
   b. Click on the **Conditional Formatting** button (*Home* tab, *Styles* group).
   c. Click on **New Rule**.
   d. In the New Formatting Rule dialog box, click on *Use a formula to determine which cells to format*.
   e. In the Edit the Rule Description section, click in the box below **Format values where this formula is true:**
   f. Type the following: **=ISODD(B4)**. The reference to cell **B4** tells Excel where the range begins. **The program requires you to click on the cell in the top left cell in the range to make this work**.

   g. Click on the **Format** button (Figure 11-126).
   h. In the Format Cells dialog box, click on the **Font** tab.
   i. Under Font Style, click on **Bold**.
   j. In the Color box, click on the down arrow and select Red.

FIGURE 11-126 Highlight Odd Values

k. Click on the Fill tab.

l. Under Background Color, select Yellow.

m. Click OK to exit the Format Cells dialog box.

n. Click OK to exit the New Formatting Rule dialog box.

o. Conditional Formatting highlighted all odd value cells (Figure 11-127).

116	-7	470	477	774	118
259	3	33	180	393	94
389	16	231	-6	220	137
387	555	98	3.16	285	333
90	24	28	47	210	230
201	0	127	360	16	475
68	35	25	105	306	400
380	222	427	42	402	111

FIGURE 11-127 Odd Values Highlighted

7. On the **Odd & Even** tab, select the range **B17:G24. Conditional Formatting** will only highlight the **even** values.

a. Click on the **Conditional Formatting** button (*Home* tab, *Styles* group).

b. Click on **New Rule**.

c. In the New Formatting Rule dialog box, click on **Use a formula to determine which cells to format**.

d. In the *Edit the Rule Description* section, click in the box below *Format values where this formula is true:*

e. Type the following: **=ISEVEN(B17)**. The reference to cell **B17** tells Excel where the range begins. The program requires you to click on the cell in the top left cell in the range to make this work.

f. Click on the **Format** button (Figure 11-128).

g. In the **Format Cells** dialog box, click on the **Font** tab.

FIGURE 11-128 Highlight Even Values

h. Under **Font Style**, click on **Bold**.

i. In the **Color** box, click on the down arrow and select **Green, Accent 6,** (Top row, last color on the right, or the 10th color).

j. Click on the **Fill** tab.

k. Under **Background Color**, select **Green, Accent 6, lighter 60%** (third option down in the green column on the far right in the middle section).

l. Click **OK** to exit the **Format Cells** dialog box.

m. Click **OK** to exit the **New Formatting Rule** dialog box.

n. **Conditional Formatting** highlighted all **Even** value cells (Figure 11-129).

116	-7	470	477	774	118
259	3	33	180	393	94
389	16	231	-6	220	137
387	555	98	111	285	333
90	24	28	47	210	230
201	0	127	360	16	475
68	35	25	105	306	400
380	222	427	42	402	111

FIGURE 11-129 Even Values Highlighted

8. On the **Duplicates & in-betweens** tab, select the range **B4:G11**.

a. Click on the *Conditional Formatting* button (*Home* tab, *Styles* group).

b. Click on **New Rule**.

c. In the *New* **Formatting Rule** dialog box, click on *Format only unique or duplicate values.*

d. In the bottom box under *Edit the Rule Description:*, make sure the word "**duplicate**" appears in the box below **Format all:**

e. Click on the *Format* button (Figure 11-130).

f. In the **Format Cells** dialog box, click on the **Font** tab.

FIGURE 11-130 Duplicate Values

g. Under **Font Style**, click on **Bold**.

h. In the **Color** box, click on the down arrow and select **Blue, Accent 1** (Fifth color in the top row).

i. Click on the **Fill** tab.

j. Under Background Color, select **Blue, Accent 1, Lighter 60%** (third option in the blue column-fifth column from left).

k. Click **OK** to exit the *Format Cells* dialog box.

l. Click **OK** to exit the **New Formatting Rule** dialog box.

m. **Conditional Formatting** highlighted all duplicate value cells (Figure 11-131).

n. On the **Duplicates and in-betweens** tab, highlight the range **B17:G24**.

116	-7	470	477	774	118
259	3	33	180	393	94
389	16	231	-6	220	137
387	555	98	111	285	333
90	24	28	47	210	230
201	0	127	360	16	475
68	35	25	105	306	400
380	222	427	42	402	111

FIGURE 11-131 Duplicate Values Highlighted

a. Click on the **Conditional Formatting** button (*Home* tab, *Styles* group).

b. Click on **Highlight Cells Rule**.

c. Click on *Between* in the right column.

d. In the *Between* dialog box, under the *Format cells that are BETWEEN*, in the left-hand box, type in **1.** In the right-hand box, type in **100,**

e. Click on the down arrow to the right of the **with** box.

f. Click on the *Light Red Fill with Dark Red Text* option.

g. Click **OK** to close the *Between* dialog box (Figure 11-132).

o. **Conditional Formatting** highlighted every number between **1 and 100** (Figure 11-133).

p. On **the Icons & Data Bars** tab, highlight the range **B4:G11**.

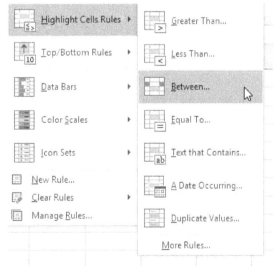

FIGURE 11-132 Highlight Cells Between

FIGURE 11-133 Formatting Cells Between 1 and 100

q. Click on the **Conditional Formatting** button (*Home* tab, *Styles* group).

r. Click on **Icon Sets**.

s. Click on **3 Symbols (Uncircled)** in the *Indicators* group (Figure 11-134).

t. On the **Icons & Data Bars** tab, highlight the range **B17:G24**.

u. Click on the **Conditional Formatting** button (*Home* tab, *Styles* group).

v. Click on **Data Bars**.

w. Click on the purple **Data Bar** in the *Gradient Fill* section (Figure 11-135).

x. Save and close your workbook. Turn in your assignment.

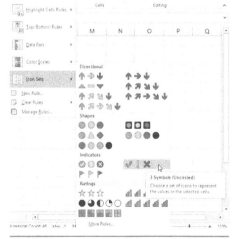

FIGURE 11-134 Icon Sets

FIGURE 11-135 Purple Data Bar Formatting

Part 4

Presentation Software

PowerPoint Part I

Introduction

A well-designed presentation provides listeners with many benefits. For visual learners, the presentation will provide the visual aspect of what the speaker is talking about. For the audience, a well-designed presentation will provide a point of reference for the topic being covered. Many of us have already seen presentations that are boring or so busy that your eyes go buggy. PowerPoint, when used effectively, is an excellent tool for highlighting key elements of a live presentation. PowerPoint presentations can have audio embedded in them, can be placed on a web page for viewing, and can be used in a host of diverse ways.

Learning Objectives

In this chapter, you will learn the basics of formatting a PowerPoint presentation. When you complete this chapter, you should be able to do the following:

1. Create, save, open, and format a PowerPoint presentation.
2. Copy, cut, paste, undo, redo and other editing features.
3. Home tab—Font, Paragraph, Styles, and Editing Groups.
4. Insert tab—New Slide, Tables, Images, Illustrations, and Text groups.
5. Design tab—Themes, Variants, and Customize Groups.

Microsoft officially released the first version of PowerPoint May 22, 1990.

The Ribbon

The first thing you will see when you open PowerPoint is the ribbon. The ribbon is one of the main tools that all users will employ when using PowerPoint or any of the MS Office programs. It is from the ribbon that you will access all the key features of PowerPoint. Figure 12-1 below shows a picture of the ribbon. As you look at the graphic (*) you will see at the top in the Title bar the title of the presentation, the author, and such items as **minimize**, **restore up/down**, and **close** buttons on the right of the title bar.

FIGURE 12-1 PowerPoint Ribbon

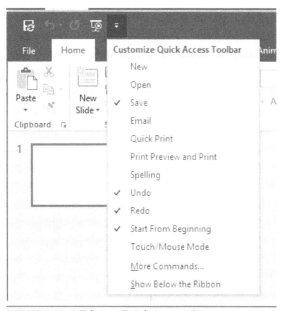

FIGURE 12-2 Editing Quick Access Bar

On the **Title bar** is the **Quick Access Toolbar**; you can see the Save icon, and, in this case, the save feature will save the presentation to cloud storage. Undo, Redo, and Slide Show icons are also available. The icon with the down arrow is a feature that will allow you to customize this area of the ribbon. To customize the Quick Access bar, click on the down arrow. In Figure 12-2, on the right, you will see the options that are available for the Quick Access bar. From this drop-down list, simply click on the options you wish to add to the Quick Access bar. Clicking on the checked options will deselect the items you do not wish to have on the Quick Access bar.

File Tab/Backstage View

The file tab provides you with the ability to open new or existing presentations, save a presentation, and, if necessary, print a presentation in a variety of formats. There are other features available in the file tab that we will cover in this section of the chapter. In Figure 12-3, there is a display of the basic information contained on the File tab. Another name you will see in the display called the file tab is the Backstage view. You will see many standard features such as Info, New, Open, Save, Save As, and Print. Each of these features will be covered in the following pages.

FIGURE 12-3 Backstage

Info

The Info option of the File tab provides you with a wealth of information and the ability to manage specific elements of the presentation information. In the graphic below, you see information on the size of the presentation, modification and creation dates, and author of the presentation. You also can modify some of the properties related to the presentation.

FIGURE 12-4 Document Properties

FIGURE 12-5 Edit Presentation Properties

Presentation1 Properties ? ✕

General Summary Statistics Contents Custom

Title: Idaho Presentation

Subject: Hells Canyon Recreational and Power Complex

Author: Cassie Daughenbaugh

Manager:

Company:

Category:

Keywords:

Comments:

Hyperlink
base:

Template:

☑ Save preview picture

OK   Cancel

FIGURE 12-6 Advanced Properties

To edit the presentation properties, you will want to click on the specific presentation property that will be changed. In Figure 12-5, you can see that the Title property is selected and that the title has been changed. Tags and Categories can be added to the presentation information. Not every item can be edited.

There are advanced properties that can also be selected and edited. Next to the Properties header, you will see a drop-down arrow. Clicking on this arrow will allow you to select the advanced properties. Figure 12-6 shows you the Summary tab of the Advanced Document Properties. For this presentation, the Subject and Comments fields have been edited.

The information on the other tabs provides limited properties to be changed. Most of the information on these tabs provides summary and statistical information about the presentation.

1. Create, Save, Open, and Format a PowerPoint Presentation

New

The first step to creating an effective presentation is to make use of many of PowerPoint's professionally designed presentation templates. To access these templates and create a new presentation, click on the **File** tab and then click on **New**. This option allows you to create a new presentation. Microsoft provides users with many free presentation templates. These templates are professionally designed and will get you started on creating a presentation that is well laid out and stylish. In Figure 12-7, on the next page, you can see the various presentations that are available. Each presentation is also designed with several color variants.

A new presentation can also be created by pressing both the CTRL+N keys at the same time.

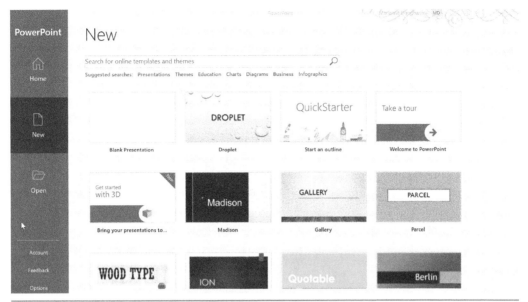

FIGURE 12-7 Creating a New Presentation

Creating a New Presentation

1. Click on the **File** tab.
2. Click on the **New** option in the navigation pane.
3. **Select** the desired template.
4. **Select** the desired variant.
5. Click on the ***Create*** button.
6. PowerPoint will now create a new presentation using the features you have selected.

FIGURE 12-8 Selecting a Theme

Save

Once a presentation is created, a generic title will be assigned to the presentation. This title will be dependent upon how many presentations you have created prior to closing PowerPoint. The initial presentation will be titled ***Presentation1***. When you create additional new presentations, the number will increment. When you close PowerPoint and open PowerPoint, the numbering will begin from ***Presentation1*** again.

Save As

There will be times when you will need to save your presentation in a different format or with a different file name, such as when you are tracking revisions. The **Save As** function will allow you to save your presentation in several different formats from older versions of PowerPoint to a .PDF format. **Table 12-1** lists a few of the many different formats available to PowerPoint users for saving a presentation.

TABLE 12-1 Presentation Formats

Formats	Extension	Use
Standard PowerPoint Presentation	.pptx	This is the standard PowerPoint presentation for versions 2007–2016 including Office 365.
PowerPoint 97-2003 Presentation	.ppt	For all versions of PowerPoint prior to 2007.
Portable Presentation Format	.pdf	This creates a presentation that is typically noneditable. This type of presentation is typically smaller in size and is frequently used in web pages and legal presentations.

Saving a Presentation

1. Click on the **File** tab.
2. Click on *Save*.
3. Navigate to the location on your computer where you want to save the new presentation.
4. Enter the name of the file.
5. Click on *Save*.
6. If you do not see the location you wish to save your presentation in, click the **More Options** link. You will be able to browse your computer for the desired location to save your presentation.

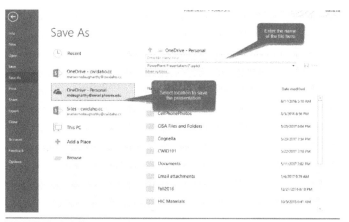

FIGURE 12-9 Saving a Presentation

1. A new presentation can be saved by pressing both the CTRL+S keys at the same time.
2. If Save is a selected option on the Quick Access toolbar, click on it to save your presentation.

Opening a Presentation

It is not uncommon for a student to have to go back and edit a presentation or make corrections and add additional information as a project evolves. Many times, this can be later in the day or on a different day. You will need to open the presentation you were working on to make changes and corrections.

The easiest method for opening a presentation is to use the recent presentations list in the Backstage view of PowerPoint. You can also browse for a presentation that you may have not opened in a while.

To open a presentation:

1. Click the **File** tab.
2. **Select** the file to be opened by clicking on the desired file name. You may have to browse for the file.
3. If you do not see the file, click on the location/drive you wish to browse for your file on. As a rule, Windows will, by default, save all presentations in the documents library unless you specify otherwise.

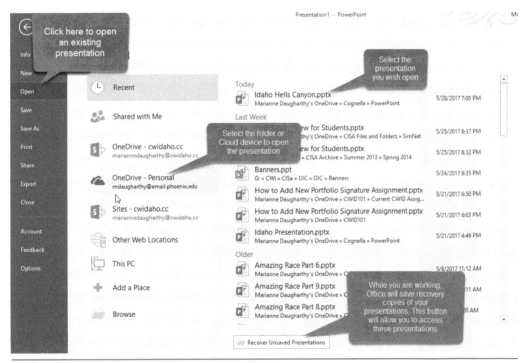

FIGURE 12-10 Opening Presentations

FIGURE 12-11 Open

FIGURE 12-12 Browse to Open File

Print

Printing a document is an important feature and one that you will use. Depending upon your program, chances are you will have to give a presentation in class. To make it easier to present your materials, you will want to print off your presentation. You may want to script your presentation and print off the slides with the scripted notes, your instructor may want you to provide a six pack so notes can be made during the presentation, and other formats may be used in the printing of a presentation. Figure 12-13 shows the different options available for printing.

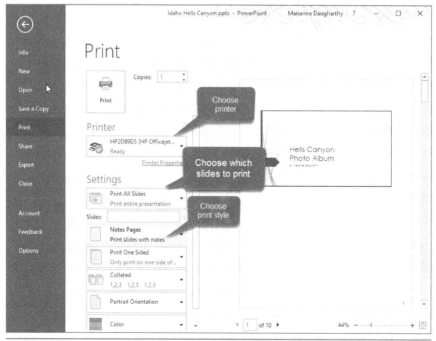

FIGURE 12-13 Printing

Here you will get a chance to test your understanding of the material covered in the chapter. You will need access to a computer with Power-Point. Using the OneDrive PowerPoint App will be a viable alternative if you do not have access to a computer with a full version of Office 2019, Office 2021, or Office 365.

In this project, you will create a presentation focusing upon the Hells Canyon Power Complex and Recreational Area covers the states of Idaho and Oregon. Your presentation will incorporate the skills you are learning in the chapter. **Note: Blue text represents typed text.**

File Needed: **None**
Completed File Name: **(Your initials) Student Checkup PowerPoint 12-1**

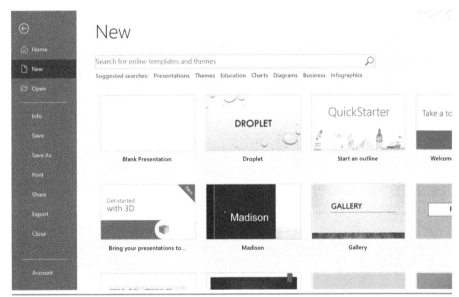

FIGURE 12-14 New Presentation

1. Create a new presentation (Figure 12-14).
   a. **Open** PowerPoint.
   b. Select the **File** tab.
   c. Click on **New**.
   d. Select a **Design theme**.
   e. Select a **color variant**.

f. On the title slide, enter the following title place holder: the Hells Canyon Power Complex and Recreational Area covers the states of Idaho and Oregon. In the subtitle place holder, enter your **First and Last Name**.

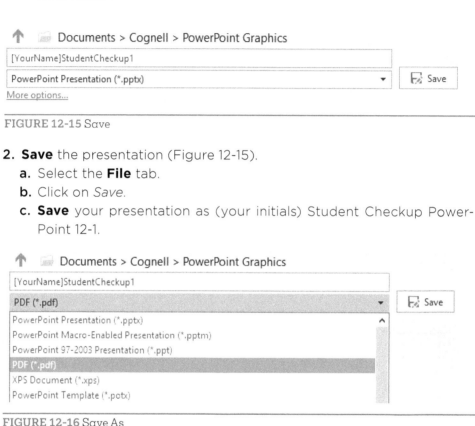

↑ 📁 Documents > Cognell > PowerPoint Graphics

[YourName]StudentCheckup1

PowerPoint Presentation (*.pptx) ▼   💾 Save

More options...

FIGURE 12-15 Save

2. **Save** the presentation (Figure 12-15).
   a. Select the **File** tab.
   b. Click on *Save*.
   c. **Save** your presentation as (your initials) Student Checkup Power-Point 12-1.

↑ 📁 Documents > Cognell > PowerPoint Graphics

[YourName]StudentCheckup1

PDF (*.pdf) ▼   💾 Save

PowerPoint Presentation (*.pptx)   ∧
PowerPoint Macro-Enabled Presentation (*.pptm)
PowerPoint 97-2003 Presentation (*.ppt)
PDF (*.pdf)
XPS Document (*.xps)
PowerPoint Template (*.potx)

FIGURE 12-16 Save As

3. **Save** the presentation in a different format (Figure 12-16).
   a. Select the **File** tab.
   b. Click on *Save As*.
   c. Using the file drop-down menu, save your presentation as a .PDF with the file name (your initials) Student Checkup PowerPoint 12-1 pdf.
4. Printing your presentation (Figure 12-17).
   a. Click on the **File** tab.
   b. Click on *Print*.
   c. Select the print format Note Pages.

5. Save and close your presentation.
  a. Press the **CTRL+S** or click on *Save* on the **Quick Access Toolbar**.
  b. Submit your presentation to your instructor

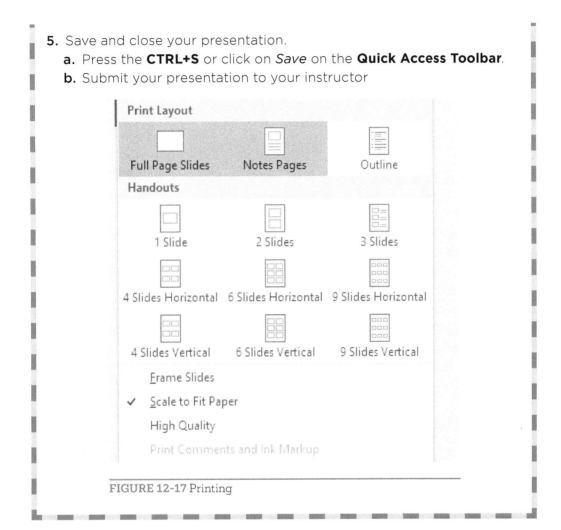

FIGURE 12-17 Printing

2. Copy, Cut, Paste, Undo, Redo, and Other Editing Features

Home Tab

For most people, the Home tab is the starting place of any project. The Home tab is the default starting point for all projects. It is here that you will find items that have been stored to the Clipboard and your copy, cut, and paste features. You will also be able to manage font and paragraph options, apply drawing tools, and edit specific items in the presentation. This section of the chapter will cover the features included on the Home tab.

Clipboard Group

Anytime you need to move, copy and paste, or delete information, the Clipboard group is the starting place for most users. Each feature provides you with specific functions that will allow you to organize information into a professional looking presentation.

Paste

The **Paste** function provides you with the ability to paste information that you wish to relocate within your presentation. The Paste function is gener-

FIGURE 12-18 Paste Options

ally combined with the **Copy** or **Cut** functions in organizing information in your presentation.

In Figure 12-18, you can see that there are several paste options available to you. In most cases, simply clicking on the paste icon without clicking on the drop-down arrow is all you need to paste the item into your presentation. There are times, though, when you need to use some of the other options such as the formatting features or the Paste Special options. These additional options are generally used when you are working with multiple presentations. The first option allows you to change the formatting of the item being copied to the format of the destination. If you are using distinctive design themes between the presentations, you can use the formatting of the destination theme.

The second option allows you to keep the formatting of the source presentation. As in the first option, if you are working between distinctive design themes, you can keep the formatting of the source of your information.

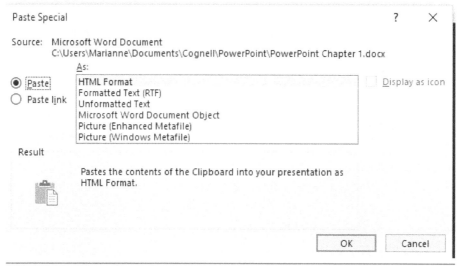

FIGURE 12-19 Paste Special

The third option allows you to paste a picture while the fourth option is for pasting the text from the source.

There are some instances where you will need to paste something that is outside of the normal, such as pasting HTML formatted information. The use of the **Paste Special** function provides the means to paste this information. Figure 12-19 provides you with a sample of the various other types of information that can be pasted into your presentation.

Cut In Figure 12-20, you will find another important function, the **Cut** function. This function will allow you to select text, pictures, or slides and cut this information from the presentation. You have the option of pasting this information in another place in the presentation or in another presentation.	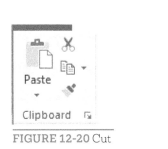 FIGURE 12-20 Cut
Copy The **Copy** function provides you with the ability to duplicate information within your presentation or information from another presentation. The duplicate option will provide you with the ability to duplicate slides easily.	 FIGURE 12-21 Copy/Duplicate
Format Painter Many times, you will find it necessary to create a presentation and then set up the formatting on one slide and then copy the formatting to the other slides. The **Format Painter** provides you with the means of copying the formatting of previously formatted information to other information in the slide. Double-clicking on the **Format Painter** will allow you to continue copying the formatting to other portions of the document. To turn off the Format Painter, simply click on the **Format Painter**.	 FIGURE 12-22 Format Painter

Clipboard

The Clipboard feature is accessible from the launcher in the lower right corner of the Clipboard group. In Figure 12-23, you will see the options available to you on the Clipboard. Any information you copy or cut is placed on the clipboard, allowing you to access information for your presentation later. Clicking on the X in the upper right corner of the Clipboard will close it.

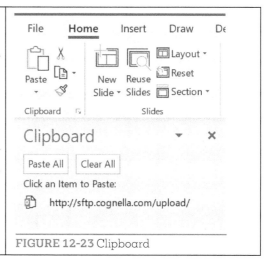

FIGURE 12-23 Clipboard

Slides Group

Most presentations are made up of various slide formats. The Slides group will allow you to create a new slide and to select the format of that slide. Figure 12-24 shows you the diverse options in the **Slides** group. You can also change the layout of a specific slide if you decide that a different format would look better.

FIGURE 12-24 Slides Group

When you are ready to add in a new slide, you can click on the icon above the word **New Slide**, and PowerPoint will insert a new slide of the same format as the one you previously you created. If you decide you need a different slide format, click on the down arrow to select one of many different slide formats. You can also reuse slides from other slide presentations. Figure 12-25 shows you the various layouts that are available for the design theme that you have chosen for your presentation. The layout drop-down menu will also present you with these same layout options if you wish to change the layout of your slide.

3. Font, Paragraph, Styles, and Editing Groups

Font Group

In each presentation, if you select a design theme, coordinating fonts will be a part of the theme. Sometimes you will want to change the fonts for the presentation, or you will want to create your own style of presentation; the Fonts group will allow for these changes. This section will cover the basic elements of the font group and how to make use of the tools located in the group. The **Font**

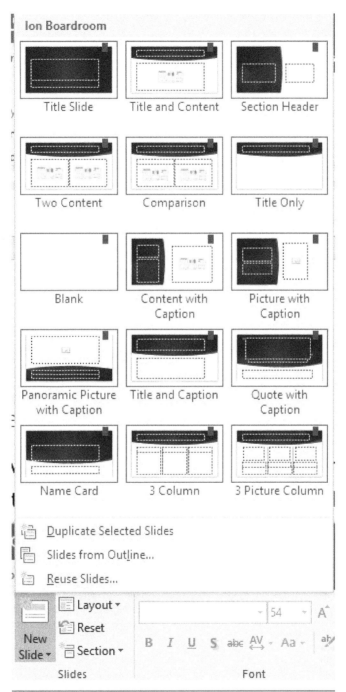

FIGURE 12-25 Slide Layouts

group is located on the Home tab. Figure 12-26 shows you all the tools in the font group.

FIGURE 12-26 Font Group

Font

Referring to Figure. 12-27, you will see the name of the font currently in use in the presentation. Using the drop-down menu next to the font name, you will be able to change the font style. There are thousands of fonts available from both Microsoft and other sources. Hovering over a font style will provide you with a preview of how the font will look in the presentation.

Next to the font, you will see the size of the font being used. A drop-down menu is also available for the font size. Adjusting the font size will add dimension to your presentation. Additionally, you will want to ensure that your font size can be seen when creating a presentation from the back of the venue in use. Keep in mind that a font size of 72 (also known as 72 points) is equal to one inch. Simple math will allow you to determine the height of the font you are choosing.

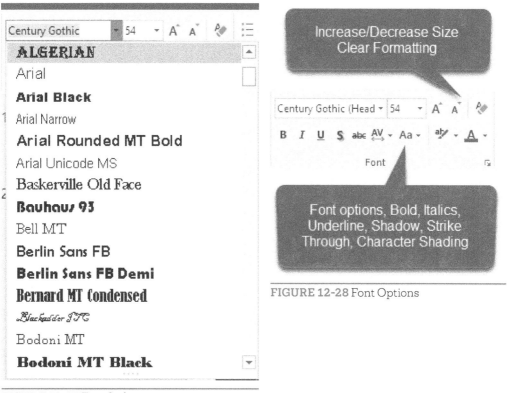

FIGURE 12-28 Font Options

FIGURE 12-27 Font Styles

Increase/Decrease Font Size

Next to the font size icon, you will see the icons for increasing and decreasing the font size. These icons allow you to quickly and easily change the size of the font one increment for each click.

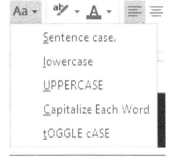

FIGURE 12-29 Change Case

Clear Formats

There are times when it becomes necessary to clear the formatting related to a font and start over. The **Clear Formats** icon will remove the formatting from the selected text and restore the formatting to the normal font.

Other Font Options

The second line in the font group provides additional formatting options for your font styles: Bold, Italic, and Underline provide a method for emphasizing specific words or text to bring them to the attention of your audience. Since a presentation is about the visual aspect of a presentation, there is an option for shadowing the text used on the slide. The shadow function will highlight behind the text to help it stand out.

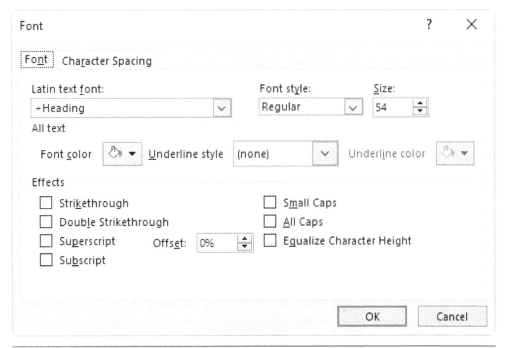

FIGURE 12-30 Font Launcher

As part of the editing features, you will find a strike-through icon. With this tool, you can strike through text that needs to be deleted. A change case icon will allow you to select from several case options. Select the text you wish to change, and then select the case style desired.

The final options in the Font group include highlighting and font color. Both options include a drop-down menu for selecting your choice of color. You can

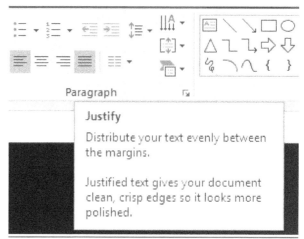

Justify

Distribute your text evenly between the margins.

Justified text gives your document clean, crisp edges so it looks more polished.

FIGURE 12-31 Paragraph Group

choose from the theme colors or the standard colors. An option is available for more colors so that additional colors can be employed in the presentation.

In the lower right corner of the **Font** group, you will find the launcher to allow you to display additional font options.

Paragraph Group

Like many other programs, paragraphs can be used in PowerPoint. The paragraph group will allow for the formatting of paragraphs in your presentation. Each line that ends with pressing the enter key is treated as a paragraph. Hovering over each icon will display a screen tip telling you what the icon does. Paragraph options include bullet and list options. These options can be changed or adjusted as needed. Drop-down arrows allow you to choose from several bullet and list choices.

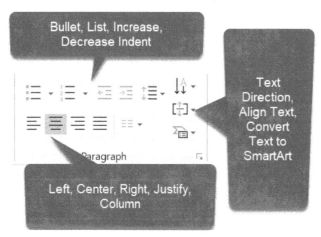

FIGURE 12-32 Paragraph Group

Increase and decrease indent icons allow you to adjust the indentation of a paragraph. The next item is Line Spacing, which will allow you to adjust the spacing between the lines in the paragraph. The second line of the paragraph group contains such functions as left align, center, right align, and justify. The other icon in this row is the Columns feature. You can add or remove columns from the selected text.

On the far right of the paragraph group are three other options. Text Direction will provide you with the tools to change the direction of the text on the slide or slide place holder. Align Text will adjust the alignment of the text vertically within a text box. The final option is Convert to SmartArt.

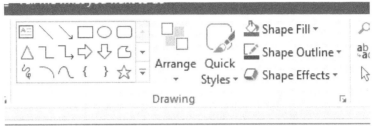

FIGURE 12-33 Drawing Group

Drawing Group

The **Drawing** group provides you with the tools that will allow you to add additional shapes and visual aids to your presentation. Tools to arrange your shapes, fill the shape, or outline the shape all work together to enhance the visual aspect of your presentation. As you work on the various projects in this chapter, you will learn about other features that you can employ to enhance your presentation with the use of shapes such as cropping a picture to a shape. The launcher in the lower right corner provides additional formatting tools to use with shapes.

Editing Group

The final group you will need to know about for the Home tab is the Editing group. There are three features in this group: *Find*, *Replace*, and *Select*. Figure 12-34 shows you the functions that are in the Editing group.

FIGURE 12-34
Editing Group

The **Find** function allows you to find a specific word or words within the presentation. When you select the **Find** function, PowerPoint will search the presentation for all occurrences of the word or words. When using the Find function, you can click on the ***Find Next*** button, and PowerPoint will move your cursor to the next occurrence of the word. At this point, you can choose to change the word, make corrections, or simply move on to the next occurrence by clicking on the ***Find Next*** button again. In Figure 12-35, Find was used to search for the word "Shapes" in the document. The first instance of the word was found and, at this point, you can make changes or you can click on the ***Find Next*** button to find the next occurrence of the word. The ***Close*** button will close the Find function.

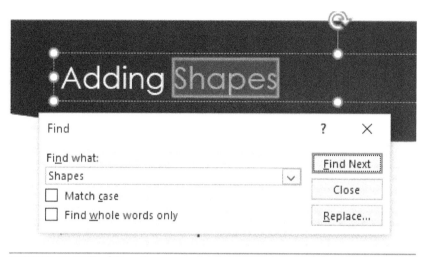

FIGURE 12-35 Find Function

The **Replace** option is an option that will take the find function further. Here, you can enter the word, phrase, or symbol you wish to find and, in the replace field, the correction. The **Replace** function will then locate the information in the **Find** field and ask you if you wish to replace the text. Another option is to replace all text. If, for example, you know that you need to change the phrase "Rotary Club" to "Kiwanis Club" throughout the presentation, you can select the *Replace All* button and PowerPoint will automatically make this replacement without requiring you to view each item. In this case, "Rotary" was inserted into the **Find what** field and "Kiwanis" was used as the **Replace with** (Figure 12-36). At this point, you can replace the next occurrence of "Rotary," or you can replace all occurrences of "Rotary" by clicking on *Replace All*.

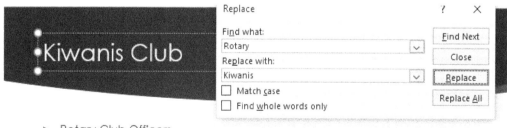

FIGURE 12-36 Replace

Here you will get a chance to test your understanding of the material covered in the chapter. You will need access to a computer with Power-Point. Using the OneDrive PowerPoint App will be a viable alternative if you do not have access to a computer with a full version of Office 2019, Office 2021, or Office 365. **Note: Blue text represents typed text.**

In this project, you will continue working on your presentation focusing upon the Hells Canyon Power Complex and Recreational Area covers the states of Idaho and Oregon. Your presentation will incorporate the skills you are learning in the chapter.

File Needed: **(Your initials) Student Checkup PowerPoint 12-1**

Completed File Name: **(Your initials) Student Checkup PowerPoint 12-2**
1. Edit a presentation.
   a. **Open** PowerPoint presentation from previous checkup.

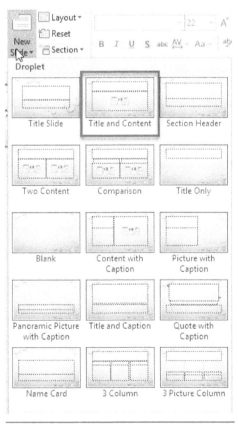

FIGURE 12-37 New Slide

2. Add new slides in presentation.
   a. **Select** the New Slide drop down from on the Home tab (Figure 12-37).
   b. **Select Title and Content**.
3. **Save** the presentation (Figure 12-38).
   a. **Select** the **File** tab.
   b. Click on **Save As** or **Save a Copy**.
   c. **Save** your presentation as (your initials) Student Checkup Power-Point 12-2.
4. Add the following to your new slide.
   a. Click on the **Title** place holder.
   b. In the **Title** place holder add **Hells Canyon Recreational Area**.
   c. In the body of the slide add **Four Campgrounds**, press Enter.
   d. **Press TAB** to indent next lines.
   e. Click in the **Content** part of the slide. Click on the **Numbering** icon (*Home* tab, *Paragraph* group, *Numbering*). Under **Numbering Library**, click on the first option in the second row. It looks like Roman Numeral upper case.
   f. Enter the following, pressing Enter after each item:
      i.   **Hells Canyon**
      ii. **Copperfield**
      iii. **McCormick**
      iv. **Woodhead**
   g. **Save** the presentation.
5. Add another slide, and enter the following information:

FIGURE 12-38 Save As or Save a Copy

   a. **Title**—**Hells Canyon Power Complex**
   b. In the body of the slide add **Three Dams**. Press Enter. Press **TAB** to indent next lines.
   c. Enter the following, pressing **Enter** after each item.
      i.   **Brownlee Dam**
      ii. **Oxbow Dam**
      iii. **Hells Canyon Dam**

6. Make the following changes to the two slides you just created.
   a. **Select** the text **Four Campgrounds** and increase the font size to **24** pt. Do the same with the text **Three Dams** on the next slide
   b. **Select** the text with the names of the four campgrounds, and increase the font size to **20** pt. Do the same with the names of the dams on the next slide.
   c. Select the titles on both slides and change the font to **Baskerville Old Face**. **Bold** title text on both slides. **Center-align** the titles on the slides.
7. Save and close your presentation.
   a. Press the **CTRL+S**, or click on **Save** on the **Quick Access Toolbar**.
8. Your presentation should be similar to Figure 12-39 below.

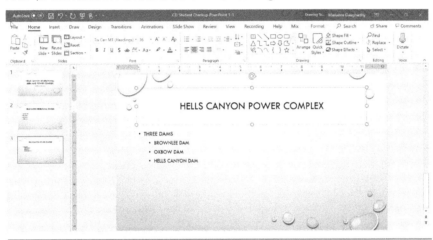

FIGURE 12-39 Completed Checkup

4. Insert Tab—New Slide, Tables, Images, Illustrations, and Text Groups

Insert Tab

The Insert tab is just as its name implies. This tab allows you to insert various items into your presentation. These items can include cover pages, tables, and illustrations. Other items you can insert from the Insert tab include hyperlinks, online videos, and text boxes. In this section, we will cover several of the more commonly used tools.

FIGURE 12-40 Insert Tab

Slides Group

Adding slides to a presentation easily is important. The New Slides group on the Insert tab provides you with another means of adding slides without going back to the Home tab. The New Slide option operates in the same manner as the New Slide option on the Home tab.

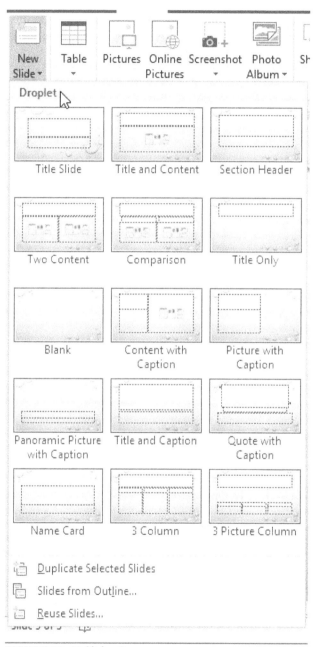

FIGURE 12-40 Slides Group

The **Slides** group (Figure 12-41) has only one option in it, and that is for inserting new slides. The drop-down menu provides you with the format options for the various slides. Options are also provided for you to duplicate selected slide, create slides from an outline, such as from a Word document, or to reuse slides from other presentation. The last feature is especially useful if you are taking a class that is a two-semester class and projects carry from one class to the next.

Tables Group

One important element of a presentation is the creation of tables. Tables provide an easy means for analyzing information in a visual format. Tables can be added easily to your PowerPoint presentation in one of two methods. You can use the Tables group, or you can use the Tables icon on a new slide. The following is an example of how to create tables on your slide.

Creating Tables

To create a table on a slide, you can employ one of two methods. The first method makes use of the features located on the slide while the second makes use of the insert ribbon.

FIGURE 12-42 Insert Table

1. The first step in creating a table is to create a new slide. Generally, the Title and Content slide is the choice you will use.

2. When you click on the **Table** icon on the slide, you will be asked some information about your table, specifically the number of columns and rows in your table. Click **OK** once you have determined the size of your table. Do not worry; you can adjust your table size if necessary.

3. Adjustments to the table can be made by using many of the formatting tools available on the Home tab. Changes in the font size, position of the text, and other formatting was completed here.

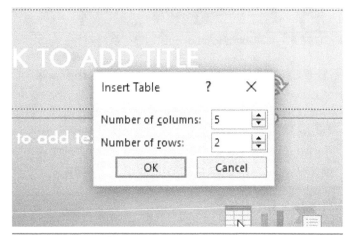

FIGURE 12-43 Table Size

4. The other method for creating tables is to use the Table option on the Insert tab. You highlight the number of columns and rows you desire in your table and then follow the same methods of using the Home tab formatting options for dressing up your table.

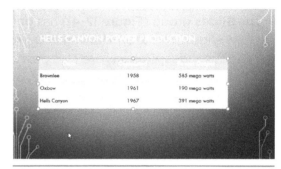

FIGURE 12-44 Completed Table

5. Design and layout contextual tabs are activated when working with tables. These tabs will allow the modification of table features to improve the readability of the information contained in the table. Figures 12-45 and 12-46 provide a glimpse of what is available on these tabs.

One of the many features of Microsoft programs is the ability to personalize anything you are working on. With the **Table Tools** contextual tabs, you can easily make changes to the layout of the tables in your presentations. The **Table Styles** group on the **Design** ribbon allows you to select from preset table formats. The options are many, and you can even create your own style.

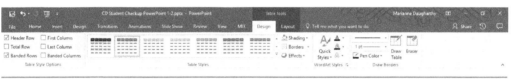

FIGURE 12-45 Table Tools Design Tab

FIGURE 12-46 Table Tools Layout Tab 1

The **Layout** contextual tab provides other tools for table formatting. You will notice on the ribbon, tools that will allow you to add and delete rows and columns. Other tools allow you to merge and split cells as needed in the slide. With a table, you can also set the alignment and position of the table on the slide.

More information on how to use these tabs will be provided as we work with the various tools and presentation features.

Images Group

The **Images** group (Figure 12-47) provides you with a variety of ways to insert images into your presentation. Pictures can be added to a presentation from either your local computer or you can search for online pictures. PowerPoint also allows you to take a screenshot of your computer to include in a presentation.

Adding pictures to a presentation:

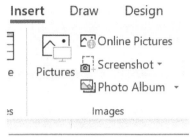

FIGURE 12-47 Images Group

1. **Select** a slide in your presentation; you can also add a new slide to add a picture.
2. Click on the **Insert** tab. and then select one of the two picture options (Figure 12-46). The **Pictures** icon is for inserting pictures from your local drive. **Online Pictures** will provide you a way to search for pictures online to use in your presentation.
3. For pictures from your local drive, navigate to the location of your pictures (Figure 12-47). Select the picture, and click **OK**. PowerPoint will insert the picture in the PowerPoint slide.
4. To find an online picture, select the **Online Pictures** from the Images group, on the Insert tab. Then enter the criteria you wish to search for (see Figure 12-48). Select the picture that relates to your presentation by clicking on the desired picture and then click on **Insert.** Microsoft also allows for you to select pictures from your online locations such as your OneDrive account.
5. You can also use the same icons located on a new slide to add photos to your presentation.

Another fun feature of the Images group is the Photo Album (Figure 12-49). This option provides you with a method of creating a photo album of photos from a trip or other activity that you wish to share with others. Figure 12-51 on the right shows a sample of a photo album.

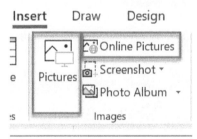

FIGURE 12-48 Insert Pictures

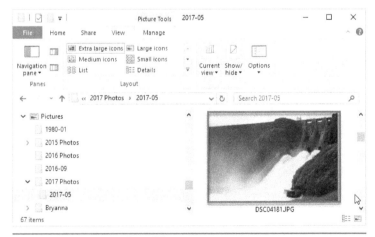

FIGURE 12-49 Insert Local Pictures

Creating a Photo Album:

1. Photo albums are a fun way to create a presentation of a vacation or other event. They can be easily added into a presentation, and you will have a variety of options for the presentation. The first step is to create a new presentation. You can use a **Blank** presentation for this feature.

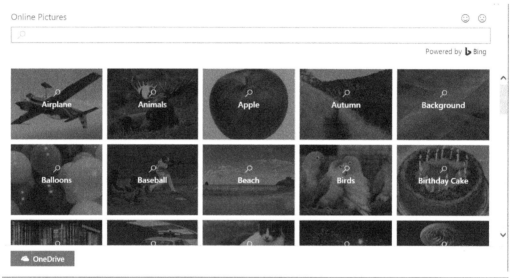

FIGURE 12-50 Insert Online Pictures

2. Click on the Insert tab and select **Photo Album** (Figure 12-50)**.**
3. The next step is to select the folder with the photos you want in your photo album. Before selecting your photos, go to File Explorer, and rename the photos something meaningful. The reason will become clear shortly. Click on the ***File/Disk*** button as you see in Figure 12-51.

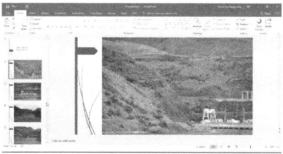

FIGURE 12-51 Photo Album

4. In Figure 12-52, you can see the photos selected for the photo album, bordered in red. Notice that each of the photos has been renamed. Once you have selected your photos, press **Enter**.

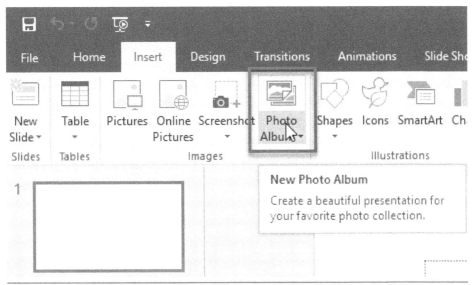
FIGURE 12-52 Create a Photo Album

5. Once you select your photos, you will come back to the screen in Figure 12-53. Now you can add in a few other touches to your photo album. From this screen, you can click on the **Browse** button to search for a design theme for your presentation. The themes available are the same design themes you have already seen in PowerPoint.

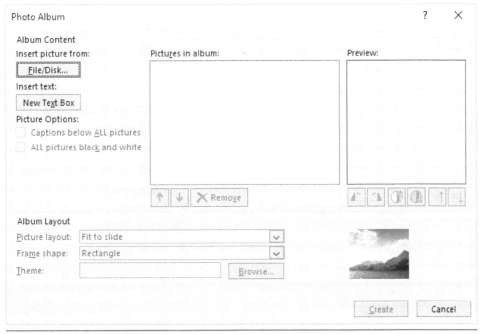
FIGURE 12-53 Insert Pictures

6. Once you have completed the settings of your choice, click on the **Create** button.
7. PowerPoint will take your photos and put them in an album. Now you can make changes to the slides with your pictures.
8. When you are finished, you will have an album like the one in Figure 12-54.

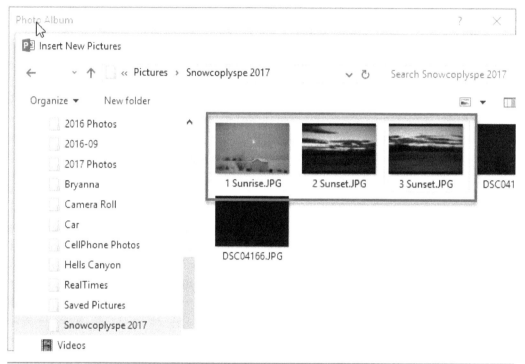

FIGURE 12-54 Select Photo Album Pictures

Illustrations Group

The Illustrations group provides additional tools for you to add other visual items to your presentation. Shapes, Icons, SmartArt, and Charts are all tools that will add to the visual impact of the presentation.

Shapes can be added to a slide to highlight a specific point or add dimension to the presentation. Shapes can be adjusted in size and location on the slide. Icons can be added to a presentation.

Adding Shapes and Icons:

1. Shapes and Icons can easily be added to a presentation. First click on the Insert tab (Figure 12-55).
2. Click on **Shapes** or **Icons.** Choose the graphic you desire to insert into your presentation.

Photo Album

Album Content

Insert picture from:
[File/Disk...]

Insert text:
[New Text Box]

Picture Options:
☐ Captions below ALL pictures
☐ ALL pictures black and white

Pictures in album:
☐ 1   1 Sunrise
☐ 2   2 Sunset
☐ 3   3 Sunset

[↑] [↓] [✕ Remove]

Preview:

Album Layout

Picture layout: [Fit to slide ▾]
Frame shape: [Rectangle ▾]
Theme: [   ] [Browse...]

[Create] [Cancel]

FIGURE 12-55 Order Photos

3. **PowerPoint** will insert the graphic on your slide. From there, you can use the sizing handles to adjust the size of the graphic, rotate the position of the graphic, or, using the directional arrows, move the graphic to a different position on the slide.

4. For some of the Shape graphics, you can insert text into the graphic (Figure 12-56).

5. When you insert Shapes or Icons, appropriate contextual tabs will be available for you to adjust your graphics to fit your presentation.

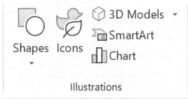

FIGURE 12-56 Paste Special

Shapes Icons 3D Models ▾ SmartArt Chart

Illustrations

FIGURE 12-57 Illustrations Group

Text Group

The last item to be discussed on the ribbon under the Insert tab is the **Text** group. The options in this group provide a way to add additional information to the slide (Figure 12-58). The **Text Box**, **Header & Footer**, and **WordArt** tools provide excellent accents to a presentation.

FIGURE 12-58 Text within Shapes

The **Text Box** will provide you with the means to add in text information on a slide.

Creating a Text Box:

1. On your slide, click the **Text Box** icon located on the Insert tab (Figure 12-59). Move your cursor to the location on the slide where you want your **Text Box** and click.

FIGURE 12-59 Insert Shapes and Icons

2. Begin typing the information in the **Text Box**. After you complete entering your information, you can then adjust the Text Box by using the sizing handles. There is a rotate handle to adjust the direction of your Text Box (Figure 12-60).
3. When you have your **Text Box** selected, you will see a **Drawing Tools** contextual tab displayed. Additional formatting features will be available to you to further enhance your **Text Box.**

FIGURE 12-60 Creating a Text Box

Many classes will require that you create a presentation and deliver it in class. As part of your slides, you will need to include **Header & Footer** information. This information may include the date, slide number, and name of the person(s) responsible for the presentation.

Creating a Header and Footer:

1. In your presentation, click on the **Insert tab** and then click on the **Header & Footer** option in the **Text** group. The **Header & Footer** dialog box will display on your screen (Figure 12-61).
2. There are two tabs on the dialog box. For your slides, you will check the boxes with the information you wish to enter, such as date and time, slide number, and footer text. You can tell PowerPoint that you do not want to display this information on your Title slide (Figure 12-62).
3. When you have entered all your information, click on the *Apply* button or *Apply to All* button.
4. The other tab allows you to insert **Header & Footer** information on your handouts and notes.

FIGURE 12-61 Completed Text Box

Because PowerP oint focuses on visual effects, the next item is the **WordArt** option. **WordArt** takes text entered in the presentation and converts it into a visually engaging format. In Figure 12-62, you will see text that has been con-verted into **WordArt.**

FIGURE 12-62 WordArt

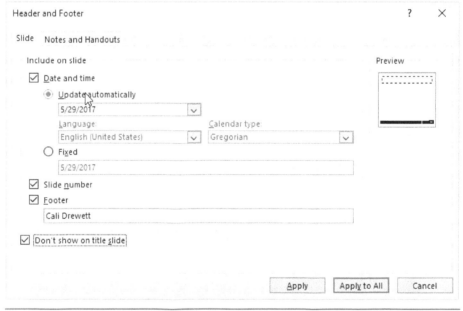

FIGURE 12-63 Header & Footer

When creating **WordArt** (Figure 12-64), there are many options. Choose the option that fits your presentation. When working with **SmartArt**, you will see the **Drawing Tools** contextual tab active.

5. Design Tab—Themes and Variants

The Design tab allows you to select from several design features. While the Normal template is the default layout, when you open a new presentation, there are times when you might want to venture to the other design formats. This section will provide you with directions on how to make these changes.

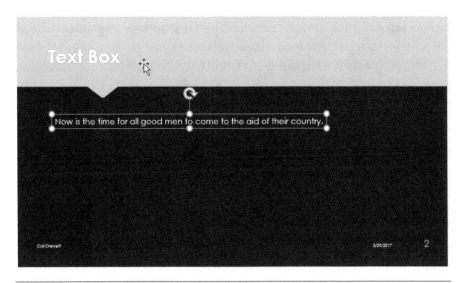

FIGURE 12-64 Footer Information on Slide

Themes Group

As you have noticed, Microsoft offers you numerous options and choices to personalize your presentations. Microsoft has incorporated the talents of graphic artists and designers to provide professional-looking presentations. The **Themes** option provides you with numerous professionally designed design options for your presentation. Many more are available to you on Microsoft.com. When you create a new presentation, you are asked to choose one of the many themes that are available. What happens, though, if you find that a theme really does not fit your presentation? The **Themes** group (Figure 12-65) on the **Design** tab will provide you with the means to change your theme for your presentation.

FIGURE 12-65 Word Art

To change your theme, simply click on the **Design** tab and select the theme you want to try from the ***Themes more*** button. If you do not see a theme that you like, try searching for a theme online at https://templates.office.com/en-US/templates-for-PowerPoint.

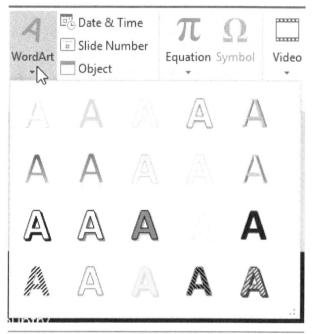

FIGURE 12-65 WordArt Options

Variants

Each theme has a set of related Variants. These **Variants** include color combinations and font combinations that work well together. Options to change the background and effects are also available in the Variants group. Changing any of the **Variants** is accomplished by selecting the ***More*** button and then choosing your **Variant** from the list. Except for the **Effects** variant, you have the freedom to create your own variants.

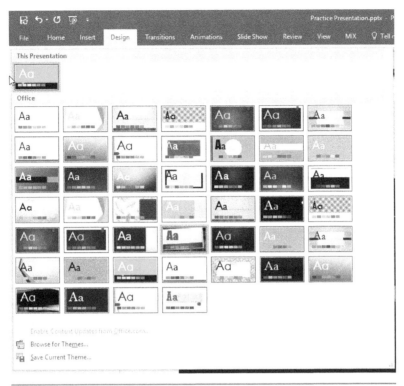

FIGURE 12-67 Presentation Themes

FIGURE 12-68 Design Theme Variants

Here you will get a chance to test your understanding of the material covered in the chapter. You will need access to a computer with Power-Point. Using the OneDrive PowerPoint App will be a viable alternative if you do not have access to a computer with a full version of Office 2019, Office 2021, or Office 365. **Note: Blue text represents typed text.**

In this project, you will continue working on your presentation, focusing upon the Hells Canyon Power Complex and Recreational Area. Your presentation will incorporate the skills you are learning in the chapter. The Hells Canyon Power Complex and Recreational Area covers the states of Idaho and Oregon.

Files Needed**: (Your initials) Student Checkup PowerPoint 12-2**

PowerPoint Checkup Files 1-1.zip

Completed File Name: **(Your initials) Student Checkup PowerPoint 12-3**
1. Open your Checkup file 12-2.
2. **Insert** a new **Title and Content** slide.
   a. In the **Title** place holder, **enter** the title **Hells Canyon Power Production**.
   b. Go to the previous slide, using the **Format Painter**, copy the format of the title, and apply it to the new slide. **Center-align** the title on the slide.
   c. Click in the body of the slide.
   d. Click on the **Insert** tab.
   e. Click on the *Table* group. Create a table that is 3 columns wide and 3 rows deep.
   f. **Press** the **Enter** key to insert the table on the slide.
3. Modify the **Table** style.
   a. Click on the table.
   b. Click on the **Table Tools Design Contextual** tab.
   c. Select table style **Medium, Style 2, Accent 1**. Use your screen tip to help you select the correct table style.

---

4. Enter table information.

    a. Enter the following table information, pressing the **tab** key to move to the next cell.

Dam	Completed	Power Output
Brownlee	1958	585 megawatts
Oxbow	1961	190 megawatts

    b. The table currently is setup for 3 columns and 3 rows. There are 4 dams and you need to create another line for the 4th dam. To do this, press the TAB key. Now you will be able to enter the last row of information.

Hells Canyon	1967	391 megawatts

5. Add three more **Title and Content** slides to your presentation.

    a. On the title of the first new slide, enter the title **Brownlee Dam**.

    b. On the title of the second new slide, enter the title **Oxbow Dam**.

    c. On the title of the third new slide, enter the title **Hells Canyon Dam**.

6. Insert pictures on each of the slides.

    a. For each of the slides, go Online and select a picture of your choice.

    b. If you have text on the bottom of your pictures, select the placeholder underneath the picture and delete it. Do this for each picture with text below it.

7. Using the **Format Painter**, click on slide 4. Highlight the title ad. Double-click on the **Format Painter**. Apply this formatting to the title place holders on the last three slides.

    a. Resize font to size **28** and bold. Resize shape if necessary.

    b. Resize font to size **28** and bold. Resize shape if necessary.

    c. Resize font to size **28** and bold. Resize shape if necessary.

8. Add Shapes and Icons to your presentation.

    a. Select slide 5.

    b. Click on the **Shapes** tool on the **Insert tab**.

    c. On each of the last three slides, insert one of the **Banners and Scrolls or Callout Shapes**.

    d. On slide 5, enter in the shape the following text: **The 1st dam heading from Idaho**.

    e. On slide 6, enter in the shape the following text: **The 1st dam in Oregon**.

    f. On slide 7, enter in the shape the following text: **The end of the road**.

    g. Using the drawing tools, modify each shape by changing the fill color.

    h. On slide 6, insert one of the **Nature** icons and change the color.

9. From the **Insert** tab, select the **Header & Footer** option.
   a. Make the entries as in Figure 12-67. Apply to all slides except the **Title Slide**, and put your name in the **Footer** field. Move the fields to an appropriate location on the slides.
10. **Save** and **close** your presentation. Submit your presentation as instructed to your instructor

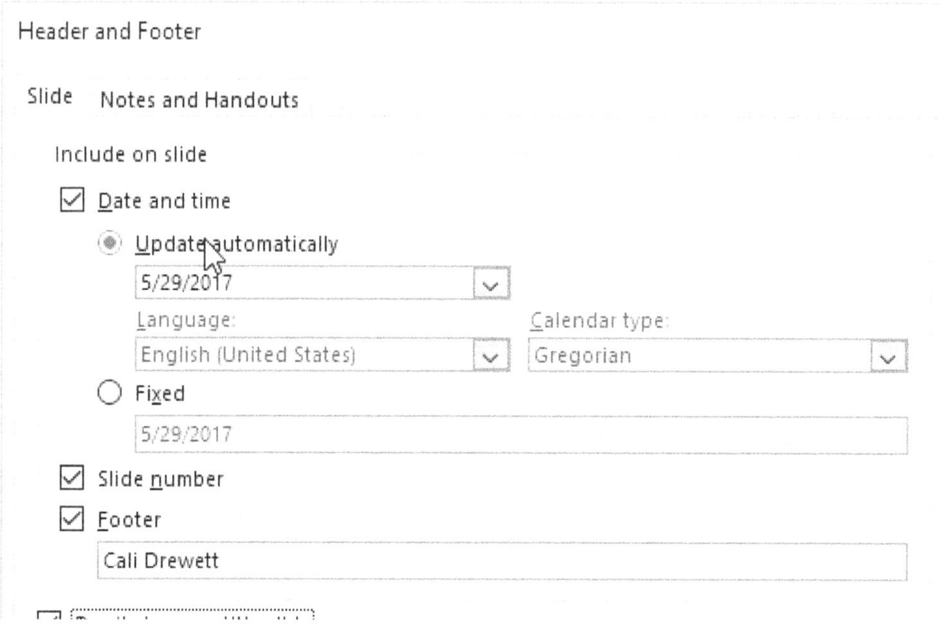

Header and Footer

Slide   Notes and Handouts

   Include on slide

   ☑ Date and time

      ◉ Update automatically

      | 5/29/2017 | ⌄ |

      Language: Calendar type:

      | English (United States) | ⌄ | | Gregorian | ⌄ |

      ◯ Fixed

      | 5/29/2017 |

   ☑ Slide number

   ☑ Footer

   | Cali Drewett |

FIGURE 12-69 Header & Footer

Completed checkup project.

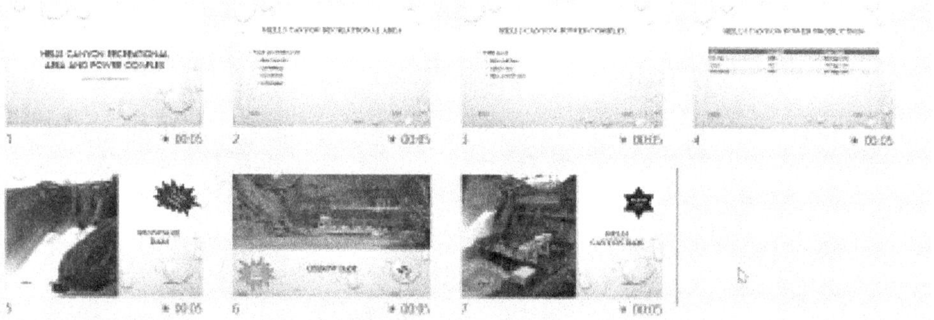

FIGURE 12-70 Completed 12-3 Checkup Project

Chapter Projects

Here you will get a chance to test your understanding of the material covered in the chapter. You will need access to a computer with Power-Point. Using the OneDrive PowerPoint App will be a viable alternative if you do not have access to a computer with a full version of Office 2019, Office 2021, or Office 365. **Note: Blue text represents typed text.**

In this project, you will create a presentation focusing upon the Hells Canyon Power Complex and Recreational Area. Your presentation will incorporate the skills you are learning in the chapter. The Hells Canyon Power Complex and Recreational Area covers the states of Idaho and Oregon.

File Needed: **PowerPointChapter12CapstoneProject1.zip**
Completed File Name: **(Your initials)_Chapter_12_PowerPoint_Capstone**
1. Create a new presentation.
   a. **Open** PowerPoint.
   b. Select the **File** tab.
   c. Click on **New**.
   d. Select the **Mesh** theme.
   e. Select a **color variant** of your choice.
   f. On the title slide enter the following title place holder: **Arlington Cemetery Tomb of the Unknown Soldier**. In the subtitle place holder enter **Washington D.C.**
2. Save the presentation.
   a. Select the **File** tab.
   b. Click on **Save**.
   c. **Save** your presentation as (Your initials) _Chapter_1_PowerPoint_ Capstone.
3. Add new slides in presentation.
   a. Select the New Slide drop-down from on the Home tab.
   b. Select **Title and Content**.
4. Add the following to your new slide.
   a. Click on the **Title** place holder.
   b. In the **Title** place holder—**Highlights of the Tomb of the Unknown Soldier**.

c. In the body of the slide, add the following bullets:

    i. **Guarded 24 hours per day, 365 days.**

    ii. **Off-season the guard is changed every hour.**

    iii. **Peak season the guard is changed every 30 minutes.**

    iv. **Wreath-laying ceremony.**

d. **Save** the presentation.

5. Add 4 more slides, and enter the following information:

    a. Slide 3—

        i. Title—**Changing of the Guard.**

        ii. Body of slide:

            1. **Relief commander announces the Changing of the Guard.**

            2. **New Sentinel unlocks bolt of M-14 rifle to signal start of ceremony.**

            3. **Relief commander walks to Tomb and salutes.**

            4. **Spectators are asked to stand and stay silent during ceremony.**

    b. Slide 4—

        i. Title—**Inspection.**

        ii. Body of slide:

            1. **Detailed White-glove inspection of the rifle.**

            2. **Relieving sentinel, retiring sentinel, and relief commander all salute the unknown.**

            3. **Relief commander commands, "Pass on your orders."**

            4. **Current sentinel commands, "Post and orders, remain as directed."**

            5. **Newly posted sentinel replies, "Orders acknowledged."**

            6. **Newly posted sentinel steps into position on black mat.**

    c. Slide 5—

        i. Title—**Guarding the Tomb.**

        ii. Body of slide:

            1. **Begins walking at a cadence pace of 90 steps per minute.**

                a. **21 steps down the black mat.**

                b. **Turn face east for 21 seconds.**

                c. **Turn face north for 21 seconds.**

                d. **21 steps down the black mat.**

            2. **The sentinel stands between the tomb and any possible threat.**

    d. Slide 6—
        i. Title—**Sentinels.**
        ii. Body of slide:
            1. All volunteers.
            2. Best of the elite 3rd U.S. Infantry Regiment.
            3. Superb physical condition.
            4. Unblemished military record.
            5. Between 5 feet, 10 inches and 6 feet, 4 inches.
            6. Sentinels know history of Arlington and grave locations of nearly 300 veterans.

6. Make the following changes your presentation.
    a. Slide 1: Change the font size of the subtitle to **32** pt.
    b. Slide 2: Change the title to **Highlights**.
    c. Slide 6: Change FT to **Feet**.
    d. Save the presentation.

7. Select slide 3.
    a. Insert a new Title and Content slide.
    b. In the title, enter the following: **Images of Changing of the Guard.**
    c. Insert the following pictures on the slide:
        i. Changing of the Guard
        ii. Inspection
        iii. Relieved

8. Select slide 6, and insert another Title and Content slide.
    a. In the title, enter the following: **Images of Guarding the Unknown.**
    b. Using the **Insert** tab, select **Online Pictures**.
    c. Search for Online Pictures using Arlington Cemetery Tomb of the Unknown.
    d. Select two images of sentinels guarding the tomb and inset them on the slide.

9. Add a Shape to your presentation.
    a. Select slide 7.
    b. Click on the **Shapes** tool on the **Insert** tab.
    c. Select the **Scroll Horizontal** shape.
    d. Enter in the scroll: **Guarding the Tomb of the Unknown Soldier Year-Round.**

10. From the **Insert** tab, select the **Header & Footer** option.
    a. Apply to all slides except the **Title Slide**, and put your name in the **Footer** field. Move the fields to an appropriate location on the slides.

2. Save your presentation and submit to your instructor

Completed chapter 1 project 1.

FIGURE 12-71 Completed Chapter 12 Project 1

Chapter 12 PowerPoint Capstone 2

Here you will get a chance to test your understanding of the material covered in the chapter. You will need access to a computer with Power-Point. Using the OneDrive PowerPoint App will be a viable alternative if you do not have access to a computer with a full version of Office 2019, Office 2021, or Office 365. **Note: Blue text represents typed text.**

In this project, you will create a presentation focusing upon the Hells Canyon Power Complex and Recreational Area. Your presentation will incorporate the skills you are learning in the chapter. The Hells Canyon Power Complex and Recreational Area covers the states of Idaho and Oregon.

File Needed: **PowerPointChapter12CapstoneProject2.zip**
Completed File Name: **(Your initials)_Chapter_12_PowerPoint_Capstone**
1. Create a new presentation.
   a. **Open** PowerPoint.
   b. **Select** the **File** tab.
   c. Click on **New.**
   d. In the search bar, **enter Nature** to view Nature based presentations.
   e. **Select** the **Serenity Nature Presentation (widescreen).**
   f. On the title slide, enter the following title place holder: **Yellowstone National Park.** In the subtitle place holder enter **Land of Fire and Ice.**
   g. Using the sizing handles, adjust the Title place holder so that the title fits on one line.

2. Save the presentation.
   a. **Select** the **File** tab.
   b. Click on **Save.**
   c. **Save** your presentation as (your initials)_Chapter_1_PowerPoint_ Capstone 1.
3. Add new slides in presentation.
   a. **Select** the New Slide drop-down from on the home tab.
   b. **Select Title and Content.**
4. Add the following to your new slide.
   a. Click on the **Title** place holder.
   b. In the **Title** place holder—**Attraction Highlights.**
   c. In the body of the slide, add the following bullets:
      i. **Old Faithful**
      ii. **Steamboat Geyser**
      iii. **Visitor Centers**
      iv. **Wildlife**
         1. **Bison**
         2. **Moose**
         3. **Bear**
      v. **Mud pots**
      vi. **Lakes and fishing**
5. **Save** the presentation.
6. Delete the remaining slides in the presentation.
7. Add a section slide with the following information:
   a. Title—Line 1—**Land of Fire and Ice.** Line 2—**A park is born.**
   b. Subtitle—

   The Yellowstone National Park Protection Act says, "the headwaters of the Yellowstone River … is hereby reserved and withdrawn from settlement, occupancy, or sale … and dedicated and set apart as a public park or pleasuring-ground for the benefit and enjoyment of the people." (NPS.gov)
8. Add 4 more slides and enter the following information:
   a. Slide 4—Two content layout.
      i. **Title—History of the Park.**
      ii. Body of slide column 1.
         1. **First national park in the world.**
         2. **Established in 1872.**

3. **First Superintendent.**
   a. **No money.**
   b. **No Rangers.**
   c. **No money to build structures.**
4. **Second Superintendent.**
   a. **Given funds for roads.**
   b. **Built the Grand Loop Road.**
   c. **Built the park headquarters.**

iii. Column 2.
   1. **Army manages the park.**
      a. **1886 the Army takes over management of the park.**
      b. **National Park Protection Act gave the Army authority.**
      c. Slide 5—Two content layout
         i. **Title—Old Faithful**
         ii. Column 1.
            1. **Predictable within 10 minutes.**
            2. **Erupts every 60 to 90 minutes.**
            3. **Length of eruption determines time between eruptions.**
         iii. Column 2.
            1. Insert a picture of Old Faithful erupting. Google Images can help you with this picture.
      d. Slide 6—Two content layout.
         i. **Title—Wildlife**
         ii. Column 1.
            1. **Bison**
            2. **Moose**
            3. **Bears**
            4. **Elk**
            5. **Bald eagles**
            6. **Fish**
         iii. Column 2
            1. Insert a picture of wildlife in Yellowstone.
9. Make the following changes to your presentation.
   a. Slide 1: Change the font size of the subtitle to **36** pt.
   b. Slide 2: Change the title to **Park Highlights**.
   c. Save the presentation.

10. Add a new Title Only slide.

  a. Insert a new Title and Content slide.

  b. In the title enter the following: **Images of Yellowstone**.

  c. Insert three pictures from Yellowstone—use a Google Image search of Yellowstone.

11. Add a Shape to your presentation.

  a. **Select** slide 7.

  b. Click on the **Shapes** tool on the **Insert** tab.

  c. **Select** the **Wave** shape.

  d. **Enter** in the wave **Elk Resting.**

12. From the **Insert** tab, select the **Header & Footer** option.

  a. Apply to all slides except the **Title Slide,** and put your name in the **Footer** field. Move the fields to an appropriate location on the slides.

13. **Save** your presentation and submit to your instructor.

Completed chapter 1 project 2.

FIGURE 12-72 Completed Chapter 12 Project 2

CHAPTER THIRTEEN

PowerPoint Part II

Introduction

In the previous chapter on PowerPoint, you were introduced to the basics of PowerPoint. You learned about the various features and tools available to you in PowerPoint and gained a basic understanding of each of these tools. There are many more tools available in PowerPoint, and in this chapter, we will apply more hands-on experiences and delve deeper into the features available in PowerPoint.

Learning Objectives

In this chapter, you will apply the basics of formatting a PowerPoint presentation and further explore the various tools available in PowerPoint. When you complete this chapter, you should be familiar with the following:

1. Transitions Tab—Preview, Transitions, Timing.
2. Animations Tab—Preview, Animation, Advanced Animation, Timing.
3. Slide Show Tab—Start Slide Show, Setup.
4. Review Tab—Proofing, Comment.
5. View Tab—Presentation Views, Show.

1. Transitions Tab

A well-developed presentation will be engaging and will keep the attention of the audience. The use of transitions and other animations will add to the effectiveness of the presentation. Transitions are the animations that add spice between slides. The use of transitions should be thought out and planned. Transitions should be of one style, with changes on the effects available to that style. Too many changes or changes that are too rapid may not have the desired effect in the presentation.

In Figure 13-1, you will find the tools necessary to add transitional animations to your presentation. The Transition ribbon will allow you to see what the transition will look like using a **Preview** function, and the *More* button will provide you with other available transitions. **Effect Options** will allow you to adjust the selected transitions for each slide. **Timing** options will allow you to automate some of the transitional effects.

FIGURE 13-1 Transitions Tab

Preview

When you make use of a transition, you will want to preview how the transition will look when you apply it to your presentation. The *Preview* button will allow you to see the transitions in action.

Preview

Transitions to This Slide

The **Transitions to This Slide** group provides you with a list of slide transitions available. The *More* button located to the right of the **Transitions** will provide you with additional transition options. Figures 13-3 and 13-4 provide you with a list of available transitions.

FIGURE 13-2 Preview

FIGURE 13-3 Transition Group

FIGURE 13-4 Transition Styles

To apply a transition to a slide, you will need to select the slide. Click on the Transitions tab, and select a transition (Figure 13-5). PowerPoint will apply the transition to the slide and then provide you with a quick preview on how the slide will transition.

FIGURE 13-5 Apply Transitions

When applying transitions, you can switch to slide sorter and then, using **CTRL+left mouse click**, select the slides you wish to apply the transition to (Figure 13-6). In the following figure, you will see that the odd-numbered slides are selected, and when you click on the desired transition, this transition will be applied to the presentation. In the above figure, the **Push** transition was selected for all the odd-numbered slides.

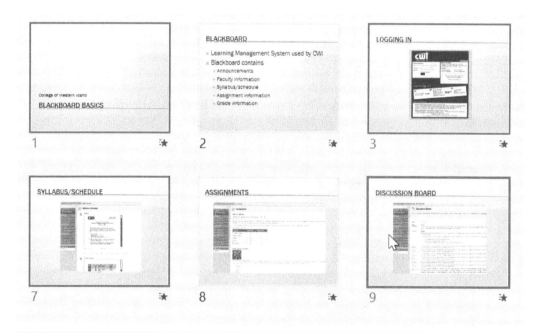

FIGURE 13-6 Selective Transition

When you apply a transition to a slide or slides, an Effect Option is applied to the slide transition. For the odd-numbered slides in our example, the Effect Option is From Bottom. To add an additional dimension to the presentation, you can change the effect option on the even-numbered slides by using From Top to give variety to the presentation.

When using transitions, do not apply a different transition to each slide. This leads to confusion for the audience and leaves them dazed with the presentation. Use the same transition on all the slides, and simply change the Effect Option to create the desired visual effect.

Timing

Many times, you will need to do a presentation and will not have a wireless mouse or have a person to advance the slides for you. The **Timing** function will allow you to set up an automatic advance on each slide. The timing can be set up to advance the slide on a click or after a specific period of time. You can apply the timing to all the slides or set up a specific timing for each slide. Figure 13-8 provides you with a view of the options available in the **Timing** group.

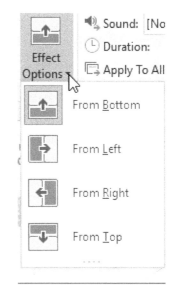

FIGURE 13-7 Transition Effects Group

Rehearsing your presentation will allow you to adjust the timing so that it will be appropriate for the presentation. You may choose to create a question slide for the end of the presentation and hold all questions until you are finished with the presentation so that your timings work appropriately with each slide. Figure 13-9 displays the timing applied to a slide.

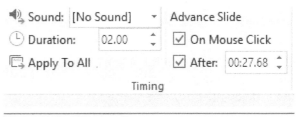

FIGURE 13-8 Timing Group

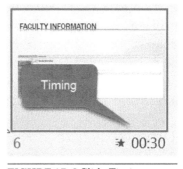

FIGURE 13-9 Slide Timing

2. Animations Tab

Another tool that is available to add pizazz to your presentation is the Animations tab. This tab will allow you to animate items within your presentation. When you are presenting information in a point-by-point manner, it can be helpful to use animations to display one point at a time. This will allow you to fully cover the points and allow for potential questions from the audience on each point. Animations can also be used to emphasize a specific point or element in the presentation. Figure 13-10 displays some of the animations available for use.

FIGURE 13-10 Animations Tab

Animation Group

The **Animation** group is the key to selecting animations for your slides. The most commonly used animations appear initially at the top of the group. The *More* button will display more animations, some of which are for entrance effects, exit effects, and others are for emphasis. At the bottom of the animation display, are options for additional animation effects (Figure 13-12). A common entrance effect would be the use of a **Fly-in** or **Appear** animation to bulleted information on a slide.

FIGURE 13-11 Animation Group

Most anything on a slide can be animated and, like the slide transitions, you will want to take care to avoid applying too many animations on a slide. Too many animations will make the slide overly busy and distract the audience from your presentation.

When you have applied an animation to a slide, PowerPoint will present you with a preview of the animation. Once you have applied all the animations to the slide, you can use the *Preview* button to do a fast preview of the animations.

FIGURE 13-12 Animation Effects

Timing

Timing can be used to manage the presentation of the animations. The length of the animation can be controlled and a delay can also be applied to the animation.

In some instances, it may be necessary to reorder the animations on a slide. The **Reorder Animation** feature will allow the animations to be placed in a modified order.

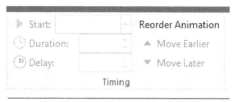

FIGURE 13-13 Timing

Here you will get a chance to test your understanding of the material covered in the chapter. You will need access to a computer with Power-Point. Using the OneDrive PowerPoint App will be a viable alternative if you do not have access to a computer with a full version of Office 2019, Office 2021, or Office 365.

In this project, you will continue working on your presentation focusing upon the Hells Canyon Power Complex and Recreational Area. Your presentation will incorporate the skills you are learning in the chapter. The Hells Canyon Power Complex and Recreational Area is located on the borders of Idaho and Oregon.

Files Needed: **(Your initials) Student Checkup PowerPoint 12-3**
Completed File Name: **(Your initials) Student Checkup PowerPoint 13-1**
1. Open your Checkup file 12-3.
2. Click on the slide sorter.
3. Using your keyboard and mouse, click on the first slide; holding the shift key down, click on the last slide.
4. Click on the **Transitions** tab; select the **Split** transition.
5. Click anywhere that is not on a slide to deselect all the slides.
6. Using the **CTRL** key, hold the key down and select the even-number slides by clicking on each of the desired slides.
7. Click on **Effect Options** and select **Vertical In**.
8. Select all slides.
9. In the **Timing Group**, adjust the timing to a duration of 02.00.
10. Click the **After** check box, and set the timing to 00:05.00. See Figure 13-14a.

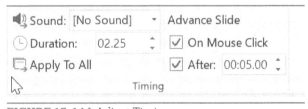

FIGURE 13-14A Adjust Timing

11. Select slide two of your presentation.
12. Click on the **Animations** tab.
13. Select the body place holder.
14. Apply the **Fly In** animation to the text.
15. Select slide 3, and select the body place holder,
16. Apply the **Float In** animation to the text.
17. Save your project and post as instructed by your instructor.

Completed checkup project.

FIGURE 13-14B Completed Checkpoint Project

3. Slide Show Tab

The **Slide Show** tab provides you with many options for presenting a slide show. It is possible to make a slide show to be viewed on a website. Companies may have slide shows that use many of the same slides for different portions of the company. A custom slide show can be created using a group of slides that have been tailored for a group or department. Rehearsing a slide show can be done to set slide timings. There are many other features that can be used to help the presenter give the best possible presentation (Figure 13-15).

FIGURE 13-15 Slide Show

Start Slide Show
Once you have completed your presentation or at any time during the creation of the presentation, you can view how your presentation will look. The first of two options is **From Beginning** to start the slide show at the first slide of the

presentation. The second option is **From Current Slide**, which will start the slide show on the current slide. When creating a presentation, it is always good to view the presentation at least once from the beginning. During the creation of the presentation, feel free to use the **From Current Slide** for simplicity.

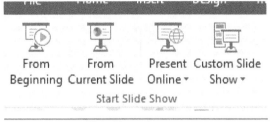

FIGURE 13-16 Slide Show Group

4. Review Tab

The **Review** tab provides you with the tools to review the spelling of your presentation, find synonyms, add comments, and show comments. If you have a tablet or other touch screen device, **Inking** tools are available to annotate your presentation.

FIGURE 13-17 Review Tab

Proofing

The **Proofing** group provides you with a spell checker and Thesaurus. To use the **Spelling** tool, move to the first slide and then click on the **Spelling** tool. The spell check will move through your slide show, scanning for spelling errors on the slide and in the notes section of each slide. Errors are displayed in a **Spelling** pane with recommended corrections. You simply choose the preferred correction and click on **Change** to implement the correction. A *Change All* button will make the correction to all similar errors.

FIGURE 13-18 Spelling Pane

Comments

Comments allow instructors or others working on the presentation to insert comments within the slide. The comments are not seen when the presentation is in **Slide Show** mode. The **New Comment** function is active when

working on a slide. The other functions are active when there are active comments within the presentation. The **Previous** and **Next** functions are active when there is more than one comment within the presentation. The **Show Comments** will display the **Comments** pane to the right of the slide (Figure 13-19). In the figure, you can see a comment balloon annotating where a comment is in the presentation. The **Comments pane** will display the comments for you. If the **Comments** pane is not active, clicking on one of the comment balloons will activate the **Comments** pane.

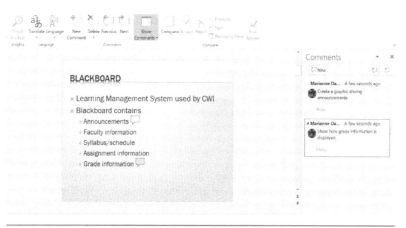

FIGURE 13-20 Presentation Comments

Translation and Language tools are available. These tools will allow you to make a translation of the slides. If you are using these tools, it is always wise to have a native speaker translation and ensure the quality of the translation.

5. View Tab

The **View** tab will provide you with tools to view your slides from different perspectives. As you design your presentation, frequently changing the view and moving to different perspectives will allow you to determine if a slide needs to be moved, if the transitions and animations work, or if you need to restructure your slides to be more effective.

FIGURE 13-21 View Tab

Presentation View

The **Presentation Views** group provides you with several ways to look at your presentation. There are five different views that you can choose from to view your presentation. If you look at the status bar on the right, you will see several of these views.

FIGURE 13-22 Presentation Views

When working with a slide show, the **Normal** view is the most common view. The **Normal** view will allow you to add text, images, graphics, and other media to enhance the presentation.

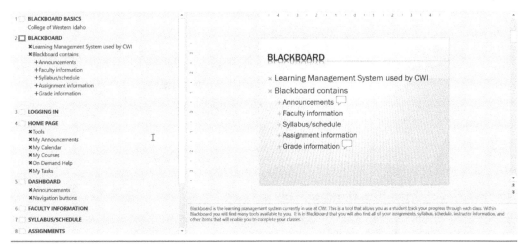

FIGURE 13-23 Outline Group

The **Outline** tab will provide a view showing an outline of the information on the slide on the left and the related slide on the right. Changes can be made within the outline to the slide or slides can be added. Pressing the ENTER key will allow you to add new bullets or slides to the presentation.

The **Slide Sorter** works the same as the slide sort on the status bar. Here you will see all the slides placed on the screen. Depending upon the size of the presentation, you may have to scroll to see all the slides. Here you can make style changes such as adding in different transitions to groups of slides at once. You can also see the flow of the slides and adjust the order of the slides in the presentation by dragging and dropping the slides.

FIGURE 13-24 Show Options

If you are taking an online class or you get very nervous when doing a live presentation or you need notes related to the slide in one place, you can make use of the **Notes** section of the slide. The **Notes Page** on the **View** tab will display your slide with the related notes. This format can be printed as needed.

The final view is the **Reading View**. With this tool, you can view your presentation with transitions and animations without going into slide show view.

Show

Another group that is useful is the show group. We all want a presentation that looks good and is engaging. Work is needed to make sure that graphics and placeholders line up properly, animations and transitions flow smoothly, and that the pre-sentation is designed in a clear and logical manner. Tools like the **Ruler**, **Gridlines**, and **Guides** all serve to help you to effectively layout your presentation. The **Notes** tool allows you to easily display and hide the notes page on your slides. A show launcher will allow you to adjust the Grid settings and Guide settings. It is here that you can also turn off the Smart guides.

FIGURE 13-25 Show Launcher

FIGURE 13-26 Zoom

Zoom

The final group is the **Zoom** group. This is a small group that will allow you to adjust your slides for easier viewing while working on your pre-sentation. When inserting graphics into a slide, it sometimes helps to **Zoom** in on the slide for more accurate placement. For those who may be visually impaired, **Zoom** will help enlarge the slide for viewing.

When you select the **Zoom** function, you will be presented with a display that will allow you to choose from several preset zoom sizes or adjust

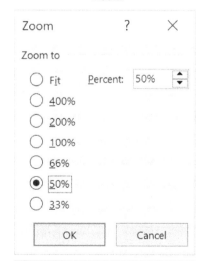

FIGURE 13-27 Zoom Options

the display using a percentage. Using the Notes pane on a slide will impact the zoom sizing.

The **Fit to Window** tool will adjust the slide to the available space.

Chapter Projects

Here you will get a chance to test your understanding of the material covered in the chapter. You will need access to a computer with Power-Point. Using the OneDrive PowerPoint App will be a viable alternative if you do not have access to a computer with a full version of Office 2019, Office 2021, or Office 365. **Note: Blue text represents typed text.**

In this project, you will continue working on your presentation focusing upon the Hells Canyon Power Complex and Recreational Area. Your presentation will incorporate the skills you are learning in the chapter. The Hells Canyon Power Complex and Recreation Area covers the states of Idaho and Oregon.

Files Needed: **(Your initials)_Chapter_12_PowerPoint_Capstone**
Completed File Name: **(Your initials)_Chapter_13_PowerPoint_Capstone**

1. Open (Your initials)_Chapter_12_PowerPoint_Capstone 1.
2. Using the **Save As** function, save the presentation as (Your initials)_ Chapter_13_PowerPoint_Capstone 1.
3. Close (Your initials) _Chapter_12_PowerPoint_Capstone 1.
4. Click on the slide sorter.
5. Select all the slides in the presentation.
6. Click on the **Transitions Tab**, select the **Glitter** transition.
7. Click anywhere that is not on a slide to deselect all the slides.
8. Using the **CTRL** key, hold the key down and select the even number slides by clicking on each of the desired slides.
9. Click on **Effect Options**, and select **Hexagons from Right**.
10. Select all slides.
11. In the **Timing Group**, adjust the timing to a duration of 04.00.
12. Click the **After** check box, and set the timing to 00:06.00.
13. Select slides two, three, five, six, and eight of your presentation. Note: You must do these steps to each slide individually.
14. Click on the **Animations** tab.
15. Select the body place holder.
16. Apply the **Appear** animation to the text.
17. Select slide four, and select the first picture.
18. Apply the **Appear** animation to the text.

---

19. Select slide four, and select the picture on the left of the slide.
20. Apply the **Appear** animation to the text.
21. Set the **Timing** as follows: **Start**: After Previous and **Duration**: 01.00,
22. Try something new, and use the **Animation Painter**, located in the **Advanced Animation** group. With the first picture selected, click on it and then click on the second picture. Repeat for the third picture.
23. Change the **Effect Options** for the middle slide to **From Top**.
24. Move to slide seven and click on the scroll. Apply one of the **Emphasis** animations to the scroll.
25. Go to the **Review** tab.
26. Run **spell check** on the presentation, and correct any errors identified.
27. Go to slide two, and create a comment on the first bullet; insert a comment to "Increase the font size to **24** pt."
28. Go to the **View** tab.
29. Turn on the **Ruler, Guidelines**, and **Guides**.
30. Set the **Presentation View** to **Slide Sorter**. Take a Snip of the display.
31. Move to the end of the presentation, and add another slide. Paste the snip in the new slide, showing the slide sorter view. In the title use **Slide Sorter Snip**.
32. Select **Zoom**, and set the slide to **Fit**.
33. Save your presentation, and submit to your instructor as directed.

FIGURE 13-28 Completed Chapter 13 Project 1

Here you will get a chance to test your understanding of the material covered in the chapter. You will need access to a computer with PowerPoint. Using the OneDrive PowerPoint App will be a viable alternative if you do not have access to a computer with a full version of Office 2019, Office 2021, or Office 365. **Note: Blue text represents typed text**.

In this project, you will continue working on your presentation focusing upon the Hells Canyon Recreation Area and Power Complex. Your presentation will incorporate the skills you are learning in the chapter. The Hells Canyon Power Complex and Recreational Area covers the states of Idaho and Oregon.

Files Needed: **(Your initials)_Chapter_12_PowerPoint_Capstone 2**
Completed File Name: **(Your initials)_Chapter_13_PowerPoint_ Capstone 2**

1. Open (Your initials)_Chapter_12_PowerPoint_Capstone 2.
2. Using the **Save As** function, save the presentation as (Your initials)_ Chapter_13_PowerPoint_Capstone 2.
3. Close (Your initials)_Chapter_12_PowerPoint_Capstone 1
4. Click on the slide sorter.
5. Select all the slides in the presentation.
6. Click on the **Transitions** tab, select the **Peel-Off** transition.
7. Click anywhere that is not on a slide to deselect all the slides.
8. Using the **CTRL** key, hold the key down and select the even number slides by clicking on each of the desired slides.
9. Click on **Effect Options**, and select **Right**.
10. Select all slides.
11. In the **Timing Group**, adjust the timing to a duration of 03.00.
12. Click the **After** check box, and set the timing to 00:10.00.
13. Select slides two, four, five, and six of your presentation. (Note: You must do these steps to each slide individually.)
14. Click on the **Animations** tab.
15. Select the body place holder.
16. Apply the **Split** animation to the text.
17. Set the **Timing** as follows: **Start**: After Previous and **Duration**: 01.00.
18. Repeat steps 13 through 17 with the other slides.

19. On slide seven, for each of the pictures, add the **Appear** animation for each picture. For the shape, apply the **Swivel** animation.
20. Go to the **Review** tab.
21. Run **spell check** on the presentation, and correct any errors identified.
22. Go to slide three, and create a comment on the first bullet. Insert a comment to "Increase the font size to 28 pt. and the font to Aparajita."
23. Go to the **View** tab.
24. Turn on the **Ruler, Guidelines**, and **Guides**.
25. Set the **Presentation View** to **Slide Sorter**. Take a Snip of the display.
26. Move to the end of the presentation, and add another slide. Paste the snip in the new slide showing the slide sorter view. In the title use **Slide Sorter Snip**.
27. Select **Zoom**, and set the slide to **Fit**.
28. Save your presentation, and submit to your instructor as directed.

FIGURE 13-29 Completed Chapter 13 Project 2

CHAPTER FOURTEEN

PowerPoint Part III

Introduction

Up to this point we have been learning how to create a PowerPoint presentation and the various tools that are available in PowerPoint. There are many other tools that have not been discussed, and in this chapter, we will cover these tools. Let's look at many of these innovative tools to enhance your presentations.

Learning Objectives

In this chapter, you will learn about some of the other tools and features that are available with PowerPoint. Office 365, PowerPoint 2019 and PowerPoint 2021 have additional features that were not available with previous versions of PowerPoint. When you complete this chapter, you should be able to use the following:

FIGURE 14-1 Media Group

1. Audio Files
2. Video Tools
3. Sway

1. Audio Files

Audio files add an element to a presentation that taps into the auditory learning centers of a person's brain. Many times, audio will enhance a presentation and provide an element that will help keep the viewers engaged. Audio can come in many forms, from background music to a narrated presentation.

Instructors make use of audio in their presentations to convey a lecture to a class in an online environment. Some instructors have had students make use of audio to create presentations to be given in the online environment. A good set of headphones with a microphone are a must if you are planning on making your own recordings. Any store that sells computer equipment will have good headphones and microphones for sale.

FIGURE 14-2 Inserting Audio from PC

Audio files can come from many places. Chances are you have a few audio tracks on your computer. Many people like to rip their compact discs to their computers so that they can listen to the music at various times. These music tracks can also be added to your PowerPoint presentation. To add a track, click on the **Insert** tab and, then, in the **Media** group, you will click on the **Audio** drop-down menu and select **Audio on My PC**.

Once you have inserted the audio, you will see the **Audio Contextual** tab. There are two tabs; this is the one you will need. Here, you can make changes to the audio clip. As you can see, the audio can be started **On Click** or **Automatically**. There are **Fade In** and **Fade Out** controls along with **Volume** controls. The audio can be set to **Play Across Slides** and can be **Looped** until stopped.

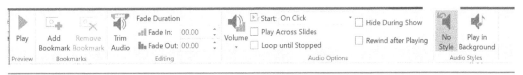

FIGURE 14-3 Audio Contextual Tab

2. Video Tools

Video also provides additional spice to a presentation. Videos can be the ones you make or from the web. It is always a good idea to limit the length of a video in a presentation to not diminish the effectiveness of the presenter.

The first method for adding a video to a presentation is by using the video tool on the slide. Click on the video tool and then select the video you wish to insert. You will then see an **Insert Video** dialog box as in Figure 14-4. This box will allow you to search videos from various sources including YouTube.

In Figure 14-5, you will select a video from your computer using File Explorer. These are videos that you may have created from your digital camera or a video

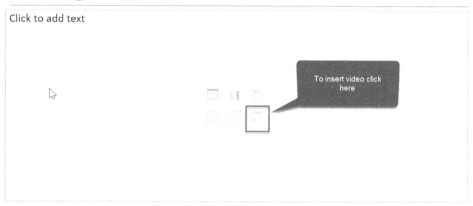

FIGURE 14-4 Inserting Video

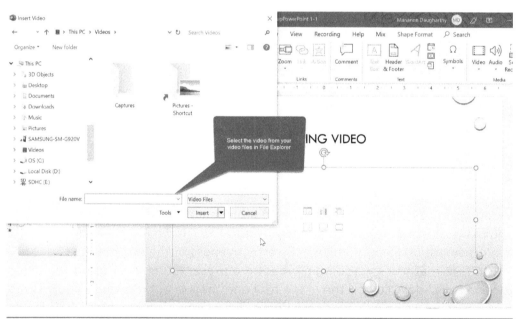

FIGURE 14-5 Video Search

that you have stored on your computer from another source. For an online video you will need the full URL of the video. In Figure 14-6, you can see that the Media group located on the Insert Tab was selected and then Online Video.

FIGURE 14-6 Selecting an Online Video

In Figure 14-7, you will see the pop-up where you will need to enter the URL for your presentation. When the slide show is being played, you can adjust

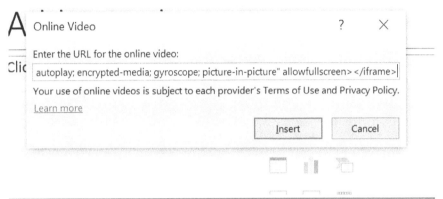

FIGURE 14-7 Online Video URL

to full-screen mode. In Figure 14-8, you can see the video we are inserting along with the Playback contextual tab. Here you can adjust how the video is used in the presentation by using features such as start automatically.

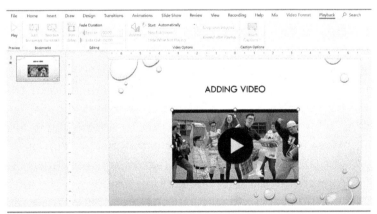

FIGURE 14-8 Inserted Video and Playback Tab

When you present your presentation, you will see the video as shown in Figure 14-9. Notice at the bottom of the video that there are control buttons will allow you to start and stop the video.

Adding Video

FIGURE 14-9 Playing the Video

Note that you may receive a warning from PowerPoint that references to external links have been disabled. You have the flexibility to enable this content. Before enabling content from external sources, always make sure that the content is from sources you trust or content that you have chosen for your presentation.

Chapter 14 PowerPoint Checkpoint

Here you will get a chance to test your understanding of the material covered in the chapter. You will need access to a computer with Power-Point. Using the OneDrive PowerPoint App will be a viable alternative if you do not have access to a computer with a full version of Office 2019, Office 2021, or Office 365. **Note: Blue text represents typed text**.

In this project, you will try your hand at creating a presentation that makes use of audio and video functions. For this project, unless your instructor tells otherwise, you can be more creative and choose some of the things to insert in this presentation.

Files Needed: **None**

Completed File Name: **(Your initials)_Chapter_14_PowerPoint_Checkpoint**

1. Open a new PowerPoint presentation using one of the design themes. Do not use the blank or plain white slide background.
2. Create a title slide; be sure that you include your name in the subtitle. For the title enter **Chapter 14 Checkpoint**.
3. On slide two, you will want to insert an audio track. You can use a song of your choosing, create your own recording by using a microphone, or you can search for an audio track on the Internet. Set the tack to begin automatically.
4. On slide three, insert a video track. Search YouTube for a video that you like, and insert the video into the presentation. Set the video to start automatically. Enlarge the video to fit the screen. Some videos will not have playback options enabled for user use.
5. For the previous two slides, be sure that you include a title for each slide.
6. Click back on slide 1, and create speaker notes for each slide.
7. Save the project, and post as directed.

FIGURE 14-10 Completed Chapter 14 Checkpoint Project

3. Sway

Up to this point we have discussed only PowerPoint. Other programs will provide users with different methods of presenting information to a live audience. One of Microsoft's newest tools is Sway. Sway provides users with another method of presenting information in an engaging manner. With Sway, you can add pictures, audio, and videos. You can choose from a multitude of templates or create your own. In this section we will explore how you can create your own Sway.

Microsoft Sway, one of Microsoft's new applications, was released in 2014.

Let's get started creating a Sway. You will need to access Sway in one of two methods. The first one is through a work or education account provided for you. If you do not have one of these, you can create a personal Microsoft OneDrive account that will give you access to Sway. From both accounts, you will access Sway in the same manner.

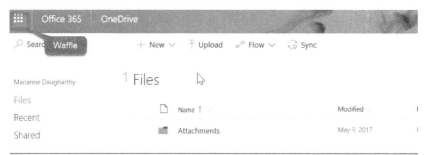

FIGURE 14-11 Office Waffle

To create a Sway, you will need to log into your online Microsoft account. Clicking on the Waffle in the upper left corner of your screen (see Figure 14-11) will bring you to a display of all the available applications associated with your account.

Please note that the Office 365 accounts have applications that are authorized by the account administrator of your institution. Figure 14-12 shows you some of the many applications that your account administrator may make available for you to use. From the available applications you can see that this institution has online applications such as Word, Excel, and PowerPoint. Added applications include OneNote, Sway, and Flow. It is from the waffle in your Office account or through your own personal OneDrive account that you will access Sway.

FIGURE 14-12 Online Office Applications

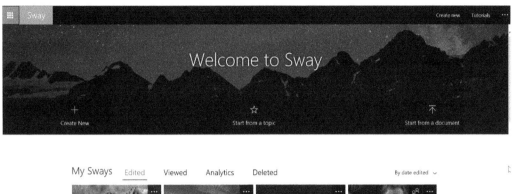

FIGURE 14-13 Sway Start Page

Once you select Sway from the Office Applications, you see the following startup screen. Here in Figure 14-13, you have the option of creating a new Sway, start from a topic, or start from a document. Each option provides you with countless ways to create a dynamic presentation or story. In the upper right corner of the screen, you will find a link to tutorials that will provide you with other ideas and help with creating your Sways.

Scrolling down the startup screen, you will see the Sway templates, featured Sways, and Sways that you have created. Templates are designed to help you get a quick start on creating your Sway. Featured Sways provide you with a host of ideas for creating a Sway. Like PowerPoint, Sway will provide you with a graphical way of presenting a report or other information. You can include videos, photos, and other graphical information within your Sway.

Creating a Sway

To create a Sway, start by sketching or outlining your idea. You might want to answer the following questions as you begin the process of building your Sway.

1. What is your topic?
2. What do you wish to convey?
3. Have you created a story board or outline?
4. What graphics or videos do you want to include?

You can easily add to this list of questions. and this list will provide you with some direction as you begin your project. Building your Sway from scratch, you want to select one of the templates.

Creating a Sway

To start creating your Sway you will need to first open Sway. 1. Scroll down on the web page to the templates. 2. Select the template you wish to use as in Figure 14-14. 3. You are now ready to begin editing the template to create your Sway.	 FIGURE 14-14 Selecting a Template
Now that you have selected your template, it is time to start editing the Sway. 1. Click on Start editing this Sway. 2. You can now start making changes to the template entering your own information in the text.	 FIGURE 14-15 Start Editing
Information is entered on cards within the Sway. Figure 14-16 shows the first two cards of our practice Sway. 1. The first card is the Title card that introduces the title of the Sway. 2. The second card in this Sway is a text card that will allow you to enter text into the Sway.	 FIGURE 14-16 Editing the Sway

In the left corner of the title card, you can see that a background can be added. Clicking here, you will be presented with a list of suggested graphics. If you do not care for the items presented, there is a search option for you to find other graphics that may work in your Sway. In the title card, a background picture was added. Since the suggested image did not fit the theme, a search for jungle pictures was performed. **Creative Commons Only** was checked to select an image that is generally available for sharing.

FIGURE 14-17 Background Images

As you edit and create your Sway, you will notice the green plus sign in a circle between the cards. This icon will provide you with other tools that are available to enhance your Sway. Figure 14-18 shows you some of the tools available. Each of the items listed at the top of the box will display additional tools when selected.	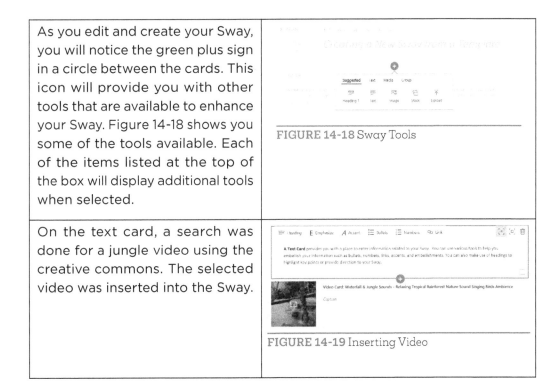 FIGURE 14-18 Sway Tools
On the text card, a search was done for a jungle video using the creative commons. The selected video was inserted into the Sway.	FIGURE 14-19 Inserting Video

As you build your Sway, periodically play the Sway to see how you are progressing. Let's look at what we have completed so far. To play the Sway press the **Play** button in the upper right corner of the display.

In the upper right corner of the Sway you will see several controls. The Edit control will allow you to go back to editing your Sway. Share gives you the ability to share your Sway with others. You can set the Share options so that others can only view the Sway, or you can allow them to edit. The edit feature is especially useful if you are creating a collaborative project. The cog will allow you to adjust the layout of the Sway. The ellipsis will provide you with many other options for working with your Sway.

FIGURE 14-20 Playing the Sway

The lower right corner of the Sway has buttons for moving the Sway forward and backward. If a vertical presentation was chosen, then direction controls will be adjusted to scroll the project. To the left of the navigation buttons is a button that will allow you to navigate to other sections within the project. In Figure 14-21, you can see the sections that were created in the Sway. Click on any of the sections and you will immediately navigate to that section of the Sway.

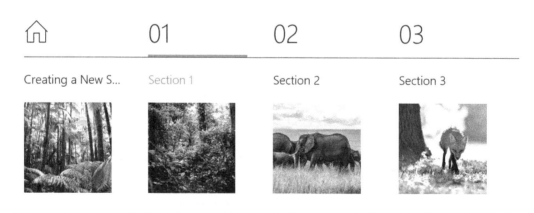

FIGURE 14-21 Navigating Sway Sections—Sway Template

In this section, we have covered creating a Sway using a template. What if you have a document with your information already in place and wish to create a

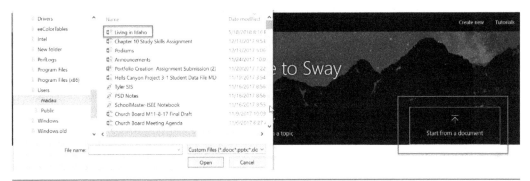

FIGURE 14-22 Start from a Document

Sway from that? You can use the option to create your Sway from that document. This is done by clicking on the Start from a Document, as shown in Figure 14-22.

When you select **Start from a Document**, you will be taken to a screen to locate your document. When you select your document, Sway will take your document and start a Sway. Your text will likely be in one Text card, and any graphics or pictures will be either included on the card or put on a card of their own.

In Figure 14-23, you can see the results of creating a Sway from a document. Notice that the title of the document is used in a text card beginning the Sway. The rest of the text in the document is placed in a text card, and you can then modify the Sway and add your own embellishments.

FIGURE 14-23 Creating a Sway from a Document

When Sway is finished with the initial setup from your document, you can begin fine tuning the Sway. The document used in Figure 14-23 had no graphics or anything special in the document. Now it is time to enhance the Sway. For the title card, a background graphic will be used, and this will be obtained from a search of the creative commons available in Sway. In the search box, the title provided many excellent choices as seen in Figure 14-24.

FIGURE 14-24 Title Card Background Photo from Creative Commons

Once a background picture was applied to the title text box, the second text-box was split into two separate textboxes. From the second textbox, we have information that will provide us with additional graphics for the Sway, again, searching creative commons for images of the lakes mentioned in the first para-graph. Pictures of each of the lakes were found and added to the Sway. When using the creative commons pictures, author credit is also applied to the picture information. Three pictures were selected and placed in a group stack.

FIGURE 14-25 Pictures Selected of Highlighted Areas from Creative Commons

The second text card created from the body of the document features pictures taken locally on a backpacking trip. Sway allows you to add your personal pictures to a Sway with no problems. If video had been taken of the various places, it too could be added to the Sway.

Text Card

As we tour Idaho, we find that mountains form a major part of the landscape. The Bitterroot Mountain and the Sawtooth Mountains are two of the major ranges that provide Idaho with many wilderness activities. Hiking, camping, fishing, are some of the many adventurous activities that a person can engage in.

FIGURE 14-26 Adding Personal Pictures

When creating photo stacks, you have a few options with the stack. The first option is to make use of Focus Points. Focus Points allow you to select a specific point in a picture for Sway to focus upon. You can also reset the Focus Point or remove it from the photo. In Figure 14-27, a Focus Point is applied to the selected photo, focusing upon the summit of the mountain.

FIGURE 14-27 Focus Point

Besides Focus Points, you can specify the type of grouping you would like with your photo stack. There are several types of grouping that you can make use of. Additionally, to the right of the ungroup option, there are three icons that will allow you to adjust your stack group intensity. Play with the options to find the style that fits your presentation.

FIGURE 14-28 Group Types

Now that we have created the Sway, let's walk through how the final Sway looks. Figure 14-29 shows a picture of the Title card.

FIGURE 14-29. Title Card

Scrolling to the next card, Figure 14-30, we see our photo stack of the various lakes selected for the Sway. The icon in the lower right corner of the stack is a full screen option.

Idaho is known as the Gem State. The name fits the state it is full of a myriad of gems. These gems are not always the precious stones that many people think of, though there are plenty of these too. Sparkling lakes such at Payette Lake in McCall, Lake Coeur d' Alane, and Lake Pend Oreille are three of Idaho's precious gems.

FIGURE 14-30 First Text Card

The second text card, Figure 14-31, presents the next Idaho gems. This card contains the text information that was moved to this card along with two different photo stacks highlighting the two mountain ranges highlighted in the text information.

As we tour Idaho, we find that mountains form a major part of the landscape. The Bitterroot Mountain and the Sawtooth Mountains are two of the major ranges that provide Idaho with many wilderness activities. Hiking, camping, fishing, are some of the many adventurous activities that a person can engage in.

FIGURE 14-31 Second Text Card

Now that you have the basics of creating a Sway, there are a few other features that will be of use to you. The three dots, Figure 14-32, will provide you with additional options for using Sway. Here you can create a new Sway. You can see that there are other options such as duplicating and printing your Sway. Other options such as setting, accessibility checker, and accessibility view provide you with other tools for using Sway in various environments.

As a student, you may have to work on a group project or submit a Sway for an assignment. Figure 14-33 provides you with the ability to share the Sway. You can share the Sway as a view only or provide the ability for others to edit the

FIGURE 14-32 Additional
Options

FIGURE 14-33 Sharing a Sway

Sway. If you are working with a web page and need to embed your Sway, you can get an embed code for your Sway.

The final option is the change layout option. You get to this option by clicking on the cog icon while playing your Sway. The default layout option is to scroll down. You can change the layout to scroll horizontally or to present the card and graphic together. Depending upon your Sway and the material in your Sway, one layout may work better than the other.

One last option that we have not discussed yet is the design tab when you are in edit mode with your Sway. The Design tab allows you to add other design features automatically to your Sway. Features such as different fonts and styles and layouts are available to add to your Sway. In Figure 14-35, you can see a variety of styles that are available for use. There are arrows at the end of each style

FIGURE 14-34 Sway Layouts

row that will provide you with additional related styles. Once you select a style click on the **Remix** button to apply the style to your Sway. The palette in the upper right corner of your display will allow you to apply other changes to the style you have chosen, such as font styles, and color changes to the style.

FIGURE 14-35 Design Styles

For our current Sway, the style was changed to Style 5, Variant 1. Remix was used to apply the design change to the Sway, and in Figure 14-36 you can see the results of the design change. The results produced changes that framed photos and a geometric background to the Sway.

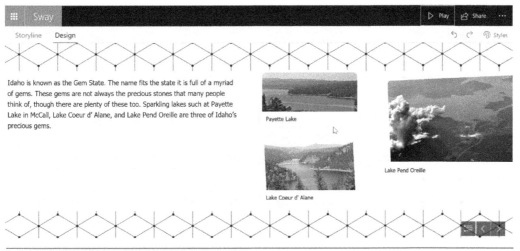

FIGURE 14-36 Sway with Design Change

Chapter 14 Sway Project

In this section we have been discussing how to use Sway to create a presentation. In this project you will try your hand at creating a Sway of your own.

Files Needed: **None**

Completed Project: Submit a Sway share link with edit capabilities.

1. Go to your One Drive account using either your institution account or your personal account.
2. Create a Sway, highlighting your favorite state outdoor activity.
3. Your Sway needs to contain the following:
    a. Title card
    b. Two text cards
    c. Two picture stacks of at least 3 pictures each
    d. One related video
    e. Apply one of the design styles
    f. Apply an intense style to one of your photo stacks
    g. Include a focus point on one of your photos.
4. Create a share link with an invite to edit the Sway.
5. Post your share link as instructed by your instructor.

Credits

Fig. 14-8: Source: https://www.youtube.com/watch?v=hZg7EBxbqSE.
Fig. 14-9: Source: https://www.youtube.com/watch?v=hZg7EBxbqSE.
Fig. 14-10: Source: https://www.youtube.com/watch?v=hZg7EBxbqSE.

CHAPTER FIFTEEN

Prezi Next

Introduction

With **Prezi**, you'll learn to use motion, zoom, and spatial relationships to help people truly engage with your message. No more clicking on slides—everything is on one slide.

You can get Prezi Classic and Prezi Next for free (Figure 15-1).

FIGURE 15-1 Prezi Sign-ups

Supported Browsers for Prezi Next

For Editing: **Prezi Next** presentations can currently be edited on a Windows or Mac computer using Chrome, Firefox 64 bit, and Safari 10. If using your phone or tablet, our ***Prezi Viewer*** app enables you to view, present, and share presentations on Android and iOS devices, however the Prezi app does not support editing at this time.

For Viewing: Presentations are best viewed with the latest versions of Safari, Firefox, Chrome, Edge, or Internet Explorer.

Prezi Next Desktop App
Installation

- The installation of **Prezi Next** requires about 650MB but can vary by 1–2MB from one release to the next.
- Minimum requirements for running Prezi Next.
  ○ **Windows**: Windows 7 SP1 with a minimum of 4 GB RAM.
  ○ **Mac**: OS X 10.10.5 with a minimum of 4 GB RAM.

Note: **Prezi Next** is not officially supported on Linux.

Prezi Sign-up
As a student, you can also upgrade to EDU Plus for $7 per month. However, for this lesson, we will be signing up for the EDU Standard (Free) version for starters.

1. Click on **Continue** in one of the boxes with the red borders (Figure 15-2).

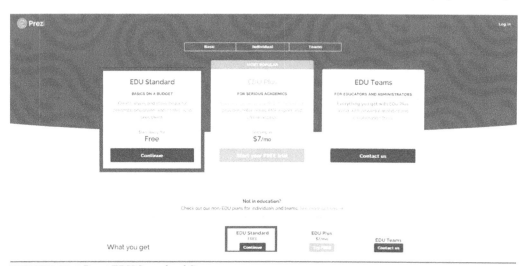

FIGURE 15-2 Prezi EDU Standard Sign-up

2. A **Prezi Student/Teacher Verification** dialog box will open. This is where you will type in your school email address in the **Email Address** box.
3. Click on **Verify**. The program will verify that your student email is valid. Once it is validated, you will receive an email in your school email (Figure 15-3).

Prezi   Log in ~

Student/Teacher Verification

Please provide the email address issued to you by your educational institution.

Email address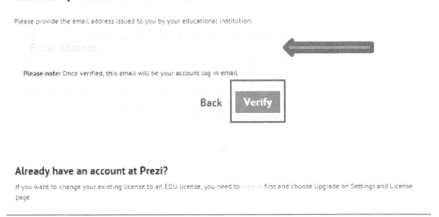

Please note: Once verified, this email will be your account log in email.

Back   **Verify**

Already have an account at Prezi?

If you want to change your existing license to an EDU license, you need to sign in first and choose Upgrade on Settings and License page.

FIGURE 15-3 Student/Teacher Verification

4. The following screen will appear. This is your dashboard for **Prezi Next** (Figure 15-4).

FIGURE 15-4 Prezi Next Dashboard

5. Note: In the lower left panel of both **Prezi Classic** and **Prezi Next**, you may also get the app for your tablet, notebook, net-book, and mobile device. This will enable you to create and present anytime and anywhere (Figure 15-5).

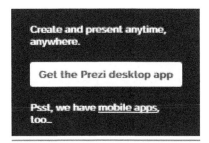

FIGURE 15-5 Prezi Next Apps

Creating a New Presentation

The overall look and feel of your presentation set the mood for your audience. Templates are a great way to start a presentation because they come ready with topics and subtopics for you to plug in your information and add images.

Once you've logged in, you'll be taken to your dashboard that has presentations you can view, edit, and create. In the left panel, you will notice two other options. The first option is to **Create from Template**, and the second option is to **Convert PowerPoint**. When you click on **Create from Template**, the following window will appear. In the left panel, you will also notice you have options for five different categories and the option to filter the templates by color (Figure 15-6).

1. *Sales and Business Development*. This option has forty-five different templates.
2. *Marketing.* This option has thirty-one different templates.
3. *Education & Non-Profit*. This option has fifteen different templates.
4. *HR & Training*. This option has thirteen different templates.
5. *General*. This option has forty different templates.

FIGURE 15-6 Prezi Next Templates

Figure 15-7 shows you what happens when you choose to **Filter by Color**. In this case, I selected a blue shade. A small white circle around the color shows you what color you selected. The program will show you templates in each of the five categories (listed above) based on the color you used as a filter.

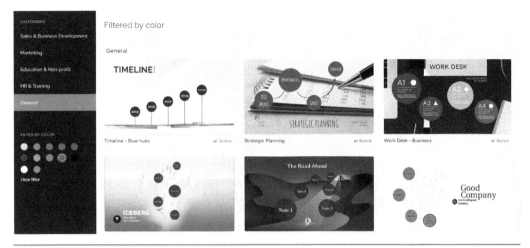

FIGURE 15-7 Filter by Color

When you click on your chosen template, a blue button will appear at the bottom of your choice that says, "**Use this Template**." If you like it, click on it. Your new presentation will open in a new tab. If you do not like it, you can click on the white "x" circled in yellow in the upper right-hand corner of the window (Figure 15-8). The program will take you back to your template page where you may make another selection.

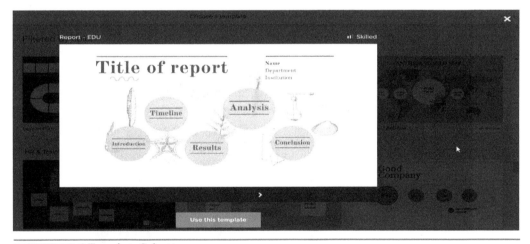

FIGURE 15-8 Template Selection

In Figure 15-9, a new template has been selected. The window will open with your "slides" in the **Overview** panel on the left side of the window. The center panel will show you your "Slide." The right panel, Background, will give you the option to upload your own image, do a **Background Image Search**, or you may select one of the **Recommended Backgrounds**. Below the **Recommended**

FIGURE 15-9 Selected Template

Backgrounds you can choose a different background color (Figure 15-10), or **Revert to the Original** (just in case you didn't like the background color).

Once you are happy with your choice of template, click on the three horizontal bars icon above **Overview** in the left panel, then click on *Save* to save your presentation (Figure 15-11).

When you are ready to name your presentation, click on the **Untitled presentation** blank to type in your presentation name then click on *OK*. You can find this just to the right of the cloud above **Overview** in the left panel (Figure 15-12).

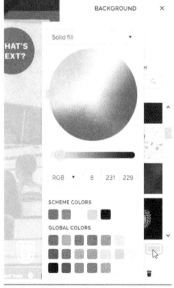

FIGURE 15-10 Background Color Options

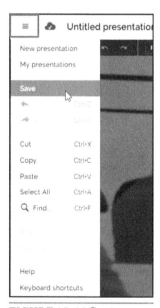

FIGURE 15-11 Saving a New Presentation

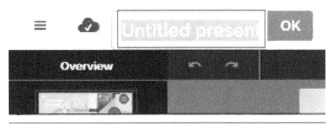

FIGURE 15-12 Naming/Renaming your Presentation

Note: If you select a template but change your mind and would like to change your template completely, you will have to create a new presentation. So, before you get too far down the road with your presentation, keep checking that your template is still working for your presentation.

If you decide to change your template, return to the Prezi dashboard page and click on **Create from Template**.

Deleting a Presentation

Deleting a presentation will remove it from your dashboard and your **Prezi Next** account. Once you delete a presentation, you will not be able to recover it. Double-check and make sure you really want to erase it. Once it is deleted, it will be gone forever (Figure 15-13).

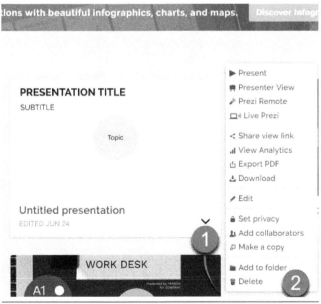

FIGURE 15-13 Deleting a Presentation

1. From the dashboard, click the **Arrow** icon in the lower right-hand corner of the presentation thumbnail to get the menu (1). **Delete** is at the bottom of the list (2).
2. Once you click on **Delete**, you will see the following window (Figure 15-14): This is your last chance to confirm that you want to delete it.
3. If you are absolutely sure that you don't want or need the presentation, click **Yes, delete** (pink button) again to confirm that you want to delete the presentation.

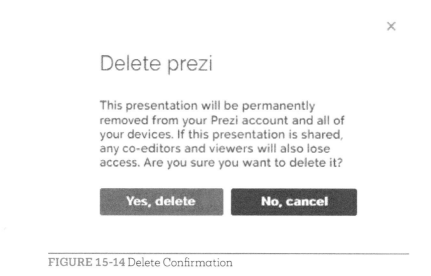

FIGURE 15-14 Delete Confirmation

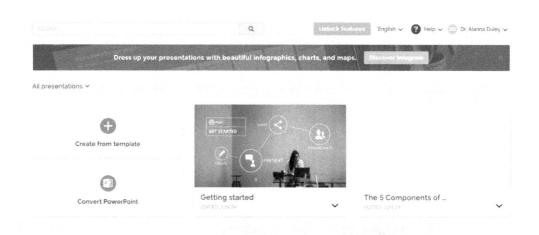

FIGURE 15-15 Dashboard after Delete

Note: The program will not allow you to delete the **Getting Started** presentation (Figure 15-15).

Select Your Language

Prezi Next is available in nine languages (Figure 15-16). You may change your language option at any time. You can set a default language to match your computer's operating system or set the language manually.

1. Click the language drop-down menu in the upper right corner of your dashboard. and select your language.

Note: To change your language, you must first select and open a presentation.

Navigating the Dashboard

The dashboard is central control, where you can find your presentations, organize them, and access additional options for sharing and presenting.

FIGURE 15-16 Selecting your Language

Once you open **Prezi Next**, you'll immediately be taken to your dashboard. The most recent presentations you've edited or viewed display at first.

To find a particular presentation, type a keyword from the title in the search field (1) (Figure 15-17). You will find this handy if you have several presentations and don't feel like searching for it yourself.

Presentation Thumbnails

You also have the option to click on the presentation thumbnail picture to open it for editing or viewing. The most recent Prezis will show up at the top of the window while the older presentations will be below them. They are ordered by date. In this case, all I have to do is click on the thumbnail for ***The 5 Components of a Computer System*** (Figure 15-17).

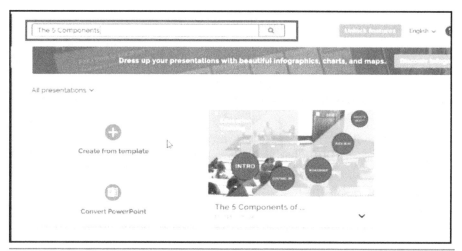

FIGURE 15-17 Using the Search Box to Find a Presentation

Name a Presentation

You will want to name your presentation once you create it (See Figure 15-12).

1. Click in the Untitled Presentation box (next to the cloud above Overview).
2. Type in the desired name for your presentation.
3. Click the blue **OK** button to the right.

Renaming a Presentation

If you have various copies of your presentation, you may want to rename it to help organize your files.

1. From the dashboard, click the little pencil to the right of the title of the presentation you want to rename.
2. The background of the title will highlight.
3. Type the new name of your presentation and press **Enter**, or click anywhere outside of its title.
4. If you change your mind, you can click on the small "**x**" to the right of the title.

Using the Editor

The editor is where you start building your presentation. It was designed to give users and team members ease in creation and collaboration.

Figure 15-18 The pencil shows you the button to click to Edit your presentation.

Figure 15-19 Forward arrow is the button to select to open your presentation quickly when you are ready to present it.

Figure 15-20 Three dots show you the button to select to Collaborate or add a link to share your presentation.

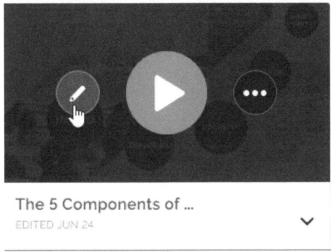

FIGURE 15-18 The Edit Button

FIGURE 15-19 The Present Button

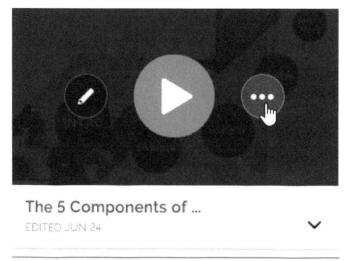

The 5 Components of ...

EDITED JUN 24

FIGURE 15-20 Add Collaborators and a Link

The editor comes with three important toolbars. They are Style, Insert, and Share.

Style Toolbar:

1. **Style** Option:

    a. Use the **Style** option (Figure 15-21) to change your background or upload your own picture. The program provides over fifty different backgrounds from which to choose. To open the **Background** gallery, click on the three little dots after **Background**.

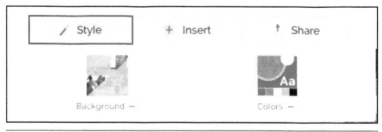

FIGURE 15-21 Style Toolbar

2. **Colors** Option:

    a. Use the **style** option (Figure 15-22) to change your colors to a selection of 22 different default colors, or choose your own. To open the **Colors** gallery, click on the three little dots after **Colors**. Each different color option is called a *Theme*.

3. **Insert** Toolbar. This is where you add all your **Topics, Story blocks, Text, Image**, and **Icons & symbols** (Figure 15-22).

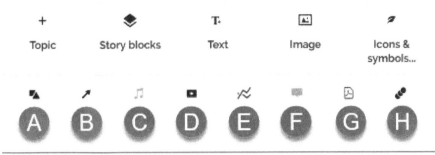

FIGURE 15-22 Insert Toolbar

Additionally, you will find the following listed buttons on the **Insert** toolbar:

a. **Shapes**
b. **Arrows & Lines**
c. **Audio**
d. **Video**
e. **Charts**
f. **Comments**
g. **Pdf**
h. **Animations**

The Share toolbar makes it easy for you to perform the following (Figure 5-23):

a. **Present Presentation**
b. **View Link**
c. **Collaborate,** or
d. **Live Prezi**! Presents your presentation Real-time.

FIGURE 15-23 Share Toolbar

Left Sidebar

The left sidebar allows you to add topics and sub-topics to your presentation. You can also preview the order of your content and how it will appear. Clicking on one of the "Slides" will automatically change to show where you are in your presentation's structure.

To navigate to a specific item or content, click on a thumbnail. You can also click and drag to reorder your topics and subtopics (Figure 15-24).

Click on the blue +**Topic** button on the bottom to add a new "Slide" (Figure 15-25). For this template, two types are available to choose from:

1. Planet Style
2. Stack Style

Note: Experiment with the different Topic Types to see what would work best for your presentation.

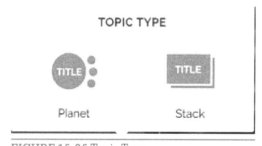

FIGURE 15-25 Topic Type

FIGURE 15-24 Left Sidebar

Animations

Animations bring your presentation to life.

Overview of the Animation Icon

From the editor, click on the **Animations** icon in the **Insert** toolbar (Figure 15-26).

Once you click on the **Animations** icon, you will see a drop-down list in the **Overview Animations** pane that lets you select where you want the animations to appear in your presentation (Figure 15-27).

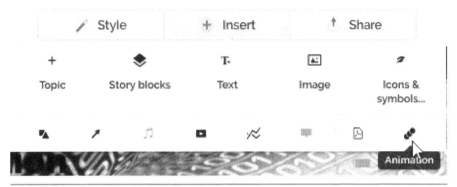

FIGURE 15-26 Animations Icon

If you are using the desktop app, go to **View > Animations** to show the sidebar.

Note: The animations sidebar view adjusts depending on where you are in your presentation's structure. This allows you to add separate sets of animations within your overview, topics, subtopics, and pages.

Adding Animations

Animations allow you to zoom in to particular areas on your canvas or zoom back out to get an overall picture of the topic or subtopic. You can also add zoom animations to an object such as text or an image, or you can add fade-in and fade-out animations to highlight specific information.

FIGURE 15-27 Overview Animations Pane

Here are the two steps to add an animation to an object in your presentation:

1. Select the object or text where you'd like to add the animation. If you do not select an object, you can still add a zoom area anywhere on your canvas. To do this, click on the down arrow next to **At the beginning of this prezi** to have the drop-down list appear. You can click on any of the listed areas of your prezi to add animations (Figure 15-27).

2. Right-click (CTRL/CMD + click) and select **Add animation** (or click the **Insert** button at the top of your screen, then select **Animation**).

3. Select the animation you would like to add. You'll see a preview of the animation before it appears in the sidebar (Figure 15-28). You will see two

groupings of animations: **Standard** and **Zooming**. **Standard** consists of *Fade in* and *Fade out options* (1), and **Zooming** allows you to add a *zoom* area (2).

4. Click + to add another animation (3).

Fade in and Fade out

To see the **Standard** and **Zooming** animations, you will need to click on the white plus sign in the blue circle to make them appear (Figure 15-28).

Fade-in animation helps you to control when the object or text appears or disappears. You can fade in or out of images, text, video, topics, and subtopics. This enables you to drive your presentation according to audience response.

In addition to selecting one object, you can select multiple objects. To select multiple objects, hold the **SHIFT** key and drag your cursor over the desired objects. You may also hold down the **SHIFT** key and click each object. The objects you have selected are outlined in blue.

You can also select multiple items and add fade in or fade out to create a more spectacular effect (Figure 15-29). To select multiple objects, hold the **SHIFT** key and drag your cursor over the items you want to select. You can also click on each object while holding the **SHIFT** key. You'll see the objects you've selected outlined in blue.

Zoom

Zooming allows you to highlight a specific area or provide more details. **Zoom** can be used with objects, text, and any area on the canvas.

Add Zoom Area

Select your object. Once you click on **Add Zoom Area**, a blue rectangle will appear

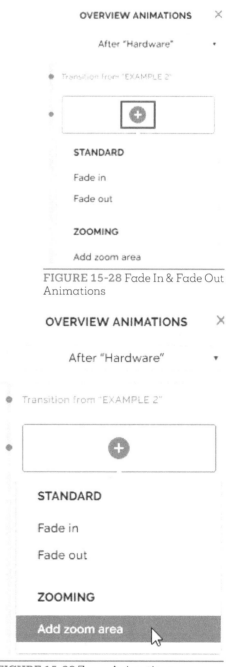

FIGURE 15-28 Fade In & Fade Out Animations

FIGURE 15-29 Zoom Animations

(Figure 15-30). You can resize it and move it to fit the area you would like to emphasize.

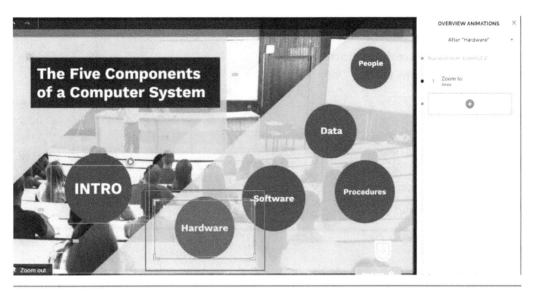

FIGURE 15-30 Zoom to Area

Zoom Out to Overview, Topic, or Subtopic

Context is vital to a good presentation. Adding a **zoom out** to the overview, topic, or subtopic will help your audience match the details to the bigger picture. Depending on the number of subtopics you use, you can make it easier for your audience to follow your presentation when you use the **zoom out**.

Note: You must add a **zoom-in** animation to be able to see the option to zoom out to your overview, topic, or subtopic.

Editing Animations

Animations can be reviewed, reordered, or deleted anytime, using the animations sidebar.

Reviewing your Animations

To preview your animations, you can play your animations in the sidebar to see how they will appear during your presentation. To see a preview, hover your mouse over one of the small black circles on the left of your animation. It will turn into a small right-facing arrow. Click on the arrow to see a preview of your animation (Figure 15-31).

Reordering Animations

Once you add an animation, you can change the order it appears (Figure 15-32). In your sidebar, click the animation you want to move, then drag and drop it to the desired position. Notice in Figure 15-32, **Zoom to** has been moved above **Fade in**.

Removing Animations

To remove an animation, right-click on an animation in the sidebar and click **Remove animation** (Figure 15-33). You will see the animation disappear from the sidebar.

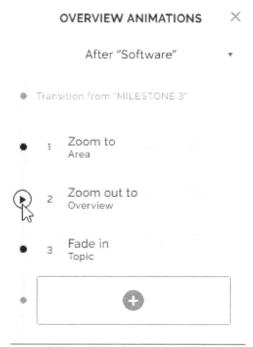

FIGURE 15-31 Reviewing Animations

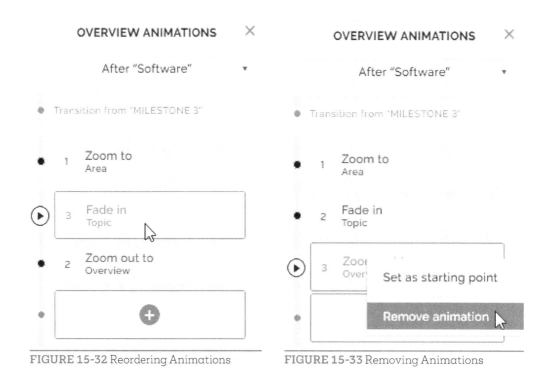

FIGURE 15-32 Reordering Animations

FIGURE 15-33 Removing Animations

Folders

Filtering Presentations

Folders act as identifiers for your presentations. You can put a **Prezi Next** presentation in any folder to help organize your presentations. Some folders may be used to sort presentations by course, topic, team, or shared.

The Left Sidebar

The left sidebar is designed to organize your presentations by using folders. In addition to sorting presentations by course, topic, team, or shared, you can create your team folder and filter those presentations by those you own and those that are shared with you.

You can add new folders in your Dashboard.

Adding Folders

1. To add a folder, click on the + **New Folder** in the left sidebar on the Dashboard (Figure 15-34).
2. Type in the new folder name, and click on **Save** (Figure 15-35).
3. Once your click Save, your new folder will appear in the Left Sidebar (Figure 15-36).

FIGURE 15-34 Adding a New Folder

FIGURE 15-35 Naming a Folder

FIGURE 15-36 New Folder Named

Adding a Presentation to a Folder

It is easy to add folders from the dashboard. The presentations you put in folders are tagged, so if you end up deleting a folder, your presentation can still be found in the dashboard. Unless you actually delete your presentation, your presentation cannot be deleted if you delete a folder.

Here's how to add a presentation to a folder:

1. From the dashboard, click the **down arrow** icon in the lower right corner of the presentation thumbnail (Figure 15-37).
2. A menu will appear to the right. Click on **Add to folder** (Figure 15-38).
3. In the pop-up window, select the folder you would like to add your presentation to. Click on it (Figure 15-39).
4. In the **Left Sidebar**, on the **Dashboard**, click on your folder, and you will see your presentation inside your folder (Figure 15-40).

FIGURE 15-37 Down Arrow Icon

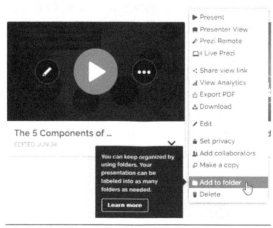

FIGURE 15-38 Add to Folder

FIGURE 15-39 Add Presentation to Selected Folder

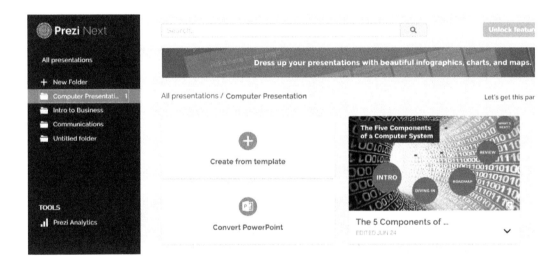

FIGURE 15-40 Contents of Computer Presentation Folder

Organizing Folders

You will use the left sidebar to organize your presentations using folders. Here you can create your team folder and filter your presentations according to those you own and those you don't own but are shared with you.

Delete Folders

When you delete a folder, no presentations will be deleted. Although the folder has been deleted, your presentation(s) may still be found with your synced dashboard or in any other folder with which they are tagged. To delete a folder, do the following (Figure 15-41):

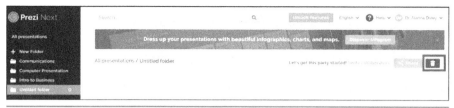

FIGURE 15-41 Delete Folders

1. Click on the folder to bring up its screen.
2. On the far right of the screen, click on the trash can icon.
3. A **Delete Folder** dialog box will appear. You can click **Delete** or **Cancel** (Figure 15-42).
4. The "Untitled Folder" (highlighted in blue) that appears in Figure 15-42 has been deleted.

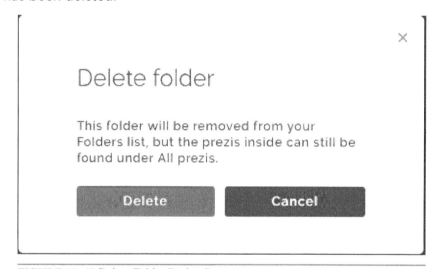

FIGURE 15-42 Delete Folder Dialog Box

Rename Folders

1. Click on the desired folder in the left sidebar to bring up its screen.
2. Hover over the folder name and the pencil will appear (Figure 15-43).
3. Click on the title, and type a new name for your folder (Figure 15-44). Then, click **Save**.

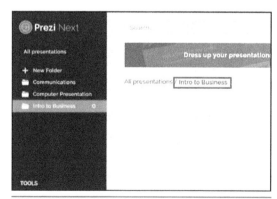

FIGURE 15-43 Rename Folder

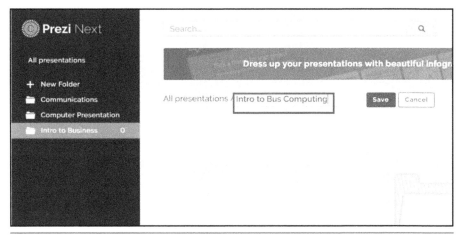

FIGURE 15-44 Type in New Folder Name

Sharing a Folder

If you want to share a folder, you can do so from your online dashboard.

Note: You will need an Internet connection to do this action.

To share a folder or invite collaborators (Figure 15-43):

1. Click on the folder that you would like to share to open that folder.
2. Click the aqua-colored **Share** button located at the upper right corner next to the trash can icon (Figure 15-45).

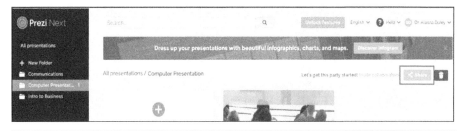

FIGURE 15-45 Sharing a Presentation

3. In the window, type the email of the person you'd like to share the folder with and click **Add**.
4. You can add other people.
5. Under the Email Address box, you will see you are listed as the Owner. To the right, you will see the word **Owner** and a crown. Your collaborators can view, add, and remove Prezis from the folder. They can also add additional collaborators, but not remove them. You, as the owner, are the only person who can delete the folder.

6. A list of you and your collaborators will appear under where you typed in their email addresses.
7. Once the email has been sent, a small green box with white text will appear.
8. When you are done sharing your folder, click **Finished** to close the window (Figure 15-47).

FIGURE 15-46 Share Folder Computer Presentation

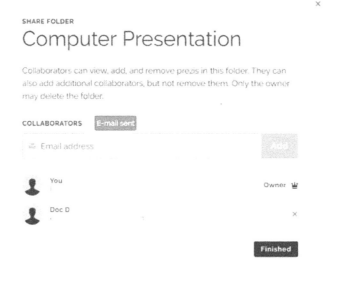

FIGURE 15-47 List of Collaborators

Once you share a folder, it will appear in the user's dashboard. Anyone y ou share a folder with will have access to all the presentations. Additionally, any user with access to a folder can create analytics and invite other users.

Added users will be added as a viewer to all presentations in the folder. To change a user's status, you have to change his or her rights or remove the user from the presentation. Refer to the **Collaborating on a Group Presentation** section.

Note: A folder can be deleted only by its owner.

Structuring Your Presentation

A **Prezi Next** presentation's structure consists of chapters that follow a path using connectors. Your overview will show the titles of each topic, and once you enter a topic, your subtopics will be revealed.

Elements of a Presentation's Structure

You will see the following when you enter a **PreziNext** presentation.

FIGURE 15-48 Overview

1. is the Overview (Figure 15-48).
2. Topics are represented by a circle.
3. Subtopics are included within Topics.

Overview

Your overview shows the title of each topic while content remains hidden until you zoom to reveal that particular information. Connectors include lines and arrows that preview the path your audience will take through your presentation. Click on a topic to show the connectors that make up your presentation's path.

Note: Before you begin, try sketching out an overview of the main points in your presentation. The overview would be similar to an outline. That way you'll have a better idea of how to structure your content. It will serve to keep you focused on your main topic without going off on different tangents.

Topic Types

Topics organize important points to convey your message. These are similar to bullet points. There are two types of topics: **Planet** and **Stack**.

Planet

Planet. Use this type if you want to break your topic up into subtopics or advanced subtopics. This type of topic presents deeper levels of a topic or subtopic. If you have a data rich presentation, the **Planet** would be a good choice. Figure 15-49 shows the main topic as Hardware. The first subtopic is ARPARNET. The three subtopics of ARPARNET are shown as slides 1, 2, & 3, respectively. When you enter a **planet** topic, you'll see only the title of each subtopic while presenting. The title is taken from the largest text on a subtopic. To reveal a subtopic's contents, just click on the numbered slide of your choice.

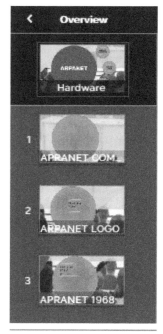

FIGURE 15-49 Planet Subtopics

Stack

Stack displays pages of content in a timeline manner. Use **Stack** if you want to reveal content to your audience in a historical reveal, in a timeline format, or step-by-step. With a **Stack** presentation, each **Stack** page will display separately and in order. Similar to PowerPoint, the left sidebar shows the number of pages in the stack and the order they will appear. The selected thumbnail is the **Current** page in stack.

You can add additional pages to a stack; however, you cannot add further subtopics. To add a page, enter the stack topic or subtopic and simply click [**+ Page**] in the left sidebar. The new page will be added to your path (Figure 15-50).

Adding Topics

Click +**Topic** to add another topic. [**+ Topic** ▼] Then in the left sidebar you may choose a topic type. The new topic will be added as the last topic in your **Prezi**.

Once you add a topic, you will have the option to choose **Planet** or **Stack** (Figure 15-51).

FIGURE 15-50
Add Topic

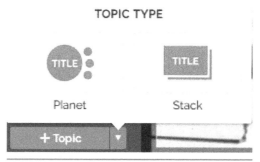

FIGURE 15-51 Topic Type

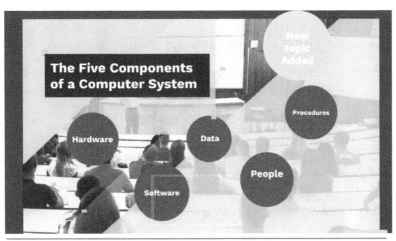

FIGURE 15-52 New Topic Added

After you click on your topic type choice, you will see your new topic *Planet* or *Stack* as your last item (Figure 15-52). Double-click on your new topic to open it to add subtopics.

Note: For a clean, uncluttered look, use as few topics as possible. Then resize them to fit your canvas, and put them in strategic positions that support your story. If a Prezi is too busy, your audience will tend to lose focus. Keep it clean and simple.

Changing a Topic's Position

To change a topic's position, click and drag, or use the arrow keys on your keyboard to move it to a new place on the canvas (Figure 15-53). Connectors automatically adjust when moving a topic.

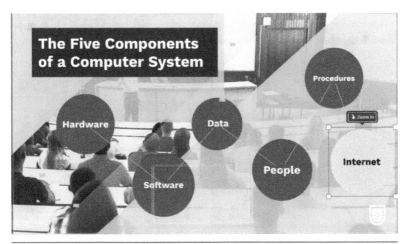

FIGURE 15-53 Changing a Topic's Position

Note: Set your background image to appear to hide your topics until they appear.

Deleting a Topic

You can easily delete a topic. There are two ways to do it:

1. Select your topic, and press **Backspace/Delete** on your keyboard.
2. Right-click, and select **Delete** from the context menu (Figure 15-54).

Editing Connectors

Click on a connector to select it, or double-click to select all of the connectors at the same time. You can change a connector's thickness (1, 2), color (3), custom color (4), and opacity (5) from the context toolbar. If you want to make a connector invisible, drag the opacity marker to the left (Figure 15-55).

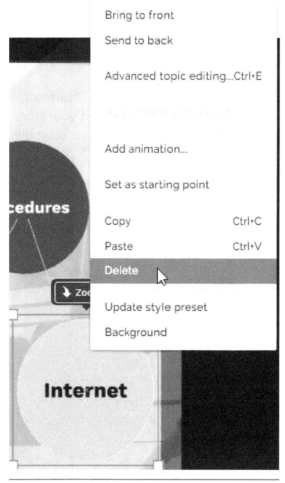

FIGURE 15-54 Deleting a Topic

FIGURE 15-55 Editing Connectors

Adding Subtopics
Adding Subtopics to Planet
With a **Planet** subtopic, new subtopics will be added to the planet's orbit. You may add both **Planet** and **Stack** subtopics to the planet's orbit (Figure 15-56). To add a subtopic, enter the planet topic or subtopic and click  in the left sidebar.

FIGURE 15-56 Two Layers of Subtopics

Advanced Subtopics
In a **Planet** structure, you can add both **Stack** and **Planet** subtopics but Prezi does not allow you to add **Planets** to a **Stack** structure.

If you want to continue to add subtopics to subtopics (Figure 15-57), it is recommended that you don't exceed three layers in your presentation. Otherwise, you may to restructure your presentation.

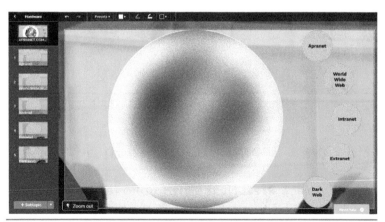

FIGURE 15-57 Three Layers of Subtopics

Note: Preview flow of your topics and subtopics as you create your presentation. You can do a dry run with a friend, classmate, or your instructor to make sure your topics and subtopics flow in a logical manner before you present your **Prezi**. This will help manage your content so you don't lose your audience while presenting.

Deleting Subtopics and Pages
If you change your mind, you can easily delete a subtopic or page. There are two ways to do it:

1. Select the subtopic or page in the left sidebar, and press **Backspace/Delete** on your keyboard.
2. Right-click, and select "delete" from the context menu.

Reordering Topics and Subtopics
To reorder topics and subtopics, click on a thumbnail in the left sidebar and drag it to a new position. The topic, subtopic, or page that you reorder will automatically update on your presentation canvas. No need to manually move subtopics when moving a main topic (Figure 15-58). Also refer to Figure 15-53 to see the original topic order.

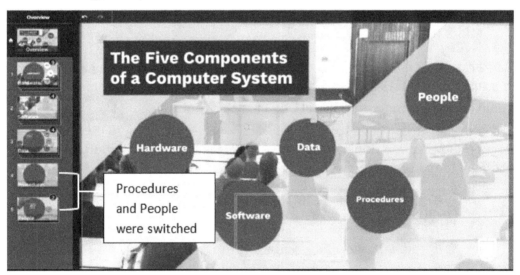

FIGURE 15-58 Reordering Topics and Subtopics

Collaborating on a Group Presentation

If you have a group project, **Prezi Next** allows up to ten users on a single presentation. This will allow you to work more efficiently by enabling you to add comments to specific topics and subtopics or pose questions in real time.

Once you create your presentation, with collaboration you can do the following:

1. Add collaborators (users) with the options you choose to edit, comment, or present your presentation.
2. You also have privacy settings for a presentation which allow only collaborators and people with a view link to access your presentation.

Adding Collaborators

To start collaborating on a presentation, its owner (you) must first give users rights to edit, comment, or view.

Note: Collaborators will need a **Prezi Next** license to be able to edit a presentation. Your collaborators may also sign up for free.

Add a Collaborator via the Dashboard:

To add **collaborators** via the dashboard, do the following:

1. Move your mouse over your presentation thumbnail. Click on the three dots of a presentation to get the detailed view screen (Figure 15-59).
2. Click on the blue **Add Collaborators** button (Figure 15-60).

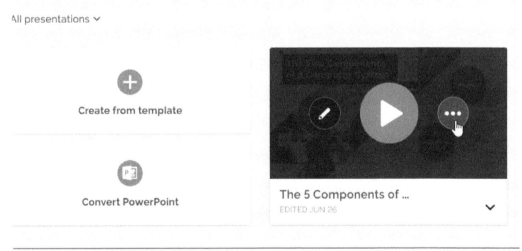

All presentations ⌄

Create from template

Convert PowerPoint

The 5 Components of ...
EDITED JUN 26   ⌄

FIGURE 15-59 Add Collaborators

3. In the **Invite People to Collaborate** window, do the following (Figure 15-61):

   a. Under **Collaborators**, type in the collaborator's email address.
   b. Click on one of the three: **Can Edit, Can Comment**, or **Can Present**.
   c. Click **Add**.
   d. You can continue to add collaborators.

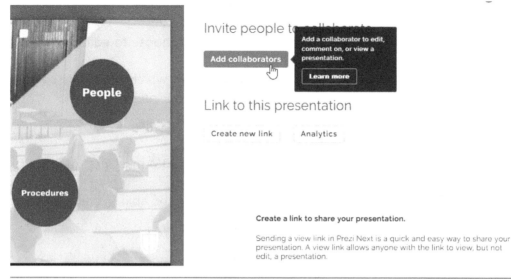

FIGURE 15-60 Invite People to Collaborate

    e. When you are finished adding collaborators, click on the **Done** button.

    f. If you change your mind, you can click on the **Done** button even if you don't add any collaborators.

Add a Collaborator via a Drop-Down List

1. Click on the down arrow at bottom right corner of the selected Prezi presentation thumbnail window.
2. You will see a drop-down menu (Figure 15-62).
3. Click on the **Add collaborators** option towards the bottom of the list. The **Invite People to Collaborate** dialog box will open (Figure 15-61).
4. In the **ADD COLLABORATOR** dialog box, follow the above steps, 3a–f.

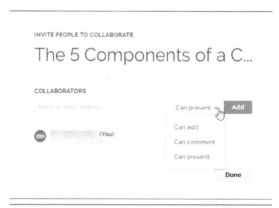

FIGURE 15-61 Invite People to Collaborate Window

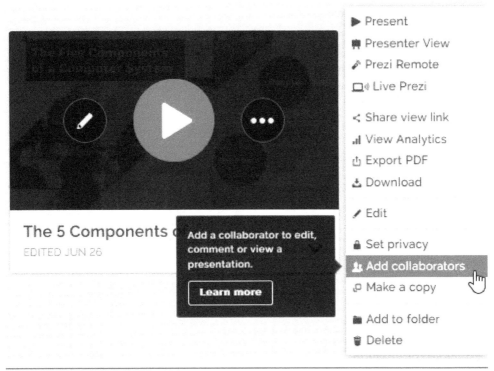

FIGURE 15-62 Another Way to Add Collaborators

Removing Collaborators

It's easy to remove a user from your presentation or to change a user's rights. From the dashboard, click the three dots (...) in the thumbnail of a presentation to get the **Invite people to collaborate** window (Figure 15-63).

FIGURE 15-63 Delete Collaborator(s)

Adding and Viewing Comments

The **Comments** feature is great way to give feedback Figure 15-64 shows you your comments features and options.

Note: The **Comments** feature is only available to teams with a Prezi Business plan. This feature is not available if you have the free EDU version.

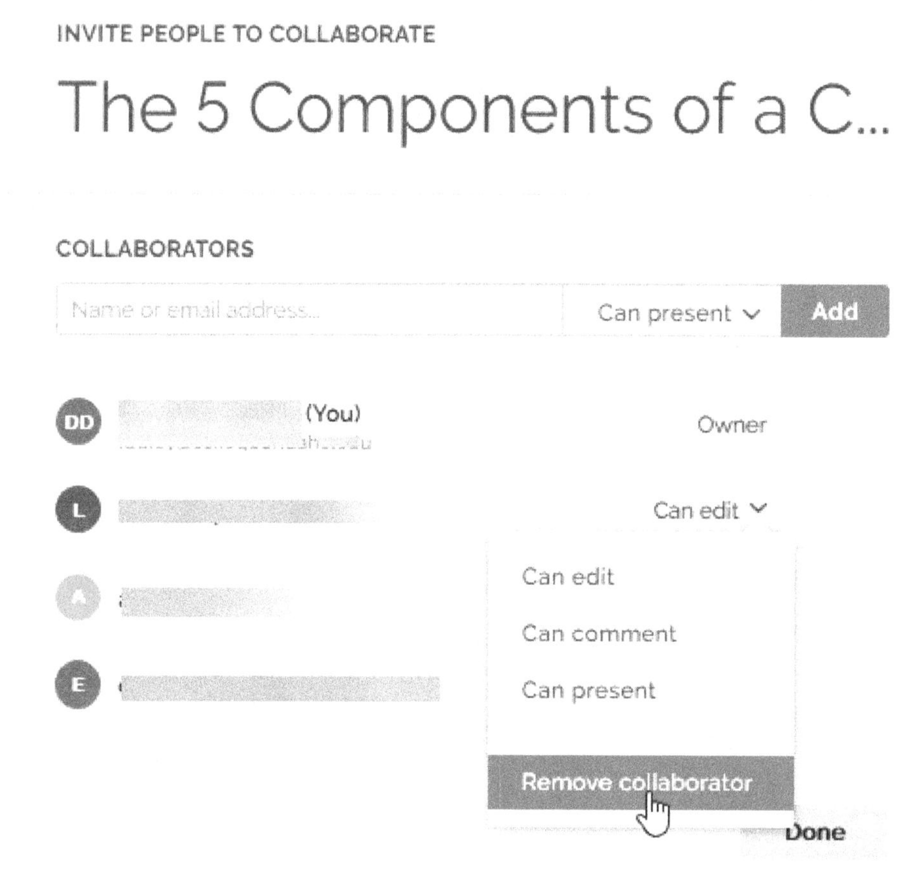

INVITE PEOPLE TO COLLABORATE

The 5 Components of a C...

COLLABORATORS

| Name or email address... | Can present ⌄ | Add |

DD (You)
_____ah__du
Owner

L _____
Can edit ⌄

A _____
Can edit

Can comment

E _____
Can present

Remove collaborator

Done

FIGURE 15-64 Collaborators Pop-Up Window

Sharing a Presentation

Once you've created your presentation, you may want to share it (Figure 15-65).

FIGURE 15-65 Share a Presentation

Sharing a Presentation's Share Present

The Present link will take you directly to present your Prezi (Figure 15-66).

FIGURE 15-66 Share Present

Sharing a Presentation's View Link

A **View Link** allows users with the link to view but not edit or modify a presentation. (Figure 15-67).

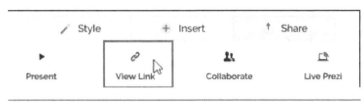

FIGURE 15-67 Share—View Link

Create a View Link

Here is the way to create **view links**:

1. Move your mouse over your presentation thumbnail.
2. Click on the **Edit** button (pencil) to open your presentation.
3. Click on the **Share** tab.
4. Click on **View Link** (Figure 15-68) or
5. Click in the blue box to **Enter the company or viewer's name for your own records** (Figure 15-69).

6. Choose if you want to track the link on Prezi Analytics or require viewers to identify themselves before viewing.

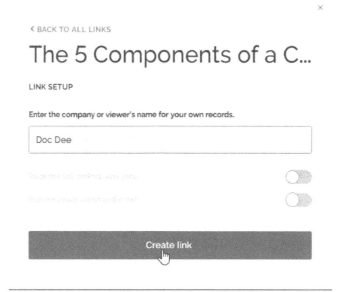

FIGURE 15-68 Link Setup

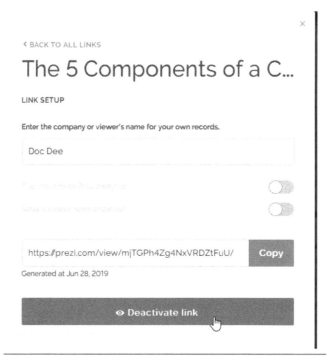

FIGURE 15-69 Deactivate Link

Note: This feature is not available in the EDU free version.

1. Click on the **Create Link** blue button (Figure 15-68).
2. You can copy the Prezi link and paste it in an email or, if you change your mind, you can click on Deactivate Link.
3. You can exit this dialog box by either clicking on **BACK TO ALL LINKS** link or click the "x" in the upper right corner.

Deactivating Links

When you decide to stop sharing a presentation, you deactivate a view link.

To deactivate a link:

1. Move your mouse over your presentation thumbnail.
2. Click on the Edit button (pencil) to open your presentation.
3. Click on the **Share** tab.
4. Click on **View Link** (Figure 15-67).
5. Click the **Deactivate link** button.
6. To stop sharing and delete the presentation's tracking data in Prezi Analytics, click **Deactivate link** and delete data. If you only want to stop sharing the presentation, click **Deactivate link**.
7. Once you click on the button, a Deactivate Link confirmation box will pop up. Click on the blue **Deactivate link** button or Cancel button (Figure 15-70).
8. The View Link dialog box will reappear. The link is gone.

FIGURE 15-70 Deactivate Link Confirmation

Create a Collaborate Link

1. Move your mouse over your presentation thumbnail.
2. Click on the **Edit** button (pencil) to open your presentation.
3. Click on **Share** tab.
4. Click on **Collaborate** (Figure 15-71).
5. This will take you directly to the **Invite People to Collaborate** (Figure 15-61).

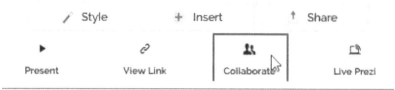

FIGURE 15-71 Share—Collaborate

Create a Live Prezi link

1. Move your mouse over your presentation thumbnail.
2. Click on the **Edit** button (pencil) to open your presentation.
3. Click on **Share** tab.
4. Click on **Live Prezi** (Figure 15-72).

FIGURE 15-72 Share—Live Prezi

1. In the **Start Live Prezi** dialog box, you can share your live link with your audience. Prezi provides you with a code you can edit (click on pencil) or copy.
2. You also have the option to **Protect with Access Code**.
3. Then you can click on either **Start Live Prezi** or click on the "**x**" in the upper right corner of the **Start Live Prezi** dialog box.
4. The presentation is ready to play. It will list the link the presentation may be accessed. Additionally, there will be a red button to press if you want to **End** the presentation.

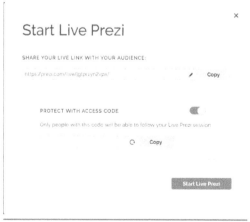

FIGURE 15-73 Start Live Prezi

FIGURE 15-74 Prezi Live Link

Convert PowerPoint

On the Dashboard, there is a button available for you to convert a PowerPoint presentation to a Prezi. This is a VERY COOL feature. Here are the steps:

1. On your dashboard, click on **Convert PowerPoint**.
2. You will see an option to either **Upload PowerPoint** or **Use Sample .ppt file** (Figure 15-75).

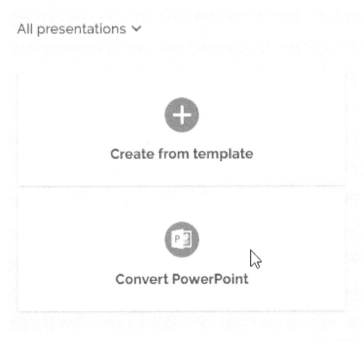

FIGURE 15-75 Convert PowerPoint

3. Click on the blue **Upload PowerPoint** button (Figure 15-76).
4. Locate the PowerPoint you want to use either in the cloud, or on your computer.
5. The PowerPoint download progress blue bar appears (Figure 15-77).

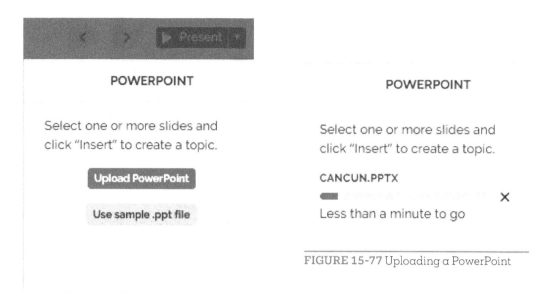

POWERPOINT

Select one or more slides and click "Insert" to create a topic.

Upload PowerPoint

Use sample .ppt file

POWERPOINT

Select one or more slides and click "Insert" to create a topic.

CANCUN.PPTX

✕

Less than a minute to go

FIGURE 15-77 Uploading a PowerPoint

FIGURE 15-76 Upload PowerPoint or Use Sample .ppt File

6. The PowerPoint appears. Select one or more slides to create a topic. Select your first slide, hold down your CTRL key then select the slide(s) you want. At the bottom of the window, click on **Insert.**

7. Several slides were selected for the first topic. A white check in a blue circle will appear in the upper left corner of each selected slide to show which slides were selected.

8. For each topic, you will select corresponding slides until you build your Prezi presentation.

9. Your PowerPoint will look like a Prezi with topics and subtopics. The download may run a little slow. You may have to do one or two at a time rather than a bunch of slides. Please be patient.

10. You can also add slides as subtopics to your topics.

11. Add your images, charts, graphs, text, and animations.

12. Enjoy! You might impress your audience with a Prezi rather than a PowerPoint. It definitely will put a spin on your presentation.

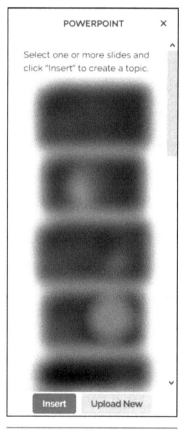

FIGURE 15-78 PowerPoint Progress Bar & Selected Slides

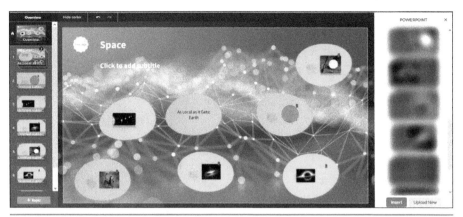

FIGURE 15-79 PowerPoint Converted to Prezi

Logging Out

To log out of **Prezi Next** online, click the drop-down menu next to your name in the upper right corner and click on **Log out** (Figure 15-80).

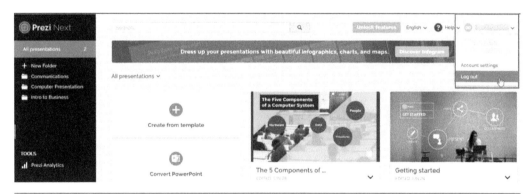

FIGURE 15-80 Log Out of Prezi

Part 5
Email

16. Outlook

CHAPTER SIXTEEN

Outlook

Introduction

Launched on July 31, 2012, Microsoft Outlook is a personal information manager from Microsoft, normally available as a part of the Microsoft Office suite. It is used mainly as an email application; however, it also includes a calendar, calendar manager, task manager, contact manager, and a journal as well as notes and web browsing.

With Outlook on your PC, Mac, or mobile device, you can:

1. Stay connected and productive wherever you are.
2. Easily manage your calendar to schedule meetings and appointments.
3. Organize email to let you focus on your most important messages.
4. Share latest versions of files from the cloud to recipients.

Note: Your institution's IT department will connect you to Outlook. If you experience any difficulties with Outlook, contact your instructor.

The Ribbon—Introducing the File, Home, and View Tabs

When you open Microsoft Outlook, you will notice many similarities between Outlook's and other Microsoft Applications Ribbons. You will also see that many features on the Ribbon you learned about in other Microsoft Applications that will enable you to navigate Outlook and allow you to easily expand your understanding of Outlook. Let's start off with the File Tab and look at the features that are unique to Outlook.

File Tab or Backstage

The **File** tab, or **Backstage** view, in Excel is very similar to the File tab in Word. The **Info** option is where you would view information regarding your workbook, such as *Account Settings, Automatic Replies (Out of Office), Mailbox Settings, Rules and Alerts, and Manage Add-ins* (Figure 16-1).

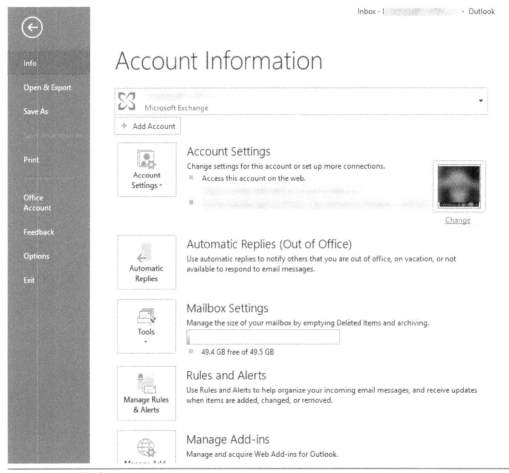

FIGURE 16-1 Backstage

The **Open & Import** feature allows you to open an **Outlook Calendar**, open an **Outlook Data File**, **Import/Export** files and settings. The **Other User's Folder** allows you to access, edit, and save Outlook files which may be shared with another user.

The **Save As** feature will allow you to save your Outlook file. This is commonly referred to as an *update save*. Normally this feature will save your updates since the last time you saved your file, but if you hadn't saved it previously, it will ask you where you want to save your file and also for a name.

The **Print** feature is where you navigate to print your files or messages. Other options include selecting the printer you want to use and the page settings.

The **Office Account** feature allows you to make changes to your account, including adding or changing a photo or avatar or changing the **Office Background** or **Office Theme**. You may also add a connected service to your **Connected Services**.

The remaining features include **Feedback** and **Options (Outlook Options)**. Take a few moments to explore those too.

The back arrow in the upper left of the Backstage will take you back to your workbook (Figure 16-2).

Home Tab

The Home tab is your main tab in Outlook. When you open your Outlook, the program will default to the Home tab. We will cover each icon on Outlook's Home tab here (Figure 16-3).

FIGURE 16-2
Back Button

FIGURE 16-3 Home Tab

New Group

The ***New Group*** provides icons that make it easy to create a **New Email** with one click, or to create **New Items** with two or more clicks. These are very handy shortcuts.

The **New Email** icon allows you to create a new email with one click (Figure 16-4).

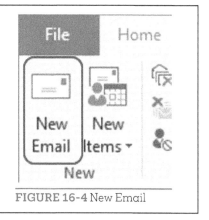

FIGURE 16-4 New Email

The **New Items** icon allows you to create new items with just a few clicks. The *More Items* option make take a few more clicks (Figure 16-5).

The menu pops up with options to create an E-mail Message, Appointment, Meeting, Contact, Task, Email Message Using, More Items, and Skype Meetings.

E-mail Message Using includes More Stationery, Plain Text, Rich Text, and HTML.

More Items include Post in this Folder, Contact Group, Task Request, Internet Fax, Choose Form, and Outlook Data File.

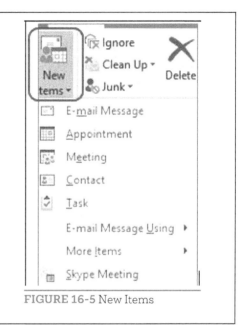

FIGURE 16-5 New Items

Delete Group

The **Delete Group** contains icons that allow you to mark items as junk, block messages, mark redundant messages, move items to an archive file, delete an item, or move an item to the Deleted Items folder.

Ignore: Moves current and future messages in the selected conversation to the Deleted Items folder (Figure 16-6).	 FIGURE 16-6 Ignore Feature
Clean Up: Removes redundant messages in the selected conversations (Figure 16-7). You have three options: 　Clean Up Conversation 　Clean Up Folders 　Clean Up Folder and Subfolders	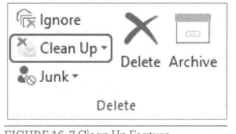 FIGURE 16-7 Clean Up Feature

Junk: Marks the selected items as junk or blocks items sent by this sender or this sender's domain (Figure 16-8). When you click on the down arrow next to the ***Junk*** button, it provides these options: 　　Block Sender 　　Never Block Sender 　　Never Block this Sender's Domain 　　Never Block this Group or Mailing List 　　Not Junk 　　Junk E-mail Options ...	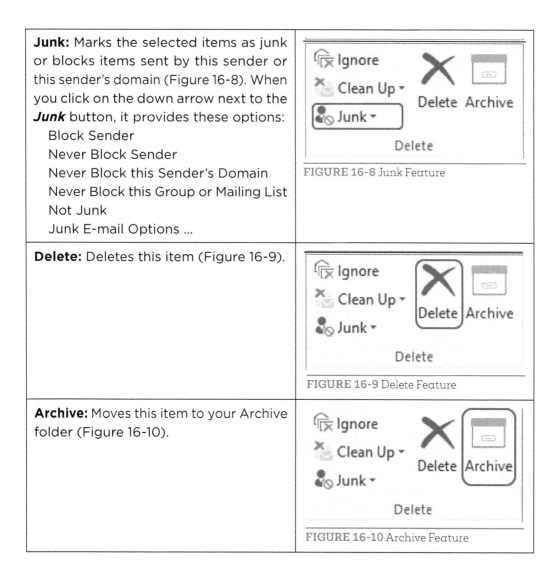 FIGURE 16-8 Junk Feature
Delete: Deletes this item (Figure 16-9).	FIGURE 16-9 Delete Feature
Archive: Moves this item to your Archive folder (Figure 16-10).	FIGURE 16-10 Archive Feature

Respond Group

Reply *(Crtl+R)*: Reply to the sender of this message (Figure 16-11).	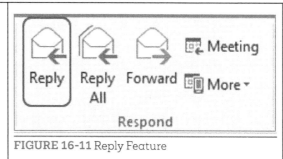 FIGURE 16-11 Reply Feature

Reply All *(Ctrl+Shift+R)*: Reply to the sender and all other recipients of this message (Figure 16-12).	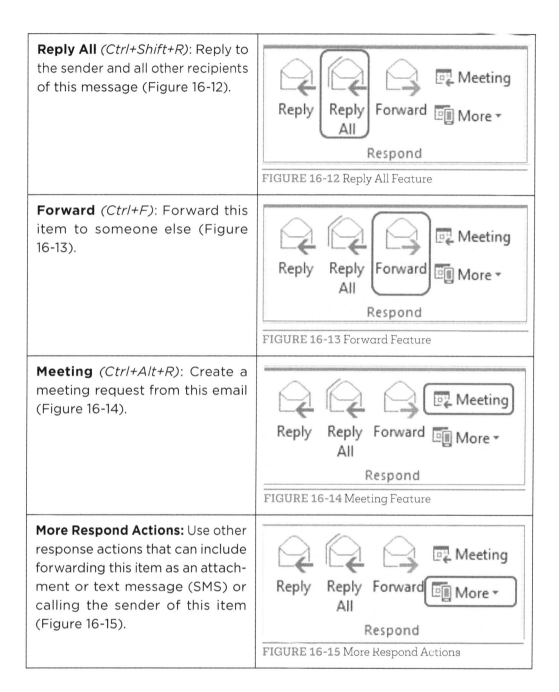 FIGURE 16-12 Reply All Feature
Forward *(Ctrl+F)*: Forward this item to someone else (Figure 16-13).	FIGURE 16-13 Forward Feature
Meeting *(Ctrl+Alt+R)*: Create a meeting request from this email (Figure 16-14).	FIGURE 16-14 Meeting Feature
More Respond Actions: Use other response actions that can include forwarding this item as an attachment or text message (SMS) or calling the sender of this item (Figure 16-15).	FIGURE 16-15 More Respond Actions

Quick Steps Group

All of the **Quick Steps** enable you to complete email tasks quickly with fewer mouse clicks. Once you begin to use these, you will find them to be great timesavers.

Move to: ?: Moves selected email to a folder after marking the email as read (Figure 16-16).	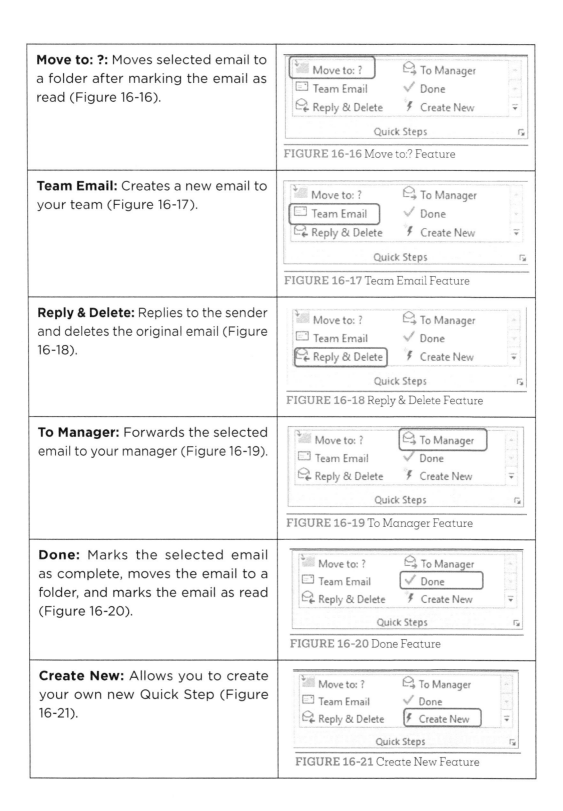FIGURE 16-16 Move to:? Feature
Team Email: Creates a new email to your team (Figure 16-17).	FIGURE 16-17 Team Email Feature
Reply & Delete: Replies to the sender and deletes the original email (Figure 16-18).	FIGURE 16-18 Reply & Delete Feature
To Manager: Forwards the selected email to your manager (Figure 16-19).	FIGURE 16-19 To Manager Feature
Done: Marks the selected email as complete, moves the email to a folder, and marks the email as read (Figure 16-20).	FIGURE 16-20 Done Feature
Create New: Allows you to create your own new Quick Step (Figure 16-21).	FIGURE 16-21 Create New Feature

Create New down arrow: If you point to **New Quick Step**, more options will open for you (Figure 16-22):
    Move to Folder...
    Categorize & Move...
    Flag & Move...
    New E-mail To...
    Forward to...
    New Meeting...
    Custom...
	FIGURE 16-22 Create New Options

Quick Steps Launcher: Opens the *Manage Quick Steps* dialog box which displays all the built-in Quick Steps in one place (Figure 16-23).	**FIGURE 16-23** Quick Steps Launcher

Move Group

The options in the ***Move Group*** will enable you to move an item to a different folder, provides rules based on sender or conversation to move items to specific folders, and the option to send files to *OneNote*.

Move: Provides shortcut options to enable you to quickly and easily move items to folders (Figure 16-24).
    Your options include:
    Other Folder...
    Copy to Folder...
    Always Move Messages in This Conversation
    Move to Clutter
	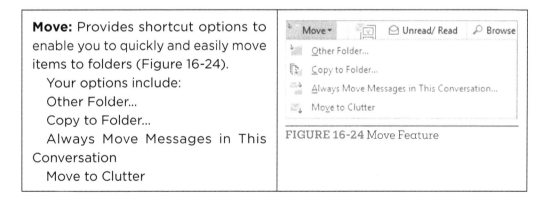
	FIGURE 16-24 Move Feature

Rules: Creates a rule based on the sender, recipients, or conversation topic of this message to always move mail to a different folder (Figure 16-25). You also have the option to create your own rule or manage rules and alerts.	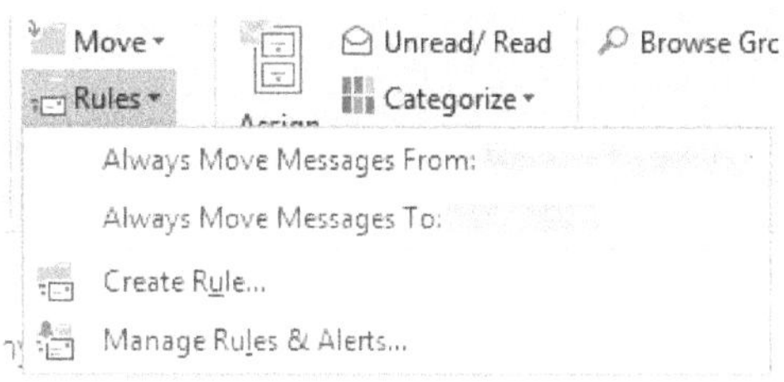 **FIGURE 16-25** Rules Feature
OneNote: This will send selected messages to *OneNote* (Figure 16-26).	 **FIGURE 16-26** OneNote Feature

Tags Group

The **Tags Group** provides automatic options on how long you want to archive and retain selected items. The Unread/Read will mark the item as unread or read; you may categorize items by color and follow-up with flags as reminders.

Assign Policy: Allows you to automatically set up a Retention Policy for selected items. Once you select a Retention Policy and change your mind, you can easily change it or set up your own timeframe (Figure 16-27).
 	
    Outlook provides a short list of commonly used timeframes to retain items.
 	
    Note: Normally, these default times are set up for you by your IT department. They may not enable you to make changes.
	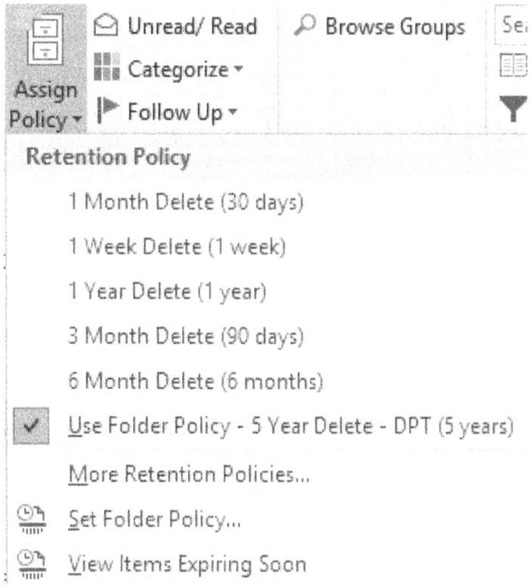
	FIGURE 16-27 Assign Policy Feature

Unread/Read: Will mark an item as *unread* or *read* (Figure 16-28). This is a toggle button. You can click on it to mark the item as *read*, then come back, click on it again, and change it back to *unread*.	 FIGURE 16-28 Unread/Read Feature
Categorize: Categories applied to a conversation will be applied to all current and future items in the conversation (Figure 16-29). Color-coding is perhaps one of the easiest, most fundamental way to group items, sort items, and find items. This tag will help you to easily keep track of conversations.	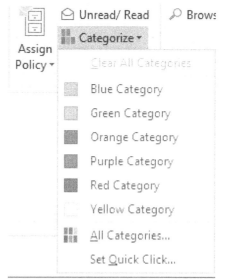 FIGURE 16-29 Categorize Feature
Follow Up: This feature will flag you to follow up on an item. Outlook provides the most common reminder timeframes from which to choose. If you prefer another follow up time, you may set up a custom one. You can add a reminder and mark it complete once done (Figure 16-30). Flagged items appear in the To-Do Bar, Daily Task List, and Tasks.	 FIGURE 16-30 Follow-Up Feature

Groups

Groups enable you to browse for existing groups. A group is a workspace for shared conversations, documents, and calendar events.

Groups: Allows you to browse for existing groups (Figure 16-31).	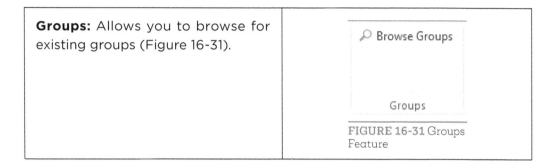 FIGURE 16-31 Groups Feature

Find Group

Items in the ***Find Group*** help you to find people, look people up in an address book, and allow you to filter your emails by a list of different categories.

Search People: You can type in the email, username, or name of a contact (Figure 16-32).	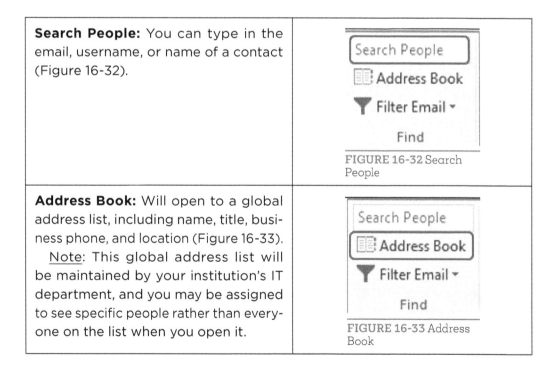 FIGURE 16-32 Search People
Address Book: Will open to a global address list, including name, title, business phone, and location (Figure 16-33). Note: This global address list will be maintained by your institution's IT department, and you may be assigned to see specific people rather than everyone on the list when you open it.	FIGURE 16-33 Address Book

Filter Email: This feature provides numerous ways to filter email to show only categorized or flagged emails, for example (Figure 16-34).

When you move your mouse over **Categorized**, you will see a list of color categories.

When you click on the arrow to the left of **This Week**, you will view the following list:

Today
Yesterday
This Week
Last Week
This Month
Last Month
This Year
Last Year

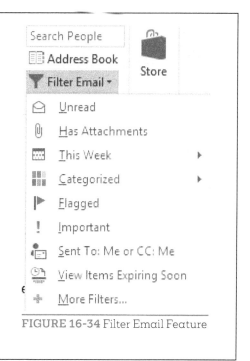

FIGURE 16-34 Filter Email Feature

Send/Receive Tab

FIGURE 16-35 Send/Receive Tab

Send/Receive Group

The **Send/Receive Group** helps you keep track of all items and folders sent and received.

Send/Receive All Folders *(F9)*: Send and receive items such as mail messages, calendar appointments, and tasks in all folders (Figure 16-36).

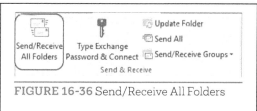

FIGURE 16-36 Send/Receive All Folders

Type Exchange Password & Connect: Enter your password to connect to Microsoft Exchange (Figure 16-37).	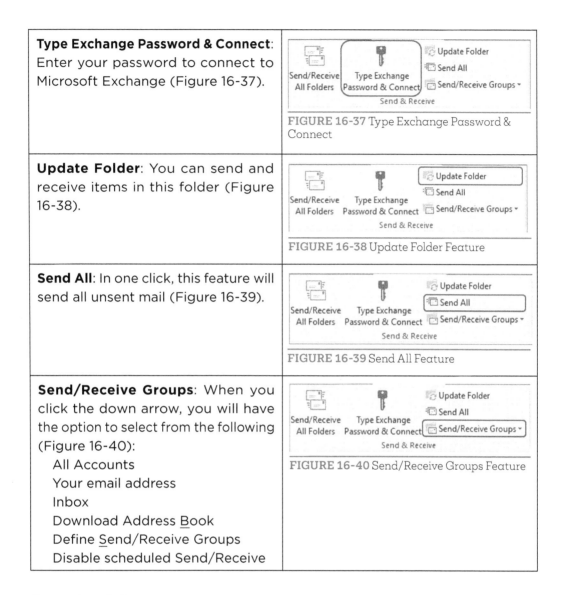 FIGURE 16-37 Type Exchange Password & Connect
Update Folder: You can send and receive items in this folder (Figure 16-38).	FIGURE 16-38 Update Folder Feature
Send All: In one click, this feature will send all unsent mail (Figure 16-39).	FIGURE 16-39 Send All Feature

Send/Receive Groups: When you click the down arrow, you will have the option to select from the following (Figure 16-40):
    All Accounts
    Your email address
    Inbox
    Download Address Book
    Define Send/Receive Groups
    Disable scheduled Send/Receive
	FIGURE 16-40 Send/Receive Groups Feature

Download Group

The **Download Group** shows you the status of the current send/receive status and allows you to quickly cancel all pending send/receive requests.

Show Progress: Shows the current Send/Receive status (Figure 16-41).	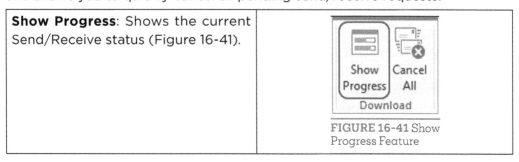 FIGURE 16-41 Show Progress Feature

Cancel All: You can quickly cancel all pending Send/Receive requests (Figure 16-42).	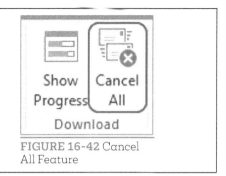FIGURE 16-42 Cancel All Feature

Server Group

The **Server Group** is a group geared toward the more advanced Outlook user. As like other groups in Outlook, it is designed to provide more shortcut options.

Download Headers: Downloads all mail headers in this folder (Figure 16-43). A mail header includes some message fields such as the email address of the sender, subject, and date.	FIGURE 16-43 Download Headers Feature
Mark to Download (*Ctrl+Alt+M*): Marks the message to be downloaded the next time marked headers are processed (Figure 16-44). When you click the down arrow, you will have the following two options: Mark to Download Mark to Download Message <u>C</u>opy	FIGURE 16-44 Mark to Download
Unmark to Download (*Ctrl+Alt+U*): This feature unmarks the message header so that it is not downloadable (Figure 16-45). When you click the down arrow, you will have the following two options: Unmark to Download Unmark All to Download	FIGURE 16-45 Unmark to Download

Process Marked Headers: This feature downloads the content of all marked headers in this folder (Figure 16-46). When you click the down arrow, you will have the following two options: Process Marked Headers Process Marked Headers in All Folders	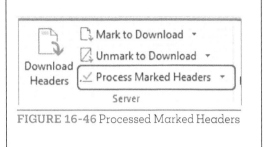 FIGURE 16-46 Processed Marked Headers

Preferences Group

The **Work Offline** feature in this group makes it easy to disconnect and work offline without the interruptions of receiving new mail.

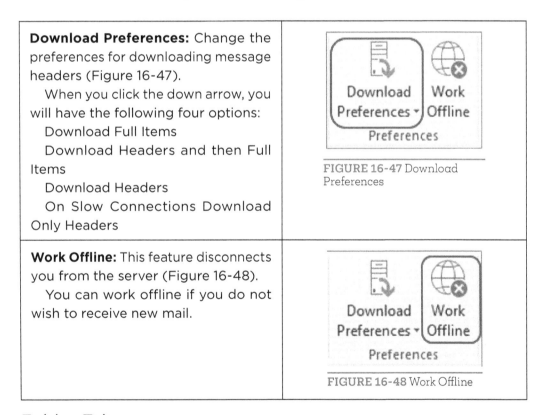

Download Preferences: Change the preferences for downloading message headers (Figure 16-47). When you click the down arrow, you will have the following four options: Download Full Items Download Headers and then Full Items Download Headers On Slow Connections Download Only Headers	FIGURE 16-47 Download Preferences
Work Offline: This feature disconnects you from the server (Figure 16-48). You can work offline if you do not wish to receive new mail.	FIGURE 16-48 Work Offline

Folder Tab

This tab is all things Folder. You can create a new folder, a new search folder, copy, move, or delete a folder, mark as read, alphabetize folders, clean up your folders, delete all your folders, and then recover them (Figure 16-49).

FIGURE 16-49 Folder Tab

New Group

The **New Group** Sets up New Folders and New Search Folders.

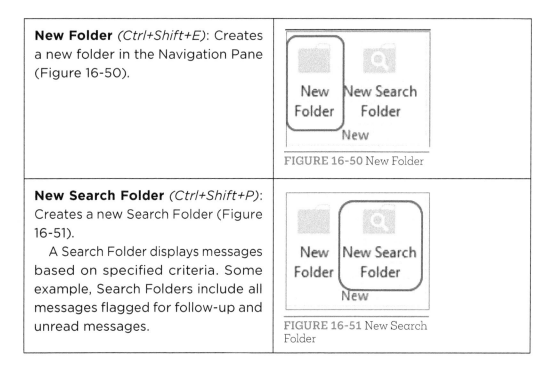

New Folder *(Ctrl+Shift+E)*: Creates a new folder in the Navigation Pane (Figure 16-50).	FIGURE 16-50 New Folder
New Search Folder *(Ctrl+Shift+P)*: Creates a new Search Folder (Figure 16-51). A Search Folder displays messages based on specified criteria. Some example, Search Folders include all messages flagged for follow-up and unread messages.	FIGURE 16-51 New Search Folder

Actions Group

The **Actions Group** provides options for you to rename a folder, copy a folder, move a folder, and delete a folder.

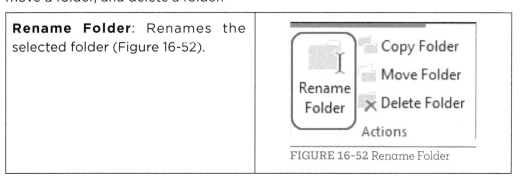

Rename Folder: Renames the selected folder (Figure 16-52).	FIGURE 16-52 Rename Folder

Copy Folder: Copies this folder to a new location (Figure 16-53).	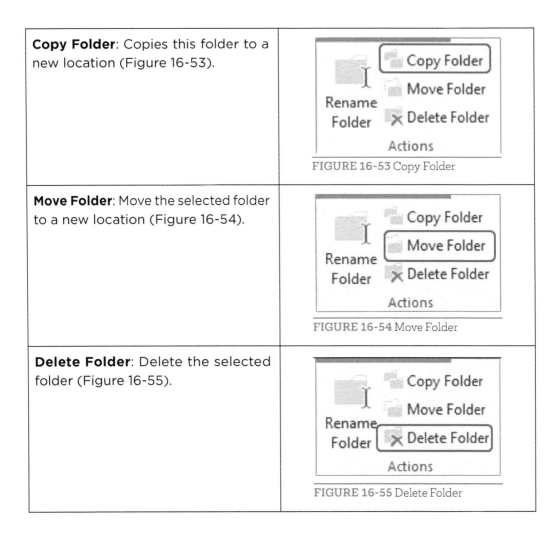 FIGURE 16-53 Copy Folder
Move Folder: Move the selected folder to a new location (Figure 16-54).	FIGURE 16-54 Move Folder
Delete Folder: Delete the selected folder (Figure 16-55).	FIGURE 16-55 Delete Folder

Clean Up Group

The Clean Up Group contains options for you to mark all as read, show folders in alphabetical order, clean up folders and subfolders, delete all items from a folder, plus the opportunity to recover items previously deleted from a folder.

Mark All as Read: Marks all messages in this folder as Read (Figure 16-56).	 FIGURE 16-56 Mark All as Read Feature

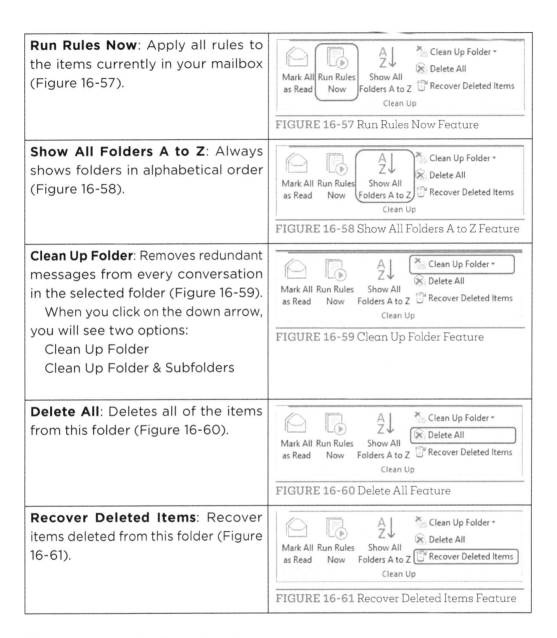

Run Rules Now: Apply all rules to the items currently in your mailbox (Figure 16-57).	FIGURE 16-57 Run Rules Now Feature
Show All Folders A to Z: Always shows folders in alphabetical order (Figure 16-58).	FIGURE 16-58 Show All Folders A to Z Feature

Clean Up Folder: Removes redundant messages from every conversation in the selected folder (Figure 16-59).
  When you click on the down arrow, you will see two options:
    Clean Up Folder
    Clean Up Folder & Subfolders
	FIGURE 16-59 Clean Up Folder Feature

Delete All: Deletes all of the items from this folder (Figure 16-60).	FIGURE 16-60 Delete All Feature
Recover Deleted Items: Recover items deleted from this folder (Figure 16-61).	FIGURE 16-61 Recover Deleted Items Feature

Favorites and Online View Groups

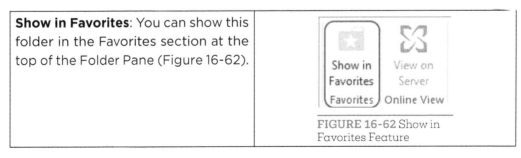

Show in Favorites: You can show this folder in the Favorites section at the top of the Folder Pane (Figure 16-62).	FIGURE 16-62 Show in Favorites Feature

View on Server: Shows older messages by loading an online view from Microsoft Exchange (Figure 16-63).	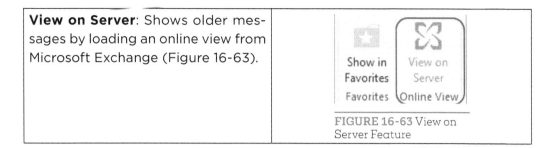 FIGURE 16-63 View on Server Feature

Properties Group

Policy: Sets the Retention Policy for this folder (Figure 16-64).	FIGURE 16-64 Policy Feature
AutoArchive Settings: Specify when items in this folder are archived, and where they are stored (Figure 16-65).	FIGURE 16-65 AutoArchive Settings Feature
Folder Permissions: View and edit the sharing permissions for this folder (Figure 16-66).	FIGURE 16-66 Folder Permissions Feature
Folder Properties: Views the properties for this folder (Figure 16-67).	FIGURE 16-67 Folder Properties Feature

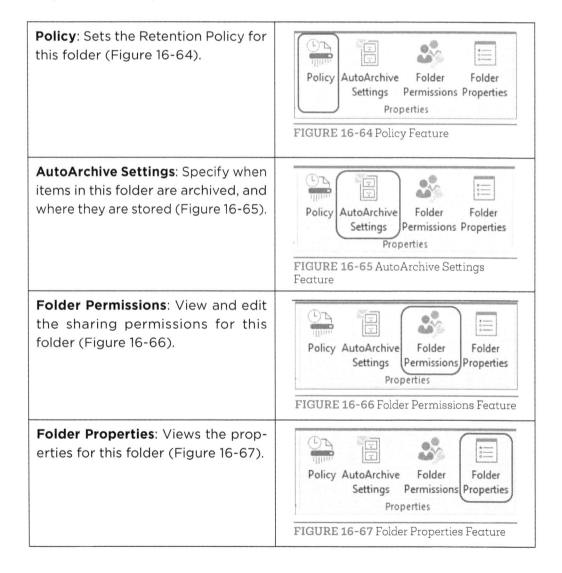

View Tab

This tab provides numerous ways to view your messages.

Current View Group

Change View: When you click on the down arrow, a window will appear. You have further options to Compact, Single, or Preview (Figure 16-68). You also have three other options: *Manage Views...* *Save Current View As a New View...* *Apply Current View to Other Mail Folders...*	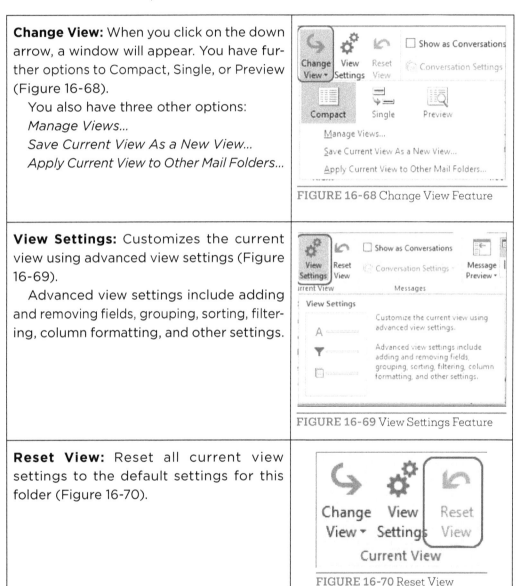 FIGURE 16-68 Change View Feature
View Settings: Customizes the current view using advanced view settings (Figure 16-69). Advanced view settings include adding and removing fields, grouping, sorting, filtering, column formatting, and other settings.	FIGURE 16-69 View Settings Feature
Reset View: Reset all current view settings to the default settings for this folder (Figure 16-70).	FIGURE 16-70 Reset View Feature

Message Preview: Use AutoPreview to quickly scan items (Figure 16-71).	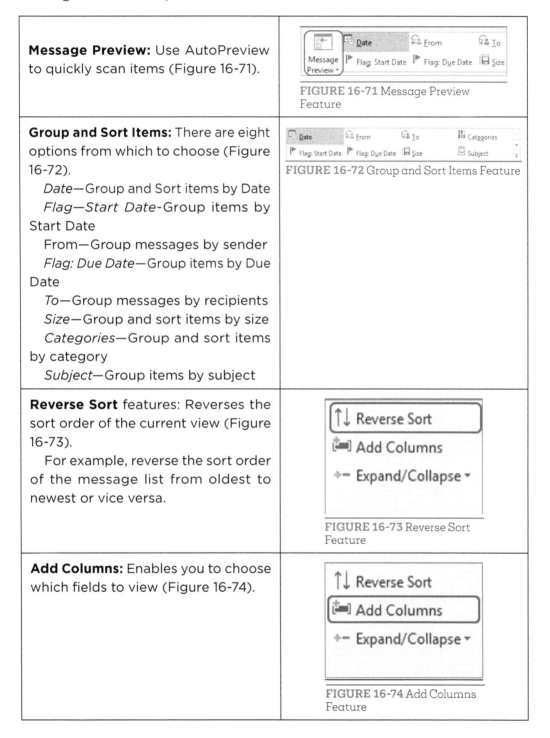FIGURE 16-71 Message Preview Feature
Group and Sort Items: There are eight options from which to choose (Figure 16-72). *Date*—Group and Sort items by Date *Flag—Start Date*-Group items by Start Date From—Group messages by sender *Flag: Due Date*—Group items by Due Date *To*—Group messages by recipients *Size*—Group and sort items by size *Categories*—Group and sort items by category *Subject*—Group items by subject	FIGURE 16-72 Group and Sort Items Feature
Reverse Sort features: Reverses the sort order of the current view (Figure 16-73). For example, reverse the sort order of the message list from oldest to newest or vice versa.	FIGURE 16-73 Reverse Sort Feature
Add Columns: Enables you to choose which fields to view (Figure 16-74).	FIGURE 16-74 Add Columns Feature

Expand/Collapse: Expands or collapses groups in the list (Figure 16-75). When you click on the down arrow, you will see four options:
    Collapse This Group
    Expand This Group
    Collapse All Groups
    Expand All Groups
	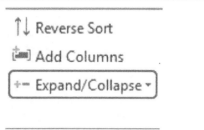
	FIGURE 16-75 Expand/Collapse Feature

Layout and People Tabs

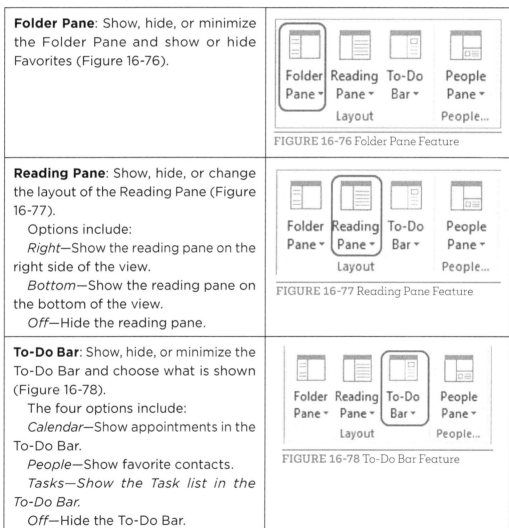

Folder Pane: Show, hide, or minimize the Folder Pane and show or hide Favorites (Figure 16-76).	FIGURE 16-76 Folder Pane Feature

Reading Pane: Show, hide, or change the layout of the Reading Pane (Figure 16-77).
    Options include:
    Right—Show the reading pane on the right side of the view.
    Bottom—Show the reading pane on the bottom of the view.
    Off—Hide the reading pane.
	FIGURE 16-77 Reading Pane Feature

To-Do Bar: Show, hide, or minimize the To-Do Bar and choose what is shown (Figure 16-78).
    The four options include:
    Calendar—Show appointments in the To-Do Bar.
    People—Show favorite contacts.
    Tasks—Show the Task list in the To-Do Bar.
    Off—Hide the To-Do Bar.
	FIGURE 16-78 To-Do Bar Feature

<table>
<tr>
<td>

People Pane: Show, hide, or minimize the People Pane and configure social network accounts (Figure 16-79).

The three options include:

Normal—Show the People Pane.

Minimized—Minimize the People Pane.

Off—Turn off the People Pane.

</td>
<td>

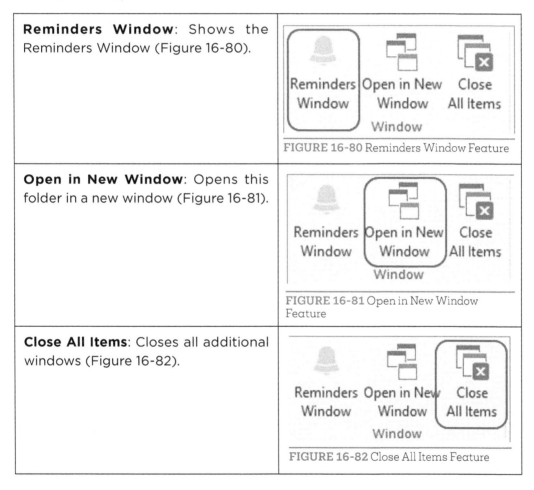

FIGURE 16-79 People Pane Feature

</td>
</tr>
</table>

Window Group

<table>
<tr>
<td>

Reminders Window: Shows the Reminders Window (Figure 16-80).

</td>
<td>

FIGURE 16-80 Reminders Window Feature

</td>
</tr>
<tr>
<td>

Open in New Window: Opens this folder in a new window (Figure 16-81).

</td>
<td>

FIGURE 16-81 Open in New Window Feature

</td>
</tr>
<tr>
<td>

Close All Items: Closes all additional windows (Figure 16-82).

</td>
<td>

FIGURE 16-82 Close All Items Feature

</td>
</tr>
</table>

Create and Send Email

1. On the Home tab, click on **New Email** to start a new message (Figure 16-83).
2. Enter a name or email address in the **To...**, **Cc** (carbon copy), or **Bcc** (blind carbon copy) field (Figure 16-84).

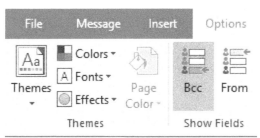

FIGURE 16-84 Blind Carbon Copy Feature

FIGURE 16-83 New Email Feature

Note: If you don't see **Bcc**, click on the **Options** tab, then click on **Bcc** in the *Show Fields* group. **Bcc** is used when you do not want those receiving the email message to see other recipient's email addresses or names. When a recipient receives an email, he or she will be able to see the address in the **To** and **Cc** fields, but the names in the **Bcc** field are hidden (Figure 16-85).

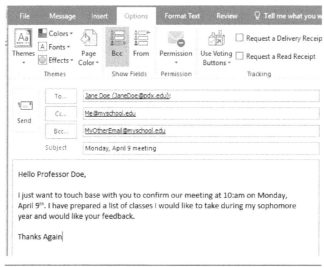

FIGURE 16-85 Email with Bcc ... field

Note: If you click on the **To...** button, you will see the contacts from your address book from which to choose. This also happens when you click the **Cc** and **Bcc** buttons. You would use this when you want to send the email to multiple recipients.

3. In **Subject**, type the subject of the email message.
4. Place the cursor in the body of the email message, and then start typing. On the Message tab, you can format font type, font size, color, bold, italicize, underline, etc.
5. After typing your message, choose **Send**.

Save an Email Draft

If you are working on an email and don't have time to complete it, or if you would like to look it over later (it is always a good idea to look it over before sending it!), you can save it as a draft. To save an email as a draft, press **Ctrl S** to save it as a draft. It will be saved in the **Folder pane** under **Favorites** (Figure 16-86).

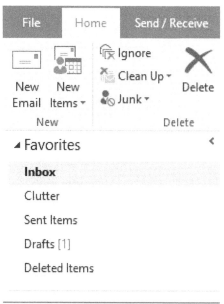

FIGURE 16-86 Save an Email Draft

Reply, Reply All, and Forward

When you respond to an email, you have three options: *Reply, Reply All*, and *Forward*. You use *Reply* to send a message to the original sender; you use *Reply All* to send a message to the original sender and all other email recipients in the *Cc* and *Bcc* lines. Forward enables you to send the email message to recipients you choose.

Attach a File or Outlook Items

Once you open the *New Email* window, you may include an attachment any time. To add a file attachment, click on the *Message* tab, then click on **Attach File** in the *Include* group.

You can also attach other Outlook items, such as a *Business Card, Calendar*, or *Outlook* item from the drop-down list (Figure 16-87). To insert a Business Card, click on **Attach Item**, and then click on the **Business Card** option. Select the items to be attached. Use the Ctrl key to select nonadjacent items or the

Shift key to select a range of items. Once you click on a contact name, his or her business card will appear. Click **OK** to attach.

FIGURE 16-87 Attach a Business Card

Share a File Instead of Sending an Attachment

1. Create a message or **Reply To**, **Reply All,** or **Forward** an existing message.
2. Click on **Attach File**.
3. Select a file from the list of recent files you have worked with.
4. If the file shows a small cloud icon, the file is saved online, and you will share the file.
5. If the file does not show a cloud, click on Browse the Web Locations, choose the small arrow, and choose **Upload to OneDrive**.

Delete or Recover a Deleted Email

Outlook enables you to delete email you no longer need or want from your Inbox or mail folders or recover those that you previously deleted but decided you wanted to keep.

Delete an Email

1. Select an email you want to delete.
2. In the Outlook ribbon, select **Delete**.
3. Or, move your mouse to the right side of the listed message. In this example, you will notice that this email has the bell icon for a *Reminder* notification, the calendar for a meeting, a Follow Up flag, and a red X. If you want to delete a message, click on the red X (Figure 16-88).

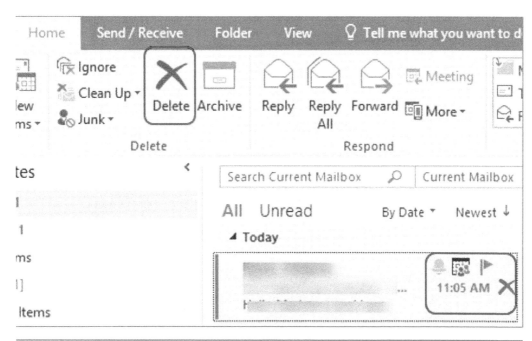

FIGURE 16-88 Delete an Email

Note: If you would like to permanently delete an email, press Shift + Delete. Be careful: you won't be able to recover this email later.

Recover a Deleted Email

Select **Deleted Items** (in your *Folder* pane in the same group as your *Inbox)*, and then right-click the email you would like to recover.

Focused Inbox

Focused Inbox helps you focus on the emails that matter most. It separates your inbox into two tabs—**Focused** and **Other**.

Outlook makes it easy to organize messages the way you want by moving them and specifying where all future messages from that sender should be delivered. You bypass the list view you would normally see and where you would have to scroll down the list to find emails from specific individuals.

1. From your inbox, choose the **Focused** or **Other** tab and then right-click the message you want to move.
2. If moving from **Focused** to **Other**, choose **Move to Other** if you want only the selected message moved. Choose **Always Move to Other** if you want all future messages from the sender to be delivered to the **Other** tab.

Note: If moving from **Other** to **Focused**, choose **Move to Focused** if you want only the selected message moved. If you want all future messages from the sender to be delivered to the Focused tab, choose **Always Move to Focused.**

Note: Not all versions of Outlook 2019 have this feature. If you do not see it in your Inbox, then the feature is not available. If you have further questions regarding this feature, ask your instructor or contact your school's IT Department.

Using Follow Up Flags

Outlook provides you with *Follow Up* flags to mark email and task items that need further attention. Instead of having a stack of to-do items, you can now do this electronically.

Outlook provides numerous flags to mark items depending on priority (Figure 16-89). The types of *Follow Up flags* available in Outlook are:

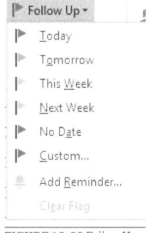

1. Today
2. Tomorrow
3. This Week
4. Next Week
5. No Date
6. Custom

FIGURE 16-89 Follow Up Flags

To Apply a Follow Up Flag

You can use a Follow Up flag in email messages and contacts.

1. Open the Outlook item (email, contact, or task).
2. Click the **Follow Up** button (Home tab, *Tags* group).
3. Select the desired *Follow Up* flag.
4. Close the Outlook item. This item is now marked and will be included in the list of **To-Do** items.
5. You can also create a **Custom Follow Up** flag (Figure 16-90).
6. Open the Outlook item (email, contact, or task).
7. Click the **Follow Up** button (Home tab, *Tags* group).
8. Select **Custom**.
9. A *Custom* dialog box will open.
10. Enter your details in the *Custom* dialog box.
11. Close the Outlook item. This item is now marked and will be included in the list of **To-Do** items.

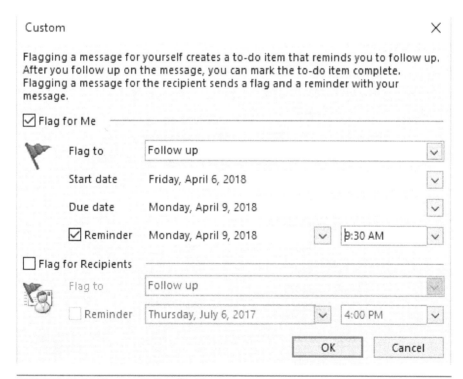

FIGURE 16-90 Custom Follow Up Flag

Completing a Flagged Item

Once an item marked with a Follow Up flag in Outlook is completed, you can use Mark Complete to indicate the item has been completed. This will replace the flag with a check mark. There are three ways to do this:

1. Click the flag icon and the **Mark Complete** check replaces the flag.
2. Right-click the item, choose **Follow Up**, and click *Mark Complete*.
3. Open the item, click on the *Follow Up* button in the Tags group, and select *Mark Complete*.

Contacts

Like a personal phonebook, Outlook provides an area to manage names, addresses, email addresses, phone numbers, birthdays, anniversaries, etc. You can even add a photo, web addresses, a notes box, and even map the contact's location.

Create a Contact

1. Click on the **Home** tab.
2. Click on the down arrow in the *New Items* icon. (Home tab, *New* group), or press *Ctrl+Shift+C* (Figure 16-91).

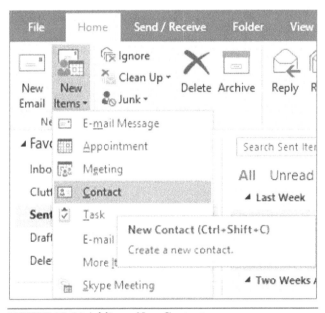

FIGURE 16-91 Adding a New Contact

3. Click on the Contact option.
4. The New Contact window will open. It will be titled as *Untitled—Contact*.
5. Type in your New Contact information. As you fill in each field, you should notice that the business card image will populate with the contact information as you enter a few fields.
6. If you look at the top of the window, you will see your contact's name in place of *Untitled*.
7. Notice that you now have a new Ribbon named *Contact*.
8. Once you complete your contact information, you have several options from which to choose. These are your options, from left to right: (Figure 16-92).

FIGURE 16-92 Contact Tab

a. **Save & Close**—Select this option when you have completed adding your new contact and don't need to add any more contacts.
b. **Delete**—Select this option if you want to delete this contact.
c. **Save & New**—Select this option when you have more than one contact to enter your address book.
d. **Forward**—Forwards this contact's information to another person.
e. **OneNote**—Create or open linked contact notes in OneNote.
f. **General**—Shows the General page where you can edit your contact.

g. **Details**—Shows the Detail page of the contact in which you can edit secondary information regarding this contact.

h. **Certificates**—Shows the Certificates page of the contact in which you can store Digital IDs used to send encrypted emails to this contact.

i. **All Fields**—Shows the All Field page of the contact in which you can edit all the information contained for the contact (all *General* information and *Detail* information for the contact).

j. **Email**—Creates a new email message addressed to this contact.

k. **Meeting**—Creates a new meeting request addressed to this contact.

l. **More**—4 more options:

   i. *Call or Instant Message* (IM) this contact.
   ii. *Web Page*—Open this contact's web page in this browser.
   iii. *Assign a Task*—Assign a task to this contact.
   iv. *Map It*—View a map of this contact's address.

m. **Address Book**—Opens the Address Book to locate names, email address, and phone numbers.

n. **Check Names**—Checks the names and email addresses you have typed to make sure that you can send messages to them.

o. **Business Card**—Add or edit a business card for this contact.

p. **Picture**—Add or edit a picture for this contact.

q. **Categorize**—Categorize contacts by color groups.

r. **Follow Up**—Sets a flag to help you follow up on this item later.

s. **Private**—Marks the item as *private* so that other people cannot see the details of it.

t. **Zoom**—Allows you to zoom in on a level that make it easier for you to read.

Address Book

Your electronic address book will include *All Address Lists, All Contacts, All Distribution Lists, All Groups, All Rooms, All Users, Offline Global Address List*, and *Public Folders*. You have plenty of options in your address book (Figure 16-93).

You can perform a search. Depending on how your global address list is set up, you can click on the radial **Name Only** button and then type in the name you are looking for.

The default address book view will list Name, Title, Business Phone, Location, Department, Email Address, Company, and Alias. Again, depending on how your global list is set up, you may be able to click on the **More Columns** radial button and see additional columns.

You can also perform an Advanced Find and use any field in addition to the Name field to find someone on your address list (Figure 16-94).

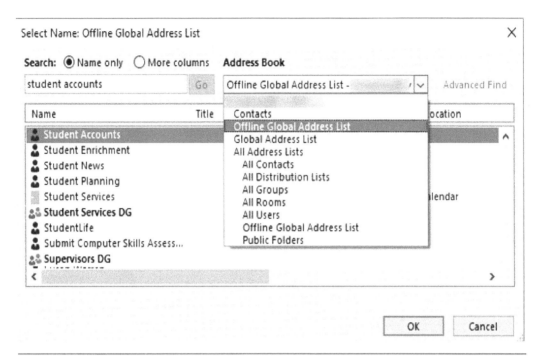

FIGURE 16-93 Address Book

FIGURE 16-94 Advanced Find

Create a Contact Group in Outlook

At times, you may need to send a message to a special group of people. In Outlook, you will use a contact group (formerly called a "distribution list") to send an email to multiple people—fellow students, your instructors, a committee, or even just a group of friends—without having to add each name each time you want to write them (Figure 16-95). To create a contact group:

1. Click on **New Items** (Home tab, *New* group).

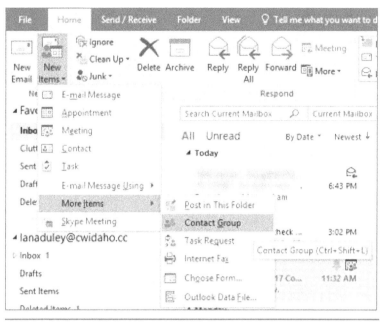

FIGURE 16-95 Create a Contact Group

2. Click on **More Items**.
3. Click on **Contact Group** or press (*Ctrl+Shift+L*). You will be on a new Ribbon tab named **Contact Group**.
4. In the Untitled—Contact Group box, type a name for your group in the name box.
5. Click on Add Members.
6. Add members from your Outlook contacts, address book, or enter an email address.
7. To add someone who is not in your address book or contacts, create or add a person as a contact.
8. When you are finished adding contacts to your new Contact Group, click Save & Close (Icon is on the Ribbon at the far left).

Add, Delete, and Update Members

As time goes on, you will add new friends, remove some friends, or make changes to members in your contact group (Figure 16-96). This is how you can add new contacts, update current contact information, and delete contacts:

1. Open your Contact Groups.

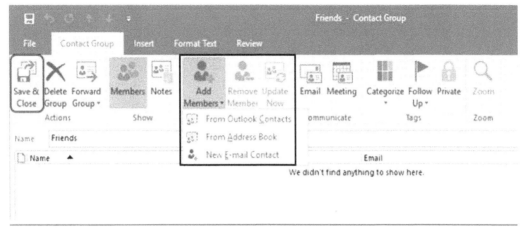

FIGURE 16-96 Add, Remove, or Update Members

2. Click on Add Members. You have the option to add members from the following places:

    a. Outlook Contacts

    b. Address Book

    c. New Email Contact

3. If you want to remove a member from your contact group, click on his or her name in the list, then click on **Remove Member**.

4. If you want to update member information, click on his or her name in the list, then click on **Update Member**.

5. Click on **Save & Close**.

To Create a Contact Group from an Email List

You can create a contact group that includes all of the recipients by using a previous email that you sent to them. Then, the next time you want to contact them or schedule a meeting with them, you can add the contact group to the **To** line of your message instead of adding each person individually.

1. Open an email that was sent to the people you want to include in the contact group.

2. In the **To** or **Cc** box, highlight all the names with your mouse.

3. Right-click your selection, and then click **Copy**, or press *Ctrl+C.*

4. Click on **New Items** (Home tab, *New* group).

5. Click on **More Items**.

6. Click on **Contact Group** or press (*Ctrl+Shift+L*).

7. In the Untitled—Contact Group box, type a name for your group in the name box.

8. Click ***Add Members***.
9. Click on ***New Email Contacts***.
10. Click on ***Save & Close***.

Calendar

You probably have multiple calendars and daily planners in your life. You use these to organize you daily, weekly, and monthly activities to keep track of activities at home or work. Most of you now have smartphones to manage the same activities.

Outlook provides an electronic version of a calendar. In addition to replicating calendar entries, you can also schedule appointments or events. Outlook also sends you electronic reminders (Oops! Almost forgot that dentist appointment!), sends meeting requests, and also gives you the ability to share calendar events with other Outlook users through your computer and/or your mobile device(s).

Outlook also makes it possible for you to synchronize your work, school, and home calendars. Many working professionals use Outlook Calendar to help keep them organized and on time. Once you get everything set up through Outlook, you will wonder how you ever lived without it.

The three main types of calendar items are appointments, events, and meeting requests. You can use the same new calendar items to create each of these different calendar items.

An **appointment** is a calendar item that has a duration of less than 24 hours, such as a meeting with your advisor, a doctor's appointment, or your child's presentation. You can use an appointment to schedule blocks of time that are less than 24 hours.

An **event** is a calendar item that lasts for 24 hours or more. Examples include Spring Break, Thanksgiving Holiday, or vacations. You can convert an **appointment** to an **event** by clicking the **All day event** check box.

A **meeting request** is used to create a calendar item and to invite others to a meeting. Although it looks similar to appointments and events, the meeting request includes a ***To*** line used to invite attendees and a ***Send*** button.

Outlook provides four main calendar views: *Day, Week, Month*, and S*chedule*. To open your calendars, click on the ***Calendar*** button in the **Navigation** bar at the bottom of the Folder pane (Figure 16-97). The Monthly calendar will appear. To see the Day View, Week View, Work Week View, and Schedule View, click in the *Arrange* group on the Home tab (Figure 16-98).

If you want to use key strokes to display different calendar views, then see the following:

Favorites

Inbox

Clutter

Sent Items

Drafts [1]

Deleted Items

◄   **April 2018**   ►

SU	MO	TU	WE	TH	FR	SA
25	26	27	28	29	30	31
1	2	3	4	5	6	7
8	9	10	11	12	13	14
15	16	17	18	19	20	21
22	23	24	25	26	27	28
29	30	1	2	3	4	5

You have nothing scheduled in the next 7 days.

Misc

FIGURE 16-97 Calendar Views

1. **Day View**:   Ctrl+Alt+1

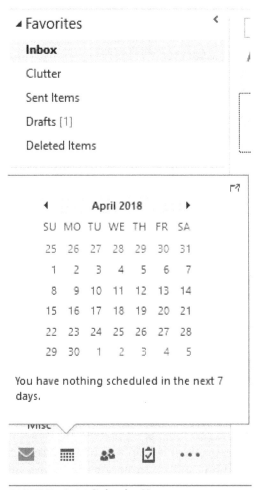

FIGURE 16-98 Multiple Calendar Views in the Arrange Group

2. **Work Week View**:   Ctrl+Alt+2

3. *Week View*:   Ctrl+Alt+3
4. *Month View*:   Ctrl+Alt+4
5. *Schedule View*:   Ctrl+Alt+5

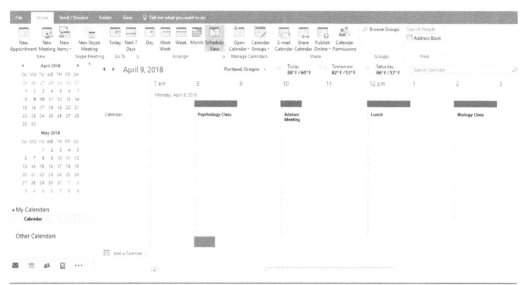

FIGURE 16-99 Day View

Schedule View

Schedule view displays your calendar in a timeline view. The timeline view is horizontal rather than vertical. In Schedule view, you are able to type in a new appointment directly in your calendar. There are two ways to do this:

1. Double-click a time slot to open a new appointment.
2. Click the **New Appointment** button on the Home tab.

Other Calendar Views

Outlook also provides other preset calendar views. The **List** view (Figure 16-100) and **Active** views (Figure 16-101) will list calendar items rather than Day, Week, or Month view.

To access these other views, click on the **View** tab. Then click on **Change View,** and choose the view you want. You will notice all 4 views from left to right.

The difference between the List and Active lists is that **List** view shows ALL calendar items while the **Active** list shows only the active ones.

Note: To go back to Calendar view, click on the Calendar icon under Change View.

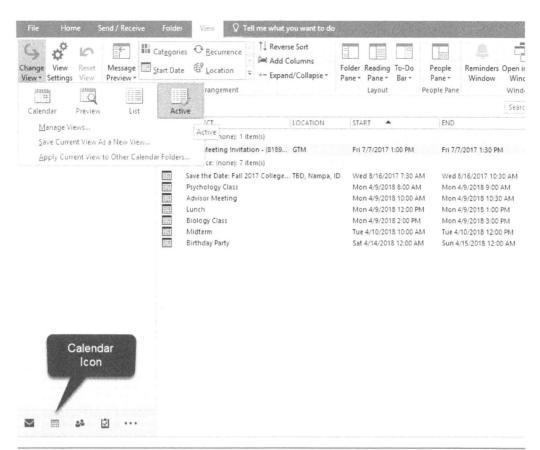

FIGURE 16-100 List View

FIGURE 16-101 Active View

<u>Note</u>: You must click the Calendar icon in the Navigation pane (bottom of Folder pane) to see this View tab and the calendar views.

Schedule an Appointment

1. Click on the **Home** tab.
2. Click on the down arrow in the *New Items* icon. (Home tab, *New* group) or press *Ctrl+Shift+A* (Figure 16-102).

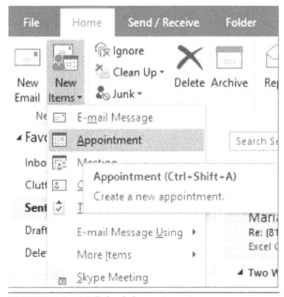

FIGURE 16-102 Schedule an Appointment

3. Click on the **Appointment** option.
4. The **Appointment** window will open. It will be titled as *Untitled—Appointment*.
5. In the **Subject** box, type a description.
6. In the **Location** box, type the location.
7. Enter the start and end times.
8. **Optional**: Type in more information regarding this appointment.
9. Notice that you now have a new Ribbon named *Appointment*.
10. Once you complete your appointment information, you have several options from which to choose. These are your options, from left to right: (Figure 16-103).

   a. ***Save & Close***—Select this option when you have completed adding your new appointment.
   b. ***Delete***—Select this option if you want to delete this appointment.
   c. ***Calendar***—Opens the calendar to see if this meeting time works for you.
   d. ***Forward***—Forward this item to someone else.
   e. ***Appointment***—Set up the details for your appointment or meeting.

f. **Scheduling Assistant**—Find out the best appointment time by checking other people's calendars.

g. **Skype Meeting**—Set up a new *Skype* meeting.

Note: The default options might allow uninvited people to join your meeting. Use meeting options to control access to your meetings.

h. **Cancel Invitation**—Cancels this meeting invitation. No meeting will be created on your calendar, and no invitations will be sent to other people.

i. **Address Book**—Open the Address Book to look for names, phone numbers, and e-mail addresses.

j. **Check Names**—Check the names and e-mail addresses you have typed to make sure that it is possible to send messages to them.

k. **Response Options—**Choose the kind of responses you want to allow for this meeting.

l. **Show As**—Changes how the time for this item is marked on your calendar. This also affects the free/busy information other people can view.

   i. **Free**
   ii. **Working Elsewhere**
   iii. **Tentative**
   iv. **Busy**
   v. **Out of Office**

m. **Reminder**—Choose when to be reminded of this item. When you click on the down arrow, you will have a long list of options. At the end of the list, you can select a reminder sound.

n. **Recurrence**—*(Ctrl+G)* Schedule this item to repeat regularly. Good for setting up weekly or monthly meetings.

o. **Time Zones**—Show or hide (toggle button) the time zone controls which you can use to specify the time zones for the beginning and end of the appointment.

p. **Room Finder**—Show or Hide the Room Finder task pane.

q. **Categorize**—Categorizes the appointment by color. The selected category will be applied to all current and future items in the conversation.

r. **Private**—Marks the item as *private* so that other people cannot see the details of it.

s. **High Importance**—Marks this item as high priority.

t. **Low Importance**—Marks this item as low priority.

u. **View Templates**—Schedule a Meeting.

v. **Collapse Ribbon**—Minimizes the Ribbon for more work area.

FIGURE 16-103 Meeting Tab

Schedule a Meeting

1. Click on the **Home** tab.
2. Click on the down arrow in the *New Items* icon. (Home tab, *New* group), or press *Ctrl+Shift+Q*. Click on the **Meeting** option.
3. The **Meeting** window will open. It will be titled as *Untitled—Meeting*.
4. In the *Subject* box, type a description.
5. In the *Location* box, type the location.
6. Enter the start and end times.
7. **Optional:** Type in more information regarding this meeting.
8. Notice that you now have a new Ribbon named *Meeting*.
9. Once you complete your appointment information, you have several options from which to choose. Refer to options A-V above.

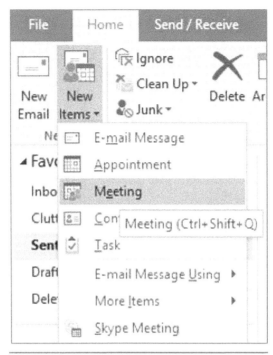

FIGURE 16-104 Schedule a Meeting

Respond to a Meeting Request

When you are invited to join in a meeting, your meeting request will appear in your Inbox along with your other emails. The Inbox icon for a meeting request will look slightly different because it will include a calendar with avatar icon.

When you open the meeting request, it will appear to be similar to an email, but the *Respond* group includes four additional options: *Accept, Tentative, Decline*, or *Propose New Time* (or a calendar icon). Once you make your choice, a dialog box will open with the following options: *Edit the Response Before Sending*, *Send the Response Now*, or *Do Not Send a Response*.

If you choose *Accept, Tentative*, or *Propose New Time*, your meeting request will be removed from your Inbox and added to your calendar, and a response email is sent to the meeting organizer. However, if you choose *Decline*, the meeting request will move from your Inbox to the *Deleted Items* folder, and a response is sent to the meeting organizer.